ROUTLEDGE HANDBOOK OF PEACEBUILDING AND ETHNIC CONFLICT

This handbook offers a comprehensive analysis of peacebuilding in ethnic conflicts, with attention to theory, peacebuilder roles, making sense of the past and shaping the future, as well as case studies and approaches.

Comprising 28 chapters that present key insights on peacebuilding in ethnic conflicts, the volume has implications for teaching and training, as well as for practice and policy. The handbook is divided into four thematic parts. Part 1 focuses on critical dimensions of ethnic conflicts, including root causes, gender, external involvements, emancipatory peacebuilding, hatred as a public health issue, environmental issues, American nationalism, and the impact of the COVID-19 pandemic. Part 2 focuses on peacebuilders' roles, including Indigenous peacemaking, nonviolent accompaniment, peace leadership in the military, interreligious peacebuilders, local women, and young people. Part 3 addresses the past and shaping of the future, including a discussion of public memory, heritage rights and monuments, refugees, trauma and memory, aggregated trauma in the African-American community, exhumations after genocide, and a healing-centered approach to conflict. Part 4 presents case studies on Sri Lanka's postwar reconciliation process, peacebuilding in Mindanao, the transformative peace negotiation in Aceh and Bougainville, external economic aid for peacebuilding in Northern Ireland, Indigenous and local peacemaking, and a continuum of peacebuilding focal points. The handbook offers perspectives on the breadth and significance of peacebuilding work in ethnic conflicts throughout the world.

This volume will be of much interest to students of peacebuilding, ethnic conflict, security studies, and international relations.

Jessica Senehi is a Professor of Peace and Conflict Studies at the University of Manitoba, Canada.

Imani Michelle Scott is a Professor of Communication at the Savannah College of Art and Design, USA.

Sean Byrne is a Professor of Peace and Conflict Studies at the University of Manitoba, Canada.

Thomas G. Matyók is a Senior Lecturer in Political Science and Executive Director of the Joint Civil-Military Interaction Research and Education Network at Middle Georgia State University, USA.

ROUTLEDGE HANDBOOK OF PEACEBUILDING AND ETHNIC CONFLICT

Edited by Jessica Senehi, Imani Michelle Scott, Sean Byrne, and Thomas G. Matyók

LONDON AND NEW YORK

Cover image: © Getty Images
First published 2023
by Routledge
4 Park Square, Milton Park, Abingdon, Oxon OX14 4RN

and by Routledge
605 Third Avenue, New York, NY 10158

Routledge is an imprint of the Taylor & Francis Group, an informa business

© 2023 selection and editorial matter, Jessica Senehi, Imani Michelle Scott, Sean Byrne and Thomas G. Matyók; individual chapters, the contributors

The right of Jessica Senehi, Imani Michelle Scott, Sean Byrne and Thomas G. Matyók to be identified as the authors of the editorial material, and of the authors for their individual chapters, has been asserted in accordance with sections 77 and 78 of the Copyright, Designs and Patents Act 1988.

All rights reserved. No part of this book may be reprinted or reproduced or utilised in any form or by any electronic, mechanical, or other means, now known or hereafter invented, including photocopying and recording, or in any information storage or retrieval system, without permission in writing from the publishers.

Trademark notice: Product or corporate names may be trademarks or registered trademarks, and are used only for identification and explanation without intent to infringe.

British Library Cataloguing-in-Publication Data
A catalogue record for this book is available from the British Library

Library of Congress Cataloging-in-Publication Data
Names: Senehi, Jessica, 1959- editor.
Title: Routledge handbook of peacebuilding and ethnic conflict / edited by Jessica Senehi, Imani Michelle Scott, Sean Byrne and Thomas G. Matyók.
Other titles: Handbook of peacebuilding and ethnic conflict
Description: First Edition. | New York : Routledge, 2022. | Includes bibliographical references and index. | Identifiers: LCCN 2021061487 (print) | LCCN 2021061488 (ebook) | ISBN 9780367428037 (Hardback) | ISBN 9781032286433 (Paperback) | ISBN 9781003000686 (eBook)
Subjects: LCSH: Peace-building--Handbooks, manuals, etc. | Ethnic conflict--Handbooks, manuals, etc. | Culture conflict--Handbooks, manuals, etc. | Social conflict--Handbooks, manuals, etc.
Classification: LCC JZ5538 .R686 2022 (print) | LCC JZ5538 (ebook) | DDC 303.6/6--dc23/eng/20220327
LC record available at https://lccn.loc.gov/2021061487
LC ebook record available at https://lccn.loc.gov/2021061488

ISBN: 978-0-367-42803-7 (hbk)
ISBN: 978-1-032-28643-3 (pbk)
ISBN: 978-1-003-00068-6 (ebk)

DOI: 10.4324/9781003000686

Typeset in Bembo
by MPS Limited, Dehradun

We dedicate this volume to our parents and children, and to Senator John Lewis (1940–2020) and Nobel Peace Prize–winner Betty Williams (1943–2020)—for their teachings and inspiration.

CONTENTS

List of illustrations   xi
List of contributors   xii
Acknowledgments   xviii

Introduction: Peacebuilding and ethnic conflict   1
Jessica Senehi, Imani Michelle Scott, Sean Byrne, and Thomas G. Matyók

PART I
Key Dimensions of Ethnic Conflicts   15

1 The roots of ethnopolitical conflict   17
   Stuart J. Kaufman

2 How gender is implicated in ethnopolitical conflict   28
   Franke Wilmer

3 Complex effects of external involvements in ethnopolitical violence   39
   Marie Olson Lounsbery and Frederic S. Pearson

4 Re-examining peacebuilding priorities: Liberal peace and the emancipatory critique   48
   Andrew E. E. Collins and Chuck Thiessen

5 Hatred is a contagious disease and public health issue in ethnopolitical conflicts   59
   Izzeldin Abuelaish

6 The environment and peacebuilding in ethnic conflict 71
Ane Cristina Figueiredo and Calum Dean

7 Deconstructing the relapse of American nationalism 83
Harry Anastasiou and Michaelangelo Anastasiou

8 How does the COVID-19 pandemic influence peacebuilding, diversity management, the handling of ethnic conflict, and ethnic minorities? 94
Mitja Žagar

PART II
Peacebuilders in Ethnic Conflicts 105

9 Indigenous peacemaking and restorative justice 107
Brandon D. Lundy, J. Taylor Downs, and Amanda Reinke

10 Interactive conflict resolution: Addressing the essence of ethnopolitical conflict and peacebuilding 118
Ronald J. Fisher

11 Core dynamics of nonviolent accompaniment and unarmed civilian protection 131
Patrick G. Coy

12 Peace leadership, security, and the role of the military in ethnopolitical conflict 141
Yvan Yenda Ilunga and Thomas G. Matyók

13 Interreligious peacebuilding: An emerging pathway for sustainable peace 151
Mohammed Abu-Nimer

14 The laughter that knows the darkness: The Mamas' resistance to annihilative violence in West Papua 164
Julian Smythe

15 The role of youth in ethnopolitical conflicts 174
Cihan Dizdaroğlu and Alpaslan Özerdem

PART III
Addressing the Past and Shaping the Future   185

16 On peacebuilding and public memory: Iconoclasm, dialogue, and race   187
    Adam Muller

17 When the past is always present: Heritage rights, monuments, and
    cultural divides   198
    Anya B. Russian

18 Voices of their own: Refugees missing home and building a future   209
    Umut Ozkaleli

19 Trauma, recovery, and memory   220
    Joseph Robinson

20 A season of reckoning for the children: Exploring the realities of
    aggregated trauma in the African American community   231
    Imani Michelle Scott

21 Peace after genocide: Exhumations, expectations, and peacebuilding
    efforts in Bosnia and Herzegovina   242
    Hasan Nuhanović and Sarah Wagner

22 A healing-centered peacebuilding approach   252
    Angi Yoder-Maina

PART IV
Approaches and Cases   267

23 Sri Lanka's postwar reconciliation: Reconciling the local and
    international   269
    S. I. Keethaponcalan

24 Emancipatory peacebuilding and conflict transformation: Mindanao as
    a case study   280
    Wendy Kroeker

25 Transformative peace negotiation   292
    SungYong Lee

26 External aid and peacebuilding 304
    Sean Byrne and Calum Dean

27 Bringing the Indigenous into mainstream peacemaking and peace-
    building in farmer-herder conflicts: Some critical reflections 315
    Surulola Eke and Sean Byrne

28 Focal points in ethnic conflicts: A peacebuilding continuum 327
    Jessica Senehi

Conclusions: Peacebuilding and ethnopolitical conflicts revisited 339
Jessica Senehi, Imani Scott, Sean Byrne, and Thomas G. Matyók

Index *355*

ILLUSTRATIONS

Figures

5.1	Hatred conceptual framework: Exposure, impact and determining factors	62
5.2	The relationship between hatred and violence	62
5.3	Exposure to hatred	63
5.4	The hexagon of hatred	64
12.1	Circle of conflict and peace efforts	145
13.1	Mapping the types of engagement with religious agencies in peacebuilding intervention	159
22.1	Systems map: Healing-centered peacebuilding approach	255
22.2	Healing-centered peacebuilding elements and subelements	256

Table

1.1	Ethnopolitical armed conflicts in 2018	20

CONTRIBUTORS

Mohammed Abu-Nimer is a Professor in the School of International Service and Director of the Peacebuilding and Development Institute at American University, Washington, DC. He has conducted interreligious conflict resolution training and interfaith dialogue workshops in conflict areas around the world, including Palestine, Israel, Egypt, Northern Ireland, the Philippines (Mindanao), and Sri Lanka. In addition to his articles and publications, he is the cofounder and coeditor of the *Journal of Peacebuilding and Development*.

Izzeldin Abuelaish, Professor, Dalla Lana School, University of Toronto, is a five-time Nobel Peace Prize nominee. *I Shall Not Hate* was inspired by the loss of his daughters, Bessan, Mayar and Aya, and cousin Noor to Israeli shelling in 2009, and in whose memory he founded *Daughters for Life Foundation*. His awards include 16 honorary doctorates, the Gandhi peace award, The Governor General's Medallion, The Order of Ontario, and the Queen Elizabeth II Diamond Jubilee Medal.

Harry Anastasiou is a Professor of International Peace and Conflict Studies at Portland State University, Oregon. His primary research and practice interest is nationalism and ethnic conflict, postnationalist peacebuilding, and international affairs. His publications include *Practical Approaches to Peacebuilding* (2016), and *The Broken Olive Branch*, Volumes I & II (2008).

Michaelangelo Anastasiou is a sociology instructor at the University of Cyprus. He specializes in political sociology and nationalism studies. His most recent publications examine the relationship between populism, nationalism and democracy. He is currently preparing a monograph that develops a poststructuralist theory of nationalism.

Sean Byrne is a Professor of Peace and Conflict Studies at the University of Manitoba, and its first program head (2005–2014). He was the first director of the Arthur Mauro Centre for Peace and Justice at St. Paul's College (2003–2018). In 2017 and 2018, respectively, he received a university Outreach Award, the Faculty of Graduate Studies award for excellence in graduate student mentoring, and the SPC Memorial Endowment Fund Award.

Contributors

Andrew E. E. Collins is a PhD candidate with the War Studies Department at King's College London, where he conducts research that focuses on local ownership of police reform in conflict-affected societies. He received his MA from the University of Canterbury and has worked for various non-profit organizations in the education sector in both the UK and New Zealand.

Patrick G. Coy Patrick G. Coy is Professor Emeritus at the School of Peace and Conflict Studies, Kent State University. He has published more than 30 peer-reviewed journal articles and chapters, is co-author of *Contesting Patriotism: Culture, Power and Strategy in the Peace Movement,* and has thirteen peer-reviewed, edited books with various publishers.

Calum Dean is a part-time faculty member at the Institute for Interdisciplinary Studies at Carleton University, and a doctoral candidate in Peace and Conflict Studies at the University of Manitoba. His scholarship has been published in *Journal for Peace and Justice* and *Peace Review*. He has been the recipient of a Kanee-Mauro Fellowship, as well as a Joseph Armand Bombardier Scholarship from the Social Sciences and Research Council of Canada.

Cihan Dizdaroğlu is an assistant professor at the Department of Political Science and International Relations at Baskent University and serves as IstanPol-HBS fellow at Istanbul Political Research Institute. He previously served as Marie Skłodowska-Curie Actions (grant no. 796053) fellow at the Centre for Trust, Peace and Social Relations at Coventry University, and as lecturer at the Department of Political Science and Public Administration at Kadir Has University. He holds a PhD in International Relations from Kadir Has University. He served as the Director of the Center for Turkish Studies at Kadir Has University between 2017 and 2018, and as the Project Coordinator to the International Relations Council of Turkey between 2009 and 2018. He also worked as a research associate in the Economic Policy Research Foundation of Turkey|TEPAV, a think-tank based in Ankara, in the Foreign Policy Studies Program between 2006 and 2010.

Jonathan Taylor Downs is a PhD student in International Conflict Management, author of *Guns or Growth: Lessons from Security-First and Civil-Society-First Approaches to Peacebuilding in East Timor* as part of the Peacekeeping and Stability Operations Institute at the U.S. Army War College and TRENDS Global Case Study Series.

Dr. Surulola Eke is a Banting Fellow at Queen's University, Canada. His research straddles international relations and comparative politics. Specifically, Dr. Eke is interested in ethnic conflict analysis, terrorism, and peacebuilding. His current research projects include the spatial variation of autochthonous conflicts and the spatial intensity variation of farmer-herder conflicts.

Ane Cristina Figueiredo is a research coordinator at the Faculty of Social Work, and a doctoral candidate in peace and conflict studies at the University of Manitoba. She is an environmental advocate and a firm believer in the importance of local environmental projects in building cross-cultural understanding and positive peace. Her scholarship has been published in The Palgrave Handbook of Positive Peace, Springer International Publishing, Third World Quarterly, and Journal for Peace and Justice Studies.

Ronald J. Fisher is a Professor Emeritus of International Peace and Conflict Resolution at American University, Washington, DC. His primary research and practice interest is interactive conflict resolution, which involves unofficial third-party interventions in ethnopolitical conflict. His publications include *Interactive Conflict Resolution* (1997) and *Paving the Way* (2005).

Yvan Yenda Ilunga is an international development practitioner and global policy analyst. His research interests include humanitarian action and security, modern violent conflicts, policy modeling, civil-military interaction, natural resources-based conflicts, and political philosophy. He earned his PhD at the Division of Global Affairs, Rutgers University.

Stuart J. Kaufman is a Professor of Political Science and International Relations at the University of Delaware. Most of his research focuses on the causes and management of ethnic conflict. He is the author of *Modern Hatreds* (2001) and *Nationalist Passions* (2015).

S. I. Keethaponcalan is a Professor of Conflict Resolution at Salisbury University, Maryland. He served as Chair of the Conflict Resolution Department between 2011 and 2018. Formerly, he was a Professor of Political Science at the University of Colombo, Sri Lanka. He also served as Head of the Department of Political Science and Public Policy. He has published extensively on Sri Lanka's politics, conflict and peace, as well as conflict resolution theories, and is the author of *Post-war Dilemmas of Sri Lanka: Democracy and Reconciliation* (Routledge, 2019).

Wendy Kroeker is an Associate Professor of Peace and Conflict Transformation Studies at Canadian Mennonite University. She brings academic interest and contextual experience to ideas of everyday peacebuilding with over 20 years of experience as a mediator, facilitator, and peace program consultant. Her work focuses on South/Southeast Asia and Latin America.

SungYong Lee is an Associate Professor at the National Centre for Peace and Conflict Studies, University of Otago. His areas of research expertise include conflict resolution and post-conflict peacebuilding processes in civil war, especially related to post-liberal peacebuilding.

Brandon D. Lundy is a Professor of Anthropology and an Associate Director of the School of Conflict Management, Peacebuilding and Development at Kennesaw State University. He serves as the editor of the journal *Economic Anthropology* and as an Associate Editor for the *Journal of Peacebuilding and Development*. He holds PhDs from the State University of New York–Buffalo and the University of Science and Technology of Lille, France. His work focuses on climate change, sustainable livelihoods, ethnoeconomics, transnational labor migration, and entrepreneurship. He is the co-editor of *Indigenous Conflict Management Strategies*, alongside Akanmu Adebayo and Jesse Benjamin, (Lexington Books, 2014, 2015) and editor of *Teaching Africa: A Guide for the 21st Century Classroom* (Indiana University Press, 2013). His scholarship is published in numerous academic journals. He has served as a country specialist (Guinea-Bissau) for the State Department.

Thomas Matyók is a Senior Lecturer in Political Science and Executive Director of the Joint Civil-Military Interaction Research and Education Network at Middle Georgia State University. His research interests are conflict analysis in complex operations, civil-military interaction, and religion in peace operations.

Adam Muller is the Director of the Peace and Conflict Studies program at the University of Manitoba, Canada. He researches and teaches the visual representation of genocide, suffering, and human rights. He is a former Vice President of the International Association of Genocide Scholars, as well as a Senior Research Fellow with the University of Manitoba's Centre for

Defense and Security Studies and founding member of the University's Centre for Human Rights Research.

Hasan Nuhanović is a PhD student at the School of Global, Urban and Social Studies at the RMIT University in Melbourne, Australia, and graduate researcher on the project "Missing people, missing stories in the aftermath of 'ethnic cleansing' and genocide in Prijedor and Srebrenica," funded by the Australian Research Council. He is also the author of the books *Under the UN Flag: The International Community and the Srebrenica Genocide* (DES 2007), and *The Last Refuge: A True Story of War, Survival and Life under Siege in Srebrenica* (Peter Owen, 2019). He serves as an adviser to the Srebrenica Potočari Memorial Centre and Cemetery for the Victims of the 1995 Genocide and works closely with the survivors' organizations.

Marie Olson Lounsbery is a Professor of Political Science at East Carolina University. Her research examines civil war peace processes, rebel group dynamics, and the impact of intervention on civil wars. Her most recent book is *Conflict Dynamics: Civil Wars, Armed Actors, and Their Tactics* (with Alethia Cook, University of Georgia Press, 2017).

Alpaslan Özerdem is the Dean of the Jimmy and Rosalynn Carter School for Peace and Conflict Resolution, and Professor of Peace and Conflict Studies at George Mason University. He specializes in conflict resolution, peacebuilding and post-conflict reconstruction. He has more than 20 year field research experience in Afghanistan, Bosnia-Herzegovina, El Salvador, Kosovo, Lebanon, Liberia, Nigeria, Philippines, Sierra Leone, Solomon Islands, Somalia, Sri Lanka, Tajikistan and Turkey. He has undertaken numerous research projects that were funded by the UK's Economic and Social Research Council (ESRC) (faith-based conflict prevention), the British Academy (youth and peacebuilding), the U.S. Institute of Peace (reintegration of ex-combatants), and various European Union funding schemes (conflict transformation and leadership). He has published extensively (16 books and numerous journal articles, book chapters, and op-eds), and is co-editor of Comparing Peace Processes, alongside Roger Mac Ginty (Routledge, 2019).

Umut Ozkaleli is an Associate Professor of Public and International Affairs at ADA University. She earned her PhD from the Social Science Department, Syracuse University-Maxwell School. Her publications are related to developing intersectional frameworks for equity in state institutions, gendered agency in democratization, gendered war memories, transborder re-making of social interactions, everyday becoming of refugees and their articulations of agency in the host country. Her articles have appeared in academic journals such as *International Feminist Journal of Politics, Women's Studies International Forum, Journal of Woman, Politics and Policy, Asian Journal of Women's Studies, Social Change,* and *Postcolonial Studies*.

Frederic S. Pearson is the Director of the Center for Peace and Conflict Studies, Professor of Political Science, and Gershenson Distinguished Faculty Fellow at Wayne State University. He was previously professor and research fellow at the University of Missouri–St. Louis and twice a Fulbright scholar in the Netherlands and UK.

Amanda J. Reinke is an Assistant Profess of Conflict Management at Kennesaw State University. She researches how slow, bureaucratic, and everyday violence undermine community peacebuilding and disaster recovery efforts. She has conducted ethnographic and rapid qualitative research in a wide variety of contexts, including: Tennessee on tornado recovery amid COVID-19, post-hurricane Florence North Carolina, on restorative justice in Virginia, post-conflict northern Uganda, and displacement and alternative dispute resolution in the San Francisco Bay Area. She serves as the Secretary-Treasurer for the Southern Anthropological Society and is a registered mediator with the Georgia Office of Dispute Resolution.

Joseph S. Robinson is a final-year postgraduate student in the Department of Geography at Maynooth University. His research sits at the intersection of critical geography, memory studies, and transitional justice, with a special emphasis on Northern Ireland. He is the author of *Transitional Justice and the Politics of Inscription: Memory, Space, and Narrative in Northern Ireland* (Routledge, 2018).

Anya Russian is a graduate student in the joint Peace and Conflict Studies Program at the Universities of Manitoba and Winnipeg in Canada. Her thesis investigates how museums in the southeast U.S. are using digital education to address contemporary issues of racial justice. Other research interests include how creative platforms can promote embodied learning, dialogue, and empathy-building in cross-cultural and identity-based conflicts. She has worked as a cultural immersion specialist with refugees, a museum content developer, a language educator, editor, translator (English/Spanish), and performing artist in dance and theater).

Through her custom-designed *Peace Begins with Truth^{TM} Workshops*, **Dr. Imani Michelle Scott** works diligently to facilitate training related to (1) appreciating the inherent values in diversity, equity, and inclusion; (2) addressing the consequences of racial conflict, oppression and violence, and (3) moving beyond racism towards reconciliation, healing and social transformation. She has also conducted research and presentations on the topics of implicit racism, unconscious bias, domestic violence, school violence and dispiriting violence related to terrorism. Scott holds a PhD in Conflict Analysis and Resolution from Nova Southeastern University. In addition to having published in numerous scholarly journals and peer-reviewed books, she is the editor of and contributing author to *Crimes against Humanity in the Land of the Free: Can a Truth and Reconciliation Process Heal Racial Conflict in the United States?* (2014), and co-editor and contributing author to the *Routledge Companion to Peace and Conflict Studies* (2019). An award-winning writer, she is also a former contributor to the *Huffington Post*, and currently sits on the Editorial Board for the *Peace Review* and *Storytelling, Self and Society* Journals.

Jessica Senehi is a Professor of Peace and Conflict at the University of Manitoba. She is co-editor of *Storytelling, Self, Society: An Interdisciplinary Journal of Storytelling Studies*. She is the founding director of the Winnipeg International Storytelling: Storytelling on the Path to Peace/*Festival international du conte: Se raconter une nouvelle histoire de paix*. Her scholarly work focuses on the role of storytelling in peacebuilding, culture, gender, and young people affected by violence.

Dr. Julian Smythe is a peace scholar, educator, and practitioner. Dr. Smythe's work focuses on peacebuilding, creativity, and West Papua.

Chuck Thiessen is an Associate Professor in the Centre for Trust, Peace, and Social Relations at Coventry University. He is currently researching international peacebuilding, the prevention of violent extremism, and conflict resolution, with a special focus on Central Asia, Afghanistan, and the Sahel.

Contributors

Sarah Wagner is a Professor of Anthropology at George Washington University. She is the author of *To Know Where He Lies: DNA Technology and the Search for Srebrenica's Missing* (University of California Press, 2008) and co-author with Lara J. Nettelfield of *Srebrenica in the Aftermath of Genocide* (Cambridge University Press, 2014). With research funded by the National Science Foundation and the National Institutes of Health, she has published numerous articles and book chapters on the subjects of war and memory, missing persons, and forensic science applied in post-conflict societies. In 2017, she was awarded a John Simon Guggenheim Fellowship and a National Endowment of the Humanities Public Scholar Award to complete her third book, *What Remains: Bringing America's Missing Home from the Vietnam War* (Harvard University Press, 2019), which won the 2020 Victor Turner Prize for Ethnographic Writing.

Franke Wilmer is a Professor of Political Science and former Department Head at Montana State University, former Chair of the Montana Human Rights Commission, and served four terms as a legislator in the Montana State legislature. Her most recent book is *Breaking Cycles of Violence in Israel and Palestine* (Lexington, 2021).

Angi Yoder-Maina, PhD is the Executive Director of the Green String Network (GSN) based in Nairobi, Kenya. GSN's programs create opportunities for people at the most local level to learn about the effects of trauma, begin to heal and come together as a community to plan community-wide activities and structures supporting social healing. Formally Angi worked for the United States Agency for International Development (USAID) in Somalia, South Sudan and Liberia on stabilization programming. Angi holds a BA in Peace Studies and Political Science from Manchester University, and an MA in Public and Social Policy with a concentration of Conflict Resolution and Peace Studies from Duquesne University. Angi recently completed her doctoral studies in Applied Conflict Transformation Studies at the Centre for Peace and Conflict Studies in Siem Reap, Cambodia. Her dissertation was entitled: *Healing-Centered Peacebuilding: A Grounded Theory using a Trauma-Informed Lens*.

Mitja Žagar is a Research Councilor at the Institute for Ethnic Studies and a Full Professor at universities in Slovenia and abroad, and was previously a member of the Scientific Council of the Slovenian Research Agency (2015–2020). His research interests include human rights, the protection of minorities, international and comparative constitutional law, comparative politics, transformation, transition, and diversity management.

ACKNOWLEDGMENTS

We gratefully acknowledge the support and participation of all the contributors to this handbook who took the time to write meaningful and significant chapters. We also acknowledge support of colleagues, students, staff, and infrastructural support from the Arthur V. Mauro Institute for Peace and Justice at St. Paul's College, and the PhD and MA programs in Peace and Conflict Studies at the University of Manitoba, the School of Liberal Arts at Savannah College of Art and Design, and the Joint Civil-Military Interaction Research and Education Network at Middle Georgia State University. We also gratefully acknowledge Routledge's Senior Editor Andrew Humphrys for his guidance and support.

INTRODUCTION: PEACEBUILDING AND ETHNIC CONFLICT

Jessica Senehi, Imani Michelle Scott, Sean Byrne, and Thomas G. Matyók

The perpetual reemergence of violence associated with protracted ethnic conflicts amid an increasingly polarized global milieu presents today's peace scholars with a sense of urgency to identify and propose enhanced approaches to peacebuilding. Joined with an unprecedented complexity of factors, including widespread fears introduced by the worldwide COVID-19 pandemic, pervasive hatreds fueled by virulent ethnonationalist movements, and prevalent concerns related to unrelenting environmental catastrophes caused by climate change, the consequences of sustained, global ethnic violence challenge all preconceived theories associated with peacebuilding. As a result, this volume has been crafted to analyze specific, contemporary challenges to Peace and Conflict Studies (PACS) by surveying the intersection of ethnic conflict and social justice through a series of peacebuilding lenses intended to support resolutions and transformation. Our goals are to (1) yield a better understanding of the root causes and ongoing stimulants for various protracted ethnic conflicts; (2) explore conventional and, in some cases, lesser-known theories for examining local agency in peacebuilding opportunities; and (3) offer fresh approaches to analyzing, intervening in, and preventing these conflicts around the world.

Since local actors often play a contentious role in perpetuating inequalities and injustices, this angle for exploring ethnic conflict has become a growing research concern and begs greater considerations of the local fabric in peacebuilding processes. Therefore, this book is one way of encouraging peacebuilding research and praxis communities to bear in mind how factors—ranging from democratization, globalization, identity politics, regime survival, structural inequalities, and the transgenerational transmission of trauma, intersect with local agency as sources and consequences of ethnic conflicts (Crocker et al., 2007; McGarry & O'Leary, 2004). Intersectionality gets at the core of conflict cleavages to include community voices that acknowledge differences to create a collaborative synergy of action; ultimately, this produces new insights including each group's strategy in a balanced intervention strategy (Chinn, 2012). Intersectionality can also provide an inclusive and plural solidarity based on cross-group collaborations. Sometimes the complexity and intersectionality of identities is exploited by those in power as a "divide and conquer" strategy; equally, when someone has loyalty to multiple social justice movements (e.g., feminism, anti-racism, and/or LGBTQ rights), one movement may be leveraged over the other.

Background

As an ongoing legacy of colonialism, ethnic chauvinist leaders repeatedly led virulent ethnonationalist movements within segmented cultural milieus to manufacture boundaries among ethnic groups and intensify polarization, competition, and violence (Anastasiou 2008; Ross, 2007; Sandole, 2003). Thus, complex and unique ethnic conflicts have leaned toward universal rather than local peacebuilding approaches, practices, and techniques as third parties are often biased as they expand their interests (Byrne, 2017; Mac Ginty, 2008). For example, "external ethno-guarantors" (Byrne, 2007) or regional third-party intermediaries like India and Pakistan play out their conflict in Kashmir, where local people's human rights are violated and external intervenors exacerbate the power asymmetry in ethnic conflicts to focus on their own interests (Bose, 2010).

Empirical studies in ethnic conflict and peacebuilding have burgeoned over the recent past to produce scholarship which is detailed in terms of conflict indicators and dimensions in specific contexts (Carter et al., 2008; Gurr, 2015; Kaufmann, 2001). The qualitative research has included specific ethnic conflict case studies, and the quantitative studies have delineated interesting patterns across numerous cases (Olson Lounsberry & Pearson, 2009). Primordialists contend that ethnic group members regularly share biological, cultural, and identity ties to a kinfolk, and a particular territory as hatred and fear of domination leads to protracted ethnic conflicts (Nasong'o, 2015). In contrast, constructionists highlight that the media and modernity were used by political elites to imagine, and culturally and socially construct, fraternal nations using ethnic identity that people are intrinsically connected to (Anderson, 2016; Smith, 2013).

The social construction of race as a global political hegemonic tool to enforce division, friction, and violence is also powerful in fueling interethnic, intercommunal, or bicommunal conflict (Björkdahl et al., 2016; Horowitz, 2000). In addition, instrumentalists report that ethnic leaders time and again use ethnic identity as a tool to mobilize their constituents to access power and resources, while denying other ethnic groups entrée as competition, inequality, and security issues drive ethnic conflict (Taras & Ganguly, 2009; Wolff, 2006). As a result, frustrations and grievances as well as ethnic identity often escalate ethnic conflict (Coakley, 2012). Chosen glories and chosen traumas are invoked in the transgenerational transmission of trauma spurring on ethnic groups to avenge the past (Volkan, 1997).

Gender also frames and constructs ethnic conflict as patriarchy reinforces oppressive structures and socially constructs gender that includes male patriots and their valued experiences and courage while excluding women from active war making and peacebuilding processes as they are objectified and killed in rape-warfare milieus, and are often treated as less than in the overall conflict and peacebuilding processes (Leatherman, 2011; Wilmer 2002).

Heteronormativity, hypermasculinity, and homonationalism reinforces ethnopolitical identities and masculinist behaviors, codes, practices, and values that are prioritized while marginalized communities like women, LGBTTQ2+, youth, people living with disabilities, the poor, and ex-combatants are ignored, bullied, and excluded so that using a queer lens could remove borders, focus on plurality, and reject the positive-negative peace binary (Byrne et al., 2018; Mizzi & Byrne, 2015; Mizzi & Walton, 2014). National state policies and practices are heteronormative and individuals, groups, and organizations are "homonationalist" so that queer persons are often estranged and detached from states (Puar, 2007).

Democracy and democratic institutions are also under attack by the rejuvenation of alt right, racist, and populist ultra nationalist ideologies coupled with global inequality and militarism that are creating the conditions for minority groups, framed and treated as adversaries, to be decimated by the state in a process that Achille Mbembe (2019) calls "necropolitics" as the state decides who lives and who dies among marginalized groups. Moreover, certain groups are unduly exposed to death and violence as a result of discursive and structural power asymmetries or "precarity vulnerability" that is intensified by class, gender, nationality, and race (McLean, 2019). For example, violence directed against racialized and queer individuals include micro-macro linkages as destructive hate crimes are a form of "ethnoviolence" (e.g., Byrne & Senehi, 2012). Ethnic conflicts and intrastate wars are also influenced by globalization as well as regional and global actors as the current Russo-Ukrainian war has expanded beyond an intrastate violent conflict.

It is challenging to create peace in societies with deep polarizing social cleavages and divisions where the fear of violence shapes community's attitudes and behavior with "representative violence and communal deterrence" entrenching deep divisions in societies trying to transition to peace through ethnic elite accommodation and powersharing governments (Guelke, 2006, 2012). The scholarship on peacebuilding and interventions in ethnic conflicts has proliferated (Darby, 2006). The international community has rediscovered the local, ofttimes proposing, instead a peacebuilding model linking international actors, and the local indigenous wisdom and peacebuilding processes of everyday people that could empower local communities (Donais, 2012; Paffenholz, 2015). Hybrid peacebuilding maintains, however, a power asymmetry as the knowledge and resources remain with the external actors (Mac Ginty, 2011; Richmond, 2016). Thus, the dysfunctions of international peacebuilding efforts can be found in the habits, practices, and stories of expatriates working in a myriad of international agencies and nongovernmental organizations (Autesserre, 2014). Ethnic conflict is a critical area to study, and it is an urgent area of concern throughout the world.

About this book

This volume explores the extent to which peacebuilding is tied to locally cultivated peacemaking as a critical message for people to consider—especially in light of the changing world order and its global security implications. This work also calls for building inclusive social justice frames into peace processes as a necessary step toward sustainable peace agreements (Byrne & Thiessen, 2019). For those in PACS, this book serves as a reference for both undergraduate and graduate students in the areas of peacebuilding, ethnic conflict, and culture. For those in professional settings, this book offers practitioners an in-depth understanding of various types of ethnic conflicts and unique ways in which theories and praxis have been and might be used to resolve and transform those conflicts. And for those in interdisciplinary studies and across global communities, this book weaves together a plethora of insights to share lessons and wisdom from those whose voices represent a spectrum of generational, cultural, educational, and social threads.

To achieve these objectives, the book is divided into four parts: key dimensions in ethnic conflicts; participation in ethnic peacebuilding; creatively dealing with the past, and social change; and specific approaches and cases. Within each part, chapters have been carefully crafted to share unique insights and relay critical information by presenting: contextual and theoretical background, key findings and insights, implications for teaching and training, and implications for practice and policy. Our hope is that this text will serve as a long-term relevant resource to those in educational, training, practice, and policy arenas.

Conceptual focus and organization of the volume

This book uses an interdisciplinary PACS approach to advance theoretical, practice, and policy contributions to peacebuilding. The following four parts outline the purpose, importance, and goals of each chapter.

Part 1: Key dimensions of ethnic conflicts

The complex dynamics of internal and external issues come into play in analyzing the deep roots of protracted ethnopolitical conflicts as a myriad of grassroots peacebuilding agents and international actors actively work across difference to strive for social change and social justice.

In Chapter 1, Stuart J. Kaufman explores the complex roots of ethnic conflicts. Social mobilization theory and symbolic politics theory provide ways for bringing these considerations together to help explain ethnopolitical cooperation, contention, and war. Discussion encompasses the following topics:

- Countries' ethnic cultural diversity is usually benign, yet it sometimes leads to conflict, violence, or even civil war. Such conflicts stem in part from hostile historical memories or group narratives, which may teach people to define another group as an enemy, leading to prejudiced attitudes and group conflict.
- Poverty, state weakness, and the political exclusion of some groups increase the likelihood of armed conflict.
- Leaders and organizations also play an important role, mobilizing their followers either for intergroup cooperation or for conflict, depending on their own values and on political pressures from followers.

In Chapter 2, Franke Wilmer reflects on how gender is implicated in ethnopolitical conflicts. She addresses the empirical evidence that answers three questions of feminist scholarship to ethnopolitical conflicts:

- Where are the women in ethnopolitical conflicts and what are they doing?
- How does the power structure gender relations in ethnopolitical conflicts?
- What does gender theory have to tell us about ethnopolitical conflict?

In Chapter 3, Marie Olson Lounsbery and Frederic S. Pearson address the complex effects of external involvements in ethnopolitical violence. They examine the processes which internationalize ethnopolitical wars, and the results of those external involvements in terms of conflict escalation and de-escalation. The analysis is based on data from the Uppsala Conflict Data Program on 112 armed conflicts occurring between 1989 and 2006, of which 83 (74 percent) are identified as "ethnopolitical."

- The 83 ethnopolitical conflicts attracted outside diplomatic, military, or economic involvement and experienced ceasefires or peace agreements, with mediation as the most effective device.
- Military interventions supported ethnic insurgents, though controversial politically and legally, also tended to facilitate agreements.
- Economic sanctions had less peacemaking success.
- External military interventions came in the most deadly and destructive cases, and that simultaneous multiple outside interventions tended to worsen peace prospects. Important policy and educational deductions can be drawn from these findings.

In Chapter 4, Andrew E. E. Collins and Chuck Thiessen speak to the need for reexamining peacebuilding priorities. The authors argue that liberal peacebuilding as an internationalized political project with wide-ranging objectives has attracted a vigorous critique that revolves

Introduction

around local ownership, and that local populations do not always aspire to build liberal societies in the aftermath of ethnopolitical conflict. They find that:

- Dominant practices within the international donor community privilege externally defined priorities above local population values and modalities of interaction, and peacebuilding activities have often failed to go beyond the superficial level to create sustainable change.
- Critical and emancipatory peacebuilding gives rise to an emergent creativity and everyday experience that plays a role in shaping teaching and training activities, along with policy building within international institutions.
- Best practices hold the potential for increasing everyday emancipation, albeit under continued international influence.

In Chapter 5, Izzeldin Abuelaish explores hatred as a contagious disease, a public health issue, and a determinant of health in ethnopolitical conflicts, and examines the prevalence of racism, discrimination, injustice, incitement, and violent civil-military conflicts across the globe that are often fueled by hatred. He finds that:

- Hatred is a contagious disease, public health issue, and a determinant of health that engenders widespread physical, psychological, or political violence.
- Hatred disturbs the homeostasis and emotional equilibrium of an individual or group leading to physical, psychological, social, and behavioral changes.
- Hatred is a pressing public health issue that should be taken seriously by the medical community, the public, and governments.
- Hatred is an intense destructive attitude whose manifestations are war, violence, and a disease that compromise the health, welfare, and functioning of human beings.
- The global community must recognize hatred as a public health issue to move from the management of hatred to the active prevention of its root causes through education and awareness.

In Chapter 6, Ane Cristina Figueiredo and Calum Dean articulate the importance of deconstructing the relapse of American nationalism. They examine how the real and perceived security threat is implicated in the recent rise of U.S. nationalism. In particular, they elaborate on the following key points:

- While the environment is a cause of conflict, it also provides a context for cooperation between ethnic groups acting as a catalyst for peacebuilding.
- The importance for educators, practitioners, and policymakers to include a consideration of emancipatory peacebuilding, environmental conflict, and critical environmental justice in their initiatives.
- The need for a critical theoretical framework that fits the environment into peacebuilding agendas is imperative since it provides potential peacebuilding opportunities through locally led environmental initiatives focused on social justice and cooperation.

In Chapter 7, Harry Anastasiou and Michaelangelo Anastasiou reference how the environment is deeply connected to peacebuilding in ethnic conflict. They examine the role of the environment in causing ethnic conflict and its relation to peacebuilding, bringing together several analytical lenses to understand the factors underlying ethnic cleavages. In particular, they note:

- Historical realities and general perceptions about the security threat have evolved in recent decades, by identifying the principal factors that contributed to its amplification: the dynamics between terrorism and the U.S. government's counterterrorist wars, the exacerbation of militant and religious nationalism, the persistent gun culture, and the successful political mobilization of the radical right.
- The politicization of security is intimately associated with the consolidation of extreme nationalism that has enabled engulfing political tendencies.

In Chapter 8, Mitja Žagar explores how the COVID-19 pandemic has influenced peacebuilding, diversity management, and ethnic minorities. He argues that, often underestimating the problem, the authorities, state, public institutions, states and their (sub)systems, international community, and organizations have been ill-prepared to deal with such crises. To explore this, he examines different responses in Slovenia and some selected countries during the first wave of the pandemic:

- The characteristics, impacts, and results in the management of the first wave of the COVID-19 pandemic are reviewed.
- Special attention is paid to the situation of ethnic minorities and ethnic relations in different environments.
- Lessons can be learned for developing successful diversity management, particularly in improving minority rights and protection, inclusion and integration of minorities and persons belonging to them.

Part 2: Peacebuilders in ethnic conflict

People differently positioned in society due to their professional role or their experiences as a member of a particular community have a unique position in society. The work of peacebuilding in interethnic conflicts requires intervention by diverse agents at many levels and in many sectors of the society.

In Chapter 9, Brandon Lundy, J. Taylor Downs, and Amanda Reinke discuss how restorative justice (RJ) and indigenous peacemaking share many similarities in practice. The authors call for:

- A paradigm shift in thinking regarding the localization of peace
- Recognition of the complexities of indigeneity
- Practitioners and policymakers to move "beyond essentialist notions of romantic authenticity"

In Chapter 10, Ronald J. Fisher discusses how interactive conflict resolution encompasses a variety of small-group methods for engaging informal representatives of conflicting groups or states in dialogue, shared analysis, and joint problem-solving facilitated by an impartial third party. He notes:

- The theory and research base of ICR can be taught in graduate level third-party intervention courses, complemented with experiential exercises.
- Professional training can be provided through interactive workshops, as illustrated by a successful multi-university consortium training program.

- Implications for practice and policy include a need to adapt to the widening context of peace work, the importance of continually improving practice, and the challenge to increase policy receptivity and influence.

In Chapter 11, Patrick G. Coy addresses the necessity of protecting civilians from the violence that occurs during wars, domestic insurgencies, civil unrest, and states of emergency when civil rights are suspended and often violated by police, military, and paramilitary. This is a task increasingly taken up by civil society organizations (CSOs). Key points include:

- The protection of civilians is increasingly being done in a nonviolent fashion through the deployment of trained, unarmed civilian peacekeepers who utilize a variety of mechanisms to protect and preserve the human rights, civil liberties, and lives of other civilians under threat in conflict situations.
- Practices of unarmed civilian protection (UCP) in repressive settings over the past 40 years, and eight characteristics of UCP that are widely embraced across the field's organizations are delineated and explained.
- The evolution of UCP training is addressed and the field's rich potential for teaching and training in a variety of courses across multiple disciplines is highlighted.

In Chapter 12, Yvan Ilunga and Thomas G. Matyók address the peace leadership and the role of the military in ethnopolitical confrontations and conflicts. They note:

- The future of peace operations is dependent on how national and international security threats are managed by the civil-military community.
- Peacekeepers should be seen as providers and consumers of security.
- Peace operations need to be carried out at policy levels as well as at strategic, operational, and tactical military levels.

In Chapter 13, Mohammed Abu-Nimer discusses the current theoretical assumptions underlining the practices of interreligious peacebuilding and the role of interreligious peacebuilding in responding to policies related to violent extremism, and explores the relevancy of interreligious peacebuilding in conflict areas in the Northern Hemisphere. He addresses the following key questions:

- What are the main components of interreligious peacebuilding?
- What is the role of interreligious peacebuilding in responding to violent extremism?
- What are the challenges faced in the field of interreligious peacebuilding?

In Chapter 14, Julian Smythe discusses the ways in which totalitarian systems engage in the annihilation of competing discourses, resulting in the destruction of people's culture and identity. Smythe discusses how women of Indonesia's innermost province of West Papua respond, resist, and survive. For example:

- Naming, honoring, and storying together the grief and violence they experience
- Finding space for togetherness in mourning and life-affirming celebration
- The hard work of striving through suffering, supporting others, preparedness, and action

In Chapter 15, Alpaslan Özerdem and Cihan Dizdaraǧlu examine the agency of youth in ethnopolitical conflicts. A discussion of the contested concept of youth is provided. The authors highlight:

- The role of youth in peacebuilding is defined by whether or not youth are perceived as a "problem" or a "potential."
- Ignoring and underutilizing young people's contributions to peacebuilding is a lost opportunity for peacebuilding.
- If youth can be recognized with equal members of the society, they can contribute meaningfully and powerfully to peacebuilding and positive social change.

Part 3: Addressing the past and shaping the future

Building on the capacity for human ingenuity to envision, design, and implement creative approaches to advance critical and emancipatory peacebuilding, this part highlights a series of varied, yet impactful global initiatives as retorts to ethnic conflict, expressions of resistance to oppression, and boosts to agency and group resilience.

In Chapter 16, Adam Muller considers how acts of protests carried out through the destruction of symbols and images which represent values and beliefs held in esteem by the elites and their institutions are more than mere expressions of anger and outrage, and instead are a type of nonverbal messaging related to group trauma. In particular:

- Peacebuilders might reimagine what would otherwise be negatively conceived of as "public vandalism" to represent a necessary expression of voice from the otherwise voiceless, powerless, and traumatized among us.
- While iconoclasmic protests may have legitimacy as a type of crying out for relief from distress and suffering, it remains incumbent upon peacebuilders to employ variations of facilitated dialogue to support the resolution of conflict between groups as a critical strategy for repair.

In Chapter 17, Anya B. Russian discusses the role of heritage rights and monuments in cultural divides in the United States. She proposes:

- The transformation of public spaces to accurately reflect historical truths is as necessary for the realization of social justice and equity as are the laws and policies of the land.
- Such historical accuracy validates the roles that spatial integrity, access, and design might offer in strategic peacebuilding techniques.
- Communities can build trust, authenticate education, and inspire healing through the strategic utilization of collective spaces.

In Chapter 18, Umut Ozkaleli shares research which offers unique and specific insights into the various ways of interpreting the concept of *home*, especially as it pertains to the experiences of a group of Syrian refugees in Turkey in 2016. In particular she explores:

- The intensely complex and contradictory ways in which place and space are characterized by the refugees, whose depictions of home are replete with paradoxes, irony, lure, and loathing.
- Peacebuilders will have a stronger understanding of the psychological complexities linked to human understandings of safety, security, and belonging, and the risks individuals are willing to take to secure them all.

Introduction

In Chapter 19, Joseph Robinson explores crucial debates on key concepts surrounding the trajectory of trauma studies and its links to peacebuilding. He highlights:

- Emergent theories related to the political elite's use of spatial relationships and realities to produce and reproduce violence in marginalized and disenfranchised communities.
- The use of geo-politics as an elitist tool of violence from the Holocaust-era to the present-day trauma-inducing violations waged against minoritized and vulnerabilized groups.
- Insight into strategic ways that space informs the political and, ultimately, social imposition of trauma and suffering on the oppressed.

In Chapter 20, Imani Michelle Scott focuses on the long-term consequences to black children who grow up in systemically racist societies and under the weight of "living while black." Key points include:

- While subjection to racism has always been consequential to the growth and development of black children in the United States, Scott proposes that such exposure is an especially harsh reality for children living in today's highly mediated milieu where children as young as four years old can be exposed to racialized violence through visual platforms.
- Community engagement workshops and programs are developing ways to contradict the consequences of childhood exposure to racism through collective empowerment and resilience-building strategies.

In Chapter 21, Sara Wagner and Hasan Nuhanović explore the complexities associated with communal mourning as reflections of group trauma emerging from the consequences of massive and lethal state violence, in the context of Bosnia. They emphasize:

- Communal mourning is key to peacebuilding since the role of the state in perpetuating any trauma—let alone a calculated type of aggression that ends in the violent demise of our loved ones and neighbors, is one of the most perplexing and tragic realities for communities to comprehend.
- Guidance for peacebuilders in reconciling communal mourning processes with the needs for social repair, reconciliation, and healing.

In Chapter 22, Angi Yoder explores how violence and distrust work together to produce unhealthy communities, and ultimately deplete the health, resilience, and capacity of larger social structures. In many parts of the world, entire generations and nations live in chronic violence and have existed in survival mode for decades. Based on a grounded theory methodological study, the author introduces the new, healing-centered peacebuilding approach to address the mental distress among peacebuilders dealing with long-term exposure to violence and trauma. In particular:

- Yoder's work confirms ways in which the unhealthy, traumatized agency transforms into the unhealthy, fractured community: an ominous cycle which proves detrimental to the well-being of larger social structure for generations on end.
- A key takeaway is Yoder's introduction of a "healing centered" approach to peacebuilding that moves beyond traditional models of mental health and psychosocial support to a healing-centered model which can be adapted by agents, communities, and the larger society.

Part 4: Approaches and cases

The chapters in Part 4 provide specific case studies and approaches to interethnic peacebuilding.

In Chapter 23, S. I. Keethaponcalan analyzes Sri Lanka's postwar reconciliation. In particular, he focuses on a disjuncture between conceptions of reconciliation at the local and international levels. He emphasizes:

- As a result of this disjunction, international actors and institutions made fundamental errors in their reconciliation strategy in Sri Lanka.
- Reconciliation requires a resolution of the conflict between ethnic groups, and simply the cessation of war where one side forces a military victory does not end the underlying conflicts and address the relationship between communities.

In Chapter 24, Wendy Kroeker examines the emancipatory peacebuilding approaches toward social justice in the context of the peace process in Mindanao, Philippines. Based on in-depth interviews and ethnographic research, she finds:

- The backdrop of the peace process holds a deeply held belief that it is in the spaces of locally based, committed conversation that persons and communities will be transformed.
- In Mindanao, peacebuilders, relentlessly push at the edges of a simple binary of "bottom-up" or "top down" peacebuilding.
- Peacebuilding goals are both proximate and global, examining the everyday grassroots peace opportunities within the foundational social processes and conceptions of peace.

In Chapter 25, SungYong Lee seeks to understand transformative peace negotiations at the national level in the context of Asia. Toward this end, he examines two sets of national peace negotiations undertaken in Aceh, Indonesia, and Bougainville, Papua New Guinea. In particular, he identifies and analyzes:

- The promotion of an inclusive process, involving meaningful participation of CSOs in Aceh.
- Culturally reflective third-party mediation in Bougainville that adopted a non-conventional process, that is, non-Western formats of negotiation.

In Chapter 26, Sean Byrne and Calum Dean critically explore external aid as a key component of liberal peacebuilding and state-building practices from the International Fund for Ireland and the European Union's Peace and Reconciliation Fund, which support 5,800 uni-identity and cross-communal CSOs tacking social exclusion, sectarianism, economic deprivation, and polarization. Based on a study with 120 semistructured interviews with organizational leaders, development officers, and civil servants with the IFI and the EU Peace 3 Fund, they found:

- Civil society organization leaders need resources to continue their peacebuilding work as Northern Ireland continues to remain a high segregated society.
- A legacy of British colonialism created a dependent culture and, as a result of internalized oppression many people lack the agency to be entrepreneurial.
- As funding resources dwindle, a culture of competition is sowed among the peacebuilding CSOs.
- Funding for CSOs has undermined the voluntary sector, which has weakened and voluntary workers felt stifled by the requirements of a top-heaving funding bureaucracy.

In Chapter 27, Surulola Eke and Sean Byrne discuss bringing indigenous approaches into mainstream peacebuilding. Concepts are illustrated with data from ethnographic research on the herder-farmer conflict in Nigeria is included. For example,

- Women draw on networking and ritual for peacebuilding and conflict prevention.
- The arts serve as a vehicle for transcultural storytelling.
- Local elders find way to understand underlying needs and address them.

In Chapter 28, Jessica Senehi integrates ideas about peacebuilding to propose a peacebuilding continuum to provide perspective on the multiplicity of approaches that may be used at multiple levels and in different sectors in a single intercommunal conflict. This is significant for both peacebuilders, peacebuilding knowledge, and the field:

- To identify projects or process that might be further evaluated, replicated, and/or scaled up.
- To help clarify connections between personal and political change, and between local efforts and societal impact.
- To balance reconciliation with justice and accountability.

Conclusion

Developing a critical and emancipatory peacebuilding framework on ethnic conflict is an important approach to comprehending core issues and are highly meaningful in terms of theory building, practice, and policymaking (Lee & Özerdem, 2015). This synergistic approach is essential toward exploring peacebuilding within an ethnic conflict context that includes adaptability, local agency, minority voices, resilience, and resistance to dominant discourses and powerful actors (de Coning, 2018). It is vital to integrate the agency of a myriad of actors absorbed in conflicts, ranging from grassroots to political elites to global actors (Özerdem & Mac Ginty, 2019). It also assists in our understanding of local cultural everyday peacebuilding practices in protracted ethnic conflicts that empower local practitioners and policymakers to furnish inclusive processes (Millar, 2014). Eliciting policy ideas from local grassroots actors with regards to peacebuilding practice plus local wisdom provide important insight regarding the dynamics and the roots causes of ethnic conflict (e.g., patriarchy, poverty) that are sensitive and receptive to local needs (Lederach, 2010; Özerdem, 2014). Addressing the gap between the causes and ramifications of ethnic conflicts as well as powerful state's conflict management processes typically ignore structural causes in contrast to critical and emancipatory peacebuilding approaches that aim to transform relationships, structures, and policies that promote equality and social justice, and empower local people (Thiessen, 2011). Exploring the role of different critical and emancipatory peacebuilding frameworks (e.g., the arts, civil society, economic aid, indigenous practices, nonviolent activism, reconciliation, etc.) is pivotal to enhancing analytical and practical peacebuilding skills.

References

Anastasiou, H. (2008). *The broken olive branch: Nationalism, ethnic conflict, and the quest for peace in Cyprus: The impasse of ethnonationalism*. Syracuse University Press.
Anderson, B. (2016). *Imagined communities: Reflections on the origins and spread of nationalism*. Verso.
Autesserre, S. (2014). *Peaceland: Conflict resolution and the everyday politics of international intervention*. Cambridge University Press.

Björkdahl, A., Höglund, K., Millar, G., Vanderlijn, J., & Verkoren, W. (Eds.). (2016). *Peacebuilding and friction: Global and local encounters in post conflict societies.* Routledge.

Bose, S. (2010). *Contested lands: Israel-Palestine, Kashmir, Bosnia, Cyprus and Sri Lanka.* Harvard University Press.

Byrne, S. (2007). Mired in intractability: The roles of external ethno-guarantors and primary mediators in Cyprus and Northern Ireland. *Conflict Resolution Quarterly, 24*(2), 149–172.

Byrne, S. (2017). International mediation: Some observations and reflections. In A. Georgakopoulos (Ed.), *The mediation handbook: Research, theory and practice* (pp. 336–343). Routledge.

Byrne, S., Mizzi, R., & Hansen, N. (2018). Living in a liminal peace: Where is the social justice for LGBTQ and disability communities living in post peace accord Northern Ireland? *Journal for Peace and Justice Studies, 27*(1), 24–52.

Byrne, S., & Senehi, J. (2012). *Violence: Analysis, intervention and prevention.* Ohio University Press.

Byrne, S., & Thiessen, C. (2019). Foreign peacebuilding intervention and emancipatory local agency for social justice. In S. Byrne, T. Matyók, I. M. Scott, & J. Senehi (Eds.), *Routledge companion to peace and conflict studies* (pp. 131–142). Routledge.

Carter, J., Irani, G., & Volkan, V. (Eds.). (2008). *Regional and ethnic conflicts: Perspectives from the front lines.* Pearson/Prentice Hall.

Chinn, P. (2012). *Peace and power: New directions for building community.* Jones & Bartlett Learning.

Coakley, J. (2012). *Nationalism, ethnicity and the state.* SAGE.

Crocker, C., Osler Hampson, F., & Aall, P. (Eds.). (2007). *Leashing the dogs of war: Conflict management in a divided world.* United States Institute of Peace Press.

Darby, J. (2006). *Violence and reconstruction.* University of Notre Dame Press.

de Coning, C. (2018). Adaptive peacebuilding. *International Affairs, 94*(2), 301–317.

Donais, T. (2012). *Peacebuilding and local ownership: Post conflict consensus building.* Routledge.

Guelke, A. (2006). *Terrorism and global disorder.* I. B. Tauras.

Guelke, A. (2012). *Politics in deeply divided societies.* Polity.

Gurr, T. R. (2015). *Political rebellion: Causes, outcomes and alternatives.* Routledge.

Horowitz, D. L. (2000). *Ethnic groups in conflict.* University of California Press.

Kaufmann, S. J. (2001). *Modern hatreds: The symbolic politics of ethnic war.* Cornell University Press.

Leatherman, J. (2011). *Sexual violence and armed conflict.* Polity Press.

Lederach, J. P. (2010). *The moral imagination: The art and soul of building peace.* Oxford University Press.

Lee, S., & Özerdem, A. (2015). *Local ownership in international peacebuilding: Key theoretical and practical issues.* Routledge.

Mac Ginty, R. (2008). *No war, no peace: The rejuvenation of stalled peace processes and peace accords.* Palgrave Macmillan.

Mac Ginty, R. (2011). *International peacebuilding and local resistance: Hybrid forms of peace.* Palgrave Macmillan.

Mbembe, A. (2019). *Necropolitics.* Duke University Press.

McGarry, J., & O'Leary, B. (2004). *The Northern Ireland conflict: Consociational engagements.* Oxford University Press.

McLean, L. (2019). Protesting vulnerability and vulnerability as protest: Gender, migration, and strategies of resistance. In S. Byrne, T. Matyók, I. M. Scott, & J. Senehi (Eds.), *Routledge companion to peace and conflict studies* (pp. 178–188). Routledge.

Millar, G. (2014). *An ethnographic approach to peacebuilding: Understanding local experiences in transitional states.* Routledge.

Mizzi, R., & Byrne, S. (2015). Queer theory and peace and conflict studies: Some critical reflections. In M. Flaherty, S. Byrne, T. Matyok, & H. Tuso (Eds.), *Gender and peacebuilding: All hands required* (pp. 359–374). Lexington Press.

Mizzi, R., & Walton, G. (2014). Catchalls and conundrums: Theorizing "sexual minority" in social, cultural, and political contexts. *Paideusis, 22*(1), 81–90.

Nasong'o, W. S. (2015). *The roots of ethnic conflict in Africa: From grievance to violence.* Palgrave Macmillan.

Olson Lounsberry, M., & Pearson, F. (2009). *Civil wars: Internal struggles, global consequences.* University of Toronto Press.

Özerdem, A. (2014). *Local ownership in international peacebuilding.* Routledge.

Özerdem, A., & Mac Ginty. (Eds.). (2019). *Comparing peace processes.* Routledge.

Paffenholz, T. (2015). Unpacking the local turn in peacebuilding: A critical assessment towards an agenda for future research. *Third World Quarterly, 36*(5), 857–874.

Puar, J. (2007). *Terrorist assemblages: Homonationalism in queer times.* Duke University Press.

Richmond, O. P. (2016). *Peace formation and political order in conflict affected societies*. Oxford University Press.
Ross, M. H. (2007). *Cultural contestation in ethnic conflict*. Cambridge University Press.
Sandole, D. J. D. (2003). Virulent ethnocentrism and conflict intractability: Puzzles and challenges for 3rd party intervenors. *Peace and Conflict Studies*, *10*(1), 72–86.
Smith, A. D. (2013). *Nationalism and modernism*. Routledge.
Taras, R., & Ganguly, R. (2009). *Understanding ethnic conflict*. Routledge.
Thiessen, C. (2011). Emancipatory peacebuilding: Critical responses to (neo)liberal trends. In T. Matyók, J. Senehi, & S. Byrne (Eds.), *Critical issues in peace and conflict studies: Theory, practice, and pedagogy* (pp. 115–143). Lexington Press.
Volkan, V. (1997). *Bloodlines: From ethnic pride to ethnic terrorism*. Basic Books.
Wilmer, F. (2002). *The social construction of man, the state, and war: Identity, conflict and violence in former Yugoslavia*. Routledge.
Wolff, S. (2006). *Ethnic conflict: A global perspective*. Oxford University Press.

PART I

Key Dimensions of Ethnic Conflicts

1
THE ROOTS OF ETHNOPOLITICAL CONFLICT

Stuart J. Kaufman

Ethnic identities have existed throughout recorded history. Even in ancient times, ethnic groups such as the Babylonians and Egyptians were important political actors (Smith, 1986). Today, ethnic groups such as the Greeks, Armenians, and Jews can plausibly trace their forebears all the way back to classical antiquity, based either on the cultural continuity of their religious tradition or their language. Most modern countries have populations that are ethnically diverse, and since ethnic groups by definition express different cultures, the typical result of this diversity is cultural friction due to language barriers or clashing religious beliefs. Such cultural friction, however, does not necessarily result in *ethnopolitical* conflict. Many ethnic identities are politically benign: Irish-Americans, for example, do not clash as a group with Cuban-Americans, nor do Catholic Germans contend against Lutheran Germans.

The modern world, however, is organized on the principle of national self-determination, and since national identities are usually conceived in terms of ethnonational identities, such as the German and the Russian, ethnic identities are often politicized. When multiple groups with different ethnic identities politicize those differences, the result is political contention. The Quebecois, for example, seek to secure the place of the French language in Quebec's public life, while Catalans seek independence from Spain. The most extreme cases of ethnopolitical conflict take the form of bloody civil wars. Upwards of two million people are estimated to have died in Sudan's civil wars beginning in 1983, for example. Indeed, the most violent civil wars, including the 21st century ones in Afghanistan, Iraq, and Syria, are to a large extent ethnic in nature. When ethnopolitical conflict is intensified it often turns brutal and deadly. Yet uniting people in one state around a single ethnonational identity may not solve the problem of conflict, either, as the result can be ethnonationalist clashes between states.

Why do groups of people sometimes clash on the basis of their ethnic identities? What are the roots of ethnopolitical conflict? There are many theories that have attempted to explain this conundrum, each of which identifies part of the problem. Constructivist theorists note that ethnopolitical identities are socially constructed, often in ways that claim that some other group is the historical adversary. Psychologists would point out that such ethnic narratives are likely to cause prejudice. International relation realists argue that, in some circumstances, the members of one group may feel threatened by members of another, generating a security dilemma in which efforts by one group to preserve their security further threaten the security of other groups. Instrumentalists note that ethnic group leaders often seize on such fears, and stoke them, in a ploy to gain power. Conflict between groups is thus a result of politics within them. Structuralists point out that such processes are likely to lead to violence only when the institutions of the state are too weak to manage ethnopolitical disagreements. Finally, social mobilization theorists note that conflict of any kind is only possible if at least one dissident group is organized enough to mobilize people to challenge the status quo.

These theories can be grouped into two categories, theories of agency and of structure, in keeping with a theme of this book. The first category focuses on agents. Why do specific political actors do what they do? Psychological and instrumentalist theories fit into this category. The other category focuses on social structures. Structuralism, mobilization theory, and international relations realism are all structural theories of sorts. This chapter explores each of these theories in turn, and then introduces one approach, symbolic politics theory, that can bring the ideas from the other theories together into a single overview.

The rest of this chapter elaborates on these themes as follows. The first section explains the background; what ethnicity is and where it comes from. It then sketches out a picture of the frequency of different kinds of ethnopolitical conflicts. The second section identifies the key insights we can gain from theories focused on agency and structure. The following section summarizes lessons for teaching and training. The final section summarizes the implications for practice and policy.

Background

Scholars disagree about what counts as an ethnic conflict. Some definitions focus primarily on conflicts between groups divided by language; others include conflicts between different racial, religious, and sectarian groups. For an anthropologist, what these cases all have in common is that the groups involved are primarily ascriptive, that is, membership in the groups is typically assigned at birth and is difficult to change. In theory, members of one religious or communal group, Indian Muslims, can convert and become Hindu, but in practice few do, and the conversion of those few is not always accepted by their new co-ethnics. Identities of this kind, then, are "sticky," hard to change even if they are not marked by the kind of obvious physical differences that are typical of "racial" conflict. Based on this commonality, I use the broader definition of ethnicity that encompasses all of these kinds of ascriptive groups. According to Smith (1986), a group is an ethnic group if its members share a common name, a believed common descent, elements of a shared culture (most often language or religion), common historical memories, and attachment to a particular territory.

In the past, experts disagreed widely about where ethnicity comes from. Some, focusing on the evidence that many ethnic identities seem to go back hundreds or thousands of years, asserted that ethnicity was a "primordial" identity, and implied that it was essentially unchangeable. They emphasized that groups often worked hard to make their identity unchangeable, sometimes carving that identity onto their bodies through tattoos or circumcision (Isaacs, 1975). Even when they do not go that far, however, people tend to stick to the identities, especially the language and religion, they learn first from their parents.

There is another more complicated side to ethnic identity, however. Most people have multiple identities that are either "nested" (as subgroups within larger groups) or overlapping. The average Cuban-American is at the same time also an American-Hispanic or Latina, an American Catholic, an American, and a member of the worldwide Catholic Church. Which identity is more important to her is likely to depend on the situation. When listening to the pope, she is likely to respond as a Catholic; when watching the U.S. president, as an American; and when thinking about U.S. policy toward Cuba, as a Cuban-American.

Further, identities do sometimes change, with new ones emerging and old ones disappearing, especially in times of crisis. Early 20th century French-Canadians, for example, emphasized not only their language but also their Catholic religious identity. After the 1960s, however, French Canadians in Quebec redefined their identity as Quebecois, de-emphasizing their Catholic heritage and emphasizing instead a claim to political power and autonomy in the province of Quebec (Meadwell, 1993).

Noticing that people shift their identity, or at least the identity they use politically, based on the situation, a second group of scholars emerged to argue that ethnic identity is not "primordial" but merely "instrumental" (Hardin, 1995). From this perspective, people follow "ethnic" leaders when it is in their interests to do so, and leaders try to create ethnic solidarity when it works for them. This view of ethnic identity implies that ethnic conflict can be blamed primarily on selfish leaders who mislead their followers in pursuit of their own power. The conflicts themselves, these scholars argue, are typically not really "ethnic" at all; in many cases, clashes are motivated by economic or criminal disputes, but are later reinterpreted as having been ethnically motivated for political purposes (Brass, 1997).

A third point of view about ethnic identity is the constructivist one, which emphasizes the degree to which groups create their identities. This view points out that ethnic identities are "socially constructed" (Hobsbawm & Ranger, 1992). They are not "natural" in the sense that a simple primordialist view would assume; even racial distinctions are just a matter of custom. For example, most African-Americans accept the label "black," but in South Africa, most would be classified as "colored" or of mixed race rather than as the darker, purely African "blacks." Most Americans would overlook the difference, yet in Apartheid-era South Africa, the difference would have shaped every aspect of people's lives, with strict laws forcing them into separate communities.

Further, constructivists point out the source of the customary definitions of group identity is "invented traditions;" scholars *create* what Smith (2009) calls a "myth-symbol complex." This myth-symbol complex establishes the accepted history of the group and the criteria for distinguishing who is a member; identifies heroes and enemies; and glorifies symbols of the group's identity. In most cases, these mythologies "mythicize" real history, taking historical events yet redefining them as the morally defining experiences of their people. In many cases, these events are what Volkan (1997) has called "chosen traumas," real historical experiences such as the Holocaust for Jews or the 1389 Battle of Kosovo for Serbs that take a central place in their group self-understanding. In other cases, however, histories and myths are invented from whole cloth to create new identities (Hobsbawm & Ranger, 1992).

These constructivist insights can be viewed as a way to settle the argument between primordialists and instrumentalists, because constructivist ideas explain both the insights and the problems of the other two views. For example, most Serbs honestly believe that their identity is primordial, forged in the fires of battle against the Turks at Kosovo in 1389, so their perception is that their conflicts with Muslims are the result of primordial "ancient hatreds." This is what Fearon and Laitin (2003) call "everyday primordialism." In fact, that view of history was the result of late 19th century Serbian politics and educational policy (Snyder, 2000); before that, most of those who would later be labeled as Serbs did not think of themselves as Serbs, but as Orthodox Christians. Similarly, Serbian politicians such as Slobodan Milosevic did indeed use Serbian ethnic identity instrumentally to pursue power in the 1980s and 1990s, yet that identity only "worked" politically because it had been socially constructed before.

Ethnic groups and ethnic conflicts are everywhere. One comprehensive survey found a total of 275 ethnic or communal groups in 116 countries around the world that were socially disadvantaged in some way as "minorities at risk." Put together, the groups included more than one billion people, or about 17.4 percent of the world's population (Gurr, 2000, pp. 9–10). Of the 50 largest countries in the world by population, only four, Poland, Tanzania, Nepal, and North Korea, did not have at least one "minority at risk." If we add to the "minorities at risk" total the members of groups not "at risk," especially majorities such as Han Chinese in China, Russians in Russia, and so on, we find that the vast majority of the world's population live in ethnically diverse societies.

Most of the time, such diversity does not lead to serious conflict. In 1995, most of the "minorities at risk" (58 percent) were either politically inactive or mobilized only for routine politics. Sometimes this quiescence reflects routine inclusion within established party systems, as for the minority Chinese and Indian parties inside Malaysia's longtime ruling alliance. More often it reflects some degree of exclusion, as for many Indigenous peoples in Latin America or Canada, or an inclusion that falls short of genuine equality, as for Blacks in the United States. Ethnopolitical conflict in these societies takes the form of group advocacy within established political channels. Another 15 percent of "minorities at risk" were a bit more volatile in 1995, engaging in demonstrations, rioting, or both (Gurr, 2000).

Still, violent ethnopolitical conflicts do occur. The peak came around 1995, when about a quarter of minorities at risk (71) were engaged in violent rebellions (Gurr, 2000, p. 28). Indeed, ethnopolitical conflict is the leading cause of civil war. One analysis identified 215 "armed conflicts" between 1946 and 2005, and found that a slight majority (110) were ethnic conflicts (Wimmer, 2013, p. 160). Since the mid-1990s, the number of such conflicts has declined. A 2018 survey lists only a dozen countries engaged in ethnopolitical-armed conflicts in which at least 100 people died (Pettersson et al., 2019). Of these only three involved more than 1,000 battle deaths: the conflicts in Afghanistan (mostly Tajiks vs. Pashtuns), Syria (mostly Alawites vs. Sunnis), and Yemen (mostly Sunnis vs. Houthi Shi'ites). The full list is presented in Table 1.1, in descending order of severity.

A form of ethnopolitical conflict that has recently regained importance is expressed as ethnonational, often aimed primarily at asserting national values against foreign adversaries, either immigrants or other states. In 2020, the leaders of four of the five most populous states in the world were leaders of ethnonationalist movements: Xi Jinping in China, Narendra Modi in India, Donald Trump in the United States, and Jair Balsonaro in Brazil. Xi's violent crackdown

Table 1.1 Ethnopolitical armed conflicts in 2018

Conflict location (group rebelling)	Estimated deaths in 2018*
Afghanistan (Pashtuns in Taliban)	22,800
Syria (Sunnis)	11,500
Yemen (Houthis)	4,500
Turkey (Kurds)	900
Iraq (Sunnis in ISIS)	800
Cameroon (English speakers)	800
South Sudan (Nuer)	500
Democratic Republic of Congo (multiple)	400
India (Kashmiris)	400
Philippines (Muslims)	300
Ukraine (Russians)	200
Sudan (groups in Darfur)	200

* Pettersson et al. (2019, pp. 598–599) best estimate, rounded to nearest 100.

on China's Uighur minority illustrates the internal effects of this trend. A prominent case of international tumult resulting from such a movement is Britain's exit from the European Union. Pettersson et al. (2019) also identify two international armed conflicts killing over 100 people that can be traced to such movements; those between Israel and Iran, and between India and Pakistan. Xi, Modi, and their ilk can be deadly both domestically and internationally.

Yet another form that ethnopolitical violence can take is the deadly ethnic riot. A major example is the Gujarat riots in India in 2002. In that incident, in response to a fire on a train that killed 58 Hindu pilgrims, Hindu rioters rampaged through the state, killing more than 2,000 Muslims whom they blamed for the fire. Many Muslim victims were burned to death; many girls and women were raped and tortured first (Nussbaum, 2007, pp. 17–21). Such savagery is not uncommon. One study found detailed descriptions of 150 riot episodes in 50 countries, ranging from minor incidents to the 1947 communal riots in India that may have killed 200,000 people. Furthermore, there is typically no remorse on the part of the killers afterward. "They had it coming" is the attitude typically expressed by rioting communities all over the globe (Horowitz, 2000, p. 29).

Key insights

One structural explanation of ethnopolitical conflict starts with where ethnic groups come from. According to Smith's "ethno-symbolist" understanding, "the cultural elements of symbol, myth, memory, […] and tradition [are] crucial to an analysis of ethnicity, nations and nationalism" (2009, p. 25). Further, in many cases "the role of cultural nationalist intellectuals was critical to the process of defining and reviving the ethnic community through the rediscovery of ancient myths, symbols and memories" (Smith, 2009, pp. 24–25). In sum, in keeping with the constructivist understanding, ethnic identities are made up. Yet they cannot be made up any which way; there typically need to be preexisting "myths, symbols and memories" that can be rediscovered, often in the context of some nationalist project.

Given that context, an ethnic or national idea being formed out of historical memories during a political struggle for group interests, the temptation is overwhelming to create what Volkan (1997) has called "chosen traumas" and "chosen glories" or historical episodes that not only define who the group is, but also who their enemies are. Conflict and rivalry can become baked into the very definition of who a group is. Armenians, for example, define their identity largely in terms of their victimization by Turks in the 1915 genocide, and Palestinians define theirs in terms of the *naqba* (catastrophe) of 1948, when most became refugees as a result of the war with the newborn Israel. Any understanding of the roots of ethnopolitical conflict must start here, with the myths or narratives that often define a group's identity as involving hostility to some other group.

Another kind of structural theory emphasizes institutions, especially the state. In a widely cited work, Fearon and Laitin (2003) showed that one of the most powerful factors making civil war more likely, whether ethnic or otherwise, was poverty; the lower a country's GDP per capita, the greater the probability of civil war. Wimmer's more fine-grained analysis partially supported this conclusion, finding that low GDP per capita is indeed one of the two most powerful influences on the likelihood of ethnic rebellions that do not aim at secession (2013, pp. 168–169). The other main structural factor he found was political exclusion; the larger the population of ethnic minorities excluded from government power, the greater the likelihood of rebellion against that government (Wimmer, 2013, p. 166). Wimmer's logic here is strengthened by a separate finding (Gurr, 1993) that if a group previously had autonomy yet lost it, the probability of ethnic civil war also goes up. Ethnic oppression, it turns out, is risky for the oppressor.

In sum, macrostructural approaches to understanding ethnopolitical conflict tell us a few important things. When a state is weak and overstretched; when society is poor and diverse; and when some groups of people are excluded from government, the chances of ethnopolitical conflict go up. Additionally, some groups define their identity as hostile to or in conflict with another group; that should make those groups particularly likely to engage in conflict.

The finding that political exclusion leads to ethnic rebellion raises a number of further questions. First, why exclude large and potentially powerful groups from a share of power when such a course of action is obviously dangerous? Power hunger is the obvious answer, yet why are some leaders or governments greedier for power, and less prudent about it, than others? Mobutu Sese Sekou in Zaire, for example, was a world champion kleptocrat who is believed to have stashed billions of dollars in overseas bank accounts while his country remained among the poorest in the world, yet even he saw the sense in sharing power with representatives of multiple ethnic groups. Why do other leaders not do likewise?

One answer seems to be prejudice. Psychologists believe that hostile narratives of the sort that Palestinians repeat about Israelis lead to prejudiced feelings (Duckitt, 2003), and certainly Palestinians and Israelis both are prone to holding nasty stereotypes about each other (Kaufman, 2009). Kaufman (2015) has found that prejudices of this type are common in cases of ethnopolitical conflict. Examples include the racist attitudes that drove Rwanda's Hutus to commit genocide against the Tutsi minority, Sudanese Arabs' racism against the blacks of what is now South Sudan, and South African Afrikaners' racism toward South African blacks. In each case, such prejudices prompted the governments to exclude the disliked group from power, and ethnopolitical violence was the result.[1] It may seem obvious to point out, but prejudice is a major reason for ethnopolitical conflict (cf. Horowitz, 1985). McDoom (2008), for example, found that the people who led groups of roving killers who carried out the Rwanda genocide were often people who were well known locally for their bigotry against Tutsis.

If feelings of dislike are one important source of ethnopolitical conflict, feelings of threat are even more important. There is a large literature claiming that the problem is "fear" (Lake & Rothchild, 1998), yet this is not quite right. Psychologists theorize that fear causes people to retreat, and that anger is what causes them to lash out (Lazarus, 1991). Political psychologists have shown that this is true of political behavior as well (Claassen, 2014).

To be more specific, feelings of threat lead to aggressive nationalism. In psychology, students of terror management theory have shown that when people are reminded of their mortality, they tend to become more ethnocentric; they rate their own group more positively, and outgroups more negatively (Greenberg et al., 1990). They also become more aggressive and punitive toward those who challenge their group values. Mortality salience, such as a reminder of the 9/11 terrorist attacks, also increases national pride and support for nationalist leaders, while decreasing concern with incidental harm to innocents (Pyszczynski et al., 2003, pp. 73–74). "Fear" does indeed lead to anger.

These feelings of threat are directly connected to ethnopolitical conflict. Every program of lashing out or rebelling against another group is justified by the claim that the targeted group is a threat. In Georgia, South Ossetians turned to separatism in 1990 when faced with a threat from the Georgian government, which had taken away their autonomy (Kaufman, 2001). Armenians launched a separatist bid in the mountainous Karabakh region of Azerbaijan based on charges of "white genocide" (i.e., ethnic cleansing). Hutus massacred Tutsis in Rwanda because the Tutsis were allegedly plotting with the Tutsi-led Rwandan Patriotic Front to take over power (Kaufman, 2015). Even the Holocaust was justified by Hitler's paranoid belief that Jews were responsible for most of the world's ills, including Germany's defeat in World War I.

One factor all of the above cases have in common is that ordinary people were able to become "ethnic activists" (Lake & Rothchild, 1998), that is, to be active agents in ethnic politics, in many cases toward violent ends. Turning grassroots activism into organized campaigns, however, requires leadership; and the leaders of ethnopolitical movements are not necessarily motivated by prejudice and anger, even if their followers typically are. According to the instrumentalist school of thought, what leaders of ethnopolitical movements have in common is a desire to gain and keep power, and a belief that promoting ethnopolitical conflict is a way to achieve that goal. The implication is what Brown (1996) has called the "bad leaders" theory of ethnopolitical conflict.

Gagnon's (1995, 2004) account of ethnic nationalism in Serbia illustrates the argument about the importance of leaders as agents in promoting ethnopolitical conflict. As Gagnon explains, whenever Serbia's conservative elites in Yugoslavia had their power threatened, they turned to making ethnonationalist appeals to try to outflank liberal opponents. The most important example is Slobodan Milosevic in the 1980s and 1990s. In the 1980s, Gagnon shows, conservative Serbian elites' grip on power was being threatened by reformers, both in Serbia and in other parts of Yugoslavia, who sought democracy and decentralization of power. In response, Milosevic led a movement alleging Serbs were under threat, primarily by ethnic Croats and Albanians. His proposed solution was a Serbian-dominated Yugoslavia; his movement's slogan was, "Only Unity Saves the Serbs." The results of this push were the wars in Croatia (1992), Bosnia and Herzegovina (1992–1995), and Kosovo (1999).

Yet another way of understanding ethnopolitical conflict is to look at "social movement organizations" that provide the connections between leaders and followers. From the perspective of a sociologist, what matters are not individuals' thoughts but rather the social ties they have with others (Tilly, 2005). In fact, the key predictor of whether someone will participate in some kind of collective action is whether he or she is asked to do so (McAdam et al., 1996). The kind of organization that matters can vary. A network of black churches, especially in the southern United States, powered the U.S. civil rights movement of the 1950s and 1960s (McAdam et al., 1996, p. 4). In the Serbian and Rwandan cases, political parties played important organizing roles. Brubaker (2004) sums up the lessons; namely that ethnopolitical conflicts are not conflicts between "groups," most of whose members typically do not participate. Rather, they are conflicts between organizations that claim, more or less plausibly, to represent those groups.

All of these approaches might seem to be in fruitless debate with each other. Some say the problem is weak states in poor societies; others blame hostile narratives or "myths"; still others focus on feelings of prejudice or threat; yet others blame aggressive leaders; and others attribute the problem to clashes of organizations. The truth, however, is that these accounts fit together because all of them are right. Ethnopolitical conflicts are likely to become severe only when most or all of these factors are present.

This is what symbolic politics theory (Kaufman, 2001, 2015) claims. At the center of the symbolic politics account is the way leaders frame issues. A frame is "a central organizing idea or story line that provides meaning to an unfolding strip of events … The frames suggest what the controversy is about, the essence of the issue" (Gamson & Modigliani, 1987, p. 143). Framing is what leaders are doing when they say that the political problems facing their people are ethnic in nature, that they are ethnopolitical. That framing is likely to work, and to result in ethnopolitical conflict, only when all of the other factors are present.

Specifically, Kaufman (2015) argues that, first, the ethnonationalist frame is more likely to "resonate" with people when that theme is familiar from existing discourse and narratives, and when people are prejudiced against the other group. It cannot result in ethnopolitical conflict unless people feel that there is a significant threat, and unless some organization can be pressed into service to mobilize them. It is likely to result in violence only if the perceived threat involves violence, and if the rival group countermobilizes in response. If the threat is to group interests, values, status, or identity, in contrast, the likely result is a contentious ethnopolitical movement. Examples of such movements include the U.S. civil rights movement and the widespread right-wing anti-immigrant nationalist movements of the 2010s. Finally, all of this is likely to happen only when the macrostructural causes are in place, typically in weak and poor states where governments exclude large or important minorities.

Implications for teaching and training

For anyone seeking to teach others about ethnopolitical conflict, the first lesson is that there are always multiple reasons. There is not one answer to the question of why ethnopolitical conflict breaks out, and certainly not any panacea to it. The roots of ethnopolitical conflict include macrostructural factors like weak states that exclude some groups from power. They typically included widespread narratives that are hostile to the rival group, and consequently prejudice and other psychological predispositions that prime people for conflict. They include feelings of threat and leaders who play on those feelings in the way they frame their messages. And they include the efforts of social movement organizations, and the strategic interaction between the sides, the security dilemma process (Posen, 1993) in which one side's efforts to increase its security threaten the other and lead to escalation.

Two teaching strategies suggest themselves in this context, both of which have been touched upon here. One option is to teach in terms of contending schools of thought, the structuralists, instrumentalists, social psychologists, etc. The other is to emphasize a theoretical perspective that brings most or all of these factors together and shows how they interrelate. The symbolic politics account is one example of such a theory. Another is social mobilization theory (McAdam et al., 2001). Mobilization theory emphasizes opportunity structures (including macrostructural factors such as state strength), mobilizing structures (organizations), and framing processes by elites, yet it also has room for narrative structures as well. What are left out are the psychological processes driven by prejudice and fear that provide the motor for human behavior in the symbolic politics account.

Implications for practice and policy

Every insight from each school of thought has implications for policymakers and practitioners. The rest of this book explores these issues, yet it is worth sketching out a few practical lessons here.

Rhetoric matters

On the one hand, aggressive talk by national or group leaders should not be dismissed as "cheap talk." Such statements are not mere words but are powerful political acts in their own right; the Israelis are right when they denounce Palestinian leaders for "incitement" when they indulge in violent rhetoric against Israel. Similarly, history textbooks, television news and talk radio stations may not be benign social structures but delivery systems for the hostile narratives that are at the root of ethnopolitical conflict. Practitioners and policymakers must take them seriously.

On the other hand, benign rhetoric also matters. What heals ethnopolitical conflict, to the extent that anything does, are narratives and frames that rise above the "us versus them" dichotomy and create a unifying identity. Psychologists call this approach the "common ingroup identity model" (Gaertner & Dovidio, 2000). An outstanding example of its application is Tanzania, where an orchestrated campaign of nation-building rhetoric and education succeeded in building the strongest national identity in Africa (Kaufman, 2015).

State structure matters

How to get state structures right is a debate of its own, yet again each side in the debate has an important point. First, state strength itself is important as actions and measures that impair the ability of the state to do its job of maintaining order should be considered suspect. Second, since we know ethnic exclusion tends to promote conflict, some sort of powersharing is essential; actions to strip groups of their autonomy must be understood as destructive. Third, since we know divisive rhetoric is destructive, constitutional engineering aimed at creating incentives for politicians to moderate their rhetoric is also necessary.

Emotions matter

Practitioners on the ground must expect people, especially during and after violent conflict, to demonstrate prejudice and anger, and they should employ all the tools at their disposal to mitigate and manage it. Similarly, mediators should expect prejudiced and angry behavior even from the diplomats and political leaders of both sides, who are expressing not only their own prejudices but also often the cruder ones of their followers. Doing so is politically the path of least resistance for elites; expecting the rational pursuit of national or group interests in conditions of hostility and fear is itself irrational.

On the other hand, mediators do have tools at their disposal to mitigate the feelings of threat that underlie much of the anger. These tools include promotion of confidence-building measures, face-saving concessions, and the introduction of observers or peacekeepers. These should be understood as tools for emotional management as much as for conflict resolution.

Look at leaders and organizations

Sometimes leaders are the problem. This does not mean that they cannot later be part of the solution. Milosevic, for example, was alternately both problem and solution. However, it points out the importance of the advice of Roelf Meyer, one of the lead negotiators in South Africa's transition from apartheid; if mediators are to succeed, they cannot want peace more than the parties do.

Sometimes, however, organizational strength or weakness is the problem. Practitioners and policymakers need to be alert to the problem that moderate leaders may be too weak to deliver peace (Haass, 1990); strengthening their organizations can strengthen them. Sometimes problems in peace implementation are the result not of leaders' bad faith but of their inability to control local leaders who may not be subordinates but unruly allies (Autesserre, 2010). Practitioners need to know the second- and third-tier leaders of the parties in conflict and to be able to identify the spoilers, those who want to disrupt peace instead of benefit from it (Stedman, 1997).

Conclusion

Practitioners generally know that reality is complicated and the problem rarely boils down to one or two issues. What they can learn from theorists is to look for issues whose importance they may not have realized before.

Note

1 The South African case is often thought of as a case of a peaceful transition to democracy, but in fact about 20,000 people died in communal violence during the transitional decade 1985–1995 (Kaufman, 2017).

References

Autesserre, S. (2010). *The trouble with the Congo*. Cambridge University Press.
Brass, P. R. (1997). *Theft of an idol*. Princeton University Press.
Brown, M. (1996). Internal conflict and international action. In M. Brown (Ed.), *International dimensions of internal conflict* (pp. 603–629). MIT Press.
Brubaker, R. (2004). *Ethnicity without groups*. Harvard University Press.
Claassen, C. (2014). Group entitlement, anger and participation in intergroup violence. *British Journal of Political Science, 46*(1), 127–148.
Duckitt, J. (2003). Prejudice and intergroup hostility. In D. O. Sears, L. Huddy, & R. Jervis (Eds.), *Oxford handbook of political psychology* (pp. 559–600). Oxford University Press.
Fearon, J. D., & D. D. Laitin (2003). Ethnicity, insurgency, and civil war. *American Political Science Review, 97*(1), 75–90.
Gaertner, S. L., & Dovidio, J. F. (2000). *Reducing intergroup bias*. Routledge.
Gagnon, V. P. (1995). Ethnic nationalism and international conflict: The case of Serbia. *International Security, 19*(3), 130–166.
Gagnon, V. P. (2004). *The myth of ethnic war: Serbia and Croatia in the 1990s*. Cornell University Press.
Gamson, W. A., & Modigliani, A. (1987). The changing culture of affirmative action. In R. G. Braungart & M. M. Braungart (Eds.), *Research in political sociology* (pp. 137–177). JAI Press.
Greenberg, J., Pyszczynski, T., Solomon, S., Rosenblatt, A., Veeder, M., Kirkland, S., & Lyon, D. (1990). Evidence for terror management theory II. *Journal of Personality and Social Psychology, 58*(2), 308–318.
Gurr, T. R. (1993). *Minorities at risk: A global view of ethnopolitical conflicts*. United States Institute of Peace.
Gurr, T. R. (2000). *Peoples versus states*. United States Institute of Peace.
Haass, R. N. (1990). *Conflicts unending*. Yale University Press.
Hardin, R. (1995). *One for all: The logic of group conflict*. Princeton University Press.
Hobsbawm, E., & Ranger, T. (Eds.). (1992). *The invention of tradition*. Cambridge University Press.
Horowitz, D. L. (1985). *Ethnic groups in conflict*. University of California Press.
Horowitz, D. L. (2000). *The deadly ethnic riot*. University of California Press.
Isaacs, H. R. (1975). *The idols of the tribe*. Harper & Row.
Kaufman, S. J. (2001). *Modern hatreds*. Cornell University Press.
Kaufman, S. J. (2009). Narratives and symbols in violent mobilization: The Palestinian-Israeli case. *Security Studies, 18*(3), 400–434.
Kaufman, S. J. (2015). *Nationalist passions*. Cornell University Press.
Kaufman, S. J. (2017). South Africa's civil war, 1985–95. *South African Journal of International Affairs, 24*(4), 501–521.
Lake, D. A., & Rothchild, D. (1998). Spreading fear: The genesis of transnational ethnic conflict. In D. A. Lake & D. Rothchild (Eds.), *The international spread of ethnic conflict* (pp. 3–32). Princeton University Press.
Lazarus, R. S. (1991). *Emotion and adaptation*. Oxford University Press.
McAdam, D., McCarthy, J. D., & Zald, M. N. (Eds.). (1996). *Comparative perspectives on social movements*. Cambridge University Press.
McAdam, D., Tarrow, S., & Tilly, C. (2001). *Dynamics of contention*. Cambridge University Press.
McDoom, O. (2008). The mico-politics of mass violence: Authority, security and opportunity in Rwanda's genocide [Doctoral dissertation, London School of Economics and Political Science]. London School of Economics, eScholarship. https://ethos.bl.uk/OrderDetails.do?uin=uk.bl.ethos.529310
Meadwell, H. (1993). The politics of nationalism in Quebec. *World Politics, 45*(2), 203–241.
Nussbaum, M. C. (2007). *The clash within: Democracy, religious violence, and India's future*. Harvard University Press.

Pettersson, T., Hogbladh, S., & Oberg, M. (2019). Organized violence, 1989–2018 and peace agreements. *Journal of Peace Research*, *56*(4), 589–603.
Posen, B. R. (1993). The security dilemma and ethnic conflict. *Survival*, *35*(1), 27–47.
Pyszczynski, T. A., Greenberg, J., & Solomon, S. (2003). *In the wake of 9/11: The psychology of terror*. American Psychological Association.
Smith, A. D. (1986). *The ethnic origins of nations*. Wiley-Blackwell.
Smith, A. D. (2009). *Ethno-symbolism and nationalism*. Routledge.
Snyder, J. (2000). *From voting to violence*. W. W. Norton.
Stedman, S. J. (1997). Spoiler problems in peace processes. *International Security*, *22*(2), 5–53.
Tilly, C. (2005). *Identities, boundaries and social tiers*. Paradigm Publishers.
Volkan, V. (1997). *Bloodlines: From ethnic pride to ethnic terrorism*. Farrar, Straus & Giroux.
Wimmer, A. (2013). *Waves of war*. Cambridge University Press.

2
HOW GENDER IS IMPLICATED IN ETHNOPOLITICAL CONFLICT

Franke Wilmer

From Boko Haram's kidnapping of Nigerian schoolgirls in 2014 to the sexual violence perpetrated against men and women in the former Yugoslavia and the Democratic Republic of Congo (DRC), to the trafficking of Rohingya women and girls in Myanmar, gender-based violence is a ubiquitous feature of chauvinistic ethnopolitical violence. What insights can applying a gendered lens to the problem of ethnopolitical violence render?

Background

First, let's clarify the term "ethnopolitical." The term "ethnic conflict" is often used as if its meaning were self-evident. I think it is more useful to talk about "identity conflicts." Identity is group-referential. Ethnicity is regarded by social scientists as socially constructed, with political consequences. Parties often believe that their identity entitles them to exercise control over their own political destiny, or that controlling their own destiny is the only way to be free from discrimination, marginalization, or oppression. A broad definition puts the sectarian conflict in Northern Ireland, the wars in former Yugoslavia, the Rwandan civil war, the expulsion and ethnic cleansing of the Rohingya from Myanmar, the atrocities committed in Darfur, and race relations in South Africa in the category of ethnopolitical conflict.

Ethnonational conflict involves at least one party who narrates its identity as constituting a nationality, Chechnya, for example, the Kurds, or all parties to the Yugoslav wars. Ethnopolitical refers to an identity group mobilized to achieve political objectives through collective action, articulated as resistance to inequality, injustice, and domination. Ethnic conflict can also include what is sometimes called "race relations" or "race conflict" in the United States. Because states are "ethnicized," as Enloe puts it, they can be parties to ethnopolitical conflict (Enloe, 1995).

Where are the women in ethnopolitical conflicts? How is ethnopolitical violence gendered? Iraqi-born Zainab Salbi founded Women for Women International (WWI) in 1993 to support women living in conflict zones by connecting them with critical economic and educational resources. Her activism arose from her own experience, escaping Saddam's brutality and the war with Iran by agreeing to an out-of-country arranged marriage. The marriage became abusive and she left, but was unable to return to her home because of the second Iraq War in 1991. She and her second husband, Amjad Atallah, founded WWI two years later, during the war in Bosnia and Herzegovina. I first learned of her work in the summer of 1995. Women's relationship with political violence is complicated. Widespread publicity of rape as a weapon of war in the former Yugoslavia prompted international recognition of sexual violence as a war crime for the first time in 1993 (Wilmer, 2002). Genocide and rape were also going on at about the same time in Rwanda. Although both were widely reported in the Western media, rapes in Rwanda seemed to get less media attention (Thompson, 2007; Tyrrell, 2015). Between 20,000 and 50,000 women were raped in the former Yugoslavia, and an estimated ten times as many in Rwanda (Aginam, 2012).

Zainab Salbi talks about women on the "backline" of war. On the frontline are the tactics, weapons, attacks, and casualties that become "interesting numbers"; percent of fatalities that are civilians, hundreds of thousands of rapes, the percent of refugees that are women and children. We have come to see the frontline as the location of war. The backline is invisible. On the backlines, women shop, prepare food, keep schools open, care for children and the elderly, bury the bodies, and clean the streets. "We are missing stories of women who are literally keeping life going in the midst of wars," she says (Salbi, 2010).

Yet women are raped in armed conflict, including ethnopolitical conflict. And they are enablers and perpetrators. They are combatants, leaders, peacemakers, and activists.

Rape

An excellent recent study of rape during civil war, by Dara Kay Cohen, examines three of the most often cited causes of rape during war: opportunism, ethnic hatred, and gender inequality (Cohen, 2013, p. 461). Using an original dataset, she finds that rape is "not more likely to occur during ethnic wars, genocides, or in countries with greater gender inequality" (Cohen, 2013, p. 461). Instead, she offers evidence to support a different conclusion: Rape is a tool of recruitment and socialization. It is used to "create bonds of loyalty and esteem from initial circumstances of fear and mistrust" (Cohen, 2013, p. 461).

Today, we must look for women in many more places, some where we would rather not find them, like perpetrators of rape, torture, and war crimes. Enloe notes in her opening chapter that:

> … One has to become interested in the actual lives – and thoughts – of complicatedly diverse women. One need not necessarily admire every woman whose life one finds interesting. Feminist attentiveness to all sorts of women is not derived from hero worship. Some women, of course, will turn out to be insightful, innovative, and even courageous. Upon closer examination, other women will prove to be complicit, intolerant, or self-serving. (2014, pp. 5–6)

Women are rape victims in ethnopolitical conflicts like the former Yugoslavia, Rwanda, and the DRC, which are among the most publicized cases. Less well known is the case of Allied soldiers, albeit an interstate rather than ethnopolitical conflict. American, Canadian, British, French, and Soviet male soldiers raped tens of thousands, and maybe millions of German women following German surrender in 1945 (Matthews, 2018). These "revenge rapes" were known, but hidden, or silenced, for 70 years, according to Phillip Kuwert and Harald Jürgen Freyburger (Kuwert & Freyberger, 2007; Matthews, 2018). The women were raped because they were German. Nazi ideology was ethnonationalist. Does that make this a case of ethnopolitical violence?

Women are also perpetrators and enablers. Enablers covers a broad range of complicity, from witnessing prisoners being sexually tortured in order to further humiliate the victim, to nurses assisting in forced sterilizations in Nazi camps (Raphaely, 2013; Sjoberg, 2016). Women's capacity for cruelty is not new. Consider this story from Wendy Lower's book *Hitler's Furies* (2013):

> Blonde German housewife Erna Petri was returning home after a shopping trip in town when something caught her eye: six small, nearly naked boys huddled in terror by the side of the country road.
>
> Married to a senior SS officer, the 23-year-old knew instantly who they were. They must be the Jews she'd heard about, the ones who'd escaped from a train taking them to an extermination camp.
>
> But she was a mother herself, with two children of her own. So she humanely took the starving, whimpering youngsters' home, calmed them down, and gave them food to eat.
>
> Then she led the six of them, the youngest aged six, the oldest 12, into the woods, lined them up on the edge of a pit and shot them methodically one-by-one with a pistol in the back of the neck. (Rennell, 2013)

In the DRC we find women who are victims and perpetrators, as well as men who are victims of rape (Karbo & Mutisi, 2012). "Rape capital of the world" is how Margot Wallstrom, UN Special Representative on Sexual Violence in Conflict from 2010 to 2012, described the scale of crimes committed in the DRC (Hatcher, 2013). Estimates in 2012 indicated that 48 women were raped per hour then (Hatcher, 2013). An estimated one-in-three women and one-in-four men in the eastern DRC have suffered sexual violence (Thust & Esty, 2020). One of the victims recounted his story after escaping to Uganda:

> It was 8 pm, and they shot open the door with a gun, yelling at us, accusing us of being rebel sympathizers […] They said, "You support the rebels. We'll show you that you are not a man."
>
> They shot me in the back. They put a cable around my neck and began choking me. The soldiers grabbed and held me down. They said, "We are going to rape you." And they each took turns.
>
> I used to be big and strong, but I couldn't fight off all three. I closed my eyes. I only heard sounds.
>
> I heard the cries of my mother and sister as they were raped in the next room. Then shots rang out, and my father was dead. (Thust & Esty, 2020, p.)

Will Storr calls men's rape "the darkest secret of war" (Storr, 2011). "Male rape is endemic in many of the world's conflicts," says Storr, citing data from Lara Stemple's (2009) study, *Male Rape and Human Rights* (Storr, 2011). Although long recognized as a violation perpetrated against male prisoners, including at Abu Ghraib, men are also raped in war. Stemple documents male rape in conflict zones, including Chile, Greece, Croatia, Sri Lanka, El Salvador, Iran, Kuwait, former Yugoslavia, the DRC, and the former Soviet Union (Stemple, 2009, p. 612).

Not only men's rape, but women perpetrators are also underreported and invisible. Harvard Professor Lynn Lawry interviewed members of over 1,000 households in eastern Congo. She asked victims of sexual violence to identify the gender of their perpetrators, finding 40 percent of the women and ten percent of men surveyed identified their assailants as women (Hatcher,

2013). One UN expert and rape victim estimated that 90 percent of armed groups included women (Hatcher, 2013). Pauline Nyiramasuhuko, who was ironically the Minister of Family Welfare and the Advancement of Women before the genocide, and her son, were found guilty of inciting rape by the International Criminal Tribunal for Rwanda in 2011 (Simons, 2011).

Laura Sjoberg takes an in-depth look at "women as wartime rapists" in her 2016 book. Her survey spans the Armenian genocide through the present, including survivors who "tell how women were involved in beating, killing, sexually violating, and selling other women and girls into sexual slavery" (Sjoberg, 2016, p. 100). Many continued sex trafficking and torture of their victims after the conflict ended (Sjoberg, 2016). Questioning whether women's increased participation as combatants reduces the incidence of rape, Meredith Loken developed a dataset on women combatants in civil wars from 1980 to 2009. She found that women's involvement had no significant impact on reducing rape by combatants (Loken, 2017). This suggests that women are socialized to conform to or uphold the combatant culture, rather than alter it.

Women combatants

In *Women and War* (1995), Jean Bethke Elshtain analyzed how men's and women's gender roles created an interlocking logic to sustain and reproduce a patriarchal system of masculinized virtuous warrior and feminized maternal innocence. Women's violent conduct undermines the "good soldier/good mother logic." Do women combatants defy this logic? Yes, and no. Yes, because, as I will argue later, more fluidity and a less exclusive conception of gender identity challenges the logic of the binary and interlocking gender roles necessary to the maintenance of patriarchal ideology. No, because women acting like men, meaning women who reproduce masculinized behavior within a patriarchal system are not a threat to its perpetuation.

Enloe's 1993 book *The Morning After: Sexual Politics at the End of the Cold War* opens this way:

> Now that the war is over, Esmeralda has had her IUD removed. What? I read the sentence again. Esmeralda is a Salvadoran woman who spent many of her young adult years as a guerrilla in the Farabundo Marti National Liberation Front, the FMLN. She pounded out tortillas and washed her boyfriend's clothes as well as wielding a gun.
> (Enloe, 1993, Kindle Locations, pp. 16–18)

The "morning after," Esmerelda returns to her role as a woman living in a patriarchal world. She turns her weapon over to the UN, reinserts her IUD, and aspires to be the good mother Elshtain expected from patriarchally socialized women. Women played an unusually large role as members of the Salvadoran rebel force, the FMLN. However, they remained confined by a gendered division of labor during the struggle (Viterna, 2013). Although El Salvador is not an ethnopolitical conflict in the narrow sense because rebels mobilized around deprivations arising from class differences, El Salvador's class distinctions are stratified primarily by ethnic identities linked to the European-descended ruling class versus the Indigenous and Mestizo peasants. Women's status seemed to improve initially after the end of the war, yet El Salvador now ranks the country below the regional average on gender equality (SDG Gender Index, 2019).

Many women also fought in the Tamil war for independence against the economically advantaged Sinhalese majority in Sri Lanka. They made up about a third of the Liberation Tigers of Tamil Eelam (LTTE) and participated as fighters and suicide bombers. A Tamil woman suicide bomber assassinated Indian Prime Minister Rajiv Gandhi in May, 1991 (Eager, 2016; Robertson, 2018). The LTTE included the women-only Malathi Brigade, named for the first woman Tiger to die in combat. The agenda of the "Women's Front" of the LTTE included the abolition of dowries, eliminating gender discrimination, and obtaining legal protection against rape, sexual harassment, and domestic violence (Alison, 2003, p. 45). When the war ended in a loss for the Tigers in 2009, women ex-combatants who had fought as equals to male combatants suffered a double disadvantage as civilians. By then, the Tigers had lost support among the Tamil people because they recruited child soldiers, and used civilians as human shields. Ex-combatants were shunned and sent to rehabilitation camps. Further, women ex-combatants who are now relegated to traditional roles in the economy are at higher risk of poverty and are more vulnerable to sexual violence (Robertson, 2018).

A group of women meeting in Dublin in 1914 to discuss how to support the nationalist Irish Volunteers decided to organize their own paramilitary organization, Cumann na mBan (the Women's Council). While explicitly recognizing the need for armed resistance, they primarily assisted the men by procuring supplies and fundraising for the nationalist cause. They mobilized with James Connolly's Irish Citizen Army and participated in the Easter Uprising of 1916 as combatants, including the sniper, Countess Constance Markiewicz (Eager, 2016; Robbins, 1977). More recently, sisters Dolours and Marian Price were arrested in connection with a 1973 car bombing and sentenced to 20 years in prison. There, the Price sisters joined other Provisional Irish Republican Army (PIRA) prisoners such as Bobby Sands and Francis Hughes on a hunger strike lasting almost seven months to reinstate Special Category Status (Vitello, 2013). Bernadette Sands-McKevitt, Bobby Sands' sister, and her husband Michael McKevitt led the Real IRA that broke off from the Provisional IRA in 1997, when it called a ceasefire. The Real IRA claims to be the only legitimate successor to the original PIRA and it merged in 2012 with Republican Action Against Drugs (RADD) to become the New IRA (Eager, 2016, pp. 158–159).

Around 30 million Kurds live in Kurdistan, the traditionally Kurdish territory including parts of Turkey, Syria, Armenia, Iran, and Iraq (Lazarus, 2020). They fight for independence and resistance to their marginalization by these states. In the case of Iraq, they also fight for survival in a country where they have been targeted by chemical weapons. An estimated 30–40 percent of Kurdish peshmerga combatants are believed to be women (Lazarus, 2020). In Syria, there is a female brigade known as the Women's Protection Unit. The Turkish- and Iraqi-based Kurdistan Workers Party (PKK) includes an all-women guerilla unit called the Free Women's Unit (Lazarus, 2020). They have fought in their units as well as with men's units against ISIS in the Kurdish area of Syria. Many believe they are fighting for greater gender equality. The leader of the PKK, Abdullah Ocalan, says that, "women's liberation is deeply rooted in P.K.K. ideology" (Lazarus, 2020).

Women leaders

In addition to being victims of sexual violence in larger proportion than men, perpetrators, although in smaller proportion than men, and combatants whose aspirations for post-conflict equality are elusive, women are also leaders in ethnopolitical conflicts. Although Aung San Suu Kyi is not a political leader of an ethnopolitical nonstate group, she is implicated in ethnic violence in Myanmar. Under her leadership, the Rohingya Muslims became victims of ethnic cleansing, leaving at least 6,700 Rohingya children dead and as many as 43,000 adults missing, presumed dead (Barron, 2018; BBC, 2020). An estimated 700,000 have fled the country, most to Bangladesh (BBC, 2020). As journalist Hannah Ellis-Petersen put it, "There are falls from grace, and then there is Aung San Suu Kyi" (Ellis-Petersen, 2018).

Recipient of the Nobel Peace Prize in 1991, after 15 years under house arrest, she opposed the military government that took control after her party won more than 80 percent of the seats in parliament. She would become prime minister in 1988. Although many have called for the revocation of the peace prize, the rules do not allow for withdrawal. The International Court of Justice heard a case charging the Myanmar military and government of genocide in 2020. Still, it was not evident that the military intended to destroy the Rohingya as a group (Sun, 2020).

Hanan Ashrawi was educated in a Quaker school for girls in Ramallah in the West Bank of Palestine, annexed by Jordan at the time, earning a bachelor's and master's degrees at the American University in Beirut, and a PhD from the University of Virginia (Horsley 2005). She was the first woman elected to the Palestinian Legislative Council, and is one of the most articulate and widely recognized spokespersons for the Palestinian Authority. She served in a variety of positions representing Palestinians in the peace process, and advocating for their human rights. She also served on the faculty of Birzeit University, including as chair of the English department. In May 2019, the United States denied her a visa just months after U.S. Middle East Envoy Jason Greenblatt said that she had an open invitation to the White House (Hackel, 2019).

Although women played key roles in resistance to the violence in former Yugoslavia, most were as nationalistic as the men (Wilmer, 2002, p. 215). There were also women in all of the irregular as well as regular forces throughout the former republics (Kešić, 1999). Silber and Little list 208 key individuals who played vital roles in the violent conflict in former Yugoslavia (Silber & Little, 1997). Four are women. Two spoke out against the nationalist-driven violence, one a Slovenian, and the other a member of the Serbian Presidency. One was Mirjana Marković, wife of the infamous Serbian president Slobodan Milošević who died in custody at the Hague awaiting trial for genocide and war crimes in 2006, and the other was Bosnian Serb Biljana Plavšić, who served as vice president of the rogue Republika Srpska during the war. Plavšić, a scientist, was known for making some of the worst eugenics-based racist statements about Bosnian Muslims (Wilmer, 2002, p. 216).

Irish nationalist women took part in violent resistance to British rule, both as combatants and terrorists.[1] They fought against British landlords in a movement known as the 1878–1903 Land Wars, and, when the men were imprisoned for nonpayment of rent, they kept the rent-resistance movement going. There were few women in leadership of the nationalist resistance, however. Maud Gonne, whose father was a British colonel stationed in Ireland, was stirred to political activism by the Land Wars evictions. She became the first president of the Inghinidhe na hÉireann (Daughters of Ireland), a women's literary organization founded in 1900 and "dedicated to complete independence" (Eager, 2016, p. 160). Under her leadership, the organization called not only for freedom for Ireland but equality for Irish women, and created a Gaelic language revival program (Eager, 2016, p. 160). She was arrested and imprisoned in Dublin and served six months in prison for seditious acts (Cardozo, 1979). Her son Sean MacBride was a prominent IRA leader and human rights lawyer.

Mothers and caregivers

I learned from elders of the Haudenosaunee (people of the Longhouse) or the Iroquois Confederacy that traditionally, women had veto power over war-making because they would be making the greatest sacrifice, giving birth to children whose lives would be at risk (Johansen, 1998). Elshtain's Spartan Mother "reared her sons to be sacrificed on the altar of civic need" (Elshtain, 1995, p. 62). Palestinian mothers praise Allah "that their child was chosen by God to achieve martyrdom," and an Iowa mother, Mrs Sullivan, becomes a "five Gold Star" mother, having lost five sons serving in WWII (Eager, 2016, p. 18). These associations between women as mothers and war contrast sharply with Zainab Salbi's (2010) "backline" of women's wartime activities that maintain daily life and some sense of normalcy in the family and community.

While women peace activists often invoke their motherhood as motivating their activism, the fact remains that many women in ethnonationalist conflicts often share the exclusionary views of their enemies that are espoused by male leadership (Wilmer, 2002). Eager writes about the pro-fascist "Mothers Movement" during World War II, and racist movements more generally where mothers and motherhood symbolically plays a central role (Eager, 2016, p. 82). Indeed, Hitler valorized motherhood and encouraged German women to have more children. One scholar found five ways white supremacist propaganda portrays white women including as "glorious mothers and naturally maternal" (Blazak, 2004, p. 165 cited in Eager, 2016, p. 83).

Women negotiators and peacemakers

Early 20th century women's peace groups were international and national rather than ethnopolitical, including the Women's League for Peace and Freedom (1918), the Madres de Plaza de Mayo (1977), and the antinuclear Greenham Commons Women's Peace Camp (1981). These emboldened women in ethnopolitical conflict zones. Israeli Jewish women started Women in Black in response to the First Intifada. Palestinian Israeli women soon joined them. When I was in Belgrade, Serbia, in 1995, during the war, Women in Black stood on Republic Square every Wednesday afternoon, holding antiwar signs, and withstanding harassment from detractors. Today Women in Black sponsor ongoing vigils in Africa, the Americas, Asia, Europe, the Middle East, and Oceana (Women in Black, 2000).

Women Wage Peace was also founded in Israel, following the 2014 war in Gaza and the Israeli military operation known as "Protective Edge." They claim to have 43,000 supporters representing all ethnic and religious groups in Israel today, and from across the political spectrum (Women Wage Peace, 2020). I joined them during an encampment outside the Israeli Knesset in 2018, where they engaged Knesset members in dialogue with their members. That day Likud member Oren Hazan joined them. More than 30,000 participated in their 2016 March of Hope (Liebermann, 2017). In addition to the simple demand that leaders commit to negotiate peacefully and resolve the conflict, Women Wage Peace now also declares as its second main goal, the inclusion of women according to UN Resolution 1325.

In 2000, the UN Security Council unanimously passed Resolution 1325, calling for women's participation in conflict resolution, peacebuilding, and post-conflict reconstruction. The Security Council has passed 12 more resolutions on women, peace, and security since then, and in 60 countries created National Action Plans to implement the framework established by the resolutions (UN, 2020). The United Nations holds annual meetings to assess progress on fulfilling the aspirations of the resolution, although progress is difficult to measure. Women seem to be playing a more significant role in peacemaking and negotiations in Mali and Colombia, in electoral processes throughout Africa, and in humanitarian and disaster relief coordinated by the United Nations. They are also more engaged in meeting the needs of refugees and displaced persons, the majority of which are women and children, in post-conflict peacebuilding in the Balkans, and greater participation in peacekeeping forces (UN Women, 2020).

Key insights

Women are combatants, rapists, ethnopolitical leaders, and traffickers as well as peacemakers and antiwar activists (Whyte, 2017). But does doing "men's work" make them equal, in combat or afterward? Eager reports on Fernando Reinares' research (2004) on women's participation in the Basque separatist movement ETA (Euskadi Ta Askatasuna) (Eager, 2016, p. 148). Reinares "found that most of the women joined ETA due to affective ties with boyfriends or husbands"

(Eager, 2016, p. 148). Barbara Victor recalls a speech by Palestinian President Arafat in 2002, when he said, "You are the hope of Palestine. You will liberate your husbands, fathers, and sons from oppression. You will sacrifice the way you women, have always sacrificed for your family" (Eager, 2016, p. 188). The next day, suicide bomber Wafa Idris killed herself, and one Israeli Jewish man on Jaffa Road in central Jerusalem (Eager, 2016, p. 188).

Like Esmerelda reinserting her IUD, many women ex-combatants return to traditional gender roles, often regarding childbearing as a postwar nationalist duty, and reestablishing the pre-conflict gendered division of labor (Luna et al., 2017). They also face special challenges during the disarmament and demobilization period because, according to activist Sanam Anderlini, they are excluded and invisible. This is partly because recognizing their participation as combatants would necessitate a number of changes existing power actors do not want to undertake and would also bring to light the fact that some were kidnapped or coerced, and were often in auxiliary roles (Anderlini, 2007, p. 108).

Rwanda is often cited as an exception. With a post-genocide population that is 60–70 percent female, 64 percent of the legislative assembly seats are held by women. The World Economic Forum Global Gender Gap report ranks Rwanda in the sixth lowest gap, following Iceland, Norway, Finland, Sweden, and Ireland. Yet feminism and equality in leadership roles are still taboo (Warner, 2016). The issue of women's equality was raised decades ago, before the genocide, but without results. Now women can own property and work outside of the home. Rwandan Justine Uvaza returned after completing her PhD at Newcastle University where she interviewed many of the women serving in public elected and appointed positions. "She found with rare exception that no matter how powerful these women were in public, that power didn't extend to their homes" (Warner, 2016). They were expected to clean house, polish and lay out their husband's shoes (socks on top), iron laundry and basically "being docile and serving her husband" (Warner, 2016). Asked if they would support a movement for women's equality, "almost all" of them said they would not (Warner, 2016).

Implications for teaching and training

The normalization of violent and dehumanizing in-group/out-group male behavior and the emulation of that behavior by some women is a product of gender roles mediated by patriarchal ideology. Not patriarchy as a social system in which men dominate women, although that is a consequence, but patriarchal ideology as theorized by Gilligan and Richards (2009). An ideology that (1) normalizes fear, domination, and control; (2) constructs and idealizes masculinity as emotionally disconnected; and (3) attributes qualities to idealized masculinity that both defend against and perpetuate fear, domination, and control. In the spirit of Elshtain's interlocking gender roles, women are socialized under patriarchal ideology to regard disconnected masculinity and selfless femininity as normal. As Gilligan and Richards put it:

> The long-standing and vaunted divisions between mind and body, reason and emotion, self and relationships, culture and nature, when viewed through the lens of gender turned out to be deeply gendered, reflecting the binaries and hierarchies of a patriarchal culture. Mind, reason, self, and culture were considered masculine and were elevated above body, emotion, relationships, and nature, seen as feminine and like women at once idealized and devalued. These splits revealed a chasm in human nature, a systematic distortion or deformation of both men's and women's natures.
> (Gilligan & Richards, 2009, p. 193)

The meaning of gendered difference is mediated by patriarchal culture. Nationalism itself is patriarchal and masculine, framed as in-group/out-group or antagonist "us" versus "them" relations. Adding insights from Gilligan and Richards, fear of otherness, and the inequalities and domination produces and sustains are also ubiquitous features of ethnopolitical conflict. Solving or at least reducing the harm cause by these conflicts will ultimately necessitate dismantling the patriarchal ideology that underlies the normalization of inequalities, binary and oppositional hierarchies, intolerance of ambiguities, and control over as a response to fear of difference. This can only be done through education and training. As a (male) student of mine once said, "I am depatriarchalizing my mind!" Gilligan and Richards also make the case that patriarchal ideology is deeply antidemocratic. Trust, not fear; equality, not domination; and liberation, not control. These are the core values of a democratic society and relations among democratic citizens.

Implications for practice and policy

UN Security Council Resolution 1325 is a good place to start. Twenty years since its passage, more women are gradually taking part in peace negotiations generally, including between or among parties to ethnopolitical conflicts. Still, as of 2015, fewer than ten percent of negotiators were women and only three women had signed peace agreements (McWilliams, 2015, p. 231). The Council on Foreign Relations reported over the entire 26-year period between 1992 and 2018, women only made up three percent of mediators, four percent of signatories, and 13 percent of negotiators (Council on Foreign Relations, 2019). It is not surprising, then, that the overwhelming majority of peace agreements since 1990 fail to address women's concerns, or even mention women at all (Council on Foreign Relations, 2019). Nilsson finds that peace negotiations that include civil society and women's groups are 64 percent less likely to fail (Nilsson 2012, p. 258).

Women's participation alone will not be enough. As this chapter shows, normalizing violence, associating it with masculinity, and regarding masculinity as the norm, is the root of the problem. This is evidenced by the gendered language of conflict, women's imitation of violent behavior, and sexual torture of men as well as women. This, in turn, is a product of social constructions of gender mediated by patriarchal ideology. Fortunately, Gilligan and Richards also identify sites of resistance that challenge and potentially transform these dysfunctional gender norms. Feminists (men and women), civil rights advocates, peace activists, and LGBTQ identities are all sites of resistance. Wherever trust replaces fear, equality replaces domination, and liberation replaces control, there is hope for transforming patriarchal ideology.

Note

1 Not being an essay on defining terrorisms, or assessing the logic, rationale, or justification for acts often characterized as terrorism, here all I mean are things like bombings of primarily civilian targets (Matthews, 2010).

References

Aginam, O. (2012). *Rape and HIV as weapons of war*. United Nations University. https://unu.edu/publications/articles/rape-and-hiv-as-weapons-of-war.html

Alison, M. (2003). Cogs in the wheel? Women in the Liberation Tigers of Eelam. *Civil Wars*, 6(4), 37–54.

Anderlini, S. N. (2007). *Women building peace*. Lynne Reinner.

Barron, L. (2018, March 8). More than 43,000 Rohinga parents may be missing. Experts fear they are dead. *Time*. https://time.com/5187292/rohingya-crisis-missing-parents-refugees-bangladesh/

BBC. (2020, January 23). Myanmar Rohingya: What you need to know about the crisis. *BBC News*. https://www.bbc.com/news/world-asia-41566561

Blazak, R. (2004). Getting it: Women and male desistance from hate groups. In Ferber, A. L. (Ed.), *Home grown hate: Gender and organized racism*, 154–172. Routledge.

Cardozo, N. (1979). *Maud gonne: Lucky eyes and a high heart*. Victor Gollancz.

Cohen, D. K. (2013). Explaining rape during civil war: Cross-national evidence (1980–2009). *American Political Science Review*, *107*(3), 461–477.

Council on Foreign Relations. (2019). Women's participation in peace processes. *Council on Foreign Relations*. https://www.cfr.org/womens-participation-in-peace-processes/

Eager, P. W. (2016). *From freedom fighters to terrorists: Women and political violence*. Routledge.

Ellis-Petersen, H. (2018, November 23). From peace icon to pariah: Aung San Suu Kyi's fall from grace. *The Guardian*. https://www.theguardian.com/world/2018/nov/23/aung-san-suu-kyi-fall-from-grace-myanmar

Elshtain, J. B. (1995). *Women and war*. University of Chicago Press.

Enloe, C. (1993). *The morning after: Sexual politics at the end of the cold war*. University of California Press.

Enloe, C. (1995). When feminists think about Rwanda. *Cultural Survival Quarterly Magazine*. https://www.culturalsurvival.org/publications/cultural-survival-quarterly/when-feminists-think-about-rwanda

Enloe, C. (2014). *Bananas, beaches and bases*. University of California Press.

Gilligan, C., & Richards, D. A. J. (2009). *The deepening darkness: Patriarchy, resistance, and democracy's future*. Cambridge University Press. Kindle Edition.

Hackel, J. (2019, May 14). Veteran Palestinian negotiator Hanan denied a visa to the US. *Public Radio International: The World*. https://www.pri.org/stories/2019-05-14/veteran-palestinian-negotiator-hanan-ashrawi-denied-visa-us

Hatcher, J. (2013, December 3). Congo's forgotten curse: Epidemic of female-on-female rape. *Time Magazine*. https://world.time.com/2013/12/03/congos-forgotten-curse-epidemic-of-female-on-female-rape/

Horsley, S. K. (2005). Hanan Ahrawi. Fem/Bio http://www.fembio.org/english/biography.php

Johansen, B. E. (Ed.). (1998). *The encyclopedia of native American legal tradition*. Greenwood Press.

Karbo, T., & Mutisi, M. (2012). Ethnic conflict in the Democratic Republic of Congo (DRC). In D. Landis & R. Albert (Eds.), *Handbook of ethnic conflict: International and cultural psychology* (pp. 381–402). Springer.

Kešić, O. (1999). Women and gender imagery in Bosnia: Amazons, sluts, victims, witches, and wombs. In S. Ramet (Ed.), *Gender politics in the western Balkans: Women and society in Yugoslavia and the Yugoslav successor states* (pp. 187–202). Pennsylvania State University Press.

Kuwert, P., & Freyberger, H. J. (2007). The unspoken secret: Sexual violence in World War II. *International Psychogeriatrics*, *19*(4), 782–784.

Lazarus, S., (2020). Women. Life. Freedom. Female fighters of Kurdistan. *CNN World*. https://www.cnn.com/2019/01/27/homepage2/kurdish-female-fighters/index.html

Liebermann, O. (2017, October 9). Israeli, Palestinian women join peace march through desert. *CNN*. https://www.cnn.com/2017/10/09/middleeast/israeli-palestinian-women-peace-march-desert/index.html

Loken, M. (2017). Rethinking rape: The role of women in wartime violence. *Security Studies*, *26*(1), 60–92.

Lower, W. (2013). *Hitler's furies: German women in the Nazi killing fields*. Chatto and Windus.

Luna, K. C., Van Der Haar, G., & Hilhorst, D. (2017). Changing gender role: Women's livelihoods, conflict and post-conflict security in Nepal. *Journal of Asian Security and International Affairs*, *4*(2), 175–195.

Matthews, A. (2010). *Renegades: Irish republican women 1900–1922*. Mercier Press.

Matthews, H. (2018, May 7). As we remember V E Day, remember too the German women who were raped. *The Conversation*. https://theconversation.com/as-we-remember-ve-day-remember-too-the-german-women-who-were-raped-96196

McWilliams, M. (2015). Women at the peace table: The gender dynamics of peace negotiations. In M. P. Flaherty, S. Byrne, H. Tuso, & T. G. Matyok (Eds.), *Gender and peacebuilding: All hands required* (pp. 229–244). Lexington Press.

Nilsson, D. (2012). Anchoring the peace: Civil society actors in peace accords and durable peace. *International Interactions*, *38*(2), 243–266.

Raphaely, C. (2013, April 14). South African police accused of routinely torturing crime suspects. *The Guardian*. https://www.theguardian.com/law/2013/apr/14/south-africa-police-accused-torture-suspects

Rennell, T. (2013, September 25). The Nazi women who were every bit as evil as the men: From the mother who shot Jewish children in cold blood to the nurses who gave lethal injections in death camps. *Daily Mail.* https://www.dailymail.co.uk/news/article-2432620/Hitlers-Furies-The-Nazi-women-bit-evil-men.html

Robbins, F. (1977). *Under the starry plough: Recollections of the Irish citizen army.* Academy Press.

Robertson, H. (2018, June 7). From soldiers to housewives: Women who fought as Tamil Tigers in Sri Lanka are forced into traditional roles. *The Washington Post.* https://www.washingtonpost.com/world/asia_pacific/the-women-who-fought-for-the-tamil-tigers-in-sri-lanka-are-being-forced-into-traditional-roles/2018/06/06/6894df7a-681a-11e8-bea7-c8eb28bc52b1_story.html

Salbi, T. (2010). Women, wartime and the dream of peace. *Ted Talk.* www.ted.com/talks/zainab_salbi_women_wartime_and_the_dream_of_peace?language=en

SDG Gender Index 2019. (2020). Equal measures: El Salvador. *Gender Advocates Data.* Hub. https://data.em2030.org/countries/el_salvador/

Silber, L., & Little, A. (1997). *Yugoslavia: Death of a nation.* Penguin Books.

Simons, M. (2011, June 24). Life sentences in Rwanda genocide case. *New York Times.* https://www.nytimes.com/2011/06/25/world/africa/25rwanda.html

Sjoberg, L. (2016). *Women as wartime rapists.* New York University Press.

Stemple, L. (2009). Male rape and human rights. *Hastings Law Journal, 60*(3), 605–645.

Storr, W. (2011, July 16). The rape of men: The darkest secret of war. *The Guardian.* https://www.theguardian.com/society/2011/jul/17/the-rape-of-men

Sun, Y. (2020, February 8). Aung San Suu Kyi comes out on top in ICJ Rohinga ruling. *Nikkei Asian Review.* https://asia.nikkei.com/Opinion/Aung-San-Suu-Kyi-comes-out-on-top-in-ICJ-Rohingya-ruling

Thompson, A. (Ed.). (2007). *The media and the Rwanda genocide.* Pluto Press.

Thust, S., & Esty, J. (2020, April 14). DRC's male and female rape survivors share their stories. *Al Jazeera.* https://www.aljazeera.com/indepth/features/drc-male-female-rape-survivors-share-stories-200412123610314.html

Tyrrell, C. (2015). *The Rwandan genocide and Western media: French, British, and American press coverage of the genocide between April and July of 1994* [Master's thesis, University of Central Florida]. University of Central Florida, eScholarship. https://stars.library.ucf.edu/etd/1188/

UN 2020. (2020). Timeline to 2020: 1325 $ the women, peace, and security agenda. *UNSCR.* http://un2020.org/timeline/timeline-unscr-1325-the-women-peace-and-security-agenda/

UN Women. (2020). Feature stories. *UN Women Africa.* https://africa.unwomen.org/en/news-and-events/stories/2015/10/women-peace-and-security.

Vitello, P. (2013, January 25). Dolours Price, defiant I.R.A. bomber, dies at 61. *New York Times.* https://www.nytimes.com/2013/01/26/world/europe/dolours-price-defiant-ira-bomber-dies-at-61.html

Viterna, J. (2013). Women in war. The micro-processes of mobilization in El Salvador. *European Review of Latin American and Caribbean Studies, 97*(1), 169–171.

Warner, G. (2016). It's the no. 1 country for women in politics – but not in daily life. *NPR Goats and Soda: Stories of Life in a Changing World.* https://www.npr.org/sections/goatsandsoda/2016/07/29/487360094/invisibilia-no-one-thought-this-all-womans-debate-team-could-crush-it

Whyte, L. (2017). *Women as wartime rapists: Beyond sensation and stereotype.* New York University Press.

Wilmer, F. (2002). *The social construction of man, the state, and war: Identity, conflict, and violence in the former Yugoslavia.* Routledge.

Women in Black. (2000). Women in black for justice, and against war. *Women in Black.* http://womeninblack.org/vigils-arround-the-world/africa/

Women Wage Peace. (2020). Women wage peace. https://womenwagepeace.org.il/en/about-eng/

3
COMPLEX EFFECTS OF EXTERNAL INVOLVEMENTS IN ETHNOPOLITICAL VIOLENCE

Marie Olson Lounsbery and Frederic S. Pearson

The international ramifications of ethnopolitical conflict have mushroomed in the "global" age. Such conflicts have long had international consequences, sometimes of immense proportions, as in the Serbian-Austrian struggle, with German and Russian involvements, which triggered World War I. However, in today's conflicts the complexities have become even more difficult to unravel and understand, as in the multiparty "conflict complexes" in and surrounding Syria, Afghanistan, Iraq, and Yemen, which include multiple local, regional, extra-regional and global actors, and in the case of Syria some thousand opposition groups.

External involvements in these struggles tend to be motivated by a variety of strategic, political, ethnic, and humanitarian concerns. Relevant motivations and resultant impacts are examined in this chapter, as we discuss the processes that internationalize ethnopolitical conflicts. Specifically, we will analyze the escalation and de-escalation effects such linkages have on the local conflicts and fighting, concentrating especially on international military interventions.

It has been argued that during the Cold War, it was perhaps easier, especially for major powers such as the Soviet Union (USSR) or even smaller states such as Tito's Yugoslavia, to isolate and contain local ethnic disputes and prevent them from spreading or attracting outside involvements. With the emerging post-Cold War multipolar system, however, and with the development of regional "crisis arcs" in zones such as Southeastern Europe, the Middle East, Central and South Asia, East Africa, Central and Southern Africa, the impacts of ethnic fighting have spread and sparked numerous external involvements, that is, interventions, of various sorts. Often these external involvements, whether by official governments or ethnic and diaspora kin, by international agencies, organizations, and peacekeepers, by nongovernmental organizations (NGOs) such as Doctors Without Borders, Engineers Without Borders, and Journalists Without Borders, or by transnational insurgent networks, are variously designed to help one or another party to the disputes, promote "regime change" or secession, or, unfortunately less frequently, to provide humanitarian relief and protection of refugees. Other motives include border modifications or offsetting security threats or economic losses (Najafov, 2017). In some rare instances, interveners also might attempt to promote ethnic integration or segregation in the affected target state.

Little is known, in general, about the impacts of such involvements on what are termed "ethnic wars," that is, impacts on the dynamics of such wars themselves, as distinct from involvements in civil wars in general (for case study-based results see Cooper & Berdal, 1993). As with all civil wars, external funds and armament can sustain fighting; pacification efforts or enforced sanctions might lead to negotiated or de facto ceasefires; external troops might prolong the conflict by strengthening or impeding certain parties; collaborative involvements by multiple external actors might hasten peace, while competitive involvements might create stalemates or massive destruction and civilian casualties (Olson Lounsbery & Pearson, 2009; Regan, 1998, 2002). However, ethnopolitical conflicts per se have added attraction and implications for kinship groups and nations abroad and can become political footballs for regional or global powers seeking to extend their influence and control across regions or to forestall ethnic outbreaks in their own countries (Carment & James, 2000). As always, intended effects might give way to unintended or unanticipated consequences, as they did in Iraq post-2003 and Libya in 2011. A systematic study of external involvement effects is due so that we know better what to expect in this complicated globalized age.

One of the impacts of external involvement can be conflict escalation both in the target state and the surrounding area, through spillover or contagion effects. Carment et al. (2009) examine three factors thought to explain the escalation of conflicts across borders, namely extension, interaction, and transformation; yet they find that none of the three is fully explanatory. They conclude that the synthesis of social and state capacity factors better determines state stability by overcoming insecurity; they maintain that a positive history of social diversity combined with limits on disruptive state actions are key factors in the positive resolution of ethnopolitical disputes. However, we lack similar categories for explaining the rebounding impacts of internationalization/intervention on the course of the domestic ethnic disputes themselves.

Saideman (2016) focuses particularly on what makes some ethnic groupings more likely to attract outside support than others. He finds, for example, that separatist groups, seeking or thought to be seeking secession, seem relatively unlikely to gain (at least overt) outside support given the prevailing international norms favoring state sovereignty and the territorial status quo, especially in regions such as Africa. Contrasting results were, however, reported by Khosla (1999), looking at interventions, albeit by third world states, and noting that secessionist or autonomy demands were more likely to engage foreign patronage. Indeed, we might note that the Eritrean struggle against Ethiopia had foreign involvements and did produce ultimate separation, as did South Sudan's long war with Sudan. Thus, proximity to the conflict and regional interests may distinguish interventions by states nearby or with global motives.

While power machinations, such as weakening regional opponents (e.g., Iran's periodic aid under the Shah to Iraqi Kurds during their struggles with Saddam Hussein), also affect decisions to support movements from abroad, according to Saideman (1997); on the whole cross-national ethnic ties, especially to powerful foreign states, seem generally to outweigh such "realist" calculations in accounting for external support. Huibregtse (2010, 2011) adds the dimension of size, number, dominance, and power of ethnic communities in the intervening and target states as worth consideration as well. For example, states with significant diversity and with a dominant ethnic group seem more prone to cross border ethnic fighting.

Variation also seems to occur on involvements in violent versus non- or less-violent disputes (Saideman, 2016). The latter, perhaps reflecting potential cost and risk calculations, seem to inspire more external support to groups in conflict, especially from states with certain regime types or in proximity to the conflict. In violent disputes, the noted effect of separatism and the relative power of the host government seem more to condition foreign involvements.

Background: Types of engagement

Thus, the complicated sociopolitical interests involved in ethnic violence require a more systematic look at the wars' circumstances and outcomes in light of external interventions. We can further examine these probabilities by disaggregating forms of uni- or multilateral intervention (Nalbandov, 2009). Involvements can vary, including funding, arms supply, diplomacy, and direct military or intelligence engagement, for example, along with intervention motives ranging from strategic interests to humanitarian, peacemaking, or kinship protection. Indeed, Lake and Rothchild (1996) distinguish noncoercive, coercive, and mediating approaches. While the most extreme form of intervention involves military support of one form or another, for example, aid packages or drone attacks or troops on the ground, states also frequently utilize diplomatic, covert, or economic measures in attempts to influence civil war actors and groups. Indeed, sometimes interveners caught up in their own wars might seek to engage ethnic opponents to weaken their local enemies, as the United States attempted to do so with the Hmong groups in Vietnam.

Diplomatic intervention tends to involve mediation. External actors offering their mediation services seek to bring the parties closer to negotiated resolution, even as ulterior motives may also exist. This may help to explain why mediation is not applied equally across the world. According to Grieg and Diehl (2012), European and Middle Eastern conflicts have tended to be "overmediated" relative to their conflict levels, whereas Asian conflict tends to be "undermediated." Strategic motives, at least among major power mediators, appear to involve trade relations and former colonial ties. The largest factor motivating state mediation interest, however, for both major and minor powers, appears to be religious ties (Grieg & Diehl, 2012, p. 85). Ethnic and linguistic ties also tend to motivate smaller power mediators and conciliators.

External actors may also seek to punish states experiencing ethnopolitical violence through the use of sanctions. In fact, this approach increased dramatically in the post-Cold War period (Morgan et al., 2014), coinciding with an increase in the number of civil wars. However, the impact of sanctions on civil disputes seems to be largely negative, exacerbating human rights (Peksen, 2009) and gender violations (Drury & Peksen, 2012). Previous work in this regard has not focused specifically on ethnopolitical disputes, however.

The basic analytical question, then, involves whether the trends outlined in the literature hold up across all or only some forms of external engagement, and whether the association between forms of involvement and effects on levels of fighting or initiation and direction of talks (Cetinyan, 2002) in the target or host state can be predicted for ethnopolitical conflict.

Specifically, based on the literature we might state the following working hypotheses:

- Null hypothesis—the pattern of interventions and effects on fighting are the same for ethnopolitical and nonethnic civil violence.
- Ethnopolitical disputes, entailing more primordial grievances and threats, are more difficult to settle through diplomatic interventions, including mediation, than other forms of disputes.
- Noting the claim that European and Middle Eastern disputes are "overmediated," the mediation of ethnopolitical disputes will vary in frequency and effectiveness by region.
- Given human rights concerns, external economic and commercial sanctions will be more frequent in ethnopolitical fighting than in nonethnic disputes.
- Military interventions backing governments will be more frequent and more effective in ethnopolitical fighting than those backing rebels in bringing conflict to conclusions and agreements.

Key insights

In order to examine the international dimensions of ethnopolitical disputes, data drawn from the Uppsala Conflict Data Program on all armed conflicts occurring between 1989 and 2006 were examined. Using the Foundations of Rebel Group Emergence (FORGE) data (Braithwaite Maves, & Gallagher Cunningham, 2019), conflicts were considered either "ethnic" or "religious" to narrow in on specifically ethnopolitical forms of disputes. There were 112 intrastate (i.e., "civil") armed conflicts during that time period, an era of decided escalation in civil as opposed to international warfare. Of those 112, 830 (74 percent) could be identified as "ethnopolitical," with either ethnic (64 percent of the ethnopolitical conflicts) and/or religious (30 percent) dimensions.

Contrary to our null hypothesis, ethnopolitical disputes did appear more likely than the other forms of civil conflict to experience or attract external involvement. We considered diplomatic,[1] economic,[2] and military interventions[3] as external involvement. On the diplomatic front, of the 83 ethnopolitical disputes, 52 percent ($N = 43$) experienced mediation at some point during the time period examined, whereas only nine of the non-ethnopolitical disputes had such intervention (31 percent of 29 cases). Economic, commercial or political sanctions also were more likely in such circumstances; 42 percent of the ethnopolitical disputes involved external sanctions compared to 28 percent for non-ethnopolitical conflicts. When we consider the most invasive form of intervention (i.e., military intervention), once again, ethnopolitical conflicts experience higher rates of hostile (pro-rebel) foreign military intervention. Just under half of those cases experienced military intervention supporting rebels ($N = 38$, or 48 percent), while only 24 percent ($N = 7$) of the non-ethnopolitical conflicts had direct rebel support. Supportive interventions, however, did not vary much between the two sets of cases. Fifty-five percent ($N = 44$) of the ethnopolitical cases had military support on behalf of the warring government compared to 52 percent ($N = 15$) of the non-ethnopolitical cases.

It does appear that some regions gain more international attention than others, confirming previous research by Wallensteen and Svensson (2014) and DeRouen and Bercovitch (2012), although not quite as expected by the "overmediated" claims regarding Europe and the Middle East. Mediation appears more likely in Africa (70 percent of the 37 cases) than in the other regions. Despite the relatively high number of disputes in Asia, only 23 percent (or eight cases) involved mediation. Africa also led other regions in attracting military intervention (in 80 percent of the cases), but had significantly less sanction presence (only 19 percent of the 37 cases). Comparatively, sanctions tend to be used more frequently in the Middle East (seven of the 11 cases, or 64 percent).

Regardless of intervention presence or type, and contradicting our second hypothesis above, ethnopolitical armed conflicts are also more likely than other types to experience peace agreements and/or ceasefires, at least during the time period studied here. Nearly 47 percent ($N = 39$) of the ethnopolitical cases saw peace agreements and/or ceasefires of at least some duration, compared to only six (or 21 percent) of the non-ethnopolitical cases. Peace agreements prove more difficult to achieve than ceasefires, yet ethnopolitical conflicts appear to reach more of these agreements than nonethnic cases (27 percent compared to 14 percent).

We can look further into just how effective various forms of intervention were in deescalating versus escalating the conflicts. Given that ethnopolitical disputes are more likely to experience external intervention, do such involvements influence these trends and does it vary by intervention type? Obviously, mediation efforts are specifically aimed at bringing about conflict resolution. Again contrary to Hypothesis 2, ethnopolitical disputes with mediation were more likely than nonmediated disputes to achieve either a ceasefire or peace agreement (or both); 65 percent ($N = 28$) of the mediated ethnopolitical disputes had such agreements, while just shy of 28 percent of the nonmediated cases that reached agreement. Interestingly, mediation in non-ethnopolitical disputes was less successful (though still better than nonmediation); only three of nine such mediated disputes reached an agreement (or 33 percent).

These trends were similar if we focus specifically on peace agreement outcomes; 44 percent of the mediated ethnopolitical conflicts reached such agreements compared to 33 percent of the mediated non-ethnopolitical conflicts. Not only do ethnopolitical disputes draw more diplomatic attention, it appears that those efforts are more fruitful. Concerns that identity-based conflicts are inherently more difficult to resolve may be unwarranted (Svensson, 2007) if we consider the effects of external diplomatic actors.

External actors have also sought to influence the outcomes of civil conflicts through economic pressure, specifically by the use of sanctions, as discussed above. The literature on sanction effectiveness has been rather harsh on this foreign policy tool, suggesting such economic pressure is not only ineffective at ending disputes, but it may make the situations worse on the ground. The findings presented here, albeit at relatively low case numbers, support this previous work. Among ethnopolitical disputes, 35 experienced external sanctions (42 percent), and of the 35 sanctioned conflicts, 17 (49 percent) also experienced a peace agreement or ceasefire. Only eight (23 percent) reached a peace agreement, specifically, however. Those without sanctions had similar experiences, with 22 (46 percent) reaching at least a ceasefire and 14 (29 percent) reaching a peace agreement.

Hypothesis 4 predicted more sanction attempts aimed at ethnopolitical than non-ethnopolitical conflicts. This is confirmed as 42 percent ($N = 35$) of the ethnopolitical cases experienced sanctions, yet only 28 percent ($N = 8$) of the non-ethnopolitical cases had such intervention. We must note, however, that contrary to what one might suppose, sanctions had a slightly higher success rate among the non-ethnopolitical disputes; three of the eight non-ethnic disputes with sanctions reached a peace agreement (38 percent).

External actors may also seek to influence conflict outcomes using the most expensive and potentially disruptive forms of intervention (Olson Lounsbery & DeRouen, 2016); foreign military intervention can involve supplying weapons, related materiel, or troops and other forces to warring parties. Previous work has found that such interventions can indeed impact conflict outcomes generally, depending on the direction of that support. "Hostile" anti-government military interventions tend to bolster rebel factions, making rebel victory and negotiated outcomes more likely (Gent, 2008). In our study, 38 cases of ethnopolitical conflict experienced intervention supporting rebels (i.e., hostile military intervention). Of those, 23 (or 61 percent) also experienced a ceasefire or peace agreement ($N = 16$). Comparatively, only two (29 percent) of the non-ethnopolitical cases experienced both hostile intervention and an agreement (both were peace agreements). Clearly in relation to Hypothesis 5, hostile, pro-rebel forms of military intervention appear more decisive at bringing about peace agreements in ethnopolitical fighting than in other types of conflicts. Given the asymmetric nature of most civil disputes, interventions that occur on behalf of the typically weaker faction, that is, the rebels, may have the effect of pressuring the reluctant warring government to the bargaining table, albeit with the caveat that under international law, pro-rebel involvements are not acceptable, though again the more recent doctrine of "Responsibility to Protect" (R2P) does call for humanitarian protection in extreme cases. It is this type of imperative that might account for more willingness to intervene militarily backing rebels in ethnic than nonethnic cases.

On the other hand, if we consider military interventions aimed at supporting struggling warring governments, and contrary to the hypothesis, intervention effectiveness seems to wane for both types of conflicts. It has previously been argued that interventions on behalf of warring governments appear to be less decisive in countering rebellion, as only the weakest of governments appear to make such requests (Gent, 2008). Fourteen of the ethnopolitical disputes in our study experienced supportive, pro-government intervention and a peace agreement (32 percent of 44), while 27 percent of the 15 non-ethnopolitical conflicts drawing intervention had the same effect. If we expand our analysis to consider those that at least reached ceasefire, both sets of cases had about 40 percent reaching some form of agreement to suspend hostilities when supportive, pro-government interventions were involved. Thus, backing governments in civil disputes appears to have about the same peacemaking efficacy (ranging from 30 to 40 percent), whether or not the dispute has ethnopolitical roots. Of course, some would argue that a 30–40 percent success rate is a considerable level of impact either way.

Finally, we also consider the impact of external intervention, in its various forms, on conflict intensity, that is, escalation/de-escalation levels. Among the 117 civil conflicts examined for the 1989–2006 time period, the mean number of cumulative battle-related deaths was 7,756, but the median conflict intensity (casualty) measure was 606. Such conflicts, though tragic, rarely ($N = 21$) reached over 10,000 battle-related deaths during the time period under study; of course, as Syria and Yemen show, since that time we have had instances of astoundingly high death rates. Nineteen of the immediate post-Cold War high intensity cases were considered ethnopolitical conflicts. Using linear regression on a logged measure of battle-related deaths to account for a skewed distribution,[4] all military intervention measures were positively associated with overall conflict intensity among the cases of ethnopolitical civil conflict. While our analysis does allow us to determine whether military intervention *causes* higher levels of intensity (no time-lagged analyses were run); we can conclude that external military interventions tend to be *associated* with the most dangerous and destructive cases. Among the 29 non-ethnopolitical cases in the study, if we lower the intensity threshold to focus on conflicts reaching at least 1,000 battle-related deaths during the time period examined, it appears that only supportive pro-government military intervention is associated with the higher casualty rates. Eight of the ten relatively intense non-ethnopolitical conflicts also had such pro-government intervention. Thus, as found previously by Regan (2000, 2002) and others, and as subsequently proven again in Syria and Yemen, military intervention, especially friendly to the government, tends to drive up casualty rates and fighting intensity.

Implications for teaching and training

In terms of teachable lessons for both students and those interested and professionally engaged in managing ethnopolitical and other civil disputes, our findings offer both hope and caution. It appears that diplomatic initiatives such as mediation, depending of course on the identity, power, and acceptance of the mediator and the timing of the initiatives (Yassine-Hamdan & Pearson, 2014), offer hope of achieving ceasefire and settlement agreements even in cases of heated ethnic warfare. Yet of course matters are complicated; Indian Prime Minister Rajiv Gandhi, for example, failed and paid a mortal price in his mediation attempts and military intervention during the Sri Lankan civil war, a highly charged long-term ethnopolitical battle that, despite periodic ceasefires, finally ended in a costly government military victory against the Tamil Tigers or LTTE. Perhaps, though one never knows with precision, some greater accompanying support for the Tamil rebels would, according to the pattern of our intervention findings, have better balanced the outcome, since pro-rebel military moves seemed to generate more ethnopolitical agreements than pro-government involvements did.

We have shown some efficacy for outside diplomatic and military involvements in ethnopolitical as opposed to non-ethnic cases, yet recent instances have shown vividly that if the involvements are multiple and competitive, the stabilization effects may be muted. In both Syria and Yemen, for example, external intervention competition, involving such actors as Saudi Arabia, Iran, Turkey, Russia, the United States, the Gulf States, and non-state groups such as Hezbollah and others, have decimated the populations, countryside and peacemaking prospects, creating massive civilian casualties and refugee flows. In our data analysis, however, no clear distinction emerged in the effects of competitive military interventions in ethnopolitical disputes. Further, dissensus among the permanent United Nations Security Council members can prevent humanitarian moves, as when Russia and China reportedly threatened vetoes of multilateral humanitarian relief in Syria out of opposition to the legitimation of external pro-rebel involvements that could apply to their own ethnic disputes regarding Chechens, Uighurs, Tibetans, and other minorities.

Future analyses also should consider the effects of external involvements, including diplomacy, sanctions, and intervention in situations where governmental authority has nearly or completely broken down, in what are termed failing or failed states. The choices of backing the remnants of government, seeking to provide external governing resources, bringing rebels and militias of various stripes to the negotiating table, or letting the situation merely deteriorate into chaos and extremist breeding grounds, are very stark. We know little about how these choices affect restabilization or peacemaking, except perhaps for anecdotal evidence in areas such as Somalia and post-Qaddafi Libya.

Implications for practice and policy

Our analysis and discussion presented above suggest that external actors are drawn to higher intensity in ethnic conflicts. Intervention efforts tend to include diplomatic, economic and military initiatives. Our findings also suggest, however, that diplomatic efforts, as well as military efforts that seek to balance out the weakness of the rebel factions may make for more effective resolution efforts (in the form of ceasefires and peace agreements). There are several implications for the practice of intervention into ethnopolitical intrastate disputes to be discussed.

If we consider all the intervention tools available for external states to consider when seeking to influence the behavior of intrastate warring ethnic factions, economic punishments appear to be most problematic. As previous literature has suggested, such efforts tend to create more painful situations on the ground with higher levels of human rights abuses and lower levels of women's rights and security (Drury & Peksen, 2012; Peksen, 2009). Research discussed here also indicates that punishing sanctions do not make for more effective outcomes in ethnopolitical civil wars, though sometimes penalizing actors for foreign involvements in such wars, such as anti-Russian sanctions regarding Ukraine, can make important international statements of solidarity, and in principle, may slow down the fighting. Not only are sanctioned conflicts more deadly, however, they appear less likely to reach lasting ceasefires or peace agreements.

The practice of diplomatic intervention does appear to be supported as a beneficial mechanism to address ethnopolitical conflict. Mediated civil disputes are more likely to experience ceasefire and agreements, even when we consider that higher intensity and longer lasting disputes seem to experience more than what might be considered their fair share of diplomacy. While it seems evident that ethnic and religious identities may complicate negotiations, our analysis suggests that such differences need not serve as barriers to resolution. However, since ethnic uprisings are a highly volatile and sensitive international political issue, and measures to intervene can be seen as undesired precedents by other powers concerned with their own internal ethnic unrest, it may be difficult to achieve international consensus for either mediation or intervention.

The internationalization of ethnopolitical conflict through more coercive measures such as military intervention or economic sanctions adds another layer of complexity for these disputes. Previous work indicates that military initiatives tend to prolong and intensify (at least in the short term) civil conflicts generally (Regan, 2000, 2002). Further, military initiatives are costly and likely to be prolonged from the perspective of the intervener, especially when such interventions occur on behalf of the typically weaker rebel group(s). It appears, however, that these types of interventions may have the beneficial effect of improving agreement prospects. Previous work (Gent, 2008) found that to be the case among all civil conflicts; the research presented here suggests this is also the case for ethnopolitical conflicts in particular. Given the costly nature of military intervention, and the negative consequences it often exhibits, increasing this practice seems unlikely since it runs the risk of "slippery slope" and quagmire involvements. Still if the regional stakes seem high enough, outside interveners, especially major powers, have shown the willingness for prolonged involvements. One does not yet know whether the significant financial and potential troop losses in such prolonged engagements will make them less likely in the future.

Conclusion

External actors will probably continue to reserve the intervention tool for the most challenging, or the most threatening, cases. That said, a lesson that can potentially be drawn here has to do with why such interventions can be effective. Asymmetric warfare tends to be resistant to diplomatic initiatives, as the more powerful government at least initially seeks to reinforce its sovereignty in the face of internal opposition (Cook & Olson Lounsbery, 2017). Hostile intervention counters this governmental power advantage thereby raising the conflict cost and pressuring authorities to consider other alternatives. While this may embolden rebel factions and encourage them to pursue victory over negotiated outcomes, their success is driven by the external actor. The conditions would seem ripe for agreement if that is in the interest of the intervener(s) who are likely to prefer to minimize their own costs (Olson Lounsbery & DeRouen, 2016). Third parties might consider other diplomatic mechanisms to assert such pressure to potentially rebalance long-running asymmetric ethnopolitical disputes and avoid costly quagmires.

Notes

1. Mediation events were identified using the Civil War Mediation Data (DeRouen et al., 2011).
2. Sanction events were identified using the Threat and Imposition of Sanctions Data (TIES) (Morgan et al., 2014).
3. External support data were drawn from the UCDP External Support Dataset (Högbladh et al., 2011).
4. Battle-death data were drawn from the UCDP Battle-Related Deaths Datasets (Högbladh, Pettersson, & Öberg, 2019) using the best estimate for battle deaths.

References

Braithwaite Maves, J., & Gallagher Cunningham, K. (2019). When organizations rebel: Introducing the foundations of rebel group emergence dataset. *International Studies Quarterly*, *64*(1), 183–193.

Carment, D., & James, P. (2000). Explaining third-party intervention in ethnic conflict: Theory and evidence. *Nations and Nationalism*, *6*(2), 173–202.

Carment, D., James, P., & Taydas, Z. (2009). The internationalization of ethnic conflict. *International Studies Review*, *11*(1), 63–86.

Cetinyan, R. (2002). Ethnic bargaining in the shadow of third-party intervention. *International Organization*, *56*(3), 645–677.

Cook, A., & Olson Lounsbery, M. (2017). *Conflict dynamics: Civil wars, armed actors, and their tactics*. The University of Georgia Press.

Cooper, R., & Berdal, M. (1993). Outside intervention in ethnic conflicts. *Survival*, *35*(1), 118–142.

DeRouen, K., Jr, & Bercovitch, J. (2012). Trends in civil war mediation. In J. J. Hewitt, J. Wilkenfeld, & T. R. Gurr (Eds.), *Peace and conflict 2012* (pp. 59–70). Center for International Development and Conflict Management, University of Maryland.

DeRouen, K., Jr, Bercovitch, J., & Pospieszna, P. (2011). Introducing the civil wars mediation (CWM) dataset. *Journal of Peace Research*, *48*(5), 663–672.

Drury, A. C., & Peksen, D. (2012). Women and economic statecraft: The negative impact of international economic sanctions visit on women. *European Journal of International Relations*, *20*(2), 463–490.

Gent, S. E. (2008). Going in when it counts: Military intervention and the outcome of civil conflicts. *International Studies Quarterly*, *52*(4), 713–735.

Grieg, J. M., & Diehl, P. F. (2012). *International mediation: War and conflict in the modern world*. Polity.

Högbladh, S., Pettersson, T., & Themnér, L. (2011, March 16–19). *External support in armed conflict 1975–2009: Presenting new data*. A paper presented at the 52nd Annual International Studies Convention, Montreal, Canada.

Huibregtse, A. (2010). External intervention in ethnic conflict. *International Interactions*, *36*(3), 265–293.

Huibregtse, A. (2011). Interstate conflict and ethnicity. *Civil Wars*, *13*(1), 40–60.

Khosla, D. (1999). Third world states as intervenors in ethnic conflicts: Implications for regional and international security. *Third World Quarterly*, *20*(6), 1143–1156.

Lake, D. A., & Rothchild, D. (1996). Containing fear: The origin and management of ethnic conflict. *International Security*, *21*(2), 41–75.

Morgan, C. T., Bapat, N., & Kobayashi, Y. (2014). The threat and imposition of sanctions: Updating the TIES dataset. *Conflict Management and Peace Science*, *31*(5), 541–558.

Najafov, Z. (2017). The internationalization of ethnic conflicts and the impact on regional and international security. *Journal of Political Sciences and Public Affairs*, *5*(4), 1–5.

Nalbandov, R. (2009). *Foreign interventions in ethnic conflicts*. Ashgate.

Olson Lounsbery, M., & DeRouen, K., Jr. (2016). The viability of civil war peace agreements. *Civil Wars*, *18*(3), 311–337.

Olson Lounsbery, M., & Pearson, F. S. (2009). *Civil wars: Internal struggles, global consequences*. University of Toronto Press.

Peksen, D. (2009). Better or worse? The effect of economic sanctions on human rights. *Journal of Peace Research*, *46*(1), 59–77.

Petterson, T., Hogbladh, S., & Oberg, M. (2019). Organized violence 1989-2018 and peace agreements. *Journal of Peace Research*, *56*(4), 589–603.

Regan, P. M. (1998). Choosing to intervene: Outside intervention in internal conflicts. *Journal of Politics*, *60*(3), 754–779.

Regan, P. M. (2000). *Civil wars and foreign powers: Outside intervention in intrastate conflict*. University of Michigan Press.

Regan, P. M. (2002). Third-party interventions and the duration of intrastate conflicts. *Journal of Conflict Resolution*, *46*(1), 55–73.

Saideman, S. M. (1997). Explaining the international relations of secessionist conflicts: Vulnerability vs. ethnic ties. *International Organization*, *51*(4), 721–753.

Saideman, S. M. (2016). ELF must die: Institutions, concentration, and the international relations of ethnic conflict and the quest for better data. *Ethnopolitics*, *16*(1), 66–73.

Svensson, I. (2007). Bargaining, bias, and peace brokers: How rebels commit to peace. *Journal of Peace Research*, *44*(2), 177–194.

Wallensteen, P., & Svensson, I. (2014). Talking peace: International mediation in armed conflicts. *Journal of Peace Research*, *51*(2), 315–327.

Yassine-Hamdan, N., & Pearson, F. S. (2014). *Arab approaches to conflict resolution: Mediation, negotiation, and the settlement of political disputes*. Routledge.

4
RE-EXAMINING PEACEBUILDING PRIORITIES: LIBERAL PEACE AND THE EMANCIPATORY CRITIQUE

Andrew E. E. Collins and Chuck Thiessen

Societies emerging from violent conflict can emerge profoundly changed, with key norms and institutions damaged, or sometimes breaking down entirely. Since the 1990s, stabilizing such societies has been a notable foreign policy focus for the United States and its allies (Helman & Ratner, 1992), with peacebuilding emerging as a prominent tool of the international community. In 1992, Boutros-Ghali famously defined peacebuilding as "action to identify and support structures which will tend to strengthen and solidify peace in order to avoid a relapse into conflict" (United Nations, 1992), yet the track record of actual peacebuilding operations has been disappointing for most observers. Debates about how best to improve efforts in this sphere have often been framed in technocratic terms within key policy documents, with issues such as programmatic sequencing, implementation, service delivery, and institutional coordination occupying the attention of many in the practitioner community. However, peacebuilding is a technical exercise, and it is also associated with a highly political form of international intervention into matters, which historically have been (at least notionally) the exclusive preserve of sovereign governments to regulate as their domestic affairs. Securing the peace and providing access to justice, for example, are fundamental to the structure of a society, and are crucial sources of legitimacy for the state, in its traditional Weberian conception. Consequently, there is a great deal at stake in debates over this deeper political aspect of peacebuilding.

Peacebuilding's political character has most frequently been discussed in relation to a dominant theoretical paradigm, known as the liberal peace, which has at its core the idea that liberal (as opposed to illiberal) societies will be more peaceful, both domestically, and in their relations with their neighbors. There is some variation among different accounts of what, specifically, comprises liberal peacebuilding, yet the essential components are generally considered to involve (Joshi et al., 2014; Lemay-Hébert, 2013):

- Promotion of human rights
- The rule of law
- Promotion of democracy and good governance principles
- Security sector/system reform
- Promotion of free market economic reforms and privatization

With such wide-ranging scope, liberal peacebuilding aims at more than simply producing an environment free of physical violence, and focuses on moving toward what Galtung termed "positive peace" (Galtung, 1975). This entails building up the foundations for a just and stable society, whatever those specific foundations might prove to be in the case at hand. Liberal peacebuilding, however, circumscribes the range of possibilities as far as which sorts of societal foundations do end up being consolidated and protected through the state's and the international community's resources. The preference of intervening actors is to focus on top-down, institutionally driven reforms as a way of impacting the wider society. Hence, the main objective of liberal peacebuilding is to bring about "a self-sustaining peace within domestic, regional and international frameworks of liberal governance in which both overt and structural violence are removed and social, economic and political models conform to a mixture of liberal and neo-liberal international expectations" (Franks & Richmond, 2008, p. 83).

Key insights

The critique of liberal peace

Problematically, however, the norms and institutions favored by liberal peacebuilding do not always resonate well with local populations living in war-torn areas of the world, and a body of literature has arisen which is critical of the norms and assumptions underpinning liberal peacebuilding. Liberal peacebuilding is accused, for instance, of being hypocritical, coercive, and unconcerned with the social welfare of communities affected by intervention (Richmond, 2009). Critiques have ranged from the fundamental to the incremental. On the one hand, some critical scholars (e.g. Chandler, 2006; Tadjbakhsh, 2011) have rejected fundamental assumptions underlying the liberal peace, such as whether democratization and marketization are indeed pacifying forces, and have advocated wholesale rethinking of the paradigm at the conceptual level. On the other hand, "problem-solvers," often writing from a practitioner perspective, are considered to prefer practical prescriptions and incremental tinkering as ways to improve how peacebuilders operate within the constraints of the current international environment. It may be tempting to conclude that problem-solving thinking is the remit of the practitioner and policymaker communities, while critiquing paradigms is the remit of academics, and this is certainly not the case. By no means are problem-solvers incapable of critical reflection, or critical scholars incapable of solving problems, and both perspectives are acknowledged to produce important insights (Bellamy, 2005). Nonetheless, peacebuilders face a genuine dilemma when determining their own positionality in the liberal peacebuilding debate. As we argue here, the norms and practices associated with liberal peacebuilding have the potential to do a great deal of good in the right contexts, yet there are convincing reasons to believe that liberal peacebuilding fails to achieve its stated goals because of more than just simple problems of implementation; rather, there are deep conceptual contradictions embedded within the approach, which manifest in ways that disrupt peaceful social relations.

Critics contend that the mechanisms chosen by interventionist actors for promoting change attempt to treat deep-seated political and socioeconomic problems as mere technical matters, amenable to technocratic solutions, through the implementation of good governance principles at the level of state institutions, for example. Politically rooted problems can necessitate actual decision-making on the prioritization of resources and reform agendas, and reframing such situations into a more comfortable bureaucratic form is, understandably, a strong temptation for practitioners and policymakers (Paris, 2009). Unfortunately, bureaucratic action at an elite institutional level is not necessarily an acceptable substitute for actual political reform permeating all levels of society. From this viewpoint, liberal peacebuilding can suffer from a lack of local legitimacy, as it aims at providing the kind of peace, which external actors believe the local society *should* have, rather than the kind of peace, which people living in a conflict-affected society might develop for themselves. Even if well intentioned, the activities of interveners may not be experienced by local populations as peacebuilding at all. Millar (2014) has observed how experiences are mediated by the concepts people hold in their minds, in contexts where democracy and the institutions of a liberal state have not historically shaped people's worldviews, it may be difficult to predict the outcomes when donors try to incentivize the adoption of liberal practices.

Consequently, critical responses to liberal peacebuilding have increasingly drawn on ideas of local ownership and agency to challenge the assumption that liberal norms and institutions, deriving from the historically particular experience of wealthy, industrialized states, are universally applicable. Part of the reason peacebuilding missions fail so often, critics argue, is precisely that they represent a set of efforts to implant liberal norms and institutions in contexts lacking the social preconditions for the formation of a liberal state (Ejdus & Juncos, 2018). Calls for greater reliance on context-specific empirical insights and the role of local agency are now fairly commonplace (Schneckener, 2016), yet in spite of significant progress in making interventions more context-sensitive and elicitive of the needs and priorities of local communities (Bøås & Stig, 2010), peace operations continue to face local resistance. In principle, it should be possible for peacebuilding to take on greater flexibility of form without fundamentally changing anything about the *liberal* character of norm exportation involved (Paris, 2010). Yet it would be remiss of peacebuilders to ignore that the liberal tradition of philosophical thinking is precisely what generated such a strong focus on institutional formalism and process-based forms of legitimacy in the first place (Richmond & Mac Ginty, 2014).

From this perspective, one contradiction embedded within liberal peacebuilding is that it asserts the benefits of specific norms and institutions, all the while incremental reformers try to bring more adaptability to those institutional forms so that they match with local appetites and hopefully engender less resistance. In other words, liberal peacebuilding lionizes the state and its constitutive institutions. At the same time, these structures automatically marginalize and exclude many local parties, generating political winners and losers, and making control of the state into a prize to be contested, often through the continuation of conflict. For example, the securitization of peace interventions has been well documented (Newman, 2010; Tschirgi, 2013), when outsiders privilege the state and channel massive resource flows through approved security structures, many informal and nonstate security provider actors are relegated and excluded from participation in the planning and implementation of peace. Williams (2010) points to donor community discourses which treat local political and social structures as dysfunctional because of their "tribal" affiliations, as a way of justifying why they should be marginalized.

The crucial theme in much of the critique of liberal peacebuilding is essentially one of inclusivity. Richmond (2009) perceives a need for "emancipatory" forms of peacebuilding, which would offer greater participatory opportunities across a broader spectrum of society, making peace into everyone's collective concern. Rather than advocating the abandonment of liberal principles, though, he envisages hybrid local-liberal alternatives, which mix elements of different peacebuilding traditions, and emphasize everyday, bottom-up participation. Similarly, Donais (2012) sees peacebuilding as a negotiated consensus, necessitating the express inclusion of both local level and elite actors to ensure the uptake of ideas.

Does liberal peacebuilding really exist?

Emancipation is a worthy goal for peacebuilders, yet what role can outsiders legitimately play in facilitating critical, multilevel negotiations within societies where they are charged with helping build the peace? As Selby (2013) has argued, the conduct of peacebuilding may have more to do with traditional concerns of strategy and geopolitics than with some overarching ideologically inspired paradigm. In other words, the influence of liberal theories over individual and institutional behavior might be overstated, with political and bureaucratic pressures accounting for the bulk of decision-making in reality. As Selby and others have noted, peacebuilding operations are often supported by multiple donor governments, intergovernmental organizations (IGOs), nongovernmental organizations (NGOs), and nonstate actors (including private sector entities). This is, clearly, far from a homogeneous group, and scholars have questioned the value of describing these institutions collectively, as though they were animated by a shared ideological strategy at all. For some (e.g., Richmond, 2010, p. 22), there is "implicit agreement" between the various institutional actors engaged in peacebuilding over the essentiality of its liberal norm promotion. For others (e.g., Duffield, 2001, p. 12), the liberal character of globalized peacebuilding lies in "complex, mutating and stratified networks," and is therefore prone to different interpretations. The solidity of international consensus about liberal norms and their role in supporting peace cannot be taken for granted, since peacebuilders' efforts to implant liberal norms and institutions into societies emerging from conflict will be shaped by the coherence of what different stakeholders envisage as an appropriate peacebuilding strategy.

Similarly, specific donor institutions involved with peacebuilding can vary with respect to their understandings of what will alleviate conflict (Zaum, 2012). In Kosovo, for example, the North Atlantic Treaty Organization (NATO) and United Nations (UN) missions have perceived a context of ethnic conflict between Serbian and Albanian communities, whereas the Organization for Security and Cooperation in Europe (OSCE) and the European Union (EU) rule of law mission have focused on corruption and the maintenance of law and order as the primary challenges to building peace. This variance has led to the adoption of multiple overlapping strategies, with donors sometimes duplicating each other's efforts or working at cross-purposes. Such fragmentation provides the opportunity for local actors to exploit coordination gaps, resist externally imposed agendas, and modify the implementation of peacebuilding policies to the point where outcomes do not necessarily resemble the intentions of any of the donors. Contestation can also emerge among international actors over political agendas, with the promotion of liberal norms increasingly clashing with illiberal priorities involved in securitization and counterterrorism activities (Thiessen, 2019).

Recognizing this diversity of actors and approaches, Heathershaw (2008) disaggregates the liberal peacebuilding edifice into three separate strands of discourse, those relating to democratization, civil society, and state-building. While it is true that these represent different agendas, and that peacebuilding has always been a conceptually contested enterprise, we do not believe that this vitiates the concept of liberal peacebuilding. There is still much to be gained from analyzing commonalities among the many peacebuilding operations, which have been deployed around the world. In fact, data from the Peace Accords Matrix dataset would suggest that, in spite of great variation in which principles are implemented and to what degree, peace accords themselves do generally enshrine core principles of the liberal peace (Joshi et al., 2014). Taken together, all of this illustrates that the phenomenon of "liberal peacebuilding" is no ideological monolith, yet it does provide analytical leverage for those committed to an emancipatory vision of peacebuilding, as something against which their efforts at promoting the inclusion of the marginalized must be able to be measured favorably.

The high stakes of connecting theory to practice

The preceding sections survey the growing critique of universalizing claims made based on liberal norms and practices within the peacebuilding sector. We have discussed how liberal interventionism may not result in locally experienced peace in contexts of violence. This insight has emerged as part of the emancipatory approach to peacebuilding, which seeks to define the contours of an intervention system that is broadly inclusive in nature, methodologically bottom-up in its approach, locally owned, and hybrid in its structures and processes (Byrne & Thiessen, 2020, p. 135; Donais, 2015; Mac Ginty, 2008; Thiessen, 2014). Emancipatory intervention systems challenge the prescriptive limits of liberal concerns for donor security interests and short-term geopolitical agendas (Smirl, 2015; Thiessen & Özerdem, 2019; Tschirgi, 2013), and take seriously the social and political agendas of local domestic groups and populations. Our hope is that some practical steps can be taken to initiate the sorts of challenges to liberal peacebuilding orthodoxy that the critical literature has been advocating.

Peacebuilders themselves are unlikely to abandon the familiarity of known and normalized intervention practice (for instance, with respect to their reliance upon "proven" templates and global expertise or the maintenance of external control over funding streams). Because of this, their domestic counterparts may feel the need to wrestle for control of project initiatives, a phenomenon we label as "local ownership meta-conflict," because of its societal pervasiveness, far-reaching structural implications, and dependence on conceptual contestation (Collins & Thiessen, 2019). This ownership meta-conflict can very easily travel down unhelpful paths that do not necessarily result in local emancipation. In response, our goal here is to discuss select intervention practices that increase the odds of emancipatory outcomes in this ownership contest. What can external interveners and their domestic partners do to navigate the contestation inside foreign-funded peacebuilding initiatives? What theoretical and practical guidance is available to support intervening actors who face scepticism at multiple levels regarding the adoption of emancipatory goals in teaching, training, capacity building, and policy advising?

Frontline intervention activities such as teaching, training, capacity building, and policy advising are our primary concern here. How do practitioners grapple with the contradictions, dilemmas, uncertainties, and disagreements highlighted by the foundational critiques leveled against liberal intervention in contexts of ethnic conflict (Chandler, 2006; Duffield, 2007; Heathershaw, 2008; Selby, 2013; Turner & Pugh, 2006)? Should these critiques inspire practitioners to pack up and leave conflict zones, requiring local groups and populations to face their future on their own? Or, can the liberal intervention machinery be turned in an emancipatory direction as peacebuilding practices are revised within the context of competition over local ownership?

Grappling with these questions is worthwhile, practically speaking. Forsaking interventionism altogether would be "tantamount to abandoning tens of millions of people to lawlessness, predation, disease and fear" (Paris, 2010, p. 338). If, instead, interventions are to continue in some shape or form, then fundamental critiques of liberal interventionism should not tear down theoretical scaffolding without offering a substitute as to do so would be likely to reproduce conventional, tried, and tested bureaucratic patterns that appeal to practitioners on grounds of safety and comfort more than for their effectiveness. Unfortunately, critiques of liberal peacebuilding have struggled to plan for a transition to postliberal praxis. A failure to initiate meaningful discussions of postliberal alternatives have left well-intentioned practitioners unsure of what to do in the face of unabashed hard power politics and raw projections of power and self-interest, clearly on display in the morass of foreign intervention in Syria and Yemen.

The evolving situation in Syria raises a difficult dilemma. Should theorists and practitioners be wary of deconstructing liberal interventionism for fear of creating a void, which could be filled by something worse? While the Syrian case suggests that more work remains to theorize postliberal peacebuilding scenarios, we are wary of allowing such a fear to temper critical exploration of emancipatory alternatives. Subversions, distractions, and crises will inevitably face any challenge to the status quo, yet failing to challenge liberal peacebuilding ensures its continued ideological hegemony, and carries the risk of failing to understand alternative sources of power and legitimacy beyond the state and its institutions. Given how contested power and legitimacy are in societies emerging from violent conflict, constructing a proposal for emancipatory peacebuilding practice should be undertaken with urgency. Urgent revisions to practice may not occur at elite levels, yet rather at the level of the "everyday," where emergent creativity produces revised practices that change the direction of intervention trends and increasingly promote an everyday emancipation (Millar, 2020; Redekop, 2019).

We now explore the possibility of emergent creativity and everyday emancipation in two areas of frontline intervention activity: (1) teaching and training and (2) policy-building and peacebuilding practice. Our analysis does not stop after deconstructing the liberal intervention project yet it takes the next analytical step to consider alternative practices that increase the odds of everyday emancipation, even if under the influence of international interveners.

Implications for teaching and training

Before venturing further, we need to lay some theoretical groundwork for the choices that practitioners make regarding the methodological and pedagogical shift away from conventional to more emancipatory practices. In particular, we return to the dichotomy between broad categories of thinking about peacebuilding practice on the frontlines, problem-solving or paradigm critique (Cox, 1981). Problem-solving is, understandably, the realm in which trainers often operate being primarily interested in supporting the status quo peacebuilding system to be more efficient and effective in essence a "quest for perfection within defined limits" (Pugh, 2013, p. 12). Problem-solving practitioners, such as technical training experts, researchers, or project designers, work for the interests of political authority, often in advising or consulting roles. Problem-solving does not mean that critique does not occur; however, critique is restrained according to liberal biases and ideological limits (Pugh, 2013, p. 12).

To contrast, emancipation requires paradigm-shifting critiques of the underlying structure and assumptions of interventionism. This sort of critique offers a way to resist conventional peacebuilding knowledge that is created and used solely to further the goals of liberal interveners (Booth, 1997, p. 111). Further, paradigmatic critique emancipates by questioning the legitimacy of political and social authority that calls upon the "common sense" of hegemonic liberal peace theories in contexts of ethnic conflict (Pugh, 2013, p. 12). "Theory is *for* someone and *for* some purpose," (italics in the original) and theory is most effectively challenged once this is fully understood (Cox, 1981, p. 128).

Herman Schmidt (1968) recognized decades ago that theorizing in the disciplines of peace studies and conflict resolution have tended to support entrenched power and be oriented favorably toward the structural status quo. In addition, North American peacebuilding scholarship and think-tank outputs have tended to be problem-solving in nature, offering up solutions for international organizations and governments (Mac Ginty, 2013, p. 3). Indeed, the publication lists of many international NGOs support the continued dominance of the liberal intervention paradigm.

To begin with, critical approaches to teaching and training are rooted in the challenge of local ownership of peacebuilding initiatives and its constitutive components. As alluded to above, ownership is not something which powerful foreign actors gift to domestic partners to remedy some supposed lack of agency on their part; rather, local ownership is acquired through constructive forms of international-domestic conflict (Collins & Thiessen, 2019, p. 16). It is inevitable that deeper forms of ownership by local counterparts will have a significant impact on the way teaching and training are practiced, with implications for the very question of who is legitimately able to conduct training. The difficult reality is that even when shifting ownership toward the "local," donors often come from wealthy, industrialized nations. Understandably, these donors often insist upon their own roster of experienced, educated, typically English-speaking consultants and trainers (von Billerbeck, 2016). These trainers carry a wealth of technical skills and form an epistemic community that can be challenging for newcomers to break into.

However, this reliance on a roster of experienced trainers and teachers helps explain why paradigm critique is rare. These trainers form a global training industry, which is heavily invested in the liberal peace model of intervention. The sustainability of this training industry is directly linked to the maintenance of liberal interventionist approaches. Maintenance requires problem-solving and do-it-yourself revisions to improve the efficiency of peacebuilding ventures in contexts of ethnic conflict. Thus, radical critique and resistance to the status quo are rare as trainers whose mindset leans toward such critiques will sit awkwardly inside the liberal intervention system, feeling the danger of "biting the hand that feeds them," and wary of jeopardizing their own livelihoods. It is difficult to imagine a World Bank trainer, for example, advising national government trainees to return to their offices and actively resist development goals set by the World Bank, in favor of a bottom-up agenda with priorities determined exclusively by local actors. Nor is it clear that this would necessarily lead to a better quality of peacebuilding, endorsing an approach with such ambiguous potential consequences for peace would naturally strain the credibility of anyone suggesting it (Donais, 2012).

There are, perhaps, ways to support the development of critical new approaches to peacebuilding in actual training. An obvious move would be to utilize trainers that are ideologically different and geographically distant from the liberal interventionist mission and its associated professional training industry. Hiring trainers from the Global South may expand the range of viewpoints and critical perspectives needed to resist excessive influence from industrialized countries and their elites. A practical and philosophical transformation of training philosophy to a "south-south" experience would have distinct advantages. Deep forms of cooperative exploration into new policy solutions are more likely to occur among actors with similar life experiences of peace and ethnonational conflict, for example. South-south interactions may also be less vulnerable to postcolonial paternalism, dependency tendencies and other ideological baggage that impede the identification of appropriate and locally owned responses to violence (Nganje, 2013, p. 4). Further, south-south teaching and training may hold special appeal because they are often perceived to involve an ethos more of knowledge sharing than of transfer and receipt (Nganje, 2013, p. 4). Vern Redekop (2019) suggests that this sort of dynamic between domestic and international peacebuilders enables "emergent creativity," and helps unearth new, context-appropriate practices, which get beyond the restrictions of template-bound bureaucratic formalism associated with the usual activities of the interventionist community.

However, south-south interactions are certainly not guaranteed to avoid the pitfalls of institutional isomorphism, centralism, and context-inappropriate knowledge transfer. To integrate the desired emancipatory spirit into training, it may be necessary to conceive of these interactions as a "sounding board," in which mutual knowledge is built and resource and power asymmetries are addressed explicitly. Viewing training interactions as a sounding board would encourage stakeholders to ask critical and incisive questions of each other regarding the discovery and development of alternative peacebuilding models not necessarily promoted by dominant liberal interventionist philosophies. This sort of reflective interrogation may support a pedagogy of liberation, as local institutions and individuals consider alternative peacebuilding practices besides those authorized by the liberal peace edifice and its champions. Often, local societies are rich sources of ideas and peacemaking capacity; alternative peacebuilding approaches could draw upon local culture, customs, manners of conflict resolution, and conceptions of justice (Mac Ginty, 2008). Open conversation and self-reflection in a training setting can also reveal blockages facing the local emancipation agenda, for example, pointing out lingering ethnic, gender or age-based power dynamics that deny agency and emancipation to whole swaths of society. Recognizing the destructiveness of such blockages is central within the liberal peacebuilding tradition, yet arriving at the same conclusions through an emancipatory conversation offers a way to build bridges and highlight common values held by both foreign and domestic actors.

Crucially, however, this depends on the value of emancipation being communicated successfully. In this way, critical peacebuilding approaches perhaps suffer from the same dilemma as liberal peacebuilding does whenever local actors are encountered whose genuine desire is to repress other members of their own society. Rather than decry or marginalize such actors as "spoilers," though, the spirit of engagement characterizing the emancipatory agenda would seek opportunities to communicate underlying values in new ways, and based on existing sources of local legitimacy (Thiessen, 2019). Whether the result is reliably a contribution to greater peace is an open question; critical peacebuilding scholars have tended to take care to avoid being overly prescriptive in this area, recognizing that peace must be locally accepted if it is to hold in the long term (Richmond & Mac Ginty, 2014).

Implications for practice and policy

Keeping in mind our task of fleshing out critical forms of intervention, this section discusses the possibility of critical stances toward policymaking and emancipatory peacebuilding practices more broadly. Critical and emancipatory approaches must grapple with an important contradiction; namely, that it has been difficult for both theorists and practitioners to imagine the resolution and/or transformation of many cases of large-scale ethnic violence without some sort of invasive external intervention. "International control is required to establish local ownership," yet this has been a debilitating contradiction for practitioners and policymakers (Paris & Sisk, 2009, p. 305). We suggest it can be approached through several key questions.

First, what roles can universal values and prescriptions play in building locally experienced and meaningful peace? While impinging on local ownership, universalist prescriptions may be well suited to counter the traditional dynamics of conflict resolution that are biased toward wealthy elderly men at the expense of the very poor, women, and youth. Second, what is the most constructive footprint for interventional intervention? While a heavy international footprint may provide short-term security in a crisis, a much less intrusive international stance may be required to promote locally owned economic, political, and social reform (Paris & Sisk, 2009, p. 307). Third, to what extent does international intervention shape and alter local political participation? Local peacebuilding actors may not have the secure space to pursue their locally derived goals without the blessing of external actors, especially local action to combat long-held ethnic divisions that might someday flare into violence if left unaddressed.

Last, to what extent can critical approaches toward specific cases of ethnic conflict be separated from global political and economic concerns? A full separation of the local from the global political economy is impossible, and that local conflict cannot be fully understood or addressed without considering global inequality, colonial and imperial conquest, looting of wealth and strategic resources, and even current forms of global capitalism (Pugh, 2013, p. 22).

These are politically charged issues, which may be uncomfortable for some, and they do highlight a risk associated with critical peacebuilding scholarship namely, that an individual practitioner is not in a position to challenge or change abstract global systems, and that insufficiently bounded critical exploration can be overwhelming, leading to inaction. We take the view that the place which a conflict-affected society holds within global systems, and the strategy it most prefers for navigating inequalities within those systems, are best seen as topics of ongoing discussion for the members of that society to explore on their own terms (Thiessen & Byrne, 2017).

As we have discussed elsewhere (Collins & Thiessen, 2019), a realistic engagement with these four questions leads to the conclusion that locally owned and emancipatory peacebuilding practices will inevitably be laden with conflict. The analytical tradition of agonism is of use here as it highlights the constructive potential of international-domestic competition and the strategic resistance that subordinate domestic counterparts put up (Björkdahl & Mannergren Selimovic, 2016, pp. 324–325; Lee, 2015; Peterson, 2013). In other words, practitioners and policymakers should be aware that despite their acceptance of permissions, resources, or other support from liberal international interveners, they should be primed for necessary and constructive conflict with external actors who, at the end of the day, are unlikely to gift meaningful ownership to them without the intensification of competition over ownership. Facilitating the competition for ownership needs to be considered carefully, yet inclusive, dialogue-based structures can be (and often have been) established to ensure conflict is managed in nonviolent ways (Thiessen, 2014). Local civil society institutions can be supported to serve as a nexus point whose primary mission is to build connections and promote dialogue and negotiation between international and domestic actors.[1]

Conclusion

This chapter has achieved two objectives. First, it has surveyed the aims of liberal peacebuilding and the corresponding critique of the liberal peace that explores how local conflict-affected populations do not always support the goals and structures of liberal peacebuilding. Second, this chapter has discussed the implications of this critique for building a critical and emancipatory stance toward teaching, training, practice, and policy formation inside international interventions to transform ethnic conflict. We have argued that emancipation requires a fundamentally critical stance as it promotes teaching and training initiatives that are locally owned in deep ways, including the use of "south-south" interactions to develop and test alternative peacebuilding models. Last, we have explored critical stances toward policymaking and other peacebuilding practices. Critical stances must grapple with difficult contradictions and dilemmas, yet they are assisted by an agonistic analytical lens.

Note

1 Insight by Andy Carl, independent expert on conflict resolution and public participation in peace processes.

References

Bellamy, A. (2005). The 'next stage' in peace operations theory? In A. Bellamy & P. Williams (Eds.), *Peace operations and global order* (pp. 17–38). Routledge.

Björkdahl, A., & Mannergren Selimovic, J. (2016). A tale of three bridges: Agency and agonism in peacebuilding. *Third World Quarterly, 37*(2), 321–335.

Bøås, M., & Stig, K. (2010). Security sector reform in Liberia: An uneven partnership without local ownership. *Journal of Intervention and Statebuilding, 4*(3), 285–303.

Booth, K. (1997). Security and self: Reflections of a fallen realist. In K. Krause & M. C. Williams (Eds.), *Critical security studies: Concepts and strategies* (pp. 83–120). Routledge.

Byrne, S., & Thiessen, C. (2020). Foreign peacebuilding intervention and emancipatory local agency for social justice. In S. Byrne, T. Matyók, I. M. Scott, & J. Senehi (Eds.), *Routledge companion to peace and conflict studies* (pp. 131–142). Routledge.

Chandler, D. (2006). *Empire in denial: The politics of state-building*. Pluto.

Collins, A. E., & Thiessen, C. (2019). A grounded theory of local ownership as meta-conflict in Afghanistan. *Cooperation and Conflict, 55*(2), 216–234.

Cox, R. W. (1981). Social forces, states and world orders: Beyond international relations theory. *Millennium: Journal of International Studies, 10*(2), 126–155.

Donais, T. (2012). *Peacebuilding and local ownership: Post-conflict consensus-building*. Routledge.

Donais, T. (2015). Operationalizing local ownership. In S. Y. Lee & A. Özerdem (Eds.), *Local ownership in international peacebuilding: Key theoretical and practical issues* (pp. 39–54). Routledge.

Duffield, M. (2001). *Global governance and the new wars*. Zed Books.

Duffield, M. (2007). Development, territories, and people: Consolidating the external sovereign frontier. *Alternatives, 32*(2), 225–246.

Ejdus, F., & Juncos, A. E. (2018). Reclaiming the local in EU peacebuilding: Effectiveness, ownership, and resistance. *Contemporary Security Policy, 39*(1), 4–27.

Franks, J., & Richmond, O. P. (2008). Coopting liberal peace-building: Untying the Gordian knot in Kosovo. *Cooperation and Conflict, 43*(1), 81–103.

Galtung, J. (1975). *Peace: Research – education – action. Essays in peace research Vol. 1*. Christian Ejlers.

Heathershaw, J. (2008). Unpacking the liberal peace: The dividing and merging of peacebuilding discourses. *Millennium, 36*(3), 597–621.

Helman, G. B., & Ratner, S. R. (1992). Saving failed states. *Foreign Policy, 89*, 3–20.

Joshi, M., Lee, S. Y., & Mac Ginty, R. (2014). Just how liberal is the liberal peace? *International Peacekeeping, 21*(3), 364–389.

Lee, S. Y. (2015). Motivations for local resistance in international peacebuilding. *Third World Quarterly, 36*(8), 1437–1452.

Lemay-Hébert, N. (2013). Critical debates on liberal peacebuilding. *Civil Wars, 15*(2), 242–252.

Mac Ginty, R. (2008). Indigenous peace-making versus the liberal peace. *Cooperation and Conflict, 43*(2), 139–163.

Mac Ginty, R. (2013). Introduction. In R. Mac Ginty (Ed.), *Routledge handbook of peacebuilding* (pp. 1–8). Routledge.

Millar, G. (2014). Disaggregating hybridity: Why hybrid institutions do not produce predictable experiences of peace. *Journal of Peace Research, 51*(4), 501–514.

Millar, G. (2020). Preserving the everyday: Pre-political agency in peacebuilding theory. *Cooperation and Conflict, 54*(2), 149–166.

Newman, E. (2010). Peacebuilding as security in 'failing' and conflict-prone states. *Journal of Intervention and Statebuilding, 4*(3), 305–322.

Nganje, F. (2013). Peacebuilding from below: The role of decentralized south-south cooperation in Africa. *The Southern Voices Network: Research Paper No. 1*. Washington DC: The Wilson Centre. https://www.wilsoncenter.org/sites/default/files/media/documents/publication/fritz_nganje_africa_program_policy_brief_7.pdf

Paris, R. (2009). Understanding the "coordination problem" in postwar statebuilding. In R. Paris & T. D. Sisk (Eds.), *The dilemmas of statebuilding: Confronting the contradictions of postwar peace operations* (pp. 53–78). Routledge.

Paris, R. (2010). Saving liberal peacebuilding. *Review of International Studies, 36*, 337–365.

Paris, R., & Sisk, T. D. (2009). Conclusion: Confronting the contradictions. In R. Paris & T. D. Sisk (Eds.), *The dilemmas of statebuilding: Confronting the contradictions of postwar peace operations* (pp. 304–315). Routledge.

Peterson, J. (2013). Creating space for emancipatory human security: Liberal obstructions and the potential of agonism. *International Studies Quarterly, 57*(2), 318–328.

Pugh, M. (2013). The problem-solving and critical paradigms. In R. Mac Ginty (Ed.), *Routledge handbook of peacebuilding* (pp. 11–24). Routledge.

Redekop, V. N. (2019). The emergence of integrative peacebuilding: A complexity-based approach to professional leadership development. *Journal of Peacebuilding & Development, 14*(3), 272–287.

Richmond, O. P. (2009). A post-liberal peace: Eirenism and the everyday. *Review of International Studies, 35,* 557–580.

Richmond, O. P. (2010). A geneology of peace and conflict theory. In O. P. Richmond (Ed.), *Palgrave advances in peacebuilding: Critical developments and approaches* (pp. 14–40). Palgrave Macmillan.

Richmond, O. P., & Mac Ginty, R. (2014). Where now for the critique of the liberal peace? *Cooperation and Conflict, 50*(2), 171–189.

Schmidt, H. (1968). Peace research and politics. *Journal of Peace Research, 5*(3), 217–232.

Schneckener, U. (2016). Peacebuilding in crisis? In T. Debiel, T. Held, & U. Schneckener (Eds.), *Peacebuilding in crisis: Rethinking paradigms and practices of transnational cooperation* (pp. 1–20). Routledge.

Selby, J. (2013). The myth of liberal peace-building. *Conflict, Security & Development, 13*(1), 57–86.

Smirl, L. (2015). *Spaces of aid: How cars, compounds and hotels shape humanitarianism.* Zed Books.

Tadjbakhsh, S. (Ed.). (2011). *Rethinking the liberal peace: External models and local alternatives.* Routledge.

Thiessen, C. (2014). *Local ownership of peacebuilding in Afghanistan: Shouldering responsibility for sustainable peace and development.* Lexington Books.

Thiessen, C. (2019). The strategic ambiguity of the United Nations approach to preventing violent extremism. *Studies in Conflict & Terrorism, 42*(1), 1–22.

Thiessen, C., & Byrne, S. (2017). Proceed with caution: Research production and uptake in conflict-affected countries. *Journal of Peacebuilding and Development, 13*(1), 1–15.

Thiessen, C., & Özerdem, A. (2019). Turkey in Somalia: Challenging North/Western interventionism? *Third World Quarterly, 40*(11), 1976–1995.

Tschirgi, N. (2013). Securitization and peacebuilding. In R. Mac Ginty (Ed.), *Routledge handbook of peacebuilding* (pp. 197–210). Routledge.

Turner, M., & Pugh, M. (2006). Towards a new agenda for transforming war economies. *Conflict, Security & Development, 6*(3), 471–479.

United Nations. (1992). *An agenda for peace: Preventive diplomacy, peacemaking and peace-keeping* (UN Doc A/47/277-S/2000/809). New York, NY: United Nations. http://www.un-documents.net/a47-277.htm

von Billerbeck, S. (2016). *Whose peace?: Local ownership and United Nations peacekeeping.* Oxford University Press.

Williams, A. (2010). Reconstruction: The missing historical link. In O. P. Richmond (Ed.), *Palgrave advances in peacebuilding: Critical developments and approaches* (pp. 58–73). Palgrave Macmillan.

Zaum, D. (2012). Review essay: Beyond the 'liberal peace'. *Global Governance, 18*(1), 121–132.

5
HATRED IS A CONTAGIOUS DISEASE AND PUBLIC HEALTH ISSUE IN ETHNOPOLITICAL CONFLICTS

Izzeldin Abuelaish

The prevalence of violent ethnopolitical conflicts across the globe that are fueled by mutual or one-sided hatred, interpersonal and especially intergroup hatred is a serious public health issue requiring a public health perspective intervention. Intergroup hatred often causes widespread physical and psychological violence or sociopolitical harm, affecting entire populations and generations of populations, including children. The harm molded by hatred includes long-term distress-related health effects caused by immune system dysregulation. Such health effects of hatred are found in the targets of hatred, and the haters. Hatred self-perpetuates through cycles of hatred, violence, counterhatred, and counterviolence. Each cycle brings in its wake increased risk of pathophysiologies.

Violence is recognized as a public health issue, preventing or managing interpersonal and intergroup hatred also makes a positive contribution to public health by addressing a significant category of violence. Hatred is a wide-spread health issue that is linked to violence as only one of its consequences. Health practitioners, researchers, educators, cultural figures, faith representatives, policymakers, governments, and members of the public must create a radical immunization program to inoculate all (first and foremost children and youth) against individual and group-based hatred to begin to heal wounds created by hatred.

Background

A disease is an impairment of an organism caused by external or internal elements that are harmful to that organism, and is recognizable by its symptoms. Hatred is a disease. Such a conceptual framework is based on the interplay of exposure, human hosts, and the environment that leads to the production of hatred. Hatred's underlying causal factors are social, political, environmental, physical, psychological or dehumanization, which could be a "psychological result of hatred," racism, discrimination, bigotry, hate crimes, hate speech, hate acts, incitement, fear, or serious atrocities. Hatred is a contagious disease and a pathological weapon that can be caused by extended exposure to harms, namely humiliation, harassment, violation, deprivation, torture, dehumanization, or victimization. Hatred of another is caused by being hated by that other, and by being exposed to hate speech from that other. One of most common triggers and symptoms of hatred is violence. The patient suffering from hatred often responds to the source of those harms with physical or verbal violence.

Hatred has been studied for centuries by philosophers, theologians, and more recently by social psychologists, anthropologists, peace scholars, and evolutionary scientists. No consensus on a definition of hatred that is scientific and comprehensive exists. Hatred is more than just an emotion; it is a "negative emotion that motivates and may lead to negative behaviors with severe consequences" (Halperin, 2008, p. 715). The prevalence of hatred is a pressing public health issue that must be taken seriously by the medical community, the public, governments, political leaders, academic and nonacademic institutions because hatred represents an existential global threat. Comprehensive and scientific studies are needed. Reliable data and evidence are essential to understand the link between violence and hatred, the long-term consequences of morbidity, and the economic costs of hatred.

To identify a condition as a disease one must identify a visible, tangible, apparent, or recognizable cause. The fundamental question of whether hatred is a contagious disease, a determinant of health, and a public health issue requires the demonstration of a physiological or pathological process leading to disturbed homeostasis. A valid scientific medical model is needed to investigate the causes, characteristics, and impact of hatred on health and well-being using a multidisciplinary comprehensive and holistic approach rather than a fragmented one. A multisystem approach is needed to include socio-biomedical, psychological, sociological, psychiatric, neurological, and endocrine variables. Hatred is an overlooked epidemic and contagious disease.

Given that hatred is a contagious disease and public health issue, then disease is an impairment of the normal state (functionality) of the person or one of its parts that interrupts or modifies the performance of vital functions. Disease is a pathological process, most often physical, sometimes undetermined in origin (Marinker, 1975), and it is a disease of the mind (Gaylin, 2003). Hatred is also a disease of the human heart, soul, and body. Hatred is a complex process that attacks humankind, and becomes a community disease. Hatred is a complex state, discrete, involving destructive intent, disturbed perceptions; a contagious disease affecting individuals, groups, and communities and is often the result of exposure to harm or chronic frustration leading to episodes of rage that go unaddressed. Hatred has causes, triggers, and risk factors that can be prevented from developing or being modified, and whose effects must be treated.

A causal relationship exists between exposure and causality. The human body is a complex and thriving ecosystem. Reasons exist for the consequences of exposure to provocative and harmful actions. When a pathological agent invades or attacks us, our body's response to the invading pathogen depends on many factors including the virulence of the pathogenic agent individual's social, cultural, immunological, and educational status. If our body cannot withstand the harm it leads to a disease with signs and symptoms. Sometimes the response may seem more powerful than the exposure. Newton's third law of action and reaction states that for every action (force) in nature there is an equal and opposite reaction. When we face atrocities and are exposed to challenges, our reaction to these challenges varies according to the type, magnitude, and duration of the challenges, individual variation, and environmental conditions. Hatred may follow a traumatic event or severe disappointment. Hatred involves the dehumanization of the other, which serves as a gateway through which moral barriers can be removed and violence can be perpetrated (Halperin, 2008). What would happen if people are exposed chronically to incitement and hate speech or an environment of humiliation, fear, and oppression where anxiety and stress prevails for a long time?

There are health and social consequences of hatred that disturbs the homeostasis and emotional equilibrium of an individual leading to physical, psychological, social, and behavioral changes.

People afflicted with hatred experience malfunction of daily activities, and several health problems. There is a statistically significant correlation between changes in clinical anxiety and the production of salivary cortisol in listeners who were exposed to hate speech on commercial radio (Garban et. al., 2012). The research reveals that hate speech could potentially have a deleterious impact on the health of listeners. Hateful speech increases clinical anxiety levels, thereby potentially disrupting immune systems and enhancing the growth of cancer and chronic inflammatory disease (DeRijk & Sternberg, 1997). This suggests that exposure to selected hate speech content could potentially influence the onset or development of pathophysiological processes or diseases such as cancer or chronic inflammatory diseases (Elenkov & Chrousos, 1999a, 1999b). They found that volunteers experienced a spike in clinical anxiety after listening to Savage Nation, and had increased levels of cortisol, the so-called "stress hormone," in their saliva. Exposure to the physical or psychological violence of hatred has worse outcomes. Some data is suggestive of the adverse health effects of hatred on the *agent of hate* as negative emotions such as depression, anxiety, anger, and hostility tend to contribute to mortality and morbidity, including cardiovascular disease, osteoporosis, arthritis, certain cancers, Alzheimer's disease, and periodontal disease via immune dysregulation (Glaser et al., 2002; Khayyam-Nekouei et al., 2013).

Stress is generated both in the target and the agent of hatred, that disturb the homeostatic balance of the body, resulting in physiological, psychological, and behavioral changes (Muir & Pfister, 1989). Stress increases the activation of the hypothalamic-pituitary-adrenocortical axis (HPAA) leading to a complex set of interactions that control many of the body's processes (Fisher, 1989). One way to assess the impact of stress is to track steroid hormones, cytokines, and immunological regulators that are produced by the HPAA in response to a stressful situation. These regulators are present in saliva, where they can be measured by noninvasive means (Arellano-Garcia et al., 2008; Vining et al., 1983a, 1983b).

Therefore, there is justification for dealing with hatred as a contagious disease employing a public health approach investigating its socio-epidemiology and pathophysiology, and identifying modifiable risk factors, prevention, and management strategies (see Figure 5.1).

Anxiety typically happens in response to circumstances in life, such as living in a war zone or living with uncertainty. Stress has an effect on the immune system and may trigger a rheumatoid arthritis flare-up or worsen its symptoms (Walker et al., 1999).

The body's balance of cytokines can determine the difference between health and disease. There is a "moderate correlation" between stress and the regulation of a cytokine that signals an antiinflammatory response (Zeki & Romaya, 2008). A pattern of brain activity occurs when the subjects felt hate viewing a hated face resulted in increased activity in the medial frontal gyrus, right putamen, bilaterally in the premotor cortex, in the frontal pole and bilaterally in the medial insula (Zeki & Romaya, 2008). They found three areas where activation correlated linearly with the declared level of hatred, the right insula, right premotor cortex, and the right fronto-medial gyrus showing that there is a unique pattern of activity in the brain in the context of hate so that the sight of a hated person mobilizes the motor system for the possibility of attack or defense.

There is a *link between violence and hatred* as hatred might be a prime and extreme enabler of direct, structural, and cultural violence. Hatred self-perpetuates, usually through cycles of hatred and counterhatred, violence and counterviolence (sometimes as revenge) (Figure 5.2).

In the 21st century hatred due to racism, discrimination, hate speech, injustice, fear, incitement, and violence is presenting an unprecedented global existential threat. Hatred contributes to the burden of disease, death, and disability among individuals and communities. A significant portion of violence in the world is based on hatred of the "other." People find so many reasons to hate one another—their class, gender, authority, religion, skin color, ethnicity,

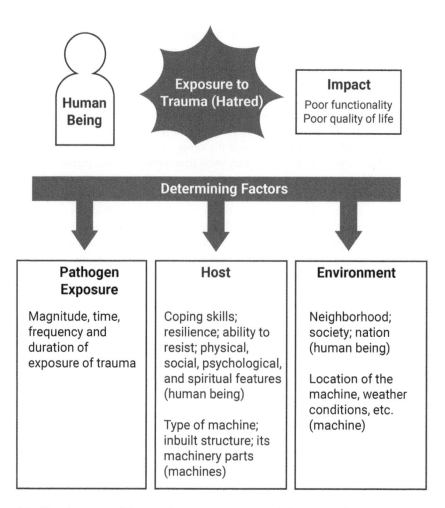

Figure 5.1 Hatred conceptual framework: Exposure, impact and determining factors

Figure 5.2 The relationship between hatred and violence

sexual orientation, creed, customs, and nationality, membership of social groups, political incitement, political opinion, physical attributes, or imagined attributes. Hatred begets hatred and violence begets violence. This is particularly true when one group hates another group and the result is mutual hatred. The current increasingly violent and cruel ethnonationalist, political, religious, or religious-sect-based civil or civil-military conflicts, many of which are either based on or fuelled by racism, incitement, supremacy, discrimination, fear, and hatred, demonstrate unequivocally that hatred is a dangerous and contagious disease.

Understanding the psychological, pathological, physiological, and neurobiological consequences of hatred suggests that the link is not just metaphoric, as it is true and measurable for the individual experiencing it. "It is plausible that the physiological arousal associated with

Figure 5.3 Exposure to hatred

chronic experiencing of hatred or blame might endanger health" (Harris & Thoresen, 2005, p. 325). There may be evidence that this physiological arousal can lead to the accumulation of stress responses and allostatic load.

The World Health Organization (WHO) defines violence as "the intentional use of physical force or power, threatened or actual, against oneself, another person, or against a group or community, that either results in or has a high likelihood of resulting in injury, death, psychological harm, mal-development, or deprivation" (Krug et al., 2002, p. 61). WHO calls violence a "leading worldwide public health problem," and global public health agencies devote entire divisions to its prevention because hatred is interconnected with violence resulting from the exposure (Abuelaish & Arya, 2017) (Figure 5.3).

WHO estimates that 1.6 million die from violent causes, including wars, gang and group murders, child abuse, youth violence, domestic abuse, sexual violence, elderly abuse, and suicide each year as 35 people are killed every hour as a result of armed conflict (Krug et al., 2002). Hatred is a public health issue, warranting the attention of practitioners and academics alike (Dahlberg & Mercy, 2009). Hatred can be conceptualized as an infectious disease, spreading violence, fear, and ignorance. Hatred is contagious and crosses barriers and borders, and no one is immune to the risk as we are all potential targets and agents (Abuelaish & Arya, 2017).

Hatred can lead to the accumulation of stress responses and allostatic load that triggers specific cases of hatred that are likely to be cumulative exposures to some kind of repetitive harm, often violent or provocative (physical, psychological, social, political, including deprivation and dehumanization), or to hate speech that thrives on greed, arrogance, racism, discrimination, and ignorance. There may be a causal relationship between exposure to these triggers and hatred as an outcome, warranting further exploration from a public health perspective. There's justification in recognizing hatred as a contagious disease, determinant of health and a public health issue by employing a public health approach investigating its societal characteristics and causes, and identifying modifiable risk factors, prevention, and management strategies (Abuelaish, 2021).

Health promotion and prevention means that in public health, the first step is prevention of disease, both at the individual and population levels. Hatred is a disease and preventive measures are essential in building immunity to hatred by emphasizing prevention policies of its upstream causes such as incitement, and structural systematic violence. We must seek immunization to hatred through a multifaceted approach that explicitly captures the social determinants of health perspectives, promotes advocacy efforts, and prioritizes the awareness and education of the population. Long-term results require elimination of the specific triggers and causes. In hatred triggered by oppression, for example, a major part of the treatment could be removing the oppression that include lifting political and economic barriers, providing concrete signs of recognition, and truth-and-reconciliation and restorative justice processes. If the hatred is ignorance based or through religious or political incitement, then superstitions and false narratives must be eliminated.

Figure 5.4 The hexagon of hatred

The components of hatred include people, actions, and behaviors, and the target of hatred can be individual or group, community or nation (Figure 5.4).

We must close the knowledge gap in the study of hatred as a contagious disease learning how to respond to this threat and its consequences on human health and stability. We have to give more attention to understanding hatred using a comprehensive, multidisciplinary, holistic, and collaborative approach like the medical model along with what we have learned about the drivers of spreading hatred. It remains linear and limited to psychology, and this urges us to adopt a broader social, ecological, and medical context.

There is hope for filling the knowledge gaps and advancing research activities. There is a need for a wakeup call to the global community to refocus attention, research efforts, and investment on hatred as a contagious disease with epidemic potential. The international community's commitment to taking it more seriously will be advanced by establishing a global network for proactive research, surveillance, rapid detection, and prevention.

A central contribution of the current conceptualization of hatred as a contagious disease, a public health issue, and a determinant of health is the recognition of this holistic approach with a focus on the physiological concomitants occurring at the time of the hatred experienced, so that researchers can explore the potential long-term chronic effects of the hate on subsequent health, including physical, mental, social, and spiritual well-being.

This chapter provides a framework for understanding the holistic model of hatred as a disease and addresses the unanswered dynamic relationship and aspects of hatred. Significant knowledge gaps in this area exist along with failures in the response to contain it. There is, as of yet, no evidence-based practice to draw upon. This lack of information is embedded in a simplistic view of the causes of hatred that are disconnected from the root causes, and their social and ecological contexts. This urges us to require a holistic socio-epidemiological and bio-medical perspective that incorporates social as well as physical, psychological, political, economic, and biological dimensions.

The notion of the bio-complexity paradigm and addition of the medical model captures the depth and richness and most importantly, the interactions between the causal agents (exposure), the human host, and the context. The promotion of a multidisciplinary approach and the insights gained by employing the bio-complexity paradigm for addressing and garnering an improved understanding of hatred as a disease is needed. In order to promote the health and well-being of people afflicted with hatred, interventions must be aimed at all levels of the model.

Key insights

Hatred is not extreme dislike, aversion, resentment, anger, rage, or resentment, even if some of those attitudes sometimes precede or accompany hatred. Hatred is an attitude that includes an intense, toxic, self-consuming, very unpleasant and *chronic* feeling, a judgment of the object of hatred as bad, immoral, disgusting, dangerous, even *subhuman*, and a tendency, desire, or intention to be violent, often to the extreme of destroying—physically, psychologically, or socially—the object of hatred. Hatred differs from hatred of things and events, for example, hatred of disease, war, violence, and cruelty. It is immoral to destroy, hurt or eliminate human beings so that an individual who chooses to act based on hatred might be morally compromised. Hatred is contagious and spreads locally and remotely. The triggers for hatred can be typified as exposure to something. Hatred is mostly triggered by (1) exposure to repetitive harm, usually violent or provocative (physical, psychological, social, political, including deprivation, racism, discrimination, incitement, hate speech, oppression, and dehumanization), and worsened by nonacknowledgement of, and nonremorse for the harm done by the harm doer; or (2) ignorance exacerbated by exposure to misinformation about another. Intergroup hatred is also triggered by prolonged exposure to expressions of hatred, either hatred by the group one belongs to of another group, or hatred by another group of the group one belongs to; and for that reason, intergroup hatred is usually highly contagious. A typical example of such expression is hate speech, fear mongering, political incitement, false narratives or superstitions that dehumanize the other, generally created by leaders or those striving for leadership.

Intergroup hatred can be chronic, sometimes passed on through generations. It is a significant challenge for those concerned with reducing hatred, and the destruction and adverse health effects it causes so hatred can continue even when the original exposure that triggered it has ceased, since it is easy to keep an inflammatory narrative alive, or rekindle it, by couching it in "revenge" or "justice" talk, especially in speeches by charismatic leaders. For that reason, treating the symptoms of hatred alone, such as the violence that expresses it, or the pathophysiologies that follow, will be ineffective and at most temporary. To reduce or cure hatred is to reduce or eliminate its root causes.

Implications for teaching and training

Understanding the psychological, pathological, physiological, and neurobiological consequences of hatred suggests that the link to disease is metaphorical, literal, and measurable for the individual experiencing it. The global community must recognize hatred as a public health issue to move from the management of hatred to the active prevention of its root causes through promotion, education, and awareness. We must measure it and if unable to prevent it, mitigate it. Preventing, mitigating, containing, managing, or treating hatred (and its health consequences) requires a comprehensive, holistic, and collaborative involvement by researchers, medical practitioners, educational and cultural institutions, policymakers, governments, peace practitioners, parents, other primary caregivers, and enlightened citizens. Health, freedom, justice, education, well-being, violence, and war depend on who you are and where you live. The context and environment are a critical determinant.

Given the same exposure, each individual's chances of experiencing interpersonal and intergroup hatred, expressing that hatred with violent acts, or suffering its pathophysiological effects are also a function of many other factors—genetic, biological, psychological, cultural, economic, political, social, as well as other environmental variables. Even in the case of intergroup hatred, contagion is not inevitable for each individual; yet some individuals are up against more odds than others.

Our research goal should be to fill the research gap and generate knowledge on the relations between hatred, health, and well-being, beginning by investigating the socio-epidemiology and pathophysiology of hatred to identify modifiable risk factors, and formulate intervention, prevention, and management strategies. Multidiscipline and interdisciplinary research into the contributing causes and health effects is needed and preventing or reducing hatred and mitigating its adverse health effects, especially in the hating subject.

Practitioners and teachers must develop "hatred and health" workshops, courses, and graduate studies; incorporate these streams into existing hate studies curricula (which currently focus on legal, political, and social justice considerations of hatred), as well as peace and conflict studies. For example, I intend to create an institute for hatred, health, well-being, and international peace (IHHWIP). Besides generating new knowledge on the relations between hatred and health, and disseminating that knowledge to the public, health organizations, and decision-making bodies, through publications, conferences, and town hall meetings, IHHWIP will be responsible for developing a new conflict resolution and peacebuilding program that is sensitive to the role that hatred plays in creating, maintaining, or inflaming certain conflicts. While a typical goal of resolving violent conflict is to reduce or eliminate the root causes of violence by replacing it with collaboration, compromise, accommodation, and empowerment, this specialized kind of conflict resolution will emphasize the importance of containing, managing, or reducing the hatred that causes violent conflicts. Elimination of war, violence, and injustice is through the language of justice, freedom, equality, and accountability for all. IHHWIP's priority will include researchers, educators, and health practitioners from past and present ethnopolitical conflicts and hatred-prone social sectors.

IHHWIP will center its activities on educating youth about hatred to enhance their problem-solving and conflict resolution skill sets. Richter et al. (2018) noted that education is "the fundamental source of a society's ideological training." Children and youth are the most susceptible to being indoctrinated with specific ideologies, whether positive or negative (Matzopoulos et al., 2010; Richter et al., 2018). Primary prevention techniques for interpersonal violence require investment in early childhood developmental stages that includes long-term educational programs through school-based learning (Matzopoulos et al., 2010). Enhancing the pedagogical curriculum with antioppression topics include understanding social categories on multiple dimensions, including individual and collective experiences, providing space for voices to be heard, and allowing for classroom dialogue (Nelson, 1999). Providing safe and healthy environments for children are effective in preventing violent outcomes in the future (Matzopoulos et al., 2010).

The educative goal, via formal curricula and other means, is to drive into public awareness the notions that (1) interpersonal and intergroup hatred is a contagious, malignant, chronic, and destructive disease to all involved, and (2) the choice to not hate is a real choice, and to mobilize everyone against its promotion and growth. The relevant education of school-age individuals and reeducation of adults should include:

> *Critical thinking skills:* Individuals must be able to distinguish between speech and speaker, fact and superstition, evidence-based history, and mythology or hearsay. They must be able to recognize a faulty generalization and *ad hominem* attacks to become less susceptible to provocative hate speech, and the influence of charismatic leaders or group-think that promotes the rapid spread of such hatred.
>
> *Moral education*: Individuals must understand the importance of mutual respect, human rights, and personal accountability for actions and inactions in every corner of private and public life.
>
> *Knowledge and know-how:* It must become essential for everyone to understand the causes and consequences of hatred, and to acquire the practical skills of (1) self-awareness in understanding one's motivations and emotional reactions; (2) resistance and resilience under stress; (3) civility; and, (4) conflict resolution.

The education categories above are the responsibility of formal institutions, family members, and social groups. The upstream and political leaders' responsibility is vital to eradicate structural systematic violence and replace it with justice and equality to bridge the gap in inequity and inequality.

The responsibility of cultural actors and faith communities are enormous as they reflect about their choices to glorify, glamorize, or trivialize hatred and revenge in their cultural works and faith messages. Cultural icons and religious leaders reach large numbers of the public to speak against individual and intergroup hatred and hatred-based violence as they have against discrimination, poverty, wars, and violence in the past. It is critical to use all of our available mediums for disseminating the message about the harms and self-harm arising from hatred, and protection against it through broadly accessible online graphics and animations, posters, and public service announcements.

To *mitigate hatred*, the goal of mitigatory or rehabilitative measures is to help individuals already suffering from interpersonal hatred in managing, reducing, and finally eliminating their hatred—particularly through learning and practicing cognitive reappraisal, emotion regulation, and conflict resolution techniques. To that end, medical practitioners must be sensitive to the possibility that stress-related immune system dysregulation and following diseases can be induced by or maintained by hatred, rather than other stressors, so that they are able to direct their patients to relevant therapists and support groups. They must develop diagnostic tests and scales to assist practitioners. Hatred mitigation measures cannot promise long-term results to eliminate the health effects of intergroup hatred that necessitate eliminating or reducing hatred's triggers.

Group-based hatred intervention is sociopolitical. First, if the hatred is triggered by oppression or another form of long-term mistreatment of one group by another, a major part of the "cure" will be in the hands of those guilty of mistreatment: for example, by eliminating political and economic barriers and replacing those with symbolic and practical signs of recognition and accountability. For permanent results, truth-and-reconciliation and restorative justice processes, whereby all who have mistreated others acknowledge their wrong-doing, will often be necessary to complete the treatment. That is a step that cannot be skipped, since hatred can continue even after the immediate triggers are lifted.

If the hatred is ignorance-based, then what must be eliminated are superstitions, myths, and false narratives of the "other." In mutual hatred there is usually superstition and false "destructive stories" on both sides (Senehi, 2002). Educational campaigns will be necessary; yet deeper self-understanding and understanding of the hated other (and why the other hates) might require working and living together, and developing projects for mutual advancement.

Second, in addition to reducing settled hatred in groups, individual-based hatred interventions provide opportunities to construct new different therapies so that individual cases will be responsive. Given the identical exposure to a hatred trigger, everyone's chances of experiencing interpersonal and intergroup hatred, of expressing that hatred with violent acts, or suffering its pathophysiological effects are a function of many other factors that without at least economic security and basic good health, some measures are bound to be only weakly effective. Good health is necessary for individuals to be able to moderate stress levels and become better listeners, critical thinkers, and conflict resolvers. Good health also provides a counterbalance against genetic, biological, social, and other environmental factors and exacerbating conditions that make some individuals more prone to becoming hateful or to expressing their hatred with violence. It is important to raise the average level of health in populations vulnerable to conflict (whether hatred based or otherwise) by allocating more health resources to those populations to prevent, mitigate, contain, manage, reduce, and eliminate hatred.

These recommendations constitute a formidable list of actions that involve most sectors of society; some will take generations to put into effect to produce results; sometimes visionary patience will be called for. A one-size-fits-all solution to a health issue that has psychological, social, ethical, economic, political, and physiological dimensions is not possible. It is important that global health and social justice groups collaborate with each other to put into effect regionalized action plans.

Implications for practice and policy

Policy responses for mitigating and preventing hatred may differ regionally especially if hatred is already present and has affected the population by means of interpersonal violence, intergroup conflict, incitement, genocide, resentment, and other manifestations of hatred. Long-term results require the eradication of specific triggers for prevention and intervention procedures to succeed (Abuelaish & Arya, 2017). The United Nations (2021) noted that countries should work toward "promoting peaceful and inclusive societies for sustainable development, provide access to justice for all and build effective, accountable and inclusive institutions at all levels." It is vital that policy solutions for social cohesion enhance the well-being for all, reduce inequalities, and "leave no one behind" by participating in a "bottom up" process (Boarini et al., 2018; Forje, 2017). "Concrete policy actions" span a multitude of social institutions including education, "fiscal instruments," labor, "public and private governance" (Boarini et al., 2018).

Prevention is the first step to target hatred through a public health perspective (Abuelaish & Arya, 2017). Tackling upstream factors are expected to have greater success regarding inequities (Matzopoulos et al., 2010), which can lead to the elimination of triggers (Abuelaish & Arya, 2017). Meso-level and local law and policy changes represent more promising results toward upstream and structural factors, in a relatively shorter time span than the highest, national law levels (Goldberg, 2020). Health systems and other social institutions can adapt their existing policies and regulations to accommodate underserved communities, and tackle distal factors (Goldberg, 2020). Effective prevention for eradicating hatred structurally includes reducing income inequality, improving social welfare services, changing cultural norms, providing school-based prevention programs catered to community and regional needs (Matzopoulos et al., 2010). Evidence-based responses and data collection across all social institutions can help us better understand the socioeconomic conditions leading to inequities and how to mitigate them (Boarini et al., 2018). Alleviating social disadvantage through policy should reduce inequalities, and include people in decision-making to achieve social cohesion (Boarini et al., 2018).

If primary prevention has not prevented harm, or if hatred is already prevalent in the region, intervention is the next step to prevent further adverse health outcomes (Abuelaish & Arya, 2017). Educational efforts to work toward peace, integration, and promoting reconciliation are effective (Al Ramiah & Hewstone, 2013; Staub et al., 2005). Reducing prejudice can be achieved by promoting "intergroup contact, inclusive common identities and social norms, social cognitive skills training, moral reasoning and tolerance" (Bekerman, 2018, p. 79). Rather than separating groups after conflict, cities with intergroup daily contact are less likely to have hatred and violence directed toward one another (Al Ramiah & Hewstone, 2013). An experimental study to measure the efficacy of a conflict group's healing and reconciliation program after the Rwandan genocide had positive results in reducing trauma and "enhancing acceptance" of the other group (Staub et al., 2005). Such intervention programs can help to address community and regional manifestations of hatred. The ultimate prevention and intervention strategies lie within the discretion of world leaders to deploy the appropriate policies and actions to tackle hatred.

Conclusion

Hatred is a health, legal, political, and social matter that needs to be taken seriously as a *pressing public health issue* by the public, governments, other institutions, and the medical community. Hatred is not a nontrivial phenomenon with nontrivial consequences for all, and it is not a mere private "feeling." Hatred is an intense attitude with intent to eliminate or destroy its object. Its appropriate objects are wars, disease, violence, and cruelty, not human beings. Interpersonal hatred is bad for the health of the hater and the hated. Interpersonal and intergroup hatred is a public health issue calling for urgent and long-term action. Hatred is a contagious, destructive disease, and is the result of exposure. It is a public health issue and a determinant of health because it often engenders widespread physical, psychological, or political violence.

References

Abuelaish, I. (2021, May 26). Why hatred should be considered a contagious disease. *The Conversation*. https://theconversation.com/why-hatred-should-be-considered-a-contagious-disease-161163

Abuelaish, I., & Arya, N. (2017). Hatred-a public health issue. *Medicine, Conflict and Survival, 33*(2), 125–130.

Al Ramiah, A., & Hewstone, M. (2013). Intergroup contact as a tool for reducing, resolving, and preventing intergroup conflict: Evidence, limitations, and potential. *American Psychologist, 68*(7), 527.

Arellano-Garcia, M. E., Hu, S., Wang, J., Henson, B., Zhou, H., Chia, D., & Wong D. T. (2008). Multiplexed immunobead-based assay for detection of oral cancer protein biomarkers in saliva. *Oral Diseases, 14*, 705–712.

Bekerman, Z. (2018). Working towards peace through education: The case of Israeli Jews and Palestinians. *Asian Journal of Peacebuilding, 6*, 75–98.

Boarini, R., Causa, O., Fleurbaey, M., Grimalda, G., & Woolard, I. (2018). Reducing inequalities and strengthening social cohesion through inclusive growth: A roadmap for action. *Economics, 12*(6), 1–26.

Dahlberg, L. L., & Mercy J. A. (2009). History of violence as a public health issue. *The Virtual Mentor, 11*(2), 167–172.

DeRijk, R., & Sternberg, E. M. (1997). Corticosteroid resistance and disease. *Annals of Medicine, 29*, 79–82.

Elenkov, I. J., & Chrousos, G. P. (1999a). Stress, cytokine patterns, and susceptibility to disease: Bailliere's best practices and research. *Clinical Endocrinology and Metabolism, 13*, 583–595.

Elenkov, I. J., & Chrousos, G. P. (1999b). Stress hormones, th1/th2 patterns, pro/anti-inflammatory cytokines and susceptibility to disease. *Trends in Endocrinology and Metabolism, 10*, 359–368.

Fisher, L. A. (1989). Corticotropin-releasing factor: Endocrine and autonomic integration of responses to stress. *Trends in Pharmacological Sciences, 10*, 189–193.

Forje, J. W. (2017). USA-Africa relations under President Trump: Towards improving socioeconomic aspects of migration, integration, development and poverty alleviation policies. *African Renaissance, 14*(1-2), 39–65.

Garban, H., Iribarren, F. J., Noriega, C. A., Barr, N., & Zhu, W. (2012). Using biological markers to measure stress in listeners of commercial talk radio. *Chicano Studies Research Center Working Paper, 3*, 1–8.

Gaylin, W. (2003). *Hatred: The psychological descent into violence*. PublicAffairs.

Glaser, R., Kiecolt-Glaser, J. K., McGuire, L., & Robles, T. F. (2002). Emotions, morbidity, and mortality: New perspectives from psychoneuroimmunology. *Annual Review of Psychology, 53*, 83–107.

Goldberg, D. S. (2020). Structural stigma, legal epidemiology, and COVID-19: The ethical imperative to act upstream. *Kennedy Institute of Ethics Journal, 30*(3), 339–359.

Halperin, E. (2008). Group-based hatred in intractable conflict in Israel. *Journal of Conflict Resolution, 52*(5), 713–736.

Harris, A. H. S., & Thoresen, C. E. (2005). Forgiveness, unforgiveness, health, and disease. In E. L. Worthington (Ed.), *Handbook of forgiveness* (pp. 321–334). Routledge.

Khayyam-Nekouei, Z., Hamidtaher Neshatdoost, H., Yousefy, A., Sadeghi, M., & Gholamreza, G. (2013). Psychological factors and coronary heart disease. *ARYA Atheroscler, 9*(1), 102–111.

Krug, E. G., Dahlberg, L. L., Mercy, J. A., Zwi, A. B., & Lozano, R. (2002). The world report on violence and health. *The Lancet*, *360*, 1083–1088.

Marinker, M. (1975). Why make people patients? *Journal of Medical Ethics*, *1*(1), 81–84.

Matzopoulos, R., Bowman, B., Mathews, S., & Myers, J. (2010). Applying upstream interventions for interpersonal violence prevention: An uphill struggle in low-to middle-income contexts. *Health Policy*, *97*(1), 62–70.

Muir, J. L., & Pfister, H. P. (1989). Psychological stress and oxytocin treatment during pregnancy affect central norepinephrine, dopamine, and serotonin in lactating rats. *International Journal of Neuroscience*, *48*, 191–203.

Nelson, B. J. (1999). Diversity and public problemsolving: Ideas and practice in policy education. *Journal of Policy Analysis and Management*, *18*(1), 134–155.

Richter, E. D., Markus, D. K., & Tait, C. (2018). Incitement, genocide, genocidal terror, and the upstream role of indoctrination: Can epidemiologic models predict and prevent? *Public Health Reviews*, *39*(1), 1–22.

Senehi, J. (2002). Constructive storytelling: A peace process. *Peace and Conflict Studies*, *9*(2), 41–62.

Staub, E., Pearlman, L. A., Gubin, A., & Hagengimana, A. (2005). Healing, reconciliation, forgiving and the prevention of violence after genocide or mass killing: An intervention and its experimental evaluation in Rwanda. *Journal of Social and Clinical Psychology*, *24*(3), 297–334.

United Nations. (2021). *Goal 16*. United Nations Department of Economic and Social Affaris. https://sdgs.un.org/goals/goal16

Vining, R. F., McGinley, R. A., Maksvytis, J. J., & Ho. K. Y. (1983a). Salivary cortisol: A better measure of adrenal cortical function than serum cortisol. *Annals of Clinical Biochemistry*, *20*(6), 329–335.

Vining, R. F., McGinley, R. A., & Symons, R. G. (1983b). Hormones in saliva: Mode of entry and consequent implications for clinical interpretation. *Clinical Chemistry*, *29*, 1752–1756.

Walker, J. G., Littlejohn, G. O., McMurray, N. E., & Cutolo, M. (1999). Stress system response and rheumatoid arthritis: A multilevel approach. *Rheumatol*, *38*, 1050–1057.

Zeki, S., & Romaya, J. P. (2008). Neural correlates of hate. *PLoS One*, *3*(10): e3556. https://doi.org/10.1371/journal.pone.0003556

6
THE ENVIRONMENT AND PEACEBUILDING IN ETHNIC CONFLICT

Ane Cristina Figueiredo and Calum Dean

Ethnic conflicts are described as complex, protracted, and intractable that are difficult to ameliorate and present themselves along ethnic lines (Wolff, 2006). Discussed through several analytical lenses, it is important to appreciate the multiplicity of factors that underly ethnic cleavages (Byrne & Nadan, 2011). As such, the role of the environment in contributing to the causes of ethnic conflict and its resolution are a dimension worth investigating. Given the current global and political dynamics involving climate change, environmental change, and resource scarcity, how the environment affects interethnic conflict, and how it can be a space for cooperation and peacebuilding, are important questions for consideration.

The argument in this chapter is that environmental issues provide space for cooperation between ethnic groups and can be a catalyst for peacebuilding (Conca, 2002) so that critical environmental peacebuilding approaches must be interwoven into greater peacebuilding frameworks. This chapter is broken down into four main sections. The first section addresses the ways the environment affects conflict and its relation to peacebuilding. The second section discusses a theoretical framework for understanding critical environmental peacebuilding through exploring critical emancipatory peacebuilding, environmental conflict, and critical environmental justice. The third section highlights four major insights that emerge from incorporating critical environmental peacebuilding into peacebuilding practices. Finally, this chapter elaborates on the implications of integrating critical environmental peacebuilding into greater peacebuilding initiatives for teachers, practitioners, and policymakers.

The environment and ethnic conflict

Interethnic conflicts involve multiple intersecting factors that influence and shape the development of conflict. Levy and Vaillancourt (2011) suggest three ways the environment is related to conflict, namely as a casualty of war; as a cause of conflict; and as a prospective tool for peace. The environment is most associated with conflict as a cause. Subsequently, environmental changes due to war and opportunities for peace receive lesser attention. Often, environmental factors that contribute to conflict are framed under the analysis of security threats stemming from environmental degradation (Barnett, 2001; Renner, 1996). However, a shift to a more comprehensive understanding of how the environment affects conflict, challenged the environmental security dilemma (Conca, 2002; Homer-Dixon, 1999; Libiszewski, 1992). Thus, as a cause of conflict, the environment is discussed within two main approaches, namely environmental security and critical perspectives.

Environmental security

Environment security approaches focus primarily on the relation between environmental degradation and insecurity. In the traditional sense, the security perspective looks at the environment as a threat to the state and its military security. The evolving and contentious security concept has also moved from a focus on traditional security to the object of security. This shift began to examine threats to people as opposed to threats to states and nations. Both traditional and human-centered security approaches have tackled the environment-security issue (Barnett, 2001; Conca, 2002). However, increasingly within the security framework, scholarship began to associate the effects of the environment with threats to human security (Deudney, 1991; Gleditsch, 1997; Wæver, 1995).

The environmental security approach emphasizes environmental degradation as the cause of increasing levels of human insecurity. The emphasis on security does not necessarily ignore the conflation of factors that lead to conflict per se. However, the focus is on how environmental threats can be incorporated into the greater security framework. For example, Fiona Rotberg (2010) discusses how the physical consequences of climate change lead to social and political consequences that affect security, and the stability of peace. Further, environmental dynamics are viewed as driving influences that along with sociocultural, political, and economic factors can lead to the development of conflict that more broadly impact human security (Nixon, 2011; Renner, 1996). The issue that environmental security exponents emphasize is the broader concern of security, and how the environmental security debate fits within the broader security framework. In comparison, critical approaches examine the relationship between the environment and conflict, emphasizing the multitude of environmental concerns that can exacerbate latent conflicts.

Critical approaches

Senehi and Byrne (2012) suggest that the effects of human activity and environmental change pose a serious hurdle for establishing peace. Critical perspectives related to effects of the environment on conflict attempt to move past what Ken Conca (2002) describes as a reductionist and misleading environmental security argument. Homer-Dixon (1999) believes the environmental security approach is broad, especially considering the breadth of what the concept of security encompasses. Instead the focus is on violent conflict, that environmental scarcity, along with compounding factors of resource capture and marginalization, can be a trigger for violent conflict (Homer-Dixon, 1999).

Bretthauer (2017) argues that conflict, in relation to resources, is located in certain economic, political, and social conditions. The dependency on agriculture for example is significant in the relation between resource scarcity and conflict (Bretthauer, 2017, p. 73). Further, certain political factors (neopatrimonial states and weak rule of law) and social factors (inequality and adaptive skills) influence the potential for environmental changes to develop into conflict (Bretthauer, 2017). In Africa, where the environmental security thesis is predominantly evoked, Williams (2016) discusses its limitations and how compounding factors influence conflict over resources. Decision-makers and leaders play particularly important roles as climate change, and the management of environmental issues, either ameliorate or exacerbate conflict. How leaders respond to these issues is an important factor to consider (Alvarez, 2017).

The relation between the environment and conflict is critical for peace scholars to understand, as direct and indirect links between the two are well established. The security and critical approaches both contend that environmental changes impact insecurity and violent conflict. The security approach, analyzing the effects of environmental degradation on human insecurity, is an important angle to consider as it goes beyond conflict to look at how the environment can cause a multitude of issues within society. However, what is made clear by critical scholarship in this area is that the issue is complex. It involves a multitude of dynamics, and there is a conflation of economic, sociocultural, and political factors that influence the environment-conflict nexus. How these issues might be a space for alleviating conflict is discussed as follows.

Environment and peacebuilding

The environment has predominantly been discussed as a cause of conflict, with its potentials for peace garnering less attention. However, according to Ken Conca (2002) environmental issues can provide opportunities to promote cooperation and potentially peace. He identifies two pathways through which this occurs, changing the strategic climate, and transforming state governance (Conca, 2002). Changing the strategic climate occurs through reducing uncertainty, promoting reciprocity, and creating long-term, mutually beneficial relationships; transforming governance structures refers to creating more transparent and accountable government institutions. Through these two means, Conca (2002) argues the environment can act as a catalyst for more peaceful relations between conflicting parties.

The environment has also been linked to issues related to peacebuilding and conflict resolution in other ways. Environmental Conflict Resolution (ECR) has looked at how conflict resolution techniques can be applied to environmental disputes (Haydon & Kuang, 2013). Brian Rice (2011) describes the interconnections between humans, nature, and animals and forms of indigenous peace leadership. In addition, Young and Goldman (2015) use the relations between natural resources, livelihoods, and peacebuilding processes as a lens for looking at peacebuilding. Moreover, Burrowes (1996) draws on the ideas of "deep ecology" to suggest that peace and security for humanity lies within our relationship with nonhuman animals and nature. These examples reveal the various relations between peace studies and the environment, and how the environment may be integrated into peace frameworks.

Although existing scholarship provides an understanding of how the environment can become a space for peacebuilding, the work in this area is limited. Building a theoretical framework that fits the environment into peacebuilding agendas is imperative. Further, how these frameworks can coincide with critical and emancipatory peacebuilding approaches that focus on local ownership, critical analysis, and social justice is important in providing holistic peacebuilding initiatives (Byrne & Thiessen, 2019).

Critical framework for environmental peacebuilding

As environmental peacebuilding emerges, it is crucial to combine efforts to achieve sustainable peace by understanding the root causes of environmental conflicts. Especially since conflict over natural resources and the environment represent one of the most significant challenges of 21st century politics (Swain & Öjendal, 2018). It is essential to enhance the critical emancipatory peacebuilding frameworks, emphasizing environmental and natural resources as alternative peacebuilding initiatives. These initiatives, focusing on civil society organizations (CSOs), local ownership, and social justice, are a critical element in transforming peacebuilding practices (Byrne & Thiessen, 2019). To this end, critical emancipatory peacebuilding, environmental conflict, and critical environmental justice provide a framework for critical environmental peacebuilding that centralizes cooperation, social justice, and local empowerment to promote sustainable peace.

Critical emancipatory peacebuilding

Critical emancipatory peacebuilding is a multifaceted peace practice focused on critical analysis and local ownership of peace processes (Thiessen, 2011). It attempts to give voice to those experiencing hardship at the grassroots level by identifying human needs (Richmond, 2005) while promoting civic engagement (Paffenholz, 2015). This process is rooted in the idea of social transformation by making visible and addressing structures of oppression. Thus, it challenges the status quo of the liberal peacebuilding mechanisms (Thiessen, 2011). While liberal peacebuilding is perceived as a process creating liminal peace, critical emancipatory models focus on sustainable forms of peace (Lederach, 1997). This mechanism is important because it focuses on ordinary people's needs (Richmond, 2005), supporting local actors, community leaders, and CSO initiatives from the bottom-up.

Lederach (1997) suggests it is necessary to create proactive practices to ensure sustainability in the peacebuilding process. He continues by suggesting that the sustainable, transformative approach "lies in the relationship of the involved parties" (Lederach, 1997, p. 75) and encompassing multiple social spheres. Meanwhile, the traditional peacebuilding framework is dominated by neoliberal methods focused on democratization, and free-market economics, where environmental and natural resources are not the primary concern (Richmond, 2005). As pointed out by Murithi (2009), peacebuilding embedded in ethics can address the root causes of conflict, of which the environment is one, while supporting dialogue between or among parties.

The critical environmental peacebuilding approach fits under the umbrella of critical emancipatory peacebuilding as an integrated and innovative method, focusing on local ownership and social justice. As described by Senehi and Byrne (2012), "peacebuilding and conflict transformation approaches need to include the ecological dimension" (p. 400) because human behavior impacts the environment in destructive ways. Environmental peacebuilding promotes opportunities for cooperation and acts as a peacebuilding catalyst by promoting efforts and dialogues among antagonist groups (Conca & Beevers, 2018). Therefore, it is essential to contextualize environmental theories and understand how environmental conflict, critical environmental justice, and critical environmental peacebuilding fits within critical emancipatory peacebuilding frameworks.

Environmental conflict

Environmental conflicts are described as "the destabilizing interferences in the ecosystem's equilibrium" (Libiszewski, 1992, p. 3). Its complex nature can have many causal relationships (e.g., political, social, economic, cultural, ethnic, religious), which can lead to violent conflict. Consequently, environmental conflict is the result of many different variables, from environmental scarcity to degradation, from human activities to population growth, and from climate change to control and access over natural resources (Diehl & Gleditsch, 2001). Thus, ecological stress has driven many nations to food insecurity, massive migration, and internal chaos (Renner et al., 1991).

In the past three decades many armed conflicts were linked to natural resources, including those financed or triggered by the access and control of resources. Also, as natural resource scarcity spreads, basic human needs are neglected, and human conflict increases as a struggle for survival ensues (Swain & Öjendal, 2018). This conflict over natural resources becomes a conflict over rights (Shiva, 2015). For instance, land tenure had a critical role in the civil war in Sierra Leone (Richards, 2005). Similarly, conflict has escalated in Israel and Palestine over land access and water resource control (Ide et al., 2018).

The abundance of natural resources can create tensions and grievances among groups struggling to access and control such resources as well (De Soysa, 2000). For example, the civil wars in Sierra Leone and Côte d'Ivoire were linked to Liberia's wars and the illegal regional trade of natural resources such as diamonds and cacao (Bruch et al., 2016a; UNEP, 2009b). Environmental transformation and renewable and nonrenewable natural resources are linked to many violent conflicts such as those emanating from oil revenues sponsoring ISIS in Iraq and Syria, to charcoal trades financing Al-Shabaab in Somalia (Bruch, 2019; Jensen, 2019a); from desertification amplifying the conflict in Syria (Dalby, 2018; Gleick, 2014), to illegal gold mining financing criminal groups in the Democratic Republic of Congo (UNEP-MONUSCO-OSESG, 2015) and Colombia (Jensen, 2019b).

These scenarios led the Security Council (SC) to consider the environment as a significant factor in the security framework, and to provide a set of specific tools to address resource-driven conflicts. These sets of tools include resolutions and presidential statements, peacekeeping mission mandates, sanctions, and panels of experts to address the environment and natural resources' impacts on conflict (Bruch et al., 2016a; UNEP, 2012). For example, these measures were applied to the Mali mission, which considered environmental factors in peacekeeping operations (UNSC, 2013), or the SC embargo and ban on Liberia's diamonds and timber extractions (Bruch et al., 2016b). Thus, it is essential to understand the triggers of environmental and natural resource conflicts, to avoid regional spillover, and create sustainable mitigation processes for peacebuilding.

In sum, natural resources are frequently connected and entrenched in violent conflicts. The broader spectrum of environmental and natural resource conflicts challenges the dynamics of conflict management, making it difficult to mitigate violence and create effective strategies to build peace. Despite its complex nature, natural resources and the environment can play numerous roles during ethnic conflict and peacebuilding processes. The key lies in whether natural resources are managed to promote consensus across a range of interests or whether the lack of cooperation and mismanagement trigger violence or escalate existing conflict (Bruch et al., 2016a). Social and ecological justice needs to be prioritized to promote sustainable peace and local ownership.

Critical environmental justice

Critical environmental justice (CEJ) was built upon interdisciplinary environmental justice studies (EJS) to produce a more robust understanding of environmental (in)justice and to promote more effective responses (Pellow, 2018). While EJS tend to focus on race and class as drivers for environmental injustice, CEJ's interdisciplinary framework creates an interaction across different fields seeking to "bridge and blur the boundaries and borders between the academy and community, theory and practice, analysis and action" (Pellow, 2018, p. 30). CEJ analyzes EJS through a multiscale process to gain a deeper grasp of different forms of social inequality while seeking transformative approaches to achieve environmental justice.

Also known as ecological justice, EJS focuses on the just and fair distribution of environmental goods and burdens (Baxter, 2005; Pellow, 2018). EJS scholar Bullard (1996) defines environmental justice in terms of equal access to environmental protection for all individuals by ensuring environmental laws and regulations. In contrast, Pellow (2000) explains that environmental injustice is the disproportion in which social groups are affected by environmental hazards. EJS provides an understanding that the existence of social inequalities by race and class are often linked to environmental injustice where marginalized groups are often more exposed to environmental burdens, as well as excluded from decision-making that directly impacts those outcomes (Pellow, 2018). However, a broader vision of EJS focuses on eliminating the root causes of environmental injustice by eradicating structural violence, and creating a more inclusive decision-making process (Gellers & Jeffords, 2018).

Pellow (2018) suggests using a CEJ framework comprising multiple intersecting causal factors of environmental injustice, focusing on alternative pathways to resolutions. CEJ seeks to understand how gender, sexuality, citizenship, and indigeneity shape these experiences, and how humans and nonhumans facing environmental threats from dominant structures respond to these injustices (Pellow, 2018). Therefore, it is essential to understand the root causes of environmental injustice and to foster a mechanism to promote CEJ through environmental initiatives and cooperation.

While environmental inequality is perceived through insufficient access and the abundance or lack of natural resources, CEJ fosters a framework to understand the multiple levels of EJS. Also, it provides lenses to respond to the oppressive mechanics of environmental injustice. Environmental initiatives at the local level are taking place to foster CEJ in places affected by environmental conflict. For example, CEJ is shaping water cooperation in Israel and Palestine (EcoPeace, 2008), and empowering women's movements and communities in Kenya (UNDP, 2014). Also, CEJ is taking place in women's participation in local mediation and natural resources management in South Kordofan, Sudan (SOS Sahel International UK, 2009), and in Rwanda with postpeace accord land reforms (Ngoga, 2012), to women's participation in Colombia's peace agreement standing for gender equality, women's rights, and natural resource management (Halle & Church, 2018).

Alternative and inclusive environmental initiatives promote justice and sustainable peacebuilding at the local level (UNDP, 2014). The environment and natural resources are being used as an instrument and catalyst of cooperation and peace, as communities are acting as change agents based on their vision of environmental rights and justice. Consequently, it is essential to recognize the benefits of using CEJ as a tool to foster sustainable peace while empowering local people. Bringing these ideas together is the framework of critical environmental peacebuilding.

Critical environmental peacebuilding

Environmental peacebuilding is defined as an opportunity to move from conflict to cooperation by using ecological nonviolent means to promote trust between different groups through a shared collective identity and interdependence (Conca & Beevers, 2018). The critical environmental peacebuilding perspective intends to enlighten the grassroots' capability, integration, and resilience to existing power relations. Critical environmental peacebuilding is a constructive and alternative tool to promote peace by using environmental initiatives, emphasizing the potential of local knowledge and empowerment while promoting socioecological justice.

While cooperation does not necessarily imply the absence of conflict, it sponsors a shared ground to overcome and negotiate mutual problems based on ecological alternatives (Swain & Öjendal, 2018). Ashley McArthur (2013) suggests that such a practice brings parties together toward mutual goals. While in the past six decades, natural resources were linked to 40–60 percent of civil wars (UNEP, 2015), it is critical to shift the focus from natural resource conflict to natural resources peacebuilding. The latter is described by Conca and Beevers (2018) as a catalyst for peace by using "the environment proactively and cooperatively, as a point of departure for strengthening the conditions for peace" (p. 54). Based on this idea, it is crucial to convert environmental conflict into long-term transformative social group dynamics to foster environmental and social justice (Conca & Beevers, 2018; Swain & Öjendal, 2018). Locally driven critical environmental peacebuilding promotes opportunities for local peace ownership by having ethnic groups cooperate in the sharing of natural resources, equitable distribution, civic engagement, sustainable practices, and local resilience.

It is essential to integrate environmental initiatives across peacebuilding practices, as they can contribute to economic recovery, to the development of sustainable livelihoods, and to dialogue and confidence-building (UNEP, 2009a). However, it is critical to strengthen community peacebuilding by using environmental cooperation practices as a form to share regional norms and needs, overcoming traditional peacebuilding frameworks, dominated by neoliberal approaches focused on short-term solutions and economic growth. Environmental peacebuilding models "tend to simplify the heterogeneity and internal dissensions that exist within local communities" (Dresse et al., 2019, p. 103). Mac Ginty (2015) describes the top-down approach as an imposition at the local level, diminishing people's societal system and problemsolving capability. High politics are important to ensure strong institutional practices related to natural resources management, however, low politics need to be integrated and tailored within each local context to convey a multilevel system to attain sustainable peace (Bruch et al., 2016b).

Conca's environmental peacemaking framework focuses on the interstate level of using ecological issues as opportunities for cooperation, and strengthening political practices and social identity (Conca, 2002). However, it is critical to focus the efforts at the local level to nurture sustainable peace. While Conca and Beever's (2018) approach creates a shared collective identity to promote a positive form of interdependence and mutual gains among states, Critical Environmental Peacebuilding (CEP) complements this by promoting local empowerment and ownership of environmental initiatives and cooperation. Since multiple forms of inequality and marginalization lead to environmental injustice and conflict, it would be beneficial for peacebuilding frameworks to integrate critical environmental peacebuilding.

Key insights

CEP provides a framework for using environmental issues as potential peacebuilding opportunities through locally led environmental initiatives focused on social justice and cooperation. Integrating environmental approaches within peacebuilding initiatives reveals several insights related to peace and the environment, namely that the environment provides a space for peacebuilding, grassroots/local ownership of the process is imperative, an emphasis on sustainable practices is crucial, and we must centralize a social justice framework.

Environment provides a space for peacebuilding

There is ample evidence to show how environmental factors influence violent conflict (Homer-Dixon, 1999). In terms of how it can facilitate peace, Conca (2002) provides the most comprehensive view of how the environment can be a catalyst for cooperation and facilitate processes that encourage peaceful relations. Environmental change essentially provides an opportunity to provoke conflict and violence or it can be used to facilitate peaceful relations. A central point in this discussion is the possibilities for peace. The environment is more than a threat to be wary of, or a resource to be depleted, it can be a space for cooperation that can result in more peaceful relations between conflicting ethnic groups (Conca, 2002).

Grassroots/local ownership of the process

Environmental change is intrinsically linked to other sociocultural, political, and economic issues. For example, Bretthauer (2017) discusses the role of social inequality, Homer-Dixon (1999) points to marginalization and resource capture, and Dalby (1999) highlights the role and exploitation by the Global North of the Global South. The environment-conflict nexus is complex and involves intricate local, as well as national and international, dynamics. As such, universal, top-down peacebuilding initiatives that devalue local knowledge, and forms of peacebuilding are unable to account for local intricacies, knowledge, and peacebuilding methods. Environmental peacebuilding initiatives should be rooted in local ownership, and further, respect and support the capacities, knowledge, and expertise of local communities.

Emphasis on sustainable practices

The concern over climate change and the risks of a rise in global temperature, show the impending danger of the unsustainable consumption of the earth's resources. Sustainability is also a key word for peacebuilding; many postviolent peace agreements have lapsed back into violence and scholars have called into question the efficacy of these interventions altogether (Mac Ginty, 2015). Sustainability in terms of environmental peace projects is, therefore, a central issue. CEP projects offer a way for peacebuilding to incorporate ecologically sustainable practices as well as providing a space for working toward sustainable peace by facilitating greater cooperation between conflicting ethnic groups (Conca, 2002).

Centralizing a social justice framework

Another commonality between critical emancipatory approaches and CEP is the focus on social justice, that is uncovering and addressing social marginalization through fair distribution of environmental goods, equal access to environmental resources, and shared responsibility over environmental burdens. Incorporating a social justice framework into peacebuilding allows for initiatives to centralize structural issues that tend to linger and prolong conflict (Byrne & Thiessen, 2019). Addressing the structural issues related to environmental change is essential because of the economic, political, and social factors that influence the environment's impact on conflict. Resolving environmental issues may not alleviate conflict on its own. However, these environmental issues can be spaces for cooperation that can challenge and change socially unjust structures that prevent the resolution of conflict or affect the sustainability of peace agreements.

The remainder of this chapter focuses on the recommendations that come from incorporating CEP into mainstream peacebuilding approaches. The first set of recommendations focuses on training and teachers, while the second focuses on policy and practitioners.

Implications for teaching and training

Teaching and training in peacebuilding practice must go beyond technocratic programs that devalue existing local capacities for peace and ignore local dynamics that are imperative to understanding conflict and its resolution (Lederach, 1997). It is important to localize training, in culturally embedded programs that elicit the solutions and lessons from the participants and local peacebuilders. In terms of pedagogical recommendations, Paulo Freire (2000) signals the importance of providing space for critical development and thinking, through education and giving students agency in the education process. As such, the following suggestions for teaching and training may prove useful:

- Teaching and training programs should promote awareness about environmental issues that can lead to, and ameliorate conflict.
- Programs should develop ecologically sustainable practices as well as encourage the development of ecologically sustainable initiatives.
- Teachers and trainers should engage with local communities' knowledge both about peace and peacebuilding as well as about their unique ecological environment.
- There should be an emphasis about how both groups relate to the environment, and processes of dialogue with one another to facilitate these connections and problem-solving strategies.
- Training programs should draw on international norms, rights, and laws surrounding the environment, yet allow for environmental issues and resolutions to emerge organically in ways that allow local people to have ownership.

Implications for practice and policy

CEP is essential to assure social justice within peacebuilding programs and protect marginalized communities who are the most adversely affected by conflict relating to the environment. Changes to policy and peacebuilding practice are important to ensure the protection of marginalized groups and must go beyond this protective paradigm. These practices must also engage local people and communities within the peacebuilding process, especially in relation to environmental issues. The connection between high and low-level politics is important to create transparency, inclusion, and trust within political systems (Lederach, 1997). Preventative systems are key in creating proactive responses to environmental change that could spark or worsen conflict (Homer-Dixon, 1999). Policies and practices are important to structure local ownership of peacebuilding processes, where those affected can engage with and benefit from the solutions to environmental issues. The following suggestions are put forward to implement these forms of change:

- Strengthening existing or transitional government's capacities in natural resource and environmental management.
- Creating sustainable economic practices that are predicated in respecting the environment and also safeguarding local people's livelihoods.
- Increased involvement of women in the management of natural resources and peace negotiations.
- Focus on the processes of transitional justice, accountability for perpetrators of environmental violence within ethnic conflict and meaningfully compensating those harmed by these forms of violence.
- Creating policies that ensure land ownership, use and access rights, and land tenure.
- Better infrastructure and mechanisms of implementation of international environmental laws and norms.
- Promoting conflict sensitive policies and practices into national environmental security frameworks such as conflict assessment, mapping, and monitoring.

Conclusion

This chapter explored the ways the environment and conflict intersect, and the possibilities for peacebuilding this intersection provides. The environment-conflict nexus has been well studied as a potential cause of ethnic conflict, and relations between environmental change and violent conflict are well established. However, the ways in which this can be a space for peacebuilding and cooperation has been undertheorized, especially as it relates to CEP. This chapter argues for incorporating a CEP framework into greater peacebuilding practices, as a way to facilitate cooperation between conflicting parties over environmental issues. Further, it argues for using a process that engages with civil society and local communities, and creates a form of local ownership over environmental peacebuilding initiatives. Centralizing social justice is essential to mitigate structural marginalization over environmental resources. Environmental change can be a catalyst for both violent conflict and peaceful cooperation. Peacebuilding processes and peacebuilders must recognize the opportunities this space provides for the amelioration of environmental issues, and also, for facilitating peaceful relations between ethnic groups recovering from violent conflict.

References

Alvarez, A. (2017). *Unstable ground.* Rowman & Littlefield.
Barnett, J. (2001). *The meaning of environmental security.* Zed Books.
Baxter, B. (2005). *The theory of ecological justice.* Routledge.
Bretthauer, J. M. (2017). *Climate change and resource conflict.* Routledge.
Bruch, C. (2019). Conflict resources and pillage. In E. Weinthal, C. Bruch, R. Matthew, M. Levy, & D. Jensen (Eds.), *Textbook for massive open online course on environmental security and sustaining peace* (pp. 74–75). SDG Academy.
Bruch, C., Muffett, C., & Nichols, S. S. (2016a). Natural resources and post-conflict governance. In C. Bruch, C. Muffett, & S. S. Nichols (Eds.), *Governance, natural resources, and post-conflict peacebuilding* (pp. 1–31). Earthscan.
Bruch, C., Slobodian, L., Nichols, S. S., & Muffett, C. (2016b). Facilitating peace or fueling conflict? In C. Bruch, C. Muffett, & S. S. Nichols (Eds.), *Governance, natural resources, and post-conflict peacebuilding* (pp. 953–1040). Earthscan.
Bullard, R. D. (1996). Symposium. *St. John's Journal of Legal Commentary, 9*(2), 445–474. https://heinonline.org/HOL/LandingPage?handle=hein.journals/sjjlc12&div=1&src=home
Burrowes, R. J. (1996). *The strategy of nonviolent defense.* University State of New York Press.
Byrne, S., & Nadan, A. (2011). The social cube analytical model and protracted ethnoterritorial conflicts. In T. Matyok, J. Senehi, & S. Byrne (Eds.), *Critical issues in peace and conflict studies* (pp. 61–80). Lexington Books.
Byrne, S., & Thiessen, C. (2019). Foreign peacebuilding intervention and emancipatory local agency for social justice. In S. Byrne, I. M. Scott, T. Matyok, & J. Senehi (Eds.), *Routledge companion to peace and conflict studies* (pp. 131–142). Routledge.
Conca, K. (2002). The case for environmental peacemaking. In K. Conca & G. D. Dabelko (Eds.), *Environmental peacemaking.* (pp. 1–22). Woodrow Wilson Center Press.
Conca, K., & Beevers, M. D. (2018). Environmental pathways to peace. In A. Swain & J. Öjendal (Eds.), *Routledge handbook of environmental conflict and peacebuilding* (pp. 54–72). Routledge.
Dalby, S. (1999). Threats from the south? In D. Deudney & R. Matthew (Eds.), *Contested grounds* (pp. 155–186). State University of New York.
Dalby, S. (2018). Climate change and environmental conflict. In A. Swain & J. Öjendal (Eds.), *Routledge handbook of environmental conflict and peacebuilding* (pp. 42–53). Routledge.
De Soysa, I. (2000). The resource curse. In M. B. Malone (Ed.), *Greed and grievance* (pp. 113–135). Lynne Rienner.
Deudney, D. (1991). Environment and security. *Bulletin of the Atomic Scientists, 47*(3), 22–28.
Diehl, P. F., & Gleditsch, N. P. (2001). Controversies and questions. In P. F. Diehl & N. P. Gleditsch (Eds.), *Environmental conflicts* (pp. 1–9). Westview Press.

Dresse, A., Fischhendler, I., Nielsen, J., & Zikos, D. (2019). Environmental peacebuilding. *Cooperation and Conflict*, *54*(1), 99–119.

EcoPeace. (2008). *Environmental peacebuilding theory and practice: A case study of the good water neighbours project and in depth analysis of the Wadi Fukin/Tzur Hadassah Communities*. Israel. https://www.eldis.org/document/A40498

Freire, P. (2000). *Pedagogy of the oppressed*. Bloomsbury Academic.

Gellers, J. C., & Jeffords, C. (2018). Toward environmental democracy? *Global Environmental Politics*, *18*(1), 99–121.

Gleditsch, N. (1997). *Conflict and the environment*. Kluwer Academic Publishers.

Gleick, P. (2014). Water, drought, climate change, and conflict in Syria. *Weather, Climate and Society*, *6*, 331–340.

Halle, S., & Church, C. (2018). *Connecting the dots*. International Institute for Sustainable Development. https://www.iisd.org/blog/connecting-dots-natural-resources-women-and-peace

Haydon, J., & Kuang, J. (2013). Using environmental conflict resolution and consensus building towards improved sustainability. *WIT Transactions on Ecology and the Environment*, *179*, 81–92.

Homer-Dixon, T. F. (1999). *Environment, scarcity, and violence*. Princeton University Press.

Ide, T., Sümer, V., & Aldehoff, L. M. (2018). Environmental peacebuilding in the Middle East. In A. Swain & J. Öjendal (Eds.), *Routledge handbook of environmental conflict and peacebuilding* (pp. 175–187). Routledge.

Jensen, D. (2019a). Welcome and introduction. In E. Weinthal, C. Bruch, R. Matthew, M. Levy, & D. Jensen (Eds.), *Textbook for massive open online course on "environmental security and sustaining peace"* (pp. 9–12). SDG Academy.

Jensen, D. (2019b). Case study. In E. Weinthal, C. Bruch, R. Matthew, M. Levy, & D. Jensen (Eds.), *Textbook for massive open online course on "environmental security and sustaining peace"* (pp. 22–24). SDG Academy.

Lederach, J. P. (1997). *Building peace: Sustainable reconciliation in divided societies*. United States Institue of Peace Press.

Levy, A., & Vaillancourt, J. (2011). War on earth? In T. Matyók, J. Senehi, & S. Byrne (Eds.), *Critical issues in peace and conflict studies* (pp. 217–244). Lexington Books.

Libiszewski, S. (1992). What is an environmental conflict? *Environment and Conflict Project*. Center for Security Studies and Conflict Research. https://www.files.ethz.ch/isn/236/doc_238_290_en.pdf

Mac Ginty, R. (2015). Where is the local? *Third World Quarterly*, *36*(5), 840–856.

McArthur, A. L. (2013). Environmental change and peacebuilding. In C. Zelizer (Ed.), *Integrated peacebuiling: Innovative approaches to transforming conflict* (pp. 173–198). Westview Press.

Murithi, T. (2009). *The ethics of peacebuilding*. Edinburgh University Press.

Ngoga, T. (2012). Empowering women through land tenure reform. OHCHR. https://www.ohchr.org/Documents/Publications/RealizingWomensRightstoLand_2ndedition.pdf

Nixon, R. (2011). *Slow violence and the environmentalism of the poor*. Harvard University Press.

Paffenholz, T. (2015). Civil society. In R. M. Ginty (Ed.), *Routledge handbook of peacebuilding* (pp. 347–359). Routledge.

Pellow, D. (2000). Environmental inequality formation. *American Behavioral Scientist*, *43*(3), 581–601.

Pellow, D. (2018). *What is critical environmental justice*. Polity Press.

Renner, M. (1996). *Fighting for survival*. W. W. Norton & Company.

Renner, M., Pianta, M., & Franchi, C. (1991). International conflict and environmental degradation. In R. Vayrynen (Ed.), *New directions in conflict theory, conflict resolution and conflict transformation* (pp. 108–128). SAGE.

Rice, B. (2011). Relationships with human and non-human species and how they apply toward peacebuilding and leadership in Indigenous societies. In T. Matyók, J. Senehi, & S. Byrne (Eds.), *Critical issues in peace and conflict studies* (pp. 199–216). Lexington Books.

Richards, P. (2005). To fight or to farm? *African Affairs*, *104*(417), 571–590.

Richmond, O. P. (2005). *The transformation of peace*. Palgrave Macmillan.

Rotberg, F. (2010). Peacebuilding and environmental challenges. In O. P. Richmond (Ed.), *Palgrave advances in peacebuilding: Critical developments and approaches* (pp. 392–414). Palgrave Macmillan.

Senehi, J., & Byrne, S. (2012). Where do we go from here? In T. Matyók, J. Senehi, & S. Byrne (Eds.), *Critical issues in peace and conflict studies* (pp. 397–404). Lexington Books.

Shiva, V. (2015). *Earth democracy*. North Atlantic Books.

SOS Sahel International UK. (2009). *Engaging youth and women in natural resource management and conflict reduction process*. Sudan. http://sahelsudan.org/program-focus-in-greater-kordofan/

Swain, A., & Öjendal, J. (2018). Environmental conflict and peacebuilding. In A. Swain & J. Öjendal (Eds.), *Routledge handbook of environmental conflict and peacebuilding* (pp. 1–14). Routledge.

Thiessen, C. (2011). Emancipatory peacebuilding. In T. Matyók, J. Senehi, & S. Byrne (Eds.), *Critical issues in peace and conflict studies* (pp. 115–140). Lexington Books.

UNDP. (2014, June 12). *Environmental justice: Comparative experiences in legal empowerment*. https://www.undp.org/publications/environmental-justice-comparative-experiences-legal-empowerment

UNEP. (2009a). *From conflict to peacebuilding: The role of natural resources and the environment*. https://postconflict.unep.ch/publications/pcdmb_policy_01.pdf

UNEP. (2009b). *Protecting the environment during armed conflict: An inventory and analysis of international law*. https://postconflict.unep.ch/publications/int_law.pdf

UNEP. (2012). *Greening the blue helmets: Environment, natural resources and UN peacekeeping operations*. https://www.unep.org/resources/report/greening-blue-helmets-environment-natural-resources-and-un-peacekeeping-operations

UNEP. (2015). *Natural resources and conflict: A guide for mediation practitioners*. https://postconflict.unep.ch/publications/UNDPA_UNEP_NRC_Mediation_full.pdf

UNEP-MONUSCO-OSESG. (2015). *Experts' background report on illegal exploitation and trade in natural resources benefitting organized criminal groups and recommendations on MONUSCO's role in fostering stability and peace in eastern DR Congo*. http://wedocs.unep.org/handle/20.500.11822/22074?show=full

UNSC. (2013). United Nations Security Council Resolution 2100. S/RES/2100. http://unscr.com/en/resolutions/2100

Wæver, O. (1995). Securitization and desecuritization. In R. Lipscut (Ed.), *On security* (pp. 46–86). Columbia University Press.

Williams, P. D. (2016). *War and conflict in Africa*. Polity Press.

Wolff, S. (2006). *Ethnic conflict: A global perspective*. Oxford University Press.

Young, H., & Goldman, L. (2015). Managing natural resources for livelihoods. In H. Young & L. Goldman (Eds.), *Livelihoods, natural resources, and post-conflict peacebuilding* (pp. 393–463). Routledge.

7

DECONSTRUCTING THE RELAPSE OF AMERICAN NATIONALISM

Harry Anastasiou and Michaelangelo Anastasiou

The relapse of populist nationalism in Western countries has precipitated into escalating conflicts, unprecedented political polarizations and even extremist politico-cultural attitudes, behaviors, and actions. In this regard, it is of utmost importance to resort to conflict analysis in historical perspective to help diagnose the underlying causes of the phenomenon of American nationalism.

In its unabashed and hyper-vocal articulations, populist nationalism has gained increasing traction as a result of several diachronic phenomena of potent historical influence that occurred throughout the post-9/11 era. These phenomena can be captured in the form of three interrelated types of threats. They are the security threat, the economic threat, and the identity threat. The analysis that follows will focus primarily on the security threat.

The security threat: Post 9/11 protracted warfare

The dark and sinister attacks of September 11, 2001, which resulted in the death of nearly 3,000 innocent people, the great majority of which were American citizens, triggered in the collective psyche of American society profound pain and anguish, as well as an unprecedented sense of vulnerability and fear. In this context, the 9/11 attacks also initiated in American political culture the emergence and crystallization of a widespread bellicose nationalism, which the Bush administration capitalized on, and amplified. Widely experienced and rationalized as a "morally justified" response to 9/11, the emergent nationalism became entrenched in mainstream America. Across party lines, with extremely few exceptions, America's political leadership and the vast majority of public opinion supported the Bush administration's launching of the so called "global war on terror." Starting with the invasion and occupation of Afghanistan in 2001 (that was the only intervention supported by the United Nations, which, however, did not entail ongoing occupation), followed by the invasion and occupation of Iraq in 2003, along with multiple other military operations in an array of countries around the world, the United States triggered a global historical dynamic of far-reaching consequences. The deployment of hard power by the United States and its coalition allies, as the primary means of defeating terrorism, continued and was sustained by subsequent U.S. governments.

While the term "nationalism" did not enter the political language of mainstream America until the 2016 presidential elections and thereafter, the phenomenon of nationalism was already driving large sectors of both America's political leadership and citizenry. Even though, in its "high" or "low" manifestations, populist nationalism is not new to America, its relapse during the post-9/11 era, brought it to the forefront as a major historical driver.

In observing the historical trajectory of the wars against terrorism, including all counter-terrorism operations since 9/11, one does not observe any definitive or substantive eradication of terrorism. According to START, the National Consortium for the Study of Terrorism and Response to Terrorism, also affiliated with, and supported by, the U.S. Department of Homeland Security, between 2001 and 2014, the number of terrorist attacks, injuries, and deaths around the world have been on the rise. While there was a decline in all three categories between 2014 and 2017, in 2017 there were over 10,900 attacks, 25,000 injuries and 26,400 deaths globally, which included 8,075 perpetrators and 18,000 victims. Significantly, START notes that "[t]errorist violence remains extraordinarily high compared to historical trends. In the decade prior to the September 11th attacks, the frequency and lethality of terrorist violence each year was less than one-third of what took place in 2017" (START, 2018).

In considering this trend, a critical question that arises is what impact terrorism had on the citizenry of America. This question cannot be fully addressed unless one takes into consideration the role played by the mass media, including social media, in reporting and disseminating news about terrorist attacks. The central issue is how coverage of terrorist attacks by the news outlets and social media highlight and make the attacks more visible, bringing information, descriptions, commentary, and potent images into citizens' living rooms. While this process occurs across nations, and often globally, it is particularly intense in the United States. The primary issue here is not about politicized fearmongering, antijihadi rhetoric, or exaggerating the terrorist threat for political expediency, which also takes place. More important is the fact that the very reporting of terrorist attacks through the power of electronic and digital media that reach millions, raises and expands the visibility of the phenomenon and the threat it poses. As a result, the issue of terrorism acquires political centrality by the mere process of reporting. This dynamic creates an impressionistic, yet potent and sustained sense of a present and unpredictable danger.

Therefore, even unintentionally, yet stunningly, the media also enhance the objectives of jihadi terrorism, by widely publicizing the very terror that the culprits intend to elicit among the populace of the west. One of the very few analysts who have grasped this problematic dynamic of terror intensification is Emily Dreyfus, reporter for *Wired*, who elaborated how sharing information about a terrorist attack on social media helps terrorists spread their message.

Moreover, the elusive and unpredictable nature of terrorist attacks renders the phenomenon more intangible and hence more difficult to manage psychologically and existentially, thereby placing sectors of the population, consciously or subliminally, on edge. Rising fear and insecurity tend to induce a portion of the citizenry to increasingly lean toward "strong men." That is, toward political leaders who exhibit the image of defiant power in defense of the nation, while criticizing the ineffectiveness of the establishment. This inclination renders a portion of the electorate fundamentally susceptible to the rhetoric of authoritarian leaning leaders and their fundamentalist nationalism.

Through these dynamics, populist nationalist leaders gain traction by establishing themselves and their agenda precisely in those "spaces" of the political landscape where the system has failed, or where the system's legitimacy has been compromised. Systemic crises, where social and political institutions become delegitimized, very often result in the waning or breakdown of "traditional" allegiances (Mouffe, 2018).

This "unravelling" of allegiances germinates new political potentials that are, however, indeterminate. This means that disenfranchised citizens are more responsive to political messages that exceed institutional norms. Relatedly, the electorate tends to respond more favorably to the political messages of leaders or parties who effectively project themselves as "independents" or "outsiders." This tendency should be understood by considering that such leaders and parties very often wage antiestablishment polemics—something that is fortified by their projected status as "outsiders." They pit "the people" against "the establishment," in what essentially amounts to a symbolic "simplification" of the political landscape. By deploying the all-encompassing notion of "the people," they are enabled in fostering allegiances across heterogeneous electoral groups. Similarly, by deploying the all-encompassing notion of "the establishment," they are enabled in symbolically conflating a wide array of grievances, and in directing them against multiple political "enemies." For example, the political messages of the ultra-Right often conflate the notions of "unemployment," "imminent terrorism," and "immigration" and project them as "failures of the establishment at the expense of the people."

This symbolic simplification of the political landscape, which is styled in the form of antagonistic political bodies, is what is very often defined as *populism* (Laclau, 2005; Panizza, 2005). Populist politics can be deployed in any context and under any conditions, but they become all the more expedient in periods of crises. Authoritarian leaders can (and often do) make use of populist politics during such "windows of opportunity." And in turn, the aforementioned type of electorate tends to not only accept, but also welcome more authoritarian styled leaders, as it finds greater "security" in authoritarian regimes. Under these conditions, authoritarianism satisfies an immediate psychological need among a portion of the electorate, however illusory its solutions may be, and however erosive it may be to democracy, to human rights, to the rule of law, and to multilateral cooperation among nations.

Extremism breeds extremism

What is often overlooked, or better, what is often ideologically and moralistically suppressed by a significant part of the leadership and citizenry in the west, and particularly in America, is that protracted wars abroad breed a generalized radicalism and militant nationalism at home (Lieven, 2004). This constitutes a subtle but potent dynamic by which wars that are fought thousands of miles away boomerang back home and impact the countries involved.

It is well established that the attacks of 9/11 have triggered a tsunami of bellicose nationalism in the United States—a nationalism that has not subsided since, but metastasized and proliferated in different forms. This broader trend of a relapsing nationalism fused with traditional self-styled nationalist extremists, many of who predated 9/11. Moreover, in combination with the increasing polarization between Republicans and Democrats on the domestic front, the general bellicose nationalism that swept mainstream America in the post-9/11 years gave rise to the radicalism of the Tea Party, and added legitimacy to America's traditional gun culture.

For example, as early as 2009, when the intelligence agency of the Missouri Information Analysis Center issued a report on the militia movement, mainstream Republican leaders immediately criticized the state government of attempting to arrest anyone with "conservative" political views. And when in 2018 a white nationalist attacked a Pittsburg synagogue, killing 11 people, the Trump administration was hesitant to outright condemn it. The reason is that for the Republican political leadership, and especially under the Trump presidency, right-wing nationalists and, relatedly, gun-bearing militia, are seen as patriotic Americans who are defending the homeland.

The Democratic Party is not absolved from having contributed to this phenomenon. As it too has contributed to the dynamic trend of a rising and sustained mainstream nationalism, which furnished the general climate within which domestic extremist groups gained traction.

Even at the height of the disastrous outcomes of the Iraq war, the Democrats' critique of the Republican administration was merely on the execution of the war, not on the war itself and its problematic consequence on Iraq and the region. Nor were Democrats critical of the bellicose nationalism, which much of its leadership adopted and employed in unison with Republicans.

For example, leaders of the Democratic Party, such as Hillary Clinton, have a track record of a bellicose nationalist approach to foreign policy. It is on the basis of nationalist driven dispositions that Clinton unreservedly supported America's involvement in all the wars, from Afghanistan to Iraq, and to Libya especially, where she played a key role in prompting the Obama administration to participate. It is noteworthy that, being dubious about Trump's personality traits, numerous Republican nationalists, known as high profile hawkish neocons, like Robert Kagan, openly endorsed and supported Hillary Clinton in the 2016 presidential elections.

A war fomenting and sustaining nationalism, a strong gun culture, armed right-wing militia, deadly attacks by mostly domestic jihadi terrorists, the spectacular dissemination of terror attacks by the media, all of these converging trends, cultivated a strong populist nationalist undercurrent, which created the perfect environment within which violent, fringe cultic groups were reawakened, or newly incubated.

In both the United States and many EU member countries, this general culture of defensive/aggressive nationalism, and more specifically of American militant nationalism, was initially discharged and released abroad through the national armies that participated in the ongoing wars against terrorism. But in time, this militancy started to be discharged and released at home through individuals and groups who, on their own initiative, resorted to acts of violence "in the nation's defense." They did so by targeting American citizens, whom they deemed as alien to, or enemies of, what they consider to be the "rightful identity" of the nation, the "rightful interest" of the nation and the "rightful security" of the nation.

It is noteworthy that the U.S. Government Accountability Office reported in 2017 that, of the 85 violent extremist incidents that resulted in death since September 12, 2001, far right-wing violent extremist groups were responsible for 62 (73 percent) while radical Islamist violent extremists were responsible for 23 (27 percent). The total number of fatalities is about the same for far-right wing violent extremists and radical Islamist violent extremists over the approximately 15-year period (106 and 94, respectively). However, 52 percent of the deaths attributable to radical Islamist violent extremists occurred in a single event—an attack on the Pulse nightclub in Orlando, Florida in 2016 (US Government Accountability Office, 2017).

And by 2018, ideological murders committed by right-wing nationalists in the United States exceeded those committed by radical jihadists.

The August 2019 El Paso, Texas, mass shooting that left 22 persons dead and over 20 wounded marked yet another case of nationalist driven violence in the United States. A professed white nationalist with antiimmigrant Trump quotes on his website, drove over nine hours from suburban Dallas to El Paso, where 80 percent of its inhabitants are Latinos, and indiscriminately started shooting people in a busy Walmart shopping mall.

Similar to other white nationalist violence, in the El Paso killings, the emergent, mainstream nationalism provided the general politico-cultural environment of negative stigmatization and toxic stereotyping, while a gun bearing individual provided the violence—a violence underpinned and galvanized by the dangerous nationalist notion of ethnonational purity. This episode of violence was directed against a community that was deemed, by the white nationalist mind, as an impurity staining America's presumed white identity. And according to the nationalist mind, such a stain on the nation had to be cleansed. The tragic irony here is that El Paso has been one of the most peaceful and violent-free towns in America.

In light of the aforementioned, it is prudent to pose the following ethical question. Is "the nation" defiled by the presence of nonwhite, non-European and non-Christian minorities? Or is it defiled by the indiscriminate, vigilante-styled murdering of innocent people, in the name of a presumed "national superiority and purity?" Indeed, it is these murderous actions that defile and stain the identity of the nation. It is this kind of violence that leaves the most abominable stain on the nation—the very nation that such extremists purport to cleanse and redeem through their violence.

Nevertheless, it ought to be noted that violent cultic nationalists operate in an emergent politico-cultural environment from which they draw legitimacy. The *Financial Times*, referring to expert analysts, rightfully stated that the extremist right-wing nationalists trend, "is being driven by social media and a dangerous mix of populist politics, economic inequality and a dissatisfaction with liberal elites and institutions" (Bond & Chazan, 2018).

This is not to suggest that mainstream right-wing nationalists endorse or condone the violence of extreme white nationalists. In fact, most of them condemn it. Yet what mainstream right-wing nationalists fail to acknowledge is that while legalistically they may deploy the law and condemn such violence, the ideological content of their own nationalism coincides considerably with that of nationalist extremists. With the exception of vigilantly violence, the ideological narrative of mainstream populist nationalists and that of cultic nationalists are fundamentally similar.

America's gun culture

There is yet another phenomenon that feeds into populist nationalism that is unique to America and that is its prevalent gun culture. Unlike any other Western society, the Second Amendment of America's constitution states that "A well-regulated Militia, being necessary to the security of a free State, the right of the people to keep and bear Arms, shall not be infringed." While there are numerous interpretations as to what this provision practically entails, and whether or not it is outdated by history, the fact remains that the vast majority of American citizens believe that gun ownership is a constitutional right. It is therefore not surprising that according to the 2018 UN report based on studies by *The Small Arms Survey,* American civilians account for 393,000,000 of firearm ownership (Small Arms Survey, 2018). There are now more guns than people in the United States.

In comparative perspective, the UN referenced report by *The Small Arms Survey* noted that, "Americans made up 4 percent of the world's population but owned about 46 percent of the entire global stock of 857 million civilian firearms" (Karp, 2018). Based on these numbers, "American civilians own more guns than those held by civilians in the other top 25 countries combined" (Karp, 2018).

As the author of *The Small Arms Survey* report, Aaron Karp provides a further stunning statistic. Namely that, the number of firearms owned by American citizens is three times as many guns as the armed forces of the Russian Federation (30.3 million), China (27.5 million), North Korea (8.4 million), Ukraine (6.6 million), United States (4.5 million), India (3.9 million), Vietnam (3.8 million), Iran (3.3 million), South Korea (2.7 million), Pakistan (2.3 million), and all the other countries (39.7 million) combined (Karp, 2018).

While for most Americans, owning guns is viewed primarily as a matter of individual freedom and safety, based on the right to self-defense, it does not diminish the fact that there is an entrenched, yet understudied, relationship between America's gun culture and mainstream American nationalism. In fact, it highlights it.

Bellicosity and assertiveness through the deployment or projection of hard power has always been integral to American nationalism, and particularly in its central hegemonic narrative of

American exceptionalism. The latter is based on the unexamined conventional presumption that American fire power, be it through the U.S. military or through the armed U.S. citizenry, is a "moral force for good" for both American society and the world. Evading all problematic aspects associated with the use of lethal force/violence in the real world, the American nationalist gun culture views fire power as a unilateral force for good, believed to be the legitimate instrument in the hands of those conventionally called "the good guys" who are deemed to be fighting and killing "the bad guys," domestically or internationally. And more importantly, this belief system assumes that in the hands of the American nation and its citizenry, the power of the gun carries an intrinsic relationship to freedom. It is believed to be, simultaneously, a supreme expression and a supreme means of protecting and propagating national and individual liberty (McCartney, 2004).

This is especially exemplary in American religious nationalism. For example, in response to the shooting at Stoneman Douglas High School in Parkland, Florida, on February 14, 2018, Wayne LaPierre, the executive vice president of the powerful National Rifle Association, asserted that the right to bear arms was bestowed upon Americans by God. Referencing the American constitution, he asserted:

> The genius of those documents, the brilliance of America, of our country itself, is that all of our freedoms in this country are for every single citizen. And there is no greater personal, individual freedom than the right to keep and bear arms, the right to protect yourself, and the right to survive. *It is not bestowed by man, but granted by God to all Americans as our American birthright* [emphasis added]. (C-SPAN, 2018)

Advocates of the view that ownership of firearms is God given, prevalent among citizens who have been identified as Christian nationalists in mainstream religious America, also argue that it is the breakdown of "Christian values" that drives gun violence in America and not easy access to firearms, or socioeconomic conditions. And as a consequence of this belief, religious nationalists, be they citizens or political leaders, have been the most ardent opponents to legislating stricter gun laws.

Historically, the gun culture of America had a perpetual association with American nationalism—a phenomenon that has not been sufficiently addressed by scholars, including Peace and Conflict Studies (PACS) scholars. The linkage between American nationalism and the prevalent gun culture is manifested in two distinct, yet interrelated strands of nationalism.

The first, which is more mainstream, prioritizes the sovereignty of America in an absolutist and fundamentalist way. It perceives the American nation as being ordained by history and/or God, rendering it thereby superior to all others in its moral standing, economic power and military might. Thus understood, this brand of nationalism bestows on the state the right to use deadly force against what the nationalist mind perceives as an enemy of America, in both the domestic and the international realms. In this perspective, America and its military might is presumed to have the role of the moral domestic and global policeman.

The second strand of nationalism that underpins America's gun culture, which is more fringe than mainstream, prioritizes the sovereignty of the individual American citizen in an absolutist and fundamentalist way. It perceives the individual as the ultimate, historically and/or divinely ordained agency from which the legitimacy of all other agencies of power and authority is derived, including that of the state, especially the federal state, and all its branches and instrumentalities. Americans who espouse this belief system, believe that they have the right to use deadly violence, even against the state and its organs, especially against the federal government, if the state is perceived to be infringing the rights of the individual citizen.

This rugged form of gun-bearing individualism is typically prevalent among cultic, white nationalists and related militia.

These two strands of nationalism frequently collide, particularly in instances where cultic nationalists break the law and commit homicide. However, they are considerably aligned in their general belief in inalienable gun rights, in American exceptionalism, superiority and supremacy, and in a deep mistrust of "foreigners," be they nations or individuals, among others. And in regard to guns, many nationalists see a seamless relationship between the American nation having the most powerful military and the American citizenry having the most firearms. This type of symbolic alignment reached a high point during the Bush administration.

The Obama administration made numerous attempts at introducing stricter gun laws within America. In response to this effort, most nationalists among the American leadership and citizenry, and especially the National Rifle Association and armed militia, saw Obama as an enemy of American freedom and the American constitution. They saw the President's approach as an attempt to seize their guns, and by so doing deprive them of their freedom. Thereby, gun-bearing nationalists considered Obama, not merely as un-American, but as anti-American, and thus as an enemy of the America nation to be fiercely resisted and removed from office. The combination of gun control efforts and the much-publicized mass shootings, resulted in an enormous increase of gun sales during the Obama presidency. According to *Forbes* the gun industry grew by 158 percent during the Obama administration (Minister, 2016). Yet, not surprisingly, even as some brands of nationalists fiercely resisted Obama's efforts at stricter gun laws, all nationalists, across political parties, tolerated, and/or explicitly supported, Obama's vast escalation of drone warfare abroad.

In light of the aforementioned analysis, one can conclude that within the broader master narrative of American nationalism, there exists an intimate relationship between mainstream nationalist bellicosity, the general gun culture and the more fringe cultic type of white nationalism.

Gun culture versus gun reality

One of the great paradoxes in America's nationalist gun culture is that while the conventional rationale for gun ownership is that it is a basic freedom, associated with the right to self-safety, self-defense, and the defense of individual and national freedom, the official statistical record of gun related casualties discloses a grim reality in regard to safety and security in American society. If the nationalist rationale for gun ownership were true, America, compared to other western countries, should have been the safest country in the world, with American citizens being the freest from violence. Official statistics, however, point to a very different reality.

According to the U.S. Centers for Disease Control and Prevention (2014), from 2001 to 2014, 440,095 people died by firearms in the United States, ranging from homicides, accidents, and suicides. During the same period, the number of Americans killed by terrorism amounted to a total of 3,412, of which 369 were killed overseas and 3,043 were killed in domestic terrorist attacks. The stunning comparative outcome from the data is that more Americans lose their life to gun violence than to terrorism. More specifically: "For every life claimed by terrorism on US soil (or where Americans abroad were killed by terrorists), more than 1,000 died from firearms inside the US" (Bower, 2016).

Further, what the hegemonic nationalist narrative conceals is that more Americans have been killed from domestic gun violence than from the wars America has been engaged in throughout the post-9/11 era. Yet, mainstream nationalism, and especially the pervasive nationalist gun culture, does not view this reality as a national security problem. Stunningly, while it views jihadi terrorism as a serious national security threat, it views gun related deaths either as a criminal phenomenon or a law enforcement phenomenon, under the presumption that "good" people with guns, kill "bad" people with guns. And while huge resources are committed to countering terrorism, very little is being done to seriously address gun related deaths, regardless of the fact that they exceed by far the number of deaths by both jihadi and white nationalist extremists.

The paradoxes of nationalism go even further, as mainstream nationalists view gun ownership as integral to American national and individual identity. Additionally, many view white nationalists, and related armed militia, as patriots defending the homeland. At this juncture, one sees the extraordinary blend of mainstream American nationalism, America's gun culture, cultic white nationalism, and armed militia, as a continuous, singular, and self-reinforcing reality. Simultaneously, all these interconnected components of nationalism jointly function as a blind spot in regard to the perilous national phenomenon of gun violence and gun related deaths in America. This general trend demarcates the political and cultural climate within which populist nationalism is sustained and thrives.

One of the rare voices asserting that gun related deaths are in essence a national security issue was John R. Allen, president of the Brookings Institution. Among other factors, his perspective was influenced by a personal paradoxical experience he encountered while fighting America's war in Afghanistan, in 2007. This was his recollection as he wrote about gun violence in America in 2019:

> I was in my command post in Al Anbar Province, the most violent region in Iraq during the most violent year in the war. In a phone call from the US, I had just been assured that my daughter at Virginia Tech was alive and unharmed, but that one of her close friends was killed and several of her friends were fighting for their lives in emergency surgery. That day 32 people were murdered on a college campus, vastly outnumbering our combined casualties in Iraq and Afghanistan on the very same day. (Allen, 2019)

As reflected in the quote above, Allen's articulation suggests that the prevailing nationalist perspective regarding security needs to be superseded by a broader, more grounded, real-world perspective. One that includes human security at home. Not surprising, Allen emphatically asserted that, "[g]un violence in America has become a national security emergency" (Allen, 2019).

Nationalism as engulfing master narrative

The political expedience of nationalism, as well as its most efficient proliferation following the 9/11 attacks, raises important theoretical and political questions for PACS. Recent scholarship has increasingly distanced itself from substantivist understandings of nationalism, where nationalism is understood in terms of presumably static and determinate characteristics. By extension, fixed definitions of nationalism are disposed of, in favor of understandings of nationalism as a dynamic and context-specific phenomenon that is constituted by plural and interacting elements (Anastasiou, 2018, 2019). The argument holds that nationalism consists in the integration of *diverse and disparate* phenomena, for example, social groups, institutions, histories, ideologies, and values, etc. under particular "master" narratives whose ultimate and most privileged point of reference is "the nation" (Anastasiou, 2019). For example, "national economy," "national military," "national law and order," "national culture," "national identity," and "national tradition," consist in remarkably heterogeneous ideological and institutional platforms. Yet they acquire certain "equivalence" as they are symbolically situated under the "umbrella" of "our nation," which *symbolically circumscribes* them as elements of "our community."

Nationalism further integrates such diverse elements historiographically, as part of political and cultural narratives that extol the nation's history and its interests. In the context of political discussions, as an example, "the military" does not solely reference an institutional platform. It references an institutional entity that is, at the level of citizens' perception, inseparable from the integrity and historical destiny of "our nation." It is the entity that, by "proactively protecting" "our national interests," guarantees "our way of life" and the perpetuity of our "historical past and destiny." American militarism thus acquires its political efficacy principally in reference to the *privileged symbol par excellence*—"the nation."

Nationalism's unique capacity in integrating such diverse elements as part of a master narrative is precisely where its power lies. It is its malleable, adaptive, diverse and multifarious diffusion in society, as it comes to "penetrate" diverse ideological and institutional platforms that afford it its political expedience and efficacy (Anastasiou, 2018). When citizens refer to "the nation," they are not merely referring to an abstract idea, but to an abstract idea that is mediated by diverse real-life references that constitute the core of their everyday life and existence. And this is the very reason why presumable "assaults" against "the nation" are very often met with "paranoid" reactions—because "the nation" is symbolically associated with a series of life modalities that constitute the fabric of citizens' existence: the state, democracy, the economy, the family, religion, etc. The nationalist narrative easily constructs images of "the enemies of the nation," thus rationalizing its militarism, fundamentalism and extremism.

The factors expounded in the preceding analysis constitute the historical dynamic that facilitated the rise of the Trump presidency, with its raw type of nationalism.

Implications for teaching and training

In October 2019, the platform Academia.com reported over 83,000 recent publications on nationalism, mostly by European scholars focusing on Europe. It is noteworthy, however, that a similar trend does not exist in the United States. More specifically, PACS scholars and practitioners lag behind in addressing American nationalism. In most cases, the phenomenon is altogether absent from American PACS scholarship, let alone in teaching and training.

The most critical contemporary challenge in peace scholarship for teaching and training is to engage in a fundamental demythologization and deconstruction of American nationalism, as a complex and powerful historical driver of far-reaching consequences. This would include an exposition of its mode of functioning, of its under examined assumptions, the parameters of its hegemonic master narrative, its tacit and explicit bellicosity, its fundamentalist absolutization of the nation, and how all these impact human values, policies, democracy, justice, and liberty in an increasingly interconnected world.

A derivative of the abovementioned will also require a demythologization of the nationalist presumption that warfare in the name of the nation is morally and legally legitimate when it serves "the interest" of the nation. PACS scholarship, teaching, and training will be required to elaborate perspectives, in specific and grounded ways that expose the nature of warfare as being the absolute antithesis of democracy and security, even, and especially, when tyrannical circumstances make it unavoidable.

Historically relevant, and up-to-date teaching and training will require a greatly increased capacity by PACS scholars and students to understand, recognize, and credibly articulate a critical perspective on nationalism, and especially American nationalism, due to its global impact and consequences. And based on this critical diagnosis, PACS scholars will be challenged to subsequently forge constructive, post-nationalist pathways forward, beyond the cul-de-sacs of polarizing, bellicose, exclusivist, and ethnocentric absolutisms.

Implications for practice and policy

By implication, the demythologization of nationalism, and all its associated traits, also entails a demythologization of the idea that war is a legitimate and effective instrument of the nation's policy approaches to national well-being and security challenges. The imperative of re-purposing policy in the interest of peace and democracy must inevitably transcend the fundamentalism, bellicosity, and nation-worship of any nationalist master narrative.

As a first step, a renewed policy approach will require the unapologetic realism that protracted warfare precipitates not only diminishing returns, yet also expands and complicates the resolution of problems, while instating the tragic into the order of society. It will entail the acknowledgement that the conventional, so called "realist" doctrine of international relations is fundamentally unrealistic in regard to the nationalist view of warfare.

Any unadulterated perspective reveals that protracted warfare relentlessly violates human life and human rights, especially of the innocent; it destroys and polarizes; it tears countries and identity groups apart, it denigrates democracy, it extends and establishes violence into a regime; it erodes the economic, social, and cultural fabric of society; it dislocates and shutters the institutions and infrastructure of society; it gives rise to and sustains extremist ideologies and actions; it corrodes and alienates the human spirit, and at the end of it all it produces a decade-long side effect that become far more difficult to manage than the original problem that warfare was intended to resolve.

In addition, policy leaders must confront the uncomfortable truth that protracted military engagements abroad boomerang back home in the form of radicalized nationalism, extremism, racism, and arrogance, which often metastasize into unilateral acts of political violence. In developing policy approaches, leaders need to factor in the impact of protracted war on the homeland at multiple levels, including the vulgarization of values and beliefs, the loss of life, domestic insecurity, citizen recourse to firearms, and a skewing of national and social and economic priorities.

In light of the above, the scale of investment in lives, human intelligence, money and energy, and the years that have been committed to warfare may be better utilized if they are methodically and systematically shifted to postnationalist agendas. The latter may include sustained engagements in peace and security seeking diplomacy; economic incentives that enhance the quality of life; investing in cooperative and peacebuilding development; establishing all-inclusive powersharing regimes and institutions of democratic governance; and cross ethno-religious citizen conciliation and society building. And crucially, policy leaders need to seriously address and institutionalize a more equitable distribution of wealth. Being resolute and staying the course on these directives ought to consistently supersede being resolute and staying the course in warfare.

In regard to gun violence, the challenge for American policy leaders is to move away from a nationalist and ideologically framed perspective, to a compassionate and more realistic approach to gun violence. The approach should frame it as an essentially national security issue, given the extraordinary levels of gun-related deaths. American policy leaders will better serve their society and constituency by acknowledging that comparatively speaking, Western societies whose constitution do not included the right to bear arms, and whose public opinion does not view gun ownership as a means of citizen safety, have very low levels of gun-related deaths. The reason why this is so, would be a great resource for American policymakers in helping them develop new and more effective approaches to addressing the uniquely American gun phenomenon.

References

Anastasiou, M. (2018). *Nation dislocation* [Doctoral dissertation, University of Victoria]. University of Victoria, eScholarship. http://dspace.library.uvic.ca/bitstream/handle/1828/9888/Anastasiou_Michaelangelo_PhD_2018.pdf?sequence=1&isAllowed=y

Anastasiou, M. (2019). Of nation and people. *Javnost*, *26*(3), 330–345.

Allen, J. R. (2019, August 5). *Gun violence in America*. Brookings Institution. https://www.brookings.edu/blog/brookings-now/2019/08/05/gun-violence-in-america-a-true-national-security-threat/

Bond, D., & Chazan, G. (2018, October 8). Rightwing terror in Europe. *Financial Times*. https://www.ft.com/content/86f2645a-c7a2-11e8-ba8f-ee390057b8c9

Bower, E. (2016, October 3). American deaths in terrorism vs. gun violence in one graph. *CNN*. https://www.cnn.com/2016/10/03/us/terrorism-gun-violence/index.html

C-SPAN (Producer). (2018, February 22). Conservative political action conference [Film; Streaming Video]. Films on Demand. www.c-span.org/video/?441475-3/conservative-politicalaction-conference-wayne-lapierre-remarks

Holton, P. & Pavesi, I. (2018). The 2018 small arms trade transparency barometer: Small arms survey 2018. Canberra, Australia. http://www.jstor.com/stable/resrep20044

Karp, A. (2018, June). Estimating global civilian-held firearms numbers. *Small Arms Survey*. https://www.start.umd.edu/pubs/START_GTD_Overview2017_July2018.pdf

Laclau, E. (2005). *On populist reason*. Verso.

Lieven, A. (2004). *America right or wrong*. Oxford University Press.

McCartney, P. T. (2004). American nationalism and US foreign policy. *Political Science Quarterly*, *119*(3), 399–423.

Minister, F. (2016, April 12). The gun industry says it has grown 158%. *Forbes*. https://www.forbes.com/sites/frankminiter/2016/04/12/the-gun-industry-says-it-has-grown-158-since-obama-took-office/#852db7b7f4e5

Mouffe, C. (2018). *For a left populism*. Verso.

Panizza, F. (Ed.). (2005). *Populism and the mirror of democracy*. Verso.

START. (2018, August). *Global terrorism in 2017*. National Consortium for the Study of Terrorism. https://www.start.umd.edu/pubs/START_GTD_Overview2017_July2018.pdf

U.S. Government Accountability Office. (2017, April 6). *Countering violent extremism*. US Government. https://www.gao.gov/products/GAO-17-300

8
HOW DOES THE COVID-19 PANDEMIC INFLUENCE PEACEBUILDING, DIVERSITY MANAGEMENT, THE HANDLING OF ETHNIC CONFLICT, AND ETHNIC MINORITIES?[1]

Mitja Žagar

The best way to promote and internalize peace, tolerance, coexistence, cooperation, inclusion, integration, solidarity, justice, equality, and the rights of ethnic and other diverse minorities is to practice and live them, particularly in times of crises.

Context

The SARS-CoV-2 virus and the COVID-19 pandemic have brought our lives to an abrupt halt. The pandemic that caused global and specific social and economic crises in most environments and their possible social, economic, political, and cultural consequences are exceptional challenges for all contemporary societies and authorities at all levels. They test the capacity, adequacy, robustness of public and private institutions, services, systems and (nation) states worldwide, confronted by challenges of amplitude unparalleled since the 1918 Spanish flu (Spinney, 2017).

Recent developments, reactions, responses and functioning of authorities, public and private organizations and institutions, systems and services showed that they have been ill prepared to deal with such crises. Obviously, contemporary societies, built upon the concept of (single) nation-states, international organizations and forums, including the UN failed to take seriously the warnings of medical and science professions who warned against global pandemics and their possible negative consequences and impacts. The absence of coherent, holistic, concerted, operational and effective approaches, crises strategies and policies were obvious. Even countries confronted by different epidemics (e.g., Ebola, SARS, bird-flu) in the past were unprepared and the World Health Organization (WHO) expected to coordinate the global management and containment of pandemics initially failed to present a coherent global strategy, and establish an operational international procedures, recommendations, criteria, and protocols.

Consequently, countries (nation-states), authorities, and communities opted for different approaches, strategies, policies, and measures. Some countries and authorities recognized the danger and severity of COVID-19 and consequent crises quickly. They started to act immediately, particularly by developing, introducing, and implementing policies and measures aimed to stop or, at least, slow down the spread of the virus and pandemic. Doing so, they followed directions and advice from epidemiologists and (national) epidemiological institutes that in the process learned about the virus and pandemic. As a consequence, sometimes they presented different, possibly opposing views and suggested different approaches, strategies, policies, measures, and recommendations. Defining the new normal, generally the medical profession agreed that the most effective measures should be social distancing, personal and public hygiene, particularly hand, cough, and sneeze hygiene.

Other countries and authorities ignored or underestimated the severity and scope of the COVID-19, crises that it provoked and their consequences. In some cases, they denied the very existence of the pandemic or compared it to annual flu epidemics and similar respiratory viral diseases. Consequently, they acted late and inadequately. Often, when they started to implement measures to contain the pandemic, the situation in those environments had already deteriorated, resulting in severe stresses and overload of their health systems, particularly intensive care units and numerous deaths of severely ill patients.

Regardless of their handling of COVID-19, their reactions and measures that they introduced, all countries and authorities are confronted by difficult questions: When and how should they introduce or end the lockdown and loosen individual restrictive measures, particularly preventive (health-related) ones? How long and how comprehensive a lockdown can they afford in our specific environment before our economies and societies collapse? What strategies and measures are needed to overcome the current crisis and to restart economies? How much will these strategies and measures cost and how can they be financed? Answering these questions seems even more difficult, considering that no effective medical treatment exists and vaccines being developed might not be available before 2021. Additionally, nobody knows how effective the vaccines will be. Simultaneously, epidemiologists warn that ending lockdowns and reopening borders and economies might cause new peaks of COVID-19 at least in some pockets.

Research of the SARS-CoV-2 virus and COVID-19 started immediately. Medical and natural sciences as well as the pharmaceutical industry focused on the development of effective drugs and vaccines. They try to shorten the necessary time for the development and clinical testing of those drugs and vaccines as much as possible. Studying all available information and learning in the process, researchers and medical professionals constantly develop protocols and medical treatments, particularly those for seriously ill patients in intensive care units. Still, the virus, severity of the SARS-CoV-2 illness and their consequences continue to surprise them.

Medicine, medical professionals, and all employees in health services, particularly robust, well-equipped, and professional public health institutions and systems prove essential in treating patients and in dealing with the pandemic, preventing, following, mapping, and limiting its spread. In this context, broad and readily available testing seems instrumental. However, everybody contributes by following preventive measures, particularly social distancing, wearing masks, and hygiene. Unfortunately, in environments where mentioned actors and measures fail, their health institutions and systems, particularly their intensive care units prove insufficient for the rapidly growing number of critically ill patients, of whom many die.

Initial comparisons confirm that tolerant, open, inclusive and well-integrated environments, built upon principles of solidarity, equality, and justice are better able to deal with the pandemic crises. Their capacity improves if they possess adequate economic and social resources and capacities, particularly developed functional, well-equipped, trained, and robust public health systems accessible to the broadest population. Equally important are other robust and functional public services and systems, such as education, welfare, social security, and public media. Their capacity to prevent crises and/or manage them successfully further increases when they promote communication and cooperation with other environments, including international communication and cooperation. A global comparison shows the following common characteristics of different environments that successfully managed COVID-19. As soon as possible they implemented general and specific health recommendations, particularly social distancing, wearing face masks, pubic and personal hygiene; when needed they restricted travel and free movement of people in, from and to the most affected towns, cities, and regions or in the whole country to reduce and control the spread of COVID-19; when necessary they closed international borders and introduced quarantine; stressing the importance of solidarity, individual and social responsibility they managed to agree upon, introduce and implement crisis management strategies, policies and measures aimed to assist the economy and different spheres of society; and, they developed specific strategies and measures that improve their capacity to overcome the crisis, reduce joblessness, and increase individual and social security.

Countries and environments that have not recognized the severity of the pandemic and failed to implement the recommendations of the medical and science professionals, such as social distancing, personal and public hygiene, quarantine, lockdown of economy, cultural and pubic life, have been less successful in managing the first wave of COVID-19. Consequently, they report higher numbers and shares of patients with severe symptoms and pandemic related deaths in their population.

Our preliminary COVID-19 related research at the Institute of Ethnic Studies (IES) shows that, globally, the implementation of predominantly restrictive and repressive approaches, strategies, policies, and measures failed to produce desired and proclaimed goals and results. These findings are consistent with our findings of studying different crises in the past, such as the Yugoslav crisis (in the late 1980s and early 1990s), the Global War on Terrorism (since 2001) and the European migrant/refugee crisis (particularly in 2015–2016) (Grafenauer et al., 2016; Medvešek & Pirc, 2015; Žagar, 2010). Our research confirmed that repressive responses, particularly those limiting and/or suspending certain human rights and basic freedoms introduced to prevent crisis and violence, increase general security and social stability as well as improve personal and social safety have not achieved proclaimed goals. Rather, they worsened the situation. Several limitations and suspensions of human rights declared in the name of security as partial and temporary at the time of their introduction have become permanent and contributed to the erosion of democracy. This new reality, coupled with the current social and economic crisis as well as ecological and climate crisis have further decreased security, personal and social safety, and resulted in pauperization and marginalization of additional segments of the population. Consequently, the public should demand that based upon the principle of proportionality authorities should consider every repressive response and measure restrictively and carefully, and introduce it with a very short expiration date only if there is no less restrictive option.

Our research confirms that restrictive and repressive approaches, limitations, and suspensions of human rights in diverse societies harm particularly diverse minorities, marginalized individuals and segments of population. For distinctive communities, particularly minority and marginalized communities and groups as well as persons belonging to them it is particularly important to assess how and to what extent such limiting and repressive measures and their implementation affect their social situation and status, inclusion, integration, and participation in all spheres of life (Medvešek & Pirc, 2015; Žagar, 2010). The working hypothesis is that they further increase their exclusion.

Some considerations and methodological issues

The amount of the relevant information and press reports on the COVID-19 pandemic and crises make it impossible to monitor and analyze them promptly and comprehensively (24UR.COM, 2020; BBC News, 2020; DW, 2020; CNBC News, 2020; MMC-RTVSLO, 2020). Understanding the importance of timely, accurate, and relevant information on the virus and effective medical treatments for the successful management of the pandemic, regardless of their workload and exhaustion medical professionals and researchers tried to communicate their findings to fellow medical workers and interested public through all possible channels. As a result of those efforts and intensified research in natural sciences and medicine, stimulated by the awareness of the urgent need to control and limit the pandemic, increased public interest and additional funding the publication of research and professional reports, papers, articles, and publications on the SARS-CoV-2 virus and the COVID-19 pandemic, the development of effective vaccines, drugs, and treatment increased immensely (Nature Research, 2020; *Science Magazine*, 2020; *The Lancet*, 2020). Consequently, it is almost impossible to follow and study them all closely. In the social sciences and humanities there have been some publishing attempts and ongoing discussions.[2] Relevant publications are expected over time, when the various social dimensions and consequences of COVID-19 will be studied in more detail. However, the first analyses show that in different settings (United Kingdom, United States, Mexico, Brazil, India, and South Africa), the poor, less educated, and marginalized, including various (social) minorities, among which ethnic, racial,[3] and religious ones were affected more by the pandemic, considering the number of patients in intensive care units and dead, increased unemployment, and social exclusion. Reports and journalistic commentaries in the main global media indicate that in the listed countries the number and share of the critically ill as well as deaths among individuals belonging to those poor and marginalized minorities, were two to four times higher in comparison with the rest of the population due to COVID-19 (BBC; DW).

There is a broad consensus that poverty, social exclusion, and marginalization are among key causes for such outcomes as they affect negatively individual's health conditions and increased risks for health conditions and illnesses. Diabetes, hypertension, and obesity cause more serious form of illness and complications in cases of infection with the SARS-CoV-2 virus and similar diseases. Usually minorities, particularly people of color are more likely to be poor, socially excluded, and marginalized than the rest of the population. Consequently, it is not surprising that they are particularly affected by COVID-19. It is important that mainstream public[4] and global media pay special attention to those issues. An important inducement to intense reporting of the U.S. and global media on the situation and particularly suffering of people of color is the murder of George Floyd by the Minneapolis police on May 25, 2020.[5] Although this was just one of numerous incidents with racial connotations in the United States recently, it showed the presence and potency of racism, particularly institutional racism in American society. The content and emotional charge of social and mainstream media coverage of this tragic event attracted broad attention, provoked public outrage and antiracist protests, not only in North America but globally. It strengthened the Black Lives Matter (2020) movement. This decentralized civic society movement in the United States and Canada advocates nonviolent civil disobedience in protest against racism, particularly against police brutality against African-Americans.[6] Public attention worldwide gave rise to antiracist outrage and movements globally;

it initiated public discussions on racism, its presence, impacts, and consequences (e.g., players taking the knee before soccer games).

Regardless of some similarities, the situation, status, and problems of diverse minorities as well as the presence and incidents of racism, xenophobia, and aggressive exclusive nationalism are specific and different in every country. Among others, they are conditioned by specific histories, historic development, traditions and perceptions, cultures and ethics, current economic, political, social, and cultural situations and developments as well as diverse ideologies and policies in those countries. Consequently, we can expect that the impacts and consequences of COVID-19 and crises related to it will differ in contrasting environments in the following years, possibly decades. Particularly, they will depend on the approach, nature, and success of measures, reactions and responses, policies and strategies of authorities in respective environments as well as on public perceptions thereof. For these reasons we should be very careful in the generalization of research results, findings, and interpretations.

Methodologically, our COVID-19 related research mainly utilizes established disciplinary and interdisciplinary approaches, research methods, and techniques. Thematically, it focuses on the situation and social processes determined by COVID-19 and related crises as well as their impact on the regulation and management of socially relevant diversities. Studying majority-minority and minority-minority relations and situation in selected diverse environments, special attention is paid to the situation, status, position, inclusion, integration, protection, and (special) rights of diverse minorities, particularly ethnic/national minorities and persons belonging to them. In this context, we review and analyze media, specifically news media reports and commentaries as well as available public documents of different authorities and institutions in selected countries, such as legislation, local and regional regulation, policies, policy, and strategy papers. Designed as a comparative study, our media analysis focuses on the mass media, particularly public broadcasters, news agencies, and their Internet services in selected regions and countries. When relevant, the analysis includes selected newspapers and social media, particularly Twitter and Facebook. In selecting the media to be analyzed, we need to consider numerous factors and circumstances, such as their situation, reach/audience/readership, status, independence, orientation, declared values and ideology, their editorial policies and practices, the ideologies and agendas of their owners, and/or authorities that control them and/or can direct them. For example, editorial policies of state-controlled media tend to avoid topics that might be unpleasant for the authorities, while private media might follow specific interests and ideologies of their owners. As a consequence, certain themes might be completely absent in certain media or they do not report about them objectively and extensively. Considering these problems and limitations as well as being aware that the very selection of included media, analyzed materials, and their contents determines the scope, orientation, and results of the analysis, we were very careful in interpreting research findings.

Our field research adjusted to specific COVID-19 related situations and conditions in diverse environments and within minority communities that is based on intense communication with relevant sources of information, individuals, associations, and institutions. Usually, the research includes phone and Internet interviews, questionnaires, and public polls. Unfortunately, specific COVID-19 measures declared by the respective authorities limited and regulated the form and process of direct personal contact and person-to-person communication that proved crucial in studying and interpreting minority-majority and minority-minority relations, and situations. Often it takes hours, days, weeks or months of direct interpersonal conversation and dialogue to establish trust and genuine relationship between researchers and persons belonging to specific minorities and majorities that enable a full insight and understanding of those complex issues and processes. Methodologically, in studying and interpreting such complex themes methodological pluralism that combines methods and techniques of different sciences and disciplines as well as multi-, inter-, and transdisciplinary approaches proves to be more successful than traditional disciplinary approaches and methodologies (Della Porta & Keating, 2008). In research, particularly in the presentation and interpretation of research results, findings, and conclusions we shall consider values, bias, and ideologies that influence sources of information as well as values, bias, and ideologies of researchers. To address these limitations, I developed a simple check-list, initially as a pedagogical tool for doctoral students. Its main steps, used in writing this study include determining (1) the topic and scope of the research, (2) the researcher's positionality, (3) the methodological approaches and the research methods used, (4) employing clear and precise language in the writing, (5) considering all relevant theoretical possibilities in data and research results interpretation, (6) understanding that the findings are not value or ideology free, and (6) clearly presenting the limitations of the study (Žagar, 2014). Focusing on the situation, and the inclusion and integration of national and ethnic minorities during the COVID-19 crisis, this study tests the hypothesis that crises affect minorities, and excluded groups, thereby increasing their exclusion. In doing so, the study aims to benefit minorities and majorities in respective environments, improving their coexistence, inclusion, integration, and equal cooperation as well as contributing to developing and strengthening democracy in those environments. In this context, decades after Gunnar Myrdal (1969) published his study on objectivity of, and in the social sciences we recognize that, regardless of all attempts to achieve and improve objectivity, science(s) and research results are always socially conditioned, and cannot be value free and absolutely objective.

Key insights

Presenting preliminary findings, we should stress that the situation is specific and different not only in every country and region where minorities live, but also within those minority communities. Minority communities are not homogenous and uniform. They are rather internally plural and diverse. Internal pluralities and diversities are reflected in a number of specific situations, internal organization, institutions, and associations of distinct communities as well as in the existence of several different, sometimes conflicting interests. Consequently, we should be very careful in interpreting the findings and conclusions, particularly in generalizing them even for a specific minority community. However, the findings confirm that usually those who are poorer, deprived, excluded, and marginalized within respective communities, including diverse minorities are more affected by different crises. The members of diverse minorities expressed that during the COVID-19 lockdown in their respective environments they felt that they were even more isolated than the rest of the population. This confirms our general conclusion that poverty, isolation, and social exclusion have an impact on the situation and position of individuals and distinct communities in contemporary societies as well as on their perceptions of their inclusion and integration in their respective social environments.

Our research, particularly the interviews conducted with members of various minorities in Slovenia and neighboring countries during the Pandemic show that most minority communities, especially traditional national minorities quickly and innovatively adapted to changing situations and circumstances with their civic, economic, educational, and cultural activities. They confirmed that during the pandemic the traditional national minorities in the region continue or even accelerate the digitalization of their activities in the fields of culture, education, religion, economy, politics, and social life in general.[7] They estimate that the public life of those national minorities was transformed as much, if not more than the life of the rest of population in respective countries, the region, Europe, and globally. However, the changed situation and digitalization within those minority communities emphasized existing internal differences and stratifications, increased marginalization, and exclusion of those that did not have the access to digital technologies and the Internet. Such problems were mentioned particularly in connection with education and distant learning as well as participation in cultural events.[8]

With regard to the lockdown and closure of international borders the members of diverse minorities, particularly traditional national minorities were affected more that had additional negative impacts on their lives. The closure of the borders with Italy after the spread of the epidemic was particularly difficult for the Italians in Slovenia and Croatia and the Slovenes in Italy. They felt isolated and cut off from their traditional cultural hinterland. The closure temporarily cut or, at least, substantially limited their traditional, permanent and intense close links and cooperation particularly with border regions of their kin-nation states. These links and cooperation include intense cross-border cooperation and exchange, daily commuting, and visiting of cultural and other institutions and public events, such as concerts, theater shows, exhibitions, and gatherings. Members of those minorities expressed their dissatisfaction with the restrictive measures during the COVID-19 lockdown introduced by respective authorities that did not consider the needs of minorities. They suggested that the Slovene and Austrian national authorities should have considered substantial regional differences in Italy, as border regions have not been impacted by the epidemic as much as Lombardy and some other regions. They pointed out that in the Spring of 2020 the situation and spread of the virus in Friuli Venezia Giulia were similar to that in Slovenia at the time. Consequently, they believed that the government of Slovenia should have allowed the inhabitants of this Italian border region or at least the members of the Slovene minority there and the members of the Italian minority in Slovenia who live along the border to cross it. In this context, in order to prevent the spread of the pandemic the Slovene government should have determined and enforced criteria, instructions, recommendations, and measures that those crossing the border should be following.

Although they were not affected as much by the closure of the borders by the Slovene and respective national authorities, similar experiences and problems were mentioned also by the Hungarians and members of the German speaking community in Slovenia as well as Slovenes in Austria, Croatia, and Hungary.

The situation of every minority and its members is specific and somewhat different. Consequently, it should not be surprising that their perceptions of the situation and problems that they experienced during COVID-19 and particularly during the lockdown differ as well. The more a specific minority is isolated and marginalized and the poorer it is, the bigger and more pronounced seem to be the problems. The Roma and their communities in Slovenia and all neighboring countries could be considered the poorest, most isolated, excluded, marginalized, economically, and socially disenfranchised minorities. Their social and economic situations further deteriorated during the Pandemic crisis. Considering their often-inadequate housing, the Roma pointed out that they find it extremely difficult to follow recommended social distancing, while it would be virtually impossible to follow the recommendations for isolation or governmental quarantine orders in the case of possible infection. Limited access to drinkable fresh water in some cases and poor general sanitary conditions in certain settlements are additional problems that the Roma are facing with regard to general recommendations for personal and public hygiene, including thorough washing and disinfection of hands declared a key preventive measure. As a consequence, we could expect that the risks of their potential exposure to the virus and its uncontrolled spread increase, at least in certain settlements and communities. Considering their existing health situation, chronic problems and related health risks, if infected with the SARS-CoV-2 virus, the Roma are more likely to experience severe illness, suffer severe and long-term health consequences or die.

An important factor of their poverty, social and economic exclusion, and marginalization, the unemployment of the Roma was enormous in comparison with that of the rest of the population already before the COVID-19 pandemic (2020). Considering past experiences, the current general social and economic situation, we could expect that their unemployment would increase further, proportionally more than that of the rest of the population contributing to their increased poverty. The Roma and scholars studying their situation particularly fear that their relative (social and economic) exclusion and marginalization might increase. As a consequence, we could expect that the number of cases of their direct and indirect discrimination in all fields of life could increase as well.

In this context, our traditional cooperation and relationship with the Roma and their communities proved instrumental in gathering the relevant information, particularly their perceptions. This cooperation was established in past decades when researchers from IES were studying the development of the Roma and their communities in Slovenia, focusing on education, housing, access to services, inclusion, integration, political participation, and representation (Bešter et al., 2017; Komac & Barle Lakota, 2015). Additionally, we cooperated with the Roma as experts and civic society activists. In our informal conversations addressing the possible consequences of COVID-19 an interesting hypothesis was mentioned that it might be less likely that the Roma catch a virus, in this case the SARS-CoV-2 virus, considering the existing isolation and marginalization of their communities, and persons belonging to them. However, once a single Roma is infected the epidemic would spread rapidly due to the specific social, economic, and health situation, and circumstances in respective Roma communities.

Discussing the present situation of minorities and ethnic relations in Slovenia and neighboring countries during COVID-19, we need to mention two historic events celebrated in 2020, namely the burning down of the "*Narodni dom/National Home*" in Trieste by the Italian Fascists (e.g., Total Slovenia News, 2019) and the Carinthian Plebiscite whose popular vote determined the border and resulted in the inclusion of this region into the (then new) Austrian state (Pleterski, 2008; Valentin et al., 2002). Traditionally, in Italy and Austria, particularly in the context of majority-minority relations both events and their official celebrations, often promoting Austrian/German and Italian nationalism and hegemony, were divisive and interpreted differently by ethnic communities as well as in Austria, Italy, and Slovenia. From the Slovene perspective, particularly from the perspective of the Slovene minorities in Austria and Italy, considering their experiences in the past century they were considered tragic. However, the official celebrations of these historic events and their nature have transformed and become more inclusive recently, giving voice also to the minorities.

To illustrate the social and historic complexity and contexts as well as current relevance of these historic events, the official centennial celebration of the burning down of the palace of "*Narodni dom*" is presented. On July 13, 2020, the presidents of Italy and Slovenia and key leaders of Slovene minority organizations in Italy symbolically signed a document of returning the palace to the minority, possibly in ten years when a school of the University of Trieste that now occupies it will move to a new building. This occasion was used to present the highest national orders of Italy and Slovenia to Boris Pahor, a 107-year-old Slovene writer from Trieste and the only surviving witness of the burning down of "*Narodni dom*." An independent and free-minded spirit, victim of fascism and Nazi concentration camp survivor, Pahor is an icon of antifascism and struggle for the rights of the Slovene minority in Trieste.[9] On that day, two presidents visited and paid respect to two symbolic places in Bazovica/Basovizza, the memorials of four Slovenes, prosecuted, and executed by the state as the first victims of Italian fascism and of those killed without due process after World War II.

The representative palace of the "*Narodni dom*" in the center of the city designed by the famous Slovene architect Maks Fabiani was the Slovenes cultural center in Trieste and symbolically demonstrated their presence in the most important multiethnic, multilingual, and open port-city of Austria-Hungary. In July 1920, before they took power in Italy, the Italian fascists burnt down the "*Narodni dom*" and destroyed other institutions and several Slovene businesses. Following their nationalist and hegemonic ideology, they wanted to erase the Slovene presence and establish Trieste as an Italian city. Especially during fascism, the Italian state and authorities discriminated against, repressed, and persecuted minorities in the Trieste area particularly the Slovenes (Čermelj, 1945). The symbolic return of the Palace to the Slovenes in Trieste 100 years after its burning down could be considered an important step in Italian minority policy.

Implications for teaching and training

The IES has been engaged in expert work, the development of concepts, policies, measures, and recommendations, public advocacy, education, and training, particularly in the context of civic education and life-long learning in crisis management, prevention, management, and resolution of crises and conflicts, peace and conflict studies, and diversity management (Klemenčič & Žagar, 2004; Žagar, 1991, 2008, 2009). Particularly important in such regard is the development of preventive approaches and strategies. Our research is constantly used at all levels of formal education, particularly in higher education as well as in formal and informal training offered to different interested audiences, including members of diverse minorities, minority organizations and institutions, civic and trade union activists, teachers at all levels, journalists, public servants, and politicians. In this context, we emphasize the importance of open and inclusive public dialogue, a concept and a process developed with Austrian and other partners in the framework of national and cross-border dialogue projects.

Open and inclusive public dialogue has proven to be an excellent approach and method for communication, coexistence, cooperation, and equal participation of different groups, communities, and individuals, regardless of their possibly conflicting views and attitudes. It enables an open discussion on topics relevant to the past, the present, and the future, the acceptance of different views and positions, and the identification and development of common interests, which are a key basis for future coexistence and cooperation (Brousek et al., 2020).

Implications for practice and policy

The research explored the impact of changed living and working conditions during and after the pandemic crisis on diverse minorities and their members, minority organizations, and institutions as well as on their social, economic, and cultural life inclusion and integration. In this context, it contributes to the development of theory, theoretical concepts, and models in ethnic and minority studies, the regulation and management of socially relevant diversities, crisis management, peace and conflict studies, particularly with regard to prevention, management, transformation, and resolution of crises and conflicts. Focusing on COVID-19 and its consequences, it aims to improve the preparedness and resilience of contemporary complex and diverse societies, particularly vulnerable social groups, and various minorities to such challenges, and crises. It contributes to the development and improvement of strategies, policies, responses, and measures as well as capacities and resources of societies and authorities at all levels to cope with such crises and overcome them in the future, by developing recommendations, crisis mechanisms, and proposals for measures and strategies.

Considering the current global situation, crises, and problems, particularly the climate and ecological crises as well as the inability of existing economic and development concepts, ideologies, strategies, and systems based upon financial capitalism and short-term profits to address those issues, we attempt to draw up new development concepts, approaches, strategies, policies, mechanisms, and measures which, based on research results, will promote sustainable, green, balanced, and just development, strengthen solidarity, inclusion, integration, and participation of minorities and their members as well as prevent exclusion, discrimination, and the deepening of social disparities.

Conclusion

These recent developments show not only positive transformations of minority policies in respective countries, but confirm also the importance of multicultural policies and the continuous process of open inclusive public dialogue in diverse environments as an effective tool for the recognition, inclusion, integration, and participation of minorities (Bašić et al., 2018; Žagar, 2020).

Notes

1 The research in this chapter is funded by Slovenia's ministries of science, the Slovenian Research Agency, EU, Council of Europe, OSCE, and the UN.
2 For example, referencing Internet conferences, online discussions, policy and research papers, and some special issues of magazines and journals (Wintersteiner, 2020).
3 In different environments these minorities, frequently victims of racism and discrimination, are called minorities of color, colored minorities, or black and brown minorities.
4 To differentiate private (for profit) and state media, I include those independent media, particularly broadcasters that have the status of public service, such as BBC, DW, and RTV SLO. Their independence, management and funding, and/or public funding are regulated by national legislation and provides for their independence from current government, authorities at all levels and different formal and informal centers of power, particularly economic.
5 See https://en.wikipedia.org/wiki/George_Floyd.
6 See https://en.wikipedia.org/wiki/Black_Lives_Matter
7 Online services were soon offered in March 2020 by the umbrella cultural organizations of the Slovene national community in Carinthia, the Slovene Cultural Association (SPZ), and the Christian Cultural Association (KKZ). Similar observations were expressed by members of the Hungarian minority in Slovenia, Slovene minorities in Italy and Croatia as well as by the Italian minorities in Slovenia and Croatia.
8 Some pupils and students were especially affected particularly those from larger families that did not have computers for every child who had to participate in distance learning as well as the elderly that did not have the access to adequate computers, phones, software, and/or Internet connections as they lacked the knowledge and skills necessary to use them successfully.
9 See https://en.wikipedia.org/wiki/Boris_Pahor

References

24UR.COM. (2020). Covid. https://www.24ur.com/
Bašić, G., Žagar, M., & Tatalović, S. (Eds.). (2018). *Multiculturalism in public policies*. Academic Network for Cooperation in South-East Europe.
BBC News (Producer). (2020). *Coronavirus pandemic*. https://www.bbc.com/news/coronavirus
Bešter, R., Komac, M., & Pirc, J. (2017). The political participation of the Roma in Slovenia. *Razprave in Gradivo: Revija za Narodnostna Vprašanja – Treatises and Documents: Journal of Ethnic Studies, 78*(2), 73–96.

Black Lives Matter. (2020). Black lives matter. *Wikipedia*. https://en.wikipedia.org/wiki/Black_Lives_Matter
Brousek, J., Grafenauer, D., Wutti, D., & Wintersteiner, W. (Eds.). (2020). Slovenija – Österreich: Befreiendes erinnern – osvobajajoče spominjanje; dialoško obravnavanje zgodovine – dialogische aufarbeitung der vergangenheit. Drava, Klagenfurt/Celovec.
Čermelj, L. (1945). *Life-and-death struggle of a national minority: The Jugoslavs in Italy*. Tiskarna Ljudske pravice.
CNBC News. (2020). California coronavirus cases surpass New York, Cuomo urges federal mask mandate. *CNBC News*. https://www.cnbc.com/2020/07/22/coronavirus-live-updates.html
Covid-19 pandemic. (2020). International, die zeitschrift für internationale politik. *Sonderausgabe*. https://international.or.at/wp-content/uploads/2020/04/International_Sonderausgabe_April_2020.pdf
Della Porta, D., & Keating, M. (Eds.). (2008). *Approaches and methodologies in the social sciences: A pluralist perspective*. Cambridge University Press.
DW. (2020). Coronavirus. *Deutsche Welle*. https://www.dw.com/en/top-stories/coronavirus/s-32798
Floyd, G. (2020). George Floyd. *Wikipedia*. https://en.wikipedia.org/wiki/George_Floyd
Grafenauer, D., & Munda Hirnök, K. (Eds.). (2016). *Raznolikost v raziskovanju etničnosti: Izbrani pogledi*. Institute for Ethnic Studies.
Klemenčič, M., & Žagar, M. (2004). *The former Yugoslavia's diverse peoples: A reference sourcebook*. ABC-CLIO.
Komac, M., & Barle Lakota, A. (2015). Breaking the glass ceiling: The case of the Roma ethnic minority in Slovenia. *Dve Domovini: Razprave o Izseljenstvu – Two Homelands: Migration Studies, 41*(2), 23–34.
Medvešek, M., & Pirc, J. (Eds.). (2015). *90 Let inštituta za narodnostna vprašanja: 1925-2015*. Institute for Ethnic Studies.
MMC-RTVSLO. (2020). Aktualno. Multimedijski Center RTV Slovenije. https://www.rtvslo.si/
Myrdal, G. (1969). *Objectivity in social research*. Pantheon Books.
Nature Research. (2020). *Coronavirus*. Nature Portfolio. https://www.nature.com/nature/research
Pahor, B. (2020). Boris Pahor. *Wikipedia*. https://en.wikipedia.org/wiki/Boris_Pahor
Pleterski, J. (2008). *Koroški plebiscit 1920*. Zveza Zgodovinskih Društev Slovenije.
Science Magazine. (2020). *Coronavirus: Research, commentary, and news*. https://www.sciencemag.org/collections/coronavirus?intcmp=ghd_cov
Spinney, L. (2017). *Pale rider: The Spanish flu of 1918 and how it changed the world*. Jonathan Cape.
The Lancet. (2020). Covid 19 resource centre. https://www.thelancet.com/coronavirus?dgcid=kr_pop-up_tlcoronavirus20
Total Slovenia News. (2019). Slovene minority in Trieste marks 99 years since burning of "Narodni Dom." https://www.total-slovenia-news.com
Valentin, H., Haiden, S., & Maier, B. (Eds.). (2002). *Die kärntner volksabstimmung 1920 und die geschichtsforschung: Leistungen, defizite, perspektiven*. Heyn.
Wintersteiner, W. (2020). The virus of "crisis nationalism." *Global Campaign for Peace Education*. https://www.peace-ed-campaign.org/the-virus-of-crisis-nationalism/
Žagar, M. (1991). Measures and mechanisms for the management or/and resolution of ethnic conflicts: Thesis for discussion. In O. Feinstein (Ed.), *Ethnicity: Conflict and cooperation: International colloquium reader* (pp. 96–109). Michigan Ethnic Heritage Studies Center.
Žagar, M. (2008). Diversity management and integration: From ideas to concepts. *European Yearbook of Minority Issues, 2006/7*(6), 307–327.
Žagar, M. (2009). Strategies for the prevention, management, and/or resolution of (ethnic) crisis and conflict: The case of the Balkans. In D. J. D. Sandole, S. Byrne, I. Sandole-Staroste, & J. Senehi (Eds.), *Handbook of conflict analysis and resolution* (pp. 456–474). Routledge.
Žagar, M. (2010). Human and minority rights, reconstruction and reconciliation in the process of state- and nation-building in the Western Balkans. *European Yearbook of Minority Issues, 2007/8*(7), 353–406.
Žagar, M. (2014). *Methodological pluralism in law and social sciences in the study of ethnicity, diversity management, minority protection and ethnic conflict*. University of Primorska.
Žagar, M. (2020). Transforming ethnic conflict: Building peace and diversity management in divided societies. In S. Byrne, T. Matyók, I. M. Scott, & J. Senehi (Eds.), *Routledge companion to peace and conflict studies* (pp. 414–424). Routledge.

PART II

Peacebuilders in Ethnic Conflicts

9
INDIGENOUS PEACEMAKING AND RESTORATIVE JUSTICE

Brandon D. Lundy, J. Taylor Downs, and Amanda Reinke

Background

Restorative justice (RJ) and indigenous peacemaking share many similarities in practice. Zion and Yazzie (2008) outline a localized hybrid peacemaking process utilized by the Navajo Nation in New Mexico, which they term "Navajo restorative justice." While this process maintains some points of intersection with RJ principles, it also diverges in places. Navajo peacemaking does not focus on one norm or rule in the process of finding justice and managing conflict. Its focus lies instead on a "relation-based and affective process rather than the application of rules by a neutral third party" (Zion & Yazzie, 2008, p. 153; see also Yazzie, 2005). The outcomes of this process de-emphasize judgment of individuals and focus instead on relationships in the community, as well as the needs of those affected by conflicts. The Navajo's different conceptions of institutions, community, individualism, and justice have made this type of peacemaking an effective approach for the Navajo, especially when compared to neoliberal models of peacebuilding and justice. "The Navajo peacemaking process is a quintessential form of restorative justice because it involves the community in restoring people and groups to well-being in a needs-meeting way" (Sullivan & Tifft, 2006, pp. 1–2). By pursuing a contextualized approach to resolving conflict that meets local needs, even if the approach maintains aspects of Western or neoliberal conceptions of justice (as Navajo RJ does), communities become invested in pursuing a sustainable and inclusive peace.

Indigenous peacemaking refers to the practices, methods, and institutions that help resolve conflict and restore relationships between individuals, families, and groups within indigenous communities. The process of indigenous peacemaking does not focus on individuals as isolated entities apart from society but instead emphasizes the importance of "communal identity, healing, and resolution" (Benjamin & Lundy, 2014, p. 4). Several scholars (Kemp & Fry, 2004; Lee, 2005; Mac Ginty, 2008; Tuso, 2016a) outline attributes of indigenous peacemaking. In her study of characteristics found in First Nations practices of conflict management, Lee (2005) discusses the importance of elders' leadership in the peacemaking process, the family and community's role in dealing with disputes, the necessity of an offender's admission of wrongdoing to the peacemaking process, forgiveness as an expected norm, ritual's role in facilitating healing, and the binding nature of agreements. Tuso (2016a),

Mac Ginty (2008, 2015), and Kemp and Fry (2004) propose similar aspects to indigenous peacemaking including peace process transparency, leadership accountability, restoration of damaged relationships, mandatory resolution, promotion of core values, discouragement of physical aggression, spiritual sanctions, and its use to "re-emphasize the purpose, identify and articulate the common goals and identity of the community" (Tuso, 2016a, p. 522). These characteristics of indigenous peacemaking constitute structures that focus less on placing guilt and instead "work to maintain harmony and balance the social order through various forms of community sanctioned social controls" (Lundy & Adjei, 2015, p. 4). With such differences in conceptualizations of peace, justice, communities, and institutions when compared to Western approaches to conflict, successful interventions into indigenous communities must reflect these localized practices, beliefs, and contexts.

The RJ process shares and further articulates these principles of indigenous peacemaking for a wider constituency. Since Howard Zehr's seminal work *Changing Lenses* was published in 1990, RJ continues to be developed and implemented in diverse settings. RJ addresses harm by restoring relationships between individuals and their communities, and is implemented in various contexts, including schools, prisons, transitional justice processes, settler-colonial states, and otherwise retributive justice systems. Despite wide popularity, debates about the paradigm and associated practices are ongoing. The most enduring debates concern the relationship of the state to RJ programs (Gordon, 2019; Silva et al., 2019), the appropriateness and efficacy of restorative models in cases of gendered violence or abuse (Daly, 2006; Daly & Stubbs, 2006; Hopkins & Koss, 2005; Keenan et al., 2016; Koss, 2014), client satisfaction rates (Armstrong, 2012; Marshall, 2014; Paul & Swan, 2018; Tamarit & Luque, 2016), and questioning the foundations of RJ, including its derivation from indigenous peacemaking (Vieille, 2013) and the cooptation of indigenous practices for use in settler-colonial states such as New Zealand (Gordon, 2019; Havemann, 1988; Moyle & Tauri, 2016; Tauri, 2014, 2016; Victor, 2015).

Situating their understandings within indigenous and religious contexts, early advocates created the RJ models and practices that have been adopted by scholars and practitioners throughout the world. Homogenized as nonviolent and harmonious, diverse and disparate indigenous groups such as the Māori, First Nations, Native American, and sub-Saharan African culture groups ostensibly serve as the source of contemporary RJ practices and as evidence attesting to the innateness of these practices (IIRP, 2016). Placing these models within the confines of ostensibly ancient human traditions throughout the world leverages the cultural capital of an idealized harmonious human past.

RJ advocates conflate indigeneity with prehistoric or ancient peoples considered long since gone but advocates also imply that culture groups and their practices are analogous. Indigenous peacemaking, regardless of the location or time-depth of the culture group, is represented as the same: universally communal, nonviolent, and harmonious. Braithwaite (1999, p. 2) characterizes restoration as "the dominant model of criminal justice throughout most of human history for all the world's peoples." Howard Zehr envisions philosophies of the harmonious interconnectedness of human beings as a cultural universal shared by indigenous groups: "for the Maori, it is communicated by *whakapapa*; for the Navajo, *hozho*; for many Africans, the Bantu word *Ubuntu*" (2002, pp. 19–20). Generalizing to diverse groups (e.g., Africans) and homogenizing them despite geographic, temporal, cultural, political, and social differences provides legitimacy by presenting all humans as working toward the universal goal of RJ. The result both feeds the conceptualization of restoration as universal and continues a dangerous stereotyping of indigenous peoples and culturally bound peacemaking processes.

Key insights

A key insight of this chapter is that all conflict is both local and social. It is local because "the local environment sets the stage" and social because local actors perpetuate the conflict and ultimately "endure the consequences" (Lundy & Adjei, 2015, p. 1). Parents make siblings apologize to one another or "hug it out" after a disagreement to restore peace in the home. Couples make pacts to "not go to bed angry" to avoid enduring animosity. Community elders require an airing of grievances and the offering of amends between disputants and the broader community that may include the ancestors to ensure acceptance, enforcement, and buy-in to the peace process. In order to be both sustainable and relevant, peacebuilding efforts must be rooted in society's traditions whether those traditions are recent inventions or an enduring legacy. Traditions are normative ideas and practices that stem from some form of historical and cultural precedent. In describing indigenous peacebuilding, Roger Mac Ginty (2011, p. 48) argues that these approaches "must be located in their wider cultural habitus, or the way that individuals and communities see and interpret the world, communicate with each other, and act." In this way, traditional peacemaking draws on both folk memories and cultural expectations to enact shared norms or mutuality through forms of social control, or inbuilt mechanisms and sanction systems that exert direct or indirect, positive or negative influence to get people to act within acceptable and agreed upon limits. However, Mac Ginty (2011, p. 51) also warns of the tendency among peacebuilders to romanticize "all things local, traditional, or indigenous." After all, "there are traditional and indigenous ways of warfare, torture, exclusion, and degradation" (Mac Ginty, 2011, p. 51).

The overromanization of localized RJ and indigenous peacebuilding practices is another key insight of this chapter and often stems from three broadly held fallacies. First, local communities are homogenous and egalitarian, which overlooks diversity and asymmetries of power. Second, that these approaches are equally effective in different local contexts, ignoring contextual factors that fashion what types of interventions might work. Third, that what may have been effective once in a local setting remains viable, even though cultures change through the exertion of both internal and external forces over time. Gearoid Millar (2014) counteracts these misconceptions by showing how an ethnographic approach to peacebuilding prioritizes localized approaches and critiques over imposed agendas. He advocates for understanding complex ground-level diversity in conceptions of "peace, justice, development, and reconciliation" and how they may change to empower local actors. Millar (2014) argues that evaluating peacebuilding interventions demands an understanding of the local and culturally variable context in process (see also Avruch, 1998, 2015).

Mac Ginty (2011, p. 52) contends that indigenous or localized traditional approaches to conflict resolution, peacemaking, and reconciliation are inherently conservative and reinforce existing authority and the status quo. "Women, minorities, and the young are often excluded, and an emphasis is placed on conformity and a numbing of activism, criticism, and radical change," thus obfuscating asymmetries of power (Mac Ginty, 2011, p. 52). When duress becomes pervasive and shared within local communities, these stressors can lead to disaffected factions who look to affect change. These culture change processes suggest that "cultural traditions are both the hallmark of conflict transformation and peacebuilding, while at the same time, they are largely illusory" (Lundy & Adjei, 2015, p. 1; see also Bayart, 2005). William Zartman (2000, p. 8) emphasizes, "Conflicts within a system occur in the context of a sociopolitical structure, under an institution of authority, and within a community of values." Any grounded approach such as indigenous peacebuilding or RJ must embrace both local and global discord as multivocal, multilocational, multitemporal, and multiscale, "involving persons and institutions with interrelated and sometimes conflicting histories, cultures, politics, needs, and ideologies" (Lundy & Adjei, 2015, p. 2).

Many indigenous leaders, scholars, and practitioners advocate for peacemaking approaches that incorporate both local and global conceptions of peace and justice. While we have touched on Navajo peacemaking's blending of Navajo and Western practices (Zion & Yazzie, 2008), other individuals and groups have taken similar approaches across North America in recent years. These include judges, administrators, and advocates like Michael Petoskey, Dave Raasch, Natasha Gourd, and others involved in the Indigenous Peacemaking Initiative (https://peacemaking.narf.org/), which seeks to revive traditional ways of dispute resolution in indigenous communities to better cope with issues that Western-model court systems fail to address. Stacey Gettig, tribal court clerk for the Pokagon Band of Potawatomi, describes the benefits to native justice: "in peacemaking you are forced to talk about what's going on, and a lot of times the reason that you're there is not the reason that these issues are occurring, there's more behind the problem, and when you're able to talk about it with one another you really break that ice and that's when you begin to solve problems" (Winchester, 2015).

In South America, groups and leaders like the Kayapo and Chief Megaron Txukarramãe utilize indigenous symbolism, ceremony, and dialogue in building alliances with both indigenous and nonindigenous groups to stop encroachment by the Brazilian state into indigenous territories and communities (Turner & Fajans-Turner, 2006). These approaches are also applied by indigenous practitioners in conflicts that experience more direct violence, such as with the nonviolent Indigenous Guard civil defense organization in Colombia (Mignone & Vargas, 2016) and the institution of jirga in Afghanistan (Thiessen, 2013). The reemergence and resilience of these practices comes about through the failures of Western-style justice systems to address community needs and to help preserve cultural identity in their respective settings. Therefore, a third key insight is that indigenous approaches to peacemaking are more effective in indigenous contexts.

Indigenous approaches to peacemaking possess great potential for progress toward positive peace in many communities and conflicts, but their application must take into consideration the asymmetries of power between indigenous and nonindigenous actors. Nonindigenous conceptions of peace, justice, and even indigeneity play a major role in how indigenous peacemaking can successfully be implemented alongside traditional Western practices (Benjamin & Lundy, 2014). The importance of power in incorporating integrated approaches is highlighted by the alliances and joint involvement of indigenous and nonindigenous actors in social movements over recent decades (Lundy, Collette, & Downs, 2022).

Interactions between indigenous and nonindigenous protesters at the Sacred Stone Camp at Standing Rock represent how these asymmetries in power affect perceptions of indigeneity and indigenous peacemaking. In April 2016, protesters flocked to the camp in response to the construction of the Dakota Access Pipeline through Indian treaty territory, which threatened sacred sites and the water supply of the Standing Rock Indian Reservation. The first of these protesters were indigenous peoples from across the United States and Canada. By fall, they were joined by a plethora of nonindigenous environmentalists, celebrities, politicians, human rights advocates, and other activists, protesters, and community organizers. While this diverse set of actors all opposed the construction of the pipeline, they held different ideas about participating in an indigenous-led movement.

In Lakota tradition, there is an expectation for women to wear long skirts as a matter of respect in ceremonial contexts, which included the Sacred Stone Camp. Some nonnative women objected to this practice, while others were unaware of it prior to their arrival at the camp. This point of conflict speaks to differences in worldviews, with nonindigenous women viewing the skirts as impractical and oppressive, while indigenous women viewed them as traditional, as well as a way to express their identity and culture (Gilio-Whitaker, 2019).

For indigenous peacemaking to work in these shared and hybrid spaces, nonindigenous participants must understand how their perceptions of peace, justice, and community vary from those of indigenous peoples (and vice versa). In solely indigenous settings, outside officials, administrators, and funders need to recognize that their expectations of measurable outcomes may need to be reconsidered. Even the use of the term "indigenous" obscures countless differences between communities and cultures across the globe. If the dominant discourse around peacemaking ignores these attitudes and biases, the potential impact of indigenous peacemaking will be limited.

Implications for teaching and training

Indigenous approaches to conflict management, resolution, and transformation are axiomatically diverse since they are localized, contextual, shared, experiential, and holistic (Lundy, Collette, & Downs, 2022). As an ad hoc approach, indigenous peacemaking can also be creative, which suggests a potential to be "transformative when it's sought and addresses conflict as it affects the community. It prioritizes the reparation of the relationships' web, and the restoration of the community's harmony" (Wahab, 2018, p. 21). According to Abdul S. Wahab (2018, p. 21), both indigenous peacemaking and RJ models provide "an experiential learning opportunity for victim, wrongdoer, and the entire community." With direct implications for personhood, these social pressures are effective because they exert historical, agentive, and structural forces on the stakeholders, which have the power to shape thoughts and behaviors and curb deviance.

Indigenous approaches still in use among indigenous peoples survive in some form or fashion because they have use-value and remain somewhat effective and relevant to the people who practice them, and possibly others. These include the now popularized and heavily critiqued practices of Jirga (Afghanistan and Pakistan), Gacaca (Rwanda), and Mato Oput (Uganda) (Adebayo et al., 2014; Adebayo et al., 2015; Mac Ginty, 2008). What these popular iterations show is that contemporary indigenous peacebuilding "is likely to have been updated, adjusted, and opened to new accretions in order to stay alive through changing times" (Zartman, 2000, p. 7). Protracted violent conflict found in many indigenous communities, however, suggests that many of these "homegrown measures at dampening escalation and preventing violence have failed" (Zartman, 2000, p. 3). On the other hand, hybrid forms of diverse indigenous voices can contribute valuable counternarratives, localized ownership, and sustainability of practice (i.e., habits).

The Kayapo Resistance has been a case study in anthropology and environmental studies for the last 30 years (Turner, 2006). It is the case of indigenous peoples of Brazil responding, "constructively to the threat of despoliation of their ecological bases or the theft of their lands" (Turner, 2006, p. 408). Resource extraction, farming, and a proposed hydroelectric dam along the Xingu River and its tributaries that would flood large areas of Kayapo land were hotly contested, physically, politically, and legally. The Kayapo leadership and their indigenous and international collaborators saw that their success depended on "international public opinion, press attention, and financial support" (Turner, 2006, p. 402). They used indigenous peacemaking techniques of reciprocity, feasting, and the building of local alliances and combined those with negotiation, legal challenges in the courts, and political outreach through media campaigns.

> The performance of cultural difference is strategic ... without such colorful performances many in the Western world would not even turn their attention to indigenous demands in conflict situations ... what these cultural performances also tell us is how such well-positioned essentialisms are trying to send a message about the devastating effects of global geo-politics. (Sen et al., 2014, p. 259; see also Conklin, 1997)

A hybrid approach can strengthen resilience and social cohesion of indigenous groups and their global partners. Implications of indigenous peacemaking and RJ rely on hybrid approaches to managing, resolving, and transforming conflict into acceptable outcomes for stakeholders within acceptable historical, societal, political, economic, and cultural limits. The teaching and training of these approaches comes from careful study of successes and failures to glean lessons learned and shared, sometimes from independently invented systems of restorative justices being used around the world (Aall & Crocker, 2017; Adebayo et al., 2014, Adebayo et al., 2015; Braithwaite, 2002; Zartman, 2000).

Lederach's innovative *Conflict Transformation School* elevated the knowledges and contexts of indigenous peoples as central to efforts of reconciliation aimed at refashioning relationships and the underlying structures of society (Lederach, 2010; Lederach & Lederach, 2010). Hybrid indigenous peacebuilding built on RJ foundations and informing contemporary efforts of restoring RJ approaches to a modern mainstream among diverse groups (i.e., schoolchildren, ethnic groups, siblings, ex-combatants and their victims, couples, and community members) are integrating local and indigenous peacebuilding knowledge and processes with those of international actors to enhance the agency of the mundane by empowering local people and their communities (Mac Ginty, 2011). As mentioned above, however, these hybrid approaches still instill power asymmetries. For example, international funders can blame local implementers when things fall apart in the peace process (Paffenholz, 2015) or they can empower locals to perpetuate longstanding injustices and inequalities (Ramsbotham et al., 2016). So, what lessons can teachers and trainers take away from the benefits and potential pitfalls associated with enacting indigenous peacemaking and restorative justice approaches?

RJ is a participatory and equitable process for addressing the harms, needs, and obligations for all parties affected by conflict (Sullivan & Tifft, 2006; Zehr, 2002). Although there are diverse RJ processes and models, they are all premised on conflict as an invitation to examine the multiple dimensions and scales of harm, accountability, and micro- and macrolevel societal change (Zehr, 2002). All RJ processes include accountability for wrongdoing by the offender, active participation of all parties, and the inclusion of community stakeholders. We first present two disparate examples of RJ practice, then proceed to discuss implications for teaching and training.

RJ has been implemented in schools to reduce criminalization of marginalized youth in the United States (Sandwick et al., 2019; Schiff, 2018). In California, the Oakland Unified School District (OUSD) implemented whole school RJ as a three-tier system for this purpose (OUSD, 2020). At tier 1, community building occurs and includes the entire school population. Tier 1 uses classroom-based restorative circles to create socially bound learning conditions by building relationships and focusing on values discussions. Circle processes emphasize sharing openly and honestly while respecting everyone's right to be heard and speak without interruption. There is a talking piece that moves from person to person to indicate who is holding conversational space. In tier 2 restorative processes are used to address harm or conflict. This may include family group conferences or restorative circles that work to identify the causes of harm, produce accountability, and promote healing for the offender, victim(s), and school. During tier 2, only those involved in the production, receipt, or construction of harm attend the circle or conference. Tier 3 RJ supports reintegration and reentry for students returning from suspension, expulsion, or incarceration. This is a welcoming process to promote accountability, celebrate achievements, and provide support as they reenter the school environment. The three-tier system is used to promote a healthy learning environment, strengthen the school community through emotional intelligence and relationship building in ways that are values-driven and inclusive, and reduce the likelihood of further youth conflict with the law (OUSD, 2020).

RJ has also been implemented in other settler colonial states where indigenous peoples are overrepresented in the courts and prisons. For example, Māori people in New Zealand make up to 14.5 percent of the total population, but represent 50 percent of its prison population (Tauri, 2009, p. 3) and are overrepresented in all stages of criminal justice proceedings (Department of Corrections, 2007). Māori cultural revitalization efforts included demands for legal system reform and Māori legal sovereignty (Jackson, 1988; Tauri, 2009). Demands were met by a government unwilling to provide true sovereignty but attempted to "indigenize" the legal system by implementing Māori-based justice practices into the existing settler-colonial criminal justice system (Tauri, 2009). In 1989, the New Zealand Government, Children, Young Persons, and their Families Act was enacted implementing a Māori-based justice mechanism—the Family Group Conferencing model (FGC)—in the Youth Justice system. FGC, a form of RJ, is a formal and mediated meeting between officials (e.g., police), family members, social care providers (e.g., social workers), and the youth in question. It was "a gift from the Aboriginal people of New Zealand" (Ross, 2009, p. 5), although it has failed to truly embody Māori values and processes (Moyle & Tauri, 2016; Vieille, 2013). While FGC was envisioned as a culturally appropriate justice mechanism for indigenous populations, Māori are often dissatisfied with the model (Moyle & Tauri, 2016; Tauri, 2014, 42); scholars highlight its failure to address systemic violence (Tauri, 2014), and "narratives of oppression" have emerged from participants (Gordon, 2019), all suggesting that the nonindigenous professionals may be culturally incompetent (Moyle & Tauri, 2016).

There are several significant insights for practitioners embedded in these two examples and in the RJ literature more generally. First, the healing and individual transformation experienced by offenders, victims, and their supporters in RJ processes does not necessarily lead to community or societal transformation (Daneshzadeh & Sirrakos, 2018; Schiff, 2018). For example, implementing RJ in the OUSD does not necessarily "scale up" to the level of undoing structural forms of inequality to dismantle the school-to-prison pipeline. Even where RJ is implemented to address systemic issues, such as FGC in New Zealand, it is clearly limited.

Second, while RJ practices may have use-value in their normative cultural contexts, they do not necessarily integrate into other systems or transfer to other spaces, places, and cultural settings. For example, FGC processes are typically facilitated by non-Māori (Pākehā) practitioners who proceed with a "one size fits all standardized approach to engaging with what is a socio-culturally diverse clientele" (Moyle & Tauri, 2016, p. 95). Research reveals that Māori participants in FGC often feel as though cultural components "sat alongside" non-Māori assessments, such as behavior and health (Moyle, 2013). These represent concerns with individual nonindigenous practitioners attempting to implement indigenous-based RJ processes, and the broader structural context of placing RJ processes within settler-colonial state structures.

Implications for practice and policy

This chapter argues for a paradigm shift when thinking about the localized nature of conflict and peace. "A complex understanding of the history and emerging modalities of being 'indigenous' in a global world" (Sen et al., 2014, p. 258) pushes practitioners and policymakers alike beyond essentialist notions of romantic authenticity. Avoiding Kevin Avruch's (1998, 2003) Type II errors of one-size-fits-all problematics or under-problematized acceptance of the way things are, cultural complexity must be engaged in a direct and nuanced way to understand indigenous, localized, and potentially effective responses to both conflict and the ways outsiders propose to manage, resolve, and transform it. According to Sen et al. (2014, p. 264), the cultural politics of indigeneity is an important avenue of further understanding and investigating, neither privileging or demoting the endeavor, but instead recognizing when human security is enhanced, when a cultural context is embraced, or when external interventions must be overlaid onto societal and cultural logics that are succumbing to infighting, division, discord, and violence.

Indigenous as a categorical concept emerged during a period of Western expansion in which local populations of original inhabitants, first settlers, and First Nations people experienced contact, "disruption, erasure, displacement, trauma, struggle, and reclamation" ultimately enmeshed in a nation-state superstructure that overlooked their concerns unless forced to engage often by the peoples themselves (Benjamin & Lundy, 2014, pp. 1–2). RJ studies discussed in this chapter indicate that where RJ is implemented to meet indigenous needs within settler-colonial states and is designed and practiced by nonindigenous actors, RJ is less effective. Indigenous participants often fail to see the idealized outcomes of such programs, but there is also little data to suggest that RJ implementation effectively disrupts systematic asymmetries of power and inequality, such as the overrepresentation of indigenous peoples in legal systems or the school-to-prison pipeline. RJ practitioners must thus take care to design and implement RJ programs that are contextualized, appropriate, and acknowledge the diversity of principles, ideologies, and practices of the target group.

Benjamin and Lundy (2014, p. 3) acknowledge "the wonderful and multitudinous diversity of cultures, languages, peoples, and cosmologies of indigenous communities" and that this tapestry shares "certain general similarities that appear to be common in many cases, and these are due more to manner of subsistence and social organization." In extensive reviews of indigenous peacebuilding (Adebayo et al., 2014; Adebayo et al., 2015; Mac Ginty, 2011; Tuso, 2016b; Zartman, 2000), common shared characteristics associated with these approaches include (1) a basis in experience over expertise; (2) a cooperative style that is inclusive and mutually engaging for a wide swath of stakeholders instead of just perpetrators and victims; (3) a dialogic, public, and open engagement ensuring buy-in and social control instead of more retributive consequences; (4) an efficient and low-cost affair allowing for broad participation; (5) a context sensitive, localized, and flexible approach instead of universal models and mandatory sentencing; and (6) a conciliatory style that encourages reintegration over separation and removal. Often through a reliance on ancestors and first-settler rights, these indigenous peacebuilding practices also rely on some form of spiritual sanction, meaning they can act beyond direct evidence to ensure that atonement for any wrongdoing is internalized and shared within a broader community of values (Lundy & Adjei, 2015; Lundy, Adebayo, & Hayes, 2018).

As relational and contextual, both indigenous peacemaking and RJ contribute normative and potentially transformative tools, one set aimed at restoring community harmony while the other focused on balancing and advancing the relationships between individuals. Although they are potentially transformative, policymakers and practitioners must ensure that these tools reflect conflict as both social and local. Indigenous peacemaking approaches are likely more effective in their originating contexts, where they can be applied dynamically and respond to local needs, changes, and shifting power dynamics. This would concomitantly reduce the likelihood that RJ and indigenous peacemaking practices would be overromanticized, fail to identify and respond to local power asymmetries or incorporate diversity, and allow for changing practice over time in response to internal and external sociocultural change. RJ and indigenous peacemaking practice and policy is best when rooted in and reflective of local realities. These interventions have a great deal of potential when the practitioners and policymakers have stakeholder buy-in suggesting that these tools are likely most effective in indigenous and local contexts where community matters and empathy is an instilled and shared value.

References

Aall, P., & Crocker, C. A. (Eds.), (2017). *The fabric of peace in Africa: Looking beyond the state*. Center for International Governance Innovation (CIGI) Press.

Adebayo, A. G., Benjamin, J. J., & Lundy, B. D. (Eds.). (2014). *Indigenous conflict management strategies: Global perspectives*. Lexington Books.

Adebayo, A. G., Lundy, B. D., Benjamin, J. J., & Adjei, K. A. (Eds.). (2015). *Indigenous conflict management strategies in West Africa: Beyond right and wrong*. Lexington Books.

Armstrong, J. (2012). Factors contributing to victims' satisfaction with restorative justice practice: A qualitative examination. *British Journal of Community Justice*, *10*(2), 39–54.

Avruch, K. (1998). *Culture and conflict resolution*. United States Institute of Peace Press.

Avruch, K. (2003). Type I and Type II errors in culturally sensitive conflict resolution practice. *Conflict Resolution Quarterly*, *20*(3), 351–371.

Avruch, K. (2015). *Context and pretext in conflict resolution: Culture, identity, power, and practice*. Routledge.

Bayart, J. F. (2005). *The illusion of cultural identity* (S. Rendall, J. Roitman, C. Schoch, & J. Derrick, Trans). The University of Chicago Press.

Benjamin, J. J., & Lundy, B. D. (2014). Introduction: Indigeneity and modernity, from conceptual category to strategic juridical identity in the context of conflict. In A. G. Adebayo, J. J. Benjamin, & B. D. Lundy (Eds.), *Indigenous conflict management strategies* (pp. 1–12). Lexington Books.

Braithwaite, J. (1999). Restorative justice: Assessing optimistic and pessimistic accounts. *Crime and Justice*, *25*, 1–127.

Braithwaite, J. (2002). *Restorative justice and responsive regulation*. Oxford University Press.

Conklin, B. (1997). Body paint, feathers, and VCRs: Aesthetics and authenticity in Amazonian activism. *American Ethnologist*, *24*(4), 711–737.

Daly, K. (2006). Restorative justice and sexual assault: An archival study of court and conference cases. *British Journal of Criminology*, *46*, 334–356.

Daly, K., & Stubbs, J. (2006). Feminist engagement with restorative justice. *Theoretical Criminology*, *10*(1), 9–28.

Daneshzadeh, A., & Sirrakos, G. (2018). Restorative justice as a doubled-edged sword: Conflating restoration of black youth with transformation of schools. *Taboo: The Journal of Culture and Education*, *17*(4), 7–28.

Department of Corrections. (2007). *Over-representation of Māori in the criminal justice system*. New Zealand Department of Corrections Policy, Strategy and Research Group.

Gilio-Whitaker, D. (2019). *As long as grass grows: The Indigenous fight for environmental justice, from colonization to standing rock*. Beacon Press.

Gordon, G. (2019). Wedded to the state's requirements: Restorative and community justice processes in Aotearoa/New Zealand. *New Zealand Sociology*, *34*(1), 27–50.

Havemann, P. (1988). The indigenization of social control in Canada. In B. Morse & G. Woodman (Eds.), *Indigenous law and the state* (pp. 71–100). Foris Publications.

Hopkins, C. Q., & Koss, M. P. (2005). Incorporating feminist theory and insights into a restorative justice response to sex offenses. *Violence Against Women*, *11*, 693–723.

IIRP (International Institute for Restorative Practices). (2016). *What is restorative practice?* http://www.iirp.edu/what-we-do/what-is-restorative-practices

Jackson, M. (1988). *Māori and the criminal justice system: He whaipaanga hou—a new perspective*. New Zealand Department of Justice.

Keenan, M., Zinsstag, E., & O'Nolan, C. (2016). Sexual violence and restorative practices in Belgium, Ireland, and Norway: A thematic analysis of country variation. *Restorative Justice: An International Journal*, *4*(1), 86–114.

Kemp, G., & Fry, D. (2004). *Keeping the peace: Conflict resolution and peaceful societies around the world.* Routledge.

Koss, M. P. (2014). The RESTORE program of restorative justice for sex crimes: Vision, process, and outcomes. *Journal of Interpersonal Violence, 29*(9), 1623–1660.

Lederach, J. P. (2010). *The moral imagination: The art and soul of building peace.* Oxford University Press.

Lederach, J. P., & Lederach, A. (2010). *When blood and bones cry out: Journeys through the soundscape of healing and reconciliation.* Oxford University Press.

Lee, G. (2005). Defining traditional healing. In W. D. McCaslin (Ed.), *Justice as healing: Indigenous ways* (pp. 98–107). Living Justice Press.

Lundy, B. D., Adebayo, A. G., & Hayes, S. (Eds.), (2018). *Atone: Religion, conflict, and reconciliation.* Lexington.

Lundy, B. D., & Adjei, J. K. (2015). Introduction: Reconciliation and conflict management in West Africa through cultural traditions. In A. G. Adebayo, B. D. Lundy, J. J. Benjamin, & J. K. Adjei (Eds.), *Indigenous conflict management strategies in West Africa: Beyond right and wrong* (pp. 1–18). Lexington Books.

Lundy, B. D., Collette, T., & Downs, J. T. (2022). The effectiveness of Indigenous conflict management strategies in localized contexts. *Cross-Cultural Research, 56*(1), 3–28.

Mac Ginty, R. (2008). Indigenous peace-making versus the liberal peace. *Cooperation and Conflict, 43*(2), 139–163.

Mac Ginty, R. (2010). Gilding the lily? International support for indigenous and traditional peacebuilding. In O. Richmond (Ed.), *Palgrave advances in peacebuilding* (pp. 347–366). Palgrave Macmillan.

Mac Ginty, R. (2011). *International peacebuilding and local resistance: Hybrid forms of peace.* Palgrave Macmillan.

Mac Ginty, R. (2015). Where is the local? Critical localism and peacebuilding. *Third World Quarterly, 36*(5), 840–856.

Marshall, J. M. (2014). (I can't get no) Satisfaction: Using restorative justice to satisfy victims' rights. *Cardozo Journal of Conflict Resolution, 15*(2), 569–596.

Mignone, J., & Vargas, H. G. (2016). Indigenous guard in Cauca, Columbia: Peaceful resistance in a region of conflict. In H. Tuso & M. P. Flaherty (Eds.), *Creating the third force: Indigenous processes of peacemaking* (pp. 299–314). Lexington Books.

Millar, G. (2014). *An ethnographic approach to peacebuilding: Understanding local experiences in transitional states.* Routledge.

Moyle, P. (2013). *From family group conferencing to whanau ora: Māori social workers talk about their experiences* [Master's thesis, Massey University], Palmerston North, New Zealand.

Moyle, P., & Tauri, J. M. (2016). Māori, family group conferencing and the mystifications of restorative justice. *Victims and Offenders, 11*, 87–106.

OUSD (Oakland Unified School District). (2020). Restorative justice. https://www.ousd.org/Page/12324.

Paffenholz, T. (2015). Unpacking the local turn in peacebuilding: A critical assessment towards an agenda for future research. *Third World Quarterly, 36*(5), 857–874.

Paul, G. D., & Swan, E. C. (2018). Receptivity to restorative justice: A survey of goal importance, process effectiveness, and support for victim-offender conferencing. *Conflict Resolution Quarterly, 36*(2), 145–162.

Ramsbotham, O., Woodhouse, T., & Miall, H. (2016). *Contemporary conflict resolution* (4th ed.). Polity Press.

Ross, R. (2009). Searching for the roots of conferencing. In G. Burford & J. Hudson (Eds.), *Family group conferencing: New directions in community-centered child and family practice* (pp. 5–14). Transaction Publishers.

Sandwick, T., Hahn, J. W., & Ayoub, L. H. (2019). Fostering community, sharing power: Lessons for building restorative justice school culture. *Education Policy Analysis Archives, 27*(145), 1–32.

Schiff, M. (2018). Can restorative justice disrupt the 'school-to-prison pipeline?' *Contemporary Justice Review, 21*(2), 121–139.

Sen, D., Danso, F. K., & Meneses, N. (2014). Culture and management: The need for a paradigm shift. In A. G. Adebayo, J. J. Benjamin, & B. D. Lundy (Eds.), *Indigenous conflict management strategies: Global perspectives* (pp. 257–264). Lexington Books.

Silva, S. M., Porter-Merrill, E. H., & Lee, P. (2019). Fulfilling the aspirations of restorative justice in the criminal system? The case of Colorado. *Kansas Journal of Law and Public Policy, 28*(3), 456–504.

Sullivan, D., & Tifft, L. (2006). The healing dimension of restorative justice: A one-world body. In D. Sullivan & L. Tifft (Eds.), *Handbook of restorative justice* (pp. 1–16). Routledge.

Tamarit, J., & Luque, E. (2016). Can restorative justice satisfy victims' needs? Evaluation of Catalan victim-offender mediation programme. *Restorative Justice: An International Journal*, *4*(1), 68–85.

Tauri, J. (2009). An Indigenous perspective on the standardisation of restorative justice in New Zealand and Canada. *Indigenous Policy Journal*, *20*(3), 1–24.

Tauri, J. (2014). An Indigenous commentary on the globalisation of restorative justice. *British Journal of Community Justice*, *12*(2), 35–55.

Tauri, J. M. (2016). Indigenous peoples and the globalization of restorative justice. *Social Justice*, *43*(4), 46–67.

Thiessen, C. (2013). *Local ownership of peacebuilding in Afghanistan: Shouldering responsibility for sustainable peace and development*. Lexington.

Turner, T. (2006). The Kayapo resistance. In J. Spradley & D. W. McCurdy (Eds.), *Conflict and conformity: Readings in cultural anthropology* (12th ed., pp. 391–409). Berghahn Books.

Turner, T., & Fajans-Turner, V. (2006). Political innovation and inter-ethnic alliance: Kayapo resistance to the developmentalist state. *Anthropology Today*, *5*, 3–10.

Tuso, H. (2016a). Creating the third force: Some common features in Indigenous processes of peacemaking, and some preliminary observations. In H. Tuso & M. P. Flaherty (Eds.), *Creating the third force: Indigenous processes of peacemaking* (pp. 509–535). Lexington Books.

Tuso, H. (2016b). Indigenous processes of conflict resolution: Neglected methods of peacemaking by the new field of conflict resolution. In H. Tuso & M. P. Flaherty (Eds.), *Creating the third force: Indigenous processes of peacemaking* (pp. 27–51). Lexington Books.

Victor, W. (2015). Indigenous justice: Clearing space and place for Indigenous epistemologies. Research paper, National Centre for First Peoples Governance. http://fngovernance.org/ncfng_research/wenona_victor.pdf

Vieille, S. (2013). Frenemies: Restorative justice and customary mechanisms of justice. *Contemporary Justice Review*, *16*(2), 174–192.

Wahab, A. S. (2018). *The Sudanese indigenous model for Conflict Resolution: A case study to examine the relevancy and the applicability of the Judiyya model in restoring peace within the ethnic tribal communities of the Sudan* [Doctoral dissertation, Nova Southeastern University].

Winchester, J. (2015). Native justice initiative – peacemaking. Vimeo video. https://vimeo.com/107772333

Yazzie, R. (2005). Healing as justice: The Navajo response to crime. In W. D. McCaslin (Ed.), *Justice as healing: Indigenous ways* (pp. 121–133). Living Justice Press.

Zartman, I. W. (Ed.). (2000). *Traditional cures for modern conflicts: African conflict "medicine."* Lynne Rienner Publishers.

Zehr, H. (1990). *Changing lenses*. Herald Press.

Zehr, H. (2002). *The little book of restorative justice*. Good Books.

Zion, J., & Yazzie, R. (2008). Navajo peacemaking. In D. Sullivan & L. Tifft (Eds.), *Handbook of restorative justice* (pp. 151–160). Routledge.

10
INTERACTIVE CONFLICT RESOLUTION: ADDRESSING THE ESSENCE OF ETHNOPOLITICAL CONFLICT AND PEACEBUILDING[1]

Ronald J. Fisher

Background

Interactive conflict resolution (ICR) is a term that encompasses a variety of small-group, face-to-face methods for bringing together informal representatives of groups or states involved in intense conflict to engage in dialogue, training, shared analysis and joint problem-solving or other constructive interactions facilitated by an impartial and skilled third party. A brief history is provided in Fisher (2002), with a chronological listing of major theoretical contributions and practice interventions from the mid-1960s to the mid-1990s, organized into streams that are related to the professional identity of the third parties. Predominating in this analysis were social psychologists and international relations specialists with additional contributions from unofficial diplomats (often retired officials) and psychiatrists. Thus, the interdisciplinary background and rationale for this form of conflict analysis and resolution shows a healthy variety, even though in practice the workshop design and facilitation techniques of the major contributors demonstrate a high degree of commonality.

The ICR term and concept itself were developed in response to a request arising from a workshop involving leading scholar-practitioners held in 1990 to assess developments in applied conflict resolution, particularly dialogue facilitation (Fisher, 2009). Nevertheless, the label coexists alongside a number of other terms coined and maintained by the major contributors, while younger scholar-practitioners show more preference for identifying their work as ICR. At the same time, the term track two diplomacy (TII) has gained considerable currency at the international level when using the interactive approach to address interstate or internationalized ethnopolitical conflict (Jones, 2015; Montville, 1987). The track two nomenclature makes sense when there is a track one of official diplomacy in operation, and also when incorporated into models of multitrack diplomacy (Diamond & McDonald, 1991). ICR or TII has also been distinguished from Track 1½ diplomacy in which unofficial intervenors engage official representatives of the parties in discussions (Nan et al., 2009), typically in their "personal capacity."

Drawing on the concept paper written for the 1990 workshop, ICR was initially defined as involving "small-group, problem-solving discussions between unofficial representatives of parties engaged in destructive conflict, facilitated by a third party of social scientist-practitioners" (Fisher, 1993a, p. 123). This definition was coterminous with the Problem-Solving Workshop (PSW), as brought forward by the pioneering scholar-practitioners in the field, including John Burton (1969), Herbert Kelman (1972), and Christopher Mitchell (1981). It also overlapped with my model of Third Party Consultation (TPC) designed to emphasize the identity and skills of the convener/facilitator and also to distinguish the method from mediation (Fisher, 1972). As the work of applied conflict resolution proliferated during the 1990s, I realized that a broader definition was required to encompass the wider range of interactive activities carried out by an increasing variety of actors, primarily nongovernmental organizations (NGOs). Thus, ICR was defined as "facilitated face-to-face activities in communication, training, education, or consultation that promote collaborative conflict analysis and problem solving among parties engaged in protracted conflict in a manner that addresses basic human needs and promotes the building of peace, justice, and equality" (Fisher, 1997, p. 8).

In line with the wider definition, I have posited but not published my construal of a number of forms of ICR in order to demonstrate that interactive methods have applicability at all points in the conflict analysis and resolution process. These forms include:

- *Dialogue:* A facilitated interchange and discussion of opposing ideas designed to seek mutual understanding and harmony while not resolving basic issues.
- *Training:* The provision of concepts and models for understanding conflict and the acquisition of skills and methods for addressing it more effectively, such as communication, negotiation, mediation, and problem-solving.
- *Problem-solving workshops:* A facilitated small-group discussion that brings together informal representatives of conflicting groups to jointly analyze their conflict and develop insights and creative options for de-escalation and resolution that can be fed back into official channels and into the public discourse.
- *Building cross-conflict teams:* Usually in conjunction with one of the above methods, a facilitated interaction to design and form project teams from conflicting groups that will work on conflict prevention, resolution or peacebuilding activities on the ground in the conflict zone.
- *Reconciliation:* Facilitated post-conflict interaction between members of conflicting groups to increase mutual understanding and empathy in order to reestablish harmony and co-operation through some combination of acknowledgments of transgressions, apologies, forgiveness, and assurances regarding future behavior.

As the domain of ICR has proliferated, its scope and power to bring about conflict resolution and political/social change have shown evidence of broadening in useful directions. An examination of nine cases of intervention from 1969 to 2000 all involved high-level influentials in PSWs, and were designed for transfer effects to negotiations in highly escalated conflicts (Fisher, 2005). A later analysis of six cases from 1993 to 2009 applied more forms of ICR, involved more participants from various levels and different sectors of society, and took place at different conflict stages (Lund & McDonald, 2015). This occurrence of mutually supportive and enhancing combinations of different forms of ICR was presaged by Louise Diamond and myself based on our experience as intervenors in the Cyprus conflict in the early 1990s (Diamond & Fisher, 1995). The interface between the conflict resolution training project led by Louise and Diana Chigas and the PSW project that I organized, involved a number of useful connections, including overlapping participants and activities and cofacilitation of training workshops and a PSW.

The broadening application of different forms of ICR to a wider swath of societal levels and sectors as well as phases of escalation is compatible with developments in the field of international conflict resolution. Since the end of the Cold War and particularly since the turn of the millennium, international conflict resolution has undergone a significant transformation (Babbitt, 2009). Included here is a shift to the peacebuilding agenda coupled with an increase in the role of nongovernmental actors, often in collaboration with governmental agencies. NGOs have been particularly adept at bringing unofficial efforts to bear on violent internal conflicts, because their identity and methods demonstrate notable advantages over official diplomacy. These include the ability to work quietly with nonofficial influentials in an exploratory manner, the capacity to work with actors considered to be illegitimate and off-limits to official intervenors and the willingness to provide consultation and training for the disputants (Babbitt, 2009).

The increasing involvement of NGOs is affirmed by Palmiano Federer (2021), whose work also demonstrates the profusion of nonofficial roles, typically in the context of multitrack initiatives. She maintains that unofficial initiatives have proliferated and professionalized over the last four decades, and that this now involves a new form of TII beyond the engagement of individual scholar-practitioners facilitating interactive conflict resolution workshops with the goal of transferring outcomes to track one. This newer form of track two or ICR typically involves professionalized, international NGOs providing a variety of facilitative, mediative, and supportive roles to conflict parties as well as to third parties (e.g., through mediation support units). However, this shift toward a more variegated and robust involvement as "NGO mediators" has given rise to a number of issues, including conceptual (if not practical) confusion and questions about the accountability and ethics of unofficial actors (see next).

My concern is that within this profusion of actors and forms of ICR, it is critical to maintain the distinctions between official and unofficial roles and between traditional mediation and ICR as a facilitative and consultative contribution to peacemaking (Fisher & Keashly, 1988). Nonetheless, as this chapter articulates key insights about ICR and their implications for practice and policy, it is evident that the field of conflict resolution has increasing insight and power to bring to bear on the global scourge of violent ethnopolitical conflict.

Key insights

As ICR has developed over the past five decades, its rationale, expression, and evaluation have seen continuing developments in power and sophistication to address ethnopolitical conflict. A number of key insights developed and supported over this time period affirm its application and effectiveness:

1   Interactive conflict resolution is uniquely suited to address ethnopolitical conflict, given that the latter is a highly subjective phenomenon very prone to escalation and intractability.

Ted Robert Gurr (1993) popularized the term *ethnopolitical conflict*, by identifying it as a particular form of ethnic conflict, defined in racial, religious, or cultural terms, in which distinct minority groups are placed in a disadvantaged economic and political position by governing majorities, and thus engage in collective protest or rebellion in order to seek redress for their grievances. The definition includes nationalist conflicts wherein minority groups seek autonomy or independence as well as communal conflicts to improve economic or political access or to defend cultural identity. The necessary conditions for ethnopolitical conflict include distinct collective identities and the perception that the conflicting groups' respective aspirations cannot be achieved simultaneously. When differences in ethnic identities are politicized, the result is political contention, often to the extreme of bloody civil wars (Kaufman, this volume). Thus, the destructive power of ethnopolitical conflict to motivate parties to achieve their aspirations by whatever means necessary is rooted in the intersection of collective social identity and incompatible political, economic, and social goals. There are a myriad of ethnopolitical conflicts scattered throughout the globe at various levels of suppression or escalation, and many of these have received attention from the conflict resolution field and from ICR practitioners (Fisher, 1997, 2005; Lund & McDonald, 2015).

The subjectivity of intense ethnopolitical conflict is revealed by a social-psychological approach that is phenomenological, sensitive to group dynamics and intergroup relations, focuses on the interaction between the parties, and achieves understanding through a multilevel systems analysis (Fisher & Kelman, 2011). Thus, in understanding and addressing ethnopolitical conflict, we need to look closely at perceptual processes, such as selective and distorted perception, negative attitudes and images, and errors in attributions, as well as group-level factors, such as the power of social identity and threats to it, norms that feed escalation and intractability, and faulty decision-making processes like groupthink that increase destructiveness (Fisher et al., 2013). This subjective emphasis is not to downplay the realistic definition of conflict as rooted in incompatible goals or values linked to sources related to economics (such as territory or wealth), power (such as in political oppression or exclusion), values (such as expressed in differing ideologies or religions), or the frustration or denial of basic human needs (Fisher, 1990). However, the point has been made repeatedly that as intergroup and particularly ethnopolitical conflict escalates and protracts, the subjective elements grow in influence, and need to be directly addressed in any efforts toward de-escalation and resolution.

ICR in a focused manner brings forward a subjective and objective analysis of a given conflict through the direct interaction of members of the parties facilitated by a skilled and impartial third-party team of scholar-practitioners. For implementing the wider definition of ICR, macro initiatives are required, such as public education campaigns, national dialogues, and symbolic gestures of reconciliation by leaders. In either case, the method sees the importance of subjective factors, such as perceptions, attitudes, and emotions, alongside objective elements represented in sources, priorities, and positions (Fisher et al., 2013). Although the subjective side of the analysis predominates in focused ICR, the objective elements of the conflict are also addressed through the processes of productive confrontation and problem-solving, in which the participants directly address the issues in the conflict as they see them and search for solutions.

The elements of ICR practice flow from the social-psychological analysis of ethnopolitical conflict that necessitates activities such as the confrontation of negative attitudes and stereotypes, the correction of errors in attribution, the reconsideration of group norms, and the joint analysis of decision-making and escalation processes (Fisher, 1999). The design and implementation of ICR workshops also follows the facilitative conditions of intergroup contact to increase the likelihood of cognitive and behavioral changes among participants with respect to the other group (Fisher, 1990). Thus, ICR takes a social or relationship orientation to conflict intervention as compared to the task orientation taken by traditional, interest-based methods of negotiation, mediation and arbitration, which when applied to highly subjective and escalated identity-based conflicts can actually exacerbate the situation rather than de-escalate and resolve it (Rothman, 1997).

2 Interactive conflict resolution has relevance to all phases of conflict causation, escalation, de-escalation, resolution, and reconciliation, and therefore to peacemaking and to both pre- and postsettlement forms of peacebuilding.

Early ICR interventions in peacemaking tended to be at the pre- or para-negotiation stages after violence had erupted between the parties, although there were a few exceptional cases of violence prevention (Fisher, 1997, 2005). The social-psychological rationale for PSWs as a prenegotiation intervention to increase the chances of successful negotiations is provided in detail in Fisher (1989). ICR interventions continue to focus on intractable conflicts that are in the violent or postviolence stages, and have not been settled by traditional peacemaking (Lund & McDonald, 2015). When protracted conflicts have been settled in a satisfactory manner with regard to tangible issues, there is still typically a need for improvement in the social (i.e., intergroup) relationship between the parties. This is where ICR work in implementation or reconciliation can be useful, and Fisher (1999) offers a rationale and analysis of how and why workshops can be useful in helping to reestablish harmony and cooperation. Thus, ICR practitioners have shown an ability to adapt the focus and design of workshops directly on the current state of the conflict.

To appreciate ICR's potential contribution to peacebuilding, it is first necessary to realize that there are two forms of peacebuilding, one occurring prior to the outbreak of direct violence that addresses structural violence and inequitable, torn relationships, and the other following the cessation of violence and the establishment of negative peace. Galtung (1976) saw peacebuilding as an associative approach that attempts to create a structure of peace both within and among nations which removes the causes of war and provides alternatives to war. This structure involves interdependent and equitable relationships among groups with built-in conflict resolution mechanisms to deal with incompatibilities. This socially orientated aspect of peacebuilding led me to define it as "developmental and interactive activities, often facilitated by a third party, which are directed toward meeting the basic needs, de-escalating the hostility, and improving the relationship of parties engaged in protracted social conflict" (Fisher, 1993b, p. 252). As such, relationship-orientated peacebuilding can provide a valuable bridge between peacekeeping and peacemaking in order to help move protracted conflicts to resolution.

In contrast, the 1992 United Nations Agenda for Peace placed a primary emphasis on post-conflict peacebuilding as involving cooperative, developmental efforts to address underlying social, economic, cultural, and humanitarian problems in order to build a foundation of peace in the positive sense. However, as Paffenholz (2010) points out, this construal of peacebuilding presents a narrow definition that focuses mainly on stabilizing negative peace by implementing activities such as disarmament, repatriation, establishing security, monitoring elections, and advancing human rights. To this list of requirements have been added others including the rule of law, constitutional reform, an independent judiciary, building civil society, a market economy, and so on in order to build a stable, functioning society in the Western image. Unfortunately, what is too often left out in this list is the repair and improvement of the social relationship between the conflicting groups, which if not moved toward a respectful and trusting one often means that the violent conflict will reemerge down the road. In order to build this stronger relationship, it is essential that the denial of basic human needs be addressed, so that issues related to identity and security threats as well as inequitable economic and political structures be addressed in a mutually satisfactory manner. Thus, intergroup conflict resolution activities should be at the center of post-conflict peacebuilding, and ICR has a critical role to play in such endeavors.

3   Interactive conflict resolution is complementary to other methods of conflict management and resolution, and needs to be sequenced and coordinated with other third-party interventions in order to achieve maximum effectiveness in resolving ethnopolitical conflict.

Since the start of my contributions to the concepts and methods of ICR (Fisher, 1972), I have maintained that this approach needs to be conceptualized and actualized in a complementary fashion with more established methods, particularly negotiation and mediation. The need for multiple methods is related to the complexity of human social conflict, especially at the intergroup and international levels, and particularly to the mix of subjective and objective factors that are expressed in ethnopolitical conflict. A clue for how complementarity might work is found in the observation that subjective elements come more to the fore as conflict escalates, and thus play a larger role in protracting the conflict and rendering it intractable.

These realizations led Loraleigh Keashly and me to develop a contingency model of third-party intervention in which the various methods were placed and sequenced in relation to the four stages of a model of conflict escalation (Fisher & Keashly, 1991). The overall strategy of the model is to de-escalate the conflict down through the stages, starting at whatever level it has reached, first by matching a specific lead intervention to a specific stage, and then by combining interventions in appropriate sequences to further de-escalate the conflict. Within the contingency model, the complementarity of mediation and ICR (in the form of consultation or PSWs) becomes immediately apparent. In general, ICR interventions can be used to analyze and de-escalate identity-based ethnopolitical conflicts rooted in both frustrated basic needs and differing interests in preparation for the mediation of both satisfiers of needs and positions on interests. In the model, there are two points of complementarity between consultation and mediation. First at a lower level of escalation, consultation or PSWs can be used to improve the relationship among parties so that pure mediation to settle interests can then be more successful. At a higher level of escalation, power mediation to control hostility is then followed by consultation to improve the relationship leading to further de-escalation.

The rationale and validity of a contingency approach to third-party intervention is now generally accepted in the field of conflict resolution. Major treatments of the field have come to generally support contingency thinking that allows for different intermediaries to make unique contributions to peacemaking in a complementary fashion (Fisher, 2012). This conclusion is mainly supported by separate case analyses as well as comparative case studies of transfer effects from ICR to peacemaking (Fisher, 2005; Lund & McDonald, 2015), rather than systematic research on a large number of cases of contingency. One small step in this direction is provided by a comparative case analysis of ICR interventions in five cases of ethnopolitical conflict resolution that generally supported the validity of the contingency model (Fisher, 2007).

Notions of complementarity and contingency imply a need for coordination among interveners, and the contingency model helped stimulate interest in this topic. Coordination was examined by Susan Allen Nan and Andrea Strimling in a special issue of *International Negotiation* that developed the conceptual base for the concept and included several case studies of different types of coordination in various situations. Nan and Strimling (2006) asserted that coordination can be advanced through the primary forms of information sharing, collaborative analysis and strategizing, resource sharing, formal partnerships, and other ways of synchronizing and/or integrating activities. I contributed an article on coordination between ICR as track two diplomacy and track one through a comparative case analysis of four successful cases where ICR workshops made pre- and para-negotiation contributions to the official peace process. Based on a document review combined with interviews with the primary ICR interveners, I concluded that coordination was limited to information sharing and indirect sequencing of efforts that was implemented by the ICR interveners. Typically, they would share information about their unofficial work, including an ongoing analysis of the conflict and options for resolution, and they would plan their interventions to complement and make contributions to the official process. Only one of the cases involved more engaging coordination through joint strategy planning and collaboration in workshop design and implementation. Moving forward it is hoped that official actors will become more receptive to unofficial contributions, and that a reciprocal relationship of increased respect, trust, and coordination will evolve (Fisher, 2006).

4   Interactive conflict resolution can have positive transfer effects in both the political and the public domains, and in the final analysis can make contributions to social movements for peace in the conflicting societies.

As the various forms of ICR have evolved over the past five decades, the scope of interventions has broadened from high-level influentials connected to the leaderships, to mid-level influentials and leaders from a variety of sectors (e.g., education, business, religion), to civil society and grassroots leaders involved in peacebuilding initiatives and the shaping of public discourse (e.g., Allen, 2021). In all these instances, the ultimate challenge facing ICR is the question of transfer, that is, how individual effects, such as attitude changes, new realizations and greater trust, as well as outcomes, such as frameworks for negotiation, principles for resolution and peace plans, are moved from the unofficial interventions to the domains of negotiations, policymaking and public opinion.

Herbert Kelman (1972) was the first to develop a nuanced picture of the transfer process by distinguishing individual changes in workshop participants from changes in policy and political discourse along with the mechanisms and challenges by which one leads to the other. Based on his decades of organizing workshops with Israeli and Palestinian participants, Kelman (1992) maintains that PSWs can help overcome common barriers to starting negotiations, to achieving settlement and to improving the parties' relationship post settlement. In addition to providing substantive inputs to negotiations, Kelman (1995) asserts that the development of a political atmosphere favorable to negotiations and to a new relationship contributed to the breakthrough of the Oslo Accord.

In an attempt to capture these various types of transfer effects, I developed a schematic model of transfer that identifies the major groupings and constituencies, lines of communication and interactions that are related to ICR interventions (Fisher, 1997). The lines of transfer run from ICR interventions to the leaders and negotiators at the official level as well as to public-political constituencies consisting of the public at large and various civil society organizations. In line with this conceptualization, a content analysis of 25 published case studies over a 30-year period revealed the types of transfer effects that were claimed by the interveners themselves. These ranged from a positive influence on the peace process to specific contributions to negotiations. In a more systematic comparative case study of nine successful programs of ICR intervention, I identified what aspects of the interventions under what conditions of conflict tend to be related to useful transfer effects to negotiations (Fisher, 2005). The interventions typically consisted of a series of workshops following existing models of practice and were directed toward ethnopolitical conflicts in which a government in power was being challenged by an opposing group over issues of participation, autonomy, inequity, and/or territory. Conflicts involving goals of integration were more receptive to intervention and transfer effects than those involving goals of separation. A variety of positive transfer effects occurred, from individual cognitive changes to ideas, options, and plans for addressing the conflict, and it was concluded that in almost all cases the ICR interventions made essential but not sufficient contributions to peacemaking.

To complement the schematic model, I later developed a flow model of the processes and outcomes of transfer in order to more fully describe and understand the phenomenon (Fisher, 2020). This model identifies eight sequential components of transfer and the necessary elements of each from the *identity of participants* to the *effects of transfer*. In between, it specifies the required *conditions of the interaction* and the *qualities of group and intergroup development* that support the occurrence of *individual changes* as well as the creation of substantive *products or outcomes*, which are then communicated through the *mechanisms of transfer* to the intended *targets of transfer* in both the political and public domains. It is hoped that this model will be useful to practitioners in designing and facilitating ICR experiences as well as to program evaluators assessing their implementation and outcomes.

Transfer effects from ICR interventions can bring about individual and collective changes in the conflicting societies that help energize and empower social movements working toward peace. This can be illustrated through my three decades of involvement in the ethnopolitical conflict on the island of Cyprus between Greek and Turkish Cypriots. During 1989–1991, I served as a research fellow at the now defunct Canadian Institute for International Peace and Security (CIIPS) (1984–1992) that had selected the Cyprus conflict to be the first focus of its new conflict resolution program. The institute held four multidisciplinary seminars in 1988–1989 on the conflict, and for the last one invited ten influential Greek and Turkish Cypriots from the island, some of whom suggested the institute should sponsor PSWs, which I subsequently and successfully proposed. With CIIPS funding, I was able to organize two workshops in 1990 and 1991, bringing together influentials first in Canada and then on the island with the effects of building the credibility of our third-party team and its relationship to the two administrations (Fisher, 1997).

After CIIPS was abolished, I was able to obtain funding for two further workshops on the role of education in the conflict from Foreign Affairs Canada, who apparently considered my proposal to continue workshops with political influentials to be inappropriate and risky. Unfortunately, I was not able to obtain funding for further PSWs, but was able to offer my experience and expertise to Louise Diamond and John McDonald, founders of the Institute for Multi-Track Diplomacy, who were exploring the potential for conflict resolution training on the island at the invitation of members of the fledgling Cypriot peace movement. After a number of single communal trainings on the island, IMTD, with the involvement of the NTL Institute, was able to carry out a ten-day bicommunal training of trainers workshop at Oxford University in the summer of 1993, with myself and Louise serving as co-trainers along with two NTL trainers. This signature event was followed with approximately 25 training workshops over the next several years that came to involve hundreds of bicommunal peacebuilders, supported by the *Cyprus Consortium* that now included the Conflict Management Group with Diana Chigas taking a lead role along with Louise Diamond.

The initial group of trainers from the Oxford workshop was expanded and institutionalized through the creation of a Trainer's Group of 30 individuals, who soon expanded their reach to approximately 25 bicommunal groups engaging participants in dialogue and training, and involving over 1,500 bicommunal peacebuilders in a variety of activities and projects (Wolleh, 2000). With further training from Fulbright Scholar Benjamin Broome in the small-group decision-making method of interactive management (Broome, 1997), the Trainer's Group was able to design a vision for peacebuilding in Cyprus and to become a major force in growing the peace movement on both sides of the Green Line (Broome, 2005). Other actors, including the Cyprus Fulbright Commission, the U.S. Embassy with USAID funding, and UNDP through its ACT (Action for Cooperation and Trust) program, played significant roles in supporting capacity building in conflict resolution and civil society. All of these contributions enabled the peace movement to catalyze political support for the 2004 comprehensive agreement known as the Anan Plan. With parallel referenda in the Greek-Cypriot and Turkish-Cypriot communities, the forces for peace in conjunction with progressive political parties were able to gain approval of the plan by Turkish Cypriots, but unfortunately not from Greek Cypriots, who were persuaded in the negative by nationalist, hardline politicians. The complex reasons for these different outcomes are discussed in a CDA report by Hadjipavlou and Kanol (2008), who conclude that peace activists will continue to play a leading role in the quest for peace on the island.

Implications for teaching and training

The field of ICR has shown little interest in ways to prepare new recruits to carry out its work, perhaps because doing so is a daunting challenge and continuing issue (Fisher, 1993a, 1997, 2014). An early exception is offered by Mandell and Fisher (1992) who describe a graduate course in mediation and problem-solving that prepared students to serve as observers and junior co-facilitators in the 1990 Cyprus workshops briefly described above. The course covered international mediation and the social-psychological approach to understanding and resolving protracted intergroup conflict focusing on the PSW method. Distinctions among third-party interventions preceded coverage of the contingency model, followed by a case of protracted ethnopolitical conflict, in this instance Cyprus. To complement theoretical coverage, a weekend skill training workshop was provided in communication skills, conflict resolution, including problem-solving, and group/intergroup processes. The students also designed and participated in a two-day role play of a Cyprus PSW. At the 1990 workshop itself, students sat in an outer ring of observers in a fishbowl design, and some had the opportunity to rotate in as members of the third-party panel for a session. Thus, the course provided an opportunity for students to see theory in practice and to gain an initial sense of their interest and capacity in serving as PSW facilitators.

Later in my career, I spent 15 years teaching in the International Peace and Conflict Resolution Program (IPCR) at American University, and I designed various iterations of the above course design to cover official and unofficial interventions in intractable ethnopolitical conflict. The practice element provided students with two options for team projects: (1) the analysis and evaluation of a case of third-party intervention in a chosen conflict, and (2) the formation of a PSW facilitation team with other class members serving as participants. The second option engaged the team in completing a succession of analytical and strategic exercises provided in a training manual covering all phases of PSW design and implementation (Mitchell, 2005; Mitchell & Banks, 1996). Two sessions of the schedule were devoted to role plays of PSW sessions focusing on introductions and the opening of proceedings.

To complement regular courses, IPCR also offered weekend skills training institutes for professional development, and training in facilitating PSWs was an occasional offering. This limited opportunity was extended in both frequency and depth in the Fall of 2009 when IPCR partnered with the then Institute for Conflict Analysis and Resolution at George Mason University (now the Jimmy and Rosalynn Carter School for Peace and Conflict Resolution) in offering a training program consisting of both introductory and advanced weekend workshops to their graduate students at the MA and PhD levels. The training consortium was later joined by faculty and students from the Negotiations and Conflict Management Program at the University of Baltimore and the Conflict Resolution Program at the University of Denver. Introductory workshop participation required an application form and process that gave preference to students with basic skill training in communication and conflict resolution as well as some professional experience. In addition, the advanced training required participation in an introductory workshop.

The design of the basic session covered PSW theory and practice, including the selection and invitation of participants, the organization of a PSW from invitations to reentry, skill practice for common interventions with feedback in the facilitator role, and typical issues that arise such as managing cultural differences. In addition to preworkshop readings on ICR and PSWs, participants received material on the conflict case to be used in the role plays as well as supportive handouts at the time of training. In the earlier designs, participants were formed into teams with one team as facilitators who designed and facilitated a role play focusing on one of four phases of the PSW process, from introductions and ground rules, to listening for underlying common issues, to reconciliation, and to reentry. Some later designs incorporated a series of discussion exercises and briefer role plays derived from the Mitchell and Banks handbook (Mitchell, 2005). The advanced workshops were offered once a year in the Spring following two introductory sessions in the Spring and Fall, and focused on challenges in facilitating PSWs, including timing of interventions, coping with power imbalances, and managing reentry issues, as well as advanced process skills such as reframing issues, encouraging creativity and engaging in reflective practice. A mixture of case exercises and role plays were used to engage participants in experiential learning about PSWs.

The training program was very well received, especially in the early years, with a high degree of demand and very positive evaluations from participants. Over the nine years of the program, hundreds of graduate students took part and the trainers group consisted of close to a dozen faculty members from the consortium institutions. Unfortunately, in the later years interest began to wane on the part of students due to increasing time and financial pressures and faculty found themselves under increasing workloads, so the program was suspended in 2018. Nonetheless, it served as an excellent example of how an experiential training program can be added to academic education in conflict resolution to start young practitioners on the road of professional development to conduct PSWs. Unfortunately, only a small number of the program's graduates were able to work on PSW projects in which training faculty were involved, including ones on Cyprus, Darfur-Sudan, and Georgia-South Ossetia. It is expected that only a similarly small number have been able to independently carry on their interest in ICR projects from an academic or NGO base.

The above exemplars demonstrate how the base of academic education in conflict resolution can be used and augmented to provide the initial expertise to design, organize, and facilitate ICR interventions, particularly PSWs. Nonetheless, the list of competencies articulated by experienced practitioners is long, and there is disagreement over how much potential facilitators need to possess innate qualities versus acquiring or extending these through training and experience (Fisher, 1997; Jones, 2015; Saunders, 2000). My prescription for an academic base enhanced by skill training and apprenticeship results in a long list of analytical skills, personal qualities, and behavioral skills, including interpersonal, group, intergroup, and consultation ones (Fisher, 2014). Without seriously addressing questions of training and professionalization, it is difficult to see how ICR can reach its full potential.

Implications for practice and policy

A broad implication for ICR is that practice needs to continually adapt to the changing context of international conflict resolution as expressed in both peacemaking and peacebuilding. The growth of NGOs and the proliferation of intervention roles mean increased demand for ICR practitioners as intermediaries as well as likely increased interaction with track one and other practitioners. At the same time, the usage of broad terms, such as "NGO mediation" or "peace mediation," to encapsulate a variety of third-party interventions, should not be allowed to create confusion in theory or in practice about distinct intermediary roles that have unique natures and purposes, such as among the forms of ICR or in their differentiation from mediation as traditionally defined. A multitrack approach requires clear distinctions and contributions among the various forms of practice so that their coordination and complementarity can be maximized and counterproductive overlaps and interferences minimized.

A related implication is for ICR to adapt effectively to the widening context of peacemaking processes so that transfer can be maximized in concert with the outcomes of other methods. Cuhadar and Paffenholz (2020) outline how the complexity and inclusivity of peace processes and negotiations have increased significantly over the last 20 years with the implementation of participative methods including national dialogues, observer roles, consultative forums, and peace commissions. At the same time, PSWs have shifted from working mainly with elite influentials to being a truly middle out intervention as well as operating more at the level of civil society with local and external facilitators playing complementary roles (e.g., Allen, 2021). As Cuhadar and Paffenholz (2020) point out, the concept of transfer should be broadened to include some of the newer modalities so that their effects can be conceptualized and studied.

More specifically related to ICR or TII itself, there are a number of implications for the continued improvement of practice, including the ongoing determination of best practices in design and facilitation in order to ensure maximum effectiveness and utility (D'Estree & Fox, 2021; Fisher, 2005; Jones, 2021a). Key issues in the field include the importance of defining intervention types clearly as well as specific projects, the continuing challenge of evaluating interventions and assessing transfer effects, and the development of a more inclusive field in terms of levels, interveners and cultures so that conflict transformation is the outcome as opposed to conflict management (Jones, 2021b).

With respect to policy implications, the continuing challenge is to increase ICR's policy influence on official actors and processes. In the early days this was more focused on leaders, diplomats, and negotiators. However, as peace processes have broadened toward greater inclusivity and government agencies have become more supportive of and engaged in conflict resolution, both the target audiences for influence and the official actors with whom to coordinate and collaborate have become more varied and greater in number. Nonetheless, there is still a great need to carry forward the key insights articulated above to educate and persuade policymakers and official actors that informal and participative forms of facilitated interaction can create useful insights and realistic options for resolving intractable ethnopolitical conflicts.

Thus, the corridor for policy influence continues to operate through the relationship between official and unofficial peace workers along with dissemination of ICR approaches and outcomes to affect public discourse toward conflict resolution. Based on significant achievements in both official and unofficial diplomacy, Harold Saunders (2000) developed a perspective for policymakers on the potential contributions of ICR that still rings true today. Noting the distinctive and yet complementary roles of the two domains, he asserts that policymakers need to realize that intractable ethnopolitical conflicts are embedded in relationships between whole bodies politic, involving elements that are beyond the reach of governments. If official actors can come to see the need for multilevel peace processes, in which unofficial and official efforts make complementary contributions, they would be more open to and supportive of ICR. Today, the greater involvement of NGOs as unofficial intermediaries working in concert with or in place of official mediators will hopefully enhance understanding, respect, and collaboration between the two domains, but it may also sow a degree of confusion and conflict over mandates and competencies. There is clearly a need to document and assess such developments so that ICR can continue to play a unique and valuable role in peace processes.

Note

1. The author thanks Christopher Mitchell and Susan Allen for helpful comments on this chapter. Enquiries may be directed to rfisher@american.edu.

References

Allen, S. H. (2021). Evolving best practices: Engaging the strengths of both external and local peacebuilders in track two dialogues through local ownership. *International Negotiation*, *26*(1), 67–84.

Babbitt, E. F. (2009). The evolution of international conflict resolution: From Cold War to peacebuilding. *Negotiation Journal*, *25*, 539–549.

Broome, B. J. (1997). Designing a collective approach to peace: Interactive design and problem-solving workshops with Greek-Cypriot and Turkish-Cypriot communities in Cyprus. *International Negotiation*, *2*, 381–407.

Broome, B. J. (2005). *Building bridges across the Green Line*. UNDP.

Burton, J. W. (1969). *Conflict and communication: The use of controlled communication in international relations*. MacMillan.

Cuhadar, E., & Paffenholz, T. (2020). Transfer 2.0: Applying the concept of transfer from track-two workshops to inclusive peace negotiations. *International Studies Review*, *22*(3), 651–670.

D'Estree, T. P., & Fox, B. B. (2021). Incorporating best practices into design and facilitation of track two initiatives. *International Negotiation*, *26*(1), 5–38.

Diamond, L., & Fisher, R. J. (1995). Integrating conflict resolution training and consultation: A Cyprus example. *Negotiation Journal*, *11*, 287–301.

Diamond, L., & McDonald, J. (1991). *Multi-track diplomacy: A systems guide and analysis*. Iowa Peace Institute.

Fisher, R. J. (1972). Third party consultation: A method for the study and resolution of conflict. *Journal of Conflict Resolution*, *16*, 67–94.

Fisher, R. J. (1989). Prenegotiation problem-solving discussions: Enhancing the potential for successful negotiation. In J. G. Stein (Ed.), *Getting to the table: The process of international prenegotiation* (pp. 206–238). Johns Hopkins University Press.

Fisher, R. J. (1990). *The social psychology of intergroup and international conflict resolution*. Springer-Verlag.

Fisher, R. J. (1993a). Developing the field of interactive conflict resolution: Issues in training, funding and institutionalization. *Political Psychology*, *14*, 123–138.

Fisher, R. J. (1993b). The potential for peacebuilding: Forging a bridge from peacekeeping to peacemaking. *Peace & Change*, *18*, 247–266.

Fisher, R. J. (1997). *Interactive conflict resolution*. Syracuse University Press.

Fisher, R. J. (1999). Social-psychological processes in interactive conflict analysis and reconciliation. In H. W. Jeong (Ed.), *Conflict resolution: Dynamics, process and structure* (pp. 81–104). Ashgate.

Fisher, R. J. (2002). Historical mapping of the field of interactive conflict resolution. In J. Davies & E. Kaufman (Eds.), *Second track/citizens' diplomacy: Concepts and techniques for conflict transformation* (pp. 61–77). Rowman & Littlefield.

Fisher, R. J. (2005). *Paving the way: Contributions of interactive conflict resolution to peacemaking*. Lexington Books.

Fisher, R. J. (2006). Coordination between track two and track one diplomacy in successful cases of prenegotiation. *International Negotiation*, *11*, 65–89.

Fisher, R. J. (2007). Assessing the contingency model of third-party intervention in successful cases of prenegotiation. *Journal of Peace Research*, *44*, 311–329.

Fisher, R. J. (2009). Interactive conflict resolution: Dialogue, conflict analysis, and problemsolving. In D. J. D. Sandole, S. Byrne, I. Sandole-Staroste, & J. Senehi (Eds.), *Handbook of conflict analysis and resolution* (pp. 328–338). Routledge.

Fisher, R. J. (2012). The contingency model for third party intervention. In S. A. Nan, Z. C. Mampilly, & A. Bartoli (Eds.), *Peacemaking: From practice to theory* (pp. 683–700). Praeger Security International.

Fisher, R. J. (2014). Intergroup conflict resolution. In P. T. Coleman, M. Deutsch, & E. Marcus (Eds.), *The handbook of conflict resolution* (3rd ed., pp. 230–252). Jossey-Bass.

Fisher, R. J. (2020). Transfer effects from problem-solving workshops to negotiations: A process and outcome model. *Negotiation Journal*, *36*, 441–470.

Fisher, R. J., & Keashly, L. (1988). Third party interventions in intergroup conflict: Consultation is *not* mediation. *Negotiation Journal*, *4*, 381–391.

Fisher, R. J., & Keashly, L. (1991). The potential complementarity of mediation and consultation within a contingency model of third party intervention. *Journal of Peace Research*, *28*, 29–42.

Fisher, R. J., & Kelman, H. C. (2011). Perceptions in conflict. In D. Bar-Tal (Ed.), *Intergroup conflicts and their resolution: A social psychological perspective* (pp. 61–81). Psychology Press.

Fisher, R. J., Kelman, H. C., & Nan, S. A. (2013). Conflict analysis and resolution. In L. Huddy, D. Sears, & J. Levy (Eds.), *Oxford handbook of political psychology* (2nd ed., pp. 489–521). Oxford University Press.

Galtung, J. (1976). Three approaches to peace: Peacekeeping, peacemaking and peacebuilding. In J. Galtung (Ed.), *Peace, war and defense, essays in peace research II* (pp. 282–304). Christian Ejlers.

Gurr, T. R. (1993). *Minorities at risk: A global view of ethnopolitical conflicts.* United States Institute of Peace.

Hadjipavlou, M., & Kanol, B. (2008). *The impacts of peacebuilding work on the Cyprus conflict.* Collaborative for Development Action.

Jones, P. (2015). *Track two diplomacy in theory and practice.* Stanford University Press.

Jones, P. (2021a). Best practices in track two diplomacy. *International Negotiation, 26*(1), 1–4.

Jones, P. (2021b). Track two diplomacy: The way forward. *International Negotiation, 26*(1), 151–156.

Kelman, H. C. (1972). The problem-solving workshop in conflict resolution. In R. L. Merritt (Ed.), *Communication in international politics* (pp. 168–204). University of Illinois Press.

Kelman, H. C. (1992). Informal mediation by the scholar-practitioner. In J. Bercovitch & J. Rubin (Eds.), *Mediation in international relations: Multiple approaches to conflict management* (pp. 64–96). St. Martin's Press.

Kelman, H. C. (1995). Contributions of an unofficial conflict resolution effort to the Israeli-Palestinian breakthrough. *Negotiation Journal, 11,* 19–27.

Lund, M., & McDonald, S. (Eds.). (2015). *Across the lines of conflict: Facilitating cooperation to build peace.* Woodrow Wilson Center Press.

Mandell, B. S., & Fisher, R. J. (1992). Training third-party consultants in international conflict resolution. *Negotiation Journal, 8,* 259–271.

Mitchell, C. R. (1981). *Peacemaking and the consultant's role.* Gower.

Mitchell, C. R. (2005). *Resolving intractable conflicts: A handbook.* LoCh Books/Institute for Conflict Analysis and Resolution.

Mitchell, C., & Banks, M. (1996). *Handbook of conflict resolution: The analytical problem-solving approach.* Pinter.

Montville, J. V. (1987). The arrow and the olive branch: The case for track two diplomacy. In J. W. McDonald & D. B. Bendahmane (Eds.), *Conflict resolution: Track two diplomacy* (pp. 5–20). Foreign Service Institute, Department of State.

Nan, S. A., Druckman, D., & Horr, J. E. (2009). Unofficial international conflict resolution: Is there a track 1½? Are there best practices? *Conflict Resolution Quarterly, 27,* 65–82.

Nan, S. A., & Strimling, A. (2006). Coordination in conflict prevention, conflict resolution and peacebuilding. *International Negotiation, 11,* 1–6.

Paffenholz, T. (2010). Civil society and peacebuilding. In T. Paffenholz (Ed.), *Civil society and peacebuilding: A critical assessment* (pp. 43–64). Lynne Rienner.

Palmiano Federer, J. (2021). Is there a new track two? Taking stock of unofficial diplomacy and peacemaking. *Policy Brief No. 1.* Ottawa Dialogue.

Rothman, J. (1997). *Resolving identity-based conflict in nations, organizations and communities.* Jossey-Bass.

Saunders, H. H. (2000). Interactive conflict resolution: A view for policy makers on making and building peace. In P. Stern & D. Druckman (Eds.), *International conflict resolution after the Cold War* (pp. 251–293). National Academies Press.

Wolleh, O. (2000). *Local peace constituencies in Cyprus: The bi-communal trainer's group.* Collaborative for Development Action.

11
CORE DYNAMICS OF NONVIOLENT ACCOMPANIMENT AND UNARMED CIVILIAN PROTECTION

Patrick G. Coy

On May 25, 2020, George Floyd, a 46-year-old black man, was killed on the streets of Minneapolis, Minnesota, United States, by four Minneapolis police officers; they were taking him into custody on suspicion of passing a counterfeit $20 bill. Offering no resistance, Floyd was nonetheless pinned face-down on the pavement by three officers, with a white police officer's knee on his neck for nine minutes. Mr. Floyd repeatedly complained that he could not breathe and that they were going to kill him. This brazen and brutal act of police violence was only the latest in a long litany of well-documented and widely publicized abuses of the human and civil rights of blacks and other people of color by police forces across the United States. It was this larger pattern of overt police violence toward blacks in diverse locales across the country that gave rise to the Black Lives Matter movement in 2013 (Clark et al., 2018). Yet it was the seemingly nonchalant and unabashed manner of George Floyd's killing, with the white police officer's knee on Floyd's neck while he begged—again and again—for his life that brought the Black Lives Matter movement more to the fore in the United States and even beyond. In the months that followed, impressive and creative nonviolent demonstrations, marches, and protests occurred in locales throughout the United States. One such locale was Portland, Oregon, which included innovative applications of the tactic of nonviolent protective accompaniment by a variety of local citizens.

The Black Lives Matter-related protests that occurred in communities large and small across the country following George Floyd's killing soon dissipated, but not in Oregon's Portland. It is the country's whitest major metropolitan area and the state's largest city, a state marked with the particularly prominent racist legacy of having been founded on white supremacy (Fuller, 2020). For more than 60 evenings in a row Portlanders demonstrated, first in protest against the killing of George Floyd, but then increasingly against the deployment to the city of unidentified federal police and military by the Trump administration.

Background

The militarized tactics of tear gas, pepper balls, rubber bullets, flash-bang grenades, and the widespread beatings of protesters with batons that the federal troops were using against citizens exercising their constitutional rights further incited the protest movement; it also motivated still others to become newly involved. One such group was one who originally called themselves the "Wall of Moms" and later reorganized under local black leadership and a new name: "Moms United for Black Lives" (Cineas, 2020).

Following successive evenings of excessive force by the unidentified federal agents and their forcefully seizing protesters and whisking them away in unmarked vehicles, a group of largely white Portland mothers organized via social media. Dressed in yellow to be easily differentiated from others, the mothers first showed up the evening of July 18 chanting: "Feds stay clear. Moms are here!" With arms interlocked in a long line between the protesters and the police and federal agents, these women were trusting that the gendered dynamics that traditionally accord motherhood—and white motherhood in particular—with a privileged status could be parlayed into creating safer spaces for the demonstrators to exercise their civil liberties in their hometown. By identifying as mothers, wearing an informal uniform, and nonviolently interposing themselves between the federal troops and the protesters, the mothers were utilizing the interposition dimension of long-established principles of nonviolent protective accompaniment to try to moderate police and military behavior toward the demonstrators.

The Wall of Moms immediately inspired a Pod of Dads wielding leaf blowers to dissipate the effects of tear gas on protesters, and a Wall of Vets (many in their old uniforms or wearing other insignia identifying them as veterans). The Vets used interposition tactics like the mothers. They were hoping that the vaulted status that their military service accords them in much of U.S. society (Coy et al., 2008) and the fraternal associations their military service grants them with the police and federal troops would moderate police behavior toward the protestors and offer them protection. The Moms United for Black Lives and the Wall of Vets in Portland were writing a new chapter in the story of nonviolent accompaniment and unarmed civilian protection.

This story has a long history; sadly, too much of that history is at worst unrecorded and at best not as critically evaluated as it deserves. Nonetheless, when members of a tribe or clan visited dangerous water sources or utilized contested travel corridors ages ago, they were at times accompanied by others whose presence was thought to increase their security. Today, when a women student is going to walk home across a campus after dark at universities around the world, she might call a campus service for volunteer escorts to walk alongside her. These campus escorts are usually fellow students whose presence enhances both her perceived and even her real security; they are doing accompaniment.

Accompaniment has not only taken many forms through human history; in the past 40 years it has also gone by a plethora of different names, each emphasizing specific strategic aspects or certain tactics. Those names include the following: unarmed civilian peacekeeping, peace teams, international accompaniment, third party nonviolent intervention, unarmed civilian protection, nonviolent accompaniment, and protective presence.[1] The civilian peacekeepers themselves are as varied as the contexts within which they operate; they may be community elders, citizen colleagues, dignitaries, campaigners, clerics, field staff of NGOs and INGOs, public sector officials, or one's next-door neighbor.

As the Portland examples demonstrate, sometimes accompaniment or civilian protection is born of immediate necessity and is somewhat instinctive in nature. In such situations it is more often marked by creative ingenuity in the face of new dangers than it is by situational analysis and strategic planning done in advance. Yet other dimensions of the field are evidenced by structure, formal organizations who have been established for nearly 40 years, effectiveness feasibility studies that are conducted in the field well before potential deployment, and regularized internal and external critical evaluations. It is these more formalized approaches that will be primarily focused upon in what follows.

Although Gandhi advocated for nonviolent peace teams rooted in local communities that would intervene in communal conflicts, it was largely left to his disciple, Vinoba Bhave, to later mount such an experiment in India: The Shanti Sena, or peace army (Weber, 1996). Decades later in the 1980s, much of central and South America was beset by military dictatorships; as a result, human rights violations and political disappearances were rampant across the region. It was then and there that organizations like Witness for Peace and Peace Brigades International developed the strategies and tactics of international nonviolent protective accompaniment to deter abuses and support the political agency of those under threat (Coy, 1993; Mahony & Eguren, 1997). Those early, pioneering efforts have subsequently given rise to a burgeoning movement on behalf of Unarmed Civilian Peacekeeping/protection (UCP) that has blossomed across the globe.

Today at least 40 organizations provide accompaniment and unarmed civilian protection services on request from activists and civil society organizations under threat in a wide variety of contexts. Some of the more prominent and experienced organizations include Peace Brigades International, Witness for Peace, Nonviolent Peaceforce, Christian Peacemaker Teams, International Solidarity Movement, and FOR Peace Presence. The organizational identities are broadly diverse. Some organizations foreground a collective identity, whether it be gender or religion or shared beliefs. Some are plainly secular in their orientation even though others are loosely spiritual and still others are overtly religious and even explicitly denominational in orientation. While some are strictly local and their sphere of operations is defined and restricted, others are regionally or nationally based and work across geographic regions. Still others are explicitly transnational by design and the demographics of their membership recruitment and staff deployment each reflect this commitment.

Between 1990 and 2014, these 40 organizations collectively fielded unarmed civilian peacekeeping teams on six continents and in at least 35 different countries (Janzen, 2014). Undoubtedly this is a conservative rendering of the work in the field, especially considering the many temporary and informal expressions of unarmed civilian protection that often pop up like mushrooms after a steady spring rain.

Notably, the evolving scholarship on unarmed civilian protection demonstrates that it can as effectively meet the traditional "core tasks" of peacekeeping as can the threat of violence that often comes with armed military peacekeepers, and in some instances, it is even more effective (Julian & Gasser, 2019; Julian, 2019; Wallace, 2017; Martin, 2009). Its impacts reach across multiple sectors of daily life and the struggles for security. Such initiatives have brought about significant drops in gender-based violence, assisted in establishing locally facilitated peace agreements or ceasefires, contributed to monitoring ceasefires and treaties, helped bring down the kinds and degrees of violence internally displaced people experience in camps, reduced the levels of humiliation experienced by civilians at military checkpoints, and helped ensure broader access to health care and education in conflict zones (Birkeland, 2016). The effectiveness of nonviolent accompaniment and unarmed civilian protection is rooted in commitments to four principles that are widely accepted across the field of practice: do no harm; honor the primacy of the local; nonviolence; and political independence/nonpartisanship (Schweitzer, 2020).

Unarmed civilian protection has finally begun garnering attention and support from governments, foundations, and intergovernmental organizations. For example, even the United Nations now recognizes the value of unarmed, civilian-based approaches to providing security and defending human rights. Indeed, in the 70th anniversary year of the United Nations in 2015, three high-level panels were created to recommend changes in three interrelated areas: UN peace operations; its peacebuilding architecture; and the highly influential UN Security Council Resolution 1325 on Women, Peace and Security. The recommendations of all three panels included explicit support for unarmed, nonviolent approaches to peacekeeping and civilian protection. This included proposing that UCP should be "at the forefront of UN approaches to protecting civilians," that the UN and member states should "scale up their support to unarmed civilian protection in conflict-affected countries, including working alongside peace operations," and recognizing that UCP is "a methodology for the direct protection of civilians and violence reduction that has grown in practice and recognition. In the last few years, it has especially proven its effectiveness to protect women and girls."[2]

Key insights

While the accompaniers in the Portland examples were from within the local communities and relied in part on the respect and stature associated with either motherhood or military service to attempt to deter state repression and police violence, this is not always the case. Often the accompaniers and intervenors are internationals from other countries whose internationalized presence may deter repression by altering even more so the cost-benefit analyses done by potential violators of human rights defenders. Over the past few decades, the use of international accompaniers has expanded the amount and kinds of safe political spaces available for local human rights defenders and activists to do their work (Mahony, 2004). When international accompaniment is chosen by local actors and when it is used with sensitive attention to power imbalances to support the primacy of local initiatives, it can have wide-ranging impacts that run in multiple directions, even eroding structures and shifting paradigms (Coy, 2019).

Some organizations have on occasion also attempted to exploit the dynamics of racism and of privilege by deploying white accompaniers and/or accompaniers carrying the passports of particularly influential countries. Although this use of privilege has been long problematized within organizations (Boothe & Smithey, 2007; Coy, 1993, 2001, 2011), and even though it is eschewed by some organizations and not as often utilized as it once was by yet others, it does still occur. This is due, at least in part, because in some situations in Latin America for example, those asking for accompaniment make this request, believing white accompaniers will have a greater deterrent effect and therefore increase their security (Schweitzer, 2019, 2020).

No matter the gender, ethnicity, or citizenship of the civilian peacekeeper, the deterrence and protective presence aspects of accompaniment rely, in part, on the Observer Effect, that is, people frequently adapt or even restrict their behavior when they know they are being watched, filmed, or documented. Each of us knows this to be true in our daily lives in a variety of ways in a range of our social settings. We have each behaved differently when alone than we would have if we knew we were being observed. Through the Observer Effect, the action choices of even politically powerful actors who may be prone to repress others or to engage in human rights violations can be restricted; they might refrain from doing what they otherwise would have done.

These deterrent aspects of accompaniment partly depend upon and can also be magnified by a deeply engaged and proactive presence by the civilian protectors. The importance of this background work to the ultimate usefulness of these initiatives cannot be overemphasized. What does this proactive presence look like in the field? There are at least eight dimensions that are common across many UCP organizations, each of which will be briefly described in what follows.

First, the nonviolent accompaniers and civilian protectors, who may be internationals or nationals, live and work within communities that are in need, potentially in harm's way, or directly suffering from violence. When asked, accompaniers quite literally walk alongside their fellow civil society activists, offering solidarity, encouragement and perhaps even added security. In this way they may help to expand the agency of civil society actors operating in trying circumstances.

Agency has to do with being able to freely make one's own political, economic, and social choices and to not have the range of those choices dramatically influenced by outside actors, forces, and even structures. An even more robust and nuanced notion of agency includes having a reasonable chance of influencing the outcomes produced by your choices (Hancock, 2016). This approach to understanding agency squares up quite tightly with how nonviolent accompaniment and unarmed civilian peacekeeping is often designed to work in practice. As the accompaniment work with threatened communities who have established Peace Zones has demonstrated (Coy, 2019; Gray, 2012), the mutually beneficial relationships that are nurtured and developed in and through the accompaniment experience make for a more potent civil society. In addition, by nurturing, protecting, and supporting civil society actors it also provides a critically needed antidote to the hegemony of state-centric politics and a potentially effective brake on future violence or repression from the state and even para-state organizations.

Second, unarmed civilian protectors are typically uniformed, intentionally highly visible and intensely socially interactive—all the better to develop the cross-cutting relationships that will not only inform their social and political analyses but increase their usefulness and even effectiveness. Third, they are always trained in nonviolent action, constructive communication techniques, dialogue facilitation, and political analysis skills (Martin and Coy, 2017), though to quite disparate degrees depending in part on the UCP organization they belong to.

Fourth, in a bid to enhance their acceptance to the widest variety of stakeholders and conflict parties and to increase their likelihood of effectiveness, accompaniers and protectors are generally at least politically independent and often even explicitly nonpartisan. That said, both concepts (political independence and nonpartisanship) are each very fluid both in theory and practice; they are also somewhat contested concepts both across UCP organizations and even among organizational staff and field workers within individual organizations (Coy, 2012; Schweitzer, 2017, 2020).

Fifth, in advance of events or confrontations, the civilian peacekeepers attempt to develop working relations founded in mutual respect and cooperation with other parties (including civil society organizations, INGOs, governmental agencies) who may be able to offer a unique tool set and expertise to the effort to protect human rights. After all, organizational missions and mandates in large part determine work in the field; as a result, the performance of that field work results in particular proficiencies that are specific to individual organizations. For example, working supportively and intentionally across organizations as Peace Brigades International did during the ethnic conflict in Sri Lanka in the 1990s, tapping into the expertise of other organizations to protect human rights and their defenders in a mutually complimentary and reinforcing fashion can magnify the impacts of unarmed civilian protection initiatives; this approach has been known as "cooperative accompaniment" (Coy, 1997).

Sixth, equally important is the same advance work done with those parties thought to threaten the security of local activists. In many situations, these are not mutually exclusive categories; for example, police and military can defend human rights and enhance overall security in one situation while violating fundamental liberties and repressing in still others.

This work of proactively being present, that is, explaining in advance the purposes of accompaniment, educating parties on civil liberties and on the political and even economic costs of repressive violence, and exploring ways for them to meet their goals without violating human rights, is time consuming and relationship dependent. Because of the hierarchical nature of police, military, and paramilitary it is best done both up and down the chains of command and even across sectors whenever possible (Mahony, 2006). Politically risky or costly orders to violate human rights often emanate from the upper tiers of the government or police or military. While such orders generally must be passed down through multiple levels, the fact always remains that individual officers or conscripts or workers, that is, those wearing the boots on the ground, must carry out the despicable deed. Having to engage with all these various levels and pressure points within and across a security system immeasurably complicates the deterrence work of unarmed civilian protectors. At the same time, however, it also occasions more opportunities for it to be effective and enhances both immediate and longer-term impacts.

Violence interruption can occur at any level within a security system, thereby breaking the delivery chain of repression; when this interruption happens, even long-established patterns of human rights violations can be disengaged. As cases where accompaniment has failed sadly demonstrate, this advance dialogue and relationship building up and down the chains of command and across multiple sectors and parties is often critical for accompaniment to be effective (for analysis of such failures see Coy, 1997, 2001).

Seventh, most all organizations providing nonviolent accompaniment and unarmed civilian protection heave closely to an empowerment ethic. This manifests itself in several ways. Believing that the agency of individual citizens and of the civil society organizations they work with must be a paramount concern, accompaniers don't so much lead as follow. They assiduously avoid creating dependencies, seeing these as counterproductive to the task of strengthening civil society to resist the constraints and excesses associated with state-based politics. For example, although their organizational mandates are frequently misunderstood and they are therefore often asked to provide material or humanitarian aid, most wisely eschew the mission creep that providing such aid would represent (Julian & Schweitzer, 2015). Indeed, accompaniers and civilian peacekeepers generally recognize that a primary task for them is supporting agency and local ownership of all aspects of political life, including locally controlled problem-solving initiatives of various sorts designed to address the causes of the injustices, and the conflicts and the violence besetting the communities with whom they are working (Furnari, 2015).

Eighth, and finally, the cross-cutting dialogues that are constitutive dimensions of the proactive presence dimension of unarmed civilian peacekeeping may include both fact-finding and investigative missions, rumor control within and between communities and parties, and the establishment and maintenance of early warning systems. All this work both revolves around and depends on an assiduous commitment to relationship building, long recognized as a central dimension of any peacekeeping endeavor (Furnari et al., 2015).

These early warning initiatives to announce imminent civil society harm or violence are by their nature cooperative, complimentary, and multitrack as advance information runs back and forth between the police/military, the nonviolent accompaniers, civil society organizations and the local activists experiencing injustice and imminent violence or its threat. Early warning systems to avoid harm to citizens and human rights defenders were used effectively by the UCP Nonviolent Peaceforce in Mindanao in the Philippines as well as in their groundbreaking work in South Sudan (Julian, 2016). These early warning exchanges can have at least four positive results, some of which even carry forward into long-range impacts.

First, they make it more likely to be able to interrupt violence before it begins and thereby effectively disengage cycles of ever-increasing violence. Second, early warning initiatives nurture burgeoning alliances and growing mutual interdependence between previously adversarial parties; in this way they help build stronger and more sustainable communities. Third, they essentially function similarly to how "confidence building measures" have historically been used in international affairs (Kriesberg & Dayton, 2017, p. 204), that is, increasing shared transparency in future interactions and therefore building trust. This, in turn, contributes to enhancing the capacities of communities to ensure their own security going forward, a critical ingredient for sustainable peace. Finally, when considered collectively, the communication-rich nature of the early warning systems implemented by civilian peacekeepers may contribute substantively to peacebuilding within and across communities.

Implications for teaching and training

The length, type, rigor, and professionalization of the training undergone by nonviolent accompaniers and unarmed civilian protectors vary dramatically depending on the following factors: the conflict context of the deployment; the anticipated length of the deployment; and the nature and experiences of the organization that is offering the training and putting the trainees in the field. For short, "pop-up" initiatives like the single tactic, solely interpositionary approach of the Wall of Moms and the Wall of Vets in Portland, there was, in fact, no training at all. People simply showed up and took their place along an interposing line between police and protestors. Of course, there was also no organizational infrastructure or experience in place to facilitate training there at that moment in a rapidly developing and escalating conflict environment.

In general, however, as the field of accompaniment and civilian protection has grown in depth and breadth, we have witnessed a growth in theory-building by both scholars and participants (some of that work has already been cited above). This increase in theorizing about how, why, when, and under what conditions specific tactics prove effective in particular contexts is itself based upon a growing body of direct evidence from civilian protection deployments in not only long-simmering and intractable conflicts but also quickly emerging flashpoint conflicts. The result is that as both theory-building and as wisdom born from widespread organizational field experience has developed, the complexity of the teaching and training for prospective field workers has grown as well. These changes have occurred along at least three dimensions.

First, trainings have generally lengthened in duration from in many cases only 7–10 days to a full month or more. Second, participant selections for participation in training have become more careful even while paying increased attention to demographic diversity of the training pool. Third, the training has become more demanding by engaging with complex and complicated cultural, social, and political issues that any team member must be ready to handle constructively once in the field. One aspect, however, that has not changed is the training methodology. Most organizations have an unwavering commitment to a deeply reflexive, interactive, participatory, experiential, and cooperative approach to both training and learning.

Teaching about nonviolent accompaniment and unarmed civilian protection in secondary college and university courses appears to be on the increase, and for good reasons. This is a topic that has an exciting, even inspiring story to tell. It is ultimately based on both compelling narratives and analytical case studies where individual activists and civil society organizations have stepped into an otherwise crippling void to help provide the safe political space and the security that all people must have in order to reach their full potential. In these ways unarmed civilian protection is essentially an exercise in positive peace. It is a story of people helping people, neighbors assisting neighbors through the power of dialogue, nonviolent action, and shared risks to constructively confront and ultimately transform the injustices and destructive conflicts negatively impinging on their lives.

In my 25 years of regularly teaching about nonviolent accompaniment and unarmed civilian protection on the university level in both political science and peace and conflict studies courses, I have found that most students are eager to hear about this story. They often find it inspiring. In fact, some are disappointed to learn that many organizations have a minimum age for working in the field of 25–30 years. Moreover, the experiential, role-play and simulation-based approach to teaching and training that is deeply integrated into the field's materials makes the topic accessible, engaging, and even exciting for nearly all students. Better still, trainers active in the movement have been collegial and transparent with the training manual and curricula that they have developed and refined over many years of training prospective civilian protectors. These freely available manuals are chock full of well-thought out exercises, activities, case scenarios, and role-plays, and they have been revised and refined due to extensive use and reuse by trainers across many organizations (for one example, see Hunter & Lakey, 2004).

Various aspects of the theories and practices of nonviolent accompaniment and unarmed civilian protection help the topic fit seamlessly into a wide variety of courses focused on any of the following topics: introductory peace and conflict studies, international relations, social movements, nonviolent action, security studies, the United Nations, human rights, ethnic conflicts, gender studies, conflict transformation, transitional justice, peacebuilding, and development studies. Indeed, I have personally taught the topic to good effect in no less than five of the courses in the above list. This is also not an exhaustive list of possible courses. Given the significant roles that nonviolent accompaniment and unarmed civilian protection have played in specific conflict zones over the past nearly 40 years, it would also be a good fit in courses focused on area studies, including: Latin American studies, Middle East studies, Asian studies, and African studies.

Implications for practice and policy

Nonviolent Peaceforce, a prominent organization in the field, is currently leading "a comprehensive global review of good practices in the field of unarmed civilian protection. The purpose of the good practices process is to strengthen and grow the field of UCP by bringing practitioners, academics, and affected beneficiaries together to reflect on the needs, successes and failure of UCP…" Partly funded by the Australian government, foundations, and individuals, the UCP good practices initiative includes four discrete but interrelated stages.

The first stage was the creation of an edited book of four in-depth case studies where UCP has been practiced: South Sudan, Colombia, the Philippines (Mindanao) and Israel/Palestine (Furnari, 2016). The second stage is the convening of six regional consultations of UCP practitioners, field partners, beneficiaries and researchers for three-day long sessions to review their field work and research, analyze some of the findings of stage one, and identify dilemmas or challenges raised but not previously answered. To date there have been five regional consultations completed, in Manila, Beirut, Nairobi, Paynesville, and Bogotá. Having participated in the Manila consultation, I came away deeply impressed with its preparation, strategic design, facilitation, and usefulness. A regional consultation scheduled in Europe for 2020 was postponed due to the COVID-10 pandemic.

Stage three will consist of a global conference in 2021 or 2022 to synthesize the findings of the case studies and the six regional consultations, validate a set of UCP good practices that can be scaled up and replicated, and establish a coordinated global network for UCP. Stage four eventually follows and will be focused on publishing the results of the earlier stages, broadly disseminating the good practices findings both within and far beyond the UCP world and integrating those principles and practices into the training and field work of all UCP organizations.

The state of the field of nonviolent accompaniment and unarmed civilian protection appears healthy. It continues to develop and expand. It has now matured and evolved to the point where the United Nations is foregrounding it as a policy commitment in its peace operations as well as in its security and development initiatives, particularly so with those UN initiatives that include a gender and security dimension. In addition, UCP is securing funding streams from foundations, intergovernmental organizations, and governments who recognize the distinctive contributions and value-added dimensions this approach brings to the peacekeeping and peacebuilding table. As the current push to develop and disseminate good practices demonstrates, this is currently less an experiment and now more a mature field of constructive conflict practice.

Notes

1 As a comparatively young and evolving area of practice for civil society, the nomenclature associated with accompaniment and civilian peacekeeping has regularly changed. While unarmed civilian peacekeeping had previously been a common term and was the referent for the acronym "UCP," Nonviolent Peaceforce and some other organizations have moved to using "unarmed civilian protection" as the preferred moniker. This shift recognizes the multitudinous methods used in the field, the fact that the work is fluid relative to hard distinctions between peacekeeping and peacebuilding, and that parts of the United Nations and the security studies field have traditional and somewhat restricted notions of the nature of peacekeeping, notions that may not include the work described herein by civilians.
2 UN Documents quoted in Duncan, M. (2016), "From Recognition to Implementation at the United Nations," February 1, on Nonviolent Peaceforce website: https://www.nonviolentpeaceforce.org/blog/advocacy-news/539-from-recognition-to-implementation-at-the-united-nations

References

Birkeland, T. K. (2016). *Unarmed civilian protection: The methodology and its relevance for Norwegian church-based organizations and their partners*. Norwegian Ecumenical Peace Platform. https://www.nonviolentpeaceforce.org/images/publications/Unarmed_Civilian_Protection.pdf

Boothe, I., & Smithey, L. A. (2007). Privilege, empowerment, and nonviolent intervention. *Peace and Change, 32*(1), 39–61.

Cineas, F. (2020, August 4). How Portland's Wall of Moms collapsed—and was reborn under black leadership. https://www.vox.com/21353939/portland-wall-of-moms-collapses-to-form-moms-united-for-black-lives

Clark, A. D., Dantzler, P. A., & Nickels, A. E. (2018). Black lives matter: (Re)framing the next wave of black liberation. *Research in Social Movements, Conflicts and Change, 42*, 145–172.

Coy, P. G. (1993). Protective accompaniment: How peace brigades international secures political space and human rights nonviolently. In V. K. Kool (Ed.), *Nonviolence: Social and psychological issues* (pp. 235–244). University Press of America.

Coy, P. G. (1997). Cooperative accompaniment by peace brigades international in Sri Lanka. In J. Smith, C. Chatfield, & R. Pagnucco (Eds.), *Transnational social movements and global politics: Solidarity beyond the state* (pp. 81–100). Syracuse University Press.

Coy, P. G. (2001). Shared risks and research dilemmas on a peace brigades international team in Sri Lanka. *Journal of Contemporary Ethnography, 30*(5), 575–606.

Coy, P. G. (2011). The privilege problematic in international nonviolent accompaniment's early decades. *The Journal of Religion, Conflict and Peace, 4*(2). https://www.manchester.edu/docs/default-source/academics/by-major/philosophy-and-religious-studies/journal/volume-4-issue-2-spring-2011/the-privilege-problematic-in-international-nonviolent-accompaniments-early-decades.pdf?sfvrsn=fd618962_2

Coy, P. G. (2012). Nonpartisanship, interventionism and legality in accompaniment: Comparative analyses of peace brigades international, Christian peacemaker teams, and the international solidarity movement. *International Journal of Human Rights, 16*(7), 963–981.

Coy, P. G. (2019). The intersections of international nonviolent accompaniment and radical local politics. In R. Kinna & U. Gordon (Eds.), *Routledge handbook of radical politics* (pp. 256–266). Routledge.

Coy, P. G., Woehrle, L. M., & Maney, G. M. (2008). Discursive legacies: The U.S. peace movement and "support the troops." *Social Problems, 55*(2), 161–189.

Fuller, T. (2020, July 24). How one of America's whitest cities became the center of B.L.M. protests. *New York Times.* https://www.nytimes.com/2020/07/24/us/portland-oregon-protests-white-race.html

Furnari, E. (2015). Relationships are critical for peacekeeping. *Peace Review, 27*(1), 25–30.

Furnari, E. (Ed.). (2016). *Wielding nonviolence in the midst of violence: Case studies of good practices in unarmed civilian protection.* Books on Demand.

Furnari, E., Olenhuis, H., & Julian, R. (2015). Securing space for local peacebuilding: The role of international and national civilian peacekeepers. *Peacebuilding, 3*(3), 297–313.

Gray, V. J. (2012). Nonviolence and sustainable resource use with external support: A survival strategy in rural Colombia. *Latin American Perspectives, 39*(1), 43–114.

Hancock, L. E. (2016). Agency and peacebuilding: The promise of local zones of peace. *Peacebuilding, 5*(3), 255–269.

Hunter, D., & Lakey, G. (2004). *Opening space for democracy: Third-party nonviolent intervention curriculum and trainer's manual.* Training for Change.

Janzen, R. (2014). Shifting practices of peace: What is the current state of unarmed civilian peacekeeping. *Peace Studies Journal, 7*(3), 46–60.

Julian, R. (2016). Unarmed civilian peacekeeping: Peacekeeping challenges and the responsibility to protect. http://eprints.leedsbeckett.ac.uk/3607/

Julian, R. (2019). The transformative impact of unarmed civilian peacekeeping. *Global Society, 34*(1), 99–111.

Julian, R., & Schweitzer, C. (2015). The origins and development of unarmed civilian peacekeeping. *Peace Review, 27*(1), 1–8.

Julian, R., & Gasser, R. (2019). Soldiers, civilians, and peacekeeping: Evidence and false assumptions. *International Peacekeeping, 26*(1), 22–54.

Kriesberg, L., & Dayton, B. W. (2017). *Constructive conflicts: From escalation to resolution* (5th ed.). Rowman & Littlefield.

Mahony, L. (2004). *Side by side: Protecting and encouraging threatened activists with unarmed international accompaniment.* The Center for Victims of Torture.

Mahony, L. (2006). *Proactive presence: Field strategies for civilian protection.* Henry Dunant Centre for Humanitarian Dialogue. http://www.hdcentre.org/publications/[10.9.2008].

Mahony, L., & Eguren, L. E. (1997). *Unarmed bodyguards: International accompaniment for the protection of human rights.* Kumarian Press.

Martin, B. (2009). Making accompaniment effective. In H. Clark (Ed.), *People power: Unarmed resistance and global solidarity* (pp. 96–97). Pluto Press.

Martin, B., & Coy, P. G. (2017). Skills, training, and activism. *Reflective Practice, 18*(4), 5151–525.

Schweitzer, C. (2017). *Good practices in nonviolent, unarmed, civilian to civilian protection and protective accompaniment: Documentation of the workshop in Manila, Philippines).* Nonviolent Peaceforce. https://www.nonviolentpeaceforce.org/component/pages_np/freeform/globalreview

Schweitzer, C. (2019). *Good practices in nonviolent, unarmed, civilian to civilian protection and protective accompaniment: Documentation of the workshop in Paynesville.* Minnesota, Nonviolent Peaceforce. https://www.nonviolentpeaceforce.org/component/pages_np/freeform/globalreview

Schweitzer, C. (2020). *Good practices in nonviolent, unarmed, civilian to civilian protection and protective accompaniment: Documentation of the workshop in Bogotá (Colombia).* Nonviolent Peaceforce. https://www.nonviolentpeaceforce.org/component/pages_np/freeform/globalreview

Wallace, M. S. (2017). *Security without weapons: Rethinking violence, nonviolent action, and civilian protection.* Routledge.

Weber, T. (1996). *Gandhi's peace army: The Shanti Sena and unarmed peacekeeping.* Syracuse University Press.

12
PEACE LEADERSHIP, SECURITY, AND THE ROLE OF THE MILITARY IN ETHNOPOLITICAL CONFLICT

Yvan Yenda Ilunga and Thomas G. Matyók

Introduction

Ethnopolitical conflicts seem the new norm. War conducted between states and restricted to engagements between militaries is now past. War occurs *among the people* seamlessly transitioning between competition, confrontation, and conflict (Smith, 2007). The current state has moved away from interstate wars to intrastate conflicts often manifested as civil wars (Levy & Thompson, 2010, p. 13). This return to intrastate conflicts where state authority is questioned points to a return to a pre-Westphalia arrangement. Militaries now operate in complex spaces jointly occupied by humanitarian and military actors (for e.g., Ukraine). Military operations can no longer be separated from humanitarian work (Ryan, 2016). Ethnopolitical tensions in societies can exacerbate economic, political, and social authorities (Anderson, 1999, p. 16). Rothman (1997) notes how "identity-driven conflicts are rooted in articulation of, and the threats or frustrations to, people's collective need for dignity, recognition, safety, control, purpose and efficacy" (p. 7). Rwanda and Kosovo initiated a shift away from the primacy of the state to the protection of the individual. The individual is now recognized as the sovereign (Gallant, 2011; Holt & Berkman, 2006). Responsibility-to-protect (R2P) doctrine has developed to outline legal processes that can guide military responses to humanitarian abuses (Gallant, 2011, p. 402). States now recognize the right to intervene to protect individuals from the abuses of their governments (Marten, 2004, p. 90) rather than outside state actors. Militaries are now routinely called upon to engage in human protection operations (Holt & Berkman, 2006, p. 5). Militaries are assuming a greater role in providing humanitarian assistance (Rocha, 2009, p. 50). Clear definitions and boundaries are needed regarding how humanitarian and military actors engage in complex environments. Needed now are clear policies on the integration of civil society and military actors in providing humanitarian assistance (Rietjens & Bollen, 2008, p. 248). The call to action should be centered on the growing ethnopolitical conflict and the challenges these conflicts present to humanitarian and military actors.

Theoretical concepts

Understanding the context

The surge of many ethnopolitical conflicts is often anchored to an imbalance of political representation and leadership, inequality in resource distributions, or the historical exploitation of selected ethnic groups by others (Theuerkauf, 2010, p. 119). Consequences of these actions result in social unrest, violent confrontation, and social polarization fueled with incendiary narratives that negatively characterizes relationships between communities and threatens peace and security. The sensible approach to address ethnopolitical conflict is always diplomacy and other peaceful, nonviolent ways to avoid or minimize violence and to establish social stability. The medium is the message; violence cannot beget sustainable nonviolent multiethnic communities.

However, it should be known that diplomatic means promoted by third parties are not often effective and have shown to be of limited value in highly volatile ethnopolitical conflicts. Grassroots peacebuilding is demonstrating a better way forward. Locally owned approaches to the development of just and stable societies are the promotion of peace leadership based on indigenous social and cultural norms and practices; where local leaders try to serve as bridge-negotiators between their communities (Byrne & Keashly, 2000, p. 111). This local approach is also used when conflicts occur between leaders who occupy high offices in the land, and who happen to be protected by political influences that effectively grant them immunity. While the latter effort is indigenous and well-articulated in local culture and norms, it has also demonstrated its limitations since power relations between communities is often characterized by exploitation, and those benefiting are not always willing to relinquish their power or lower their hands. As reflective of Track 3 of multitrack diplomacy, those in positions of influence sometimes see their power as transactional tools for business and deal making rather than a sign of responsibilities to deliver upon.

Even though diplomatic and local peace leadership initiatives continue to fail, they still have not lost their merit in peacebuilding. However, in this study we find it necessary to reconsider approaches to peace leadership and security by considering the expanding role of the military in violent political or ethnic conflicts. Moving forward in this analysis, our aim is to understand the correlation between ethnopolitical conflicts vis-a-vis military peace efforts. This cannot be achieved without revisiting and redefining military actors from warfighter to peacemaker, keeper, builder, etc. Additionally, transitioning military actors to take on more constabulary roles allowing peacebuilding experts—political, economic, cultural—to do their work is vital to peace leadership.

The circle of conflict and peace efforts

Failed diplomacy precedes the outbreak of every violent conflict. Traditional wisdom speaks to how wars begin and end with diplomacy where negotiation is the primary diplomatic tool. This is also true for ethnopolitical conflicts that fall short of war.

While it is important to look at the correlation between ethnopolitical conflict and military peacebuilding efforts, it is still necessary to argue that the cycle of violence and instability does not call directly for military intervention. Violent military intervention must always be considered as the last resort. We should always be cautious to not *let slip the dogs of war*. But when others cry havoc—to paraphrase Shakespeare—and violent, kinetic action occurs, military intervention becomes an important component of peacebuilding, peace restoration, peace recovery, and the future of fragile communities. In such a context, where military peace efforts have been engaged, it is not possible to rethink stability without rethinking the presence and role of the military.

In this context, the projected circle of conflict and peace efforts can be framed as "Power-Control/Exploitation-Frustration/Violence-Military Effort-Leadership Structure."

Power

With or without political ambitions, societies and their actors are structures built around the idea of possessing power. Outside the quest and ambitious behavior of some rogue actors, the fundamental reasons of power in local communities are to maintain local peace and stability. In other words, power is seen as the articulation of a community's ability to determine its own future and enjoy peace without losing control of its destiny. Maintaining sovereignty is at the center of every ethnic group's desire for power.

However, power relations between groups become an issue when the idea of "authority" comes into play and is introduced into the conflict narrative. In fact, the concept of authority brings in a hierarchical view of community structure, which is at the center of many, if not most, ethnopolitical conflicts in multiethnic settings. This arrangement leads to top dogs who can employ their power over to exploit and control those less powerful.

Hence, the question shifts from the basic existence of power for survival of the community to "who owns the power?" This itself creates a conflict of representation, control, and influence which unfortunately too often escalates to a tipping point resulting in direct violence. And direct violence is merely the end of the conflict continuum. Direct violence is made manifest and legitimate by first establishing cultural violence—establishment of a dominant culture and the elimination of competing cultures—to initiate structural violence which is found in the institutions of the state (Galtung, 1996). In this scenario restoring peace would not come with the promotion of a "power sharing" approach between ethnic groups; instead, there is need for strengthening local ownership of the future with peace defined in local contexts. Hence, the transitioning of power from local tool to hierarchical structure is at the center of violence and ethnopolitical conflict.

Control/exploitation

The second significant dilemma in the circle of conflict and peace efforts is the issue of control and exploitation. Shifting the power from being a local tool of peacebuilding to hierarchical structure, the new owner of power, also ends up being considered as *the* "authority figure." In multiethnic societies those seeking to assume controlling influence work to do so through unequivocal control of power relationships. In a classic sense, the existence of structures such as democracy are based on the transfer of responsibility for good governance to society's political, economic, and cultural elites and representatives who defend local interests and remain accountable to their local communities since power has always remained at the local level, thus limiting the possibility of exploitation.

However, in the context of dysfunctional systems where the governance style is not well established and the accountability mechanisms are not strong, there is an easy path to usurpation of power by elites who then impose their views and oppressive lifestyles on their subjects. These constitute a form of social, economic, and political control which ultimately leads to multifaceted exploitation. It is this systemic control based on elitism, power, ethnicity, and political influences that communities and countries must end to lower the risk of violent ethnopolitical conflict.

Frustration and violence

Ultimately the excessive use of power for control and exploitation can only lead to social frustration and malaise. Violence is not far from occurring when the call for protest multiplies among the oppressed and the irresponsiveness of government persists. In the case of a dominant ethnic group, and the perception of superiority on one side and the feeling of inferiority on the other, the deep roots of social frustration are set. Furthermore, when dehumanization takes place in social interactions between dominant and exploited groups, violence proves to be the only logical outcome.

In fact, throughout history, this type of frustration was displayed in different forms and shapes. Sometimes it was based on race, at other times on class, and still in other times religion. So, studying social frustration based on power, control, and exploitation is not new. However, what is novel in the 21st century cosmopolitan world is the increasing intercultural coexistence in many urban spaces throughout the globe. This cosmopolitanism, globalism, requires peace scholars and practitioners to revisit the dynamics of ethnopolitical conflicts, which in the past were violent conflicts and physical confrontations between groups primarily conducted outside of cities (on the battlefield), today they have the capacity to disrupt the social, economic, and political dynamics of large urban centers by bringing violence to them. Such disruption and the consequences of violence in large cosmopolitan cities is hardly being addressed through military peace efforts. Nor, when violence breaks out, will political negotiation succeed before major damage is caused to people and infrastructures.

Military effort

For decades, the traditional course of action in peacekeeping and peacebuilding has been characterized by military intervention as the means to stop violence and restore peace and security. Military-centric operations lack the long-term capacity to build peace; they remain limited beyond ending direct violence. The military demonstrates its merits in ending gun shots and sometimes establishing mechanisms of transitional justice. This is not enough. The wisdom in the field of peace and conflict studies shows how the worst outcome for civilians in an ethnopolitical conflict is a prolonged military leadership in a post-conflict community. In fact, either expressed explicitly or not, the hope and effectiveness of military intervention in ethnopolitical conflict, as per civilians' perceptions, is assessed based on how fast power is transitioned to civil society.

The need for power transfer is critical in peacebuilding since the presence of the military in civilian leadership contexts, mainly political, symbolizes limitations on individuals' freedom. Even if this might not always be the case in practice, the psychological perception of military leadership often maintains memories of oppression and control. Hence, within the circle of conflict and peace the quicker the transition from violence to stability is accomplished, the easier it will be to promote and conduct peacebuilding. However, it is also important to highlight that the transfer of power from military to civil actors should be conducted responsibly and with no rush. In many cases, the military effort is the guarantor of stability, but not the generator and sustainer of change.

Leadership structure

The ultimate change for military peacebuilding efforts is to guarantee peace through inclusive civilian leadership. This does not mean minimizing ethnic differences and tensions, but instead promoting the presence of leadership that is fully equipped and committed to end ethnic

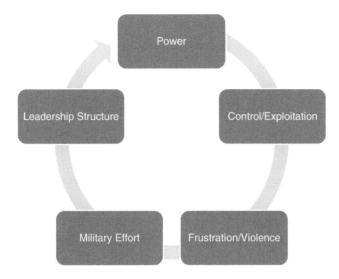

Figure 12.1 Circle of conflict and peace efforts

conflicts and promote peaceful coexistence. Past failures in attempting to achieve such an effort were due to the ideology of building systems and governmental entities focused on power sharing, rather than promoting the narrative for peace and hope within local communities.

As is well documented, the volatility of ethnopolitical conflict is often maintained by the social narratives in communities and the nature of communication that is polluted by hate speech and similar actions. Hence, every effort to restore peace through institutional leadership that is not rooted in local grievances and popular ethnic opinions will be short lived. The same way social disruptions that lead to ethnopolitical conflict emerge from political manipulations and propagandas with the use of incendiary narratives, it can only make sense that countering these destabilizing factors and promoting peace will also be made possible by the intentionality in reconstructive acts from the new civilian leadership, as well as by the effectiveness of public communication that would strengthen inclusive narratives of peace and tolerance. With such an approach, leadership is not only seen as a strong and functional structure, but also the symbol of positive messaging and a reflection of unity and humanity that emerges amid ethnic differences and antagonisms (see Figure 12.1).

The military as a national institution

The most used approach in the examination of military performance is the study of institutional and systems theory. This approach tends to analyze the military simply as an institution in which a chain-of-command is clear and established to be followed. Using this vertical and bureaucratic structure it becomes easy to assume that failure on the battlefield is most likely due to the nature of command, which is often depicted to be wrong or ineffective. This view promotes and validates the quote "there are no bad troops, but bad leaders" in the military context. This oversimplification of the military and its performance is dangerous and inaccurate as it ignores or downplays the complexity and dynamics of human behavior and the nature of troops on the battlefield, and more specifically in the context of identity conflict or violent ethnopolitical conflict. This complexity goes far beyond the structure of the military and its chain-of-command approach to leadership. It covers the background of men and women composing the troops, their education, their ethnicity, their political views, their readiness, etc. It is only when such an inclusive assessment is rigorously completed that one can objectively identify the weakness or reasons of underperformance of certain troops. This argument does not exonerate the leaders, but it expands the conversation to unfamiliar territories.

External influence

It is always ideal to have troops that are not being affected, or infected, by political or identity crises. This aspiration is in practice difficult to experience since every man and woman in uniform represents a specific identity background, identities which sometimes compete. Even in extreme cases of a monolithic society, constructed with a homogenous ethnic group, there are always identity challenges or political influences that impact the functioning of the military, which necessitates continuous attention.

The effort to increase performance of the military and strengthen its institutional abilities can only be achieved when negative political externalities are minimized, and objectivity becomes the controlling paradigm. It is also a fair assessment to mention that this political tension will never completely go away. It is also true to argue that promoting a moral and unrealistic view that the military must be completely *apolitical* is in the realm of utopia. It is true that the military, as institution, must be above political cleavages and maintain its objectivity in ensuring and promoting national security. The challenge of objectivity and maintaining an apolitical dimension of the military is that the institution serves and operates in the frame of national interest and security as defined by an elected political leadership. This is the case for many democratic regimes in the Western world where the ultimate security decision is in hands of elected politicians. Hence, maintaining the apolitical nature of the military would most likely be possible if the civilian political class promotes the independency of institutions, as well as value, in their political decisions, the integrity of pillars that ensure national security and sovereignty; among which is the military.

Also, the awareness of ethnicity as an externality in the construct of the military institution must be viewed as critical in the context of ethnopolitical conflict. Critical not in the sense of assuming less loyalty to the national cause by members of certain ethnic groups serving in the army, but critical in the sense of mobilizing resources and rules that will serve to create fairness, equality, and respect for all active-duty personnel, as well as their civilian family and ethnic groups. While this external influence is applicable in many cases, in the context of ethnopolitical conflict, one should always see ethnicity as an external influencer in the performance and composition of the military which must always be well managed.

Misleading neutrality

In fact, even with an identity as objective actors, people in the military bring their ethnicities to the institution and a conflict, and individual and group identities cannot be "left-at-the-door," so to speak. It is problematic to believe that anyone can remain neutral; especially, in identity conflicts. In promoting neutrality, or blind obedience, eliminating ethnic identity definitions can become disempowering and dehumanizing. An assumption of neutrality and the effort to disconnect people from their social identities is what we call a *misleading neutrality*.

It is misleading because it makes people adhere to an ideology of disassociation and isolation from what makes them truly human. Even when ethnicity cannot be expressed or promoted during their active-duty military service, it does not mean their sense of ethnic affiliation no longer exists. There is always the place one can call home and a group that can still be called "my people." This human need to belong cannot be overlooked or ignored, especially in identity conflict. It will always be to the benefit of the military and the country it shows support and manage the *feelings of belonging* people have for their ethnic groups. While the primary benefit is that it consolidates group dynamics and strengthens cohesion, it is also critical when many people in the military feel their ethnic groups are either being mistreated by the government, they show loyalty to, or by other groups while their own government cannot provide support to stop such violence.

In such a case, the dilemma between loyalty to the nation and the moral obligation to serve and protect their ethnic groups will be evident. And of course, throughout history we have seen that the tendency has always been that of choosing one's ethnic group above the nation. The rationale of such a decision is sociologically and politically justifiable. While institutions can be built and dismantled, ethnic groups, once extinguished, will never come back in a new form or shape. Hence, the dilemma of loyalty to the military institution is somehow solved and the ideology of neutrality cannot stand in ethnic conflict.

This move to dismantle the neutrality argument through the behavior of the troops could be considered as "just cause." Just cause because those in services, while serving their countries, also have moral obligations to defend their families or ethnic groups when and if they find themselves at risk. At risk from both their own government and external enemies. One cannot easily disassociate themself with their ethnic social realities and expecting them to do so is not realistic.

Positive ethnicity in peacebuilding: New direction in R2P?

In its essence, ethnicity is not an obstacle to peace, nor is it a guarantor of security and good governance. However, it has been over reported that major conflicts and instabilities across Africa and throughout the Middle East are due to ethnic tensions. While ethnic tensions might be one of the layers of these multifaceted conflicts, circumscribing and limiting ethnopolitical conflicts to a narrative of ethnicity alone does not create a complete picture. Yes, in some cases ethnicity has been at the center of violent conflict, but this is often a response to other types of frustration such as economic exclusion, social exploitation, or dehumanization of one's ethnic group. While there are efforts to address this imbalance among members of civil society, it is also important to project the same sense of reparation onto the troops.

In conflict, military, and security studies there is always the idea of seeing the military only as provider of security, and not as receiver of security. The notion of the military as security providers has traveled over time and across generations. Many in civil society have difficulty thinking of individuals' needs and identities outside of uniform. It is easy to identify them with their military grades, services, war experiences, etc., but hardly do we see the human in the uniform possessing a clear ethnic identity (Gezari, 2013). The fear to do so is motived by the idea of segregating the troops. But not doing it undermines every objective effort to have a more inclusive and well-represented army.

It is with this unusual way of reflecting the dynamics of ethnopolitical conflict that we argue for employing positive ethnicity in peacebuilding. To illustrate this, we speak to the growing idea of responsibility to protect (R2P), which is a civil concept and victim centered.

R2P stipulates that a country can have an obligation to intervene in another country to stop or prevent possible humanitarian crises and human rights violations conducted by the state. Within this context, and in many other narratives, these violations are orchestrated by unethical leaders and perpetrated by their troops—"the military." This places the military at the level of tools for the security or insecurity of the state. The military is not seen as a group of people expecting and needing protection, too. Protection of individual military members is not always the business of the international community nor national authorities. This is true in many developing countries where defection from the ranks and creation of either rebellions or militias based on ethnicity and social frustration result. And many of these defections are due to a sense of ethnic vulnerability of troops in and outside of the military context. Bringing this conversation into the study of ethnopolitical conflict and expanding a narrow understanding of R2P becomes critical in this age of complexity, asymmetric, and unpredictable violent conflict. The same way ethnic conflict and violence is a result of unaddressed social malaise in society, ethnic vulnerabilities in the ranks can also lead to underperforming militaries and possibly divided armies.

While this positive ethnicity might sound like a foreign conversation in many developed countries, countries such as South Sudan, Iraq, and Afghanistan which have experienced internal conflicts with opposing forces based on religion and ethnicity deserve a more serious consideration of such an approach. This is even so because some of the international suggested strategies of demobilization, disarmament, and (re)integration of these different forces into one republican army can be problematic if approached simplistically. What the strategy means in practice is an infusion of diverse ethnic groups into one army and under one chain-of-command. Such an approach is important as it promotes peace, ends violence, and engages countries in the path of peacebuilding and institutional reconstruction. But what it also does is it exposes these countries and institutions to potential internal ethnic conflicts and institutional disasters if an intentional approach of positive ethnicity is not developed and integrated into security sector reform initiatives. And this could be a new form of R2P within the military ranks and among the troops. We must protect the military as an institution and its personnel as individuals who deserve the full attention of the state and its protection. Those serving in the military are not only providers of security, but also as recipients of the same security they provide.

Key findings

As highlighted in the introductory paragraphs of this chapter, the conversation of ethnopolitical conflict has been limited over the years. The focus has been on group conflicts, ethnic conflicts, and the use of the military to address the violence that result from each. Even when the approach to conflict resolution and peacebuilding was based on diplomacy and negotiations, the presence of the military as standby forces or persuasive institutions was always envisioned, hence using the military as provider of security and guarantor of peace. While this has been effective and efficient in many contexts and over time, in this chapter we demonstrate that the study of ethnopolitical conflict will not be complete if the military are exclusively seen as providers of security. They must also be viewed as beneficiaries. Hence, we contend that the long-term peace and stability of states experiencing, or coming from, ethnopolitical violence and conflicts will be guaranteed when the military, through the lens of R2P, are receivers of security as well as guarantors. This means making sure that while the troops are working in providing security for the victims of conflicts in fragile regions, they should also be at the center of the security framework that states develop to protect civilians. In other words, the framework of national security, protection of civilians, and promotion of harmonious relations between ethnic groups should also include the consideration of those in the military as citizen-beneficiaries of security within their distinctive ethnic affiliations; either wearing their uniform or not. Doing so will necessitate a new paradigm shift in peace leadership.

Implications for teaching and training

The traditional security approach to training within military spaces is based on building capacity of the military to prevent insecurity, react to the threats, and maintain security using force and diplomatic means. In contrast to this approach used by many in the diplomatic profession, the approach in the military brings, explicitly or implicitly, the possibility of using forces when negotiations do not lead to peaceful settlement of conflicts. This means, the use of force to "provide" and "lead" *to security* is a critical element in military training. Additionally, the training provides a relational approach to security in the sense that it assumes a "from the military to the civilians" projection of security. As pointed out in the findings and previous sections in this chapter, this approach is incomplete. Such a training misses a critical element in which those working on developing security frameworks and training ignore that the military should also benefit from the security. This is different from the idea of training the military for self-defense, rather than being a receiver of the national protection. Hence, this chapter is important in the consideration of the military as provider *and* receiver of security in the sense that it lays the foundation for future development and reflects on how to readjust training manuals and rethink security and insecurity as integral parts and needs for those in the military as well as for those in civil society.

Implications for practice and policy

The implication for practice and policy is enormous. In this age of complexity, asymmetric use of forces, and uncontrolled ethnic and political polarization, rethinking security, the military, and leadership within the context of policy development becomes a considerable task that requires dedication, flexibility and seriousness for both policy makers and security practitioners (see Theuerkauf, 2010). In fact, history has shown that human nature likes the comfort of the "known" rather than the uncomfortable journey into the "unknown." This is to say that within the development and implementation of security policies, states tend to be hesitant in using new or innovative strategies to address insecurity and promote peace. Such a rigid approach continues to demonstrate that peace will continue to be far away if we do not try new ideas and expand our imagination in the development and implementation of security strategies and policies. What this chapter offers is the opportunity to see a new approach to seeing the military as simultaneous provider and recipient of peace within the growing field of peace leadership, and the necessity to innovate in our strategic thinking during ethnopolitical conflict. And, in practice this conversation raises the need for reallocation of resources to the training of military leadership, and security of the troops.

Conclusion

With such an approach and consideration of ethnopolitical conflict and the role of the military in it, a well-informed Peace Leadership would be that which combines these factors within one integral security and peacebuilding framework to serve civilians and that does not forget the military. This chapter demonstrates that the future of effective peace operations depends on how well we manage the complexity of current national and international security threats. This management will mostly be at theoretical, strategic, and tactical levels. At the theoretical level, the study of ethnopolitical conflict would have to develop a new framework for civil-military dynamics in which peace leadership is anchored in the consideration of both civilians and militaries as beneficiaries of security. In fact, while the practice of protecting civilians has gained ground in peace, military and humanitarian studies, the world seems to ignore the importance of protecting the military outside of their active duties. This chapter therefore calls for the theorization of an inclusive framework for this end.

At the strategic level, the chapter also argues that it requires military doctrine to adapt to the new and changing configuration of ethnopolitical conflict. This adaptation should consider the fact that violent conflict is not only happening on the battlefield but has transposed to new territories such as cosmopolitan cities where the potential of identity-based conflicts has become higher, hence impacting general civil societies as well as civilians who are related to the military. This shift in doctrine, at the strategic level, would therefore mean finding a way to guarantee safety and well-being of military families and those related to them. While it is true that the narrative of taking care of dependents of the military exists in the general sense, the lack of a well-developed doctrine in the context of ethnopolitical conflict exposes communities and nations to an unprecedent form of fragility and security where the security providers are unsecured and unprotected. While the chapter does not intend to be prescriptive, it does however make a case for the need to develop a doctrine that speaks to this issue with well detailed guidelines with civil-military considerations at the center.

Finally, at the tactical level, in this chapter we argue that everyone needs security and protection. Ethnopolitical conflict and tensions destabilize the social and institutional fabric of societies which in the 21st century rely on multicultural and multiidentity structures. Hence, it is of great interest that the dynamics and practice of peace leadership in the context of ethnopolitical conflict be implemented by all stakeholders as a new form of building societies in an era of heterogeneity.

References

Anderson, M. (1999). *Do no harm: How aid can support peace or war.* Lynne Reinner Publishers.
Byrne, S., & Keashly, L. (2000). Working with ethno-political conflict: A multi-modal approach. *International Peacekeeping, 7*(1), 97–120.
Gallant, M. (2011). Law and legal processes in resolving international conflicts. In D. J. D. Sandole, S. Byrne, I. Sandole-Staroste, & J. Senehi (Eds.), *Handbook of conflict analysis and resolution* (pp. 396–406). Routledge.
Galtung, J. (1996). *Peace by peaceful means: Peace and conflict, development and civilization.* Sage Publications Ltd.
Gezari, V. (2013). *The tender soldier: A true story of war and sacrifice.* Simon & Schuster.
Holt, V., & Berkman, T. C. (2006). *The impossible mandate: Military preparedness, the responsibility to protect modern peace organizations.* The Henry C. Stimson Center.
Levy, J. S., & Thompson, W. R. (2010). *Causes of war.* Wiley-Blackwell.
Marten, K. Z. (2004). *Enforcing the peace: Learning from the imperial past.* Columbia University Press.
Rietjens, S., & Bollen, M. (2008). Trends and dilemmas of civil-military cooperation. In S. Rietjens & M. Bollen (Eds.), *Managing civil-military cooperation: A 24/7 joint effort for stability* (pp. 231–249). Taylor & Francis.
Rocha, S. (2009). Humanitarians and the military: Reality beyond manuals and guidelines. In E. Hamann (Ed.), *Revisiting borders between civilians and military: Security and development in peace operations and post-conflict situations* (pp. 50–55). Viva Rio.
Rothman, J. (1997). *Resolving identity-based conflicts in nations, organizations, and communities.* Jossey-Bass Publishers.
Ryan, A. (2016). The strategic civilian: Challenges for non-combatants in 21st century warfare. *Small Wars Journal.* https://smallwarsjournal.com/jrnl/art/the-strategic-civilian-challenges-for-non-combatants-in-21st-century-warfare
Smith, R. (2007). *The utility of force: The art of war in the modern world.* Vintage Books.
Theuerkauf, U. G. (2010). Institutional design and ethnic violence: Do grievances help to explain ethnopolitical instability? *Civil Wars, 12*(1–2), 117–139.

13
INTERRELIGIOUS PEACEBUILDING: AN EMERGING PATHWAY FOR SUSTAINABLE PEACE

Mohammed Abu-Nimer

Background: Religion in peacebuilding: A force for change

The field of peacebuilding (research and practice) has witnessed tremendous growth and development in the last three decades. Since the early 1990s, over a hundred new graduate and undergraduate programs on peace and conflict resolution have been developed around the world, especially in the Northern Hemisphere. In addition, major governmental and nongovernmental agencies have invested a great deal of funds in the development of peace and conflict resolution programs as part of their domestic and international operations (Alliance of Peacebuilding, n.d.; Peace and Development Network, n.d.). The overwhelming majority of these programs and initiatives are secular in their orientation and foundations. Rarely do such institutions systematically address religion and religious dimensions in their operational frameworks.

Nevertheless, religion and religious identity remain an integral part of life for the 84 percent of the world population (*The Global Religious Landscape*, 2012). In addition, there are many conflicts around the world in which religious identities and agencies have been manipulated to justify violence and other conflict dynamics. The chain of events surrounding the September 11 attacks in 2001 and its postattacks politics is only one example of such dynamics.

In response to this reality, faith-based organizations (FBOs) and other agencies have intensified their intervention efforts and advocacy to highlight the relevancy of making peace with faith. Such groups have endorsed the hypothesis that the sacredness and spirituality elements present in every religious identity are an asset for peacebuilding and inclusion, as opposed to violence and exclusion. The efforts of these practitioners and scholars are being channeled in building and strengthening the subfield of religious and interreligious peacebuilding.

Key insights: Attributes of religious and interreligious peacebuilding

As stated above, interreligious peacebuilding is an emerging field of scholarship and practice. It focuses on the role of religious actors, agencies, and stakeholders in any given conflict and on their attempts to promote deeper understanding and cooperation when responding to common or separate challenges on interpersonal, community, organizational, national, regional, or global levels.

For the purpose of this essay, the religious peacebuilding approach can be defined as: any type of efforts made by individuals or organizations *motivated by their faith values and belief systems* to jointly enhance their mutual understanding, trust, and cooperation.[1] This approach can be put in practice in violent conflict or in any other context. Such definition does not apply to those peacebuilding efforts that, bringing in people from different faith traditions, conduct intervention utilizing secular tools without any intentional consideration of the participants' faith identity.

It is not enough to bring Muslim and Christian together and classify such an encounter as an interreligious peacebuilding activity. While many of the secular interventions focus on the mechanics of peacebuilding and dialogue, the language of faith is absent from these meetings, and the space constructed by the practitioners or the convening agency is often framed as a place for learning technical skills and for the individual to become an agent of change divorced from his/her spirituality.

There are certain attributes or conditions which need to be in place for such category of intervention to be identified as interreligious peacebuilding. What makes it unique or distinct from secular or nonreligious peacebuilding are the following attributes:

Motivation

The participants take part in the activity because of their faith, religious affiliation, institutions, or belief systems. Thus, the act of participation is described by a Muslim participant as: "It is my duty to Allah and his commandment to do peace." However, this does not mean that the participants during the intervention will only focus on their faith or theological belief system; on the contrary, the majority of the interreligious peacebuilding intervention are focused on nontheological issues, that all community members have in common such as health, climate, governance, security, etc. The motivational aspect of interreligious peacebuilding is deeply connected to the ways in which the participants chose to express their faith while discussing daily issues and challenges faced by their communities.

Intentional integration of faith in the design

Similar to any other peacebuilding interventions, interreligious and religious peacebuilding (IRPB) have the typical components of any peacebuilding operation: preparation, design, intervention/implementation, monitoring and evaluation, follow up and sustainability. In the case of IRPB, the intervention is shaped/influenced by the religious identity or the participants' affiliations. Thus, the preparation, delivery, and follow-up of the intervention are rooted and affected by the faith of the participants. Even in the analysis stage, practitioners in such context need to be able to deal with possible responses to the question of what are the causes of the conflict, such as: "God caused it." In addition, in many cases there are participants who perceive the roles of conflict structures and systems (economic, political, social, etc.) as "secondary or earthly," as opposed to the primary cause of all events, a divine intervention.

The design should consider the interreligious dynamics of the conflict, for example when designing an intervention of interfaith dialogue between Muslim and Jews in Europe and focusing on their common issues as religious and ethnic minorities in such context, it is essential in the preparation stage that the intervention considers how each of the participants theologically perceives members of the other community. The articulation of these perceptions can also be an integral part of the interaction throughout the process. Similarly, when Hindu, Muslim, and Christian groups meet to discuss their common concerns in north Sri Lanka, their religious identity is not an obstacle to confronting their common concerns; on the contrary, it should be viewed as an asset that will facilitate the creation of their common bond.

The third-party role in the IRPB intervention is as important as in secular peacebuilding initiatives or settings

Unfortunately, there are cases in which the third party who conducts the intervention is afraid of introducing various aspects of the faith and religious identity of the participants. Thus, the facilitator, mediator, or convener avoid any mention of the faith identity or affiliation of the members despite the fact that participants might have no resistance to such an approach. It should be noted that, on the contrary, in many communities around the world, participants often expect to and they themselves frame conflict issues in a religious framework.

For example, in Sierra Leone when an international agency conducted a workshop between Muslim and Christians to address the common concern of integration of child soldiers in their communities in the postwar reality, the third party avoided any conversation on how Hinduism, Islam, and Christianity deal with this issue. At some point during the intervention, the participants themselves asked each other: how does your faith instruct you to deal with this issue?

For an intervention to consider IRPB, the third party intentionally creates sufficient space for faith and religious identities to be expressed and practiced to serve the purpose of peacebuilding. In fact, spirituality is considered an essential component of the intervention, with activities that include, for example, prayer, fasting, social justice, etc.

In IRPB, religious institutions and agencies constitute an integral part of the stakeholders and beneficiaries of the peacebuilding process. Such attributes can be reflected in the various phases of the project or intervention (selection of participants, plans of actions, measurement of success, etc.); however, it should be noted that this condition does not exclude the convening of individual participants in IRPB. People do not necessarily need to be institutionally affiliated in order to participate in IRPB. Even when third parties or implementers are operating based on a professional Results Based Management (RBM), in faith-based intervention participants can attribute their achievements to different sets of criteria of success, which are often framed by their spirituality. Some examples of this framing: participants stating that "we succeeded because we were blessed by God"; "I have become a better Muslim/Christian/Jewish/Buddhist/Hindu as a result of this peacebuilding work"; "I am achieving good peace"; or "emphasizing deep personal transformation, and individual spiritual growth and development."

In IRPB, the pedagogies, tools, and skills introduced and utilized in the intervention are also adapted and even rooted in the faith tradition and are not simple recycling of secular conflict resolution tools and approaches. For example, when conducting capacity building seminar/workshop/training on mediation and arbitration in Abrahamic setting, the design of the initiative and the third parties involved have to integrate questions such as: How did the prophets mediate and arbitrate conflicts? What does your faith say about mediation? What does it mean to listen in your faith?, etc. Thus, the training cannot be considered as IRPB if the main focus is on the question of: how secular diplomats, United Nations, or think-tanks leaders deliver mediation?

Obviously, there are many overlaps and commonalities between secular and religious peacebuilding in terms of intervention and ethics. The purpose of this section is not to create artificial boundaries between the two areas of practice. The objective is to clarify the few unique aspects of interreligious peacebuilding in order to assist practitioners and policymakers to better understand the dynamics of such intervention. This can also enhance our capacity to design and deliver peacebuilding intervention in such a context.

Although the above conditions and attributes attempted to define the uniqueness of the IRPB, the interreligious peacebuilding field has fuzzy boundaries, based on the faith and values of the participants or/and practitioners. During these past decades, the secular peacebuilding world has seen rapid growth and professionalization, while some religious peacebuilding networks have carried on using the same time-tested modus operandi. Therefore some assumptions are simply not shared. At the same time, these distinctions are not absolute, and the interconnections between religious and secular peacebuilding networks are growing rapidly. There is an increase in the faith-based peacebuilding organisztions that begun requesting and adopting professional methods of program development and integrating theories of change and other guiding frameworks into their operations. Thus, their challenge is how to keep the uniqueness of their faith identity in their operations (Garred & Abu-Nimer, 2018).

Internally, the field of interreligious peacebuilding has moved significantly in terms of outside/external legitimacy (less denial of the need to deal with religion and peace); however, there are many areas that are still in need for exploration and developments. For example, the development of academic journals and research agenda for interreligious peacebuilding is warranted. Furhter, there is need for more systematic and professional toolkits that policymakers and practitioners of secular peacebuilding can utilize when they wish to engage with religious actors and agencies in the field.

In terms of the secular peacebuilding field, interreligious peacebuilding actors and agencies are moving toward further linkages and integration; however, the path for such institutional linkages is still uncharted and requires further research and practice. The level of coordination and synchronization between these two areas of practice remains very limited at the levels of funding, opportunities for professional capacity building, development of theoretical frameworks for intervention, and the general research agenda (Abu-Nimer, 2020).

Interreligious peacebuilding and violent extremism: Trap and opportunity

Despite the historical evolution of politics, technology, and international relations, we continue to see systematic linkages between religion and political violence. Such linkages are often made by politicians as well as religious actors. In the past three decades, violent extremism and extremism in general have been often linked or correlated with religion and in particular Islamic faith and Muslim communities. As a result, it is essential to address the question of how interreligious peacebuilding responds to the issue of violent extremism. The next section explores this link between interreligious peacebuilding and countering or preventing violent extremism through the peace and justice lenses and not through security and intelligence frameworks.

Many governmental and nongovernmental agencies have invested a great deal of resources in counter-terrorism (CT), counter-violent extremism (CVE), and the prevention of violent extremism (PVE). Unfortunately, and despite the good intentions, many of these efforts approached the issue from a security and defense intelligence framework, this may have contributed to further stigmatization of religion and faith as a source of violence.

However, at the same time, religious identity as a source of peace and not only of violence and extremism has increasingly become an integral part of the efforts to counter and prevent violent extremism (CVE and PVE). While the association of religion with conflict has been strengthened due to post-Cold War dynamics (the rise of ethnic and religious identity conflicts within states and in interstate settings), the notion that religion should also be taken into consideration not only in conflict resolution but also in broader peacebuilding processes as a whole continues to gain weight.

In the past decade, the UN, like numerous other secular governmental and development actors, appears to be rediscovering the power of religion and of engaging local religious actors to improve the "reach" of its work. Secular partners who choose to increase their engagement with faith-based practitioners reflect a broad trend toward taking seriously the potentially constructive role that religion can play in building stronger social cohesion in divided societies (Garred & Abu-Nimer, 2018).

Thus, in the last two decades, religious identity and religion in general have been pushed in the center of the Western governments' public and political debate regarding violent extremism, refugees, migration, and political governance, especially in relations to conflict areas such as Afghanistan, Syria, Egypt, Yemen, etc. This process has resulted in growing interests in developing systematic and effective intervention frameworks to strengthen the role of religion and religious agencies in promoting peaceful coexistence, nonviolence, access to equal citizenship, and pluralism. Such efforts are being supported by governmental agencies, private donors, and foundations; additionally, interreligious organizations and FBOs continue to implement their activities on elite and grassroots levels. However, this relatively generous support is accompanied with a clear pressure of the intergovernmental and governmental organizations to engage with religious agencies on the specific agenda of countering terrorism, violent extremism, and only protecting rights of certain religious minorities. This approach puts at great risk the credibility and relevance of the FBOs and the greater field of interreligious peacebuilding. Practitioners both in direct violent conflict areas (both in Southern and Northern Hemispheres) run an even higher risk of credibility loss, especially among their local communities whose members already hold a deep suspicion of foreign governments, national policies or regimes, and civil society (Abu Nimer, 2020).

Types of intervention and challenges in engaging policymaking agencies

There is no doubt that greater engagement of policymakers with religious agencies is an important step in responding and including marginalized stakeholders, nevertheless, interreligious peacebuilders have to develop clearer terms of engagement and intervention frameworks to prevent instrumentalization and cooptation by the governments (Abu-Nimer 2017).

There are a number of core problems and limitations when responding to religious violent extremism from a nonreligious peacebuilding framework: first, when the intervention is founded on the basis of lack of sincere engagement with or even denial of religion and its identity components. This has been a programmatic limitation of many CVE/PVE initiatives. As a result, in most cases IGOs and government agencies have historically relied on secular international, regional, or local civil society entities to implement their programs (Abu-Nimer & Kadayifci, 2008). Denying the need for positive, constructive engagement of religious actors has been, until recently, a characteristic of many international policy agencies (Abu-Nimer 2003; Appleby, 2000; Gopin, 2000).[2]

Not recognizing the need to engage religious agencies is largely due to the fact that most organizations operate within secular or nonreligious governance frameworks. As a result, their officers and managers are not aware of the need to engage religious leaders in the community. When they design their programs, they therefore tend to build partnerships with secular civil society groups and professionals, who share with them the same secular ideological assumptions of promoting diversity, human rights and sustainable development.

Second, beyond the lack of awareness, there is a basic sense of resistance toward engaging religious leaders by policy and development practitioners, who are themselves secular and believe that religion and religious institutions should be confined to their primary function of providing theological and spiritual services to communities. In fact, many would argue that any engagement beyond these parameters constitutes a violation of the principle of separation of church and state. When such an approach is taken while designing an intervention, the authentic read of the local context, including major players and power relations is missing from the analysis and intervention.

Third, lack of religious and interreligious literacy among secular policymaking circles: due to the nature of the relationship between church and state systems, public socialization agencies avoid dealing with religious belief systems and spirituality. In northern Hemisphere communities contexts, students and adults have no opportunity to formally learn even the basics religious or interreligious literacy about other faith groups or even their own faith traditions. Therefore, often officers who work with major donors and development agencies have very limited tools, lack them completely, or have only a basic understanding of the role of religion and religious agencies and their complex and diverse structure in any given society. Obviously without such basic literacy it is very challenging to constructively engage with religious actors and their institutions.

Fourth, on the other hand, religious agencies themselves are in need to acquire basic skills and understanding of the world of policymaking and its complex dynamics and processes. The overwhelming majority of religious leaders and agencies lack such opportunities to gain this needed knowledge and skills.

Overcoming the above challenges is the first step in setting up a constructive and cooperative engagement between these two agencies in any given society or setting. In addition, these challenges dictate in many cases the nature and scope of the relationship between interreligious peacebuilding and policymakers.

In the past decade, a wide range of examples can illustrate the ongoing process of overcoming the above forms of resistance for mutual engagement within policymakers and religious agencies, the section below explores several selective initiatives that focus on the role of religion in responding to global challenges such as climate change, violent extremism, and health.

The Network for Religious and Traditional Peacemakers (n.d.) was launched by the Finnish foreign ministry and in collaboration with Finn Church Aid (FCA) with strong support the UN Mediation Support Unit of the Department of Political Affairs and the UN Alliance of Civilization. The network core group includes organizations such as Religions for Peace (RFP), the Organization of Islamic Cooperation (OIC); the United States Institute for Peace (USIP) and KAICIID (King Abdullah Centre for Interreligious and Intercultural Dialogue). With almost 50 different partners who work on religion and peacebuilding, the Network managed to develop a number of initiatives to advocate for a greater role for religious leaders in peacebuilding in various region, in particular in the Central African Republic (CAR), Nigeria, and Myanmar. Additionally, the mere fact that UN bodies such as the Mediation Unit and the Alliance of Civilization have supported the foundation of a network, which also counts on the collaboration of an additional five UN bodies indicates a greater interest and willingness of the greater international community to explore ways to engage the religious agencies in peacemaking processes. In addition to the above-mentioned country-specific work, the network's most recent endeavors include training on Religion and Mediation, projects on inclusivity such as a woman on the frontline retreat in South-Sudan with the Anglican Church, and research—most recently with the USIP on inclusive peace processes in Libya, the Philippines, and Myanmar.

The Partnership for Religion and Sustainable Development (PaRD), launched by the German government in 2016, is another network of governments, multilateral organizations, faith-based organizations (FBOs) and development agencies who work on advocating for consistent and institutional engagement of religious agencies by governmental and secular development and relief agencies. PaRD focuses its work on three UN Sustainable Development Goals (SDGs): SDG 16 (Sustaining Peace), SDG 5 (Gender, Equality and Empowerment), and SDG 3 (Health). In addition to the network's focus areas, the PaRD governance structure itself displays an immense amount of interest and collaboration on the intersection of religion and development, as well as religion and peacebuilding. The network is governed through an elected steering group comprising governments, international organizations and faith-based organizations. An international secretariat is supported by the Deutsche Gesellschaft für International Zusammenarbeit (GIZ), the German Federal ministry for Economic Cooperation and Development (BMZ), and the United States Agency for International Development (USAID). A decade ago, a network governed by a triumvirate of three vastly diverse entities dealing with the topic of religion and peace and development would have hardly been imaginable. Yet, the strong governmental and multilateral interest of engagement, collaboration, and cooperation with numerous faith-based organizations shows a strong shift in this direction. Three years since its inception, PaRD membership has grown over 100 members. Based upon the focus areas of PaRD members, the network has established three working streams that correspond with the three SDGs above. Regardless of the challenges that face PaRD launching and identifying its action plan, the Network mere existence illustrates the growing need for a shared space to connect policymakers, donors, FBOs, and secular development agencies.

The Faith Advisory Council to the UN Inter-Agency Task Force on Religion and Development is a newly created forum that aims to provide the various UN agencies with input and guidance on ways to engage with religious actors and agencies. The Advisory Council includes around 40 members and is chaired by KAICIID (KAICIID Secretary General Bin Muaammar to cochair the Faith Advisory Council of the United Nations Interagency Taskforce on Religion and Development, 2018) and Finn Church Aid (Finn Church Aid's Board Chair Tarja Kantola to cochair the Faith-Based Advisory Council of the United Nations Interagency Task Force on Religion and Development, 2018). The group is hosted by the UN Inter Agency Taskforce on Religion and Development. This advisory group has also focused on identifying ways to enhance the advocacy efforts and impact of religious actors on policymakers. Their plan of action reflects a greater ambition to raise the awareness and utility or effectiveness of religious actors in advancing peace and sustainable development in collaboration with policymakers.

In another important gesture, in 2018 the Organization for Security and Co-operation in Europe (OSCE) commissioned a policy paper to guide its engagement with religious actors (McDonagh, 2018). The report provided several recommendations, among which the creation of an advisory group to assist the various OSCE agencies in engaging with religious leaders (McDonagh, 2018, p. 25). The report also recommends that such a structure be considered to be long term and not an ad hoc structure with a one-time mandate. Despite the above important steps, actors in both the peacebuilding and development fields as a whole have been slow to engage with religious agencies largely because of their secular frameworks and the principle of separating "Church and State." This is a trend that was neither unique to one area of peacebuilding, nor development, but has also been the case with programs on citizenship, democracy, education, and post-conflict resolution to name a few (Abu-Nimer, 2003, 2017; Abu-Nimer & Kadayifci, 2008).

In the past, these frameworks have resulted in not only a lack of engagement, but in many cases have constituted engagement with religious agencies and the incorporation of religion into programmatic structures to be a general taboo. Nevertheless, the recent trend is to explore ways to engage with religious actors.

Mapping the types of engagement with religious agencies in peacebuilding intervention

There is no doubt that the engagement of religious agencies in peacebuilding is an essential step in a successful intervention while responding to any issue facing diverse communities. As in other areas, the process of engaging FBOs and religious agencies in the field of international peacebuilding and policymaking, including CVE/PVE, is evolving from denial toward a more integrative approach, which could be described as one fundamental necessity of a transformative approach. These steps are as follows:

1 *Instrumentalized ("token") engagement:* In response to the pressure exerted on the centers of power (supporters of hegemonic discourse and/or dominant majority institutions) to include women and ethnic and racial minorities, new but slow steps of engagement were taken. The early steps were mostly in the form of symbolic involvement of gender, racial minorities and now religious agencies or paying lip service to peacebuilding discourse (the token minority representative syndrome) through programs that highlight only the harmonious and ritualistic features of the relations and avoid any structural aspects of the conflict.
2 *Compartmentalization:* The dominant discourse and its institutions partially recognize gender analysis, racial and ethnic perspectives, peace and conflict analysis, etc. as relevant or necessary frameworks. During this phase, the institutions might even allocate resources or personnel to handle race, ethnicity, gender, or peace, while continuing business as usual in the remaining units or in the dominant institutional culture. Academic or policy institutions thus create ethnic, racial, gender, or peace studies departments. However, the primary paradigm and its operational structure continue to exist in the dominant group's norms. The racial, ethnic, minorities-sensitive structure continues to be exclusive in its functions.[3]
3 *Integration:* Some institutions have moved from the compartmentalization phase to the integration phase, in which ethnic, racial, gender, or peacebuilding frameworks and lenses have become an integral part of the structure. Their affiliation is no longer an obstacle to their integration or advancement in the structure. This means that academic and policy institutes have adopted ethnic, gender, racial, etc., analysis as an integral part of their framework and operation (Abu-Nimer, 2018).[4]

As seen above, there are three stages toward the complete integration of engagement with religious agencies: (1) instrumentalization, which is largely reflected by symbolic engagement; (2) compartmentalization, which encompasses the creation of specialized departments or experts on the issue of religion and peacebuilding; and (3) integration, which entails the incorporation of religion and the analysis of religion as a key part of all operations (Abu-Nimer, 2017). For the full process, see Figure 13.1.

While more and more organizations are recognizing the need to engage religious actors and institutions, as well as to understand the role of religion in peacebuilding processes, many are still very much at the symbolic stage, where they invite religious leaders to speak at events or appear in programs to display their involvement in peacebuilding processes. However, the secular peacebuilding actors working on religion and peacebuilding or religion and development in an integrative manner can be used as an example for more institutionalized and sustainable ways of engagement. One such example is the work that is being done by certain governmental agencies of Switzerland, Finland, and Germany. Whether we look at development or peacebuilding, the Swiss FDFA, German GIZ, and the Finnish government's support

Interreligious peacebuilding

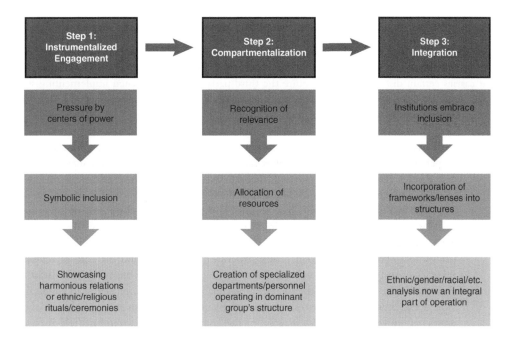

Figure 13.1 Mapping the types of engagement with religious agencies in peacebuilding intervention
Source: Abu-Nimer, 2017, p. 8.

of both Finn Church Aid and the Network for Traditional and Religious Peacemakers, these governments are analyzing the role of religion in conflict and development, and involving religious actors and institutions at various stages of their project phases. As stated above, there are increasingly intergovernmental actors that have moved toward the integration of faith-based organizations and religious actors in their work.

The UN Office on the Prevention of Genocide and the Responsibility to Protect partnered with faith-based and interreligious organizations including the KAICIID Dialogue Centre, the Network for Religious and Traditional Peacemakers and the World Council of Churches in the creation of a two-year-long process that involved more than 200 religious leaders and actors worldwide in developing a global Plan of Action for Religious Leaders and Actors to Counter Hate Speech that could incite to violence.[5] The United Nations Population Fund developed a report that analyzed the gap between faith-based actors and the United Nations, which has resulted in the establishment of an interagency task force for engagement with faith-based organizations (Karam 2016). In addition to the establishment of the Task Force, the drive for an enhancement of partnerships between faith-based organizations and multilateral organizations has most recently initiated an advisory body of more than 50 faith-based and interreligious organizations, which aims at strengthening collaboration between these highly different types of entities and establishes a standing advisory body for UN agencies to be able to learn how to better partner with FBOs to enhance their work. Furthermore, there is the ongoing UN Strategic Learning Exchange, which is a peer learning exchange between UN staff and faith-based actors, which consists of workshops for representatives of FBOs, multilateral organizations and governments, and whose aim is learning how to work together and enhance existing partnerships (Abu-Nimer, 2020).

Implications for policy and practitioners

As discussed earlier, the art of interreligious peacebuilding is not totally different from any peacebuilding intervention, on the contrary it overlaps and they have many commonalities. Yet it carries certain distinctions that require the third party to consider when implementing such processes. In designing and implementing interreligious peacebuilding programmes, there are several guidelines to keep in mind, such as:

1. *De-religionize the relationship* and the conflict among participants. Conflicts are caused and perpetuated by multiparty forces. It is rare that a conflict is driven and shaped by one driver only. Thus, it is not accurate or useful to exclusively explain and frame a conflict by religious identity or theological differences. Religion and religious actors do not operate in a social or political vacuum. There are many other actors who contribute to the process and outcome of a conflict. In addition, often participants discover many commonalities between them when they jointly engage in multifactor analysis of their conflicts or relationships. *Delve deeper* into analyzing structures of violence and the role of religious agencies in sustaining them and not only simple exploration of the symptoms. Insist on analysis of the root causes of the interreligious relationship problems. Thus, in countering violent extremism, it becomes essential not to Islamize the analysis and the solution of the problems. For example, *de Islamization* of the counter-violent extremism field is an essential reframing step that conveners and the third party have to engage in in order to gain credible entry in any given Muslim community.

2. *De-securitize the conflict analysis and the proposed solutions:* Interreligious tension and conflicts cannot be fully resolved and peacefully reconciled if the approach to counter violent extremism is solely founded and devised on the principle of defense, intelligence, and security. Maybe this approach is effective in developing short-term and immediate response to the threat of violence, but in the long term such approaches contribute to communal divisions and harm the social fabric of local communities. When working in interreligious peacebuilding, *adopt human security lenses* by using a human security framework instead of the narrow military and Realist security framework. Human security strategies and analytical frameworks can assist in preventing the silencing and manipulation of communities through the security-driven agenda of counter-religious terrorism or violent extremism. It is a more constructive approach if based on and driven by the needs and faith of the interreligious and religious local communities.

3. Instead of using lenses of security, threats, and fears, *integrate a "culture of peace" discourse*. Allocating a programmatic space for a "culture of peace" discourse injects optimism and human connectedness. The interreligious peacebuilding network is an integral part of the global movement and actions to achieve a culture of peace and challenge the Realist paradigm that assumes selfishness, competition, and violence as a necessary part of human nature.

4. *Follow the principle of inclusivity* in representation by insisting on multireligious and multi-intrafaith group designs. In any given conflict that has a religious dimension, there is a complex web of religious stakeholders, thus there are many religious entities and representations in each region which need to be included in the process.

5. *Integrate spirituality and faith language* in the program design and framing of the intervention. Adopt a language of faith as a way to capture the spirit of the initiative. Using mainly technical and mechanical or security approaches to peace and conflict resolution affects religious leaders' credibility. When interreligious peacebuilders avoid their own language

of faith, derived from their spiritual and religious traditions, they lose part of their constituency. For example, when we invite religious leaders to work on a specific project related to health or women's/girls' education, we should not shy away from integrating an intentional space for prayer or other rituals. But conveners can go beyond symbolic integration and systematically bring the spiritual dimension of the participants' identity.

6 *Provide space for religious actors to utilize their religious rituals and sacred texts* to enhance the comprehension, motivation or application of the program in their communities. For many secular donors this means finding a way to resolve any governmental policies that stipulate strict conditions on working with one faith group or on using scripture.

7 *Include space for intrareligious dialogue* and platforms that focus on internal and critical examination of the current and historical religious interpretations that facilitate peacebuilding and cooperation, and denounce the justification of violence. Often there are intrafaith challenges that prevent or obstruct peaceful change and engagement with outsiders. Intrafaith forums can be a tool to avoid the classic limitation of "preaching to the converted," by allowing the inclusion of less moderate voices, in particular those who oppose dialogue with outsiders.

8 *Adopt an institutional approach* instead of creating "individual stars": The hierarchical and authoritative nature of many religious institutions can be a unique feature that often impedes the capacity of the participants and partners to fully engage with the policymakers and development agencies without the full endorsement of their highest authorities. Seeking endorsement is thus a first step to ensure institutional and sustained impact.

9 *Start with the obvious interreligious commonalities:* Build the relationship and engagement on a strong foundation of assurance that all religious and spiritual traditions in general have positive values, especially that the main messages of all faiths emphasize peace and justice. Skipping this step weakens the participants' capacity and space to constructively confront and overcome their mutual suspicion, skepticism, and grievances.

10 *Start from within the faith groups:* Members of the faith community are the expert on their faith, not the outside third party. For sustainable change to take place in interreligious peacebuilding it is necessary to be from within rather than being a third-party agent imposing external religious interpretations or framing.

11 *Keep it real:* When interfaith and faith-based representatives and policymakers meet, they often like to emphasize a discourse of harmony based on the notion that there is or was strong and peaceful coexistence between religions in the context. This tendency to avoid discussion of controversial issues, especially those relating to national policies regarding religious freedom, self-determination, etc., can damage the authenticity of the program for participants who are affected by the conflict on a daily basis.

12 *Develop practical interreligious peacebuilding tools* that can respond effectively to challenges when dealing with policy officers and programmers who lack basic religious literacy, causing them to be tense and apprehensive when asked to approach or engage religious agencies. Building tools and frameworks that reflect the uniqueness of interreligious peacebuilding, can bridge this gap.

Conclusion

Religion and spirituality are integral parts of human interactions. All civilizations through human history have included some forms of spiritual dimensions. Religious identities and belief systems will continue to guide people's ways of relating to each other and to their environments. Thus, it is not possible to avoid the question of how faith identity can support peacemaking. The answer to this is being gradually developed through the emerging field of religion and interreligious peacebuilding.

Like other peacebuilding frameworks and approaches, interreligious peacebuilding is about the art of engagement with one's own and others' faith groups. Overcoming the resistance to engage with those agencies and actors that are different and even opposing to one's faith becomes the first step that interreligious peacebuilding has to deal with.

Our human, social, political, and cultural structures are still in the process of experimenting with different modalities of handling religious identity in public and private settings. For example, policymakers and religious agencies around the world are still struggling to find a healthy and balanced formula to work together and constructively engage in ways that allow the potentially positive role of religious agencies to fully materialize in an independent governance system and bridge the divide between secular and religious approaches to governance. It is difficult to point out to one ideal and effective system in constructively managing interreligious and religious relationships, especially in conflict areas.

Nevertheless, new opportunities and pathways are being explored on national, regional, and global levels for how to engage religious agencies in responding to current challenges facing our humanity. Such efforts are crucial for contributing to the development of peaceful, diverse, and just systems of human relations. Interreligious peacebuilding is one of these promising pathways.

Notes

1 Another proposed definition of "faith-based peacebuilding": interactive peacebuilding process in which one or more of the parties is motivated or influenced by religious identity or experience. It is important to pay attention to some ways in which Westernized notions of religion may limit our understanding of religion in peacebuilding (notion of "religion," "faith," and "spirituality"). Faith-based peacebuilders (both practitioners and participants) believe in a form of spiritual reality that transcends the material world, and that belief can have a profound effect on the way that they do peacebuilding. (See further details on the debates of defining faith peacebuilding in Garred & Abu-Nimer, 2018).
2 This section is based on an earlier work that examine in more details the implications of counter-terrorism and a violent extremism approach on Muslim communities and on the field of peacebuilding and possible ways to engage with religious peacebuilding agencies in dealing with such challenges (Abu-Nimer, 2018).
3 Between 2014 and 2017, the author facilitated over 25 consultations with policymakers and religious leaders in the context of UN, EU, OSCE, African Union, and various government agencies. In each of these settings, religious leaders wondered whether the recent intense increase in policymakers' interest in engaging religious agencies to support their fight against VE would become an institutional commitment to work with the religious agencies on other issues, building long-term partnerships that could contribute to the transformation of troubled and complicated relationships between secular and religious stakeholders and their respective institutions.
4 The institutional implications of such transformation are the fundamental changes in the balance of power, decision-making centers, representation on boards, allocation of resources, public discourse, etc.
5 The Plan of Action was adopted by the UN Secretary General on July 14, 2017.

References

Abu-Nimer, M. (2003). *Nonviolence and peacebuilding in Islam: Theory and practice*. University of Florida Press.

Abu-Nimer, M. (2017). Alternative approaches to transforming violent extremism: The case of Islamic peace and interreligious peacebuilding. In B. Austin & H. J. Glessmann (Eds.), *Transformative approaches to violent extremism*, Berghof Dialogue Handbook Series No. 13 (pp. 1–20). Berhof Foundation. http://image.berghof-foundation.org/fileadmin/redaktion/Publications/Handbook/Dialogues/dialogue13_violentextremism.pdf

Abu-Nimer, M. (2018). *Alternative approaches to transforming violent extremism*. Berghof Foundation.
Abu-Nimer, M. (2020). Religion in peacebuilding: An emerging force for change. In J. Mitchell, L. Orr, M. Percy & F. Po (Eds.), *Companion to religion and peace*. Wiley Blackwell.
Abu-Nimer, M., & Kadayifci, A. (2008). Muslim peacebuilding actors in Africa and the Balkans. *Peace and Change: A Journal of Peace Research*, *33*(4), 549–581.
Alliance of Peacebuilding. (n.d.). https://www.allianceforpeacebuilding.org/
Appleby, R. S. (2000). *The ambivalence of the sacred: Religion, violence, and reconciliation*. Rowman & Littlefield.
Finn Church Aid. (2018.) *Finn Church Aid's Board Chair Tarja Kantola to co-chair the Faith-Based Advisory Council of the United Nations Interagency Task Force on Religion and Development*. https://www.kirkonulkomaanapu.fi/en/latest-news/news/finn-church-aids-board-chair-tarja-kantola-to-co-chair-the-faith-based-advisory-council-of-the-united-nations-interagency-task-force-on-religion-and-development/
Garred, M., & Abu-Nimer, M. (Eds.). (2018). *Making peace with faith*. Rowman & Littlefield.
Gopin, M. (2000). *Between Eden and Armageddon: The future of world religions, violence, and peacemaking*. Oxford.
International Partnership on Religion and Sustainable Development, PaRD. (n.d.). http://www.partner-religion-development.org
KAICIID. (2018). *KAICIID Secretary General Bin Muaammar to co-chair the Faith Advisory Council of the United Nations Interagency Taskforce on Religion and Development*. https://www.kaiciid.org/news-events/news/kaiciid-secretary-general-bin-muaammar-co-chair-faith-advisory-council-united
Karam, A. (Ed.). (2016). *Realizing the faith dividend: Religion, gender, peace and security in agenda 2030*. United Nations Population Fund.
McDonagh, P. (2018). *Religion and security-building in the OSCE context: Involving religious leaders and congregations in joint efforts*. OSCE.
Peace and Development Network. (n.d.). https://pcdn.global/
The Global Religious Landscape. (2012). Pew Research Center. https://www.pewforum.org/2012/12/18/global-religious-landscape-exec/
The Network for Religious and Traditional Peacemakers. (n.d.). https://www.peacemakersnetwork.org

14
THE LAUGHTER THAT KNOWS THE DARKNESS: THE MAMAS' RESISTANCE TO ANNIHILATIVE VIOLENCE IN WEST PAPUA

Julian Smythe

Background

Totalitarian systems are systems which intentionally dismantle identity (Arendt, 1958; Fontaine, 2010), replacing communal or clan identity with the identity of either citizens or "others" (Marchak, 2003). Effective citizenship in totalitarian systems requires that there be an "other" against which the dominant group can define itself (Marchak, 2003). The philosophy behind a totalitarian system is to erase the bonds that connect to each other and to this undesirable "other."

Genocide is the most extreme form of this system where both the physical and cultural identities of the "other" are disappeared (see Lemkin in Power, 2002). This can be seen in Stalinist Russia, Nazi Germany, West Papua, Cambodia, and in colonial Canada and the United States (Fontaine, 2010; Power, 2002; Rutherford, 2012).

Architects of such a system, termed bureaucrats and secret agents (Arendt, 1958), follow no law but the law of expansion; hold no commitment to anything except expansion; becoming hidden gods who create and sustain the system of expansion. Arendt (1958) lays out the way in which the law of never-ending expansion underlies empire that unroots the bureaucrat and the secret agent from place, from human laws, and from relationship.

This othering discourse combined with the law of expansion is central to systems, such as totalitarianism, that seek to remove people and the idea of people for the sake of acquiring land and wealth. It is here that annihilation, "act of reducing to nonexistence" (Harper, 2020), comes in. Annihilative violence does not honor the other with the emotion to hate. Annihilative violence seeks to reduce the other to nonexistence, as if that group was never there, as if people were never there. That the land and resources may be taken.

Nowhere are annihilative systems, the devastating expansion of empire against an inhuman other, more visible than in the lives and deaths of Indigenous peoples, especially post Portuguese maritime expansion. Disease and direct and indirect violence resulted in the physical erasure of Indigenous peoples. Other forms of violence intentionally crafted to remove identity have also been in place. These include residential schools, removal of food sources, removal of land, forbidding of the use of language, songs, dances, even "potlach" from whence we get our seemingly innocuous celebration of community and eating together, the potluck (Cole & Chaikin, 1990). Lemkin explained that genocide includes both physical and cultural erasure (Assembly, 1948).

Theodore Fontaine (2010) tells of residential schools in Canada which not merely physically abused, but more potently abused identity, attempting to eradicate the Indian from the child. Identity abuse, or attack on the inner life was, he states, more difficult to overcome than an attack on the physical or sexual self (see also internalized oppression discussed by Fanon, 1965). Leaders of totalitarian bureaucracies knew this, and their efforts resulted in what Arendt terms a "radical efficiency" through which "the inner spontaneity of people under its rule was killed along with their social and political activities, so that the merely political sterility under the older bureaucracies was followed by total sterility under totalitarian rule" (Arendt, 1958, p. 245). This is the golden bullet of totalitarian rule. And it is this golden bullet which the Mamas counteract in West Papua—the internal passivity imparted by totalitarian bureaucracy. Although the physical removal of persons through killing cannot be reversed, the way that a community in the throes of being "othered" for purposes of removal from existence remembers, mourns, and comes together around such action is the way that they continually assert identity in the face of annihilation.

Context: West Papua and the Mamas

West Papua

Indigenous West Papuans have experienced systemic erasure or annihilation since 1962 (International, 2013; Kirksey, 2002). The exotic othering of the New Guinea native/cannibal (Banivanua-Mar, 2008) for the sake of annihilation is unrivaled in current discourse.

The provinces of Papua and Papua Barat make up the Indonesian half of the island of New Guinea. Culturally, its Indigenous people identify with Melanesia. About half of its population is Indonesian settlers from other islands.

Because of its remoteness, Papua largely escaped Dutch colonialism, but during the Cold War, it became a pawn in play between China/Russia and the United States. Underlying the interest in the region was its unparalleled natural resources, including oil, gold, nickel, and natural gas (Poulgrain & Wardaya, 2015). Papua was sought for what lay beneath its land. Its people were inconsequential.

The richness of Papuan resources resulted in political machinations to gain Papua (ultimately Indonesia did) and in military campaigns the removal of Papuans. The violence included bombing campaigns, chemical warfare, forced removal, and imprisonment—resulting in the deaths of between tens and hundreds of thousands of Papuans from 1962 to the present (Elmslie & Webb-Gannon, 2013). What was under the ground put Papuans in the ground.

The Papuan response has been an ongoing movement of identity: Scholar Eben Kirksey (2002) writes, "Amid campaigns of state violence, West Papuans embraced the sort of hope that arises only in times of complete hopelessness ... Indigenous activists began to find small cracks in the architecture of power" (p. xiii). Although the Land of West Papua has never known political freedom, the Papuan people are "already sovereign as a people" (Webster, 2001–2002, p. 598). David Webster (2002) contends that while a nation state has never existed, an ideological "notion-state" has been present for over 50 years—a state which holds the land of Papua in the consciousness of its people (see Anderson, 2001).

It's here that the Mamas come in. They guard life and keep identity going in Papua.

What is a Mama?

"Women are the guardians of life." Ibu Noreen tells me. "These words must be spoken, Julian. Men hold the power and women hold life" (personal communication, January 15, 2014).

Ibu Noreen further describes her Mamaness to her students: "You are my children. That is why I am angry now. Because you are not doing everything that you can do. I am your Mama" (Ibu Noreen, personal communication, April 11, 2013).

"Mama means someone who is close to us, Julian. Who will be there if we need something," says Rev. Morgana. "A Mama is someone who will feed the neighborhood children. Who has her door open" says her mother, Mama Koinonia.

A Mama is someone who is called Mama. The neighborhood children, the young people, will eventually start calling a woman Mama when they feel she is close to them. That she is there for them, to listen to their stories, to share food, to offer comfort and advice (Rev. Morgana, personal communication, May 5, 2014).

The participants are a self-identified group of Mamas working together to care for each member in situations of economic, domestic, and political duress (Wospakrik et al., 2015). Women (or Mamas, as they are known in the community) living in a parish in Lincoln City (not its real name) vary in age from mid-20s to late 60s. Most are married with children, grandchildren, and/or other children that they care for. Many have husbands absented by violence.

The Mamas have strategies of life and identity within a system of annihilative violence. I would like to focus here on three that touch annihilation most closely. These are breaking the silence—telling stories of the suffering; laughter and celebration within the suffering; and *perjuangan*, a hard work that strives through struggle to care for family and community.

Key insights

The effectiveness of the Mamas resides in their maintenance of identity, their will to maintain connections, and their ability to say, in the face of systems of annihilation, "We are still here" (Fontaine, 2010). The Mamas' humor, voice and agency allow them to resist totalitarian rule by maintaining their own stories and identity. Through creativity, they "detourne" (Swedenburg, 2004) each act of annihilation, as trickster traditions—"the uncertain humor of shadow survivance that den[y] the obscure manoeuvres of manifest manners, tragic transvaluations, and the incoherence of cultural representation"—do (Vizenor, 1993, pp. 7–8, see also King, 2010, for North American trickster stories).

Silence is the first step of terror, and countering the silence, even in small ways, is the first act of affirming the reality, the existence of the person who is no more. Breaking the silence of the violence, telling the stories, even stories of death, affirms the connection of a loved one and to others who have known loss. Hannah Arendt speaks of terror's ability to "atomize" or to break apart the me from the we. This isolation, this living the suffering in silence, is horror itself. "It is the breaking apart of what it means to be human ... love is gone" (Erickson & Jones, 2002, p. 147). In not only the telling, but in the communal celebration of love for one who has died, the Mamas find the power to overcome this atomization to become "we" once more. This is their work. This is their *perjuangan*.

List of cases

I called Mama Koinonia yesterday, and she answered with joy. She stated that her son Ferdinand was marrying Agnes whom he has loved for seven years. And she asked me the question she always asks,

"Julian, when will you come back?" When I joined the community in Lincoln City as a woman alone, all my neighbors, but particularly Mama Koinonia, invited me to "story" with them (The Papuan word *"cerita"* or "story" serves as both a noun and a verb). Mama Koinonia told me that in the afternoon, we are to leave our doors open (she did qualify that if soldiers are present, doors are allowed to be closed), and as people come, we drink tea and we "story" together. And so, one lonely afternoon, remembering Mama's words, I walked across the yard between our houses (Mama Lula's yard) and stood on the edge of her porch wondering if I was welcome, until the dogs found me, and their barking drew the family to the terrace. Then we engaged in acts of communal connection. We sat and we drank tea. We laughed at the grandchildren. But it did not end there.

We heard the cries coming from next door as Mama Lula and her son screamed at each other. We sat, silent, holding our teacups and listening for an escalation into physical violence that, this day at least, did not come. Not long after, Mama Lula, dressed in Sunday clothes, slowly walked through the hedge to join us. Her face carried the torment of drunken sons. Her eyes, the quiet hunger of granddaughters. Her face mirrored grief—as if a smile would betray the stories carried in that bit of sacred skin that was her face. But it was the way she carried this face that I will remember. Her head was high, her chin strong, and her face held the grief that her land and nation and family lived. She held this grief with dignity, sitting like a queen in Mama Koinonia's rattan chair, gazing, head high at the road and the soldiers and the vegetable vendors selling on the street because Papuans do not merit market space. We sat with her as she carried the grief of her land in every muscle of her face. We handed her a cup of tea, and we watched the motorcycles and military convoys and mosquitos going by.

During my time in Papua, the tea and intentional acts of story and connection that the Mamas invited those around them into was characterized by a laughter and a togetherness which could be called celebration. But Mama Lula's face and Mama Koinonia's quiet, knowing acceptance of her suffering adds another facet to the celebration. Benny Giay, Papuan activist and writer has captured the desperate, grief-filled elegance in Mama Lula's face. Giay says that we must "celebrate the suffering" (personal conversation, August, 2007). And I feel that the Mamas' stand against annihilation does this. For it is for celebration and for mourning that the Mamas come together, and it is into these spaces that they invite their families and community members who are still there.

The Mamas explain below some of their own experiences of suffering, interspersed with their tales of strength. I have gathered them here that we may hear them together, and as you read, perhaps you will see, like I did, the pathways by which the Mamas' journey and *berjuang* through suffering to strength. A journey of *perjuangan* that travels through pain and survives.

The implications for teaching and training and for practice and policy arise out of the Mamas stories. For the sake of clarity, I have divided the implications elicited from the stories into three thematic sections. These are breaking the silence, suffering and laughter, and *perjuangan*/hard work. I will present their stories here and then explicate the implications at the end of each section.

Breaking the silence

Mama Viki: "Don't stay alone with your burdens"

Mama Viki a childless widow who runs a kiosk. She lives with her sister Mama Tika, and cares for her nieces and nephews and many others. Mama Viki is also a deaconess at the church and quietly cares for many parishioners in this role. A woman who has faced many of her own sufferings, Mama Viki speaks about the difficulty of parishioners who bear their suffering alone.

Because they don't want to share. Their thoughts and feelings, you see, are hidden. They must tell stories, but the stories are the same. We see people who <u>can</u> (*bisa*), and we tell our stories, and they help us, and give us a path, right? But don't tell your stories to someone who hears and then immediately tells someone else. All of this, it is also something that, in our home, our thoughts can become a burden, you see. So, I go out. I gather with other women. For worship. We walk together. Don't stay alone. With your burdens (*pikiran*) [Mama laughs...]. If there's a problem, don't hold onto it yourself. We must learn much. Papuan women learn many things from others. Don't stay silent. Don't stay silent and alone. Where will you learn?[1]

Mama's phone rings. She unzips her purse. It is one of the many children she has cared for calling her from university on another island. Mama's face lights up. She answers, "My beloved, how are you?"

Mama Josefina: "The first time I set foot in the city of Sorrow[2] it was embracing the corpse of my son"

I thought for the longest time that Oliver was Mama Josefina's only son, but she explained one Sunday afternoon as we sat on a screened porch eating bananas and drinking hot chocolate that Oliver had once had an older brother. Below, Mama Josefina tells of a journey, in which she tried to save her sick child and ended up clutching him dead to her chest as she waited for her ship to arrive in port.[3] Here is Mama Josefina's story.

And then he grew ill, a hernia, I think. I called his father, "What do I do?" The pediatrician was in another city. They gave me a referral and I brought him by ship. We intended to go to Sorrow city [...] to the pediatrician, you see. But he died on the ship. At that time, Ibu Tutalatty[4]—we were together on the ship. Ibu Tutalatty, because my child was sick, brought us to the ship attendants [and Mama Josefina was placed in the infirmary with her child]. Not with Ibu Tutalatty.

Finally, the little one, he died. I was alone with just him there. And so, the first time I set foot in the city of Sorrow, it was embracing the corpse of my son.

And so, the passengers disembarked on one gangplank. One gangplank was kept for me—to go to the ambulance that they had already called to come. But where would I go? It was far, and expensive. But there was a younger brother of my husband. He has passed away now. Ahh, his [her husband's] birth brother (*adik kandung*). But he saw me sitting in the ambulance, and he ran. He chased us, because in the city of Sorrow, the hospital and the harbor are near, and so he chased the ambulance. When he arrived, he saw that I was the one getting out [...] and he wept. The child was already dead.

They [her husband's younger brother and family] prepared their house, and we went there.

I wrote about it—my experience with Oliver's older brother when he died on the ship—some of it in the form of poems, some in the form, in the form of regular descriptions [...]. Before, when Oliver's brother died, I returned from Sorrow to City B by ship. From there, I wrote poems about that story. But from then until now, I write poems. Because those ideas that I share, it's important that I write them.

Mama discovered her love of writing through this experience and shares her dream for her future where she can continue to write, and where she can live simply.

Implications for teaching and training

From Mama Viki, we learn that telling the story helps reduce burdens—sharing the load with others so we are not alone. From Mama Josefina, we learn how sharing through writing, even in loneliness is one way to survive through the darkness. When we teach and train practitioners who live or work in locations where annihilative violence is present, the telling of personal stories of suffering or of listening to stories of others' suffering remembers during the dismembering of violence (Cavanaugh, 2007). When training and teaching, providing spaces and time for stories to be told allows practitioners to practice both the telling of their own stories of suffering and listening to the stories of others (Lederach, 1996).

Implications for practice

The telling of such stories—the breaking of the silence as presented by Mama Josefina and Mama Viki—is vital to the survival of connection to others and to the one who has been lost. However, those who receive the stories, as Mama Viki reminds us, must receive them with care. Kathe Weingarten's (2003) compassionate witnessing, characterized by listening and responding from our connection with another provides a model to respond to stories of violence and suffering. As a practitioner living and gathering stories in a location that has known annihilative violence, this is one of the methods that I use both to honor the teller of the story and to tell my own grief in the hearing of it. That the silence may be broken.

I am haunted by this image of you holding the corpse of your baby, waiting for the ship to arrive in the city of Sorrow, alone in the ship clinic. This image has come to me at different times of day, over many months. I double over, and inside I scream, although it is not my pain, and I am not the one who bears it.

Dignity—walking through the darkness and molding it into light. You take the darkness and hold it inside of you. You keep walking, keep working, keep loving, keep holding a dead child on a ship going somewhere once, nowhere now. They prepare a special gangplank for you and the ambulance meets you and your child is taken away from you, and you are alone in a strange city, with empty arms.

I cannot imagine your pain, dear Mama. You tell me about the ship ride home, and how you wrote poems. You have a book of them that you wanted to share with me but in the haste of my leaving, I did not get to read them. You write poems now. You wrote one when I left, and your dream is to write. Not to think about cooking and caring for the yard and for the pigs, but to write in a small house by the sea or on a mountain. I dream that your dreams will come true.

Implications for policy

Truth and reconciliation commissions have provided the spaces for stories to be told, and in theory, for those stories to impact policy (Oduro, 2012). While a clear avenue for stories of annihilation to impact policy remains elusive what is clear is that such stories must impact policy, that the real effect of annihilation be told.

Walking through suffering: Celebration of the suffering

Mama Bunia: "Whatever life's challenges, however heavy, she will keep walking through"

Mama Bunia tells of her experience of sustained illness and despair. She weeps as she describes to me her *perjuangan*—her striving through chronic illness and suffering that she does not name. "You know Julian, you know," she says of this suffering. Ivan, who lives up the hill and has known her for 30 years, calls her "a sweet woman. Ibu Bunia is good. But she suffers." "She has been sick for many years," says Mama Koinonia. "In and out of every hospital. But she is strong." Mama Bunia takes the power of words to her suffering.

So, we must always keep giving thanks and accepting what God wants to give to us. Because of trials, our faith will grow stronger and sturdier, and our faith will grow more. But if people don't have faith—if a storm of life comes just one time like suffering, we will be destroyed [...]. But if a person who is strong has faith, whatever life's challenges, however heavy, she will keep walking through—even through suffering. There is [pain], but she keeps smiling. She keeps smiling even though she experiences suffering. But she keeps smiling because everything is God. Because of God, she can smile.

Mama Koinonia: "So we face everything but have to smile"

Mama Koinonia is the heart and leader of the Mamas. She knows each community member, has been in their homes, and they frequently occupy her terrace in search of tea, a listening ear, and the comfort of her renowned humor. She speaks of the time her husband was arrested for preaching about human rights. She was newly married, pregnant, and supporting hers and her husband's extended families as well as feeding many of those in prison with her husband. I asked her how she did this.

Achk! [Mama laughs] It was heavy. But I faced it with laughter, and every kind of difficulty that we face. But we must face it with peace. Yes, and what I always like to say is that we must smile. That's what Boeting wrote in one song that eh, how do you say? [...] If I'm not wrong, "Put your difficulties away into a box and smile,[5] wherever you go ... or whatever..."

This song often, Mama ... Achk! But always, eh, whatever your difficulty, like that—Mama remembers, eh, the song that was in—it was in what do you say? Written by Rev. Boeting. You see, there is meaning there. So, we face everything but have to smile [...].

You see, at that time, I truly felt heaviness facing that. So, Mama journeyed through it. From when I was pregnant until I gave birth [...] alone in the hospital—in the house, not in the hospital, in the house. Bapak was still in prison. Noel was three months before Bapak came out of prison, because he had done no wrong.

So, that's it. You have to be strong in everything. And at that time, our salary was 50 Rp, 150 Rp. Yes, how do we manage? If there's money or there isn't money, we give thanks because we are not alone.

Later, Mama illustrates her words. She tells a story of her own laughter during death. I write to her using the model of compassionate witnessing.

You tell me about Mama Lula's death—your good friend, our neighbor, who starved in the house next door. You describe how her granddaughter Bella found her and started screaming, and how you ran over, and your friend was lying in her room, her Bible on the floor near her, open to the Psalms. She had been there since the morning, her family thought. You called the Mamas, called Mama Maybel, and asked her to buy clothes. The Mamas came down, and you sat in her room and bathed her, but her body kept falling over as you washed her and you said, "Xena, I need you to do this one last thing for me, I need you to sit up here and help me, eh Xena. You will be so beautiful!" And you laughed as you described to me your dead friend's head lolling to the side as you laughed with her one last time. Maybe that is your way. Maybe you share, live, speak, and laugh even with the dead.

Implications for teaching and training

Mama Koinonia models laughter. When her husband is in prison and when washing the no longer living body of her friend. It's not, she explains, that you don't feel the pain, but you put it away and you smile. Teaching and training within annihilative settings can intentionally listen for stories of humor and laughter that face down the darkness as well as providing spaces for that courageous laughter to be shared.

Implications for practice and policy

From Mama Bunia, we learn how having faith, firmly and without doubt, that we are fiercely loved by someone more powerful than we can give the strength to not just survive, but to smile. Mama Bunia's living faith brings her daily through her suffering. She shares this faith and the love that she receives from it with her community. Within annihilative systems, Mama bears witness that faith can be vital to survival and to bearing unbearable and unspoken pain with a smile. Practitioners from secular contexts may be tempted to discount the role of faith. Mama Bunia reminds practitioners of the importance of faith for not only survival, but also dignity.

It is impossible to codify laughter. To make a law requiring humor to be present. The Mamas, do however, in their practice, both of retelling stories of pain and of the processes of annihilation and of experiencing them, find space for humor, for a smile, and for laughter. The practice of laughing in the face of darkness is powerful. The Mamas remind us of this.

Perjuangan: The hard work of striving through suffering

Mama Tika: "We must continue to be prepared"

Mama Tika, businesswoman extraordinaire, often receives others when they are in circumstances of difficulty and walks with them through their journeys of sadness. Here, she explains some of her philosophies on suffering. She speaks of preparedness and action. Mama explains how she has told Bapak and her family,

If I die, I remind you that when the time comes, when Mama dies, just kidding here, but please, eh? […] People bring flowers, I don't want those flowers, the flowers—flowers that say "our condolences." If you bring live flowers, it's ok [she laughs]. Fresh flowers. Fresh flowers [Mama draws in breath through her nose and smells the air as if she's imagining the fresh flowers]—instead of buying arranged artificial flowers. One arrangement is 100 thousand. Now, they are expensive. Some are 500—the fancy ones. Just put the money in an envelope […]. And later for example, if I die, I ask you to be ready, to prepare a donation, and there write "a donation for widows and orphans." Aaaaauhaaa! [Mama cackles]

I am also like that. Bapak says like this, "Oh, and if you're already dead, what will you care?" So, it's like that, we have to talk, you see, Julian, even about the place where we will be buried, we have to talk, right?

And so, I always think of that. I had already thought about it. When I said before that we must be mentally prepared, that means that we must be strong. So that in the future, in facing difficulty, we perhaps won't need to be too sad. Because we were already sad and we have to become a *perjuangan*, and become an example for others to see us, right? …

I ask her, "You are not sad, Mama?" She replies, "Sadness as a human being, ok, but it can't be for looooong. Yes. Because when you are sad for a long time, then what else can you do? All of your time is lost sitting being sad."

Here is my response informed by compassionate witnessing.

As I write this, I have just heard the news that your house has burned down. The house where you spent 30 years, building your family and your business. Where you displayed your pictures with presidents and queens, appliances from your travels, and a television where everyone would come to watch the World Cup.

A house with indoor and outdoor kitchens that feed the neighborhood. Your wall of vines and flowers which kept your porch cool.

Your daughter tells me you are staying in the Pearl Hotel with your grandchildren. I call her, and she tells me that she wept about her house burning down until she spoke to you, and you gave her strength. The neighbors tell me that your husband collapsed because all his books had been burned, but you came home and encouraged him, telling him that they are only things.

I remember how I would come to you in my own struggles, when I was so lonely, I could barely stand and when my heart was broken, and you pointed to the bamboo that you had planted 40 years before, and you told me, "Julian, consider the bamboo. The taller and taller it grows, the more and more it bows its head and the lower it gets to the ground. We must be like that, the more and more we grow, the humbler we must become." You told me another time, when I came to you in tears. "Consider the banana tree, Julian. How every part of it can be used—the banana fruit, the heart, the leaves to wrap our food, the stalk to roast food in and for children to play with." I told you that when I was a child, my friends taught me how to make noise makers out of the stalk of the banana tree. You smile and tell me that the whole tree is useful, and that we also must be like that tree, every part of us can be useful.

Implications for teaching and training

Mama Tika teaches the importance of planning for death. She offers a practice to preemptively navigate the grief of death, an occurrence all too frequent in systems of annihilative violence. She teaches that the grief must not stop the continued caring for family, the doing of life that is so vital for survival in systems of annihilative violence. In locations where annihilative violence continues, training in emotional preparedness for impending death and loss can mitigate the pain of the loss and allow for some level of functionality.

Mama Tike also teaches that whatever the pain, we must continue to work and to serve those around us. Teaching and training within annihilative contexts can include practical skills for making a living.

Implications for practice and policy

Systems of annihilative violence are far from ideal. Mama Tika is a Mama who continues to *berjuang*, to strive in the face of the destruction of her house, her impending death, and the pain that many carry to her. She emphasizes hard work within whatever constraints are present, and a pragmatic preparedness for the worst that might happen, so that when it does happen, we are not crippled by it.

Mama Tika gives the specific example of making sure she has a place to be buried and makes sure that the celebration of her upon her death will benefit others. These are two simple actions that could be implemented into policy in communities experiencing increased death due to annihilative systems. Policies determining a place for bodies and some sort of communal effort to help the living even as the dead are remembered will allow for some dignity to remain, even in death.

Conclusion

Perjuangan—carrying laughter, a certainty that you will survive. *Perjuangan*—carrying a dead child across a sea. *Perjuangan*, the practice of being a guardian of life. Of holding to the body of a baby even after its life is gone. This walking through darkness and surviving. This survivance (see Vizenor, 1993)—through laughter, through planning, through openness, through faith—these are the practices that maintain and hold life. Annihilative systems work to erase being. The Mamas work to affirm being. Annihilative systems work to dissolve connections, from the spark of being in the self and from the spark of being in another. The Mamas journey through suffering to seek out and affirm these connections. Annihilation is a serious business. So is laughing at it.

Notes

1. Taken from an interview with Mama Viki, February 17, 2014.
2. I have changed all place names to protect participants identities.
3. Annihilative violence is not always outright killing, it can also be a systemic lack of available medical care.
4. Another Mama from the community.
5. Be in a state of smiling.

References

Anderson, B. (2001). *Violence and the state in Suharto's Indonesia.* Cornell University.
Arendt, H. (1958). *The human condition.* University of Chicago Press.
Assembly, U. G. (1948, December 9). Convention on the prevention and punishment of the crime of Genocide. *United Nations, Treaty Series, 78,* 277.
Banivanua-Mar, T. (2008). "A thousand miles of cannibal lands": Imagining away genocide in the re-colonization of West Papua. *Journal of Genocide Research, 10*(4), 583–602.
Cavanaugh, W. T. (2007). *Torture and Eucharist: Theology, politics, and the body of Christ.* Wiley.
Cole, D., & Chaikin, I. (1990). *An iron hand upon the people: The law against the Potlatch on the Northwest Coast.* Douglas & McIntyre.
Elmslie, J., & Webb-Gannon, C. (2013). A slow-motion genocide: Indonesian rule in West Papua. *Griffith Journal of Law and Human Dignity, 1*(2), 143–165.
Erickson, V. L., & Jones, M. L. (2002). *Surviving terror: Hope and justice in a world of violence.* Brazos Press.
Fanon, F. (1965). *Wretched of the earth.* Beacon Press.
Fontaine, T. (2010). *Broken circle: The dark legacy of Indian residential schools: A memoir.* Heritage House Publishing Company.
Harper, D. (2020, February 15). *Online etymology dictionary.* https://www.etymonline.com/word/annihilation
International, S. (2013, April 22). *Indonesian military 'development' program spreads fear in West Papua.* https://www.survivalinternational.org/news/9173
King, T. (2010). *A coyote Columbus story.* Groundwood Books.
Kirksey, E. (2002). Anthropology and colonial violence in West Papua. *Cultural Survival Quarterly Magazine, 26*(3). https://www.culturalsurvival.org/publications/cultural-survival-quarterly/anthropology-and-colonial-violence-west-papua
Lederach, J. P. (1996). *Preparing for peace: Conflict transformation across cultures.* Syracuse University Press.
Marchak, M. P. (2003). *Reigns of terror.* McGill-Queen's University Press.
Oduro, F. (2012). *Transitional societies, democratic accountability and policy responses: The formulation of the truth commission approach to a transitional justice policy: South Africa, Nigeria, Ghana* [Doctoral dissertation, Carlton University].
Poulgrain, G., & Wardaya, F. B. (2015). *The Incubus of intervention: Conflicting Indonesia strategies of John F. Kennedy and Allen Dulles.* Strategic Information and Research Development Centre.
Power, S. (2002). *A Problem from hell: America and the age of genocide.* Basic Books.
Rutherford, D. (2012). *Raiding the land of the foreigners.* Princeton University Press.
Swedenburg, T. (2004). The "Arab wave" in world music after 9/11. *Anthropologica, 46*(2), 177–188.
Vizenor, G. (1993). The ruins of representation: Shadow survivance and the literature of dominance. *American Indian Quarterly, 17*(1), 7–30.
Webster, D. (2002). Already sovereign as a people: A foundational moment in West Papuan nationalism. *Pacific Affairs, 74*(4), 507–528.
Weingarten, K. (2003). *Common shock: Witnessing violence every day.* Dutton.
Wospakrik, J., Wospakrik, M., & Smythe, J. (2015). Economies of Papuan women. Unpublished paper.

15
THE ROLE OF YOUTH IN ETHNOPOLITICAL CONFLICTS

Cihan Dizdaroğlu and Alpaslan Özerdem

The world has witnessed a proliferation of new modes of conflict in the wake of the Cold War: intrastate civil and ethnic conflicts rather than traditional interstate wars. While the nature and causes of armed conflicts have changed significantly, their devastating impact on people has remained without change. The quest for the prevention of war and conflict has questioned the roles of different actors within such phenomena, including those of youth. Debates on the aversion of child and youth mobilization, recruitment and retention to violence, and the human impact of conflict in particular have become the subjects of a growing research agenda among scholars and practitioners. In contrast, discussions around the roles and contributions of youth—either positive or negative—in the post-conflict environment have only recently commenced, hence the literature on this specific topic is comparatively underdeveloped.

Today, youth represent almost a quarter of the global population. According to the UN World Population Prospects (2019), 1.8 billion of the 7.8 billion global population are between the ages of 15 and 29. This demographic reality is constantly changing, and the size of the youth population is growing. Nearly 1.6 billion youth live in less developed countries, where armed conflict is more likely. This means that at least one in four youth is, in some way, affected by violence or armed conflict (UNFPA & PBSO, 2018). Therefore, these individuals are an important constituency, not only in conflicts and violence, but also for peace, stability and societal changes.

Although their agency is often overlooked, youth have always been at the forefront in driving changes in society. Historic youth-led movements, such as the leadership of South African youth in ending segregation in their nation, have proven the significant impact youth have on societal developments (Dizdaroğlu, 2021). The most recent mass youth-led social mobilization erupted in global climate change demonstrations to protest ruling elites, corruption, and inequality in numerous countries, such as Sudan, Tunisia, Iraq, and Libya, demonstrating how youth can be active agents. This also triggers a specific focus on youth, since they voiced their demands, through violent and nonviolent means, against the challenges they face.

Therefore, the goal of this chapter is to investigate the relationship between youth, peace, and conflict to present the perceptions of youth that are contrary to those such as "troublemakers," "victims," and "agents of change," particularly in ethnopolitical conflicts. First, it provides brief information about the contested concept of youth and then examines the dominant perceptions of youth in the nexus of peace and conflict. Then it focuses on some of the challenges ahead of youth's recognition as agents of change. Finally, the chapter argues that, to a large extent, the role of youth in peacebuilding is defined by whether or not youth are perceived as a "problem" or a "potential." If youth agency can be recognized with equal rights, they can contribute meaningfully and become powerful agents of change. Otherwise, their contributions to peacebuilding will continue to be ignored or underutilized.

Background

Who are youth?

The term youth is highly contentious, as it has no universally accepted definition. It is, however, necessary to define the concept to understand the roles of youth in ethnopolitical conflicts. Fundamentally, we can classify the definitions within three main categories: "age-defined perspective," "social construct," and "psychological perspective" (Özerdem & Podder, 2015, pp. 1–3). No single age range exists for youth in the first perspective. The United Nations Security Council's (UNSC) landmark Resolution 2250 (2015) on "Youth, Peace and Security" established youth as being aged between 18 and 29, acknowledging the discrepancy between definitions, and noting that "variations of definition of the term that may exist on the national and international levels" (S/RES/2250, 2015). This age range can drop, for instance, to as low as 12 in Jordan and rise up to 35 in countries such as Cyprus, South Africa, Sierra Leone, and Rwanda. Likewise, it varies by government, agency, and organization. While the United Nations Educational, Scientific and Cultural Organization (UNESCO) has adopted the range of 15–24, the European Commission defines the same category with the range of 15–29. However, these conflicting—or overlapping—age-defined boundaries are inconsistent with social and cultural contexts.

The second perspective focuses on "socially constructed" characteristics, arguing that these categories are unnatural and are embedded in personal relationships, social practices, politics, laws, and public policies (Honwana, 2012, p. 11). Here, youth are characterized by assorted social attributes that differentiate them from other social groups. Among these attributes are age, authority, social position, power, ability, rights, dependence/independence, knowledge, and responsibility (Durham, 2004, p. 593).

The "psychological perspective" relates to the period of transition between childhood and adulthood. This perspective entails no clear-cut transition, though there are some markers such as marital status, childbirth, land ownership, and ritual or spiritual initiation. Accordingly, a person may still be considered a youth even after having outgrown the official age range. In some African countries, this period of transition can be prolonged: Honwana (2013) defines this phase as "waithood," and even a 40-year-old unemployed or unmarried person can still be considered a "youthman."

Regardless of its definition, youth is far from a homogenous entity. A myriad of factors—gender, class, race, ethnicity, and age—make this group of actors highly heterogeneous. To be succinct, youth can be defined in different ways, as seen from these perspectives, but this chapter focuses instead on those whose societies do not yet consider them adults.

Youth, peace, and conflict nexus

In addition to these definitional challenges, people have ascribed multifaceted roles to youth. The "perpetrators" and "victims of violence" dichotomy has long dominated academic perceptions of youth. As McEvoy-Levy (2006) points out, young people are often protagonists or victims and often play both roles in protracted ethnopolitical conflicts and civil wars. On the other hand, youth have also begun to be viewed as potentially acting as "agents of change" and "peacebuilders."

Youth as potential troublemakers

Despite the dominance of the "youth bulge" thesis in recent debates over youth roles, scholars have started to question the links between the "youth cohort" and "violence" in the 1960s. While Moller (1968) claims, "Irrespective of social and economic conditions, an increase in the number of youth in any society involves an increase in social turbulence" (p. 256), Choucri (1984) associates the issue with the economic factors, arguing, "The greater the unemployment among the educated youth, the greater are the propensities for dissatisfactions, instabilities and violence." This understanding mainly seeks to explain the underlying reasons for youth involvement in violence and conflict. The structural challenges that youth face, such as poverty, inequalities, unemployment, and unhealthy lifestyles, produce the ideal conditions for their voluntary participation in violence and conflict (Oyefusi, 2008). Weak and failing states also spawn the appropriate circumstances for the germination and survival of rebel movements, in which youth are recruited, mobilized, and retained in civil and ethnonational conflicts (Özerdem & Podder, 2015).

This negative trend has persisted, while attention paid to the topic reemerged in the late 1980s, accompanying rapid population growth, especially in less developed countries. The large number of—predominantly male—youth is deemed a potential source of instability and linked to global security concerns. For example, focusing on the role of youth to explain political violence throughout human history, Jack A. Goldstone (1991, 2001) argues that an excessive youth population has been instrumental in many instances of social unrest. Similarly, Henrik Urdal (2006) asserts in an empirical study that "youth bulges" significantly increase the risk of three different forms of internal political violence: domestic armed conflict, terrorism, and riots and violent demonstrations. While he notes that regime type and the level of development explain this violence more effectively, he reiterates the risk of violence in countries where youth constitute a high proportion of the populace—places such as the Middle East, Africa, and parts of Asia. Mesquida and Wiener (1996) also deduce that "the relative abundance of young men is associated with occurrence of aggression and the severity of conflicts" (p. 187), though it is not the only condition.

Many of these studies focus on youth involvement in violence and conflict regardless of context. Oftentimes, youth are recruited—either voluntarily or forcibly—into armed militias, paramilitaries, and gangs and find themselves on the front lines of armed conflicts. Different theoretical explanations illustrate the process of youth mobilization and recruitment, including sociocultural explanations, structural variables, coercion and gender dimensions.

This chapter limits itself to the motivations of youth involvement in violence in ethnic or religious conflicts, which are mainly driven by political or other collective grievances—self-determination, regional autonomy, fear of assimilation and discrimination (Horowitz, 1985). In ethnopolitical and religious conflicts such as in the former Yugoslavia, Sri Lanka, Kosovo, Cyprus, South Sudan, and Northern Ireland, the most compelling motivations behind recruitment are mainly political, communitarian, and religious. Some scholars differentiate the type of conflicts and argue that the "youth bulge affects the onset of non-ethnic wars, but not the onset of ethnic wars," which erupt more often due to ethnic grievances (Yair & Miodownik, 2016, pp. 38–39).

These studies, which scrutinize the negative aspects of youth, usually use the concept in reference to young men. While this literature depicts male youth as active and aggressive agents of violence, it conventionally portrays female youth at the opposite end of the spectrum, treating them as victims—sex slaves or bush wives. These simple male/female stereotypes overlook the agency of female youth. The reality of this situation, however, is starkly different. Evident from Mckay and Mazurana's (2004, p. 21) global data on the involvement, use and role of females in armed forces and militant groups worldwide, women have also been active in fighting.

This understanding of youth involvement in conflict may hold merit, particularly in developing and fragile contexts. But it has other limitations, not the least of which being the disregarding of youth contributions in post-conflict environments. There exist numerous instances that illuminate how youth participated in peacebuilding and contributed positively to post-conflict processes. Though these arguments are used to decipher political violence in countries with youth bulge populations, they fail to distinguish between youth during times of war and times of peace, as most male youth in conflict-affected countries have never been involved in violence (Bangura, 1997, p. 140; Sukarieh & Tannock, 2015, p. 107). To the contrary, the vast majority of youth take initiative to support peace rather than becoming entangled in violence (UNFPA & PBSO, 2018, p. 95). Perceiving youth as troublemakers by portraying them as irate and violent naturally results in the overlooking of the diverse roles of youth. In terms of ethnopolitical conflicts, youth involvement in violence is quite rare, even in cases when the country has a youth bulge population. As Yair and Miodownik (2016) argue, a large group of youth "may not by itself increase the motivations of members of any one ethnic group to engage in conflict" (pp. 28–29) since the concerns that trigger ethnic conflicts are not unique to one age cohort or another.

Youth as victims

The other generalized perception of youth views them as victims of direct and structural violence. Youth are not exempt from the devastating impacts of conflicts, as they too are subjected to displacement, death, injury, loss, disability, fear, and physical and psychological violence. The World Youth Report (2005) defines youth as "an important period of physical, mental and social maturation" (p. 150); hence, conflicts affect their maturation in addition to their physical and psychological health. The lives of youth are also disrupted due to conflicts and violence, and they suffer loss in their families, jobs, education, health services, and traditional livelihoods. Moreover, in situations of conflict, they can be conscripted into armies and militias or compelled into forced labor.

In post-conflict situations, youth face difficulties in reintegrating into civilian life. As such, they struggle with challenges such as unemployment, a lack of education and social rupture along with problems in transitioning to adulthood. The concept of the "lost generation," for instance, refers to poorly educated and dropouts—"inable to get jobs and unprepared to make constructive contributions to society" (Seekings, 1996, p. 110): it is used to identify African youth who are actively involved in violent and nonviolent protests.

Gender issues contribute to the further victimization of female youth, as they are often portrayed as sex slaves and bush wives, or in supporting tasks such as cooking and cleaning, denying their agency and reducing their roles to auxiliary functions. Female youth face a disproportionately high risk of sexual and gender-based violence in conflict, post-conflict and fragile settings (Women, 2018, p. 10). However, the stereotypical roles of dependency or victimhood bolster the perception that women are vulnerable and in need of protection. Forms of violence are closely related to notions of femininity and masculinity, in which the former denotes submission, and the latter aggression and superiority (UNFPA & PBSO, 2018, p. 95).

The discrete roles attributed to male and female youth force the underestimation of their roles of agency and participation in conflicts. And, as a result, they are often neglected in peace negotiations, demobilization programs and post-conflict reconstruction (Özerdem & Podder, 2015). These stereotypes are reflected in processes of disarmament, demobilization, and re-integration (DDR) in post-conflict periods, as female combatants are expected to return to traditional family roles—wives and mothers (Özerdem & Podder, 2011).

These two extremes of "infantilizing"—the perception that youth are vulnerable, powerless, and in need of protection—and "demonizing"—the notion that youth are dangerous, violent, apathetic, and security threats—shroud and inhibit youth in peace and general decision-making processes (Özerdem & Podder, 2015, p. 7). As a consequence, decisions related to youth are often taken on their behalf rather than with them.

Key insights: Youth as agents of change

In times of conflict, youth may assume different roles, such as perpetrators or victims. But once conflicts end, like adults, they return to normal. There is a pattern, which McEvoy-Levy (2019) defines as adult territoriality, in which politically active youth are expected to return to their roles, as adults are reluctant to share power and, accordingly, subordinate youth. Nevertheless, youth contribute to post-conflict environments in different ways.

Only in the past two decades has the body of research shifted its focus toward youth agency and potential in post-conflict societies, and adjusting the negative discourse on youth roles. As the most recent addition to the international community's repertoire of conflict resolution, the concept of peacebuilding challenged previous approaches toward security and peace "by taking people, rather than states, as the referent of security" (Tschirgi, 2013, p. 197). The realization that state-centered approaches were insufficient sparked greater attention to critical views. Accordingly, the "local turn" in peace and conflict studies raised awareness about the "everyday" and the "agency," which are often overlooked (Mac Ginty, 2015; Mac Ginty & Richmond, 2013; Richmond, 2006).

Agency may be best described as the "capacity of individuals to think and act independently, make choices and impose or operationalize these choices in their everyday lives" (Özerdem & Podder, 2015, pp. 23–24). Although critical studies have paid increased attention to "agency," scholars recently began to acknowledge the voices and experiences of youth. Recent studies have also offered more grounded and inclusive theorizations and engagement of children and youth (Berents & McEvoy-Levy, 2015). However, because youth defines a homogenous group of people, their agency may appear in different forms: civilians, former combatants and the displaced, traumatized and disabled. Though it is difficult to discuss the needs, challenges, and capabilities of this homogenous group, their agency is paramount in the context of their role, as they are the future holders of power. Accordingly, youth experiences in conflict and post-conflict environments will directly impact their understanding of peace and conflict, as well as their influence on the future of their country.

This shift in the focus on the perspective and the position of youth in society accentuated the importance of their potential roles as agents of change in peacebuilding (Özerdem & Podder, 2015, pp. 6–8). McEvoy-Levy (2001) suggests that "youth are the primary actors in grassroots community development/relations work; they are at the frontlines of peacebuilding" (p. 21). As Altiok and Grizelj (2019, p. 9) stressed in their study, in coordination with the UNFPA and the Peacebuilding Support Office, youth can positively contribute to post-conflict reconstruction environments. They do this by "monitoring the implementation of ceasefire agreements, mediating intra-ethnic disputes, supplying legal and logistical support for peace negotiations, providing psychosocial support for former combatants, and using mass media and online social platforms to promote peace messages to the broader public constituencies." Moreover, youth also play key roles in the prevention of, and reaction to, violent extremism. A UNDP report on the issue provides concrete examples of youth-led initiatives that address the root causes of violent extremism, and highlights the importance of actively supporting youth for successful outcomes (UNDP, 2019). Therefore, accepting youth agency in post-conflict settings is essential for enduring and sustainable peace.

The positive contributions of youth are reflected in UN Security Council Resolutions and in reports from institutions such as the United Nations Development Program (UNDP) and United States Agency for International Development (USAID). All these efforts to direct attention toward the ability of youth to positively influence peace and conflict culminated in the adoption of UNSC Resolution 2250 on "Youth, Peace and Conflict" on December 9, 2015. This resolution sets a framework for action through five key pillars: participation, protection, prevention, partnership and disengagement, and reintegration (S/RES/2250, 2015). The UN Security Council reaffirmed its commitment to implement UNSC Resolution 2250 (2015) June 6, 2018, by adopting the UNSC Resolution 2419 (2018), which seeks to include youth representation for conflict prevention and resolution.

There are concrete examples of meaningful youth contributions in ethnopolitical and religious conflicts such as South Sudan, Cyprus, Sri Lanka, Syria, and Nigeria. In many countries marred with conflict, youth have stood at the forefront in creating hope for their communities through tremendously important work in peacebuilding and reconciliation (Özerdem & Podder, 2015, p. 208). In South Sudan, for instance, where they constitute an overwhelming majority of the population, youth have been crucial in fostering social harmony for public unity and tackling the deep and divisive generational wounds exacted by tribal and ethnic hatred (Chatham House, 2016). Although the long-lasting dispute has not yet been resolved in Cyprus, youth and youth organizations continue to engage in peacebuilding activities to meet with their peers from the other community, to learn from each other, to eliminate prejudices and fears and to promote peacebuilding and intercultural dialogue (United Nations, 2019). Likewise, Sri Lankan youth have contributed to the erection of trust between different ethno-religious groups to promote reconciliation and lasting peace (United Nations, 2016). In Nigeria, several peacebuilding projects mobilize youth to shift the false narratives toward a peaceful future and to bridge divides between different ethnic and religious groups, which are often presented as the source of violence and division (Peace Direct, 2020). In Syria, young peacebuilders established platforms for neighborhood dialogue to prevent the escalation of violence between different sectarian and ethnic communities in the country (Altiok & Grizelj, 2019).

In addition to ethnopolitical and religious conflicts, many examples from around the world highlight youth contributions to peacebuilding, transparent and inclusive governance, counterterrorism, development, and preventing violent extremism (Agbiboa, 2015; Drummond-Mundal & Cave, 2007; Turner, 2015; UNDP, 2019). The youth-led United Network of Young Peacebuilders, which was founded in 1989 and contains more than 100 youth peace organizations in 55 countries, is a powerful example of how youth can contribute effectively in countries devastated by conflict.

We can thus argue that academic research and subsequent UNSC resolutions precipitated this departure from former boundaries and raised awareness about the roles of youth in peace and security. But the active involvement of youth in the processes of politics, decision-making and peacebuilding is still rarely welcomed, since UNSC resolutions do not automatically equip youth with agency. So, there remains a need to discuss the steps necessary to expand positive perspectives of youth.

Implications for practice and policy

The literature focusing on the potential of youth continues to grow among academics and practitioners, but there is still much to do to effect broader change and to constructively incorporate youth voices. As reflected in the UN Secretary-General's report on the implementation of the UNSC's landmark Resolution 2250, recognizing the "essential role" of youth in peace and security has grown in the five years since the resolution was adopted. However, some core challenges must be addressed, including the "structural barriers limiting the participation of young people and their capacity to influence decision-making; violations of their human rights; and insufficient investment in facilitating their inclusion, in particular through education" (UN Secretary General, 2020, para. 10).

The inclusion of youth in local, national and international decision-making and peacemaking and post-conflict reconstruction processes would not be possible without recognizing youth as political actors. As Berents (2020) points out, "Discourses are shifting to recognise youth not only as social actors, in need of support for education and employment; but also as political actors, capable and deserving of inclusion in decision making processes." However, existing hierarchical structures and the tension between youth and their elders have caused their marginalization and exclusion from decision-making bodies. The general belief that youth lack experience or political apathy triggers the assumption that adult (male) elites make decisions or sign peace accords to address the needs of society. This, as a result, reflects in the lower youth turnout, growing dissatisfaction and mistrust toward democratic structures (UN Secretary General, 2020, para. 25). Ongoing youth-led demonstrations around the world demonstrate youth demands in more inclusive, transparent, and accountable bodies. Regarding peace processes, Altiok and Grizelj's (2019, pp. 7–16) work reveals that the influence of youth does not always correlate to a seat at the negotiating table, as outside activism may be more powerful than their presence in negotiations. It is essential that we treat youth as political actors and provide them a platform in governance to deliver their needs best and directly in order to implement the policies that affect them.

Post-conflict DDR and peacebuilding processes must understand the trajectories of youth, particularly of those who have participated in armed conflict as combatants. Successful peacebuilding initiatives prove the importance of youth inclusion in these processes—especially in ethnopolitical and religious conflicts—for bridging divides between different ethnic and religious groups. As reflected in the latest UN Secretary-General implementation report (UN Secretary General, 2020, para. 47), former youth combatants should be actively included in the design, planning and implementation of DDR processes rather than being passive beneficiaries. Viewing youth, as a group, as vulnerable or the victims of conflicts forces us to overlook their specific needs and challenges. However, without considering the challenges youth face due to armed conflicts, such as the loss of education, a lack of employable skills and the destruction of a stable environment, it would be impossible to include them in peacebuilding and DDR processes as active agents (Özerdem, 2016).

Finally, inadequate resourcing remains a central challenge to the effective implementation of the UNSC resolutions. While meeting funding challenges requires the mobilization of additional and novel resources (UN Secretary General, 2020, paras. 66–67), international funding might precipitate a top-down effort in peacebuilding and loosen the local design and implementation process (Özerdem & Podder, 2015). Donor funding models therefore must rely on "radical flexibility"—an approach focused on grassroots-driven needs and developing longstanding and mutually beneficial partnerships with local actors (Berents, 2020; Peace Direct & Kantowitz, 2020). Moreover, if member states, rather than external donors, can provide this funding to implement the youth, peace, and security agenda, then it can be used directly to include youth in peacebuilding processes. This will affirm the intentions of member states to support this agenda.

Conclusion

This chapter presented the contradictory perceptions of youth in the nexus of peace and conflict, particularly in ethnopolitical conflicts. While two negative perceptions—"troublemakers" or "victims"—have long dominated the literature, scholars and practitioners have, in the past two decades, institutionalized the positive roles of youth as "agents of change" and "peacebuilders." Both the literature focusing on the potential roles of youth as agents of change and subsequent UNSC resolutions have contributed to the growing international acknowledgement of youth in post-conflict environments.

In ethnopolitical and religious conflicts, the negative roles attributed to youth, in general, may be irrelevant in understanding their roles in violence. As the main motivations for violence vary substantially in ethnopolitical conflicts, the "youth bulge" thesis fails to explain any correlation between youth and violence. This also reflects in Yair and Miodownik's (2016) study, which argues that the youth bulge does not affect the onset of ethnic wars. To the contrary, youth-led peacebuilding programs in conflict-affected countries demonstrate the meaningful contributions of youth as agents of change. Evident from various ethnopolitical and religious conflicts, youth have played leading roles in eliminating ethnic and religious differences, increasing dialogue, building trust between conflicting parties and promoting reconciliation and lasting peace.

The role of youth is mainly shaped around perceptions of them and whether they are considered a "problem" or a "potential." As the past decade has shown, youth have already proven their significant impact on societal developments. The latest UN Secretary-General implementation report on youth, peace and security emphasized the growing recognition of the "essential role" of youth in peace and security, though some challenges still lie ahead. Many of these challenges can easily be eliminated through the recognition of the agency and contributions of youth. Otherwise, they will most likely continue to be ignored in politics.

References

Agbiboa, D. E. (2015). Youth as tactical agents of peacebuilding and development in the Sahel. *Journal of Peacebuilding & Development*, *10*(3), 30–45.

Altiok, A., & Grizelj, I. (2019). *We are here: An integrated approach to youth-inclusive peace processes*. United Nations website: www.un.org/youthenvoy/wp-content/uploads/2019/07/Global-Policy-Paper-Youth-Participation-in-Peace-Processes.pdf

Bangura, Y. (1997). Understanding the political cultural dynamics of the Sierra Leone War: A critique of Paul Richard's "Fighting for the Rain Forest." *Africa Development*, *22*(3/4), 117–148.

Berents, H. (2020). Taking stock: The Secretary-General's report on youth, peace and security. United Nations website: hmberents.com/2020/04/24/taking-stock-the-secretary-generals-report-on-youth-peace-and-security/

Berents, H., & McEvoy-Levy, S. (2015). Theorising youth and everyday peace(building). *Peacebuilding*, *3*(2), 115–125.

Chatham House. (2016). *Peacebuilding, reconciliation and community cohesion in South Sudan: The role of youth.* Chatham House website: www.chathamhouse.org/sites/default/files/events/130216-peacebuilding-reconciliation-community-cohesion-south-sudan-meeting-summary.pdf

Choucri, N. (1984). *Multidisciplinary perspectives on population and conflict*. Syracuse University Press.
Dizdaroğlu, C. (2021). Youth leadership in conflict response in South Africa. In A. Özerdem, S. Akgül-Açıkmeşe & I. Liebenberg (Eds.), *Routledge handbook of conflict response and leadership in Africa* (pp. 313–323). Routledge.
Drummond-Mundal, L., & Cave, G. (2007). Young peacebuilders: Exploring youth engagement with conflict and social change. *Journal of Peacebuilding & Development, 3*(3), 63–76.
Durham, D. (2004). Disappearing youth: Youth as a social shifter in Botswana. *American Ethnologist, 31*(4), 589–605.
Goldstone, J. A. (1991). *Revolution and rebellion in the early modern world*. University of California Press.
Goldstone, J. A. (2001). Demography, environment, and security. In P. F. Diehl & N. P. Gleditsch (Eds.), *Environmental conflict* (pp. 84–108). Westview.
Honwana, A. (2012). *The time of youth: Work, social change and politics in Africa*. Kumarian Press.
Honwana, A. (2013). *Youth, waithood, and protest movements in Africa*. Kumarian Press.
Horowitz, D. L. (1985). *Ethnic groups in conflict*. University of California Press.
Mac Ginty, R. (2015). Where is the local? Critical localism and peacebuilding. *Third World Quarterly, 36*(5), 840–856.
Mac Ginty, R., & Richmond, O. (2013). The local turn in peace building: A critical agenda for peace. *Third World Quarterly, 34*(5), 763–783.
McEvoy-Levy, S. (2001). Youth as social and political agents: Issues in post-settlement peace building. *Kroc Institute Occasional Paper*, Occasional Paper No. 21, 1–40.
McEvoy-Levy, S. (Ed.). (2006). *Troublemakers or peacebuilders? Youth and post-accord peace building*. University of Notre Dame Press.
McEvoy-Levy, S. (2019). Youth and the challenges of "post-conflict" peacebuilding. Retrieved from UNICEF-IRC website: https://www.unicef-irc.org/article/1067-youth-and-the-challenges-of-post-conflict-peacebuilding.html
Mckay, S., & Mazurana, D. (2004). *Where are the girls?* Rights & Democracy.
Mesquida, C. G., & Wiener, N. I. (1996). Male age composition and severity of conflicts. *Politics and the Life Sciences, 18*(2), 181–189.
Moller, H. (1968). Youth as a force in the modern world. *Comparative Studies in Society and History, 10*(3), 237–260.
Oyefusi, A. (2008). Oil and the probability of rebel participation among youths in the Niger Delta of Nigeria. *Journal of Peace Research, 45*(4), 539–555.
Özerdem, A. (2016, October). *The role of youth in peacebuilding: Challenges and opportunities*. Oxford Resarch Group. www.oxfordresearchgroup.org.uk/blog/the-role-of-youth-in-peacebuilding-challenges-and-opportunities
Özerdem, A., & Podder, S. (2011). How voluntary?: The role of community in youth participation in Muslim Mindanao. In A. Özerdem & S. Podder (Eds.), *Child soldiers: From recruitment to reintegration* (pp. 122–140). Palgrave Macmillan.
Özerdem, A., & Podder, S. (2015). *Youth in conflict and peacebuilding: Mobilization, reintegration and reconciliation*. Palgrave Macmillan.
Peace Direct. (2020). *Preventing violence and recruitment to extremist groups in Northern Nigeria*. Retrieved from https://www.peacedirect.org/wp-content/uploads/2020/03/PD-Nigeria-Summary.pdf
Peace Direct, & Kantowitz, R. (2020). *Radical flexibility: Strategic funding for the age of local activism*. website: www.peacedirect.org/us/wp-content/uploads/sites/2/2020/02/PD-Radical-Flexibility-Report-v2.pdf
Richmond, O. P. (2006). The problem of peace: Understanding the 'Liberal Peace.' *Conflict, Security & Development, 6*(3), 291–314.
S/RES/2250. (2015). UN Security Council Resolution 2250 (2015). Retrieved from https://undocs.org/S/RES/2250(2015)
Seekings, J. (1996). The "Lost Generation": South Africa's "Youth Problem" in the early-1990s. *Transformation, 29*, 103–125.
Sukarieh, M., & Tannock, S. (2015). *Youth rising? The politics of youth in the global economy*. Routledge.
Tschirgi, N. (2013). Securitization and peacebuilding. In R. Mac Ginty (Ed.), *Routledge handbook of peacebuilding* (pp. 197–210). Routledge.
Turner, R. L. (2015). Youth, 'tradition' and peace building: Mobilising for just governance in rural South Africa. *Peacebuilding, 3*(2), 126–140. https://doi.org/10.1080/21647259.2015.1052628

UN Secretary General. (2020). *Report of the Secretary-General on youth and peace and security.* (S/2020/167) [EN/AR/RU]. https://reliefweb.int/report/world/youth-and-peace-and-security-report-secretary-general-s2020167-enarru

UNDP. (2019). *Frontlines: Young people at the forefront of preventing and responding to violent extremism.* website: https://www.undp.org/publications/frontlines

UNFPA, & PBSO. (2018). *The missing peace: Independent progress study on youth and peace and security.* https://www.unfpa.org/resources/missing-peace-independent-progress-study-youth-and-peace-and-security

United Nations. (2005). *World youth report.* https://www.un.org/esa/socdev/unyin/documents/wyr05book.pdf

United Nations. (2016). *In Sri Lanka, UN chief highlights key role of young people in building peace and sustainable development.* UN News Centre. website: https://www.un.org/youthenvoy/2016/09/sri-lanka-un-chief-highlights-key-role-young-people-building-peace-sustainable-development/

United Nations. (2019). *Report of the Secretary-General on his mission of good offices in Cyprus.* website: https://digitallibrary.un.org/record/522514?ln=en

United Nations Department of Economic and Social Affairs. (2019). *World population prospects 2019.* https://population.un.org/wpp/Download/Standard/Population/

Urdal, H. (2006). A clash of generations? Youth bulges and political violence. *International Studies Quarterly, 50*(3), 607–629.

Women, U. (2018). *Young women in peace and security: At the intersection of the YPS and WPS agendas.* www.unwomen.org/sites/default/files/Headquarters/Attachments/Sections/Library/Publications/2018/Research-paper-Young-women-in-peace-and-security-en.pdf

Yair, O., & Miodownik, D. (2016). Youth bulge and civil war: Why a country's share of young adults explains only non-ethnic wars. *Conflict Management and Peace Science, 33*(1), 25–44.

PART III

Addressing the Past and Shaping the Future

16
ON PEACEBUILDING AND PUBLIC MEMORY: ICONOCLASM, DIALOGUE, AND RACE

Adam Muller

> Sometimes in the face of my own/our own limitations, in the face of such world-wide suffering, I doubt even the significance of books.
> —*Cherrie Moraga (October, 1983)*

Background

In what follows I will be offering a series of related reflections amid and in response to the current moment of global protest, social and political struggle, and repression. In North America, where I live and work, protest has coalesced particularly around concerns with sexism and racism as these concepts have been marshaled by the twin forces of the Me Too! and Black Lives Matter (BLM) movements. These together and alongside other emancipatory social and political projects have shed much light on the ubiquity and destructiveness of racial and sexual violence not just in North America, but globally. My immediate concern will be with the destruction or vandalism of public statues and monuments, a longstanding practice that became highly conspicuous again in the wake of the murder by police of 46-year-old Minnesotan George Floyd in May 2020. As is now well known, for nearly nine minutes Minneapolis policemen kneeled on Floyd's neck while he verbally protested his suffocation, and died. The police's treatment of Floyd, a black man suspected of having used a counterfeit $20 bill to buy some cigarettes, has been described by some commentators as an extrajudicial execution, one speaking loudly for the toxic character of the present state of American policing practices and wider network of race relations. In the immediate aftermath of Floyd's death, protests broke out across the United States as well as around the world, not just in response to events in Minnesota but out of more general frustration with the lengthy and seemingly intractable institutional and private histories of racism and racialized injustice throughout the modern, putatively multi-cultural, West. The destruction of public monuments celebrating individuals in various ways complicit in these racist and colonial histories has been one of the more prominent features of these protests.

The fallout from Floyd's killing was immediate, turbulent, and varied. It includes violent and nonviolent protests and counterdemonstrations, many ongoing months later, a great deal of soul-searching at many different levels of society, personal and corporate *mea culpas* and apologies, as well as many loud and overlapping commitments to change (or else not to). Doing explanatory justice to the complexity of "now" requires more space than a single article allows, as well as (if I'm honest) more of what the Ancient Greeks called *nous* than I possess in such intersecting fields as critical race studies, postcolonial studies, criminology, and law. My own background is as a critical theorist working on some of the thornier "big-picture" questions relating to the representation and commemoration of war and atrocity (e.g. "What is genocide?" "How can we be made more empathetic?", etc.). I'm therefore well versed in many of the ways public structures such as museums and memorials interact aesthetically and politically with the past and what architects call their "adjacencies" in order to create meanings that transform the world around them.

Even so, I admit to feeling on very shaky ground when it comes to making sense of the struggles of the present moment. First and foremost, as a white and in many ways highly privileged person I'm unsure exactly what my standing is in public discussions of the way racialized thinking and practices damage lives, pollute memories, and weaken the institutions, habits, and conventions responsible for nourishing our collective existence. I don't mean to sound platitudinous. It isn't exactly news that the personal is at the same time political, or that it matters profoundly who speaks, for whom, and from what particular vantage point. Nor should it be surprising that even the best intentions (to learn, to advocate on behalf of, etc.) can be experienced as oppressive and unwelcome by those in need of aid and other kinds of understanding. As Donna Kate Rushin complains in "The Bridge Poem" that helps open Cherríe Moraga's and Gloria E. Anzaldúa's foundational collection *This Bridge Called My Back: Writings by Radical Women of Color* (1981):

> I do more translating
> Than the Gawdamn U.N.
> Forget it
> I'm sick of it
> I'm sick of filling in your gaps
> Sick of being your insurance against
> The isolation of your self-imposed limitations
> Sick of being the crazy at your holiday dinners
> Sick of being the odd one at your Sunday Brunches
> Sick of being the sole Black friend to 34 individual white people
> Find another connection to the rest of the world
> Find something else to make you legitimate
> Find some other way to be political and hip
> I will not be the bridge to your womanhood
> Your manhood
> Your human-ness
>
> —*Rushin (1981, pp. xxi–xxii)*

Rushin's point is at least partly that the job of constantly having to explain one's identity to others is exhausting, not to mention weird and frequently alienating. Most seriously, undertaking this kind of work can serve to rob minorities of resources required for the projects of self-knowledge, resistance, and self-love that a continuing existence in conditions of racialized inequality requires in order to be survived. As Rushin insists, rather than depend on the kindness of strangers, or serve their needs:

> The bridge I must be
> Is the bridge to my own power
> I must translate
> My own fears
> Mediate
> My own weaknesses
> I must be the bridge to nowhere
> But my true self
> And then
> I will be useful

I have had Rushin's words and perspective on utility ringing in my ears since before Floyd's murder as I've tried to make sense of the long list of racist atrocities perpetrated by police against minorities throughout the United States (and elsewhere). They have also sounded loudly as I've worked to identify the requirements of inclusive antiracist activism and policymaking. More recently, and perhaps even more pointedly, I was again reminded of them when I encountered the words of a young black activist speaking in July 2020 to a crowd protesting police brutality that had gathered in the Capitol Hill Autonomous Zone in Seattle, Washington. Looking out over the diverse group arrayed before him the young man said: "I'm tired of white people talking for me … I love you guys—you're all my allies, and I love you all—but I would love for all the Black people to talk up here. I'm really sorry. … But this is not a movement for you to be politically active, for you to be politically correct and for you to gain all these votes. Please stop taking advantage of us" (Kang, 2020).

Too often, it seems, self-styled "allies" proceed to intervene in social justice struggles in ways that, although perhaps motivated by the right kinds of concerns, nevertheless strike those on the receiving end of such "kindness" as ill-advised, inept, or else simply presumptuous. As Anthony Beckford, president of Black Lives Matter Brooklyn put it in an interview in the *New York Times* in June 2020, "Our fight is our fight. [White] privilege can amplify the message, but they can never speak for us … There have been moments where some have wanted to be in the front. I've told them to go to the back" (Stewart, 2020). What the secondary literature suggests is that it may finally not actually matter very much whether or not my intentions are good (at least by my lights), or that I am trying through my scholarship and other supportive acts to become a better citizen of the world as well as a more effective "ally" to groups seeking dignity and demanding justice. Even my best efforts to do the "right" thing may be found wanting and compromised by latent racist sentiments or privileges that can interfere with the emergence of exactly the kinds of understandings I am reaching for.

This perception of the limited utility of good intentions is shared by Robin DiAngelo, author of the highly influential nonfictional polemic *White Fragility* (2018). In a 2019 interview, when asked about the defensiveness of some white progressives when confronted with evidence of their own racist biases and complicities, DiAngelo explains that "to the degree that our identities are very attached to this idea of being free of racism, we're actually going to resist any of the critical examinations that we need to be engaged in for our entire lives" (DiAngelo, 2019). In other words, the more people think that they are somehow above or outside of a racist frame, the less likely they will be able to actually see that frame and understand the ways it shapes every aspect of their lives, including the terms and limits of their moral and political agency. According to DiAngelo, "As a result of being raised as a white person in this society, I have a racist worldview. I have racist biases. I have developed racist patterns as a result, and I have investments in the system of racism. It's incredibly comfortable. It's certainly helped me with the barriers that I do face. And I also have investments in not seeing anything I just said—because of what it would suggest to me about my identity as a good person, ... and what it would actually require of me in action" (DiAngelo, 2019).

This way of thinking is now fairly ubiquitous in progressive scholarship as well as in the left-wing political vernacular, notwithstanding the fact that it revolves around assumptions that can seem at times either premature or presumptuous (people tend not to enjoy or appreciate having their moral integrity impugned or their agency questioned a priori, regardless of the legitimacy of any such critique). It represents a politically nuclearized version of "standpoint theory," an agglomeration of perspectival epistemologies given new resonances in the late 20th century via their adoption by a growing number of philosophers and social theorists concerned with understanding identity, notably the feminist philosopher Sandra Harding and sociologist Patricia Hill Collins. For Harding,

> The starting point of standpoint theory ... is that in societies stratified by race, ethnicity, gender, sexuality, or some other such politics shaping the very structure of a society, the activities of those at the top both organize and set limits on what persons who perform such activities can understand about themselves and the world around them. (Harding, 1992, p. 442)

Accordingly, and with a view to overcoming any such limits, we can learn a great deal by trying hard to listen to those located at the bottom of a culture's social hierarchies—the dispossessed, disenfranchised, and mistreated—a task which requires a kind of "quieting" in order for those voices to become discoverable and properly heard.

Writing of the difficulty "hearing" the lowest of the low in India's rigidly stratified social hierarchy, an extremely vulnerable group she labels "the subaltern," postcolonial theorist Gayatri Spivak explains that what is needed in order for marginalized perspectives to be acknowledged and understood is a process of "unlearning," of stripping away the biases and privileges responsible for distorting perspectives and judgments and therefore preventing the apprehension of alternative ways of being and knowing. It is precisely this kind of "unlearning project" that standpoint theory represents since it emerges from the desire by especially feminist, queer, and antiracist scholars to escape the twin dominations (usually experienced simultaneously) of patriarchy and brute analytical reason. Harding for example holds that attention to marginality and subalternity helps us discover what the real problems are in the world, the ones that we must confront and overcome if we truly care about justice. She explains that:

> The activities of those at the bottom of social hierarchies can provide starting points for thought—for everyone's research and scholarship—from which humans' relations with other and the natural world can become visible. This is because the experience and lives of marginalized peoples, as they understand them, provide particularly significant problems to be explained or research agendas. These experiences and lives have been devalued or ignored as a source of objectivity-maximizing questions—the answers to which are not necessarily to be found in those experiences or lives but elsewhere in the beliefs and activities of people at the center who make policies and engage in social practices that shape marginal lives (Harding, 1992, p. 443).

Relatedly, in an interview during which she was asked to clarify the meaning of "unlearning" Spivak explains that for her it designates an informal process unfolding "in the field," some distance away from traditional sites of knowledge accumulation and exchange like universities. Unlearning, says Spivak, consists of the ability to

> check out [one's] theoretical presuppositions by testing them in areas as unlike the institution of learning/certification/validation/information retrieval as possible. Urban radicalism of various sorts, and then step-by-step alternative development work, becomes nothing more than an alibi for the opportunity to see the object of politics as the judges of ethical positions. (Spivak, 1993, p. 25)

Although this interview first appeared in 1993, it is in Spivak's reference to street politics that we find an important connection to BLM and other activism of this present moment. Both demand that society "unlearn" the racist past in order to remove structural and other impediments to the "mattering" of black and other minority lives. Unlearning facilitates recognition of these impediments, and requires that we try to understand others' lives as they see and live them.

Every unlearning project is at one and the same time also an education. Every education thus entails the twin experiences of acquiring new understanding and jettisoning what we know that is unreliable, outdated, or wrong. It is squarely within this positive and negative pedagogical dialectic that my own ideas and remarks in the present context may be located.

Key insights

As noted above, the insights I'm presenting here are the by-products of my attempts to think about how public monuments have been addressed and treated in the context of recent antiracist activism. My thoughts are rooted in a highly tentative set of impressions, rather than anything like crystalline certainties. I therefore present them here somewhat nervously and in a spirit of constructive engagement fully aware of how fundamentally provisional anything I assert or conclude must be. I hope by nevertheless speaking up to raise some issues in a way that may either be taken up and further developed, rejected, or reframed afterwards as part of the much longer (and necessarily uneven and risk-filled) process of collectively working-through racial and other traumas.

I mean "working-through" here in the specialist sense of the phrase as it is elaborated in the work of historian Dominick LaCapra (2001). In his account of the nature of trauma and traumatic memory as it affects primary and secondary witnesses to events, LaCapra argues that in the aftermath of great distress human beings typically either "act-out" or "work-through" what it is that has damaged us. Drawing on Freud's idea of "transference," or repetition (i.e., the process that permits the return of infantile Oedipal trauma in adult life), LaCapra explains that "Acting-out is related to repetition, and even the repetition-compulsion – the tendency to repeat something compulsively. This is very clear in the case of people who undergo a trauma. They have a tendency to relive the past, to exist in the present as if they were still fully in the past, with no distance from it" (LaCapra, 2001, p. 153). We find evidence of acting-out in what we now recognize as the experience of PTSD—in the nightmares of trauma sufferers, in flashbacks, blackouts, etc. As LaCapra points out, those acting-out "tend to relive occurrences, or at least find that those occurrences intrude on their present existence" (LaCapra, 2001, p. 143). In virtue of this repetition acting-out tends to reaffirm and leave intact prior beliefs and understandings. It therefore comprises experiences that are morally and politically non-transformative. Accordingly, and as a brute expression of psychic damage and pain, acting-out possesses only very limited educational value.

Working-through trauma, on the other hand, is what LaCapra terms a "countervailing force" (LaCapra, 2001, p. 153) to acting-out. He explains that

> In the working-through, the person tries to gain critical distance on a problem, to be able to distinguish between past, present, and future. For the victim, this means his ability to say to himself, "Yes, that happened to me back then. It was distressing, overwhelming, perhaps I can't entirely disengage myself from it, but I'm existing here and now, and this is different from back then." There may be other possibilities, but it's via the working-through that one acquires the possibility of being an ethical agent. (LaCapra, 2001, p. 143)

Several strands need to be teased out of this way of explaining working-through. Most importantly we must acknowledge and come to terms with LaCapra's claim concerning the link between working-through and ethical agency. On his view, this link exists owing to the epistemic richness of the working-through process. In order to work-through a difficult experience, that is, we must somehow acquire enough critical distance from it in order to be able to see and understand it clearly enough to know how best to proceed. The term "best" here signifies ethically since it stands as a placeholder for actions undertaken in order to do justice to trauma sufferers (i.e., dignify them, offer succor and redress, etc.), whether they are primary experiencers or secondary witnesses to others' distress. Absent any direct access to (and so "thick" understanding of) what Freud would consider a trauma's "primal scene" (*Urszene*) or originary moment, there is no possibility of proceeding to address suffering in a morally attuned way. While acting-out always remains to some extent agonic and characterized by irreducibly painful struggle precisely because of the kind of understandings its epistemic thickness enables, there can be something redemptive and restorative about the process of working-through. For this reason, working-though is associated—for LaCapra as well as for Freud—with the specificities and rituals of mourning. In LaCapra's words: "When one comes to certain problems, such as that of mourning – which can be seen in Freud as one important mode of working-through – one may never entirely transcend an attachment to a lost other, or even some kind of identification with a lost other, but one may generate countervailing forces so that the person can reengage an interest in life" (LaCapra, 2001, p. 151). This renewed interest is made possible by the performative qualities of mourning and specifically

> a relation to the past that involves recognizing its difference from the present – simultaneously remembering and taking leave of or actively forgetting it, thereby allowing for a critical judgment and a reinvestment in life, notably social and civic life with its demands, responsibilities, and norms requiring respectful recognition and consideration for others. (LaCapra, 2001, p. 70)

What the categories of acting-out and working-through then allow me to do in this particular explanatory context is distinguish between some of the different ways that public monuments have been treated by members of the public concerned that they are racist. This includes assaults on Civil War monuments in the United States, a matter that has received a great deal of news coverage over the last few months, yet also assaults on statues all over the world that have been linked to other historical traumas such as slavery, violence against women, and colonialism. In Canada, statues and buildings connected to this country's own history of slavery and treatment of its Indigenous peoples have been spray-painted and damaged; statues and buildings associated with racist figures (including Mohandas Gandhi) throughout formerly colonized nations such as

South Africa and Ghana have been vandalized or removed; and in formerly colonizing countries such as Belgium and Britain statues associated with figures such as King Leopold II linked to the perpetration of atrocities have been targeted by protesters attempting to promote reconsideration of the present-day effects of earlier modes of dehumanization and cruelty.

The distinction between acting-out and working-through historical trauma helps me to advance the following two related points, each presented here schematically and so as a down payment on more sustained and nuanced analysis. First, I would like to suggest that what may be found in all of these recent monument protests is a dynamic and occasionally interrelated mix of acting-out and working-through the traumatic past and present. Mostly, however, what we have witnessed are various examples of acting-out. These reactions have been intended to communicate rage, hurt, discontent, and the desire for change; they have not been designed, nor are they well-suited, to the much more demanding work of educating or explaining that rage, etc. per se. Much of what has occurred in and around public monuments and memorials signifies nothing so much as an inchoate cry of pain. Hence the violence attending some of the protests, such as the destruction of a statue honoring Christopher Columbus in June, 2020, in Richmond, Virginia. There protesters targeted a century-old statue located in a public park because of Columbus's association with the genocidal aspects of Europe's colonization of the Americas. In the context of a discussion of acting-out, the Richmond case is useful since protesters not only removed Columbus from his pedestal but set the statue on fire prior to dumping it in a nearby lake. The oddness, if that's the right word for it, not to mention the desperation involved in (and futility of) attempting to set a stone effigy on fire helps to mark this protest as an instance of acting-out. What matters about the flames is their function as a metonym for the protesters' own rage and recognition of the intractability of the prevailing moral and political order responsible for their ongoing vulnerability and abuse. The disposal of the statue in the lake, which extinguished its flames and in a way decisively (if symbolically) "buried" the problem(s) it represented, may be seen as successful only to the extent that it enabled protesters to say "No!" loudly and conspicuously enough to have them feel that they were able to do a measure of justice to their outrage. Such success is one of the hallmarks of street-level activism, which is a blunt instrument applied to problems that otherwise admit no public redress or even acknowledgment as such.

That said, it is worth noting the difference between doing justice to one's anger and doing justice *simpliciter*. The former arises from our search for a means to represent what we feel; the latter is a moral and political challenge requiring not so much anger as strategic resolve, along with the willingness to meaningfully dialogue with opponents and potential allies. Surely this is something that peace scholars know all too well: namely that building just and equitable communities requires somehow leaving our anger behind. As Marija Spanovich and her colleagues explain in an article considering aspects of the phenomenology of conflict, particularly the connection between anger and fear: "Although feelings of trust can only arise when one is not feeling aggrieved and angry over past injustices, it seems even more vital to reduce feelings of fear and ensure a sense of order and predictability in the process of conflict negotiation" (Spanovic et al., 2010, p. 14).

Second, then, I wish to suggest that Peace and Conflict Studies (PACS) scholarship and practice may contribute substantively to the moral and political work of our present moment by designing and/or refining methods and strategies more finely tuned to assist in our working-through the traumatic past. This is not to suggest that there aren't already highly effective antiracist and other epistemologies and reconciliatory initiatives available or in place that seek to provide individuals and communities with the resources required to understand what it means to live more justly (and why some people feel like they aren't able to). Quite the contrary: it is precisely the achievements of PACS, both as an academic discipline and as a set of practical approaches to facilitating conflict resolution, which makes it worth advocating for in this context.

Implications for teaching and training

Above all, peacebuilding revolves around the creation of opportunities for dialogue (Richmond, 2018). Establishing meaningful dialogue between disputants is a primary technique used by peacebuilders to resolve conflicts. While asking a great deal of us, dialogue produces profoundly transformational effects. According to Paulo Freire, "dialogue is the encounter between men[sic], mediated by the world, in order to name the world" (Freire, 2005, p. 88). That is, it is through dialogue that we enter into a relation with one another and the world such that we can come to know both well enough to either change or reconcile ourselves to them. For Freire, dialogue is thus a crucial part of any process reasonably considered educational. As he puts the matter in his landmark 1970 study *Pedagogy of the Oppressed*, "without dialogue there is no communication, and without communication, there can be no true education" (Freire, 2005, pp. 92–93). Accordingly, historian Peter Stearns argues that dialogue

> contrasts with efforts simply to state a real or imagined truth or dictate some set of conditions without discussion; it differs as well from many forms of argument, where winning takes precedence over mutual interaction. Dialogue requires a deeper kind of communication, some recognition at least for a time that whatever topic is involved— an idea, a dispute—it merits examination from different vantage points. (Stearns, 2019, p. 8)

It is very difficult, if not impossible, to locate a "deeper kind of communication" or concern with "different vantage points" in situations characterized by acting-out. Such situations may be expressive and semantically rich (in so far as they speak for the rage resulting from traumatization or injustices), yet they are not intended to facilitate conversation. Indeed, they represent an end to dialogue and a concrete and powerful delegitimation of the power of a privileged racialized majority to insist that the past be understood in only one way.

In a 2009 report, the United Nations Development Program (UNDP) identifies four reasons why dialogue is able to assist in resolving conflict. First, dialogue is inclusive. It helps opponents cultivate "a sense of joint ownership of the process," and along with it a shared understanding of what the problems requiring solutions actually are. Second, dialogue is a learning—and not just a communication—process. "Unlike other forms of discussion, dialogue requires self-reflection, spirit of inquiry and personal change to be present" (United Nations Development Program, 2009, p. 2). Dialogue can be seen to facilitate—through our discursive encounters with others—self-knowledge, curiosity (which I introduce to my university students as one of the cardinal intellectual virtues), and our resulting understanding that change is not just possible but, properly curated and directed, a means for achieving better lives. Third, and relatedly, dialogue allows us to acknowledge the full extent of one another's humanity. This is because one of the prerequisites of dialogue is empathy, which allows us to enter into others' lives in order to see and feel things as they do. Empathy assists in guaranteeing the mutuality required to establish a framework within which disputants can properly recognize one another as the same kinds of beings-in-the-world, and so worthy interlocutors (for philosopher Charles Taylor (1994), racism results in large part from failures of recognition). Empathy goes beyond ensuring that those in conflict share a common language capable of sustaining dialogue; it facilitates the understanding of what we care about, and why. Such understanding is vital if conflicting beliefs and desires are to be somehow reconciled. Finally, fourth, dialogue transcends its moment. It unfolds over time and via its circumlocutions considerable ground may be traveled, some of it only relevant to *later*. Dialogue encourages patience and restraint, and so is conducive to distinguishing between the symptoms and causes of problems. The difference is crucial: tackling the symptoms of a disease may provide short-term relief but it entails long-term risks and more suffering unless the underlying cause(s) of those symptoms are identified and addressed. According to the UNDP, "To find sustainable solutions requires time and patience. ... one-off interventions very often do not work to address deeply-rooted causes of conflict or to fully deal with complex issues" (United Nations Development Program, 2009, p. 3).

My affirmation of the value of dialogue is not meant to suggest that I view it as a peacebuilding panacea. I would also hate to come across as thinking that there is no value to acting-out in response to historical and other trauma. Far from it. Acting-out can be an important safety valve responsible for ensuring longer-term individual or societal equilibrium, particularly when access to other outlets for expressing anger or dissent is limited. But by itself, acting-out is explosive and rudderless since by definition it lacks any substantial epistemic and programmatic core. It thus serves very well to announce the fact of a problem or discontent without providing much by way of a plan for the way forward. In this sense acting-out may be understood to be politically obstructive, dramatic and at times spectacular to be sure, but a response to trauma. By contrast working-through engages our empathetic faculty and requires listening and understanding. It is not the work of a moment. Unlike acting-out, it requires that a robust groundwork be laid first in order to establish a mutually understood and agreed to framework that serves as a prerequisite for cooperative (rather than competitive) discussions of the future. Acknowledging the vital necessity of this collaboratively derived moral, political and epistemic foundation, the UNDP report observes "When violence, hate, and mistrust remain stronger than the will to forge a consensus, or if there is a significant imbalance of power or a lack of political will among the participants, then the situation might not be ripe for dialogue" (United Nations Development Program, 2009, p. 3).

Implications for practice and policy

I have worked in this chapter to develop the outline of an argument that public monuments and memorials have served as sites of posttraumatic acting-out and working-through. Both responses to traumatic experience have value, yet the goals and procedures of working-through dovetail more neatly with those of the vast majority of PACS scholars and practitioners. Acting-out is neither a new nor an especially rarefied feature of how people have chosen to take exception to what they view as the monumentalization of past wrongs. Any time there is a political point to be made, it seems probable that someone will try to make it by destroying a public structure of some kind. Doing so, as American art historian Erin Thompson has rightly noted, allows disaffected members of society not just literally to attack the representation of an objectionable person or thing, but to express their dissatisfaction or disgust with the ideas this person or thing represents. According to Thompson,

> Throughout history, destroying an image has been felt as attacking the person represented in that image. Which we know because when people attack statues, they attack the parts that would be vulnerable on a human being. We see ancient Roman statues with the eyes gouged out or the ears cut off. It's a very satisfying way of attacking an idea—not just by rejecting but humiliating it. (Bromwich, 2020)

In addition to humiliation, assaulting a public monument can be undertaken so as to publicly demonstrate a lack of fear and therefore the powerlessness of the person or idea attacked. Such behavior also signifies that the worm has turned, so to speak, and that a new moral or political dispensation has emerged (or is emerging). At the very least, the destruction or damaging of monuments is a way for those in the present to demonstrate that they either question or reject the past, and by so doing seek to restore to themselves a measure of the agency and dignity denied to them by those in charge. In Thompson's words, "The current attacks on statues are a sign that what's in question is not just our future but our past, … as a nation, as a society, as a world" (Bromwich, 2020).

And yet if the vandalism of public monuments remains an essentially annihilatory gesture tied to anger and fear yet isolated from a concern with learning and rapprochement, then it is unlikely to contribute positively and productively to all but the initial shockwave upstream of genuine moral and political reform. I therefore loudly and explicitly reject the triumphalist zero-sum view of those like Fox News commentator Cal Thomas, who recently opined that, "The purpose of politics is to win and to demonstrate one party's ideas and policies are superior to those of the other party" (Thomas, 2020). I prefer instead the conception of 19th-century German Iron Chancellor Otto von Bismarck, who famously (if probably apocryphally) viewed politics as "the art of the possible, the attainable—the art of the next best." By linking futurity and the possibility of changing things for the better (i.e. the "next best thing"), Bismarck conceives of politics as revolving not so much around domination as betterment. While we might not always agree about what counts as "better" or "worse" politically, or in our understanding of "a good life," we can all surely support the idea that more and more empathetic dialogue, underpinned by a genuine interest in others' experiences and coupled with recognition that things can in fact be improved, however slowly, seems likelier than the other available options to yield a fairer world in which fewer people feel discounted, disenfranchised, and oppressed. Creating this world will go a long way toward achieving one of the main goals of the BLM movement, namely "a culture where each person feels seen, heard, and supported" (Black Lives Matter, 2019).

References

Black Lives Matter. (2019, September 7). *What we believe*. https://blacklivesmatter.com/what-we-believe/

Bromwich, J. E. (2020, June 11). We asked an art historian who studies the destruction of cultural heritage. *The New York Times*. https://www.nytimes.com/2020/06/11/style/confederate-statue-columbus-analysis.html

DiAngelo, R. (2019). What's my complicity? Talking white fragility with Robin DiAngelo. Interview by A. Van der Valk. *Teaching Tolerance*, 65(2). https://www.tolerance.org/magazine/summer-2019/whats-my-complicity-talking-white-fragility-with-robin-diangelo

DiAngelo, R. J. (2018). *White fragility: Why it's so hard for white people to talk about racism*. Beacon Press.

Freire, P. (2005). *Pedagogy of the oppressed* (3rd ed.). Continuum International Publishing Group.

Harding, S. (1992). Rethinking standpoint epistemology: What is "strong objectivity"? *The Centennial Review*, 36(3), 437–470. http://www.jstor.com/stable/23739232

Kang, J. C. (2020, July 2). Can we please talk about Black Lives Matter for one second? *The New York Times*. https://www.nytimes.com/2020/07/02/magazine/can-we-please-talk-about-black-lives-matter-for-one-second.html

LaCapra, D. (2001). *Writing history, writing trauma*. JHU Press.

Moraga, C. (1981). Refugees of a world on fire: Forward to the second edition. In C. Moraga & G. E. Anzaldúa (Eds.), *This bridge called my back: Writings by radical women of color* (3rd ed., pp. xxi–xxii). Persephone Press.

Moraga, C., & Anzaldúa, G. (Eds.). (1981). *This bridge called my back: Writings by radical women of color* (1st ed.). Persephone Press.

Richmond, O. P. (2018). Rescuing peacebuilding? Anthropology and peace formation. *Global Society*, *32*(2), 221–239. https://doi.org/10.1080/13600826.2018.1451828

Rushin, D. K. (1981). The bridge poem. In C. Moraga & G. E. Anzaldúa (Eds.), *This bridge called my back: Writings by radical women of color* (pp. xxi–xxii). Persephone Press.

Spanovic, M., Lickel, B., Denson, T. F., & Petrovic, N. (2010). Fear and anger as predictors of motivation for intergroup aggression: Evidence from Serbia and Republika Srpska. *Group Processes & Intergroup Relations*, *13*(6), 725–739. https://doi.org/10.1177/1368430210374483

Spivak, G. C. (1988). Can the subaltern speak? In C. Nelson & L. Grossberg (Eds.), *Marxism and the interpretation of culture* (pp. 271–313). University of Illinois Press. https://doi.org/10.1007/978-1-349-19059-1_20

Spivak, G. C. (1993). An interview with Gayatri Chakravorty Spivak. Interview by S. Danius. *Boundary 2*, *20*(2), 24–50.

Stearns, P. N. (2019). *Peacebuilding through dialogue: Education, human transformation, and conflict resolution*. George Mason University Press.

Stewart, N. (2020, June 26). Black activists wonder: Is protesting just trendy for white people? *The New York Times*. https://www.nytimes.com/2020/06/26/nyregion/black-lives-matter-white-people-protesters.html

Taylor, C. (1994). *Multiculturalism*. Princeton University Press.

Thomas, C. (2020, August 20). Republicans' problems can be sourced to this Eisenhower legacy they must reject. *Fox News*. https://www.foxnews.com/opinion/republicans-problems-eisenhower-legacy-cal-thomas

United Nations Development Program. (2009). *Why dialogue matters for conflict prevention and peacebuilding*. www.undp.org.dam.undp.library.crisisprevention

17
WHEN THE PAST IS ALWAYS PRESENT: HERITAGE RIGHTS, MONUMENTS, AND CULTURAL DIVIDES

Anya B. Russian

Background

There are over 700 Confederate monuments that stand outside of courthouses, legislative buildings, libraries, parks, town squares, or on college campuses throughout the United States, though concentrated predominantly in the southeast region of that country (Southern Poverty Law Center [SPLC], 2019a, 2019b, 2021). To some, these monuments are nostalgic testimonials to the sacrifices of soldiers who fought for the cause of states' rights during the U.S. Civil War (1861–1865). To social justice advocates, however, these monuments reflect a brutal history of racial subjugation that betrays American ideals and undermines the necessary work of building a more progressive 21st century society.

Since the spring of 2020, the largest social protest movement in U.S. history (Buchanan et al., 2020) has reignited deep-seated debate about what constitutes just and socially responsible policy regarding the fate of controversial cultural heritage sites. Confederate monuments quickly became the symbolic centerpiece of a now global movement demanding substantive changes to systemic forms of racialized inequities.

Many regard transforming public spaces of commemoration that mark colonial legacies as a necessary step in achieving this goal. This raises larger questions about the ways that heritage sites can mediate contemporary struggles for social justice in societies where certain ethnic or racialized communities have been historically marginalized. However, popular legal and cultural assumptions guiding what and how we commemorate often limit the ways difficult history is acknowledged and collectively negotiated.

Heritage practices are ultimately a litmus for the willingness, preparedness, and capacity of multiethnic societies to address these challenges, and in many cases, to evolve with conflicting memory scripts as they are being renegotiated. Examining the case of Confederate monuments brings into relief the psychocultural and legal obstacles that often underride this decision-making. In particular, it demands new evaluations of what is legitimate heritage-protection and what are alternative pathways of heritage engagement, particularly in asymmetric conflicts.

Locating commemorative controversy

Concerns about the integrity of commemorative spaces are neither recent, nor unique to the American context. The African American community and press vigorously protested Confederate monuments dating back to their original construction over a century ago (Watson, 2020). Native Americans have for years resisted public figures of colonial icons such as Christopher Columbus ("Confederate and Columbus," 2020) and Juan de Oñate (Mars, 2020) on the grounds that those representations erase their experiences of cultural genocide. Contemporary struggles ensuing between ethnic Estonians and ethnic Russians over the removal of Soviet occupation era monuments (Brüggemann & Kasekamp, 2008) invoke similar problems when ideological projects of the past contest liberation movements of the present. In 2018, India's Prime Minister Narendra Modi erected the world's tallest statue—"The Statue of Unity"—while the Muslim minority has seen its historical landmarks stripped of their names, its history removed from textbooks, and citizenship laws and deadly mob violence reinforcing a culture of exclusion (Gettleman & Abi-Habib, 2020; Kidangoor, 2018).

What has changed is the speed at which distinct forms of social protest that cut across cultural and international borders have become visibly catalyzing to others. They have converged around the shared question of what should be done with symbols that simultaneously harm, erase, remember, and celebrate in the public landscape. In South Africa, the 2015 #Rhodes Must Fall student movement fought successfully to remove statues of colonizer Cecil Rhodes from the University of Cape Town campus ("Rhodes Statue," 2015). This spawned similar protests at Oxford University in the United Kingdom, which gained traction again amid the wave of global protests in 2020 (Mackey, 2015). In that same year, growing protest culminated in the removal of statues of colonial leader King Leopold II in Belgium (Pronczuk & Zaveri, 2020).

In Canada, statues of the first Prime Minister John A. MacDonald and Queen Victoria have been decapitated or covered in paint in response to decades of forced removals of Canada's Indigenous youth into state-sponsored residential schools (Shingler, 2020) and British expansion that stripped Indigenous people of land. Thousands marched in the summer of 2021 in Winnipeg, Canada in peaceful mourning for the hundreds of recently discovered, unmarked remains of such children (Bergen, 2021). The pedestal of Queen Victoria is now lined with red handprints and a sea of staked, orange flags converting the site from an homage to a citizen-made countermemorial.

These cases are just a few examples of the ways commemorative choices in multiethnic societies can inflame division, yet also be keystones to shape new meaning-processes among communities. Monuments that reinforce power of dominant groups can also be used to recalibrate the agency of communities whose experiences have been historically marginalized. Often, the question of alternative monuments, and alternative spaces that engage the public with history in more complex ways, lurks in the shadows.

Collective identity and rites of omission

Heritage practices like flags, parades, holidays, plaques, or statues reveal how collective group identities are maintained, emboldened, and differentiated through the act of public performance (Ross, 2007; Volkan, 1997). Power over public space can be exercised through various identities such as class (Lefebvre, 1974), gender (Massey, 1994), or race and ethnicity (Wilson, 2012). It may be justified by claims to security or social justice (Mitchell, 2003) or by an act of public mourning (McIvor, 2016). Commemorative power is sometimes articulated by an original connection to or current occupation of land (Ross, 2007) or by rapid ideological projects and social movements aimed at altering the social order or governing authority (Brüggemann & Kasekamp, 2008; Lixinski, 2018; Mitchell, 2003; Savage, 2017; Upton, 2015).

In spaces of deep-seated conflict or structural inequity, these identities often produce competing narratives that vie for authorship over a linked physical and psychological territory. Stories shared in the family, in schools, or in cultural spaces are the links that build and sustain inclusive or exclusive community identities (Senehi, 2011).

Monuments are symbolic expressions of these stories. They typically present the preferred, or official, narratives of a community, while concealing the unwanted ones—what James C. Scott (1990) calls the "hidden transcripts" (p. 4). In entrenched intercommunal conflicts, communities often compress their particular history into "chosen traumas" (Volkan, 1997). Vamik Volkan (1997) explains that these can take on mythic proportions. The culture and values of a community then cohere around experiences and events that individuals may have never experienced directly and dismiss traumas perceived to lie outside of that experience.

Monuments are one way to ensure that valued cultural narratives maintain their moral, political, or cultural authority over time. They lend a visual certainty to the emotions that connect people to each other and to the places they know (Ross, 2007). As distinguished spaces, they facilitate rituals that transport shared meaning passed down across generations (Volkan, 1997). In this sense, monuments are existential objects. However, because identity is neither static nor uniform (Cook-Huffman, 2011) heritage monuments are landmarks that are always under threat (Chidester & Linenthal, 1995).

Mainstream American debate about whether to remove or to preserve Confederate monuments reflects entrenched ideological divides that have been shaped by histories of selective narration passed over generations. Civil War reenactments, most Confederate memorials, and accompanying museums typically venerate a glossy image of the pre-Civil War American South. They often neglect to mention the four million black Africans and their descendants who were enslaved at the start of the Civil War by an elite group of white landowners, or they portray slavery as a benevolent institution (Letson, 2018; Palmer & Wessler, 2018; Southern Poverty Law Center, 2019a).

Confederate monuments were a way to sanction an evolving system of white supremacy that reimagined ways to deprive African Americans of equal legal, civil, and political rights in the American South. The majority of these statues were constructed 30–50 years after the end of the Civil War, during the repressive Jim Crow period, when states legally enforced segregation between blacks and whites, voter suppression, and labor restrictions. Thousands of African Americans as well as many white citizens were lynched during this period when the Ku Klux Klan terrorized communities and those suspected of violating segregationist policies (Equal Justice Initiative, 2017).

To many racialized communities, Confederate or colonial monuments are living testimonies of how resilient prejudice can be when there is a culture of denial around histories of violence. For instance, subsequent spikes in Confederate monument construction coincided with the Civil Rights Movement in the 1950s and 1960s. Thirty-two were erected or rededicated during the 21st century, coinciding with the presidency of the nation's first African American president Barack Obama from 2008 to 2016 (Lixinski, 2018). Voices from Black Lives Matter and antiracism movements are quick to point out that disproportionate incarceration of African Americans in the world's largest prison system (Alexander, 2010; Wagner, 2012), disproportionate police violence targeting African Americans and other racialized communities (Goff et al., 2016; Hansen, 2017), systematic state voter disenfranchisement (Abrams, 2020), as well as ongoing income equality (Inequality.Org, n.d.), redlining (Glantz & Martinez, 2018), and housing segregation in cities across the country ("Segregation in America," 2018) are expressions of normalized racism that is still celebrated in stone.

Despite the poor optics of continual memorializing in the face of well-documented civil and human rights violations, southern states have largely resisted changes to the status quo. Seven of them have forbidden any modifications to current Confederate monuments whatsoever (Bissell, 2019), although Virginia rescinded this law as of March 2020 (Rankin, 2020). Meanwhile, recent polls suggest a rapidly increasing majority of Americans favor removal of the monuments (Quinnipiac University Poll, 2020). The recent surge in the toppling of Confederate statues in the American South as well as statues in Europe and Canada, are in part reactions to cultural practices that remain deaf to context and sheltered by cemented laws.

What the law does get right are the intrinsic difficulties of equitably brokering commonly circulated discourses against the backdrop of histories that are richly complex. Consider that 75 percent of white Southerners at the time of the Civil War did not own any slaves at all but chose to support slavery and the war fought, at least in part, for its preservation (Hall et al., 2019). Certain Native American groups, themselves victims of American settler expansionism—owned black slaves, and some defended the Confederacy (Healy, 2020). Meanwhile, the industrial economy of the North enslaved vast numbers of Africans itself, transported the enslaved to and across the United States, and provided vital machinery for the slavery-driven southern cotton economy (Ross, 2018). This leads Marc Howard Ross (2018) to the conclusion that an elapsed conversation about the complexities of race in America ultimately bridges, rather than divides, the North and the South. Unanswered questions remain about what can be done individually and collectively to account for past wrongs, to repair their ongoing legacies, and to support new types of relationships between blacks and whites as well other racialized communities.

Ideally, monuments can provide a scaffolding to explore these questions and to reflect upon the paradoxes of historical memory. However, this is complicated by the fact that heritage landmarks often serve conflicting purposes. To communities whose likenesses and stories have historically been omitted from the symbolic landscape, embodied representations of significant figures through traditional forms of commemoration can be a powerful form of truth-telling, public acknowledgment, or reparation. However, simultaneously maintaining old monuments that glorify the difficult histories new monuments respond to can further the myth that there are two separate heritages that can comfortably coexist without implicating each other (Upton, 2015). This view ensures that monuments omitting violent chapters of history remain permanent arbiters of the public record. Meanwhile, a well-documented history of police or other systemic violence that is disproportionately experienced by marginalized racial or ethnic communities often remains off the formal record where it can be readily denied. Heritage law and commemorative practices should strive to account for those discrepancies, especially when they create barriers to transformative peacebuilding and transitional justice processes.

Key insights

The struggles over Confederate monuments expose problems of power, representation, and human security that emerge when nonnegotiable accounts of history are subjected to a critical lens. Attempts to reincorporate memory that has been ritually sacrificed frequently aggravate ethnic conflict, often to the point of violence. Monuments become both the shield and the sword for diverse social grievances, adopting new meanings as culture changes. They are frequently entangled in legal precedents that compromise efforts to rectify representation of minority group heritage.

Demographic shifts and cultural violence

Violent reaction to changes in the commemorative landscape often converges with wider unrest around symbolic shifts in power that are threatening to dominant groups. Steadily increasing nonwhite and immigrant populations in the United States (Vespa et al., 2020) have produced malaise among many in the country who find demographic changes threatening to their ideas of American culture (Klein, 2020). Proposed changes to Confederate monuments, some as simple as moving them from the front of public courthouses to Confederate graveyards, have been likened to terrorism (Lixinski, 2018) or cultural genocide (Kennedy, 2019; Marusak, 2020). These sentiments were violently expressed during a 2017 protest against the removal of the Robert E. Lee Confederate statue in Charlottesville, Virginia, where a counterprotestor was killed after being intentionally run over by a vehicle. This coincides with record increases in hate crimes against members of many racialized communities since the election of the nation's first black President Barack Obama in 2008 (Southern Poverty Law Center, 2019b).

Monumental concepts in law

Violence can also take more covert forms such as laws that thwart efforts to reimagine prevailing cultural narratives. Bissell (2019) articulates how restrictive heritage laws passed by many southeastern American states in recent years fall squarely within an international legal precedent that regards heritage as an intrinsic cultural good that should be continually preserved. This paradigm emerged in global reaction to widespread looting and destruction of cultural heritage after World War II, followed by similar incidents in the former Yugoslavia in the 1990s and in Afghanistan in 2001.

While the preservation of cultural heritage can often protect the rights of minority or marginalized populations, it can also undermine those efforts. One problem is that heritage laws are often blind to the context they wish to protect. They are built on an understanding of heritage and heritage decision-makers as intrinsically neutral (Bissell, 2019; Lixinski, 2018). In this view, heritage can only enrich the collective human experience, not detract from it. However, this frame fails to account for the "cultural violence" (Galtung, 1990) committed in the act of protecting heritage that commemorates or validates internationally recognized human rights violations (Bissell, 2019) nor does it account for heritage that is lost due to omission (Lixinski, 2018). When interpreted in isolation, controversial heritage can play a role in silently perpetuating what peace scholar Johan Galtung (1996) calls "negative peace." This includes indirect violence that results from covert discrimination endorsed by certain monuments or structural patterns like class inequality, unequal hiring in the workplace, and disparate access to quality health care, housing, or education.

Preservationist frames also fail to clarify to *which* community heritage law should hold itself accountable. Maintaining existing historical monuments may protect rights to free expression for certain communities, while violating the cultural, civil, and expressive rights of others. Protectionist law does not speak to the social justice question of whether heritage is equitably represented. Nor does it offer any guidance on how to achieve a more diverse public rendering of heritage. Toppling of statues by protestors across the United States, Europe, and Canada responds to the fact that ostensibly neutral laws have for too long narrowed their audience and ignored protest by those whom they do not see belonging to it.

Lastly, preservationist policies ignore the long history of heritage destruction across cultures. Bissell (2019) points out that this can offer symbolic, cathartic, and practical impacts, particularly for historically marginalized racial or ethnic groups. Certain events like the 1989 toppling of the

Berlin Wall or the 2003 destruction of a statue of Saddam Hussein during the Iraq war are often celebrated. Moreover, the practice of destroying monuments of old regimes frequently accompanies political or cultural transitions. For instance, in the American colonies, a statue of King George III was torn down, paraded through the streets of New York, and then melted after the signing of the American Declaration of Independence. The wave of current and ongoing protests against Confederate and colonial statues may be better appreciated as another example of previous historical attempts to secure greater freedoms and inclusivity. By their very nature, such efforts are frequently forced to bypass laws that were fashioned for the opposite purpose.

Implications for teaching and training

There are no perfect algorithms for countries such as the United States to reconcile freedom of speech with the "difficult knowledge" (Britzman, 1998, p. 118) that ultimately lies at the heart of their controversy over statues. Even if there were, these formulas would necessarily have to adapt with time. Yet grappling with paradoxes that implicate the past and the present, as uncomfortable as it may be, is the honest work of any multiethnic society with a history of intercommunal conflict. What may be a better barometer for assessing public policy on monuments and controversial history in general, is therefore the quality of the knowledge-platform that is produced. Creating curious citizens who embrace complexity as an asset and appreciate reflexive processes of meaning-making are skills that transcend context and generation.

When plaques on certain monuments are scripted into law, the job of historical reckoning then becomes the task of more porous spaces such as online discussion groups, museums, radio, art, or social protest. Conflict transformation theorist John Paul Lederach (2005) views these flexible structures as critical instruments to support relationship building across communities while accommodating the unpredictable nature of conflict. Spaces that facilitate interactive, multifaceted, or ambivalent encounters with history help to practice different ways of seeing. They encourage individuals to not only reflect back on history but to locate themselves in its making. This is a powerful form of resistance to systems, leaders, or cultural artifacts that promote ideas that the past is unalterable.

This might involve devising new ways of telling history. For instance, a typical chronological timeline or physical likenesses of a single heroic figure, whether the multiplied images of a Confederate soldier or of Civil Rights leader Martin Luther King, have a tendency to exclude the contributions of women or of more disperse grassroots activism. Traditional commemorative forms reinforce the notion that history, like our present, is made of great individuals rather than of complex partnerships and collaborations across intersectional groups and coalitions. These are the ultimate building-blocks for sustainable transformation of conflict and positive peacebuilding.

Flexible platforms

In the last 20 years, and with increasing momentum, a plethora of notable civil society initiatives in the United States have been supporting processes that foster alternative knowledge-building. By inviting open participation in democratic reflections about the commemorative landscape and the interpretations that compose history, they help to create what David McIvor (2016) calls a "circuitry of civic recognition" (p. 164). This emphasizes that official rights and cultural acknowledgment are only real in so far as they are mirrored in everyday practices and spaces.

Monument Lab, based in the U.S. city of Philadelphia, facilitates collaborations among artists, researchers, students, historians, activists, and local municipalities across the United States and with global partners. Site specific, creative initiatives develop commemorative spaces that challenge prevailing perspectives, methods, and mediums through which history is frequently articulated. This might be an impermanent monument that invites public comments or modification (Farber, 2019) or custom posters detailing lesser-known aspects of local history posted on the windows of abandoned houses (Farber, 2018). These methods of community engagement educate on many levels. They reach a broader audience and interrupt traditional expectations of how knowledge is produced and where it is found. By doing so, they elicit the contingent meanings of the past in a shifting present.

Other civil society initiatives such as Hope in the Cities serve as models for how communities can critically engage with monuments when removal is forbidden. This was the case until recently in the project's home state of Virginia. Founded in 1993, this organization was an early grassroots leader in bringing underacknowledged histories to civic life. Hope in the Cities has now grown into a multipronged collaboration that incorporates diverse community stakeholders and works across other cities within the United States and abroad. It highlights how counternarratives and countermovements can emerge amid stagnant or incendiary social prescriptions that often obscure the complex labor of history-telling.

Another nonprofit, the Equal Justice Initiative, demonstrates how truth-telling about unsettling history can mobilize individual stories into broader networks that support cultural reckoning. The organization collaborates with communities throughout the United States to gather information about the over 4,000 racial terror lynchings that occurred in the country between 1877 and 1950 (Equal Justice Initiative, 2017). Community partners host local forums to examine and discuss the meaning of these atrocities, and in turn, the Equal Justice Initiative assists in erecting a commemorative plaque detailing the lynching in their county. Soil from the site is included in a growing collection at the Initiative's Legacy Museum, based in Montgomery, Alabama, which dedicates itself to documenting the violence of that era. This work recognizes that expanding the commemorative landscape is not merely a case of substituting one story with another. It is about tapping local resources and knowledge to create infrastructures of long-term community engagement prepared to independently grapple with those stories and with future ones.

American museums are also increasingly recognizing their role in equipping citizens for processes of social change. Countless local, regional, and national museums have used online exhibits, interactive webinars, storytelling, and recommended resource lists to interrogate American experiences of race and to encourage cross-community discussion and learning about its impact on civic life. These efforts help to make a combustive moment of widespread social protest and racial reckoning more legible.

These types of civil society and cultural initiatives embody a "moral imagination" (Lederach, 2005), which can leverage community knowledge to help build a new web of relationships. They also center process over mere outcome, a consideration that conflict resolution or neoliberal peacebuilding agendas sometimes bypass. Through these processes, new rituals that allow for the creation of a shared identity may occur—what Benjamin J. Broome (2011) calls a "third culture" (p. 195). In cultures divided by violence, vitriol, and fragmentation of public spaces, this work is more important than ever.

Implications for practice and policy

Unfortunately, initiatives like these are only able to influence the public to the degree that they are known. They compete with well-funded productions of mainstream media that often profit off a theater of violence and with social media platforms that often privilege quickly digestible ideas or polarizing rhetoric. It is important for funding organizations, especially those interested in antiracism efforts, to consider donating to initiatives that propel creative entrepreneurship in memory practices. Business leaders and corporations have donated unprecedented amounts since 2020 to historically black colleges and universities (Bunn, 2021). Supporting spaces that nurture critical engagement with history and that bring together ethnic and racial communities are an important spoke of wider education efforts. In the meantime, public schools, educators, and parents should be proactively partnering with these organizations, not only to take advantage of the learning opportunities they facilitate, but to inspire the next generation to creatively advocate for deeper forms of historical engagement. By partnering with alternative public history-telling projects, social justice advocates are more likely to compel changes to heritage law that currently forbid such movement.

However, transformation of minds often takes time in systems that incentivize injustices toward minoritized populations. More than 160 Confederate symbols, including over 90 monuments, have been removed since the nation-wide protests began in May 2020, although not always through force (SPLC, 2021). Book sales by black authors have soared in the United States (Harris, 2020), yet racial schisms persist in more covert forms such as voter disenfranchisement laws and the attack on the poor or stymied changes to school curriculums. It is critical to recognize these obstacles and particularly the history of heritage destruction as it articulates the complicated relationship all societies have with their monuments. This should ideally enlarge governmental and public considerations of what constitutes vandalism and violent destruction of cultural property. Moreover, it should cultivate greater understanding of the role of large-scale protest, not merely as a form of public disturbance, but as a form of public commemoration that challenges the ownership Confederate monuments and others like them have over official meaning-making.

The United States might look to South Africa which has employed a wide array of strategies to reimagine the symbolic landscape erected during the apartheid years (Lixinski 2018; Ross, 2007), yet whose efforts also testify to their limited impact on pervasive structural inequities and residual traumas dividing communities (Holmes & Loehwing, 2016). Ukraine provides insight into how total removal of statuary influences historical memory, as that country destroyed thousands of Lenin statues after the fall of communism (Lixinski, 2018). Meanwhile, Spain's 2007 law requiring the removal of statues of dictator Francisco Franco provides a glimpse into the sometimes unintended impacts heritage destruction has on memory practices working in the service of national reconciliation (Hadzelek, 2012).

Countries like the United States could also benefit from a national task force with regional and local chapters dedicated to determining clear parameters for addressing the past. Formal participation by government and civic leadership is critical to fulfilling broader processes of national reconciliation. (Scott, 2014). Currently, in the United States, irregular allegiances result in schizophrenic heritage orientations. Existing state laws forbidding modifications and removal of heritage sites have led some Southern governors, municipalities, and universities to take extralegal steps to try to remove Confederate monuments they no longer want on their property, in the name of protecting them.

Meanwhile, state-sponsored attempts to widen the lens of commemorative practices do exist. Examples include the array of Civil Rights monuments erected starting in the 1990s (Upton, 2015), the African Burial Ground National Monument, dedicated in 2006, and a plethora of municipal efforts across diverse cities to erect monuments to African Americans who have contributed to the life of the nation. In 2016, the National Museum of African American History and Culture formally opened a physical site in the nation's prestigious Smithsonian Museum complex. This was a culmination of over a century's worth of efforts by community leaders and memory entrepreneurs in the black community (Wilson, 2012). However, during the last decade, over $40 million federal U.S. taxpayer dollars have gone to Confederate sites and organizations like the Sons and Daughters of the Confederacy, many of which redact a history unapologetically devoid of slavery and its ills (Letson, 2018).

Coherent heritage policy is ultimately an important metric to assess national commitment to acknowledging the unique experiences of racial or ethnic minoritized groups. This requires attention to considerations such as the value distinctions between a unique historical landmark and a popularized one like Confederate monuments, which were mass-produced for both the North and the South by companies who profited off their popularized iconography (Savage, 2017). International heritage law should also help tackle the challenging question of whether and when monuments have a date of expiration. Should Confederate monuments constructed in recent decades or during the 1960s receive equal protections as those constructed around the turn of the century, even then, long after the close of the U.S. Civil War? Or, in cases like this, should additional monuments be required to add something new to the collective memory? If so, how are such decisions to be enforced or encouraged?

Ultimately, laws are to monuments what monuments are to history, both convene the spirit and highest aspirations of a people. They seek to erect a certain version of a good or just world into public practice, a version that is unfortunately never complete. Laws, like monuments, are subject to the vagaries of power and historical interpretation. They tell as much about the messenger as they do about the message, both of which change over time, while laws and monuments remain mostly bound to their form.

Meanwhile, history is an ever-changing experiment subject to infinite lenses and scripts. There is no one-size-fits-all formula for grappling with contested symbolic landscapes and historical memory. Our monuments, like laws, would be better understood as palimpsests, able to accommodate new stories, old stories, and promote hybrid stories that have yet to take form. Perhaps there is space in the symbolic landscape for a little more doubt and curiosity, the right kind of forgetting, that doesn't have to compromise worthwhile convictions yet that can lead us to ask different questions. In the absence of consistent, state-sponsored agendas for reconciling with living history, citizen-led or nongovernmental spaces which curate responsive platforms are critical to the work of preparing social actors for this paradigm shift.

References

Abrams, S. (2020). *Our time is now: Power, purpose, and the fight for a fair America*. Henry Holt and Company.

Alexander, M. (2010). *The new Jim Crow: Mass incarceration in the age of colorblindness*. New Press.

Bergen, R. (2021, July 7). Mother figure or colonial oppressor? Examining Queen Victoria's legacy after Winnipeg statue toppled. *CBC*. https://www.cbc.ca/news/canada/manitoba/queen-victoria-winnipeg-statues-residential-schools-colonialism-british-empire-1.6090322

Bissell, V. E. P. (2019). Monuments to the confederacy and the right to destroy in cultural-property law. *Yale Law Journal, 128*(4), 1130–1172.

Britzman, D. P. (1998). *Lost subjects, contested objects: Toward a psychoanalytic inquiry of learning*. State University of New York Press.

Broome, B. J. (2011). Building relational empathy through an interactive design process. In D. J. D. Sandole, S. Byrne, I. Staroste-Sandole, & J. Senehi (Eds.), *Handbook of conflict analysis and resolution* (pp. 184–200). Routledge.

Brüggemann, K., & Kasekamp, A. (2008). The politics of history and the "War of Monuments" in Estonia. *Nationalities Papers, 36*(3), 425–448. https://doi.org/10.1080/00905990802080646

Buchanan, L., Bui, Q., & Patel, J. K. (2020, July 3). Black lives matter may be the largest movement in U.S. history. *The New York Times*. https://www.nytimes.com/interactive/2020/07/03/us/george-floyd-protests-crowd-size.html

Bunn, C. (2021, February 19). From Covid aid to record donations: Influx of funding helps keep HBCUs' doors open. *NBC News*. https://www.nbcnews.com/news/nbcblk/covid-aid-record-donations-influx-funding-helps-keep-hbcus-doors-n1258357

Chidester, D. & Linenthal, E. T. (1995). Introduction. In D. Chidester & E. T. Linenthal (Eds.), *American sacred space* (pp. 1–42). Indiana University Press.

Confederate and Columbus statues toppled by US protesters. (2020, June 11). *BBC News*. https://www.bbc.com/news/world-us-canada-53005243

Cook-Huffman, C. (2011). The role of identity in conflict. In D. J. D. Sandole, S. Byrne, I. Staroste-Sandole, & J. Senehi (Eds.), *Handbook of conflict analysis and resolution* (pp. 19–31). Routledge.

Equal Justice Initiative. (2017). *Lynching in America: Confronting the legacy of racial terror*. https://lynchinginamerica.eji.org/report/

Farber, P. (2018, October). Designing justice in New Orleans with paper monuments (Bryan C. Lee Jr. And Sue Mobley) (No. 3) [Audio Podcast Episode]. *Monument Lab*. https://monumentlab.com/podcast/designing-justice-in-new-orleans-with-paper-monuments-bryan-c-lee-jr-and-sue-mobley

Farber, P. (2019, October). Public noise with Paul Ramírez Jonas: New monuments for new cities (No. 17) [Audio Podcast Episode]. *Monument Lab*. https://monumentlab.com/podcast/public-noise-with-paul-ramirez-jonas-new-monuments-for-new-cities

Galtung, J. (1990). Cultural violence. *Journal of Peace Research, 27*(3), 291–305. https://doi.org/10.1177/0022343390027003005

Galtung, J. (1996). *Peace by peaceful means: Peace and conflict, development and civilization*. SAGE Publications.

Gettleman, J., & Abi-Habib, M. (2020, March 1). In India, Modi's policies have lit a fuse. *New York Times*. https://www.nytimes.com/2020/03/01/world/asia/india-modi-hindus.html

Glantz, A., & Martinez, E. (2018, February 15). Modern-day redlining: Banks discriminate in lending. *Reveal*. https://www.revealnews.org/article/for-people-of-color-banks-are-shutting-the-door-to-homeownership/

Goff, P. A., Lloyd, T., Geller, A., Steven, R., & Glaser, J. (2016). *The science of justice: Race, arrests, and police use of force*. Center for Policing Equity. https://policingequity.org/images/pdfs-doc/CPE_SoJ_Race-Arrests-UoF_2016-07-08-1130.pdf

Hadzelek, A. (2012). Spain's "pact of silence" and the removal of Franco's statues. In D. Kirby (Ed.), *Past law, present histories* (pp. 153–176). ANU Press.

Hall, A. B., Huff, C., & Kuriwaki, S. (2019). Wealth, slave ownership, and fighting for the Confederacy: An empirical study of the American Civil War. *American Political Science Review, 113*(3), 658–673. https://doi.org/10.1017/S0003055419000170

Hansen, E. (2017, November 10). The forgotten minority in police shootings. *CNN*. https://www.cnn.com/2017/11/10/us/native-lives-matter/index.html

Harris, E. A. (2020, June 5). People are marching against racism. They're also reading about it. *The New York Times*. https://www.nytimes.com/2020/06/05/books/antiracism-books-race-racism.html

Healy, J. (2020, September 8). Black, Native American and fighting for recognition in Indian country. *The New York Times*. https://www.nytimes.com/2020/09/08/us/enslaved-people-native-americans-oklahoma.html

Holmes, C. E., & Loehwing, M. (2016). Icons of the old regime: Challenging South African public memory strategies in #RhodesMustFall. *Journal of Southern African Studies, 42*(6), 1207–1223. https://doi.org/10.1080/03057070.2016.1253927

Inequality.Org. (n.d.) *Racial economic inequality*. https://inequality.org/facts/racial-inequality/

Kennedy, J. R. (2019, January 9). *The cost of southern cultural genocide*. Abbeville Institute. https://www.abbevilleinstitute.org/blog/the-cost-of-southern-cultural-genocide/

Kidangoor, A. (2018, October 31). India unveils the world's tallest statue amid controversy. *Time*. https://time.com/5434131/worlds-tallest-statue-unity-india-patel/

Klein, E. (2020). *Why we're polarized*. Avid Reader Press.

Lederach, J. P. (2005). *The moral imagination: The art and soul of building peace*. Oxford University Press.

Lefebvre, H. (1974). *The production of space*. Blackwell.

Letson, A. (Host). (2018, December 8). Monumental lies [Audio Podcast Episode]. *Reveal*. https://www.revealnews.org/episodes/monumental-lies/

Lixinski, L. (2018). Confederate monuments and international law. *Wisconsin International Law Journal, 35*(3), 549–608.

Mackey, R. (2015, November 6). Oxford students want statue of Cecil Rhodes removed. *New York Times.* https://www.nytimes.com/2015/11/07/world/europe/oxford-students-want-statue-of-cecil-rhodes-removed.html

Mars, R. (Host). (2020, June 30). Return of Onate's foot (no. 404) [Audio Podcast Episode]. In *99% Invisible.* https://99percentinvisible.org/episode/return-of-onates-foot/

Marusak, J. (2020, August 7). Moving NC Confederate statue 'smacks of ethnic genocide,' woman says ahead of protest. *Charlotte Observer.* https://www.charlotteobserver.com/news/local/article244787957.html

Massey, D. B. (1994). *Space, place, and gender.* University of Minnesota Press.

McIvor, D. W. (2016). *Mourning in America: Race and the politics of loss.* Cornell University Press.

Mitchell, D. (2003). *The right to the city: Social justice and the fight for public space.* Guilford Press.

Palmer, B., & Wessler, S. F. (2018, December). The costs of the Confederacy. *Smithsonian Magazine.* https://www.smithsonianmag.com/history/costs-confederacy-special-report-180970731/

Pronczuk, M., & Zaveri, M. (2020, June 9). Statue of Leopold II, Belgian king who brutalized Congo, is removed in Antwerp. *New York Times.* https://www.nytimes.com/2020/06/09/world/europe/king-leopold-statue-antwerp.html

Quinnipiac University Poll. (2020, June 17). 68% say discrimination against black Americans a "serious problem," Quinnipiac University national poll finds; slight majority support removing Confederate statues. https://poll.qu.edu/Poll-Release?releaseid=3786

Rankin, S. (2020). Lawmakers pass bill allowing Confederate monument removals. *Canadian Press.* http://uml.idm.oclc.org/login?url=http://search.ebscohost.com/login.aspx?direct=true&db=rch&AN=MYO425690837320&site=ehost-live

Rhodes statue removed in Cape Town as crowd celebrates. (2015, April 9). *BBC News.* https://www.bbc.com/news/world-africa-32236922

Ross, M. H. (2007). *Cultural contestation in ethnic conflict.* Cambridge University Press.

Ross, M. H. (2018). *Slavery in the north: Forgetting history and recovering memory.* University of Pennsylvania Press.

Savage, K. (2017). *Standing soldiers, kneeling slaves: Race, war, and monument in nineteenth-century America.* Princeton University Press.

Scott, I. M. (Ed.). (2014). *Crimes against humanity in the land of the free: Can a truth and reconciliation process heal racial conflict in America?* Praeger.

Scott, J. C. (1990). *Domination and the arts of resistance: Hidden transcripts.* Yale University Press.

Segregation in America. (2018, April 4). *The Economist.* https://www.economist.com/graphic-detail/2018/04/04/segregation-in-america

Senehi, J. (2011). Building peace: Storytelling to transform conflicts constructively. In D. J. D. Sandole, S. Byrne, I. Staroste-Sandole, & J. Senehi (Eds.), *Handbook of conflict analysis and resolution* (pp. 201–214). Routledge.

Shingler, B. (2020, August 31). Montreal considers next move for toppled John A. Macdonald statue. *CBC.* https://www.cbc.ca/news/canada/montreal/john-a-macdonald-montreal-1.5706485

Southern Poverty Law Center. (2019a, February 1). *Whose heritage? Public symbols of the Confederacy.* https://www.splcenter.org/20190201/whose-heritage-public-symbols-confederacy

Southern Poverty Law Center. (2019b, February 19). *Hate groups reach record high.* https://www.splcenter.org/news/2019/02/19/hate-groups-reach-record-high

Southern Poverty Law Center. (2021, February 23). *SPLC reports over 160 Confederate symbols removed in 2020.* https://www.splcenter.org/presscenter/splc-reports-over-160-confederate-symbols-removed-2020

Upton, D. (2015). *What can and can't be said: Race, uplift, and monument building in the contemporary south.* Yale University Press.

Vespa, J., Medina, L., & Armstrong, D. M. (2020, February). *Demographic turning points for the United States: Population projections for 2020 to 2060.* United States Census Bureau. https://www.census.gov/library/publications/2020/demo/p25-1144.html

Volkan, V. D. (1997). *Bloodlines: From ethnic pride to ethnic terrorism.* Westview Press.

Wagner, P. (2012, August 28). *Incarceration is not an equal opportunity punishment.* Prison Policy Initiative. https://www.prisonpolicy.org/articles/notequal.html

Watson, D. M. (2020, December 11). The racial reckoning with Confederate monuments seems new. But it dates back more than a century. *Virginian Pilot.* https://www.pilotonline.com/history/vp-nw-confederate-monuments-africanamerican-resistance-20201211-t6hw67kwvjdc5ggjm2kh7izkeu-story.html

Wilson, M. (2012). *Negro building: Black Americans in the world of fairs and museums.* University of California.

18
VOICES OF THEIR OWN: REFUGEES MISSING HOME AND BUILDING A FUTURE

Umut Ozkaleli

The concept of *home* is spoken of every day, and yet, what *home* entails is much more complex than a general, one-dimensional description. As the COVID-19 pandemic changes our daily routine, alters lives and threatens to overload health-care systems, our struggle against the virus was accompanied by the slogan, "stay home, stay safe." While its conceptualizations vary, ideals of *home* carry a strong mental image, almost singular and quite homogenous, projected through visuals and discourses. Such ideals of *home are* deeply rooted in the middle- and the upper-middle-class experiences. Hence, throughout the world there is a middle- and upper-middle-class depiction of *home*: windows that allow bright light to come into a living room that provides a sense of tranquility; a garden, even if small, to allow fresh air; a balcony to enjoy the sun or the singing of the birds; fridges that are full with food and drinks; children and adults whose only struggle is to adjust to challenges posed by work at home conditions. Despite there being numerous complaints about living in lockdown (e.g., boredom and gaining weight from excessive eating and immobility), sharing meals and spending time with family are stressed as the most important values. This ubiquitous image of *home* is not only fed to us via informal social media platforms but also through the policymakers as they encourage people to stay home to stay safe.

Safe *homes,* of course, are at the core of communal peace and harmony; yet, they are not readily available to everyone. What happens to people who do not have a safe shelter that can be called *home*? Can one be safe if confined with an abuser? Are all homes designed for us to spend long hours in them? Do they meet safety regulations? Do they get enough light and air? Do they have clean running water? What about heat for the cold winter days? Is there a room, or at least breathing space, for everyone? If all these are attained by wage workers, do the majority of them have job security to sustain their homes? Do blue-collar workers have any chance to work at home? What are the tangible and intangible necessities that make a place a *home*?

How do we relate the slogan of "stay home stay safe" to uprooted refugees who are struggling with finding a proper shelter? How do we understand *safety* when *home* is in places that do not recognize you as a citizen and when even citizens' rights are being violated? What happens to the refugees who do not have the proper documentation in these times when even the citizens are denied at the hospital doors due to the overwhelmed health-care systems? What happens to refugees who need regular health-care attention even when citizens', particularly senior citizens' health rights are perceived as less important than the economy? How can we understand "safe," and how do we need to examine this too readily available image of *home*?

As the COVID-19 pandemic has made even the most privileged feel a loss of personal security, it has become even more urgent to scrutinize refugee experiences and locate complexities that the word *home* entails. In confinement and isolation, when the sense of security is fundamentally challenged, understanding meanings of security and home, and losing home, becomes even more important to refugees. Our current situation may help us to empathize and relate with refugees, who live in constant uncertainty while being kept away from loved ones without any chance of being close to them. Further, it may lead us to explore new ways of community building by facing the reality of how we are all interlinked.

Refugee experiences show us that we cannot turn our backs and pretend that others' insecurities and lack of basic needs are none of our concern. Reading about the refugees' experiences of insecurity and losing *home* may be instrumental in helping us gain insight into the "safe homes" slogan and discern new ways to achieve a more equitable future. This chapter aims to discuss the Syrian refugee experiences with a special focus on the meaning of having (and not having) a *home*, along with some of the policy implications of such experiences.

Background

After the Syrian civil war erupted in 2011, approximately 5.6 million Syrians became refugees, mostly in the neighboring countries of Turkey, Lebanon, Jordan, and Iraq; a total of 3.6 million refugees are registered in the host country Turkey (UNHCR, 2020). While 2.4 percent live in the camps in Turkey, the majority live in urban areas, of which over 64 percent live close to or below the poverty line (Karasapan, 2019). Although there are approximately 2.1 million working-age Syrians in Turkey, between 500,000 and one million Syrians are actively working. Most of these are in irregular and informal jobs, as only around 65,000 work permits have been issued by the Turkish government (Kirisci & Kolasin, 2019). In other words, only three percent of working age Syrians have work permits. Owing to poverty, the need for work, and language barriers (not able to speak Turkish), 40 percent of Syrian refugee children remain out of school (Karasapan, 2019).

The voices that will resonate in this chapter are from Gaziantep, Turkey, where the Syrian refugee population was approximately 400,000 at the time when the interviews herein were conducted, comprising 20 percent of the total city population (Erdogan et al., 2017). Gaziantep is a border city to Aleppo, Syria, and hence, it hosts a considerable number of refugees from Aleppo. While most Syrian refugees share the Sunni Islamic faith with the dominant group in Turkey and the landscape of Gaziantep is similar to that of Aleppo, there are linguistic and cultural differences between the host community and the refugees. As the Turkish economy faced more challenges, tensions, and hostility toward refugees increased in Turkey along with the growing number of refugees in the country (Cagaptay & Yalkin, 2018; Cagaptay & Yuksel, 2019; Kirisci, 2014; Saracoglu & Bélanger, 2019), resembling the virulent ultra-nationalist xenophobic reactions toward refugees and immigrants in the European Union and the United States (Byrne *et al.,* 2019).

The refugees interviewed in this study came from different walks of life. There were refugees who lived in villages when they were in Syria and faced poverty as urban refugees in Gaziantep. There were middle- and upper-middle-class Syrians who spoke fluent English, which enabled them to either study at the universities or work in nongovernmental organizations (NGOs) related to Syrian refugee issues. Further, there were women who lost their husbands during the conflict and struggled to survive with their children. Additionally, there were refugees who left professional jobs in Syria but were struggling to survive, as they could not continue their old professions. In sum, Gaziantep resembled home for thousands of Syrian refugees, yet not as many of them were feeling at home in Gaziantep.

Key insights

Home is a complex yet crucial concept; it encompasses contradictory aspects, pulling us in different directions and making us struggle to locate ourselves in it. The complexity of *home* is that it is "experienced both as a location and as a set of relationships that shape identities and feelings of belonging," which makes the concept of home dynamic and mobile yet also rooted (Al-Ali & Koser, 2002; Ralph & Staeheli, 2011, p. 518). *Home* carries notions of security and belonging along with those of insecurity and oppression; home cannot be expressed only in terms of safety, familiarity, and freedom yet also in terms of struggle and conflict (Brickell, 2012). What is missed and not missed provides clues about how to organize our communities for creating a sense of belonging and security, thus defining ways to overcome injustice and oppression. "Home reflects both reality and ideal" (Moore, 2000, p. 209; cf. Brickell, 2012); hence, to get an insight into how "home is dreamt, conceptualized and experienced" (Ralph & Staeheli, 2011, p. 517), I asked participants what they missed about their left behind homes. What people miss (and do not miss) about a place is closely related to what they have left behind: the meaning of the place, their attachment to it, and what they are experiencing and struggling to find in their present moment.

By locating home through the voices of refugees, I aim to encourage the reader to converse with them about the idea of "home." I examine how close we are to what we imagine a home should be like, and how we conceptualize the existing and imagined *home* with the articulation of our experiences. Positive peace is deep and inclusive social justice experienced in everyday life (Byrne & Thiessen, 2019; Galtung, 1996), which can be achieved through emancipatory engagement by minority populations (Byrne et al., 2019b; Mac Ginty, 2008, 2011). In this case, refugee experiences and articulation of home can be instructive to become one of the pathways for us to reimagine and rebuild peace in societies in a relational approach to the concept of home.

Missing home is missing family and loved ones

For some refugees, home was directly related to being close to their loved ones—a combination of all the people they have known, loved, and interacted with in their everyday lives. Whether it is a 42-year-old widow homemaker (Amina) from Baniyas, or a 42-year-old single man (Firas) who was a merchant in Aleppo, several refugees stated that what they missed the most were gatherings and being surrounded by family and friends. Akila, a 24-year-old college student and NGO worker from Aleppo captures how not having all the family members together is the biggest challenge to her sense of home:

> Life for me was 4 o'clock in the afternoon. My Dad finished his work at four and for all of us, wherever we were, we had to come and sit at the table because we were having food together. Everyone must gather around the table. And we would sit around the table, not just for eating. My Dad has a sense of humor. At the table, we made fun of each other and laughed from our hearts. I really miss that. My world before the war was 4 o'clock, all of us sitting at the same table. Now, even Ramadan [holy month for Muslims] is without my parents. In Syria, Ramadan is when everyone gathers together and cooks; now, I am doing it all by myself.

As Alika suggests, religious rituals are meaningful for many in the company of family and friends. The month of Ramadan and *iftar* (breaking the fast) was a continuous theme for some of the refugees who are believers. The meaning of coming together to eat was explained by Salwa:

> Ramadan was very beautiful. But now, we are alone, just one family; earlier, it was 20 people eating from the same *sufra* (i.e., gathering around a meal). [*Sufra*] is on the floor. In the Arabic house, there are trees and flowers around you, and you create the *sufra* on the ground and eat together.

While food provides nutrition for the body, gathering together to share a meal nourishes people's sense of security and belonging. In Zeinan's (a 40-year-old teacher from Rakka) narration, food is the symbol of meaningful and peaceful existence:

> I miss everything. I miss my family. None of my sisters and brothers are here [in Gaziantep]. When I cry, I do not want anything or anybody to ask me why you are crying. I am angry. I hate to eat when I am alone. [That is why] sometimes I do not eat for one or two days. I remember once my home was full of people, with my family, my sisters and brothers, and their families. Here, there is no one, so, I do not eat. Every day, I write [poems] that war is bad, do not kill the other, you want to live, and so do the others. I want a child and [a] good future for my child, and so do the others.

Zeinan's description of missing being with her family blends with her view of war and need to find common ground between opposing sides. She stresses how all parties on different sides of the conflict need a similar sense of sharing and security, surrounded by people they love, with the hope of a good future for themselves and their children. Hence, in Zeinan's words, the missed home is intertwined with achieving positive peace.

For some people, like Joumana, a 28-year-old woman from Damascus, places were important so long as they were part of the interaction and sharing. Missing Syria or a city is connected to the memories she had in places with people she loved and their families and friends.

> [I miss] friends, of course, family gatherings, those are the main things. If I mention the streets, I think they belong to our memory, not to itself. I like some places and miss them. It is not related to the places but the gatherings and sharing.

From another angle, 23-year-old Haya's words resonate with Joumana's yearnings to locate home in connection and sharing with loved ones. Haya, who is also from Damascus, describes her home by intertwining it with her sister's feelings:

> You never run away from your home, it is always here, it is always there. Maybe I left the country, but I think of my sister who is in Damascus now. We have a farm in Damascus. Whenever she is in the farm, she says "you are not the ones who are the refugees, I am the one who is a refugee. I go to the same places without you and live in the house that I was raised, but you are not around."

The meaning that home entails becomes extremely complex when people face different dimensions of loss. Some lose the place and people simultaneously, whereas others lose the people while still living in the place. Nevertheless, all have the same feeling of no longer having a home. Here, the common point for analysis is how essential the integrity of families is for someone's sense of belonging, regardless of their location.

Missing home is missing the space and place, the familiarity, and culture

While for some refugees the concept of home is only meaningful when being surrounded by loved ones, for others, home is the articulation of feelings that are tied to the place. Some people miss not only family and friends but also being in that geography and being part of the long history of the land (cf. rootedness in Malkki, 1992, 1995). They miss the landscape and nature, the sea of Syria, the red color of dirt that felt distinct, and the trees that they nurtured like their children. Further, some miss the smell of their country, including, as Malak argued, "even the smell of the garbage." Smell symbolizes the "unobtainable," which "requires looking beyond [lost home's] material form to consider its multifaceted sensory qualities" (Petridou, 2001 cited in Brickell, 2012, p. 230).

The sense of familiarity is closely associated with home. Losing that familiarity was at the center of their sense of longing. Ramez, a 40-year-old man, missed the feel of living in his hometown of Aleppo. He longs for the time when the cities were lively and active until late at night. He nostalgically remembers the ability of abruptly deciding to go to Damascus or Homs for a visit at 9 pm. Some people miss their favorite restaurant and the market, while others yearn for their old room and pillows. Nawar, a 27-year-old man from Damascus, narrated his longing for the simplest of objects and mundane daily activities:

> [I miss] everything. Just being home. I would be happy to go, not even to my apartment but to my [childhood] room in my parents' apartment, which is not even my room anymore. I just want to go to that room and close the door for an hour. I would be so happy if that would have happened. You cannot describe home even if you try to devote an entire book. Somehow, it is not going to be enough to explain it. [I miss the] friends, whom I lost—who disappeared, died, traveled, and fled the country. I miss the family. [I miss] just my previous life, and if I had the chance to re-live it, I would have done the same stupid things.

Further, 18-year-old Anas explained the meaning of missing the places as "missing a room or a bunch of stones. [It might] sound odd. Yet, I have relations with places because I like to remember the things that happened inside of them."

While their social location and experiences in Syria were different, 47-year-old Genwa, who worked in a women's rights NGO, has similar longings. Although she showed high spirit and optimism throughout her conversation with me, when she spoke of what she missed about home, she had silent tears, and her bright voice cracked:

> [I miss] everything. I used to work in a place next to the Great Mosque in Aleppo. When I wanted to relax, I used to go and sit in [the bench outside of] that mosque. Next to it, there is the biggest *souq* (market) in the world, called *Al-Madina Souq*. I used to enter that place and smell the peppers and the spices and feel that I am smelling an entire civilization. Aleppo is really beautiful. I miss walking and seeing people walking. Ramadan was really beautiful there.

Being part of the home culture and feeling part of a place was repeated by others as their greatest longing. While 42-year-old Malek, who is from Latakia and worked in an NGO, explained that being away from Syria was like "a tree taken away from its root," Badia simply stated that she missed "being attached to Syria."

Home is often identified with the space and history of the land, talking about places like the bridge in Deir ez Zor and *Tadmor-Palymra* in Homs, or the old city of Aleppo. Kamal, a 50-year-old from Aleppo, stated that, as an architect, he had "a lot of memories and passion about Aleppo's old city. Aleppo especially has many amazing historical buildings and monuments, and for me, it represents the whole world."

Kamal's words echoed experiences shared by other refugees who were devastated by the destruction of historical sites in their country and hometowns. A shared sense of loss of home, due to war and destruction, surfaced in the recollections of 30-year-old Majed who recently became a father:

> I miss Aleppo and Idlib most of the time. Aleppo had a lot of markets and old buildings and areas. We cry about them when we see them. We cannot go back. These buildings and monuments had lasted for thousands of years and gone through a lot of force, but they were destroyed in this war. We had many old streets that aged through hundreds of years, and in one minute, an airstrike destroyed it all.

Sadness of participants such as Kamal, Majed, and Badia reveals a longing for what was lost and is now unattainable. Along with his narrative of the destruction of the places he loved, Majed talked about his mourning for his dead brother, whom he lost in the conflict. He also talked about a library that was destroyed and mentioned *Jabal al-Arba'in*, "the fortune mountain" as he called it, where he "used to go to heal people." This was the location where his brother was killed. The despair from seeing places being destroyed becomes the embodiment of feelings about everything and everyone that is lost.

How places make people feel also constitute crucial parts of a sense of identity and belonging. Refugees either witness the destruction of the most cherished places such as homes, worship places, historical sites and neighborhoods, or they see them besieged and made inaccessible to them. Their longing and sense of loss are closely related to the places being part of their identity and belonging. As Appadurai (1996) argues that the development of local life and neighborhoods creates "their own self-reproduction process that is fundamentally opposed to the imaginary of the nation-state, where neighborhoods are designed to be instances and exemplars of a generalizable mode of belonging to a wider territorial imaginary" (p. 191). Neighborhoods are under severe and deliberate attack, as such localities "may not meet the needs for spatial and social standardization that is prerequisite for the disciplined national citizen" (Appadurai, 1996, p. 191). That is why "the memories and attachments that local subjects have of and to their shop signs and street names, their favorite walkways and streetscapes, their times and places for congregating and escaping are often at odds with the needs of the nation-state for regulated public life" (Appadurai, 1996, p. 191; cf. Brickell, 2012). This articulation calls for continuous exploration about the ways different communities (e.g., refugees, immigrants, and racial, gender, and disabled minorities) are faced with policies that distance them from their sense of belonging and alienate them from their imagined home.

Missing home is missing being a part of change

Home can mean how people felt when they were working for the change that they wanted to see in Syria. They missed the feeling of being part of change, either through their profession or their voluntary work, and felt at a loss for home when they could not be part of a change within

Syria. Fatima, a 27-year-old college graduate who worked in an NGO as a case officer for Syrian refugee women's rights, explained that while her work in Turkey was also for Syrian women, working for change in Syria when she lived there felt different. Many refugees from different walks of life felt, like Fatima, a longing to be a part of the change they hoped and worked for. One of them was Ziyad, a newly married 27-year-old man, who worked as a journalist to uncover corruption:

> I miss the old work I had there [in Syria]. When I was doing the work [internet journalism], I was proud of it. I was working on issues related to poverty. Cancer patients' medication was very expensive, so the patients were getting state aid by going to hospitals to get the medication. Nevertheless, some could not get their medication ... We went after such issues. I miss those days. If I had the chance, I would have still done this job here. It was a job with high risks involved. There were gun threats to us, and our office was surrounded with guns. Still, if one day I would get a chance to tell my children, this would be something I was proud to have done.

Home is a politicized space (Blunt & Dowling, 2006; cf. Brickell, 2012), and social and political identities are constructed through place (Massey, 2001; cf. Moore, 2000). Some refugees had strong political identities and affiliations. Their political agency and how they located their identities through their politics created the context of where the idea of home was deeply connected. Let it be Leftist politics, or the desire to create an Islamic state and society, the phrase "back home" expressed a yearning that could not be completely fulfilled in the host community for the people with strong political commitments.

Missing home is not missing the insecurity and social collapse

There were also aspects of home that people did *not* miss. It is also important to analyze what drives people away from home. Two refugees missed being in their village, for they were close to the poverty line as urban refugees in Gaziantep. However, they did not consider going back to Syria because of a lack of security. Aisha, a 46-year-old homemaker who was struggling to survive in Gaziantep while her husband suffered serious health issues and was unable to work, missed her home in the village in Syria. However, she said the following:

> I miss my home, village, and childhood. Sometimes I sleep and dream about my village, but planes come, and they shoot, and I get scared and start running. Then, I wake up and feel relieved that it was a dream.

Displacement severely impacts people with limited means, placing an extra burden on their shoulders (Reinders & van der Land, 2008 cited in Brickell, 2012, p. 232). Indeed, an upper-class person, Alaa, who had a comfortable and well-decorated apartment in Gaziantep, told me,

> Even though I lived in this apartment for two years, cleaned it, and put stuff in it, I do not feel it is my home; there is something missing inside. I do not feel real happiness ... We [with her husband] built our life in Syria step by step.

Unlike Alaa, the challenge for Aisha was to feed and shelter her family. For her, "people with money ended up having comfortable homes just like they did in Syria, which meant that people with money had the opportunities wherever they were."

Many people said that they did not miss the insecurity, the war, especially the barrel bombs. Some expressed their strong objection to the Assad regime and the impossibility of living under it. For some, what led to the destruction of Syria was the social collapse, which was something they did not miss. Jamal's voice was low and broken when he talked about what he did not miss:

> […] If you ask me what I do not miss: it is the social collapse. Syria went through a social collapse […] and it is very dangerous. When such total social collapse happens, unfortunately, it ends the unity and togetherness.

Jamal was a well-educated, upper-class man. Unlike many other refugees, he had most of his family united; his wife, parents, and siblings were with him in Turkey. Nevertheless, for people like him, home meant the combination of loved ones, memories, and a sense of unity in society. Missing home, then, does not eliminate "power-laden relationships that are part of home's construction" (Ralph & Staeheli, 2011, p. 520). Although many refugees whom I interviewed had different life experiences and ideologies, many stressed a deep desire to reclaim their "dignity." They all wished an end to injustices. The aspects of home that brought suffering and oppression and attacks on their human dignity were things that they experienced simultaneously with their complex reflections of missing home.

Implications for teaching and training

People have strong voices. The more they experience oppression and injustice, the stronger their voices become as their identities become more politicized (Yuval-Davis, 2016). However, mainstream classrooms from K-12 to the graduate level do not put a spotlight on people's voices. People who have access to diverse voices are located in specialized departments (e.g., Gender and Queer, Disability, Peace, Black and Native American Studies), with only a few students who are already inclined to appreciate diversity. Even then, certain voices are not finding their fair share of attention. For example, Peace and Conflict Studies (PACS) as a discipline is not adequately addressing "systemic racism in the United States," although the discipline "has a moral responsibility to" effectively work on issues related to "African American struggles for rights, justice and security" (Scott, 2020, p. 428). The majority of the human population is not allowed to converse with those people who are located at a distance from them. The organization of society leads to a fragmented structure where different segments of society are constantly and systematically denied the chance to interact peacefully and meaningfully.

The majority of the mainstream classrooms are not transformative. Critical thinking is not the driving force of the mainstream classroom. On the contrary, mainstream education systems perpetuate the existing disconnection among differently located groups. In my journey to different continents' and different countries' mainstream classrooms, when I was showing videos of modern slavery, I came across a question "but if there were no slaves, who would do these jobs for us?" As devastating as this question was, I also had many students rejecting such a statement who had had their first awakenings to other people's plights and lack of human rights after listening to accounts of oppression. The life journeys of people through injustice and oppression, their everyday becoming and experience of concepts like "home," "belonging," "identity," "suffering," and "discrimination" need to be told and heard in their own voices. Classroom teaching and training for any human-related occupation needs to deeply engage with relating to others, finding different ways within our different circumstances that can create the connections needed for empathy. Such connection can happen through engaging in conversation with narratives and stories that others generously and bravely share with us. Storytelling can be an effective tool for emotional connection among different identities (Senehi, 2002, 2009). For seeing refugees with their subjectivity, understanding and locating them in different points in time in different contexts, hearing their stories from their experiences needs to take a central stage (Benezer & Zetter, 2014; Harrell-Bond & Voutria, 2007; Zetter, 1991) in teaching.

Implications for practice and policy

While missing home as a refugee has unique aspects, in many ways, people in host communities who have never been positioned as refugees can find meaningful connections with those communities. A lot of people know what it feels like to face racial, ethnic, class or gender discrimination and to experience being alienated in their homes when their human dignity is not respected. People who experience discrimination in different ways can relate to different refugee experiences of exclusion and discrimination. Some can find a connection with refugees when they experience the loss of space due to urbanization and change in the landscape sweeping away what is cherished, feeling as though *home* is no longer *home*. Some may lose their home due to financial hardships or natural disasters, or they may lose their sense of home upon the passing of a loved one. Still, host communities are usually fragmented, preventing any possibility of connection at the level of sharing experiences.

Two things in the above insights from refugee voices open a path for policy change. First, we must open discussion about how neighborhoods are created and marked with the expression of one's identity and how dominant institutions or militarization intervene and besiege them. Second, space is politicized; this, in turn, creates politically engaged people, and such engagement increases people's sense of belonging to home.

Building diverse neighborhoods needs to be politicized through people engaging in the space, relating to others' experience and formulating a *home* together in practice through listening to each other's stories, life journeys, and home imaginings. Collective community building needs to be collectively done. Just as researchers are encouraged to "write with people rather than about them" (Senehi, 2020), policymakers need to create policies with people rather than about them. Research and policy, rather than organizing neighborhoods, needs to be accessible for different segments of society to engage more with one another, envision neighborhoods together and discuss how they will share the public space, events, and diverse rituals.

Coupled with enduring racism toward racial minorities, there is growing tension, discrimination and dehumanization toward refugees in host communities. Policies are fragmented, keeping minority populations segregated. In many ways, not only dominant groups, but different minority populations are kept detached and disconnected from each other. Such policy prevents people's access to one another's emotional state. The creation of new places and neighborhoods needs to be fully engaged and reflective of unique identities that refugee groups bring to the host communities. Rather than being fractured, dispersed and dehumanized, refugees need to be provided a space for sharing the meaning of home, and given access to connect with the established communities to rearticulate home as a collective experience.

References

Al-Ali, N., & Koser, K. (2002). Transnationalism, international migration and home. In N. Al-Ali & K. Koser (Eds.), *New approaches to migration? Transnational communities and transformation of home* (pp. 1–14). Routledge.

Appadurai, A. (1996). *Modernity at large: Cultural dimensions of globalization* (Vol. 1). University of Minnesota Press.
Benezer, G., & Zetter, R. (2014). Searching for directions: Conceptual and methodological challenges in researching refugee journeys. *Journal of Refugee Studies, 28*(3), 297–331.
Blunt, A., & Dowling, R. (2006). *Home*. Routledge.
Brickell, K. (2012). 'Mapping' and 'doing' critical geographies of home. *Progress in Human Geography, 36*(2), 225–244.
Byrne, S., Matyók, T., Scott, I. M., & Senehi, J. (2019a). Peace and conflict studies in the 21st century: Theory, substance, and practice. In S. Byrne, T. Matyók, I. M. Scott, & J. Senehi (Eds.), *Routledge companion to peace and conflict studies* (pp. 3–22). Routledge.
Byrne, S., Matyók, T., Scott, I. M., & Senehi, J. (2019b). Critical peace and conflict studies emancipated? In S. Byrne, T. Matyók, I. M. Scott, & J. Senehi (Eds.), *Routledge companion to peace and conflict studies* (pp. 493–503). Routledge.
Byrne, S., & Thiessen, C. (2019). Foreign peacebuilding intervention and emancipatory local agency for social justice. In S. Byrne, T. Matyók, I. M. Scott, & J. Senehi (Eds.), *Routledge companion to peace and conflict studies* (pp. 131–142). Routledge.
Cagaptay, S., & Yalkin, M. (2018). Syrian refugees in Turkey. August 22, Policywatch 3007. Policy Analysis, The Washington Institute. https://www.washingtoninstitute.org/policy-analysis/view/syrian-refugees-in-turkey
Cagaptay, S., & Yuksel, D. (2019). *Growing anti-Syrian sentiment in Turkey*. August 5, Policywatch 3159. Policy Analysis, The Washington Institute. https://www.washingtoninstitute.org/policy-analysis/view/growing-anti-syrian-sentiment-in-turkey
Erdogan, M., Kavukcuer, Y., & Cetinkaya, T. (2017). Turkiye'de yasayan Suriyeli multecilere yonelik medya algisi [Media perceptions towards Syrian refugees in Turkey]. Freedom Research Association. http://ozgurlukarastirmalari.com/pdf/rapor/OAD_c2lGWsK.pdf
Galtung, J. (1996). *Peace by peaceful means: Peace and conflict, development and civilization*. SAGE Publications.
Harrell-Bond, B., & Voutira, E. (2007). In search of 'invisible' actors: Barriers to access in refugee research. *Journal of Refugee Studies, 20*(2), 281–298.
Karasapan, O. (2019). Turkey's Syrian refugees—the welcome fades (November 25). Brookings Institute. https://www.brookings.edu/blog/future-development/2019/11/25/turkeys-syrian-refugees-the-welcome-fades/
Kirisci, K. (2014). *Syrian refugees and Turkey's challenges: Going beyond hospitality*. Brookings Institute.
Kirisci, K., & Kolasin, G. U. (2019). Order from chaos: Syrian refugees in Turkey need better access to formal jobs (July 18). Brookings Institute. https://www.brookings.edu/blog/order-from-chaos/2019/07/18/syrian-refugees-in-turkey-need-better-access-to-formal-jobs/
Malkki, L. H. (1992). National geographic: The rooting of peoples and the territorialization of national identity among scholars and refugees. *Cultural Anthropology, 7*(1), 24–44.
Malkki, L. H. (1995). *Purity and exile: Violence, memory, and national cosmology among Hutu refugees in Tanzania*. University of Chicago Press.
Mac Ginty, R. (2008). Indigenous peace-making versus the liberal peace. *Cooperation and Conflict, 43*(2), 139–163.
Mac Ginty, R. (2011). *International peacebuilding and local resistance: Hybrid forms of peace*. Palgrave Macmillan.
Massey, D. (2001). *Space, place and gender*. University of Minnesota Press.
Moore, J. (2000). Placing home in context. *Journal of Environmental Psychology, 20*(3), 207–218.
Petridou, E. (2001). The taste of home. In D. Miller (Ed.), *Home possessions: Material culture behind closed doors* (pp. 87–106). Berg.
Ralph, D., & Staeheli, L. A. (2011). Home and migration: Mobilities, belongings and identities. *Geography Compass, 5*(7), 517–530.
Reinders, L., & van der Land, M. (2008). Mental geographies of home and place: Introduction to the special issue. *Housing, Theory and Society, 25*(1), 1–13.
Saracoglu, C., & Bélanger, D. (2019). Loss and xenophobia in the city: Contextualizing anti-Syrian sentiments in Izmir, Turkey. *Patterns of Prejudice, 53*(4), 363–383.
Scott, I. M. (2020). And what about the African Americans? Peace and conflict studies neglect of the intractable conflict related to systemic racism in the United States. In S. Byrne, T. Matyók, I. M. Scott, & J. Senehi (Eds.), *Routledge companion to peace and conflict studies* (pp. 427–437). Routledge.
Senehi, J. (2002). Constructive storytelling: A peace process. *Peace and Conflict Studies, 9*(2), 41–63.

Senehi, J. (2009). Building peace: Storytelling to transform conflicts constructively. In D. J. D. Sandole, S. Byrne, I. Sandole-Staroste, & J. Senehi (Eds.), *Handbook of conflict analysis and resolution* (pp. 201–214). Routledge.

Senehi, J. (2020). Theory-building in peace and conflict studies: The storytelling methodology. In S. Byrne, T. Matyók, I. M. Scott, & J. Senehi (Eds.), *Routledge companion to peace and conflict studies* (pp. 45–56). Routledge.

UNHCR. (2020). Syria emergency. https://www.unhcr.org/en-us/syria-emergency.html

Yuval-Davis, N. (2016). Power, intersectionality and the politics of belonging. In W. Harcourt (Ed.), *The palgrave handbook of gender and development* (pp. 367–381). Palgrave Macmillan.

Zetter, R. (1991). Labelling refugees: Forming and transforming a bureaucratic identity. *Journal of Refugee Studies, 4*(1), 39–62.

19
TRAUMA, RECOVERY, AND MEMORY

Joseph Robinson

Background: Critical trauma strands

This chapter explores contemporary debates centered on "critical trauma studies." Trauma studies is an interdisciplinary paradigm that steadily and persistently challenged the psycho-medical model of trauma that dominated intellectual and social discourse in the latter half of the 20th century. While trauma studies is internally quite diverse, it hinges on a set of debates regarding the nature of psychological wounding, its causes, effects, and the scope of existing theories (Wertheimer & Casper, 2016).

This chapter will trace three interrelated threads of trauma studies that arose in the past 30–40 years. I refer to them as the "psychotherapeutic" strand, the "cultural" strand and the "historical" strand, respectively. To these I propose a fourth strand, an "ecological" strand that examines spatial violence and its impact on traumatized spaces and places. The ecological strand combines a renewed focus on ongoing violent injustice and a demand to "decolonize" the existing corpus of trauma studies. The final two sections discuss some implications of decolonial and spatial perspectives for trauma pedagogy and trauma-informed practice.

Trauma studies is a distinctly modern paradigm, one that derives from a particular set of intellectual traditions influenced by the work of Freud (Fassin & Rechtman, 2009; Leys, 2000). Prior to Freud, the "trauma neuroses" variably referred to as hysteria, shell-shock, or "railway brain" were seen as the explicit fault of the sufferer. What today we would recognize as sexually abused women and children, traumatized soldiers returning from the trenches, and workers witnessing or experiencing catastrophic industrial accidents were seen, alternately, as weak-willed women, cowards, or malingerers whose symptoms were manifestations of a lesser-developed psyche. While Freud's initial studies on the etiology of female hysteria seemed to recognize the "neurosis" roots in sexual abuse, he abandoned that theory in favor of what Fassin and Rechtman (2009) refer to as an "eventless" theory of trauma. Hysteria, in Freud's second theory of trauma, was not caused by abuse, but from the traumatic childhood psychosexual development experienced by everyone. While from our modern vantage point, it can be difficult to see an eventless theory of trauma as a progressive shift, Freudian thought gradually began to free at least traumatized workers and soldiers from mainstreamed social opprobrium and recognize trauma neuroses as legitimate afflictions (Fassin & Rechtman, 2009).

By the 1970s, psychoanalysts returned to theories of trauma centered around violent or catastrophic events. Perhaps no text had quite as much an impact in this vein as Judith Herman's (1992) *Trauma and Recovery*. Grounded in Herman's practice-based work with survivors of rape and incest, *Trauma and Recovery* positions the study of trauma (and psychoanalysis generally) within larger political discourses. Her explicitly feminist text argues that recovery from trauma, and with it, the future of psychoanalysis as a discipline, depends on the ongoing struggle for "the liberation of women" (p. 32). She also positions recovery within larger social ecologies, arguing that recovery is only possible within a wider nexus of healthy relationships and supportive social milieus (see also Janoff-Bulman, 1992). In addition to cementing trauma studies' focus on violent events, Herman also helped to catalyze the shift away from a purely psychomedical paradigm (Humphreys & Joseph, 2004).

While Herman's focus is primarily on interpersonal violence, a somewhat parallel psychotherapeutic approach focuses on collective violence, chiefly the monumental traumatic legacies of the Holocaust. Laub (1992) argues that the Holocaust was an "event without a witness." Not only had the genocide succeeded in exterminating the vast majority of eyewitnesses, but the overwhelming violence "precluded its own witnessing, even by its very victims" (1992, p. 80). Laub's is a deconstructivist reading of Freud that accepts a "temporal lag" between the etiological event and the manifestation of traumatic symptoms. Freud referred to this as the fundamental "afterwardness" [*Nachträglichkeit*] of trauma (Caruth, 2014; Laplanche, 2005). Published in 1985, Scarry's influential *The Body in Pain* theorizes that extreme political violence overwhelms and destroys the physical and linguistic capacities of human representation. Following Scarry and Holocaust-based trauma studies, by the early 2000s, the psychotherapeutic strand of emergent trauma studies adopted a consensual understanding of trauma as an unrepresentable afterward, as the limits of human language (Caruth, 1996; Felman & Laub, 1992; Langer, 1991). The pathways to both individual and social recovery in the psychotherapeutic strand coalesced around "speaking" and "witnessing." Traumatic testimony collectively recreated anew the language that had been shattered and forced the unspeakable into the open, where individuals could heal through being surrounded by a larger supportive context and societies as a whole would be forced to confront their own violent pasts. The psychotherapeutic strand was subsequently incorporated into transitional justice, most prominently in the South African Truth and Reconciliation Commission (Boraine, 2001; Hayner, 2001), from which it spread rapidly to other TRCs and institutional attempts to reckon with mass violence (Humphrey, 2013; Stover & Weinstein, 2004).

While the psychotherapeutic strand does focus on both interpersonal and collective traumas, it hinges on the impact of violence on individual survivors and bereaved. Theories of cultural trauma, first developed by Eyerman (2001) and his colleagues (Alexander et al., 2004), define trauma more collectively and sociologically. Cultural trauma theories coalesce around an event that collapses a cultural group's system of collective meaning-making (Smelser, 2004). They also accept the Freudian temporal lag between etiological event and the collective manifestation of cultural trauma, yet the lag is placed in the production of collective memory, rather than in Freudian theories of memory repression and disassociation. Cultural trauma is the outcome of social contestation over the public memory and collective interpretation of the traumatic event. It is located in the representation, contestation, and performance of the event, not the event itself (Alexander, 2012). Through its focus on collective memory and public interpretation, cultural trauma is able to engage systems of historical violence, such as slavery (Eyerman, 2001), the sudden collapse of political and cultural systems (Sztompka, 2000), and the AIDS epidemic (Sturken, 1997).

Theories of traumatic etiologies in the 20th century thus gradually shifted from the Freudian nonevent through the demand for the return of the event and then again to seeing trauma as the psychological and cultural "afterwardness" of the event. This renewed focus on afterwardness raised questions of trauma's persistence across generations, or what has come to be known as "intergenerational" trauma. In clinical psychology, "intergenerational trauma" has a number of proposed pathways, ranging from epigenetic explanations (Lehrner & Yehuda, 2018) to more traditional attachment theory approaches (Van der Kolk, 2014). From cultural studies, Hirsch's (2012) study of "postmemory" argues that inherited trauma is shared across generations by the aesthetic reactivization and reembodiment of cultural memory.

However, for Indigenous, decolonial, and Queer theorists, there exists no temporal or generational break between traumatic violence. "Historical" (Brave Heart, 2000) or "lasting" (hooks, 2003) trauma theories maintain that trauma must be seen as an unfinished continuum of suffering rooted in ongoing sociostructural conditions. Thus, while foundational traumatic events or systems may have occurred in the past, the historical effects of the trauma persist due to ongoing structural and cultural violence endemic to colonial, racialized, patriarchal, and heteronormative societies (Cvetkovich 2003; Duran & Duran, 1995; Evans-Campbell, 2008).

What I term "ecological" theories of trauma have emerged comparatively recently. They fuse decolonial criticisms of trauma studies with an added concern for the spatial relationships and realities in which traumatic violence and traumatized bodies are invariably situated. An ecological perspective on trauma views traumatic violence through a spatial lens, as ordinary, continuous, and radically present.

Key insights—radically present ecologies of trauma

In the postwar United States, the U.S. urban policy destroyed thousands of vibrant, historically black neighborhoods and displaced over 300,000 people between 1950–1966 (Digital Scholarship Lab, 2020). Fullilove (2004) uses a botanical metaphor, root shock, to describe the traumatic effects of this massive forced displacement. For Fullilove, these destroyed communities provided an "emotional ecosystem," one built on customary mobilities, social bonds, and shared memories, what she refers to as "mazeways." For Till (2012, p. 7), mazeways are "embodied spaces" that "provide a personal and social shell."

The destruction of communities, their ecosystems and mazeways, through war or ethnic cleansing, through forced migration, and/or "urban renewal," must be understood as traumatic spatial violence. While the discipline of trauma studies has examined the traumatic effects of violence in its interpersonal, political, structural, cultural, and colonial forms, it has generally overlooked spatial violence. Spatial violence is the uneven production, distribution, withdrawal, devaluation and/or destruction of resources, forms of capital, infrastructure, and caring, supportive networks, across space (Shaw, 2019). Considering spatial violence provokes questions that mainstream trauma studies largely fails to consider. Why is traumatic suffering so unevenly distributed? Could "intergenerational" or "historical" trauma also be *the shared experience of inhabiting wounded places,* or the entanglements of memory and forced displacement (Kuusisto-Arponen, 2017; Till, 2012)? Is persistent trauma not merely the afterward of war and ethnic conflict, *but the ongoing injustices of the peace* (Mueller-Hirth, 2017; Robinson, 2020)? Pain (2020) argues that "geotrauma" evokes the "relational clasping of place with the experience and impacts of trauma." Till argues that "wounded cities" are "locales ... harmed and structured by particular histories of physical destruction, displacement, and individual and social trauma resulting from state-perpetrated violence" (2012, p. 6). Drawing on these perspectives, I argue that ecological theories of trauma are those that focus on spatial violence which attacks the "social ecologies of place" (Till, 2012, p. 5), shared senses of community self-esteem (hooks, 2003), and shared senses of memory and meaning-making humans and nonhumans depend on to sustain meaningful, healthy lives (Berlant, 2016; Laurie & Shaw, 2018; Shaw, 2019).

The ecological strand also challenges trauma studies to engage with the work of feminist geopolitics over the past several decades. One major project of feminist geopolitics has been to critically link the everyday gendered realities of women and subaltern people with the national and global contexts that produce the constraints of embodied social reality and the possibilities of political action (Hyndman, 2001; Staeheli, 1994). Work within this perspective critically situates embodied trauma and interpersonal violence within national and geopolitical contexts and oppressive colonial historiographies (de Leeuw, 2016; Mountz & Hyndman, 2006). A feminist geopolitical lens is especially useful in looking at spatial violence, allowing us to see wounded places as sedimented with interweaving types and scales of violence (Pain, 2020). From the geopolitical and historical violence of colonialism, to the environmental destruction of unfettered resource extraction, to national and subnational policies and institutions steeped in racism and heteronormativity, to gendered spaces of intimate violence, these are all "part of the same complex of harm and control" (Pain, 2014a, p. 352; Pain, 2014b).

In the remainder of this section, I focus on two decolonial criticisms of existing trauma studies, namely its focus on the aftermath of a temporally bounded event(s) and the event's subsequent unrepresentability. Rothberg (2008, p. 230) argues that "canonical trauma theory tends to locate trauma in the completed past of a singular event, while colonial and postcolonial traumas persist into the present." This fixation with a singular, catastrophic event that collapses either individual or group cognitive assumptions (Janoff-Bulman, 1992) or cultural systems of meaning-making (Alexander, 2012) may be a persistent vestige of the medicalized trauma model. Traumatic stress disorders were first officially classified as a recognizable mental disorder only in 1980, with the publication of the American Psychiatric Association's *Diagnostic and Statistical Manual of Mental Disorders, 3rd edition* (DSM-III). DSM-III defined them as a "serious injury or a threat to the physical integrity of the self in the form of an overwhelming, sudden, and unassimilable experience" (cited in Visser, 2015, p. 252). Subsequent DSMs, taking into account Herman's (1992) call for the recognition of "chronic" and "repeated" traumas, did pluralize the aetiological event(s), yet the more compelling criticism relates to trauma studies dependence on the exceptional or catastrophic event itself.

Caruth's (1996) work has especially come under fire from decolonial scholars. Caruth argues that the study of traumatic history allows for new insights into the representation-defying traumatic experience common to humankind (see also Felman & Laub, 1992; Hartman, 1996; LaCapra, 1998). Writes Craps (2010): "Trauma theory confidently announced itself as an essential apparatus for understanding 'the real world' and even as an essential apparatus for changing it for the better" (p. 52). However, Das (2006), in her anthropological study of everyday suffering in India, points out stridently that the psychoanalytic, deconstructivist, Holocaust-based understanding of trauma is not rooted in any "real world" she or her research partners recognize. Das is especially critical of Caruth's (2014) universalizing and event-based understanding of traumatic violence, characterizing it as a "frozen slide" (p. 80) of historical events bounded by circumscribed time. Das instead sees traumatic violence as a "descent into the ordinary," and not the result of an exception or sublime catastrophe (pp. 101–107). This move allows Das to focus her work on "how violence is produced and lived with" which "constitute(s) the way everyday life is engaged in the present" (p. 205). Caruth's (2014) extraction of violence from the ordinary lifeworld, her excessive focus on the afterward, silences the devastated streets and terrified geographies into which sectarian violence in urban India is indelibly inscribed and consistently performed.

Elizabeth Povinelli's friends in the Northern Territories of Australia, similarly, have not experienced a time-bounded set of catastrophic events. Rather, the suffering of her friends is "ordinary, chronic, and cruddy" (2012, p. 3) rather than catastrophic, crisis-laden and sublime. Povinelli roots this suffering in "quasi-events," or how "extraordinary events of violence are folded into everyday routines, and vice versa." A quasi-event "never quite achieves the status of having occurred or taken place" (p. 13); the recognition and imprint of its individual and social impact is not registered or felt in dominant geopolitical spaces. For Aboriginal Australians, traumatic quasi-events that escape the event-based gaze of mainstream trauma studies are manifold. A washing machine, the only washing machine for her friends to use, might finally break down. The traumatic imprint of that quasi-event can be read on the staphylococcus sores emerging on her and her friends' bodies. Or they could possibly be read in the fines they receive for driving an illegal pick-up truck or piloting and unseaworthy boat. These traumas are not an afterward, they are the radically present choice between sacrificing food or abandoning an alternative social project to meet the legal strictures of a colonial state. Pain (2019), through her work with survivors of intimate-partner violence in Northern England, reminds us that these criticisms of trauma-as-afterward are not merely confined to decolonizing spaces. For Pain's research partners, even those who have escaped deeply abusive relationships, trauma is not an uncanny return or unclaimed experience, but rather it is "an ongoing relational dynamic between abuser and abused" (Pain, 2019, p. 388).

These temporal and event-based criticisms also intertwine with the critique of unrepresentability, or what Luckhurst (2008, p. 2) dismisses as the "flat contradiction in trauma theory." West (2003), for example, describes a series of unexpected encounters with men tortured by the Portuguese during the Mozambican War for Independence. These men approached the white anthropologist without prompting (West was not intending to study their experiences), insistent on narrating their stories. They spoke of being "twice silenced," first by the torture itself, then by the "triumphant historical portrait" (p. 356) of the FRELIMO regime. By "whispering to foreigners," West argues, these men kept alive the story of what had happened to them in the face of a regressive architecture of transitional silencing with a hope they would be "remembered by the living" (p. 361). Ultimately rejecting Scarry (1985) and Caruth's conceptualization of torture as the end of language, West simply and eloquently eviscerates the "flat contradiction" at the heart of the theory:

> The contradiction in this is readily apparent ... for *I* know of these things only because I was *told* them. Knowing, then, that there is something communicable in the experiences of these men, I have been left to wonder to whom I might speak of them, and to what ends. (p. 345, original emphasis)

Caruth's oft-cited remark that "trauma itself provides the link between cultures" (1996, p. 11), despite the fact that her work is grounded in the European Holocaust and its aftermath, can be seen as a dangerously familiar "twice"-silencing assumption (Marshall & Sousa, 2017; Visser, 2015).

In short, thinking spatially and ecologically about trauma further expands our understandings of its multiple violent etiologies. Violence is not restricted to an exceptional, time-bounded shock or a catastrophic rupture. In its spatial iterations, violence can also be "slow" and "attritional," a "gradual unfolding" (Nixon, 2011 cited in Pain 2019, p. 8). It can be small and repeated, what Brown (2008) calls "insidious trauma." It can manifest as a series or a continuum of quasi-events that erode or eventually destroy social ecologies. Ecological theories of trauma tend also to collapse arbitrary breaks between temporalities and geographical scales. They avoid an exclusive focus on the Freudian "afterward" in both its psychoanalytic and cultural forms, instead preferring to think of trauma as radically present and hardwired into the realities of everyday life.

Implications for teaching and training: Repoliticizing trauma

Ecological trauma contains a number of potent implications relevant to how trauma is taught in university classrooms. First, the questions of violence, trauma, memory, and recovery are never purely medical, psychotherapeutic, or cultural; they are also pressing political questions (Cvetkovich, 2003; Edkins, 2003). Second, while bodies, memories, literary texts, and cultural artifacts are and can be compelling sites of trauma, the sources and effects of trauma are not confined to these objects, rather, they are also located in the "social, environmental and structural contexts" surrounding us in the present (Pain, 2020, p. 3). This is especially important to keep in mind when we study the aftermath of war and ethnic conflict. Most mainstream peacebuilding approaches confine trauma to a "legacy," an "afterward" of violence (Hinton, 2018); few consider the ongoing and radically present trauma survivors feel as a consequence of regressive peace architectures that "sociotemporally marginalize" survivors of violence through calls to "close the books" on the past, and to artificially circumscribe the appropriate time in which the wounds of the violent past can be considered (Castillejo-Cuellar, 2014; Mueller-Hirth, 2017; Robinson, 2018, 2020).

Learners may come to trauma studies through the deep cultural well of materials produced in the North American and European contexts after the Vietnam War and after the Holocaust became a pedagogical duty in the 1960s–1970s (see Novick, 1997). Yet the implicit and explicit perspectives formed from these materials often bear little to no similarity to either modern epidemiological perspectives (Purtle, 2016) or the "cultural turn" in trauma studies. Part of the reason for this is that the utterance "trauma" is a floating signifier (Fassin & Rechtman, 2009), or as Stevens (2016) puts it: "Trauma is as trauma does." As Herman (1992) presciently identifies, the signifier of trauma is always a product of powerful social discourses, changing moral obligations, and emergent political duties toward survivors and survival. As Fassin and Rechtman (2009, p. 276) put it: "The truth of trauma lies not in the psyche, the mind, or the brain, but in the moral economy of contemporary societies." Trauma's pervasiveness in contemporary Western discourse is not the successful dissemination of empirically based medical, or psychotherapeutic understandings; rather, it is the *name* our discourse has given to surround changing attitudes to violence, endurance, and survival.

Understanding that trauma is not necessarily attached to or bound by any dominant, Eurocentric discourse suggests the real potential to decolonize, pluralize, and spatialize trauma studies. But doing so requires that instructors open up trauma studies to a more diverse set of perspectives outside of the canonical texts. Cvetkovich's (2003) work is especially important here. She came to trauma studies believing she could find a language for speaking about everyday Queer and lesbian experiences and heteronormative and heteropatriarchal violence. Yet, she argues, she simply failed to find them. This was not as simple as a failure of recognition, or a failure to simply include Queer and lesbian bodies and perspectives into the corpus, rather, it was an epistemological failure to give form, material texture, and expression to the traumatic realities of lesbian and Queer lives. What Cvetkovich's work suggests is that simply diversifying the authorship of the trauma studies corpus may be insufficient; we as instructors must work to identify scholarship that resonates with the types of everyday, ordinary, quasi-event-based traumatic violence experienced in our students' lives.

Edited collections such as Cindy Milstein's *Rebellious Mourning* (2017) are a powerful place to begin. Beginning from Judith Butler's (2006) well-known provocation: "What counts as a liveable life and a grievable death?" Milstein brings together a diverse range of essays on life, death, and the potential transformative politics of individual, communal, and historical pain and trauma. Crucially, the essays do not accept grief and trauma as a diagnosis, a pathology, or a barrier to speaking, rather, they use the surfeit of grief, loss, and collective trauma within severely marginalized communities to demand political and institutional change. The essays echo Muñoz (1997, p. 74), who writes that grief and trauma "for blacks and queers of any color, is not a pathology but an integral part of our everyday lives … a mechanism that helps us re(construct) identity and take our dead to the various battles that we must wage in their names—and in our names." While the experience of violent trauma can certainly shatter individual voices, trauma studies as a whole has tended to treat traumatized subjects as broken people in need of interventions, rather than as potentially active political agents and groups capable of advancing their own public politics of trauma and memory.

Implications for practice and policy—hierarchies of pain

Fassin (2011a) argues that trauma has become an essential aspect of "humanitarian reason," or a mode of moral thinking that demands compassion toward the suffering of the other. Humanitarian reason in turn is deeply embedded in the Western social imaginary, or how Western societies imagine themselves to be, to behave. Yet humanitarian reason is a way of thinking that allows Western societies to cognitively insulate themselves from the contradictions between their imaginary and specific political actions, not to mention the relationships of power between those extending compassion and those "lucky" enough to receive it (Nguyen, 2012). Humanitarian reason is not simply an empty affect. It is "a language … [that] serves both to define and to justify discourses and practices of the government of human beings" (Fassin, 2011a, p. 2).

The real-world implications of Fassin's study are profound. Ascendant Eurocentric, psychotherapeutic, and medicalized models of trauma create a hierarchy of traumatized bodies that directly influences the government and control of precarious lives (Loyd et al., 2018). This hierarchy places the survivors of recognizable, catastrophic events that correspond to the imaginaries of humanitarian reason at the top of the pyramid and everyone else below. It privileges those who manifest traumatic symptoms in expected ways, who can demonstrate, often, on their very bodies (Fassin & d'Halluin, 2005), exactly how they have been wounded (i.e. as part of a recognizable "event"). These criticisms are especially pronounced among scholars who study the experiences of refugees and asylum seekers across international borders, scholars of carceral confinement, and scholars who focus on the everyday, slow violence characteristic of colonial and late liberal governance (Espiritu, 2014; Fassin, 2011b; Hyndman & Giles, 2017; Loyd et al., 2018; Pain, 2019; Povinelli, 2012, 2016).

Fassin's criticism is not an indictment of an urge to compassion and solidarity. But it is a demand that practitioners recognize that Western, Eurocentric, psychomedical, and psychotherapeutic models of trauma preselect the sorts of violence that can be understood as traumatic, and thus, what sorts of bodies governments, regimes, and nongovernmental organizations (NGOs) bear a duty toward, to intervene, to witness, to aid, to treat compassionately (Loyd et al., 2018). This in turn can insulate governments, regimes, and NGOs from reckoning with their own ongoing infliction of, or complicity in, spatial violence. In Palestine, for example, Marshall and Sousa (2017) argue that NGOs who work with Palestinian survivors studiously work to separate trauma treatment and trauma recovery from the pressing political questions of ongoing occupation and everyday spatial violence.

Trauma is a floating signifier, a powerful yet malleable moral and discursive tool signifying a set of ethical duties toward human compassion and the suffering of the other, yet it is rarely turned to critically examine the structural, spatial, colonial, and everyday violence produced by late liberal capitalism and Western settler-colonial states. This violence is not limited to the production of cruel, racist, and dehumanizing sites of concentrated traumatic violence such as the refugee camp and the prison (Coddington, 2017; Mountz, 2017; Peterie, 2018), it is also found in the traumatic impacts of eviction and economic displacement (Desmond, 2016; Sullivan, 2017), the normalization of permanent economic precarity (Berlant, 2011), the intimate crises surrounding the quasi-events of deepening austerity (Hall, 2019), and the gradual destruction of our ecosystems (Nixon, 2011). These are all forms of traumatic spatial violence, violence that perniciously attacks our social ecologies of place. These attacks do not come in the form of a catastrophic event, they are ongoing, everyday hardships that slowly and insidiously wear the body down and narrow the human ability to imagine and work for alternative spatial worlds (Povinelli, 2012). Trauma practitioners and policymakers must consider policies and actions focused on the sorts of suffering and violence that are felt "less as a catastrophe or shock, but as a continued deterioration into a life less liveable" (Wilkinson & Ortega-Alcázar, 2018, p. 156). Spatial violence can be "slow violence," "a violence that occurs gradually and out of sight … an attritional violence that is typically not viewed as violence at all" (Nixon, 2011, p. 2).

Whether after war and ethnic conflict and/or within the violent lifeworlds of late liberal capitalism, perhaps some pessimism about the potential scope and reach of trauma and trauma-informed practice is warranted. Are the goals of trauma-informed research and practice merely to provide better mechanisms for the management of psychomedicalized trauma symptoms or is it to work toward the resurrection of lives worth living? If it is the latter, then the work of recovery from trauma is not separable from the work of political (re)building. The work of recovery and memory, in trauma's ecological strand, is to (re)create the sorts of places where "individuals and groups may confront and take responsibility for the failure of the democratic state and its violences" (Till, 2012, p. 7). To resurrect lives worth living, we need models of trauma that do not stop at the question of how individuals recover from trauma, but continue to ask, "What sorts of worlds will we be recovered into?"

References

Alexander, J. C. (2012). *Trauma: A social theory*. Polity Press.
Alexander, J. C., Eyerman, R., Giesen, B., Smelser, N. J., & Sztompka, P. (Eds.). (2004). *Cultural trauma and collective identity*. University of California Press.
Berlant, L. (2011). *Cruel optimism*. Duke University Press.
Berlant, L. (2016). The commons: Infrastructures for troubling times. *Environment and Planning D: Society and Space*, *34*(3), 393–419.
Boraine, A. (2001). *A country unmasked: Inside South Africa's truth and reconciliation commission*. Oxford University Press.
Brave Heart, M. Y. H. (2000). Wakiksuyapi: Carrying the historical trauma of the Lakota. *Tulane Studies in Social Welfare*, *21–22*, 245–266.
Brown, L. S. (2008). *Cultural competence in trauma therapy: Beyond the flashback*. American Psychological Association.
Butler, J. (2006). *Precarious life: The powers of mourning and violence*. Verso.
Caruth, C. (1996). *Unclaimed experience: Trauma, narrative, and history*. Johns Hopkins University Press.
Caruth, C. (2014). Traumatic temporality: An interview with Jean Laplanche. In C. Caruth, (Ed.),

Listening to trauma: Conversations with leaders in the theory and treatment of catastrophic experience (pp. 131–152). Johns Hopkins University Press.

Castillejo-Cuellar, A. (2014). Historical injuries, temporality and the law: Articulations of a violent past in two transitional scenarios. *Law and Critique, 25*(1), 47–66.

Coddington, K. (2017). Contagious trauma: Reframing the spatial mobility of trauma within advocacy work. *Emotion, Space and Society, 24*(1), 66–73.

Craps, S. (2010). Wor(l)ds of grief: Traumatic memory and literary witnessing in cross-cultural perspective. *Textual Practice, 24*(1), 51–68.

Cvetkovich, A. (2003). *An archive of feelings: Trauma, sexuality, and lesbian public cultures*. Duke University Press.

Das, V. (2006). *Life and words: Violence and the descent into the ordinary*. University of California Press.

de Leeuw, S. (2016). Tender grounds: Intimate visceral violence and British Columbia's colonial geographies. *Political Geography, 52*(1), 14–23.

Desmond, M. (2016). *Evicted: Poverty and profit in the American city*. Penguin.

Digital Scholarship Lab. (2020). Renewing inequality. In R. K. Nelson & E. L. Ayers (Eds.), *American panorama*. Online Resource. http://dsl.richmond.edu/panorama/renewal/#view=0/0/1&viz=cartogram&text=citing

Duran, E., & Duran, B. (1995). *Native American postcolonial psychology*. SUNY Press.

Edkins, J. (2003). *Trauma and the memory of politics*. Cambridge University Press.

Espiritu, Y. L. (2014). *Body counts: The Vietnam war and militarized refugees*. University of California Press.

Evans-Campbell, T. (2008). Historical trauma in American Indian/Native Alaska communities: A multilevel framework for exploring impacts on individuals, families, and communities. *Journal of Interpersonal Violence, 23*(3), 316–338.

Eyerman, R. (2001). *Cultural trauma: Slavery and the formation of African-American identity*. Cambridge University Press.

Fassin, D. (2011a). *Humanitarian reason: A moral history of the present*. University of California Press.

Fassin, D. (2011b). The trace: Violence, truth, and the politics of the body. *Social Research, 78*(2), 281–298.

Fassin, D., & d'Halluin, E. (2005). The truth from the body: Medical certificates as ultimate evidence for asylum seekers. *American Anthropologist, 107*(4), 597–608.

Fassin, D., & Rechtman, R. (2009). *The empire of trauma: An inquiry into the condition of victimhood*. Princeton University Press.

Felman, S., & Laub, D. (1992). *Testimony: Crises of witnessing in literature, psychoanalysis, and history*. Taylor & Francis.

Fullilove, M. (2004). *Root shock: How tearing up city neighborhoods hurts America and what we can do about it*. New Village Press.

Hall, S. M. (2019). A very personal crisis: Family fragilities and everyday conjectures within lived experiences of austerity. *Transactions of the Institute of British Geographers, 44*(3), 479–492.

Hartman, G. H. (1996). *The longest shadow: In the aftermath of the Holocaust*. Indiana University Press.

Hayner, P. (2001). *Unspeakable truths: Transitional justice and the challenge of truth commissions*. Taylor & Francis.

Herman, J. L. (1992). *Trauma and recovery: The aftermath of violence from domestic abuse to political terror*. Basic Books.

Hinton, A. L. (2018). *The justice facade: Trials of transition in Cambodia*. Oxford University Press.

Hirsch, M. (2012). *The generation of postmemory: Writing and visual culture after the Holocaust*. Columbia University Press.

hooks, b. (2003). *Rock my soul: Black people and self-esteem*. Washington Square Press.

Humphrey, M. (2013). *The politics of atrocity and reconciliation: From terror to trauma*. Routledge.

Humphreys, C., & Joseph, S. (2004). Domestic violence and the politics of trauma. *Women's Studies International Forum, 27*(5-6), 559–570.

Hyndman, J. (2001). Towards a feminist geopolitics. *Canadian Geographer/Le Géographe Canadien, 45*(2), 210–222.

Hyndman, J., & Giles, W. (2017). *Refugees in extended exile: Living on the edge*. Routledge.

Janoff-Bulman, R. (1992). *Shattered assumptions: Towards a new psychology of trauma*. Free Press.

Kuusisto-Arponen, A.-K. (2017). Self, place, and memory: Spatial trauma among British and Finnish war children. In T. Skelton, C. Harker, & K. Hörschelmann (Eds.), *Conflict, violence and peace. Geographies of children and young people* (Vol. 11, pp. 308–325). Springer.

LaCapra, D. (1998). *History and memory after Auschwitz*. Cornell University Press.

Langer, L. L. (1991). *Holocaust testimonies: The ruins of memory*. Yale University Press.

Laplanche, J. (2005). *Essays on otherness*. Routledge.

Laub, D. (1992). An event without a witness: truth, testimony and survival. In S. Felman & D. Laub (Eds.), *Testimony: Crises of witnessing in literature, psychoanalysis and history* (pp. 75–92). Taylor & Francis.

Laurie, E. W., & Shaw, I. G. R. (2018). Violent conditions: The injustices of being. *Political Geography, 65*(1), 8–16.

Lehrner, A., & Yehuda, R. (2018). Cultural trauma and epigenetic inheritance. *Development and Psychopathology, 30*(5), 1763–1777.

Leys, R. (2000). *Trauma: A genealogy*. University of Chicago Press.

Loyd, J. M., Ehrkamp, P., & Secor, A. J. (2018). A geopolitics of trauma: Refugee administration and protracted uncertainty in Turkey. *Transactions of the Institute of British Geographers, 43*(2), 377–389.

Luckhurst, R. (2008). *The trauma question*. Routledge.

Marshall, D. J., & Sousa, C. (2017). Decolonizing trauma: Liberation psychology and childhood trauma in Palestine. In T. Skelton, C. Harker, & K. Hörschelmann (Eds.), *Conflict, violence and peace. Geographies of children and young people* (Vol. 11, pp. 288–307). Springer.

Milstein, C. (Ed.). (2017). *Rebellious mourning: The collective work of grief*. AK Press.

Mountz, A. (2017). Island detention: Affective eruption as trauma's disruption. *Emotion, Space and Society, 24*(1), 74–82.

Mountz, A., & Hyndman, J. (2006). Feminist approaches to the global intimate. *Women's Studies Quarterly, 34*(1/2), 446–463.

Mueller-Hirth, N. (2017). Temporalities of victimhood: Time in the study of the postconflict societies. *Sociological Forum, 32*(1), 186–206.

Muñoz, J. E. (1997). Photographies of mourning: Melancholia and ambivalence in Van der Zee, Mapplethorpe, and looking for Langston. In H. Stecopolous & M. Uebel (Eds.), *Race and the subject of masculinities*. Duke University Press.

Nguyen, M. T. (2012). *The gift of freedom: War, debt, and other refugee passages*. Duke University Press.

Nixon, R. (2011). *Slow violence and the environmentalism of the poor*. Harvard University Press.

Novick, P. (1997). *The Holocaust and collective memory: The American experience*. Bloomsbury.

Pain, R. (2014a). Gendered violence: Rotating intimacy. *Area, 46*(4), 351–353.

Pain, R. (2014b). Everyday terrorism: Connecting domestic violence and global terrorism. *Progress in Human Geography, 38*(4), 531–550.

Pain, R. (2019). Chronic urban trauma: The slow violence of housing dispossession. *Urban Studies, 56*(2), 385–400.

Pain, R. (2020). Geotrauma: Violence, place, and repossession. *Progress in Human Geography*. Advanced online publication. https://doi.org/10.1177/0309132520943676

Peterie, M. (2018). Deprivation, frustration, and trauma: Immigrant detention centres as prisons. *Refugee Survey Quarterly, 37*(1), 279–306.

Povinelli, E. A. (2012). *Economies of abandonment: Social belonging and endurance in late liberalism*. Duke University Press.

Povinelli, E. A. (2016). *Geontologies: A requiem to late liberalism*. Duke University Press.

Purtle, J. (2016). "Heroes' invisible wounds of war": Constructions of posttraumatic stress disorder in the text of U.S. federal legislation. *Social Science & Medicine, 149*(1), 9–16.

Robinson, J. S. (2018). *Transitional justice and the politics of inscription: Memory, space and narrative in Northern Ireland*. Routledge.

Robinson, J. S. (2020). 'We have long memories in this area': Ulster Defence Regiment place-memory along the Irish border. *Memory Studies*. Advanced online publication. https://doi.org/10.1177/1750698020921455

Rothberg, M. (2008). Decolonizing trauma studies: A response. *Studies in the Novel, 40*(1-2), 224–234.

Scarry, E. (1985). *The body in pain: The making and unmaking of the world*. Oxford University Press.

Shaw, I. G. R. (2019). Worlding austerity: The spatial violence of poverty. *Environment and Planning D: Society and Space, 37*(6), 971–989.

Smelser, N. J. (2004). Psychological trauma and cultural trauma. In J. C. Alexander, R. Eyerman, B. Giesen, N. J. Smelser, & P. Sztompka (Eds.), *Cultural trauma and collective identity* (pp. 31–59). University of California Press.

Staeheli, L. A. (1994). Empowering political struggle: Spaces and scales of resistance. *Political Geography, 13*(1), 387–391.

Stevens, M. E. (2016). Trauma is as trauma does: The politics of affect in catastrophic times. In M. J. Casper & E. Wertheimer (Eds.), *Critical trauma studies: Understanding violence, conflict, and memory in everyday life* (pp. 19–36). New York University Press.

Stover, E. E., & Weinstein, H. M. (Eds.). (2004). *My neighbour, my enemy: Justice and community in the aftermath of mass atrocity*. Cambridge University Press.

Sturken, M. (1997). *Tangled memories: The Vietnam war, the AIDS epidemic, and the politics of remembering*. University of California Press.

Sullivan, E. (2017). Displaced in place: Manufactured housing, mass eviction, and the paradox of state intervention. *American Sociological Review*, *82*(2), 243–269.

Sztompka, P. (2000). Cultural trauma: The other face of social change. *European Journal of Social Theory*, *3*(4), 449–466.

Till, K. E. (2012). Wounded cities: Memory-work and a place-based ethics of care. *Political Geography*, *31*(1), 3–14.

Van der Kolk, B. (2014). *The body keeps the score: Brain, mind, and body in the healing of trauma*. Penguin.

Visser, I. (2015). Decolonizing trauma theory: Retrospect and prospects. *Humanities*, *4*(1), 250–265.

Wertheimer, E., & Casper, M. J. (2016). Within trauma: An introduction. In M. J. Casper, & E. Wertheimer (Eds.), *Critical trauma studies: Understanding violence, conflict, and memory in everyday life* (pp. 1–17). New York University Press.

West, H. G. (2003). Voices twice silenced: Betrayal and mourning at colonialism's end in Mozambique. *Anthropological Theory*, *3*(3), 343–365.

Wilkinson, E., & Ortega-Alcázar, I. (2018). The right to be weary? Endurance and exhaustion in austere times. *Transactions of the Institute of British Geographers*, *44*(1), 155–167.

20
A SEASON OF RECKONING FOR THE CHILDREN: EXPLORING THE REALITIES OF AGGREGATED TRAUMA IN THE AFRICAN AMERICAN COMMUNITY

Imani Michelle Scott

We are ridiculed for being angry.
We are pressured to quietly pacify our pain.
We are mocked for feeling victimized.
We are urged to 'forgive' in the face of incessant wounding.
Our hearts hurt. Our souls weep.
But our minds whisper: *Stay woke. Still rise.*

—*Imani Michelle Scott*

For nearly two years, I struggled to execute the writing of this chapter about the realities and consequences of living in the midst of perpetual and systemic antiblack racism in the United States. Yet instead of the cathartic-fueled exuberance I typically feel when given an opportunity to write about and propose resolutions to this enduring conflict, an unexpected heaviness weighted my soul with despair. As a result, what used to be a personally motivational and significant act (my writing), was on the verge of becoming my burden.

For months on end, and despite a wealth of subject matter, events and research about which to write, my mind became increasingly clouded by a humbling duality of experiences. On the one hand, I was being exposed—seemingly bombarded, with an influx of highly publicized, visual stimuli featuring daily, racist-fueled aggressions and assaults against people who looked like me and my loved ones. On the other hand, I was being exposed—seemingly bombarded, with an influx of highly publicized, imagery featuring daily, racist-fueled aggressions and assaults against people who looked like me and my loved ones. In other words, I was overwhelmed with intense levels of stimuli and emotion while feeling compelled to *objectively* think and write about both. Only after periods of dedicated and sustained introspection would I discern that the cloud in my mind was a thinly veiled blanket of fear based on my here-to-fore unacknowledged and unarticulated feelings of distress that in writing anew about this painful subject matter I would be allowing even more punctures to infiltrate my existing psychic wounds related to racial trauma. After all, it is complicated: while I may be considered a contemporary scholar of conflict resolution, I am in no way absolved from my own battles with the deep pain my African American ancestors and brothers and sisters of today continue to experience as a result of near daily racist assaults on our minds, bodies, and spirits.

In 2020, and now in 2021 I am still overwhelmed with near-daily stimuli affirming the realities of social, institutional, and structural racism against African Americans in the *Land of the Free*; accordingly, I find myself perpetually haunted with more questions than answers as I wonder: *How do I write yet another chapter about ethnic violence against African Americans when I am so personally and profoundly exhausted by that violence? Is this how rape victims feel when asked to repeatedly explore and share the violations levied on them, while knowing they remain susceptible to subsequent violations? Will it matter that I write more words to be read by more academics whose conferences will facilitate more panel discussions likely yielding more questions (than solutions) about relief for my very personal "Post Traumatic Slave Syndrome"* (see DeGruy, 2005)? *Given the deeply embedded fallacies about white supremacy and all of the twisted travesties they continue to generate, will this chapter have even a minimal impact for positive change?* I soon learned that I was not alone in facing this conundrum.

Shortly following the murder of George Floyd by then police officer, Derek Chauvin, Jessica Murrey, a social change communication expert wrote: "I am Black. I am grieving ... here I was, in the digital crowd, watching a black man being suffocated in broad daylight by the people sworn to protect him. I feel stripped raw. Despair and rage both threaten to swallow me whole. But here's the thing: I'm also a peacebuilder" (Murrey, 2020, p. 1). One might presume that as a trained expert, Ms. Murrey would be equipped with sufficient resources to work through the emotive and provocative circumstances of Mr. Floyd's death with resilience; however, this would not be the case. In unveiling the depths of her vulnerability, Ms. Murrey laid bare her humanity. Afterall, even the most highly trained and emotionally rigid among us will become exhausted with repetitive mental and emotional battering. And if this indeed, is where an African American adult—trained in social change and peacebuilding found herself in 2020, it is not difficult to presume how African American children might falter under the similar strain of unrelenting, systemic, race-based oppression (Young, 2020).

In an ideal world, all children would be afforded healthy and wholesome childhoods where they might grow into their best adult selves. But for too many African American children, life is anything but idyllic; they see too much violence, injustice and inequality, and they do not have the maturity to process or make sense of the biases that the world shows them. They live in a world where their brown skin causes them to endure aggregated traumas of living in a perpetually racist society, even though the entire concept of race is based on a fallacy. In this chapter, I review a series of recent events as examples of provocations of racial trauma and discuss the mental health consequences to members of the African American communal group. This chapter concludes with a series of recommendations, including the implementation of compassionate, community-based initiatives for building a healthier African American community, and ultimately, a healthier safer and more secure world for our children.

Background: Racism as a "socially transmitted disease"

In the introduction to her groundbreaking book, *Post-traumatic slave syndrome: America's legacy of enduring injury and healing*, Dr. Joy Degruy (2005) began by spotlighting a centuries-long greeting ritual of the powerful Maasai Tribe of East Africa. Known for its warrior-stance against 18th century colonialism and slavery, the Maasai Tribe is extoled by Degruy (2005) for its standard tribal greeting: "*Kasserian Ingera?*" which translated into English means: "And how are the children?" This Maasai greeting ritual is nothing less than fascinating in its deep wisdom, for it confirms that the security, status, and welfare of the children must be *everyone's* first order of business. Indeed, on any given day the status of the children *is* the foremost indicator of a society's future. If the children are not well, the social structure is fragile, unstable, and deeply at-risk; it cannot grow, prosper, or lead because its future is too ambiguous. In the words of Nelson Mandela, "There can be no keener revelation of a society's soul than the way in which it treats its children," (1995, para. 1). And this focus on the well-being of the children, I suggest, should be a dire concern to U.S. leaders, communities, and families since in the end, too many of *our* children, the African American children specifically, are not well.

A 2021 report published by the Children's Defense Fund (CDF) (2021) documented a series of startling statistics to give insight into the contemporary life experiences of African American children. Included in the CDF report were the following:

- More than one in four Black children are poor compared with one in 12 white children; the youngest children are the poorest.
- While representing less than 15 percent of the youth population, Black youth are 2.4 times more likely to be arrested than white children.
- Black youth are nine times more likely than white youth to receive prison sentences slated for adults.
- In 2018, 52 percent of Black youth were prosecuted in adult criminal court, and
- Black teens are four times more likely to die from gun violence than their white peers.

The CDF report also surmised that the year 2020's combined experiences of a world-wide health pandemic along with the unending toxicity of racial violence in the United States made Black youth especially vulnerable to suicide. For many, this was not surprising since in 2019 members of the Congressional Black Caucus (CBC) had already become so concerned about data indicating drastic increases in suicide rates for Black youth and teens that it convened an Emergency Task Force on Black Youth Suicide and Mental Health (CBC Task Force) to study the phenomenon.

According to the CBC Task Force, the trending increase in suicide rates among Black youth ran counter to traditionally lower rates of suicide in the Black community (when compared to other communities) at large. Add to that, the study confirmed that Black youth under 13 years of age were twice as likely to commit suicide as their non-Black counterparts.

While startling, I propose that none of the above should be dumbfounding, especially given the recent saturation of video documented racist assaults targeted at African Americans in nearly every aspect of our daily lives in the United States. For despite denials of systemic racism by some elected leaders (i.e., Senator Tim Scott, 2021; Vice President Kamala Harris [Brown, 2021]; Senator Lindsey Graham [McEvoy, 2021]; former Governor and Ambassador Nikki Haley [Yam, 2020]), the reaches of racism are so vast that even in today's America we are confronted with bizarre reintroductions of Jim Crow-like practices such as race-norming (see Hobson, 2021), voter suppression (see Tensely, 2021), and redlining (see Perry, 2020), amid proclamations of white supremacy.

In his article, titled: "Is the United States a racist country?", distinguished sociologist and David M. Rubenstein Fellow, Rashawn Ray affirmed that, "systemic racism seems to ripple through our social institutions and into our daily social interactions, whether in Congress or at a coffee shop down the street from the Capitol. These types of experiences—racialized cuts and hurdles—have a cumulative effect on [our] health" (2021, para. 8). Citing research that documents the dire health consequences for Blacks living with "daily racialized trauma," Ray goes on to propose that regardless of class status, there are painfully chronic conscious and subconscious effects on those of us who are living while Black in the United States because "systemic racism is not simply a thing of the past. It is up close and personal in the present," (2021, para. 15). Against the backdrop of exposure to recurrent racialized encounters with Karens (see Greenspan, 2020) and deadly confrontations with police are Black adults who agonize daily with their own efforts to remain mentally well, safe, and secure, while enduring heightened levels of concern about passing along their trauma to their children (see Osborne et al., 2021).

For Black children living in today's America, the situation is so alarming that a recently released policy statement by the American Academy of Pediatrics (AAP) proclaimed the chronic stress of living with racism to be a *socially transmitted disease*. Confirming what we already know scientifically, that "biologically, we are truly just one race, sharing 99.9 percent of our genes no matter what the color of our skin or what part of the world we come from" (2019, p. 1), the Academy argued that for children and adolescents, living in a racist society poses serious public health risks (Trent et al., 2019). Further, it acknowledged that in the United States, racism has been and continues to be used for the specific purposes of propagating oppression, justifying slavery, and bolstering false claims about white racial superiority. After the release of this unprecedented policy statement, the AAP further condemned racism when its president pled with pediatricians throughout the United States to actively support the dismantling of structural racism. Acknowledging that our children's futures depend on "these moments of reckoning," AAP President Sara Goza (Jenco, 2020) argued that dismantling racism is *essential*.

Key insights

> It is totally natural and normal for us to be upset, confused, [and] scared about what's going on in our society and what we are seeing.
> —*Dr. Monnica T. Williams (2019)*

To be clear, the haunting of the African American psyche began centuries ago, as the children then also saw too much; and the haunting continues today. The transgenerational transmission of trauma (see Scott, 2000, 2014; Volkan, 1997) began more than 400 years ago when children witnessed their elders being ripped away from their homes and chained in the bowels of a ship to endure a treacherous transatlantic journey to the United States. Later, more children would witness their mothers and fathers stripped of their humanity and auctioned into slavery where they were beaten, subdued, and forced to work like animals. Then, the children witnessed their father's powerlessness to save the women he loved from being raped, and his humiliated frustration at being unable to protect even the youngest among them from a broad and generalized series of violent acts rendered by their white oppressors.

In time, the children witnesses to widespread, legally sanctioned, and targeted violence against those who shared their skin color would become adults. As such, they would begin to endure traumas of their own in a world of convict leasing, peonage, and Jim Crow/Apartheid. Here, they also experienced a substandard quality of life while living under constant threats and realities of domestic terrorism such as lynching, medical experimentations, and deadly riots. Ultimately, the traumatic memories these children inherited from their fathers were compounded by their own personal experiences of victimization, powerlessness, and humiliation to the degree that some who would become mothers would eventually pass the traumas through their genes to their unborn children (Cross et al., 2017).

Ultimately, the African American children of today know what the children of yesterday knew: that the hatred, the disrespect, the sheer disregard for their humanity is all too palpable for them to expect a true *childhood*. At very young ages, they must accept that they cannot afford to be a "child" for too long; their ability to survive in this world and in this violent place we call America—it mandates that they grow up, fast. And so, if they are wise, they must also be hypervigilant. After all, they must learn early the lessons of who to trust and who to fear, when to walk and when to run, when to fight and when to cower. Maybe they know the story of John Felton who was stopped and ticketed by police in Ohio because according to the officer, Felton dared give him direct eye contact. Or maybe they heard Charnesia Corley's story of being stripped and cavity-searched in a gas station parking lot because Houston police said she possessed marijuana; she did not. And then, they may have seen the video of the bullets fired by a South Carolina police officer into Levar Jones' body, as Jones—who was obeying the officer's request to show his ID—was shot when he reached for his ID. Yet it does not end there.

The children today know how 17-year-old Trayvon Martin was profiled as he walked along a Sanford, Florida street with a can of iced tea and a box of candy, and then killed by a neighborhood watch captain whom the justice system would eventually exonerate for Trayvon's murder. They saw images of 12-year-old Tamir Rice playing with a toy gun moments before a Cleveland, Ohio police officer shot and killed him, and they heard reports that unarmed 18-year-old Michael Brown had his hands in the air when he was shot dead by a St. Louis, Missouri police officer. The children may have seen the video where 28-year-old Sandra Bland dared question an officer's reasons for pulling her over while driving, only to end up dead in her Waller County, Texas jail cell hours later. They know that 24-year-old Jonathan Ferrell had just walked away from a traffic accident where he had to kick out a window to escape, only to be shot dead by Charlotte, North Carolina police officers as he approached them for help. They saw pictures of 43-year-old Eric Garner's last moments as he struggled under a Staten Island, New York police officer's chokehold to breathe. And they heard how 31-year-old Corey Jones was shot and killed by an undercover police officer as he sat aside his stranded car along a Palm Beach, Florida, highway awaiting a tow truck. Then too, they may have seen the video of 25-year-old Ahmad Arbery fighting for his life against three white men (one, a former police officer) who hunted, and then shot him dead like an animal for jogging in a Brunswick, Georgia neighborhood.

In Georgia, many of our children have heard the strange story of 17-year-old Kendrick Johnson who supposedly killed himself in a wrestling mat while his white teammates lingered nearby in their Valdosta high school gymnasium, and the even stranger story of 26-year-old Air Force Veteran Anthony Hill—who was newly returned from Afghanistan when he was killed by a DeKalb County police office as Hill wandered naked and unarmed in his neighborhood. Yet even if the children did not know about any of the stories above, they likely saw pictures taken of a smiling and proud 26-year-old emergency medical technician named Breonna Taylor before her bullet-riddled body would be pulled out of her apartment after Louisville, Kentucky police officers killed her, unarmed and innocent of any crimes. And surely, our children saw the images of 46-year-old George Floyd crying out for his mother as he was pinned under the weight of a police officer's knee while struggling to breathe his last breath on a street corner in Minneapolis, Minnesota. So, of course, it makes good sense that the children could not possibly be well (McCaig, 2021).

African American children live with unaddressed wounds of victimization and losses of identity and dignity from the long ago past of their ancestors and the recent past of their parents. Then, they reexperience the victimization every day in their present. This is aggregated trauma.

Compounding their awareness of the too often deadly consequences of "living while Black," African American children are more—than their non-Black peers, likely to live in poverty, to be in ill health, to have fewer educational resources, to be negatively stereotyped, and to endure transgenerated psychological trauma: and this latter reality with its powerfully cyclical nature, may be the scariest travesty of them all. Although, we, in the African American community, have not reached agreement on what to name it, we know that it exists.

- Dr. Joy DeGruy (2005) calls it *posttraumatic slave syndrome*.
- Author and attorney Barbara K. Ratliff (2014) refers to it as *battered race syndrome*, an expression also frequently used by the reverend Dr. Al Sharpton.
- In the book, *Crimes against Humanity in the Land of the Free: Can a Truth and Reconciliation Process Heal Racial Conflict in America?* (2014) Dr. Trina Brown and Dr. Bentley Wallace call it *collective neuroticism*.
- Some call it *Emmett-Tillism*, referencing psychological reactions to the brutal 1955 murder of 14-year-old Emmett Till in Mississippi.
- It was officially labeled: *continuous traumatic stress syndrome* by the mental health community in Apartheid-era South Africa.

Ultimately, the label matters far less than the experience. For determinedly, what each marker attempts to verbalize is an appropriate characterization of the perennial, trauma-infused responses endured by persons of African ancestry living in the United States.

For many in the African American community, perpetual revictimization leads to a collective sense of psychosocial powerlessness, and I propose that this aggregated trauma is what provokes and disallows the effective treatment of intense emotional and psychological pain experienced by the collective. Our children cry out for relief as their anger spills over into violence. Unchecked, the internalized aggression located in raw and infectious mental agony, can derail the structure of a society; the Maasai know this. And while it is true that not *all* members of the African American community—or any communal group for that matter, may experience a collective sense of victimization or absorb the bitter acidity of racialized wounding, it is undeniable that generational transmissions of psychic, emotional, and dispiriting aggregated trauma have a sure influence on multitudes.

Implications for teaching and training

I asked an African American man: "where does a Black man with a gentle heart go for support?" And he burst into tears.
—Ms. Vanessa Jackson, Licensed Clinical Therapist

In my quest to better understand the mental and emotional dynamics of the aggregated trauma associated with living as an African American in a too often violent and perpetually racialized United States, I interviewed three distinguished African American mental-health-care professionals, Dr. Monnica T. Williams, associate professor and clinical psychologist, University of Connecticut, Ms. Vanessa Jackson, psychotherapist and owner of Healing Circles, Inc., and Dr. Matthew Smith (2019), licensed psychologist, Atlanta Consulting and Psychological Services, LLC. Below are brief, selected excerpts and paraphrased comments from our discussions, which were only about their experiences with their African American clientele:

Question: What feelings have been reported to you, or have you observed, by those seeking counseling for mental distress associated with racism?
Responses:

- Anger, outrage, and a sense of alienation
- Feeling crushed, confused, and victimized
- Grief, sadness, and fear
- Feeling deceived and constricted
- Guilt—about any or all, of the above

Questions: How about children and teens? What have you learned about their feelings or coping mechanisms?
Responses:

- Our children's mental health is impacted by all aspects of racism in our society.
- Young Black men may hide emotions under the veil of hypermasculinity.
- Our children feel they don't have traditional opportunities to connect, so they do things like joining gangs to have a sense of belonging; this ends up creating more opportunities for trauma.
- Parents must be careful to "control the narrative" by contextualizing violence and racism to create safe zones for children to talk about their feelings.

Question: What are examples of problematic and unhealthy responses to coping with racism?
Responses:

- An inability to be optimistic or function well enough to find joy and happiness
- Hypervigilance
- Sleeplessness and low energy
- Fear of going to work and/or anxiety about interacting with white people
- Internalizing painful emotions
- Withdrawing inward
- A tendency to "stuff anger"—a habit proven to contribute to the higher propensity for hypertension, diabetes, stroke, and other illnesses

Question: What about healthy resilience strategies? Are there any you recommend?
Responses:

- There are racism-related resilience strategies that we have historically passed on to our children for their survival.
- The "double-consciousness" coined by Dr. W. E. B. Du Bois is a legitimate part of our resilience toolbox.
- We must continuously assure our children that they are strong and resourceful enough to overcome a deck stacked against them.
- Trauma genes are genetically transmitted from parents to unborn children as survival mechanisms (see *The Grady Trauma Project, 2020*).

Question: What are your thoughts on feeling of guilt and anger as consequences of living in a racialized society?
Responses:

- Stereotypes of the *angry* Black woman and *angry* Black man are projections that white people put on us to control us and validate their violence against us.
- Anger is a survival skill. Sometimes, to survive we draw on anger as a tool.
- There is no evidence that Black people are angrier than white people or any other group.
- We have a right to be angry.

Question: I keep reading about the stigma associated with seeking mental health support in the African American community. What are your thoughts?
Responses:

- There is a fear of being perceived as "crazy" in a world where Blacks are historically more likely to be forcibly institutionalized and more likely to be overmedicated and diagnosed with a psychotic disorder than non-Blacks.
- There is the fear of appearing weak in a society that only rewards the strong.
- There is a long-standing belief within the dominant community that Black people do not have or feel pain.

At the conclusion of my interview, a host of suggestions were made by these three experts to support the mental health and wellness of African American adults, teens, and children caught in the web and pain of racialized trauma. These suggestions included:

- Allow ourselves to "be human" and to experience the full range of emotions that come with that allowance.
- Detach from media and external stimuli to periodically reboot.
- Seek social support from persons who empathize with what we're feeling.
- Involve ourselves in targeted self-care and pampering moments (e.g., meditation, massages, exercise, and yoga).
- Link to safe spaces like churches and community groups.
- Establish and/or participate in peer support movements (e.g., soul and healing circles).
- Join an activist group whose values and goals align with our own.
- Give ourselves the "right to pull out" of activism when it becomes overwhelming.
- Permit ourselves to work through our personal experiences of emotion without judging or timing the process.
- Allow ourselves "righteous rage" and other emotions to the degree that we don't hurt ourselves or others.
- Contact a mental health professional. The Association of Black Psychologists is a good resource for African American practitioners.
- Encourage the study of mental health; there are far too few African Americans in the mental health field.

In addition to the recommendations made by these three mental-health-care professionals, there exists a wealth of community-based health and wellness programs to support the needs of African American children. In 2011, Child Trends—a nonprofit/nonpartisan center which focuses on the developmental stages of all children, facilitated an extensive evaluation of over

50 community-based programs designed specifically to support the overall wellness and life experiences of African American children. Based on eight identified outcomes, the goal of the study was to determine which types of community-based programs worked best to support the needs of these children, and which types proved less effective. According to the researchers, there were no programs which met all outcomes identified as necessary for the wellness needs of African American children; however, the researchers did find that (1) "programs that foster partnerships between the community and schools tend to work, (2) strategies that garner family buy-in appear to be a critical component to program success, and (3) high-intensity programs that meet on a consistent basis and frequently result in impacts for African American children and adolescents" (Bandy & Moore, 2011, p. 1). And although the outcome areas did not focus specifically on the emotional and mental health consequences of living in a racist society, taken together the eight outcome areas (which included externalizing behaviors, physical health, and social skills) are relatable components to mental well-being. The greatest benefits of this study were its rigor and comprehensiveness; in fact, it identified over 20 specific programs as "proven to work" in accomplishing many of the outcomes identified as most valuable to the wellness of African American children and teens. This is important since these programs might serve as models for replication in other communities. Equally important are those programs designated by the study as either "not proven to work" or having received "mixed reviews"; this material should also inform community-based program designs and initiatives going forward.

Implications for practice and policy

Building on what I learned in the Child Trends (2011) report, and in my own effort to offer opportunities for adults and children to work through the painful and complicated consequences of racism, racial conflict, implicit bias, and social injustice, I developed the Peace Begins with Truth (PBT) workshop as a community-based model, which might be easily replicated. The concept for PBT workshops is based on the belief that all humans are created equally, and that by virtue of sharing the gift of life with other humans we have a mutual, collective responsibility to (1) build and maintain a society where each person's existence is rendered the utmost respect; (2) value and support different worldviews based on cultural backgrounds and historical realities, and (3) cultivate an existence where harmonious, equitable, and peaceful human interactions are the enduring principles upon which practices, programs and policies are established. Ultimately, I have found through my work with PBT that in the process of assisting others work through their challenges with racism, I am able to work through my own.

At the beginning of this chapter, I shared my very personal challenge to move past fears about my own rewounding and once again, write about the realities of "living while Black" in the United States. While sharing such personal information may seem a bit odd and even contrary (in some circles) to academic writing, I felt it necessary to do so; after all, beyond being peace scholars and practitioners, we are human beings (Reed, 1990). Consequently, it would be disingenuous to write about trauma as if we are always on the outside looking in when, in fact, we are very much in the midst of the madness. In closing I believe it is important for academicians, especially those of us who represent the traditionally oppressed and marginalized masses, to humanize our own journeys as a way to connect with our fellow human beings, the majority of whom are not academics and scholars.

To summarize, many African Americans are fully aware that but for the grace of God our father could be the next Eric Garner, our brother could be the next Laquan McDonald, our sister could be the next Sandra Bland … and we could be any of them. Our angst is only exacerbated when we see the men caught on video assassinating those who look like us and our loved ones not being held accountable by a seeming "injustice" system. It all hurts, very deeply, and it impacts our children, most of all.

References

Bandy, T., & Moore, K. (2011). What works for African American children and adolescents. Child Trends. *Publication 2011–04.* https://www.childtrends.org/wp-content/uploads/2013/05/2011-04WhatWorkAAChildren.pdf

Brown, M. (2021). Kamala Harris agrees with Tim Scott that America is 'not a racist country' but says we 'must speak truth' on racism. *USA Today.* https://www.usatoday.com/story/news/politics/2021/04/29/kamala-harris-responds-tim-scott-saying-america-not-racist-country/4886682001/

Children's Defense Fund. (2021). The state of America's children. https://www.childrensdefense.org/state-of-americas-children/

Cross, D., Vance, L. A., Kim, Y. J., Ruchard, A. L., Fox, N., Jovanovic, T., & Bradley, B. (2017). Trauma exposure, PTSD, and parenting in a community sample of low-income, predominantly African American mothers and children. *Psychological Trauma: Theory, Research, Practice, and Policy.* Advance online publication. https://doi.org/10.1037/tra0000264

DeGruy, J. (2005). *Post-traumatic slave syndrome: America's legacy of enduring injury and healing.* Uptone Press.

Greenspan, R. (2020). How the name 'Karen' became a stand-in for problematic white women and a hugely popular meme. *Insider.* https://www.insider.com/karen-meme-origin-the-history-of-calling-women-karen-white-2020-5

Hobson, W. (2021). NFL says it will end controversial 'race-norming' in concussion settlement with players. https://www.washingtonpost.com/sports/2021/06/03/nfl-concussion-settlement-race-norming/

Jackson, V. (February 11, 2019). Personal communication.

Jenco, M. (2020). Dismantle racism at every level: AAP President. *AAP News.* https://www.aappublications.org/news/2020/06/01/racism060120

Mandela, N. (1995). Speech by President Nelson Mandela at the launch of the Nelson Mandela Children's Fund. http://db.nelsonmandela.org/speeches/pub_view.asp?pg=item&ItemID=NMS250&txtstr=Mahla

McCaig, A. (2021). Digital divide disproportionately affected education for Black and Hispanic children during pandemic. https://news.rice.edu/2021/03/29/digital-divide-disproportionately-affected-education-for-black-and-hispanic-children-during-pandemic/

McEvoy, J. (2021). Senator Lindsey Graham tells Fox he doesn't believe systemic racism exists in the U.S. *Forbes.* https://www.forbes.com/sites/jemimamcevoy/2021/04/25/sen-lindsey-graham-tells-fox-he-doesnt-believe-systemic-racism-exists-in-the-us/?sh=22e3482ef92b

Murrey, J. (2020). I'm black. I'm a peacebuilder. I want your help. https://sfcg.medium.com/im-black-im-a-peacebuilder-i-want-your-help-8ab32f84c572

Osborne, K. R., Caughy, M. O., Oshri, A., Smith, E. P., & Owen, M. T. (2021). Racism and preparation for bias within African American families. *Cultural Diversity and Ethnic Minority Psychology, 27*(2), 269–279. https://doi.org/10.1037/cdp0000339

Perry, A. (2020). *Know your price: Valuing Black lives and property in America's Black cities.* Brookings Institution Press.

Ratliff, B. (2014). *The battered race syndrome and the habit of racism: A case for reparations and global reconciliation.* Point of View Publishing Company.

Ray, R. (2021). How we rise: Is the U.S. a racist country? https://www.brookings.edu/blog/how-we-rise/2021/05/04/is-the-united-states-a-racist-country/

Reed, I. (1990). *Writing is fighting: Thirty-seven years of boxing on paper.* Atheneum.

Scott, I. (Ed.). (2014). *Crimes against humanity in the land of the free: Can a truth and reconciliation process heal racial conflict in America?* Praeger ABC-CLIO.

Scott, K. (2000). A perennial mourning: Identity conflict and the transgenerational transmission of trauma within the African American community. *Journal of Mind and Human Interaction, 11*(1), 1–24.

Scott, T. (2020). Senator Tim Scott delivers the Republican response to the State of the Union. Available at: https://www.youtube.com/watch?v=RzOfR5Rp5bc

Smith, M. (personal communication, February 11, 2019).

Tensely, B. (2021). America's long history of Black voter suppression: A timeline of new and old efforts to limit the political power of Black Americans and other voters of color. https://www.cnn.com/interactive/2021/05/politics/black-voting-rights-suppression-timeline/

The Grady Trauma Project. (2020). http://thegradytraumaproject.com

Trent, M., Dooley, D., & Dougé, D. (2019). The impact of racism on child and adolescent health. *Official Journal of the American Academy of Pediatrics.* https://pediatrics.aappublications.org/content/144/2/e20191765

Volkan, V. (1997). *Bloodlines: From ethnic pride to ethnic terrorism.* Basic Books.

Williams, M. (February 11, 2019). Personal communication).

Yam, K. (2020). Nikki Haley claims 'America is not racist,' later says she faced discrimination. *NBC News.* https://www.nbcnews.com/news/asian-america/nikki-haley-claims-america-not-racist-later-says-she-faced-n1238025

Young, S. (2020). Deaths shape how Black parents navigate "The Talk." *WebMD.* https://www.webmd.com/mental-health/news/20200608/deaths-shape-how-black-parents-navigate-the-talk

21
PEACE AFTER GENOCIDE: EXHUMATIONS, EXPECTATIONS, AND PEACEBUILDING EFFORTS IN BOSNIA AND HERZEGOVINA

Hasan Nuhanović and Sarah Wagner

Background: Peace after genocide

If the absence of armed conflict or sustained violence measures peace, then Bosnia and Herzegovina is, by such metrics, a peaceful society.[1] Twenty-five years have passed since the end of the three-and-a-half-year war that left 100,000 people dead—31,500 of them as "missing persons"—and two million displaced, without the return of violent conflict.[2] Yet peace in the sense of security—social, economic, and political—has failed to materialize in the everyday lives of most Bosnian citizens (Henig, 2020; Jansen, 2015; Kurtović, 2016), and less tangible forms of violence persist, from structural inequities in education and health care (Hromadžić, 2015; Jašarević, 2017) to overt attempts to deny genocide and justify war crimes (Karčić, 2020).

In this chapter, we examine the unfinished business of peacebuilding efforts through the specific lens of missing persons and the legacy of mass graves. In the context of post-conflict societies, these efforts of exhumation and identification are often framed in interventionist terms, as part of a larger agenda of transitional justice work, human rights advocacy, and democracy building; scholars attuned to the necropolitics of post-conflict repair note how initiatives to recover and name the missing constitute a particular form of governing the living through the bodies of the dead (Rojas-Perez, 2017; Sant Cassia, 2005; Stepputat, 2014). Bosnia and Herzegovina is no exception, and its example illustrates how the missing and the identified are not only bound up in aspirational projects of peace and reconciliation but also become operationalized within narratives of victimhood and perpetration. Posthumous conscripts of peacebuilding, Bosnia's missing are rarely left to rest in peace.

Any discussion of postwar peacebuilding in Bosnia and Herzegovina must begin by acknowledging the failures of *peacekeeping*—namely, the failed United Nations (UN) wartime peacekeeping mission (Nuhanović, 2005; Power, 2003) during the 1992–1995 war. From the siege of Sarajevo to the fall of the UN "safe areas" of Srebrenica and Žepa, the international community's failure to protect civilians and prevent atrocities during the war set the table for its compromised position as arbiter of peace in the years that followed.

Second, in any discussion of peacebuilding, timeframes matter. While the phrase "peace after genocide" makes sense in terms of a chronological order where two things happen in a succession, placing those two words next to one another obviously creates a conflict; for many Bosnians, they are jarring to the ear. Certainly, the postwar circumstances in Bosnia and Herzegovina suggest that peace can take various forms and does not always mean the same thing to people. Nevertheless, among that variation of experience and conditions, a common denominator exists in the absence of war. Indeed, most Bosnians, from ordinary citizens to academics and journalists, use this term of peace (*mir*) when describing the situation of this postwar society.

The combination, however, of the three words—*peace after genocide*—opens other questions, such as at what point can we say that genocide is over? The word *aftermath* contains within it the word *after*, and as Wagner and Nettlefield point out, "One of many challenges of studying and writing about genocide is how to define *aftermath*. What constitutes this period and what signals its end, the transformation of post-conflict into a normalized state?" (2014, p. 27).

One way of tackling this problem of beginning and ends is to recognize the stages that exist along that span. Academic and activist Gregory Stanton outlines eight stages of genocide: classification, symbolization, dehumanization, organization, polarization, preparation, extermination, and denial, with the final one continuing after the perpetrators kill their last victim (Stanton, 1996). Extending Stanton's schema, authors have come up with a definition of yet another stage of genocide: triumphalism, a phenomenon that has typified Bosnia and Herzegovina's period of postwar reckoning (Halilovich, 2017). Halilovich analyses instances of triumphalism taking place in Bosnia and Herzegovina during the past two decades, long after official peace was signed into existence: for example, the slogan "*Nož, žica, Srebrenica*" ("Knife, wire, Srebrenica") at football stadiums displayed on huge banners by the supporters of the Serbian football clubs, and the university dormitory named in honor of convicted war criminal Radovan Karadžić.

All the while, in that aftermath and amid these protracted stages of denial and triumphalism, mass graves are unearthed and victims' remains are exhumed. The work of recovering and identifying the missing continues year after year. In examining the clash between campaigns of denialism and triumphalism and the dogged pursuit of the unnamed dead, this chapter poses three central questions: (1) What problems are addressed and resolved by conducting the exhumations? (2) What problems arise after the exhumation of mass graves, identification, and burial of the genocide victims? (3) If we accept that *peace* and the *aftermath of genocide* are possible (as this situation has been present in Bosnia and Herzegovina from the end of the armed conflict to this day), at what cost do those two phenomena exist together?

Background: Genocide in GPS coordinates and a landscape of mass graves

In order to point at the cause-effect relationship between the events from the past and the problems arising in the present time, more than two decades later, including amid the country's frustrated efforts at peacebuilding, we have to revisit the historical context. The exercise reveals a distinct correlation between war's inhumanities and postwar attempts at their redress. While past and present exhumations occur as a humanitarian response to atrocity, they were necessitated by another, inhumane process—namely, the mass executions of thousands of innocent victims, many of whom were dumped into primary, secondary, and even tertiary mass graves as part of the perpetrators' efforts to hide evidence of their crimes.

Typically, when one speaks of such mass graves in postwar Bosnia and Herzegovina, the conversation centers on Srebrenica, the UN "safe area" that fell to the Bosnian Serb army in July 1995. It is a location now synonymous with genocide and known as the single worst atrocity to occur on European soil since World War II, the massacre of 8,372 Bosniak men and boys that took place between July 10–19, 1995.[3] Much of the early (and unsuccessful) postwar attempts at "truth and reconciliation" in Bosnia and Herzegovina touched on Srebrenica in some form or fashion (Dragovic-Soso, 2016, pp. 304–307).

If you zoom in at the eastern corner of Bosnia and Herzegovina, the town of Srebrenica will appear at 44.06 degrees N of Latitude and 19.17 degrees E of Longitude. These same digits were the coordinates of suspected locations of mass graves containing the remains of the Srebrenica genocide victims transmitted to the Implementation Force (IFOR),[4] the NATO-led international forces, upon their deployment to the country at the beginning of 1996. By that time, some six months after the so-called safe area had fallen, media reports about the Srebrenica massacre had already spread across the globe; its perpetrators were already well known to the international community and specifically the UN peacekeeping forces. Indeed, a few days after the fall of Srebrenica in July 1995, the International Criminal Tribunal for the former Yugoslavia (ICTY), based in The Hague, Netherlands, issued indictments against the Bosnian Serb political and military leaders, Radovan Karadžić and Ratko Mladić, which included counts of genocide. A few weeks later, the U.S. Ambassador to the UN, Madeline Albright, released aerial images of several suspected mass grave sites near Srebrenica (Power, 2003).

The public exposure of the UN peacekeepers' failure at Srebrenica and shortly thereafter the nearby "safe area" of Žepa marked a turning point in the war. In August 1995, after several mortal shells were fired from the Bosnian Serb army positions above Sarajevo exploded at the Markale market, killing and injuring dozens,[5] NATO launched its Operation Deliberate Force, a sustained air-strike campaign which, combined with other military developments on the ground, led to a ceasefire and the signing of the Dayton Peace Agreement. The mass executions of men and boys after the fall of the Srebrenica "safe area" was one of the last episodes of mass atrocities perpetrated during the 1992–1995 war.

While Srebrenica's atrocities and network of mass graves stand apart from other events of destruction and extermination, they also represent the culmination of a concerted campaign by Serbian and Bosnian Serb forces to clear and control territory in the eastern, northwestern, and central regions of the country.[6] The mass killings, and incarceration in torture camps, as part of "ethnic cleansing" campaigns were the recognizable modus operandi that the authorities of the self-proclaimed Republika Srpska embraced from the outset of the war. These efforts to displace, dispossess, and destroy non-Serb populations resulted in missing persons (*nestale osobe*) on a mass scale.[7] In most instances, the surviving family members of the missing narrowly escaped the same fate. For example, Bosniaks of the Prijedor municipality, located at the western corner of Bosnia and Herzegovina, were victims of atrocities perpetrated during the spring and summer of 1992. By the end of July 1992, more than 3,000 Bosniaks of Prijedor were either killed or missing, while the rest of the Bosniak population was deported to the Bosnian government-controlled territory.[8] During the same period, in the initial months of the war, a very similar scenario unfolded in the eastern region of the Podrinje, in which Srebrenica is located, as well as in other parts of the country.

The legacy of those missing persons, killed but unrecovered, from the earliest incidents of violence in the spring of 1992 and extending through the Srebrenica genocide, presents one of Bosnia's most formidable challenges for building a peaceful society. A large part of that challenge stems from the fact that the work of recovering, exhuming, and identifying the remains of the missing takes place amid persistent efforts to deny or even triumph in the systemic campaigns of destruction and extermination that resulted in their disappearance.

Key insights

Searching for the missing in the aftermath

Exhumations are the midpoint in the process of resolving the missing persons issue. Before remains can be exhumed, they must first be located; after exhumation, recovered remains must be identified. In postwar Bosnia and Herzegovina, locating sites of clandestine burial, such as the primary and secondary mass graves containing the victims of the Srebrenica genocide, has been a complicated, at times, uneasy task because searching for the missing has often followed the wartime logic of ethnonational antagonisms and division (Jugo & Wagner, 2017). Thus, at its most basic level, exhumations constitute a success: the location of a grave or a set of remains has become known and in turn actionable.

Again, context is crucial. During the war, the mass graves and locations of executions were out of reach as the territory remained under the control of the Bosnia Serb authorities throughout the war. For the most part, the remains of those killed and missing in 1992, and those in 1995, as well as those who were killed or "went missing" in the intervening three years, therefore could not be recovered until the conflict ceased. After the Dayton agreement signing and deployment of IFOR, pressure quickly mounted as the survivors demanded from both the local authorities and the international organizations that information about their missing relatives be released. The division of labor, responsibility, and corresponding political will at the national level further stymied the process. With postwar Bosnia and Herzegovina divided into two entities (the Bosniak and Bosnian Croat-controlled Federation of Bosnia and Herzegovina and the Bosnian Serb-controlled Republika Srpska or RS), initially, the exhumation and identification efforts were the responsibility of the respective ethnonational entity-level commissions; these were eventually subsumed into a single, federal-level organization, the Missing Persons Institute.

These local institutions notwithstanding, it was primarily thanks to the heavy international presence, with strong mandates both in its political and military components, and the support it provided to the teams of local and international forensic experts, that the exhumations of mass graves were eventually undertaken in the early postwar years. On the one hand, these efforts flowed directly from legal investigations into war crimes. From its headquarters in The Hague, the ICTY issued dozens of indictments against suspected war criminals. The Tribunal delivered its first binding judgment that included counts for genocide, convicting a Bosnian Serb army General Radislav Krstić in 2001; forensic documentation of detention, execution, and mass graves provided critical evidence for the conviction.[9] On the other hand, the humanitarian initiative of gathering data on the missing, and later recovering and identifying their remains fell to international nongovernmental organizations (NGOs), the International Committee of the Red Cross, Physicians for Human Rights, and finally, what would become the international organization spearheading identification efforts throughout the Western Balkans from 2000 onward, the International Commission on Missing Persons (ICMP).

Despite the significant resources levied by the international community to support the work of the ICTY and ICMP and the establishment of the federal-level Missing Persons Institute, obstacles in locating gravesites, securing the necessary domestic political and material resources, not to mention public support, persisted and indeed continue to this day. The ethnic composition of Republika Srpska, the so-called smaller entity,[10] that had been turned into an exclusive Serb territory by ethnic cleansing and genocide during the war, remained both figuratively and literally a Serb land after the Dayton agreement; the return of the prewar non-Serb population to this part of the country has never reached the level that would reverse the results of the wartime "ethnic cleansing." Moreover, the demographic purge allowed denialist claims and obstructionist practice to flourish. For example, in the case of Srebrenica, it took years of investigation to locate primary, secondary, and tertiary mass graves containing the remains of the genocide victims, and forensic experts working on the cases suspect that at least one more major mass grave exists yet undetected, given that there are approximately 1,000 victims still missing. In the village of Tomašica in the Prijedor municipality of the Republika Srpska, one of the largest mass graves in the country, containing 596 bodies of Bosniak and Bosnian Croat victims killed by Bosnian Serb forces in 1992, was not unearthed until 2013—eighteen years after the war ended.

The protracted process of searching for the missing has exacted a particular toll from surviving kin. As the years passed, the families' hopes shifted from waiting for the missing to appear alive to the hope that the mass graves will be found and skeletal remains will be identified. In this regard, the Bosnian families of the missing are not alone: the desperate outcry by the victims' mothers to have "at least one bone of my child" identified and buried mirrors the experiences of surviving relatives in post-conflict societies across the globe (Edkins, 2011; Halilovich, 2013; Jennings, 2013; Rosenblatt, 2015; Sant Cassia, 2005; Wagner, 2019). In the face of these shifting expectations, survivors nevertheless have continued to press for accountability and action, demanding exhumation and identification of the victims' mortal remains, and criminal prosecution of the perpetrators.

To forgive or to forget, none or both

If searching for and recovering remains pose their own unique material challenges in postwar Bosnia and Herzegovina because of the continuing political antagonisms between the country's two entities, what problems arise on a societal and individual level *after* the exhumation of mass graves, and the subsequent identification and burial of the genocide victims? Put more simply, does the return of remains forge peace? We address these questions from the perspective of one of the authors, Hasan Nuhanović:

> It was in 2010, fifteen years after the Dayton agreement, that I received a "last-minute" notification that my brother's remains were identified through DNA testing. The notification came just in time for his remains to be prepared for the collective burial on July 11 at the Srebrenica-Potočari Memorial Centre and Cemetery, and to be buried on the same day with my mother's remains, identified in the previous year. Both were interred next to my father, whose remains had been exhumed from a secondary mass grave and identified five years before. As the notification procedure demanded, I visited the office of the Podrinje Identification Project in the city of Tuzla.[11] An additional confirmation by a traditional forensic method was needed because the DNA match was below the percentage required for positive identification on its own,[12] I confirmed my brother's identification, based on his Adidas sneakers, which I recognized immediately, and 'Levi's 501' label of his jeans, which I had procured for him at Srebrenica through a UNCHR liaison officer. Both the shoes and the jeans were purchased in Belgrade.

Upon returning home to Sarajevo that evening, I wrote an essay devoted to my brother.[13] The essay included my reflection on the fact that fifteen years had passed after the Srebrenica genocide, that new children were born in the meantime, and that both Serb and Bosniak children deserved a better future. It also included the line "no amnesty for the murderers."

Is what I wrote—that line of refusal—part of the problem or part of the solution, from a "peace and conflict resolution" perspective? I would argue that it is neither, and that such stark either/or, all-or-nothing, equations cannot be applied to my public outcry, or that of the victims' mothers, whose voices have echoed throughout the region for decades. Our resistance to any notion of amnesty can only be understood when placed in context with the counter-narratives created by genocide deniers and the false dilemma of whether we can move toward a better future if we keep recalling the past.

Our refusal also speaks to the limited options of remembrance and amnesty imposed on the Srebrenica survivors through public discourse and by the survivors' own self-reflection—that is, that we must somehow choose a future from among four paths: *to forgive and forget*; *to forgive but not forget*; *to forget but not forgive*; and *to neither forget nor forgive*. These four narrow tracks contend with another broader call to action issued by the genocide's survivors, namely the slogan *Da se nikada ne zaboravi Srebrenica* (Never Forget Srebrenica). It's a mantra that has itself undergone subtle transformations over the years and is now commonly accepted; the words headline the official pamphlet of the program to commemorate July 11, the Srebrenica genocide. The public exhortation to "never forget" invokes pledges born from past atrocities, including the "Never Again" of the Holocaust. In fact, the "Never Forget Srebrenica" message has become further enshrined in public speech, as almost every public address by the Srebrenica survivors includes the phrase, "*Da se nikada nikome ne ponovi Srebrenica*" ("That Srebrenica never happens to anyone again"). So, from the peace and conflict resolution perspective, we must acknowledge that both phrases contain the word "never"; that both phrases insist on remembrance of the past as a necessary step into the future; and that both have been coined as a result of a dynamic public discourse and have been accepted and endorsed by the survivors. It is in the space created by those two "nevers" that we should look for solutions for peace and conflict resolution.

What happens after the exhumation?

Such solutions must also take into account the complex experiences of those who survive the missing. Exhumations and identifications reattach names to remains; they do not immediately—or necessarily—stitch up the grief that prolonged absence has inflicted on families of the missing. Bosniak survivors of the massacres the Bosnian Serb forces perpetrated at and around Prijedor provide ample proof of the far-from-straightforward route from past atrocity to redress and a resumption of peace. Once again, we draw on Hasan's own experience and his engagement with members of the Prijedor community as part of his PhD research project[14]:

> Not long ago I interviewed one of the survivors of Prijedor, who had been a teenager back in 1992. The man had lost several members of his family, relatives who were either killed or went "missing."[15] Several years after the war he and his mother decided to return to their village, and they continue to live there to this day. Describing the situation that developed in the Prijedor area after the war, he uttered exactly the same sentence I did so many times when describing my life as survivor of the Srebrenica genocide: "I live two parallel lives: one of the 'normal' person living through the challenges of today, and one of someone stuck in the past, haunted by my memories." Admittedly, his experience has differed from mine in that after the war he returned to Republika Srpska, to live at his pre-war address, while I have not.

The man described the day when he and his mother buried his younger brother's remains, and another eight of his immediate and extended family members, including his father, grandmother, and grandfather at the local cemetery[16]:

> But, after the burial it became even worse, instead of having some sort of closure. And my mother, who had been saying 'I pray to find at least just one finger,' on that day said that something snapped inside her as earth was being thrown into my brother's grave.

He also describes how difficult it is to cope with such loss to this day, especially for those who returned to their prewar homes:

> The location at which I rebuilt the house is very close to the place at which my brother was executed. I drive there every day. I sometimes take time to think of it, and I say a prayer for the dead as I drive by, but sometimes I forget, and I have music playing in my car, simply because, at that moment, I failed to remember what had happened there. And, later when I recall that moment, I ask myself—how could you? But it is inevitable, as life goes on. I have two kids and a wife. And then it comes back on me. I know I literally drove with the wheels of my car over the spot at which my brother was killed. I blame myself; I have that feeling of guilt, but then I tell myself the only solution would be to build another road that would bypass that spot …. The greatest concern has been that one would never find the remains. But then when that happens, it is only then that something collapses within you. You want to bid farewell to your dead family members, but you just cannot. Your mind does not accept that. And, I vowed to myself, I will find out who killed them, and I will make sure they are brought to justice.

He is caught between the tracks of the present and the past. Beyond his own troubling memories and bouts of guilt for lapses in remembering, this survivor has also to contend with repeated attempts by others, including neighbors, to deny the past violence and its victims. Many of the perpetrators of those atrocities still live with impunity in Prijedor (they have not yet been "brought to justice"), and it is very likely that he has walked past them in the street, just as the survivors of atrocities perpetrated in Srebrenica and many other locations in Bosnia and Herzegovina claim has happened to them.

Implications for teaching and training: Numbers, names, individual identity

While there are multiple lessons to take from the example of Bosnia and Herzegovina's mass graves and missing persons, critical to analyzing either within the context of "peace after genocide" is the recognition that recovered remains are never merely objects of scientific scrutiny or vehicles for post-conflict repair. They are, instead, the material vestige of a human being whose life denied by violence, and the guardians of that life, its memory, as well as the physical remains and artifacts recovered with them, are the relatives.[17] Recognizing that order of intimacy constitutes one of the most fundamental steps in restoring dignity to the missing.

This has not always been the case in Bosnia and Herzegovina. Families have not always trusted the local and international authorities dedicated to recovering and identifying their missing loved ones. Some of the survivors' groups, both in Srebrenica and Prijedor, feel that—as part of transitional justice and reconciliation initiatives—there has been a "hidden" agenda aimed at suppressing their voices in their fight against impunity, and that the process of exhumations and identifications cannot compensate for the violations perpetrated against their missing relatives. And yet they continue to push for action and accountability. Edkins (2011) describes similar circumstances in Argentina when the authorities finally announced they would begin opening the mass graves. The Madres de Plaza de Mayo,[18] the association gathering the victims' relatives, publicly opposed the government's plan to start the exhumations, a position captured by their famous slogan: "They took them alive, we want them back alive" (Rosenblatt, 2015, pp. 93–99). As one of the mothers explained,

> How and when they died too many of us still don't know, but no one, no one shall deny that our children lived. These very particular lives should not be subsumed in any abstract category, even one as legally and morally potent as *desaparecido*. Their disappearance was someone else's crime, not our children's identity. (Edkins, 2011, p. 155)

Thus, although the recovery and identification of the victims' remains begin with and are made possible through numbers—for example, GPS coordinates for locations of suspected mass grave sites; exhumation reports detailing numbers of bodies and body parts; remains referred to as numeric "cases"; DNA profiles extracted from victims' bones and distilled into dual-digit loci—the process culminates in the production of an individual name and the reconstitution of a recognized individual social being. Numbers are a necessary means to an end: they stand in for a human life until the moment of positive identification when the victim's name is finally attached to the remains. That endeavor takes years, even decades between the moment of "disappearance" and the moment when the victim's name is etched onto a tombstone or engraved upon a memorial wall.

Conclusion: Implications for practice and policy

The processes of searching for the missing, pursuing criminal justice, and memorializing human loss are fundamentally intertwined in their aim of rehumanizing the victims of violent conflict and, in particular, genocide. In that regard, marked graves cannot achieve peace alone, as placing the identified remains into a proper grave is only one step toward this rehumanization. In postconflict societies such as Bosnia and Herzegovina where denialism and triumphalism work in direct opposition to these efforts at restoring human dignity, exhumations and identifications have achieved only limited success. For example, victims of the Srebrenica genocide, have yet to be "rehumanized" in the eyes of many Bosnian Serb citizens, whose political leadership have consistently and concertedly denied the crimes of July 1995. In the words of Šefik Džaferović, the Bosnian Muslim member of the tripartite Presidency, in his address at the 25th-anniversary commemoration and mass burial, "The Srebrenica genocide is being denied just as systematically and meticulously as it was executed in 1995." Denialist counterclaims undermine the interwoven attempts at recovering and remembering Bosnia's missing. They do irreparable damage to surviving kin, who, like the relative in Prijedor, drive past sites of execution, sometimes remembering the past, sometimes living in the present, but always aware that there are perpetrators who have eluded accountability amid a contested yet resilient culture of impunity.

How long then will "peace after genocide" continue to jar ears and elicit doubt? For the surviving family members, the process of grappling with the fate of their loved ones—missing and identified, or still missing—lasts through the end of their own lives. If anyone cherishes life and appreciates peace to its fullest meaning, it is those who survived atrocities such as these, those who lost their closest relatives. For the society, as a whole, the answer to "how long?" is more complex; and when the past remains contested, the timeline for meaningful, or even possible, reconciliation extends to future generations. As Yael Danieli has argued, trauma suppressed by the survivors and kept away from the second generation is inevitably transmitted to the third generation (Danieli, 1998). Unearthing the truth of mass graves and building memorial sites to house and honor recovered remains become part of a longer, at times unsettling, process in a post-conflict, post-genocide society moving along its path toward conflict resolution and stability. These steps of "facing the past" do not end at commemoration. Rather, as places of mourning, remembrance, and dignified rest for the victims, memorials and cemeteries have become—at least in postwar Bosnia and Herzegovina—the last, newest frontier in the fight against denial.

Notes

1 Bosnia and Herzegovina, one of the six former federal Yugoslav republics, became a member state of the United Nations on May 22, 1992, as an open aggression and war in the country raged on, by which time more than half of its territory was ethnically cleansed, and thousands of its citizens murdered.
2 More than 100,000 people were killed (Tokača, 2014), and among them 31,500 were listed as missing persons (International Commission of Missing Persons). Almost half of the number killed were civilians. Of the three major ethnic groups of Bosnia and Herzegovina (Bosnian Croat, Bosnian Serb, and Bosniak), the victims of Bosniak ethnicity comprise over 82 percent of the civilian losses (Tokača, 2012).
3 Prosecutor v. Radislav Krstić, Judgment, International Criminal Tribunal for former Yugoslavia, https://www.icty.org/x/cases/krstic/tjug/en/krs-tj010802e-1.htm. To date, the remains of 14 female victims of Srebrenica July 1995 have been recovered, including a newborn and a woman in her 90s; both were buried in a mass grave outside the UN peacekeepers' compound in Potočari (Sorguc, 2018).
4 IFOR succeeded the UN "peacekeeping troops," UNPROFOR (United Nations Protection Force), deployed to the country between 1992 and 1995. IFOR's deployment was written into the Dayton Peace Accord (i.e., The General Framework Agreement for Peace in Bosnia and Herzegovina, also known as the Dayton Peace Agreement (DPA), Dayton Accords, Paris Protocol, or Dayton-Paris Agreement). The peace agreement was reached at Wright-Patterson Air Force Base near Dayton, Ohio, United States, in November 1995, and formally signed in Paris on December 14, 1995. https://www.osce.org/bih/126173.
5 This incident is known as the "second" Markale massacre. The first Markale massacre occurred some eighteen months before.
6 These forces were the Yugoslav People's Army (JNA) and the Army of Republika Srpska (VRS).
7 There is a total of 35,000 missing persons with 23,000 missing people found. See https://balkaninsight.com/2011/02/04/bosnia-s-central-records-on-missing-persons-introduced/
8 According to the association, Udruženje Prijedorčanki "Izvor," the number of the Bosniak victims at Prijedor was 3,176 (2000).
9 General Krstić was one of a few war crime suspects arrested in the American zone of operation until the American troops withdrew from Bosnia in 2002.
10 This phrase of the "smaller entity" is a euphemism that became a part of political rhetoric and vocabulary, used mostly by the Bosniak politicians seemingly as an attempt to downplay the fact that Republika Srpska occupies almost 49 percent of the country's territory.
11 The Podrinje Identification Project is the forensic facility responsible for the Srebrenica 1995 cases. At that time (2010) it was part of the ICMP; it now is affiliated with the Tuzla Canton-run Commemorative Center.
12 According to the ICMP protocol, a DNA match must reach the 99.95 percentage threshold in order to advance the case to the final stages of identification (Wagner, 2008, pp. 115–116).
13 The essay was later published in the *Washington Post* on July 11, 2010 (Nuhanović, 2010).
14 The interview was conducted as part of Nuhanović's dissertation research as PhD candidate at RMIT University, School of Global, Urban and Social Studies, Melbourne, Australia; his research is part of the ARC Discovery Project, "Missing people, missing stories in the aftermath of genocide and 'ethnic cleansing' in Srebrenica and Prijedor."
15 The term most commonly used by the Prijedor survivors is not *nestali* (missing) but *odvedeni* (taken away).
16 The burial took place on July 20, 2014, 22 years to the day after the massacre that was perpetrated in 1992. The burial was organized following the exhumation of the Tomašica mass grave in September 2013.
17 For example, for that very reason, the case managers at the Podrinje Identification Project, the staff tasked with communicating news of identification to the Srebrenica families, referred to the missing person as a person, by his name and by his relation—son, brother, husband, father—and never as a case, a body, or set of remains.

18 The Mothers of the Plaza de Mayo (Asociación Madres de Plaza de Mayo) is an association of Argentinian mothers whose children "disappeared" during the state terrorism of the military dictatorship, between 1976 and 1983.

References

Danieli, Y. (1998). *International handbook of multigenerational legacies of trauma.* Springer Science & Business Media.

Dragovic-Soso, J. (2016). History of a failure: Attempts to create a national Truth and Reconciliation Commission in Bosnia and Herzegovina, 1997–2006. *International Journal of Transitional Justice, 10*(1), 292–310.

Edkins, J. (2011). *Missing: Persons and politics.* Cornell University Press.

Halilovich, H. (2013). *Places of pain: Forced displacement, popular memory and trans-local identities in Bosnian war-torn communities.* Berghahn. DOI 10.1007/978-3-319-31816-5_1304-1

Halilovich, H. (2017). Globalization and genocide. In A. Farazmand (Ed.), *Global encyclopedia of public administration, public policy, and governance.* Springer.

Henig, D. (2020). *Remaking Muslim lives: Everyday Islam in postwar Bosnia and Herzegovina.* University of Illinois Press.

Hromadžić, A. (2015). *Citizens of an empty nation: Youth and state-making in postwar Bosnia-Herzegovina.* University of Pennsylvania Press.

International Commission of Missing Persons. (2014). Missing persons from the armed conflicts of the 1990s: A stocktaking report. https://www.icmp.int/wp-content/uploads/2014/12/StocktakingReport_ENG_web.pdf[Accessed 26 November 2021].

Jansen, S. (2015). *Yearnings in the meantime: 'Normal lives' and the state in a Sarajevo apartment complex.* Berghahn.

Jašarević, L. (2017). *Health and wealth on the Bosnian market: Intimate debt.* Indiana University Press.

Jennings, C. (2013). *Bosnia's million bones: Solving the world's greatest forensic puzzle.* St. Martin's Press.

Jugo, A., & Wagner S. E. (2017). Memory politics and forensic practice: Exhuming Bosnia and Herzegovina's missing persons. In Z. Dziuban (Ed.), *Mapping the 'forensic turn': Engagements with materialities of mass death in Holocaust studies and beyond* (pp. 121–139). New Academic Press.

Karčić, H. (2020). How denial of Bosnian war crimes entered the mainstream. *Balkan Insight.* https://balkaninsight.com/2020/06/30/how-denial-of-bosnian-war-crimes-entered-the-mainstream/

Kurtović, L. (2016). Future conditional: Precarious lives, strange loyalties and ambivalent subjects of Dayton BiH. In S. Jansen, Č. Brković, & V. Čelebičić (Eds.), *Negotiating social relations in Bosnia and Herzegovina: Peripheral entanglements* (pp. 142–156). Ashgate.

Nettelfield, L. J., & Wagner, S. (2014). *Srebrenica in the aftermath of genocide.* Cambridge University Press.

Nuhanović, H. (2005). *Pod zastavom UN-a: Međunarodna zajednica i zlocin u Srebrenici.* Preporod.

Nuhanović, H. (2010). 15 years after the Srebrenica massacre, a survivor buries his family. *Washington Post,* July 11, 2010. https://www.washingtonpost.com/wp-dyn/content/article/2010/07/09/AR2010070902351.html

Power, S. (2003). *"A Problem from hell": America and the age of genocide.* HarperCollins.

Rojas-Perez. I. (2017). *Mourning remains: State atrocity, exhumations, and governing the disappeared in Peru's postwar Andes.* Stanford University Press.

Rosenblatt, A. (2015). *Digging for the disappeared: Forensic science after atrocity.* Stanford University Press.

Sant Cassia, P. (2005). *Bodies of evidence: Burial, memory and the recovery of missing persons in Cyprus.* Berghahn Books.

Sorguc, A. (2018). Females were 'youngest and oldest victims' of Srebrenica. *Balkan Insight.* https://balkaninsight.com/2018/07/05/females-were-youngest-and-oldest-victims-of-srebrenica-07-04-2018/

Stanton, G. (1996). *The eight stages of genocide.* Genocide Watch.

Stepputat, F. (2014). *Governing the dead: Sovereignty and the politics of dead bodies.* Manchester University Press.

Tokača, M. (2012). *Bosanska knjiga mrtvih: Ljudski gubici u Bosni i Hercegovina 1991–1995/.* The Bosnian book of the dead: Human losses in in Bosnia and Herzegovina 1991–95. Istraživač dokumentacioni centar.

Udruzenje Prijedorcanki "Izvor." (2000). *Ni krivi ni dužni: Knjiga nestalih općine Prijedor.* IPC Patria.

Wagner, S. (2008). *To know where he lies: DNA technology and the search for Srebrenica's missing.* University of California Press.

Wagner, S. (2019). *What remains: Bringing America's missing home from the Vietnam war.* Harvard University Press.

22
A HEALING-CENTERED PEACEBUILDING APPROACH

Angi Yoder-Maina

Background

Trauma and pain afflict not only individuals. When they become widespread and ongoing, they affect entire communities and even the country as a whole. […] [T]he implications are serious for people's health, the resilience of the country's social fabric, the success of development schemes, and the hope of future generations. (Cabrera, 2003, p. 1)

In the late 1990s, Martha Cabrera and her team traveled to the worst violence-affected regions of Nicaragua with a goal of better understanding their psychological health post-conflict and post-hurricane Mitch. What the team discovered was surprising. "They found high levels of apathy, isolation, aggressiveness, abuse, chronic somatic illness and low levels of flexibility, tolerance and the ability to trust and work together" (Yoder, 2013). Nicaragua, the team realized, "was a multiply wounded, multiply traumatized, multiply mourning country," and had "serious implications for people's health, the resilience of the country's social fabric, the success of development schemes, and the hope of future generations" (Cabrera, 2003, p. 3). Cabrera stated, "it is hard to move forward, to build democracy, when the personal and communal history still hurts" (Cabrera, 2003, p. 4). In situations of chronic violence, systems, structures, leaders, and communities find it difficult to just "move on" when a peace accord is signed. Regional and national peace agreements may bring hope and new ways of thinking, but unless the institutional structures are transformed people find daily life remains the same, or at times gets worse (Rokhideh, 2017). John Paul Lederach (2005) wrote, "[t]he difficulties of attaining a durable peace in contexts of protracted violence suggest we know more about how to end something painful and damaging to everyone but less about how to build something desired" (p. 41). The systems and structures impacted by decades of violence do not change overnight because of a ceasefire. And people's ways of operating and functioning in society remain, with the same mistrust, anger, and hatred of the "other."

Collective responses are negative and appear in the form of apathy, isolation, and aggression. Yet what is clear is everyone is impacted—from the people who remained in the violence, the refugees and Internally Displaced Persons (IDPs) who fled, both civil society and government leaders involved in the reconstruction activities, the men and women serving in the security services, and even outsiders, such as donors and humanitarian and development workers who are meant to support the recovery (Cabrera, 2003; Mollica et al., 2004; Search for Common Ground, 2017; World Bank, 2019). Initially, peace agreements are negotiated and signed, and the process of rebuilding begins. But when both individual and community recovery are impeded by high unemployment rates, limited and/or no social services, and the lack of opportunities to rebuild—people become depressed and suicide rates climb (Rokhideh, 2017).

The social, economic, and human costs of violence are visible and increasingly documented by research. Today, more than a quarter of the world's population lives in violence and protracted conflict environments (Adams, 2017; Greenberg et al., 2012; World Bank, 2011). In 2016, there were 53 conflicts ongoing in 37 countries (meaning 12 percent of the world's population was living in an active conflict zone), According to the World Health Organization (WHO), this is an all-time high. "Moreover, the fact that nearly 69 million people globally have been forcibly displaced by violence and conflict, makes it the highest global number since the Second World War" (UN News, 2019). Research published in the medical journal *The Lancet* determined "the burden of mental disorders is high in conflict-affected populations" with one-in-five people living in violence-affected areas suffering from depression, anxiety, or post-traumatic stress (PTS) (Charlson et al., 2019).

Key insights

Violence and its adversity are one of our biggest threats as it impacts our global wellbeing, our behavior toward each other, our ability to learn and develop, and even the global economy. Taken to the extreme, resulting traumas from violence increases instability, poverty, and all forms of extremism. Every violent act begins with a thought which is cognitively processed, yet we ignore how trauma influences attitudes, behavior, and choices.

Chronic violence impacts systems, structures, leaders, and the ability of communities to recover from violence and rebuild a peaceful and nonviolent society. It is difficult to just "move on" when a peace accord is signed, or a cease-fire has been declared. And when chronic violence is a part of the fabric of society, as happens in many of our cities across the world, it is almost impossible to address. The healing-centered peacebuilding theory was developed organically by several programs, interventions, and organizations across the globe in response to deep structural issues. It focuses on how to break the cycle of violence by examining the link between victims and perpetrators. It develops a system of supports and buffers to help people bounce back in the face of adversity, marginalization, and chronic violence in ways that break cycles of violence and promote peace.

The healing-centered approach addresses the complexity of chronic violence. It recognizes that systems and structures which should be supportive of recovery are often greatly damaged and/or broken by the same chronic violence. Healing-centered peacebuilding refers to ways in which leaders, programs, and organizations mitigate the impact of violence, bring trauma awareness, knowledge, and skills into their organizational cultures, practices, and policies (Yoder-Maina, 2020).

The systems map

As the systems map developed, it became clear that what is being done in practice is not only an individual approach for individual healing but includes collective and social healing practices as well. Healing-centered peacebuilding is a multisectorial and multidisciplinary approach linking chronic violence to issues of stability, transitional justice, governance, and development. It also became obvious that what was being done in practice across the globe did not have a theoretical framework and approach. Thus, one of the biggest challenges for peacebuilding practitioners designing and developing programs was in explaining why a healing-centered peacebuilding approach was critical to both donors and policy experts. How can you explain something that does not exist? See Figure 22.1.

Implementation responses

There are three mainstream responses to the problem: the mental health approach, the psychosocial approach, and the "ignore it" approach. A summary of the three approaches is given below.

The mental health approach

The first approach is the mental health approach. This approach is used by specialized mental health nongovernmental organizations (NGOs) and governments. Overall, there is a lack of funding, national capacity, and infrastructure. Additionally, Western-style mental health services are visible only during the humanitarian intervention phase. Such programs usually downscale during the "post-conflict" stage (Rokhideh, 2017) when the initial post-conflict boom ends and the funding support for such programs wane.

The psychosocial support approach

The psychosocial support approach is the most common. The approach is used by the United Nations (UN), NGOs, and others primarily during the humanitarian phase, immediately after conflict, and is regulated by established norms and frameworks such as the Inter-Agency Standing Committee's *Guidelines on Mental Health and Psychosocial Support in Emergency Settings* (2007). But like the mental health approach, psychosocial support interventions are usually unsustainable after initial emergency funding ends. Often in the post-conflict period when the focus transitions to reconciliation, institutional building, and governance, psychosocial support programs end (Rokhideh, 2017).

The "ignore it" approach

The final approach is the "Ignore it" approach, which includes people working in environments in conflict or emerging from conflict for a wide variety of actors, including donors, the UN, and other multilaterals, international and national civil society, as well as the host government and security actors like national and international military and police. The lack of engagement with these issues appears in policy, as there is no established clear set of guidelines for effective social healing activities for war and violence-affected populations, even though "up to 80 percent of conflict-affected populations may be affected by mental and psychosocial disorders" (Baingana et al., 2005, p. 22).

The healing-centered approach

The three mainstream approaches highlighted earlier do not sufficiently address the effects and the impacts of chronic violence; thus, a new framework was necessary. Practitioners claimed an

A healing-centered peacebuilding approach

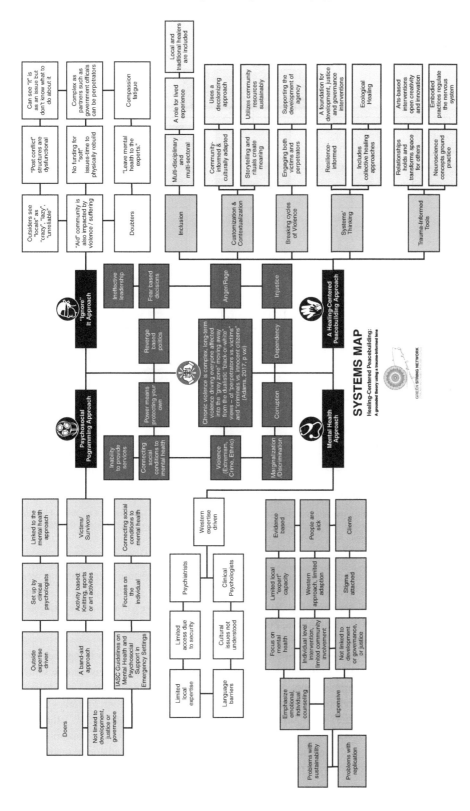

Figure 22.1 Systems map: Healing-centered peacebuilding approach. See https://green-string.org/grounded-in-theory/

Reprinted from "Wellbeing and Resilience: A Grounded Theory Using a Trauma-Informed Lens for a Healing-Centered Peacebuilding Approach" by A. Yoder-Maina, 2020, Siem Reap, Cambodia: Centre for Peace and Conflict Studies. p. 86. Copyright 2020 by A. Yoder-Maina.

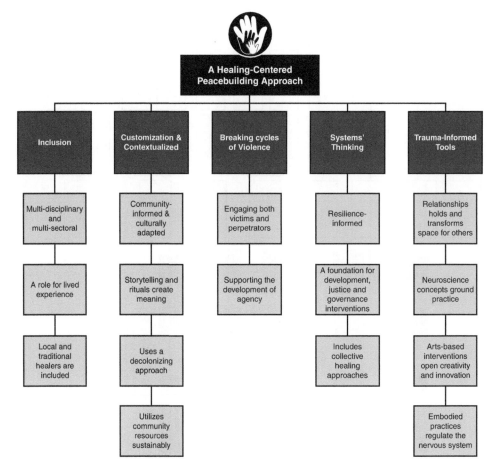

Figure 22.2 Healing-centered peacebuilding elements and subelements

Reprinted from "Wellbeing and Resilience: A Grounded Theory Using a Trauma-Informed Lens for a Healing-Centered Peacebuilding Approach" by A. Yoder-Maina, 2020, Siem Reap, Cambodia: Centre for Peace and Conflict Studies. p. 96. Copyright 2020 by A. Yoder-Maina.

alternative approach existed in practice but was nameless, and existing interventions were primarily associated with psychosocial approaches. Consequently, the healing-centered approach was developed by interviewing 30 trauma-informed and peacebuilding practitioners with vast practical experiences in Africa, Asia, Australia, Europe, North, and South America (Figure 22.2) (Yoder-Maina, 2020).

Yet the healing-centered approach brings more than just awareness, it also brings behavior change which supports social transformation and change from a violent society to one which values peace. A healing-centered approach requires important variations in how government policies are designed, and communities deal with the past, live in the present, and plan for the future. The five elements and their subelements are explained in greater detail later. The healing-centered approach addresses trauma fueled by cycles of violence and comprises key elements of the practice-based approach such as inclusion, customization and contextualization, breaking cycles of violence, systems thinking, and trauma-informed tools.

Inclusion

The inclusive component of healing-centered peacebuilding has three subcomponents, which include the following:

1   Multidisciplinary and multisectoral
2   A role for lived experiences
3   Local and traditional healers

Peacebuilder practitioners work in chronic violence environments where nothing seems to work because of the complexity of the situation. Often the complexity is triggered by the layers of trauma that activate mistrust, fear, and hate, impacting the ability to build peace and lay a foundation for social justice.

Multidisciplinary and multisectoral

Rarely are psychologists or counselors present and even if they were, it would have been unlikely that they would speak the local language(s). The community may also have been suspicious of outsiders. To create a coordinated and integrated approach for both prevention and intervention, an inclusive process of all stakeholders is critical when dealing with chronic violence. A strength of the healing-centered peacebuilding approach is the multidisciplinary and multisectoral nature which includes peacebuilders, community development workers, teachers, psychologists, artists, police officers, academics, mothers, fathers, volunteers, researchers, as well as people with lived experience.

A role for lived experiences

Lived experience is an important and welcomed aspect of the healing-centered peacebuilding approach. The underlying divergence between expertise and lived experience appears to be a common global occurrence in low-resource and conflict-prone communities. This has been highlighted as an issue by both mental health psychosocial support (MHPSS) practitioners as well as peacebuilders. Healing requires a holistic model utilizing cultural resources, individual and community agency, and peer-peer support in encouraging resilience-building from those with lived experience. Lived experience is often the only long-term support available.

Local and traditional healers are included

The healing-centered peacebuilding approach works to identify and support hundreds of grassroots traditional healers. In traditional cultures, such agents support healing in their communities and help sustain community resilience. They are accessible and stay in the communities for the long term.

Customization and contextualization

The customization and contextualization component of healing-centered peacebuilding has four subcomponents:

1   Community-informed and cultural adapted
2   Importance of storytelling
3   Uses a decolonizing approach
4   Utilizes community resources sustainably

Cultures adapt to changes and are not stagnant. Johan Galtung's theory of violence shows how beliefs, attitudes, and symbols are used to enhance hatred, mistrust, and fear of the "other" because of deep cultural practices that are often not spoken about (Galtung et al., 2002). However, cultural influences for healing and peace are just as powerful, and when combined with the healing-centered approach can have a great impact on social transformation processes.

Community-informed and cultural adapted

When the healing process is a foundational part of a larger peacebuilding platform, interventions must be adapted to ensure they are relevant in the local context. Concepts and frameworks developed in other contexts and with different populations must be critically examined for their applicability, adaptability, and utility for the local context to engage with both individual and collective trauma.

Importance of storytelling

Rituals and stories encourage resilience through the development of meaning-making. An Austrian psychiatrist and an Auschwitz survivor, Viktor E. Frankl (1949), wrote in his book *Man's Search for Meaning*, "We must never forget that we may also find meaning in life even when confronted with a hopeless situation, when facing a fate that cannot be changed" (p. 114). When conflict occurs, those impacted hand down their stories from one generation to another. Often mistrust, division, and hate are transferred along with a toxic story. When healing has taken place, stories transmit peace and trust between generations as well (Lederach & Lederach, 2010). In the healing-centered approach, stories have a quality of bringing people together and cementing good relations between neighbors. In African folklore, it is said you cannot hate people once you have heard their stories.

Uses a decolonizing approach

A key trait of colonialism is it devalued Indigenous people, their knowledge, and cultures while the healing-centered approach is intentional about integrating and utilizing indigenous healing practices. "Embedded in decolonization are colonial wounds crying out for healing. Decolonization encapsulates potentialities and possibilities of creating another world" (Omanga, 2020). Peacebuilding activities are often targeted at postcolonial societies, where structural injustices, conflict, and violence are underlying root causes of active and latent conflict. Peacebuilders are trained to develop projects, programs, and impact at the community level, but rarely focus on unraveling the tragic aftereffects of colonization. Healing-centered peacebuilding recognizes that such environments are trauma-organized and use trauma-informed interventions to develop programs challenging colonial assumptions, structures, and teachings.

Utilizes community resources sustainably

Adversity, violence, and conflict leave individuals and communities feeling depleted and without hope. Hopelessness and helplessness are common feelings expressed by communities in chronic violence. Moreover, "[m]ental health issues are compounded by exposure to conflict and violence and embedded in a larger context of adversity" (World Bank, 2016). As noted earlier, trained experts are not present in such settings as there are not enough trained counselors, psychologists, or social workers in violence-prone communities to help people deal with the high levels of distress they face (Mednick, 2019; Mumin & Rhodes, 2019). In the healing-centered peacebuilding approach, instead of relying on trained experts, the approach seeks to build on existing strengths found within communities.

Breaking cycles of violence

The breaking cycles of violence component of healing-centered peacebuilding has two subcomponents:

1. Engaging both victims and perpetrators
2. Supporting the development of agency

The cycle of violence theory is based on the writings of Olga Botcharova (1988), Vamik Volkan (2004), and Walter Wink (1992). Carolyn Yoder (2005) utilized these theorists when she initially developed the Strategies for Trauma Awareness and Resilience (STAR) at Eastern Mennonite University (EMU) after the 9/11 attacks in the United States. The practice-based healing-centered approach was birthed by the STAR Framework and the cycle of violence was a key element to the approach, especially the adage that trauma not transformed is transferred (Rohr, 2008). People who have been hurt can at times justify the use of violence to seek justice.

Engaging both victims and perpetrators

The healing-centered peacebuilding approach acknowledges there is often not a clear distinction between victim and aggressor, and everyone affected by trauma should have access to a support system to break the cycle of violence. Frank Ochberg (2008), a medical doctor with experience working in trauma situations, distinguishes "between 'victimization,' trauma that results from human cruelty, and 'traumatization,' brought on by natural disasters" (pp. 201–203). Stress and trauma often lead victims to think negatively about themselves as well as others, which in turn affects their relationships with others.

Supporting the development of agency

The impact of trauma and chronic violence causes people to feel powerless and hopeless without agency (Adams, 2017; Herman, 2015; Saul, 2014; Van der Kolk, 2014). The agency from a healing process assists in unlocking the innovation and creativity needed to address the challenges of one's life and those of one's community; it also helps in changing outlooks associated with a depressed mindset, often focused on obstructions and boundaries to achieving personal and community objectives. For the healing-centered peacebuilding approach, broadening perceptions about options of what can be realized and accomplished within a given context is critical. There will always be structural limitations and underlying inequity, yet structural transformation is driven by people, and thus increasing agency and empowerment are critical elements to addressing chronic violence. The healing process can give those who have broken the cycle of violence the agency required to share with others how to do it. There is power in being able to tell such a story to others and help them do the same.

Systems thinking

The systems thinking component of healing-centered peacebuilding has four subcomponents:

1   Resilience-informed
2   Social healing as a foundation for development, justice, and governance interventions
3   Includes collective healing approaches
4   Promotes ecological healing

Systems thinking views all experiences as interrelated. People are not isolated and are connected to their context and their environment. In systems theory, trauma is viewed as an extreme aspect of change and is not viewed as either negative or positive but as something that happens in life. This does not mean that trauma is not overwhelming for people (Connors, 2008).

Resilience-informed

Resilience is that ineffable quality allowing some people to be knocked down and come back stronger. Resilience is not a trait that people either have or do not have. It involves behaviors, thoughts, and actions that can be learned and developed by anyone.

> Resilient people [...] possess three characteristics: A staunch acceptance of reality; a deep belief, often buttressed by strongly held values, that life is meaningful; and an uncanny ability to improvise. You can bounce back from hardship with just one or two of these qualities, but you will only be truly resilient with all three. (Coutu, 2002, para 12)

Rather than letting failure overcome them and drain their resolve, people find a way to overcome adversity, trauma, tragedy, threats, or significant sources of stress. Even toxic stressors such as family and relationship problems, serious health problems or workplace, financial stressors, and communal issues such as civil war, torture by state authorities, and mass displacement and upheaval. It means coming back from difficult experiences.

A foundation for development, justice, and governance interventions

Chronic violence and adversity impact global wellbeing, our behavior toward each other, the ability of children to learn, communities to develop, and even the global economy (Kleinfeld & Muggah, 2019). Healing-centered peacebuilding is a foundation for improving the outcomes of development, justice, and governance interventions. "Extreme political trauma is not just a health problem, but a social-political problem. [Thus] [...] attempts to heal trauma [are] associated with efforts to build peace and sustainability in societies affected by political violence" (Clancy & Hamber, 2008, p. 10). The negative impact of trauma on the ability of people to constructively participate at work and school has been apparent in numerous countries and regions experiencing chronic violence. Several noted that this includes high levels of absenteeism from both work and school, high levels of unemployment, and general antisocial behaviors (Adams, 2017; Davis et al., 2019).

Includes collective healing approaches

During the global Collective Trauma Summit in October 2019, Dr. Christine Bethell noted, "we're a society organized based on trauma, so we need to go from being trauma-organized to being trauma-informed—and then, eventually, healing-centered." Thus, in a trauma-organized society, the system is ineffective and limited. However, globally trauma-informed practices create a foundation for transformation and social healing by influencing the different aspects of recovery from violence and conflict, impacting daily life, and resulting in changes in social behavior and norms. Advocacy and change-making work and healing are all connected. A healing-centered peacebuilding approach happens when we take collective responsibility for creating structures and practices that enable healing and challenge the root causes of the violence and/or abuse that caused the trauma in the first place (Lederach & Lederach, 2010).

Promotes ecological healing

Natural disasters and climate change have damaging effects on mental and social health as well as on peace and security. On the surface, many people are impacted by harsh and intense environmental events. The mental health effects of events linked to a changing global climate include mild stress and distress, high-risk coping behaviors such as increased alcohol and drug use as well as depression, anxiety, and PTS. Climate change-related impacts can also lead to job loss, force people to move, or lead to a loss of social support and community resources—all of which have mental health consequences and impact security and peace.

Trauma-informed tools

The trauma-informed tools component of healing-centered peacebuilding has four subcomponents:

1   Relationship holds space and transforms space for others
2   Neuroscience concepts ground practice
3   Embodied practices regulate the nervous system
4   Arts-based interventions open creativity and innovation

Trauma-informed is characterized as understanding the physiological, emotional, cognitive, behavioral, and spiritual impact of traumatic events (current or historic) on recipient populations, and how unaddressed trauma contributes to cycles of violence (Adams, 2017; Barge-Zook, 2011). Using established trauma-informed tools allows the healing-centered approach to go beyond traditional mental health diagnosis and symptoms of PTS in measuring trauma, by recognizing community and societal dynamics and behaviors are indicators of unaddressed trauma.

Relationship holds and transforms space for others

"Our brains are wired for connection, but trauma rewires them for protection. That's why healthy relationships are difficult for wounded people" (North, 2019). When we experience trauma, we do not have a choice. No one chooses trauma; it is a consequence of things that are done to or have happened to us, not things that we actively chose. Trauma takes away the ability to make choices, to make decisions, and to have some sense of control. When we think about healing, one of the key aspects we want to work on is regaining a sense of control and our capacity to choose. The healing process is about opening the ability to choose again. For us to be more in control, we need to be able to make decisions for ourselves. This is an important element in the healing-centered peacebuilding approach (Van der Kolk, 2014) and one supported by holding space for one and other to help rebuild broken connections with humanity. Trauma isolates people. When the trust is broken, relationships are also broken. People who experience trauma need a system of support to help them heal.

Neuroscience concepts ground practice

In the past decade, advancements in neuroscience have brought new understanding into the peacebuilding field. For example, we have learned that the brain's functioning can be altered in significant ways when trauma has taken place and that the way we react to trauma is determined by our brain (Van der Kolk, 2014). In survival mode, the stress hormones of adrenaline and cortisol rush in, while blood rushes to our large muscle groups to help us act quickly. But we are less able to think clearly, with our language and memory structures less assessable and compromised. For people and communities with a trauma reaction, the fear response happens whether the danger is real, or whether we believe the danger is there when there is none.

Embodied practices regulate the nervous system

The nervous system is the involuntary regulatory process of the Autonomic Nervous System (ANS). It regulates the body's process which we do not require conscious control to maintain a healthy body such as our heart rate, breathing, digestion, and the body's temperature among other things. These processes do not require instructions from the brain to keep you alive. Rather they are monitored collaboratively by the body and the brain and are not directly influenced by consciousness.

Arts-based interventions open creativity and innovation

Healing-centered approaches use arts-based interventions to inspire renewed creativity and innovation. Creating different types of art, such as music/sound, dance/movement, enactment/improvisation, storytelling/narrative, play, and imagination helps develop a sense of emotional safety and wellbeing, both of which are essential when trying to stabilize our brains and our nervous system (Cohen et al., 1995). Expression through the arts supports the creation of safety and the ability to separate oneself from the horrifying experience of trauma without relying on words (which are often ineffective) (Morrissey, 2013).

Implications for teaching and training

Today trauma is a buzzword within the peacebuilding field while at the same time it is becoming recognized as a critical element of the field (Gitau, 2018). The impact of trauma matters because traumatic experiences "complicate [one's] capacity to make sense of their lives and to create meaningful consistent relationships in their families and communities" (Substance Abuse and Mental Health Services Administration, 2014, p. 5). Yet there is no common understanding around a framework, the terminology used, nor best practices within peacebuilding for engaging in work with trauma and its individual and collective impact. While there are a variety of phrases, such as trauma awareness, trauma sensitization, trauma healing, and more recently trauma-informed and responsive intervention, the peacebuilding field does not have a consistent way of talking about the issues around trauma. Moreover, peacebuilders are confused if we should be in this complex space or if this space is better reserved for those from a more traditional mental health background.

Yet how do peacebuilders continue business as usual when we can tell things are not working? The best-planned "on paper" peacebuilding programs often do not work when implementation starts because there is no inbuilt method for participants to deal with their painful past. There is a lack of transitional, post-conflict justice, wounded leaders are ineffective, and structural inequalities and conflict are rarely and substantially addressed. How do peacebuilders support holistic and inclusive processes if social healing is not a foundational element of our work?

While some progress has been made to combine peacebuilding with mental health and psychosocial support (MHPSS) programs, mainstream approaches have not fully integrated the fields effectively (Tankink & Bubenzer, 2017; Wessells, 2007). The two fields have integrated "only in a piecemeal way, appending or inserting useful elements from the other discipline at one or maybe two specific points in the project cycle, rather than throughout" (Tankink & Bubenzer, 2017, p. 207).

Prepare students to meet trauma and to include healing

A healing-centered approach is a starting point to help both individuals and communities identify the drivers of adversity which are relevant to them and their context, engage with lived experiences while developing programs spanning multiple sectors including security, community peace mechanisms, the education system, health actors, and the criminal justice system. It becomes a foundation for other stabilization, development, justice, and governance initiatives in that it supports individuals and communities to come out of their survival brains. Peace and Conflict Studies programs need to incorporate foundational elements of healing-centered approaches within both undergraduate and graduate programs.

Trauma-informed organizational training

Training for peacebuilding organizations at field levels should focus on working with management and staff to make sure everyone understands the impact of trauma, how to respond to trauma within the culture and the context, and how it affects program participants and the communities they engage with. When Sandra Bloom (2011) developed the Sanctuary Model, she wrote that:

> […] our systems inadvertently but frequently recapitulate the very experiences that have proved to be so toxic for the people we are supposed to help. Just as the lives of people exposed to repetitive and chronic trauma, abuse and maltreatment become organized around the traumatic experience, so too can entire systems become organized around the recurrent and severe stress of trying to cope […] when this happens, it sets up an interactive dynamic that creates what are sometimes uncannily parallel processes. (p. 141)

Specifically, this means developing responsive organizations that develop trauma-informed, inclusive recruitment processes and human resource policies while encouraging wellbeing and debriefing of all levels of staff who are impacted by both their work and the contexts, they work and live in.

Implications for practice and policy

One of the main objectives of the healing-centered approach is to develop policy recommendations applicable to stabilization, justice, peacebuilding, development, and programming. Trauma is an obstacle to peace yet is largely ignored by policymakers, donors, and governments. Peace is as much a cognitive process as it is a political and military one. The ability to reconcile, forgive, and not conform to dehumanizing ideas of rivals requires a healthy mind. Trauma symptoms predispose sufferers to reasoning which justifies violence. Conflict, lack of services, and economic instability result in high exposure to traumatic events; this exposure is a key predictor of PTS (López, et al., 2019).

Localization must be authentic

Local peacebuilding is what started the peacebuilding movement in the 1980s. As the field professionalized, local civil society groups and social movements transformed into NGOs (Schirch, 2019). Today the relationship between professional peacebuilders who operate INGOs and the grassroots verges on being hierarchical and at times both condescending and patronizing. Donors continue to fund and enable mostly international agencies, yet these bodies are more accountable to their donors who often are very removed from the insecurity they face than the people in violence-prone communities (Bojicic-Dzelilovic & Martin, 2016; Donais, 2009).

Prioritize evidence-based research

Tools for measuring the results and unintended consequences of healing-centered peacebuilding are critical. Yet they are infrequently undertaken because they are expensive and underdeveloped. Moreover, it is often noted that "soft" data cannot be systematically gathered at community levels for a variety of reasons, including capacity. Even so, there have been two excellent pieces of impact evaluation research published within the framework of healing-centered peacebuilding programming in Kenya by the Green String Network, in Rwanda by Interpeace, and their Rwandese partner Never Again Rwanda (Davis et al., 2019; López et al., 2019). More evidence-based research of similar quality is required for the approach to become widely utilized within the peacebuilding, transitional justice, development, and governance fields.

Thus, tools like the implementation must be designed and tested within the context they will be used, increasing the cost of such impact evaluations. Additionally, tools measuring the impact of trauma are critically needed to begin to understand the impact of healing-centered peacebuilding programs. Now most tools that have been developed have been drawn from Western-based measurement instruments such as diagnosis level posttraumatic stress disorder (PTSD) scales and the Harvard Trauma Questionnaire (HTQ) which has been adapted for post-conflict environments, yet everything we know about trauma tells us that symptoms, while universal in that they are always there, are also culturally specific. Thus, it is a priority to invest in the contextualization of such measurement tools.

References

Adams, T. M. (2017). *Chronic violence and its reproduction: Perverse trends in social relations, citizenship and democracy in Latin America.* Woodrow Wilson International Center for Scholars.

Baingana, F., Bannon, I., & Thomas, R. (2005). *Mental health and conflicts: Conceptual framework and approaches.* World Bank. http://documents1.worldbank.org/curated/en/829381468320662693/pdf/316370HNP0BainganaMHConflictFinal.pdf

Barge-Zook, E. (2011). *Village STAR: Breaking cycles of violence: Building healthy individuals and communities.* Eastern Mennonite University.

Bethell, C. (2019, October 12). We are the medicine: Implementing research to heal adverse childhood experiences. *Collective Trauma Summit*. (R. Alfred, Interviewer).

Bloom, S. L. (2011). *Destroying sanctuary: The crisis in human service delivery systems*. Oxford University Press.

Bojicic-Dzelilovic, V., & Martin, M. (2016). *Local ownership challenges in peacebuilding and conflict prevention*. London School of Economics and Political Science.

Botcharova, O. (1988). Implementation of track two diplomacy: Developing a model of forgiveness. In R. G. Helmick, R. L. Petersen, & D. Tutu (Eds.), *Forgiveness and reconciliation: Religion, public policy and conflict transformation* (pp. 279–304). Templeton Foundation Press.

Cabrera, M. (2003). *Living and surviving in a multiply wounded country*. Presentation, Kalgenfurt, Germany.

Charlson, F., van Ommeren, M., Flaxman, A., Cornett, J., Whiteford, H., & Saxena, S. (2019, June 11). New WHO prevalence estimates of mental disorders in conflict settings: A systematic review and meta-analysis. *The Lancet, 394*(9441), 240–248. doi:10.1016/ S0140-6736(19)30934-1

Clancy, M., & Hamber, B. (2008, September 9–11). *Trauma, peacebuilding, and development: An overview of key positions and critical questions*. https://www.researchgate.net/publication/228774195_Trauma_peacebuilding_and_development_an_overview_of_key_positions_and_critical_questions

Cohen, B., Barnes, M., & Rankin, A. (1995). *Managing traumatic stress through art*. The Sidran Press.

Connors, J. (2008). *Trauma as change process: A systems theory view*. https://www.academia.edu/2994272/Trauma_as_Change_Process_A_Systems_Theory_View

Coutu, D. (2002). Organizational structure: How resilience works. *Harvard Business Review*. https://hbr.org/2002/05/how-resilience-works

Davis, A., Nsengiyumva, C., & Hyslop, D. (2019). *Healing trauma and building trust and tolerance in Rwanda*. Interpeace. https://www.interpeace.org/wp-content/uploads/2019/04/Trauma-Trust-Tolerance-and-Peace-activism-Web1.pdf

Donais, T. (2009). Empowerment or imposition? Dilemmas of local ownership in post-conflict peacebuilding processes. *Peace and Change, 34*(1), 3–26.

Frankl, V. (1949). *Man's search for meaning*. Beacon Press.

Galtung, J., Jacobsen, C.G., & Brand-Jacobsen, K. F. (2002). *Searching for peace: The road to transcend*. Pluto.

Gitau, L. W. (2018). *Trauma-sensitivity and peacebuilding: Considering the case of South Sudanese refugees in Kakuma refugee camp*. Springer.

Greenberg, M., Mallozzi, E., & Cechvala, S. (2012). *Peacebuilding 2.0: Mapping the boundaries of an expanding field*. The Alliance for Peacebuilding.

Herman, J. (2015). *Trauma and recovery: The aftermath of violence–from domestic abuse to political terror*. Basic Books.

Inter-Agency Standing Committee. (2007). *Guidelines on mental health and psychosocial support in emergency settings*. IASC.

Kleinfeld, A., & Muggah, R. (2019, October 14). *No war, no peace: Healing the world's violent societies*. https://carnegieendowment.org/2019/10/14/no-war-no-peace-healing-world-s-violent-societies-pub-80034

Lederach, J. (2005). *The moral imagination: The art and soul of building peace*. Oxford University Press.

Lederach, J. P., & Lederach, A. J. (2010). *When blood and bones cry out: Journeys through the soundscape of healing and reconciliation*. Oxford University Press.

López, B., Nagda, B., Yoder-Maina, A., Beti, B., Spears, H., & Yassin, H. (2019). *Growing connection, agency, and resilience: The impact of community-led trauma-informed peacebuilding in response to violent extremism in Kenya*. Green String Network.

Mednick, S. (2019, July 12). Mental health–the lasting scars of crisis–South Sudan: "The whole country is traumatised". *The New Humanitarian*. https://www.thenewhumanitarian.org/news-feature/2019/01/21/south-sudan-whole-country-traumatised

Mollica, R. F., Cardozo, B. L., Osofsky, H. J., Raphael, B., Ager, A., & Salama, P. (2004). Mental health in complex emergencies. *The Lancet, 364*(9450), 2058–2067.

Morrissey, P. (2013, May–June). Trauma finds expression through art therapy. *Health Progress: Journal of the Catholic Health Association of the United States, 94*(3), 44–47.

Mumin, A., & Rhodes, T. (2019, July 12). Mental health – the lasting scars of crisis – inside Somalia's mental health emergency. *The New Humanitarian*. https://www.thenewhumanitarian.org/feature/2019/07/12/mental-health-crisis-war-conflict

North, R. (2019, November 24). *The Minds Journal*. https://themindsjournal.com/our-brains-are-wired-for/

Ochberg, F. T. (2008). The victim of terrorism: Psychiatric considerations. *Terrorism, 1*(2), 147–168. doi:10.1080/10576107808435404

Omanga, D. (2020, January 14). *Decolonization, decoloniality, and the future of African studies: A conversation with Dr. Sabelo Ndlovu-Gatsheni*. Social Science Research Council. https://items.ssrc.org/from-our-programs/decolonization-decoloniality-and-the-future-of-african-studies-a-conversation-with-dr-sabelo-ndlovu-gatsheni/

Rohr, R. (2008). *Things hidden: Scripture as spirituality*. Franciscan Media.

Rokhideh, M. (2017). Peacebuilding and psychosocial intervention: The critical need to address everyday post conflict experiences in northern Uganda. *Intervention, 15*(3), 215–229.

Saul, J. (2014). *Collective trauma, collective healing: Promoting community resilience in the aftermath of disaster*. Routledge.

Schirch, L. (2019, December 24). *State of peacebuilding 2019: Seven observations*. https://lisaschirch.wordpress.com/2019/12/24/state-of-peacebuilding-2019-seven-observations/

Search for Common Ground. (2017). *Transforming violent extremism: A peacebuilder's guide*. Search for Common Ground. https://www.sfcg.org/wp-content/uploads/2017/04/Transforming-Violent-Extremism-V2-August-2017.pdf

Substance Abuse and Mental Health Services Administration. (2014). *SAMHSA's concept of trauma and guidance for a trauma-informed approach*. HHS Publication No. SAMHSA.

Tankink, M., & Bubenzer, F. (2017). Building sustainable peace through an integrated approach to peacebuilding and mental health and psychosocial support: A literature review. *Intervention, 15*(3), 199–214.

UN News. (2019, June 12). *One-in-five suffers mental health condition in conflict zones, new UN figures reveal*. https://news.un.org/en/story/2019/06/1040281

Van der Kolk, B. M. (2014). *The body keeps the score: Brain, mind and body in the healing of trauma*. Penguin Books.

Volkan, V. (2004). *Blind trust: Large groups and their leaders in times of crisis and terror*. Pitchstone.

Wessells, M. G. (2007). Post-conflict healing and reconstruction for peace: The power of social mobilization. In J. White, & A. Marsella (Eds.), *Fear of persecution: Global human rights, international law, and human well-being* (pp. 257–278). Lexington.

Wink, W. (1992). *Engaging the powers: Discernment and resistance in a world of domination*. Fortress Press.

World Bank. (2019). *Strategy for fragility, conflict and violence 2020–2025 concept note*. https://consultations.worldbank.org/consultation/world-bank-group-strategy-fragility-conflict-and-violence

World Bank. (2016, May 9). *Psychosocial support in fragile and conflict-affected settings*. https://www.worldbank.org/en/topic/fragilityconflictviolence/brief/psychosocial-support-in-fragile-and-conflict-affected-settings

World Bank. (2011). *World development report: Conflict, security and development*. World Bank. https://openknowledge.worldbank.org/handle/10986/4389

Yoder, C. (2013, May). *Being sensitive to trauma in humanitarian and development aid*. http://emu.edu/now/peacebuilder/2013/05/being-sensitive-to-trauma-in-humanitarian-development-aid/

Yoder, C. (2005). *The little book of trauma healing: When violence strikes and community security is threatened*. Good Books.

Yoder-Maina, A. (2020). *Wellbeing and resilience: A grounded theory using a trauma-informed lens for a healing-centered peacebuilding approach*. Centre for Peace and Conflict Studies.

PART IV

Approaches and Cases

23
SRI LANKA'S POSTWAR RECONCILIATION: RECONCILING THE LOCAL AND INTERNATIONAL

S. I. Keethaponcalan

When former UN General Secretary Boutros-Ghali theorized his idea of peacebuilding in 1992, he viewed it as a postwar strategy for peace in war-ravaged societies. In his *An Agenda for Peace*, he promoted peacebuilding as a useful instrument to "avoid a relapse into conflict" (Watson, 2004, p. 82). Despite the reality that peacebuilding could be taken advantage of to make peace even during the conflict, many others also viewed it primarily as a postwar strategy. For example, Pugh (2000) argued that peacebuilding strategies are used to "prevent recurrence of war" (p. 3). One of the significant issues peacebuilding could encounter in postwar milieu is reconciliation between former warring factions. Hence, there has been an unavoidable nexus between postwar peacebuilding and reconciliation in ethnonationalist conflicts.

In some cases, reconciliation could be treated as a subset of peacebuilding. Targeting the top-down social engineering of contemporary peacebuilding, or what could be termed liberal peacebuilding, critics emphasized the lack or absence of local ownership in peacebuilding projects, leading to the notion called hybrid peacebuilding (Uesugi, 2020). The concept of hybrid peacebuilding exposed the tension between the local and the international in regions where liberal peacebuilding is undertaken (Brown, 2018; Smith, 2014). A similar tension between the local and international could also emerge concerning reconciliation (Hoglund & Orjuela, 2016).

Sri Lanka's ethnopolitical war ended in May 2009. With the termination of the Liberation Tigers of Tamil Eelam (LTTE) as a military force, reconciliation between the ethnic Tamils and Sinhalese transformed into one of the primary pursuits of international peacebuilding actors. The internationals had their preconceived notion of reconciliation, while the local imagination of the postwar order differed significantly from international expectations. This chapter critically examines the interface and conflict between the "locals" and "international" with regard to postwar reconciliation in Sri Lanka.

Background: Terminating the war

The ethnonationalist conflict between Sri Lanka's majority Sinhala community and the Tamils, which turned into a highly destructive war since the mid-1980s, was a globally known and well-studied issue (Wilson, 2000). International and local peacebuilding communities in Sri Lanka believed that the conflict could not be resolved through military means; hence, the unwavering support for a negotiated solution. Increasingly, the Tamil rebels, the LTTE, also began to believe that they were invincible (Balasingham, 2004). Based on this assumption, the LTTE engineered the electoral victory of Mahinda Rajapaksa, who was already contemplating a military solution to the conflict (Moorcraft, 2012). The election of Mahinda Rajapaksa as the Executive President of Sri Lanka in 2005 proved to be a turning point in the trajectory of the war.

As president, Rajapaksa unleashed a concerted military campaign against the LTTE, which resulted in the termination of the Tamil rebels as a military force and the war in May 2009 (Gokhale, 2009). The government forces first focused on the Eastern Province, one of the strongholds of the LTTE, freed the territory from rebel control, and then moved into the Northern Province, the nerve center of the LTTE operations. The weaknesses of the LTTE—for example, the split that occurred during the peace process where part of the movement left the mainstream faction and the quasi-universal support the government gained from major international actors, such as the United States, India, China, Pakistan, and the United Kingdom—enabled the government to overpower the LTTE successfully. However, it was the military strategy of the regime that remained central to the successful military campaign (Hashim, 2013). The government used unfettered forces in the two provinces, which resulted in the death of thousands of LTTE cadres and civilians. The war officially concluded with the demise of LTTE leader Velupillai Prabhakaran (Gerharz, 2014).

The end of the war influenced many researchers to call Sri Lanka a post-conflict society (Derges, 2013). This was erroneous because there are clear distinctions between war and conflict. The main characteristic of war is large-scale organized violence (Kallen, 1939). Conflict, on the other hand, is caused by incompatible goals and values and may or may not entail violence (Bartos & Wehr, 2002). What was resolved in Sri Lanka with the termination of the LTTE in May 2009 was the problem of violence. The fundamental issues of the conflict between ethnically divided communities remain unresolved to date. This is precisely what made calling Sri Lanka a post-conflict society problematic. Sri Lanka was and is only a postwar society (Keethaponcalan, 2019).

Key insights: Reconciliation

Regardless of these nuances, the international community embarked on a campaign to promote reconciliation in the immediate aftermath of the war. The United Nations, the European states, and the United States held the view that Sri Lanka should move toward ethnic reconciliation. For example, Ban Ki-moon, the General Secretary of the UN when the war ended in 2009, stated it was "most important that every effort be undertaken to begin a process of healing and national reconciliation" (quoted in Udalagama & de Silva, 2014, p. 103). The Obama administration was also "pressing the Sri Lankan Government to take meaningful steps toward political reconciliation" (Committee on Foreign Relations, 2009). Local communities, however, remained indifferent to the issues of reconciliation, resulting in a mismatch or rather a conflict between the local and the international. This incompatibility was one of the reasons why reconciliation failed in this country. Later we discuss how the international and the local communities imagined and responded differently to the question of reconciliation.

International campaign

The Western states chose the United Nations Human Rights Council (UNHRC) as the venue to direct their campaign to promote reconciliation in Sri Lanka. Two factors played a significant role in the decision to make use of the UNHRC: (1) the internationals believed that the warring parties, especially the armed forces of Sri Lanka, were involved in serious human rights violation against the Tamil community during the last phase of the war, and (2) accountability is central to ethnic reconciliation (Seoighe, 2017).

Although the international community, including many of the Western European states, the United States, and the UN were supportive of the military campaign of the Sri Lankan government against the LTTE and were relieved by the fact that the war was brought to an effective end, they could not wholly ignore the reports of serious human rights violations that started to come out in the immediate postwar period. Domestic interest groups such as the Jaffna University Teachers for Human Rights (JUTHR) and international organizations such as Amnesty International and Human Rights Watch (HRW) played a prominent role in exposing the alleged human rights violations (Grant, 2014). Under pressure from international human rights advocacy groups and leading members of the UN, Ban Ki-moon appointed a panel of experts to advise him on accountability issues in Sri Lanka. The panel report entitled *Report of the Secretary-General's Panel of Experts on Accountability in Sri Lanka*, published on March 31, 2011, found the allegations credible (United Nations, 2011). According to the report, "the Panel found credible allegations, which if proven, indicate that a wide range of serious violations of international humanitarian law and international human rights law were committed both by the Government of Sri Lanka and the LTTE" (United Nations, 2011, p. ii).

The West also believed that accountability for the alleged human rights violations could serve as the primary vehicle for reconciliation (Kuwali & Frans, 2017). Although allegations were leveled against both the government of Sri Lanka and the LTTE, the focus was on the government, because the LTTE as a military force was already decimated. Sponsoring a resolution on Sri Lanka at the UNHRC, the United States argued that accountability established through a credible, preferably international, investigation, would promote ethnic reconciliation in Sri Lanka. The internationals headed by the United States and some of the leading Western European states imagined the international investigation as a transitional justice mechanism necessary to repair ethnic relations in the postwar period (Leman, 2013).

Based on these convictions, since 2012, a series of resolutions were introduced and adopted at the UNHRC. The 2012 resolution called upon the Sri Lankan government "to take all necessary additional steps to fulfill its relevant legal obligations and commitment to initiate credible and independent actions to ensure justice, equity, accountability and reconciliation for all Sri Lankans." The 2013 resolution urged the Sri Lankan government to conduct "an independent and credible investigation into allegations of violations" of international human rights and humanitarian law. In 2014, the resolution called upon the Office of the Human Rights Commissioner to "undertake a comprehensive investigation" into the alleged abuses and violations. In response, the UN High Commissioner for Human Rights appointed a team of experts to look into the matters referenced by the 2014 resolution. The team concluded that "reconciliation and addressing root causes of systematic human rights abuses and entrenched impunity are critical to securing the new government's vision for Sri Lanka. Accountability must be part of that vision, including processes of truth-telling, justice, and reparations" (Human Rights Council, 2015, p. 246).

Therefore, it was clear that the international community relied mainly on accountability, which encompassed elements such as truth-telling and justice, to promote reconciliation. The UNHRC served as a center of international operations on this issue. The main protagonists in Sri Lanka, the Sinhalese and the Tamils, responded differently to the international call for reconciliation. The government, which represented the Sinhala sentiments, refused to buy into the argument for an investigation as the primary tool for reconciliation. On the other hand, the Tamils endorsed the idea of an international investigation not as a tool for reconciliation, but as retribution for what they considered excessive brutal force used by the armed forces (Keethaponcalan, 2019).

Government response

The majority Sinhala community did not share the imagination of the international community in relation to postwar sociopolitical realities and the need for ethnic reconciliation. They were not too enthusiastic about reconciliation with their Tamil counterparts for two specific reasons. One, the majority of Sinhalese traditionally believed that Tamils did not have any specific problems in Sri Lanka due to their ethnicity. In this paradigm, the real problem was the terrorism unleashed by the LTTE (Mahindapala, 2005). Hence, according to their belief, the real problem was resolved with the termination of the LTTE in 2009. The notion that Sinhala-Tamil relation is not a problem anymore is still prevalent within the Sinhala community (Keethaponcalan, 2019). Two, reconciliation with the Tamils entailed making concessions. In the backdrop of a solid military victory, they were not willing to make any concessions, especially political concessions, in the name of reconciliation.

The Sri Lankan government headed by President Mahinda Rajapaksa shared this view of the Sinhala people and resisted the pressure created by the internationals (Vaiamon, 2012). Multiple factors contributed to the government's outright rejection of the demand for an investigation, whether internal or international. First, the government argued that the UNHRC resolutions and the associated demands of the international community were unnecessary interference by the Western states in the internal affairs of Sri Lanka (Kingsbury, 2012). They were motivated by hidden agendas of these states, argued the government. For example, when the Secretary-General's Expert Panel report was published, the President asked the people of Sri Lanka to resist the international agenda in Sri Lanka (Seoighe, 2017). Second, the government pointed out that an investigation was unnecessary because the military campaign was undertaken with "zero civilian casualties" (Wallace, 2017, p. 133). Calling the military campaign against the LTTE a "humanitarian operation," the government argued that it was undertaken to liberate the Tamil masses from the clutches of the LTTE, not to harm them. Going one step further, President Rajapaksa claimed that his "troops went to this operation carrying a gun in one hand, the Human Rights Charter in the other" (Keethaponcalan, 2016, p. 11). Third, President Rajapaksa could also not accept the demand for an international investigation due to the self-image he was promoting in the postwar period. There had been a concerted effort to promote him as a great national hero and a liberator (Perera, 2016). Fourth, an investigation into the conduct of the armed forces would have amounted to a betrayal of the national heroes, the tri-forces, who played a pivotal role in the military victory against the LTTE. Rajapaksa declared that he would rather sacrifice his own life than betray the armed forces and the country. Finally, the government, not without reasons, also argued that an investigation would rekindle memories of the war and contribute to further polarization of ethnic communities in the country. Therefore, the government remained firm on its stance against an investigation, especially international inquiries.

Nevertheless, in order to deal with international pressure, the government established a domestic mechanism called the Lessons Learnt and Reconciliation Commission (LLRC) in 2010 (Amnesty International, 2011). The LLRC was mandated to "enquire and report" on incidents that took place from 2002 to 2009. The period covered not only the last phase of the war but also the peace process facilitated by Norway. Critics argued that this was a strategy undertaken to dilute the focus. The international community wanted to focus on the last phase of the war. It was also pointed out that the Commission was filled with the President's personal friends and loyalists (Leman, 2013). Hence, neutral observers did not expect too much from the Commission. It was only a pressure-absorbing mechanism.

The LLRC delivered its report in November 2011. Predictably, the report dismissed all allegations of human rights violations by the armed forces, while condemning the LTTE for deliberately targeting the civilian population (Large, 2016). Clearing the armed forces of any wrongdoing, the report claimed that "the Commission is satisfied that the military strategy that was adopted to secure the LTTE-held areas was one that was carefully conceived, in which the protection of the civilian population was given the highest priority" (Lessons Learnt and Reconciliation Commission of Sri Lanka, 2011, p. 328). The report further reiterated that "protection of civilian life was a key factor in the formulation of a policy for carrying out military operations" (Lessons Learnt and Reconciliation Commission of Sri Lanka, 2011, p. 328). It is imperative to note that the government did not fully implement any of the recommendations the Commission made to support the promotion of ethnic reconciliation.

Nevertheless, the internationals were not happy about some of the conclusions of the Commission, especially conclusions made about the alleged human rights violations committed during the last phase of the war and accountability issues. For example, Amnesty International claimed that "Sri Lanka's LLRC is not a credible accountability mechanism" (Amnesty International, 2011, p. 6). The Secretary-General's Expert Panel indicated that the Commission's work was inadequate to deal with accountability issues. Robert Black, the former U.S. ambassador to Sri Lanka, maintained that "the LLRC did not address serious allegations of violations of international law, particularly at the end of the war" (The Sunday Times, 2017, p. 14). It is safe to assume that the failure of the LLRC to address international concerns adequately led to the UNHRC resolutions on Sri Lanka.

However, the disagreement between the internationals and the Sri Lankan government did not mean that the government was completely ignorant of the need to move toward ethnic reconciliation. The government was keen to prevent a recurrence of the conflict. The Rajapaksa government's imagination of the primary vehicle for reconciliation was markedly different from the international conceptions. The government believed in economic inducements, especially infrastructure development, as the fundamental strategy for postwar reconciliation (Venugopal, 2015).

There were philosophical as well as practical reasons for focusing on infrastructure development rather than political issues. Philosophically, the government believed that economic underdevelopment and poverty were among the top issues common to all Sri Lankans, including the Tamils. Hence, the focus on economic development and reconstruction to win the loyalty of the Tamils made total sense (Walton, 2015). This was the philosophical dimension of the economic development strategy. From a practical perspective, infrastructure reconstruction was a safe alternative to political concessions, notably the devolution of political powers to the Tamil regions. The Tamils were emphasizing the need for devolution of power to the North and East provinces. The government did not agree, as they believed the infrastructure development programs in the North-East rendered the political concessions irrelevant.

The government initiated two mega projects, *Neganahira Navodaya* (Eastern Revival) and *Uthuru Vasanthaya* (Northern Spring), for the Eastern and Northern provinces, respectively. The stated objectives of these programs included, for example, demining, livelihood recovery, resettlement of internally displaced people from the war zone, and so on. Infrastructure development was a significant part of both programs, which proposed to improve roads, transportation, water and electricity supply, education, and sanitation (Keerawella, 2013). Since war-affected areas were deprived of development opportunities and necessary facilities for a long time, these programs gained international approval and support. Japan, China, and the

United Kingdom made considerable contributions to many of the programs undertaken within the frameworks of *Neganahira Navodaya* and *Uthuru Vasanthaya* (Devoić, 2013).

It is imperative to note that the infrastructure fundamentalism failed to bring the two ethnic communities together, as the Tamils rejected the government's economic incentives. Instead, the approach exacerbated the rift. The Tamils found the program problematic for various reasons. From a Tamil perspective, the government's development-oriented reconciliation program deprived them of political autonomy and assisted the government to compound its politico-military control over the Tamil population (Devoić, 2013; International Crisis Group, 2011).

However, it would be erroneous to assume that the government's excessive focus on infrastructure development was the only factor responsible for the failure of reconciliation. The government's national security concerns and policies equally contributed to the disappointing outcome. For many members of the government and Sinhala nationalist groups, the end of the war in May 2009 did not mean the total elimination of the LTTE. They believed that the LTTE could reemerge. They also believed that activities of the Tamil diaspora in the West continued to pose serious threats to the national security of the state (Rajapaksa, 2014). Hence, in the immediate aftermath of the war, national security concerns overrode the desire for reconciliation.

These concerns pushed the government to adopt hard military strategies in relation to the Tamil people and their issues. For example, the government forced about 300,000 Tamils who lived in the LTTE-controlled areas into what were called welfare camps. Many Tamils were held in these camps for about three years (Janmyr, 2014), which they called internment camps. People in these camps did not have the option of leaving until freed by the military (Wijeyeratne, 2014). The forceful detention of a massive number of Tamils created an extreme level of suspicion and frustration within the Tamil community regarding the intentions of the government (Boyle, 2010). The continued presence of a large military contingent and the expanding nature of security zones also contributed to dissatisfaction within the Tamil community (Walton, 2015). Hence, during this period, the Tamils were not even in the mood to discuss and debate reconciliation, let alone repair relations with the Sinhala people.

The Tamil attitude

Although the Tamils were not in the mood to reconcile, they were highly supportive of the international moves, especially the UNHRC resolutions. The crushing nature of the defeat and the destruction of the last phase of the war forced the Tamil people into a defeatist mentality. They viewed themselves as oppressed victims (Somasundaram, 2014). Initially, they did not have the confidence to ask for an investigation against the government or the armed forces. The ideas of an international investigation and the need for accountability did not emerge from the Tamil community.

However, when the internationals came up with the notion of an investigation to ensure accountability, the Tamils jumped onto the bandwagon (Amarasingham, 2016). Soon, the slogan transformed into a significant demand of the Tamil people. They wanted an "international" investigation as they did not have confidence in internal mechanisms. In a way, the demand for an international investigation had become one of the central tenets of the postwar agenda of Tamil political parties. For example, the Tamil National Alliance (TNA), the main political party representing the Tamil people in parliament, contested the local and national elections on the slogan of securing an international investigation into war crimes. In 2014, the Northern Provincial Council, the only Tamil-dominated provincial council in Sri Lanka, adopted a resolution calling for an international investigation into human rights violations allegedly committed during the last phase of the war and what it called the ongoing ethnic cleansing in Tamil regions. Tamil leaders and political activists flocked to Geneva during the UNHRC sittings to lobby for harsh resolutions and action against the government (Large, 2016).

Now, the demand for an international investigation has become an integral part of Tamil politics and discourse. However, it is imperative to note that the Tamil apathy toward reconciliation remains strong as ever. The apathy indicates that the Tamils do not necessarily view accountability as a reconciliation mechanism. In their view, accountability is an instrument for justice.

Change of strategy

The Rajapaksa government, which resisted the international scheme for reconciliation in Sri Lanka, lost both the presidential as well as parliamentary elections in 2015. The new administration, which called itself the *yahapalana* government (government for good governance), was amenable to the suggestions of the internationals. On the issue of reconciliation and the future of postwar Sri Lankan society, the yahapalana government wanted to work with the international community rather than resist it. Hence, in a significant shift in strategy, the new government cosponsored the 2015 UNHRC resolution on Sri Lanka (Large, 2016).

The resolution titled *Promoting Reconciliation, Accountability and Human Rights in Sri Lanka* welcomed the Sri Lankan government's "proposal" to establish a judicial mechanism to investigate allegations of human rights abuses and violations of international humanitarian law; establish a commission for truth, justice; reconciliation and nonrecurrence; and the creation of an office of mission persons and an office for reparations (General Assembly, 2015, pp. 3–4). The resolution also welcomed the Sri Lankan government's "commitment" to take the necessary steps in order to find a political settlement (General Assembly, 2015, p. 5).

In essence, by cosponsoring this resolution, the Government of Sri Lanka agreed to (1) reform the Constitution in order to devolve political authority, (2) establish a truth-seeking mechanism such as a truth commission, (3) create a domestic mechanism to investigate human rights abuses and violations of international humanitarian law, and (4) create additional institutional mechanisms for reconciliation, including an office of missing persons and an office for reparations.

Unfortunately, none of the promises made were fully delivered. On the constitutional reform front, the government moved into action. The parliament was converted into a Constitutional Assembly in January 2016 (Shah, 2017). A steering committee consisting of 21 parliamentarians was appointed to navigate the constitutional reform process. The steering committee was expected to present the draft constitution to the Constitutional Assembly. In addition, six subcommittees were constituted to study the following subject matters, fundamental rights, judiciary, law and order, public finance, public service, and center-periphery relations (Breen, 2018). The constitutional reform process stagnated with no further progress with the release of what was called the interim report of the subcommittee deliberations in September 2017. No concrete action was taken to establish the proposed truth-seeking mechanism. The promised South-African style truth and reconciliation commission did not become a reality (Subramanian, 2014). In Geneva, the government promised an "internal" war crime investigation. Eventually, no investigation was undertaken as the President himself started to oppose any inquiry, whether internal or international. Although the Office on Mission Persons Act (2017) was enacted and the Office was constituted, no meaningful actions were undertaken. The Office has nothing to show as concrete actions or achievements (Lewer, 2017).

Back to national security?

Although the change of strategy by the new yahapalana government brought the internationals and locals closer, it failed to make any positive impacts on postwar reconciliation. One of the main reasons why the promises could not be delivered was the nationalist backlash. Sinhala nationalist groups opposed every single action promised to promote reconciliation. Leading the protest was Mahinda Rajapaksa who formed a new political party called the Sri Lanka Podujana Peramuna (SLPP). The party performed exceptionally well in the 2018 local authority election signaling the preferences of the Sinhala people (Freedom House, 2020). As expected, the party won the presidential election held in November 2019. Mahinda Rajapaksa could not contest the election as the Constitution prevented him from seeking the office for the third time. Hence, the SLPP fielded Mahinda Rajapaksa's younger brother Gotabaya Rajapaksa as the candidate and won the election convincingly. He was sworn in as president of Sri Lanka on November 18, 2019.

During the last phase of the war, Gotabaya Rajapaksa led the military operations against the LTTE and was credited for the military victory (Chanradprema, 2012). He was also responsible for many of the military and national security decisions made in the immediate aftermath end of the war (Gunaratne, 2016). Hence, it is highly likely that the government headed by Gotabaya Rajapaksa would return to national security-oriented policy priorities while overlooking ethnic reconciliation. The first signal in this regard came when the new government decided not to allow the national anthem to be sung in the Tamil language, one of the official and national languages of Sri Lanka. The new government decided to sing the national anthem only in Sinhala in the 2020 independence day official celebration. More such decisions could be unveiled in the future. The government has also decided not to support the cosponsored 2015 UNHRC resolution. In other words, none of the measures promised by the Sri Lankan government in 2015 will be implemented. This policy decision has the potential to reignite the tension and conflict between the internationals and the Sri Lankan government.

Implications for Practice and Policy

The internationals made many fundamental errors concerning their reconciliation strategy in Sri Lanka. First, they invested too much in an instrument, accountability through a credible investigation, which was difficult to achieve in Sri Lanka. The history of the country and the sociopolitical realities indicated that the Sinhala people, who form an inviolable majority, would not agree to an investigation, especially an investigation undertaken by international actors. Many political leaders in Sri Lanka understand this reality, and they effectively use it to retain power. Even if naive ones succumb to international pressure, an actual investigation cannot be undertaken because they would be unseated from political power in the next election.

Prime Minister Ranil Wickremesinghe was defeated in 2004 mainly due to the peace process he spearheaded and was seen as antinational by the Sinhala constituency (He, 2007). The government that cosponsored the UNHRC resolution in 2015 was also defeated in 2019. Therefore, as expected, a credible investigation into alleged human rights and humanitarian law violations did not become a reality. When the demand for a credible investigation was rejected and became an impossible task, the internationals did not have a fallback option. From a policy perspective, the Sri Lankan experience indicates that it is essential not to invest too much in impossible instruments to promote reconciliation. It is also essential to have alternative options. In a way, the postwar reconciliation dilemma has become more problematic as the Tamils have adopted the demand for an international investigation as a precondition for any concessions.

Second, accountability and international investigations as strategies for reconciliation are founded on the general belief that truth would lead to reconciliation. While resisting the international reconciliation project in Sri Lanka, the government argued that an investigation would further widen the gap between ethnic communities. The government preferred "selective amnesia" as it constantly talked about the alleged atrocities committed by the LTTE while expecting the Tamil people to forget what happened during the last phase of the war. However, there is an element of truth in the argument that "truth" unearthed through an investigation would have created new tension between ethnic communities. This possibility stems from Sri Lanka's unique history and sociopolitical realities. This was one of the reasons why a truth commission did not materialize in Sri Lanka. Instruments such as genuine conflict resolution and reparation could have been more useful in Sri Lanka. A truth commission could have helped in the long run as a "secondary mechanism" for reconciliation, especially after core issues of the communities are resolved. Therefore, the internationals should be extremely cautious when prescribing "truth" as the primary strategy for reconciliation.

Third, the nature and the origin of the demand for accountability were also problematic. The end of the war generated an international euphoria because the internationals believed that the termination of the LTTE would facilitate peaceful conflict resolution. They believed that the Sri Lankan government would move on to resolve the political problems of the Tamil people in the post-LTTE era (Keethaponcalan, 2019). Reports of serious human rights violations and a humanitarian catastrophe started to emerge after the military victory (Grant, 2014). It was the shock and pressure created by these reports that influenced the internationals to demand accountability from the government. For the Sri Lankan government at least, it was a hostile act. Reconciliation cannot be achieved through hostile acts, in other words, reconciliation cannot be forced. What the international community should have done is to undertake consultation with all local stakeholders and subsequently come up with a plan that reconciled international and local concerns and expectations. The lack of consultation with local stakeholders and the inherent hostile nature of the plan produced a new conflict, rather than reconciliation. The accountability issue could have been pursued as an independent issue without a concrete nexus with reconciliation.

Implications for teaching and training

There are apparent differences between war and conflict. This factor should be emphasized while training people in conflict resolution. At times, reconciliation is talked about as a postwar issue. Strictly speaking, reconciliation cannot be a postwar problem. It is a post-conflict problem. One can talk about postwar reconciliation only when war cessation includes conflict resolution. For instance, when wars are terminated through peace talks and with the conclusion of peace agreements, reconciliation becomes a postwar issue. However, when wars are terminated through military means or violence where one party completely loses and underlying issues of the conflict remain unresolved, parties cannot reconcile with their opponents, especially the losing party who would have little interest in and incentive to reconcile. The fact that true reconciliation can be achieved only when underlying issues of the conflict are resolved should be emphasized. From a theoretical viewpoint, this factor is crucial to understand. The proponent of reconciliation should understand whether underlying issues of the conflict have been resolved before expecting the parties to reconcile.

Conclusion

The international community was jubilant when the Sri Lankan armed forces decisively defeated the LTTE in May 2009. Influenced by the reports of serious human rights violations which allegedly took place during the last phase of the war, the internationals, mostly leading Western states, decided to seek accountability from the government and turned to the Geneva-based UNHRC to force the Sri Lankan government to undertake a credible, preferably an international investigation, into the alleged human rights violations. A series of resolutions was adopted since 2012, and the internationals conceived the proposed investigation and accountability as reconciliation mechanisms. Locals, especially the Sri Lankan government and the Sinhala people, did not agree with the international plan leading to considerable hostility between the internationals and the locals. The Tamils preferred accountability from the government, but only as a tool to punish the wrongdoers, not as a tool for reconciliation. The international plans failed as former warring ethnic factions in this country remain divided with a minimal prospect for a reunion. The West adopted a flawed approach as it treated Sri Lanka as a post-conflict society when, in reality, it was only postwar society. The internationals also failed to realize that one cannot bring former enemies together through hostile tactics. Sri Lanka also proved that truth could not be the fundamental approach for reconciliation in all postwar or post-conflict societies.

References

Amarasingham, A. (2016). *Pain, pride and politics: Social movement Activism and the Sri Lankan Tamil diaspora in Canada*. University of Georgia Press.

Amnesty International. (2011). *When will they get justice? Failures of Sri Lanka's lessons learnt and reconciliation commission* (Report). Amnesty International.

Balasingham, A. (2004). *War and peace: Armed struggle and peace efforts of Liberation Tigers*. Fairmax.

Bartos, O., & Wehr, P. (2002). *Using conflict theory*. Cambridge University Press.

Boyle, F. A. (2010). *The Tamil genocide by Sri Lanka: The global failure to protect Tamil rights under international law*. Clarity Press.

Breen, M. G. (2018). *The road to federalism in Nepal, Myanmar and Sri Lanka: Finding the middle ground*. Routledge.

Brown, A. (2018). The hybrid turn: Approaches and potentials. In J. Wallis, L. Kent, M. Forsyth, S. Dinnen and S. Bose (Eds.), *Hybridity on the ground in peacebuilding and development: Critical conversations* (pp. 21–36). Australian National University Press.

Chanradprema, C. A. (2012). *Gota's war: The crushing of Tamil Tiger terrorism in Sri Lanka*. Ranjan Wijeratne Foundation.

Committee on Foreign Relation (U.S. Senate). (2009). *Sri Lanka: Recharging U.S. strategy after the war*. U.S. Government Printing Office.

Derges, J. (2013). *Ritual and recovery in post-conflict Sri Lanka*. Routledge.

Devoić, B. (2013). Sri Lanka: Physical reconstruction and economic development as conflict prevention factors. *CIRR, XIX*(69), 55–75.

Freedom House. (2020). *Freedom in the world 2019: The annual survey of political rights and civil liberties*. Rowman & Littlefield.

General Assembly. (2015). *Resolution adopted by the human rights council on 1 October 2015* (Press Release). United Nations.

Gerharz, E. (2014). *The politics of reconstruction and development in Sri Lanka: Transitional commitments to social change*. Routledge.

Gokhale, N. A. (2009). *Sri Lanka: From war to peace*. Har-Anand Publications.

Grant, T. (2014). *Sri Lanka's secrets: How the Rajapaksa regime gets away with murder*. Monash University Publishing.

Gunaratne, K. (2016). *Road to Nandikadal: True story of defeating Tamil Tigers*. Vijitha Yapa.

Hashim, A. S. (2013). *When counterinsurgency wins*. University of Pennsylvania Press.

He, B. (2007). Democratization and federalism in Asia. In B. He, B. Galligan, & T. Inoguchi (Eds.), *Federalism in Asia* (pp. 1–32). Edward Elgar.

Hoglund, K., & Orjuela, C. (2016). Friction over justice in post-war Sri Lanka: Actors in local-global encounters. In A. Bjorkdahl, K. Hoglund, G. Millar, J. Lijn, & W. Verkoren (Eds.), *Peacebuilding friction: Global and local encounters in post-conflict societies* (pp. 120–137). Routledge.
Human Rights Council. (2015). *Report of the OHCHR investigation on Sri Lanka.* Human Rights Council.
International Crisis Group. (2011). *Reconciliation in Sri Lanka: Harder than ever.*
Janmyr, M. (2014). *Protecting civilians in refugee camps: Unable and unwilling States, UNHRC and international responsibility.* Martinus Nijhoff Publishers.
Kallen, H. M. (1939). *Of war and peace.* New School for Social Research.
Keerawella, G. (2013). *Post-war Sri Lanka: Is peace a hostage of the military victory?* International Center for Ethnic Studies.
Keethaponcalan, S. I. (2019). *Post-war dilemmas of Sri Lanka: Democracy and reconciliation.* Routledge.
Keethaponcalan, S. I. (2016). North–South relations and human rights. *Bandung: Journal of the Global South, 2*(1), 1–15.
Kingsbury, D. (2012). *Sri Lanka and the responsibility to protect: Politics, ethnicity and genocide.* Routledge.
Kuwali, D., & Frans, V. (2017). *By all means necessary: Protecting civilians and preventing mass atrocities in Africa.* Pretoria University Law Press.
Large, J. (2016). *Sri Lanka's dance with global governance.* Zed Books.
Leman, E. (2013). Litmus test of our resolve: War crimes and international humanitarian law in Sri Lanka. *Elon Law Review, 5*(2), 301–328.
Lessons Learnt and Reconciliation Commission of Sri Lanka. (2011). *Report of the Commission of Inquiry on Lessons Learnt and Reconciliation.* Lessons Learnt and Reconciliation Commission of Sri Lanka.
Lewer, N. (2017). Tensions between short term outcomes and long term peacebuilding in post-war Sri Lanka. In V. Rosoux & M. Anstey (Eds.), *Negotiating reconciliation in peacemaking quandaries of relationship building* (pp. 277–304). Springer.
Mahindapala, H. L. D. (2005). Origina of the North-South conflict. In *Peace in Sri Lanka, Obstacles and Opportunities*, edited by WAPS, 49–89. World Alliance for Peace in Sri Lanka.
Moorcraft, P. (2012). *Total destruction of the Tamil Tigers.* Pen & Sword Military.
Perera, S. (2016). *Survival media: The politics and poetic of mobility and the war in Sri Lanka.* Palgrave Macmillan.
Pugh, M. (2000). *Regeneration of war-torn societies.* Macmillan.
Rajapaksa, G. (2014). Sri Lanka's national security. *From the Field, 4*(4), 139–155.
Seoighe, R. (2017). *War, denial and nation-building in Sri Lanka: After the end.* Palgrave.
Shah, D. (2017). *Constitutions, religion and politics in Asia: Indonesia, Malaysia, and Sri Lanka.* Cambridge University Press.
Smith, C. Q. (2014). Illiberal peacebuilding in hybrid political orders: Managing violence during Indonesia's contested political transition. *Third World Quarterly, 35*(8), 1509–1528.
Somasundaram, D. (2014). *Scarred communities: Psychological impact of man-made and natural disasters on Sri Lankan society.* Sage.
Subramanian, S. (2014). *This divided island: Life, death, and the Sri Lankan war.* St. Martin's Press.
The Sunday Times. (2017, July 2).*Last stages of war: Blake discloses secret plan.*
Udalagama, T., & de Silva, P. (2014). Group violence against the state: The hindsight story of the thirty-year war in Sri Lanka. In J. Hawdon, J. Ryan, & M. Lucht (Eds.), *The causes and consequences of group violence: From bullies to terrorists* (pp. 91–108). Lexington.
Uesugi, Y. (2020). Introduction. In Y. Uesuji (Ed.), *Hybrid peacebuilding in Asia* (pp. 1–14). Palgrave Macmillan.
United Nations. (2011). *Report of the Secretary General's panel of experts on accountability in Sri Lanka.*
Vaiamon, S. (2012). *Pre-historic Sri Lanka to end of terrorism.* Trafford.
Venugopal, R. (2015). Democracy, development and the executive presidency in Sri Lanka. *Third World Quarterly, 36*(4), 670–690.
Wallace, M. S. (2017). *Security without weapons: Rethinking violence, nonviolent action, and civilian protection.* Routledge.
Walton, O. (2015). *Timing and sequencing of post-conflict reconstruction and peacebuilding in Sri Lanka.* Center for Research on Peace and Development.
Watson, C. A. (2004). *Nation building: A reference handbook.* ABC-CLIO.
Wijeyeratne, R. (2014). *Nation, constitutionalism and Buddhism in Sri Lanka.* Routledge.
Wilson, A. J. (2000). *Sri Lankan Tamil nationalism: Its origin and development in the nineteenth and twentieth centuries.* UBC Press.

24
EMANCIPATORY PEACEBUILDING AND CONFLICT TRANSFORMATION: MINDANAO AS A CASE STUDY

Wendy Kroeker

Ethnic conflict situations require comprehensive approaches that involve multiple methods and a diverse set of actors for the best possible chance for success. This chapter will examine the emancipatory peacebuilding approaches toward social justice embedded in the conflict-impacted island of Mindanao in the Philippines. Mindanao is a context rich in learnings toward the creation of a sustainable peace via its long narrative of diverse peace efforts and actors in addition to its more recent peace agreement process. That backdrop holds a deeply held belief that it is in the spaces of locally based and committed conversation that persons and communities will be, or can be, transformed.

This chapter will begin with a brief overview of the Philippine context in order to establish the key contextual dynamics from which has emerged a complex and diverse set of actors enmeshed in a struggle for self-determination. To fully contemplate the emancipatory impacts of peacebuilding, it is crucial to acquire an understanding of the context in which these efforts have occurred. The complexity of the Philippine context entails a web of ethnic and religious dimensions. The following section will explore key peacebuilding theories and insights that assist in exploring contested spaces. Resultant implications for teaching and practice will probe movements and theories that emerge from Philippine peacebuilder experiences as guides for enhanced efforts and practices.

Background: Philippine context

The history of the Philippines, and the island of Mindanao, in particular, is complex and is the basis toward understanding peace possibilities in the region. War, the struggle for colonial and imperial domination, movements of resistance, and the pushing of identities and boundaries are entrenched within the story involving the inhabitants of the region. Stories of violence, corruption, discrimination, injustice, and exploitation are the fabric of the communities. Calls for justice, attention to root causes, the right to self-determination, basic needs to be met, inclusion in peacebuilding processes, or simply opportunities to go to school and sleep at night are at the heart of the peacebuilding work in this region. This history of Indigenous peoples, Muslims, and settlers—the ethnic complexity in this country—is necessary knowledge in any attempt to conceptualize avenues for meaningful and sustainable peacebuilding.

The Philippines is a country of about seven thousand islands and has three diverse geographic regions: Luzon, the Visayas, and Mindanao. The Mindanao area—one that has suffered decades of violence and conflict—sits at a strategic position in the center of the shipping lane between the Far East and the Malayan world. The region is extremely fertile and rich in agricultural commodities and marine and mineral resources. The enormity of resources and the disparity regarding their distribution in this area of the country has placed Mindanao in the center of attention on political and economic fronts.

The Philippines has been hit by two forms of colonization: conquest and settlement. Foreign-owned corporations now own and control huge tracts of available agricultural land on which pineapple, banana, coffee, copra, and rubber are cultivated and processed—for export. Consequently, despite Mindanao's abundance of resources, it remains the poorest region in the country. Human Rights Watch/Asia (1992) deems Mindanao a "Laboratory of Counterinsurgency," given the conditions of disparity regarding wealth and access (p. 12). The factors of "greed and grievance" play a significant role in this setting.[1]

Until the early 1900s, thirteen Islamicized Indigenous groups known collectively as the Moros accounted for 90 percent of Mindanao's population (Human Rights Watch/Asia 1992, p. 12). After decades of American colonization and the following imperialist years of "Philippine conquest and encroachment," the make-up of Mindanao had changed (p. 12). Currently, it is the Christian settlers and their ensuing generations who dominate the region in terms of both population and resources. Almost three-quarters of Mindanao's population is now first- or second-generation immigrants from neighboring islands (Goodno, 1991, p. 241). As well, the vast majority of the population is now Roman Catholic. This context sets the stage for peacebuilding work in the Philippines.

Understanding the colonial history and journey toward independence is crucial for understanding the events of today. The Philippines is a complex land—a varied set of islands, languages, and terrains as well as a narrative mix of early fisher communities and the experience of colonization by Spain, the United States, and Japan. The roots of the conflict in Mindanao can be traced back to the colonial periods, but precolonial history is essential for understanding the undertones of the tripartite relationships involved (Quimpo, 2001, p. 274). During the time of the Spanish colonization, an intense rift emerged between the Christians, predominantly Catholic, and the Muslims, or Moros, of Mindanao. The Lumads, the Indigenous peoples, were often caught in the middle of these conflicts since the Spaniards, who converted them to Christianity, "compelled […] [them] to fight with them against the Muslims" (p. 274).

Once the Philippines gained their independence from the United States in 1946, the national government became a factor in the tensions between these groups, as "most Muslims could not identify themselves with the new republic, whose laws were clearly derived from Western or Catholic moral values and whose public school system was too Americanized and alien to Islamic tradition" (Quimpo, 2001, p. 274). For more than four hundred years, Mindanao has been a landscape of conflict as different players have postured for power at the expense of the local inhabitants. Over the past decades, numerous peace processes were initiated to settle grievances between the different stakeholders in the region.

The tri-people dimension: Multiethnic conflict

In the Philippine islands beyond Mindanao, inhabitants "found their place" in this Christianized context (Neumann, 2010b, p. 186). With Christianity emerging as the national cornerstone, it symbolically marginalized religious minorities. Consequently, a "new collective counter-identity" took shape and unified the different Islamicized ethnic and tribal groups under the grouping "Moros" who began to fight for their autonomy in what was perceived to be a hostile Christian nation (p. 186). This is often referred to as the "Mindanao conflict."

Alongside this conflict, the term "tri-people" emerged to describe the relation of the Moros, Christians, and Lumads living in Mindanao (Baybado, 2018, p. 106). Although historically the conflict has depicted Moros and Christian settlers as the key actors in this conflict, the Indigenous peoples, the Lumads, have by their very proximity to the communities of the Moros and Christians been absorbed into the struggle (p. 107). The context is far from simplistic designations of ethnicity or religion. Both Moros and Lumads are struggling for self-determination—whether political or cultural—"against the persistent policy of integration and assimilation of the Christian-centered central government" (p. 108).

Philippine President Duterte, elected in May 2016, inherited the peace process between the Moro Islamic Liberation Front (MILF) and the government of the Philippines that had stalled when Congress failed to pass the Bangsamoro Basic Laws (BBL) legislation, which would have created an autonomous region for Muslims in key parts of Mindanao and the southern islands.[2] His administration created a new peace panel in order to move forward, maintaining the momentum for an agreement. On 24 July 2018, just over two years into his presidency, President Duterte signed the Bangsamoro Organic Law (BOL) after it was ratified by the House of Representatives. This move created "the Bangsamoro Autonomous Region in Muslim Mindanao" (BARMM), providing self-determination to the minority Muslims in the region (Marcelo, 2018). The BOL is the result of negotiations over many decades between Muslim groups (Moro National Liberation Front [MNLF] and MILF) and the Philippine government (Marcelo, 2018). The journey to the negotiated national-level settlement has been long and difficult, and the journey to a durable peace will require the same effort and energy to produce a sustainable and final settlement.

The history of the Philippines outlined earlier is one of struggle—a struggle for resources, acknowledgment, preservation of identity, and emancipation. It is a struggle between distinct ethnic and religious groups with competing narratives toward self-determination. That history includes a colonial legacy that has encompassed the entrenching of inequalities and the pacification attempts of peoples through force and political structures, as well as years of martial law and decades of war and violence in Mindanao.

Muslims, the Lumad, and Christians are the current fabric of Mindanao and all are seeking to create durable peace in their island. Many voices are required for both the telling of this history and for participation in peacebuilding activities. The country is at a fragile point in terms of stabilizing its peace and making decisions that will affect next generations. Many players are working on creative measures for ensuring that a wide variety of voices are involved and that the structures that emerge provide space for multiple stakeholders. Many of these stakeholders work at the local or grassroots levels and it is at these levels that creative peace thinking is taking place. This chapter will explore frameworks and tactics utilized as bottom-up initiatives in the quest for sustainable peace in the region.

Key peacebuilding insights: Contested spaces

Examination of the geopolitical context of the Philippines reveals several key peacebuilding themes worthy of deep exploration. To open, ethnicity, at its most basic level, is a "form of cultural distinctiveness" (Bush & Saltarelli, 2000, p. 2). Kusuma Snitwongse and W. Scott Thompson's (2005) work has examined ethnic conflicts in Asia. They indicate that five distinctive dimensions frame ethnic settings: "demographic patterns and ethnic geography; precolonial and colonial legacies; the histories, fears, and goals of ethnic groups in the country; economic factors and trends; and regional and international influences" (p. viii). Identity is connected to a particular place and time and is impacted by the proximate events. Thus, understanding the context for analysis is crucial as an avenue for developing insights into ethnic conflict and its burdens. Bush and Saltarelli (2000) purport that "[o]nce violence becomes fuelled by hyper-politicized identity," the stakes begin to rise and cannot easily be met (pp. 4–5). The consequence is that a group's very existence is deemed to be vulnerable and conflict patterns begin to set in.

In the Mindanao context, these types of dynamics all "supported the formation of a deep cleavage" that, according to Philippine political scientist Miriam Coronel-Ferrer (2005), were "tapped to support a secessionist war" (p. 120). Thus, the place of emancipatory peacebuilding is significant within the challenges of dealing with cleavages emerging from the throes of ethnic conflict. Oliver P. Richmond (2001) opines that "[m]aking peace in 'intractable' conflict is a fundamental challenge" (p. 317). Recognizing this, current peacebuilding theory has moved toward an approach focused on emancipation and social justice for all stakeholders. Consequently, a vision of peace has emerged that has at its foundation a strong value placed on peace at the everyday and local levels.[3] Emancipatory-oriented peacebuilding requires meaningful listening to the issues at the heart of contested community spaces.

Moving from antagonistic relationships to some kind of restoration of those relationships requires deliberate efforts. These are not dynamics that can be resolved quickly or with "cookie cutter" frameworks. Into these types of contested spaces, according to Andrew E. E. Collins and Charles Thiessen (2020), "[i]nsights from the analytical tradition of agonism are helpful here" (p. 231). The framing of agonistic peacebuilding is specifically oriented toward transformational possibilities and "opens up the peacebuilding venture to constructive interactions between competing groups" (p. 231). Additionally, Aggestam et al.'s (2015) peacebuilding work in the Middle East indicates that utilizing "agonistic peace politics favours the opening up of institutions and arenas for interaction that allow for the development, articulation and contestation of different political alternatives that can exist in parallel" (p. 1739). This allows for a dynamic evolution of thoughts and ideas pertaining to the flourishing of communities. The agonistic framework allows for a pluralist agency—multiple and creative actors—seeking ways to articulate the issues such that it does not exacerbate antagonistic perspectives that rely on friend/enemy articulations.

Adding to the aforementioned frameworks, de Coning's (2018) work is helpful as it seeks out an approach to peacebuilding that takes into account the complexities of conflict contexts. His adaptive peacebuilding approach utilizes "iterative cycles of learning" that acknowledge the dynamic spaces in which conflict lives (p. 305). Similar to the agility of adaptive peacebuilding, Michel de Certeau developed the concept of the "everyday" arguing that it is possible to resist the structures of the day via a deliberate focus on one's daily practices (Richmond, 2011, p. 127). These "tactical" efforts of the everyday can then become a disseminated—yet noninstitutional—form of doing politics. Richmond (2011) entitles this as "an everyday agency" for its ability to "shape, resist and choose" its own strategies (p. 128).

This emancipatory orientation to the concept of the "everyday" has been examined in a wide range of disciplines. According to Highmore (2002), the concept of the everyday refers to "those practices and lives that have traditionally been left out of historical accounts. […] It becomes shorthand for voices from 'below': women, children, migrants and so on" (p. 1). In the face of unpeace, the literature of the everyday[4] that includes the concepts of the application to both resistance and peacebuilding studies is especially helpful.

The everyday is simply the context where the dynamics of local needs are being considered by locals and unconsciously, or consciously, where the strategies and problem-solving activities are implemented. Although the temptation is to describe the everyday peacebuilding as banal activities, the stakes are, in fact, high and the potential for transformation, when efforts are deliberate, immense. Being attuned to the potential of everyday peacebuilding requires developing lenses to notice emergent spaces that hold potential for change within everyday actions. Roger Mac Ginty (2014) defines everyday peace as "the routinized practices used by individuals and collectives as they navigate their way through life in a deeply divided society" (p. 2). Yet, it is not simply a matter of repeating one's daily activities and hoping for change to occur.

This everyday peace is "a form of agency. It is not something that people always and necessarily engage in. It relies on opportunities and context, as well as the ability of individuals and groups to exploit these" (Mac Ginty, 2014, p. 3). This might appear, initially, to be "beguilingly simple," but requires nurturing a mindfulness toward the desire for change and openness to observing the potential for peacebuilding in any given interaction (p. 3). The following section will examine the implications—springing from peacebuilding theories—within teaching and training for the expansion of emancipatory frameworks toward communities seeking to alleviate the existent conflicts.

Implications for teaching and training

The key peacebuilding insights that emerge out of contemplating the challenges of ethnic conflict and the resultant contested spaces give shape to possibilities for teaching and training toward an enhanced vision of peace and peacebuilding efforts. Philippine peacebuilders have struggled to find hope and direction in the face of antagonistic relationships. Two key contextual insights stand out as assistive for teaching and training: Father Bert Layson's committed approach to building an inclusive and caring community and Catholic Relief Service's (CRS) attention to interconnectedness.

Community spaces: Building the caring collective

Father Bert Layson, a member of the Oblates of Mary Immaculate (OMI) working in Mindanao, has significantly altered his way of working in his parish because of the violent conflict he has experienced and witnessed in his community. Senehi (2002) asserts that, as peacebuilders, we must create opportunities whereby we "facilitate cultural spaces" that assist communities to "work together to shape the future" (p. 57). There exists such a space in a well-loved indigenous story that describes the necessity for all peoples to work together to create the peace they seek in Mindanao:

> Peace in Mindanao is like cooking food in the pot. You need three stones to provide support to the pot before you could actually cook the food. You could not cook with only one stone, not even with two stones. You need three. And these three stones are the Muslims, Christians and the indigenous people. Only then can you cook the food. Only then can we have peace in Mindanao. (Local Manobo elder, cited in Layson, 2003)

Father Bert Layson (2003) relays this story to acknowledge that he began his parish work with entrenched biases toward the military and Muslims—work that was eventually transformed through the diversity of stories he heard.

Being assigned in an area that required networking within multiple groups when war broke out explains his transformation to identifying as a peacebuilder. Layson says:

> And that's when I really experienced the suffering of people in various evacuations centers—Muslims, Christians—but especially Muslims, even children. It was very, you know, as a missionary priest, when you hear the sounds of mothers weeping and children crying in the night, you don't anymore ask whether they are Muslims or Christians. If there's any little humanity left in you, you have to do something to alleviate them from their suffering. I remember I would just cry and shed my tears alone by myself. So, that's when I was able to become a good missionary [of peace], you have really to transcend biases and hatred and anger to be an instrument of God's peace and compassion to every human being. (Kroeker, 2021, p. 150)

Father Bert embraced this transformation of thinking and being and consequently shifted his parish work emphasis from the church, narrowly defined, to encompass his broader community. Today he is widely loved as a priest for all of the people.

Father Bert is recognized as someone embedded within the community conflict space and dedicated to teaching from a stance of appreciation and respect for all in his community. Philippine peacebuilders, specifically those directly lodged within ethnic conflict, have emerged as innovative in thinking through teaching and training concepts applicable to the context and as able to build a caring collective.

3B theory: Relational and structural interconnectedness

Out of peacebuilding work in the Philippines, deep reflection has emerged regarding the necessity of relational and structural interconnectedness for effective peacebuilding. The 3B framework emerged directly from the work of local peacebuilders as an educational intervention in the face of overt conflicts over self-determination. The CRS, which has a long history of presence in the Philippines, promoted a training and education project entitled "Applying Binding, Bonding and Bridging: A3B" that, initially, was a framework to address land conflict in Mindanao (Leguro & Kniss, 2013, p. 10). This project rests on the CRS-developed "3B theory"—a three-step reconciliation and conflict transformation process. This localized peacebuilding orientation is framed within a long narrative of community conflict and provides a basis for applying peacebuilding interventions in Mindanao.

The first stage, "Binding," focuses on personal change and trauma healing. The process encourages personal reflection, introspection, and healing to break down prejudices and stereotypes and helps individuals gain skills to address conflict in nonviolent and healthy ways. Second, "Bonding" is aimed at building internal group cohesion within respective or single identity groups, preparing them for constructive dialogue, engagement, and collaboration with other groups. Through safe intragroup settings, they work through their own commonalities and differences.

Lastly, "Bridging" works on making connections across groups to build trust and positive relations. Intergroup dialogues enable diverse—and conflicting—groups to interact in a safe space to do joint analysis of issues, generate collective information, increase understanding of conflict/issues, explore resolution of conflicts, build a common vision, and plan for collective action. The 3B framework emerges from long experienced peacebuilders who have observed the key cultural workings toward peace. This is a framework built on locally embedded peacebuilding.

The investment of Mindanaoan peacebuilders into the emergent space surrounding the current peace agreement uncertainty was enriched through decades of honing peace instincts and relationship building. Numerous communities have spent considerable energies educating communities regarding the benefits of restored relationships, using the 3B framework. The training processes developed by Mindanaoan peacebuilders have generated new practices within contested community contexts and have shaped planning processes within local government units.

Implications for practice and policy

The Philippine context is a rich environment for models of practice emerging out of conflict environments that are deliberately working from emancipatory frameworks. Philippine psychologist Cristina Jayme Montiel (2007) stresses that the "social power of peaceful structural transformation emanates from collective human actions, mobilized into a synchronized social force, purposefully directed toward disequilibrating vertical structures and building new egalitarian systems" (pp. 12–13). This orientation toward structural transformation practice is embedded in the work of many peacebuilders in Mindanao.

The peacebuilders that this section will highlight are working toward caring and respectful collective actions. They possess strength, diversity, and a will to remain invested. They are embedded in the social context and are valued for their connections to the community. This type of insider-partial role is characterized "not in distance from the conflict or objectivity regarding the issues, but rather in connectedness and trusted relationships with the conflict parties" (Wehr & Lederach, 1991, p. 87). Without trust as the foundation, positive relationships are quickly dismantled, and the essential "go-between" peacebuilding work becomes impossible (Kroeker, 2021). The multilevel role is essential to peace work in Mindanao and it occurs through the work of the locally lodged actors in that space. Two examples of particular practices/programs—Bantay Ceasefire and Christians for Peace Movement—have emerged in Mindanao that highlight the peacebuilding directions possible with a trust in local influence and frameworks focusing on emancipatory foundations in the quest for social justice for a broad range of stakeholders.

Bantay Ceasefire

Civil society activities are strongly associated with the development and nurturing of intersectionalities and the analysis of spaces that can provide possibilities for action. The potential range is immense and can include community-based organizations (CBOs), religious leaders, student groups, women's groups, revolutionary societies, professional bodies, and more. Catherine Barnes' (2005) research reveals that there are several types of orientations that motivate civil society organizations (p. 12).

One of these designated motivations is the desire to specifically address the conflict of a region and to respond in ways to involve civil society. An example of this motivation is the Bantay Ceasefire team formed in Mindanao to monitor a ceasefire in the conflict between the Philippine government and the MILF in 2003. This began as an unofficial group but, at the same time, "mandated by grassroots people living in conflict areas" (Eviota, 2005, p. 389). Its composition was broad-based across religious and ethnic lines and provided keen vigilance in order to prevent the outbreak of war. Diomedes Eviota, Jr.'s (2005) assessment of the success of the Bantay Ceasefire group is based on the fact that, in addition to its local mandate, it was also "underpinned by the participation of surrounding countries from the Southern Hemisphere" and its partnerships with the monitoring activities of nongovernment organizations (NGOs) and humanitarian groups in Mindanao (p. 389).

Bantay Ceasefire has modeled the strength of grassroots initiatives and the capacity that can be enhanced through the creation of strong networks—networks that would not have emerged without broad-based local initiation and participation. The Philippine context has produced events and organizations that are willing to push at the urgent edges. The Bantay Ceasefire volunteers' ceasefire monitoring activities have had significant impact on the local stakeholders.

As a result of their work, the conflict parties have become more cautious in their actions on the ground given the presence of a civilian-led ceasefire monitoring team watching their actions. These volunteers work in the highly conflicted areas and risk their lives in order to hold the conflict actors accountable to the maintenance of a ceasefire. As well, community people have been empowered when realizing that they can do something to prevent the escalation of conflict. They do not need to wait until conflict approaches them; they can respond with the strength of their work (Mindanao People's Caucus, 2015). Local practices require both vision and courage in the process of organizing.[5]

Christians for Peace Movement

It has been clear within studies of peace processes that "[f]ragmentation and competing identities within a society, coupled with real or perceived exclusion, can fuel violence and undermine peacebuilding efforts" (Rausch & Luu, 2017, p. 2). Rausch and Luu (2017) argue that inclusive processes are the pathway for providing an opportunity for outcomes to be accomplished: Mari Fitzduff opines that "[t]here is little point in developing just [inclusive] relationships if you're not prepared to also develop [and maintain new] structures" (cited in Rausch & Luu, 2017, p. 2). Within this post-conflict landscape in Mindanao, developing the ability to see possible links across sectors and build meaningful involvement are crucial aspects in moving forward into a post-conflict space.

The Philippines context holds great potential for observing peacebuilding methodologies because "[p]eacebuilding in Mindanao mobilizes different levels of society, engaging multiple actors" (Leguro & Kniss, 2013, p. 5). Inclusivity as a foundational practice for Mindanao peace work is also substantiated in the research of Jalali and de Guzman (2013):

> For Muslims, Christians, and Badjaos alike, people attain peace by ensuring that all sectors in a community are properly represented in relation to important economic, political, and social matters. (p. 52)

This inclusive framework highlights the place of localized efforts.

As work began in readiness for the ratification of the BBL, Christian leaders observed that the sentiments and perspectives of Christian communities seemed less visible and unarticulated at both the local and national levels in comparison to their fellow Muslim citizens in the region. Most of the debates on issues leading to signed peace agreements took place in political centers and academic conferences—spaces not easily accessible to the Christian grassroots constituency. Leaders also observed that the sentiments and perspectives of Christian communities were less visible and unarticulated both at the local and national levels. This gap resulted from a lack of consensus among the Christian constituency in the Bangsamoro region.

This concern served as the initial motivation for key individuals from the Catholic, Evangelical, and Episcopalian churches in Cotabato City to come together—as a first internal step—to mobilize Christian settler communities. The aim was to advocate for a more inclusive

Bangsamoro peace process through the "17-point Peace and Development Agenda for the Bangsamoro Peace Process" and to—as a second step—jointly create, as Christian and Muslim leaders, a "Manifesto" calling for inclusive peace and development; denunciation of violent extremism; sustained peace education and dialogue among grassroots; institutionalization of political dialogue in the context of interfaith cooperation; ratification of the BOL; and effective information dissemination of the BOL (PBCI InfoComm Team, 2018).

The mobilization gathered momentum in large part when, in March 2018, Edgar Ramirez, a well-known local peace and human rights advocate, was appointed to serve as Deputy Governor for Christian Affairs "in a bid to also enhance interreligious understanding and harmony between Muslims and Christians in the volatile region whose growth was stunted by the decades-old Moro rebellion to establish an independent Muslim state in the south" (Sarmiento, 2018). This was a significant move in a historical context rife with misunderstandings between Muslim and Christian communities. Key church leaders organized consultation meetings in three cluster areas which focused on the review of the BOL and cultivating unity and consensus as a constituency. These meetings resulted in the formulation of the "17-Point Christian Settlers Peace and Development Agenda" (Mellejor, 2018).[6]

The result of the consultations was that the group was able to position itself as a significant Christian settler platform in the Bangsamoro region through these local level consultations. This development was crucial, modeling that effective peacebuilding work must go beyond the official political agreements. With substantial input and participation from local church and community leaders in various parts of the Bangsamoro territory, the process culminated in a high-level meeting with leaders of the MILF and the MNLF in September 2018. High-level religious leaders from the Catholic, Episcopal, and Evangelical Churches led the delegation for CfPM. The result of the summit was the creation, and signing, of a "Manifesto" between these Bangsamoro (Muslim/Moro) and Christian Leaders.

The manifesto articulated important commitments on behalf of the leaders. This marked a significant milestone toward the building of constructive relationships between parties often in disagreement during decades of war—an agreement marked solely by local initiatives. The legacy of the Bantay Ceasefire efforts and the current work of the CfPM have spawned numerous other peacebuilding practices and have initiated changes[7] in the structures by which communities operate in the face of substantial tensions.

Conclusion

Rufa Cagoco-Guiam (2016)—former Director of the C-Institute for Peace and Development in Mindanao at Mindanao State University–General Santos City—asks: "Is reconciliation possible for Mindanao's diverse peoples, amid the suspicion and distrust embedded in their collective consciousness, and among groups that have fought each other on the battlefield?" (p. 31). She asserts that it will only occur with "a more holistic transformation of relationships" (p. 32). The work of the Bantay Ceasefire and CfPM emphasize that relationship building ability is a strong peace asset in Mindanao. This ability has emerged with the strength it has from a two-pronged belief that relationships do not flourish without engaging those within the community and without dedicated attention to structural justice dynamics. Consequently, the peacebuilding energies in Mindanao relentlessly push at the edges of a simple binary of "bottom-up" or "top down" peacebuilding.

Cagoco-Guiam (2016) stresses the need for peacebuilders "to talk to each other [within] and outside of their immediate circles to enlarge the windows of opportunity" (p. 36). This back-and-forth agility requires a foundation of deep wisdom regarding how social change emerges—hard-earned wisdom gleaned from decades of war and losses of loved ones. The Christians for Peace Movement leaders have seen paths and bridges where some might see despair. Working as a go-between is a challenging position in a context where antagonistic anxiety regarding the "other" is often nurtured by community leaders, politicians, and religious institutions. Emancipatory peacebuilding—as "the process where the individuals and communities which peacebuilding is targeted at are involved in the peacebuilding process in authentic ways"—is the constructive counterpoint to the oft present antagonistic approach (Oloke et al., 2018, p. 74). Thus, the insights arising from the Mindanao context of transformative approaches can significantly enhance the emancipatory peacebuilding discourse.

Notes

1 Regarding the theoretical framework of greed and grievance as it pertains to conflict analysis, see Collier and Hoeffler (1998), Collier (2000), and Collier and Hoeffler (2000).
2 Peace talks did resume in 2010 under the administration of President Benigno Aquino III. On 15 October 2012, the Philippine government and the MILF signed a Framework Agreement on the Bangsamoro (FAB), which provided a roadmap to a final peace deal between the central government and the Muslim rebels in Mindanao. On 27 March 2014, the Philippine Government and the MILF signed the "Comprehensive Agreement on the Bangsamoro" (CAB), the culmination of many efforts since peace talks started between the two parties in 1997. The next steps included the framing of a "Bangsamoro Basic Law" (BBL). Indigenous peoples' groups began to organize to analyze the impact of this on their communities. On 25 January 2015, amid Congressional deliberations on the BBL, the Philippine National Police Special Action Force launched an operation into the Bangsamoro Autonomous Region controlled by the MILF to capture two terrorist targets. In the midst of this operation, there was an exchange of fire between the police, the Bangsamoro Islamic Freedom Fighters, and a unit of the MILF. In the end, 44 Special Forces police officers, eighteen MILF members, and a number of civilians were dead. This encounter has become known as simply "Mamasapano" or the "Mamasapano clash/incident." The shift in the peace process was immediate. Politicians quickly distanced themselves from the peace process in order to avoid being seen as supporting the violence that had just occurred (Arguillas, 2015). The movement toward peace slowed as many scrambled to declare themselves as "hardline nationalists" (Abuza, 2016). President Aquino lost considerable influence in the process. Aquino's term as president ended without the passing of the BBL despite strong efforts by many.
3 For a deeper discussion of the concepts of the "local turn" and everyday peace/building, see the work of Donais (2009), Mac Ginty and Richmond (2013), and Mac Ginty and Firchow (2016).
4 For further reading on the everyday, see Friedan (1963), especially the chapter on "The Problem That Has No Name." She introduced the notion of the banality of everyday activities as defining for a particular sector. For the literature of everyday resistance, see Scott (1985, 1990), Foucault (1978), de Certeau (1984), Abu-Lughod (1990), and Vinthagen and Johansson (2013). For literature on everyday peacebuilding, the work of Mac Ginty (2011, 2014) and Richmond (2011, 2016) is helpful in creating concepts for reflecting on the types of spaces existent for peacebuilding work.
5 Further local practices would also include the development of Zones of Peace as community-initiated peacebuilding strategies (Avruch & Jose, 2007, pp. 51–70).
6 Christian leaders from the core territory of the then soon-to-be-created Bangsamoro Autonomous Region in Muslim Mindanao (BARMM) initiated a series of dialogues that produced an agenda entitled: the "17-point Christian Settlers Peace Agenda for the Bangsamoro Peace Process." It was presented to Moro leaders on September 27–28, 2018 with the aim of addressing concerns affecting Christian communities in the BARMM.
7 Through the Bangsamoro Organic Law, the Bangsamoro Transition Authority (BTA) can create an office for settler communities under the Office of the Chief Minister. These provisions created space to ensure that settlers and Indigenous peoples (IP) enjoy the rights guaranteed in this new Organic Law. Given the opportunity that the BOL provides, the recognized Christian representative in the BTA—MP Susana Anayatin—authored Bill No. 10 to endorse the formal establishment of an Office for Settler Communities.

References

Abu-Lughod, L. (1990). The romance of resistance. Tracing transformations of power through Bedouin women. *American Ethnologist, 17*(1), 41–55.

Abuza, Z. (2016, November 25). Can Duterte bring peace to the Philippines? Forging peace in Mindanao is a far more challenging task than many appreciate" *The Diplomat*. http://thediplomat.com/2016/11/can-duterte-bring-peace-to-the-philippines/

Aggestam, K., Cristiano, F., & Strömborn, L. (2015). Towards agonistic peacebuilding? Exploring the antagonism-agonism nexus in the Middle East peace process. *Third World Quarterly, 36*(9), 1736–1753.

Arguillas, C. O. (2015, January 26). Mamasapano clash between SAF and MILF/BIFF: how to explain this tragedy? *MindaNews*. http://www.mindanews.com/peace-process/2015/01/26/mamasapano-clash-between-saf-and-milfbiff-how-to-explain-this-tragedy/

Avruch, K., & Jose, R. S. (2007). Peace zones in the Philippines. In L. E. Hancock & C. R. Mitchell (Eds.), *Zones of peace* (pp. 51–70). Kumarian Press.

Barnes, C. (2005). Weaving the web: Civil-society roles in working with conflict and building peace. In P. van Tongeren, M. Brenk, M. Hellema, & J. Verhoeven (Eds.), *People Building Peace II* (pp. 7–24). Lynne Reinner.

Baybado, Jr., P. A. (2018). Tri-people dialogue: Prospects for peace building in the Philippines. *Studies in Interreligious Dialogue, 27*(1), 105–126.

Bush, K. D. & Saltarelli, D. (2000). *The two faces of education in ethnic conflict: Towards a peacebuilding education for children*. UNICEF, United Nations Children's Fund, Innocenti Research Centre.

Cagoco-Guiam, R. (2016). Grounding reconciliation: Transforming relationships in Mindanao. In M. Salter & Z. Yousuf (Eds.), *Transforming broken relationships: Making peace with the past* (pp. 30–36). Conciliation Resources.

Collier, P. (2000). *Economic causes of civil conflict and their implications for policy*. World Bank.

Collier, P., & Hoeffler, A. (2000). Greed and grievance in civil war. *Policy Research Working Paper 2355*. World Bank.

Collier, P., & Hoeffler, A. (1998). On the economic causes of civil war. *Oxford Economic Papers, 50*(4), 563–573.

Collins, A. E. E. & Thiessen, C. (2020). A grounded theory of local ownership as meta-conflict in Afghanistan. *Cooperation and Conflict, 55*(2), 216–234.

Coronel-Ferrer, M. (2005). The Moro and the Cordillera conflicts in the Philippines and the struggle for autonomy. In K. Snitwongse & W. S. Thompson (Eds.), *Ethnic conflict in Southeast Asia* (pp. 109–150). ISEAS Publications.

de Certeau, M. (1984). *The practice of everyday life*. University of California Press.

de Coning, C. (2018). Adaptive peacebuilding. *International Affairs, 94*(2), 301–317.

Donais, T. (2009). Empowerment or imposition? Dilemmas of local ownership in post-conflict peacebuilding processes. *Peace & Change, 34*(1), 3–26.

Eviota, D., Jr. (2005). Grassroots and South–South cooperation: Bantay Ceasefire in the Philippines. In P. van Tongeren, M. Brenk, M. Hellema, & J. Verhoeven (Eds.), *People Building Peace II* (pp. 388–393). Lynne Reinner.

Foucault, M. (1978). *The history of sexuality. Vol. 1: An introduction*. Random House.

Friedan, B. (1963). *The feminine mystique*. W.W. Norton.

Goodno, J. B. (1991). *The Philippines: Land of broken promises*. Zed Books.

Highmore, B. (2002). Introduction: Questioning everyday life. In B. Highmore (Ed.), *The everyday life reader* (pp. 1–34). Routledge.

Human Rights Watch/Asia. (1992). *Bad blood: Militia abuses in Mindanao, the Philippines*. Human Rights Watch/Asia.

Jalali, J. A. & de Guzman, J. M. (2013). Meanings of peace among the Tri-People of Jolo, Sulu. In C. M. Inzon, M. A. P. Ofreneo, & T. Casal de Vela (Eds.), *Meaning making in Mindanao: Everyday violence, ordinary people, finding peace* (pp. 48–55). Notre Dame of Jolo College.

Kroeker, W. (2021). *Multidimensional peacebuilding: Local actors in the Philippine context*. Lexington.

Layson, R. (2003, September 18). *Reflections on public participation in peace processes in Mindanao*. Paper presented in a panel discussion during the seminar workshop on "Learning from Public Participation in Peacemaking." General Santos City.

Leguro, M. & Kniss, S. (2013, November 12). *Back to the land: Structuring peace from the grassroots in Mindanao*. Presented at the Asia-Pacific Peace Research Association conference, Bangkok, Thailand.

Mac Ginty, R. (2016). What do we mean when we use the term 'local'? Imagining and framing the local and international in relation to peace and order. In T. Debiel, T. Held, & U. Schneckener (Eds.), *Peacebuilding in crisis rethinking paradigms and practices of transnational cooperation* (pp. 193–209). Routledge.

Mac Ginty, R. (2014). Everyday peace: Bottom-up and local agency in conflict-affected societies. *Security Dialogue, 45*(6), 1–17. doi:10.1177/0967010614550899

Mac Ginty, R. (2011). *International peacebuilding and local resistance: Hybrid forms of peace*. Palgrave Macmillan.

Mac Ginty, R., & Firchow, P. (2016). Top-down and bottom-up narratives of peace and conflict. *Politics, 36*(3), 308–323.

Mac Ginty, R., & Richmond, O. P. (2013). The local turn in peace building: A critical agenda for peace. *Third World Quarterly, 34*(5), 763–783.

Marcelo, V. (2018, July 24). The Bangsamoro Organic Law: Everything you need to know. *CNN Philippines*. http://nine.cnnphilippines.com/news/2018/07/24/bangsamoro-organic-law-primer-everything-you-need-to-know-bbl.html

Mellejor, L. (2018, September 28). Christians in Bangsamoro "core areas" push for 17-point peace agenda. *Philippine News Agency*. https://www.pna.gov.ph/articles/1049390

Mindanao Peoples' Caucus. (2015). What is Bantay Ceasefire? *MPC Website*. http://www.mpc.org.ph/index.php?option=com_content&view=article&id=105&Itemid=87

Montiel, C. J. (2007). Toward a psychology of structural peacebuilding. In D. J. Christie, R. V. Wagner, & D. A. Winter (Eds.), *Peace, conflict, and violence: Peace psychology for the 21st century* (pp. 282–294). Prentice-Hall.

Neumann, H. (2010a). Identity-building and democracy in the Philippines: National failure and local responses in Mindanao. *Journal of Current Southeast Asian Affairs, 29*(3), 61–90.

Neumann, H. (2010b). Reframing identities and social practices despite war. *Peace Review, 22*(2), 184–191.

Oloke, I. , Lindsay, P. , & Byrne, S. (2018). The intersection of critical emancipatory peacebuilding and SE. *Journal of Ethnic Studies, 81*, 67–86.

PBCI InfoComm Team. (2018, September 30). "Christians for Peace" initiate Moro-Christian leaders' dialogue. *Peacebuilders Community*. https://peacebuilderscommunity.org/2018/09/muslim-and-christian-leaders-call-for-inclusive-peace-development-in-mindanao/

Quimpo, N. G. (2001). Options in the pursuit of a just, comprehensive, and stable peace in the southern Philippines. *Asian Survey, 41*(2), 271–289.

Rausch, C., & Luu, T. (2017). *Inclusive peace processes are key to ending violent conflict*. PeaceBrief 222. United States Institute of Peace.

Richmond, O. P. (2016). *Peace formation and political order in conflict affected societies*. Oxford University Press.

Richmond, O. P. (2011). *A post-liberal peace*. Routledge.

Richmond, O. P. (2001). A genealogy of peacemaking: The creation and recreation of order. *Alternatives: Global, Local, Political, 26*(3), 317–348. http://www.jstor.org/stable/40645022

Rudy, J., & Leguro, M. (2010). *The diverse terrain of peacebuilding in Mindanao*. Collaborative Learning Projects.

Sarmiento, B. S. (2018, March 8). ARMM designates deputy governor for Christians. *MindaNews*. https://www.mindanews.com/top-stories/2018/03/armm-designates-deputy-governor-christians/

Scott, J. C. (1990). *Domination and the arts of resistance: Hidden transcripts*. Yale University Press.

Scott, J. C. (1985). *Weapons of the weak: Everyday forms of peasant resistance*. Yale University Press.

Senehi, J. (2002) Constructive storytelling: A peace process. *Peace and Conflict Studies, 9*(2), 41–63.

Snitwongse, K., & Thompson, W. S. (2005). Introduction. In K. Snitwongse & W. S. Thompson (Eds.), *Ethnic conflict in Southeast Asia* (pp. vii–xii). ISEAS Publications.

Thiessen, C. (2011). Emancipatory peacebuilding: Critical responses to (neo)liberal trends. In T. Matyok, J. Senehi, & S. Byrne (Eds.), *Critical issues in peace and conflict studies: Implications for theory, practice, and pedagogy* (pp. 115–142). Routledge.

Vinthagen, S., & Johansson, A. (2013). "Everyday resistance": Exploration of a concept and its theories. *Resistance Studies Magazine* (1), 1–46.

Wehr, P., & Lederach, J. P. (1991). Mediating conflict in Central America. *Journal of Peace Research, 28*(1), 85–98.

25
TRANSFORMATIVE PEACE NEGOTIATION

SungYong Lee

How can a national-level peace negotiation reflect the social and cultural needs of various social actors? Over the past decades, efforts have been made by the peace-supporting actors to make peacebuilding more inclusive, emancipatory, locally driven, and ultimately promote sustainable peace. In the academic debates, themes like local ownership, hybrid peace, everyday peace, and resilience have been explored in pursuit of this objective. In field practice, mechanisms to identify and reflect community actors' perspectives have been developed. At least in principle, the local turn emerged on the mainstream agenda in the contemporary peacebuilding sector.

Despite the new trend in international peacebuilding, peace negotiation at the national level has remained under the dominant influence of the conventional approaches favoring elite-driven and liberal models. Academic studies on this topic tend to conceptualize peace negotiation as a process mainly for a small number of elites and adopt the rationalist theories developed from Western cultural backgrounds. Many studies on peace negotiation "do not take account of the long-term processes that shape the outcome of peace" nor consider the link between the negotiation process and the larger peacebuilding in the relevant societies (Eriksson & Kostić, 2013, p. 9, 17; Lehti, 2019). From early examples in Mozambique and Cambodia to more recent examples in Mindanao and in Myanmar, a majority of contemporary peace negotiations in ethnic conflicts have been conducted within this framework. Although more recent studies began to seek the transformation of such a rigid format of negotiation, the debates are still at an early stage of development (Paffenholz & Zartman, 2019).

This chapter considers the relatively understudied topic of transformative peace negotiation. Its primary objective is to help readers who are not familiar with the relevant topics by providing an overview of the recent academic debates and introducing relevant case studies. Moreover, this chapter aims to contribute to the ongoing academic debates by articulating a few practical and theoretical implications demonstrated by the case studies of Aceh and Bougainville. Specifically, the following discussions focus on two thematic areas of academic debates that attempt to make peace negotiation more reflective of local needs: inclusive negotiation, and cultural reflection. While the former aims to expand the scope of participants that was once limited to elite groups, the latter intends to move beyond the liberal-rational framework of conventional negotiation.

Background

The theories and practice of peace negotiation have traditionally been under the dominant influence of the so-called problem-solving approach, which understands negotiation as interest-based bargaining. Many studies also rely on the positivist perspectives that seek to discover the universal principles or conditions for successful negotiations. The negotiation strategies presented in these studies are based on the distinctive features of Western culture, including individualism, egalitarianism, and low-context communications (Ting-Toomey, 1999). Especially, the assumption of the "rationality of humankind" is widely accepted as the most fundamental framework. Moreover, individualist societies tend to have the "outcome-oriented" model, which emphasizes the importance of interests and tangible rather than "process oriented" outcomes. Many theories' models like game theories, ripeness theory, and integrative bargaining have been proposed and explored in Peace and Conflict Studies (PACS) from these perspectives (Jeong, 2010).

Nevertheless, with the emergence of *conflict transformation* as a new paradigm in the early 1990s, an increasing number of studies began to explore new approaches to peace negotiation in PACS. Moving beyond its conventional objective to mitigate the conflictual interests and perspectives between parties, researchers adopting the new paradigm to conceptualize peace negotiation as a process "to get to the root causes of a conflict and not merely to treat its episodic or symptomatic manifestation, that is, a particular dispute" (Avruch, 1998, p. 26). Since then, a variety of studies have explored ways to transform peace negotiation and conflict resolution so that they better contribute to long-term peacebuilding. Within these debates, two prominent directions, among others, are those calling for inclusivity in the process and cultural adaptability.

First, these studies found that, due to its Western-oriented and elite drive format, conventional peace negotiation usually alienates the wider population in the conflict-affected societies from its process and does not reflect their priorities in the final agreements. Accordingly, the outcomes usually focus on military security, distribution of power, and institution building, failing to acknowledge and reflect the priorities of the social actors who are excluded in the negotiation process. Due to this limitation, the agreed settlements face many challenges during the implementation process or often play counterproductive roles in consolidating peace in conflict-affected areas (Lehti, 2019; Wanis-St-John, 2008). Especially in the societies with ethnic conflicts that faced fragmented and competing identities, such elite-drive negotiation intensifies people's sense of exclusion and marginalization (Rausch & Luu, 2017; Ross, 2007; Volkan, 1997).

In this regard, an increasing number of studies propose to open up the negotiation process to the participation of wider social groups (Paffenholz & Zartman, 2019). Inclusion is often further conceptualized articulating the difference between horizontal inclusions (between the political and military groups who engaged in the conflicts) and vertical inclusions (between the elite groups and the actors who are under their influence). The critical scholarship in the peacebuilding discourse pays primary attention to vertical inclusion, especially the inclusion of marginalized groups like women (Bell, 2019). Some studies examined the dynamics of such vertical inclusion based on the types of participation that include direct representation in negotiation: As an observer for selected groups, consultation, inclusive commissions, involvement in high-level problem-solving workshops, public decision-making processes, and mass action (Paffenholz, 2015).

It should not be assumed, studies argue, that a more inclusive negotiation process automatically brings about more transformative outcomes. Nevertheless, an inclusive process is expected to offer important platforms for enhancing the overall peace process. An immediate benefit of such wide participation is enhancement of the legitimacy of the process. The increase in legitimacy is particularly emphasized in the studies that call for the inclusion of hard-line actors who are skeptical about the peace process. Moreover, the negotiating parties can utilize participating actors' mediating skills, expert knowledge on the relevant agenda, and communication channels to the general population (Paffenholz, 2016; Rausch & Luu, 2017). From the participating actors' perspectives, more importantly, such inclusive negotiation offers a great opportunity to build their capacity for mobilizing collective voices, networking with other social groups, engaging in public discussions, and utilizing their leverages for negotiation. Moreover, empirical studies confirmed that the participation of a wider group of actors has positive correlations with the durability of peace processes, especially when such participation is *meaningful* (Nilsson, 2012; Paffenholz, 2015).

Second, another major line of debate concerns the dominant framework of peace negotiation that mostly reflects Western worldviews. Especially between the early 1980s and the mid-1990s, a serious question was raised about the Western-oriented approaches to conflict resolution and the assumption of its universality. The problem is, since many countries that require peace negotiation are non-Western, the key actors involved in the negotiation process have considerable difficulty in relating to the nature of the negotiation. Vice versa, by placing too much emphasis on Western approaches, mediators and facilitators are destined to fail to understand local people's core motives for conflicts and negotiations (Brett, 2000; Schirch, 2005, p. 35).

In ethnic conflicts, especially, cultural and perceptual issues are deeply embedded in the violent conflicts, and thus, the studies argue, negotiation in this context should be understood as a "matter of perception and belief, of cognition and affect" (Avruch, 1998, p. 27). A mismatch in the norms and understandings of conflict resolution between groups is likely to create unnecessary disruptions during the negotiation and may generate resistance from the national/local actors involved in the process. Such a discrepancy may be an important barrier to the implementation and settlement of peace agreements as well (Lee, 2011). Hence, theorists in this tradition believe that understanding the cultural traits of actors is "the first step in a successful intervention" (Avruch et al., 1991 cited in Fisher, 2001, p. 17), and the debates have been developed in various ways.

From this standpoint, a large number of empirical studies have examined various culturally embedded norms and behavioural patterns that affect the dynamics of conflict resolution (Avruch, 1998; Avruch & Black, 2009; Lederach, 1995; Zion, 1998). For instance, a group of studies pay attention to the psychosocial aspects of negotiation and examine people's perceptions toward negotiation in different cultural contexts. These cultural and structural contexts include hierarchical relations versus horizontal relations, individualism versus collectivism, high-context communication versus low-context communication, and homogeneity versus heterogeneity (Chew, 2001; LeBaron, 2003). More recent studies clarify the diversities and discrepancies in the cultural contexts within an area or society and the impact of such diversities on conflict resolution. Some of these studies pay particular attention to understanding various indigenous practices from postcolonial perspectives. Reflecting on these perspectives, numerous empirical studies have introduced and examined the negotiation and mediation practices that are more inclusive and culturally reflective. To risk overgeneralization, many of these studies fall into one of the following categories: the amalgamation of Western and non-Western practices; revitalization of preexisting indigenous practices; and external actors' elicitive trainings for local actors (Pearson D'Éstrée, 2018).

Indeed, the studies introduced earlier have made significant contributions in explaining nontraditional forms of negotiation that can be adopted and the strengths and limitations of such forms. Nevertheless, it should be noted that the extensive empirical discussion on such non-traditional peace negotiation mostly focuses on the practice at substate levels. Regarding the official peace negotiation at national/international levels which is still facilitated as one of the most important elements of the peace process, it is also valid and important to explore the possibility of transforming such conventional negotiation to be more emancipatory. This chapter, in this regard, is a modest step to address this gap by examining two sets of national peace negotiations undertaken in Aceh and Bougainville. The case studies which follow will focus on two particular questions: What do nonconventional forms of peace negotiation look like in practice? In what sense do the new forms bring about better opportunities for successful peace negotiation that can contribute to long-term peacebuilding?

Key insights

Promotion of an inclusive process in Aceh

This section examines how civil society groups in Aceh created the opportunity to take part in the national peace negotiation and managed their contribution throughout the process. For a civil society actor, it is not easy to have *meaningful* participation in peace negotiations as many decision-makers and negotiators are concerned about the potential challenges that may arise from the new formats. Probably the most important issue is the ongoing conflict itself. Many peace negotiations are initiated while violent conflicts are still active and the process for mobilizing wide participation in the new initiatives may face many practical challenges. Moreover, the increase in stakeholders may complicate the negotiation process as the coordination of dissimilar interests, behaviors and strategic grouping can be extremely tricky. Many negotiation strategies and tactics developed in the business sectors and traditional diplomacy are not compatible with the inclusive conflict resolution process itself. From a more fundamental level, the selection of the new representatives may intensify the resentment and suspicion of groups still marginalized from the process (Özerdem & Lee, 2016; Paffenholz & Ross, 2015).

For making meaningful participation, therefore, social groups need to overcome this perceptual and systemic resistance. The Acehnese civil society's participation in the peace negotiation on Aceh, Indonesia, in 2005 (which is often called the Helsinki Process) offers insights relevant to such an endeavor. The civil conflict in Aceh is rooted in the Indonesian independence process that left many Acehnese feel marginalized from the new nation state. Acehnese' anxiety intensified when the promise of the first Indonesian president, Sukarno, to implement Islamic Law in the area was reversed by the next leader, Suharto. Among the military resistance groups mobilized, the most notable one was the Free Aceh Movement (*Gerakan Aceh Merdeka*, GAM), established by Hasan di Tiro in 1976, which called for a democratic and federal governance system that acknowledges the differences of Acehnese. The peace process between the Government of Indonesia (GoI) and GAM started in the early 2000s only after the authoritarian Suharto regime was challenged by reformist movements. During the early process, the civil society actors were also mostly marginalized. While many civil society organizations like KontraS Aceh and CORDOVA as well as student movements had conducted various campaigns and programs, these actors were not acknowledged by either GoI or GAM until the mid-2000s. However, the process of negotiation also faced many challenges and did not come to fruition for years.

It was ironic that a new opportunity for a more inclusive peace process was opened by the massive tsunami that hit Indonesia in December 2004. With its devastating impact, both GoI and GAM prioritized relief activities, often collaborating with each other for the implementation of recovery programs. Moreover, a large number of foreign NGOs came to the tsunami-affected areas including Aceh. Through interaction with such international actors, and as it became more deeply involved in talks with GoI, GAM gradually realized the importance of gaining legitimacy as the representative of Acehnese and as an organization open to the voices of civil society in order to win support from the international community (Wandi & Patria, 2015).

Hence, when a new series of peace talks started in January 2005, GAM invited civil society actors in Aceh to a consultation. The first consultation meeting took place in May 2005 in Saltsjobaden, Sweden, immediately before Round 4 of the peace talks and was supported by a Swedish NGO, the Olaf Palme International Center (OPIC). The communication process, led by GAM, focused on presenting a document that summarized the progress and explained its position on a few key issues. In response, the civil society representatives raised questions about a number of key issues like independence, self-government, and democratization in Aceh. Moreover, the majority of the participants called for a referendum to enable Acehnese to determine their future, and demanded mechanisms for ensuring democratization and freedom of speech (Kingsbury, 2006, p. 93). In addition, during their stay in Sweden, the civil society actors lobbied some international NGOs for a ceasefire as a condition of their material support for rehabilitation and reconstruction. At the end of the meeting, the civil society actors issued a statement, which expressed their support for the ongoing negotiation and reaffirmed their demands.

From GAM's perspective, it was a "considerable success," as stated by OPIC, in that it consolidated the civil society's support for GAM's legitimacy as the representative of Aceh. Moreover, the official backing of the civil society actors for the continuation of the peace process meant an additional pressure on the Indonesian government to stay at the negotiation table, which was GAM's hope. From the civil society's perspective, it was the first ever opportunity to directly speak to the GAM negotiators and present their opinions. They had similar discussions over key agenda items, considering various risks and expected benefits of having a referendum. In this regard, it was an opportunity for the civil society actors to understand and "socialize" the significance and implications of the ongoing negotiation (Kingsbury, 2006).

The second GAM-civil society meeting took place in July 2005 in Lidingo, Sweden, and it was closer to a *meaningful* participation of civil society in a number of ways. First, the meeting was initiated and organized by GAM who appreciated the benefits of having such a consultation process. Nur Djuli, a key figure in the negotiation team, took the lead in organizing the meeting while OPIC still offered logistical support. Second, while the first meeting invited the civil society actors who had maintained a collaborative relationship with GAM, the second one expanded the scope to include the actors critical to GAM's directions. Third, GAM was more willing to reflect the civil society's voices and to present a show of unity with it. Moreover, compared to the first meeting, the communication was more reciprocal. Both GAM representatives and the civil society actors had an opportunity to present "official reports" at the beginning of the meeting. Concerns were raised that the ongoing negotiation did not consider a referendum or any agenda on social issues such as education, public health, and women's rights. Although their demand for a referendum failed to be included on the agenda, all participants engaged in an extensive dialogue with the GAM representatives. The participants agreed to make a joint statement from GAM and the civil society when concluding the discussion (Kingsbury, 2006, p. 110).

After the final round concluded with the signing of the Helsinki Memorandum of Understanding (MOU), GAM and the civil society in Aceh had another meeting in August 2005 in Malaysia. Some 230 individuals representing different social groups attended the meeting. GAM requested that these representatives support the peace agreement (Kingsbury, 2006). The contribution of civil society became more significant during the process of drafting the Law on Governing of Aceh. As the MOU had no legal ground and the GoI, GAM and the Acehnese public often presented significantly different interpretations of some provisions (especially on the scope of Aceh's autonomy), the MOU had to be enacted into a law. GAM requested four local universities to draft the law, and these universities and other involved organizations hosted and participated in a large number of public forums to get input from various communities in Aceh (Taqwaddin, 2013). Once the ideas were integrated into a draft law, it was circulated to thousands of representatives from various social groups for feedback, before Aceh's local government confirmed it as its official proposal (May, 2008; Wandi & Patria, 2015).

The participation of the Acehnese civil society obviously does not present an ideal type of meaningful participation. Their roles during the negotiation were limited to observer and consultation group. While they pushed forward their demands to GAM, many of them were shut out or compromised at the levels of GAM's internal decision-making and the bargaining between GAM and the GoI. Even the draft law made by the civil society actors and approved by GAM had gone through a substantial revision in the final enactment process. Having said this, the role of the civil society in Aceh during the peace process presents two types of inclusion: consultation and inclusive commissions. Moreover, this transformation of their roles in the peace process in a sense meant the growth of the Acehnese civil society into a meaningful actor in the governance. It is noticeable that the civil society actors who were largely marginalized throughout the negotiation process created the opportunity to take part in the process as an official consultation group to GAM. Then, it concretized its presence and expanded its role during the third and fourth rounds of the peace talks. For instance, their two main goals—protection of human rights and the mechanisms for transitional justice—were extensively discussed during the fourth round of the Helsinki process, and ended up with the agreement to have a human rights court and a truth and reconciliation commission. During the postagreement enactment process, civil society played key roles in developing and revising the legal draft that would determine their own future.

Culturally reflective third-party mediation: Bougainville

This section considers how nonconventional forms of peace negotiation can be facilitated by external mediators, and examines New Zealand's involvement in the Bougainville peace negotiation in 1997 and 1998. The mediation team adopted many formats for confidence building and bargaining, reflecting both Bougainville's traditional customs and New Zealand's Indigenous Māori traditions.

The civil conflict in Bougainville was largely related to the development of mineral resources (especially copper) since the 1960s, which had generated various issues like breach of land ownership, environmental destruction, economic polarization, and tensions with local communities and with new laborers from other areas of Papua New Guinea. A group of landowners organized the Panguna Landowners Association in 1979, and some of its splinter groups mobilized military frontlines like the Bougainville Revolutionary Army (BRA), the Bougainville Resistance Force (BRF) in the late 1980s. BRA declared Bougainville's independence and established the Bougainville Interim Government (BIG) in 1990. After many failed peace initiatives throughout the 1990s, a new peace process started in 1997 with the mediation of New Zealand, Australia, and the Solomon Islands. I pay particular attention to the first three rounds of negotiations that took place at the Burnham army camp and Lincoln University in Christchurch, New Zealand, in 1997 and 1998, where an important foundation for further negotiation was established and tentative agreements on a few major issues were made.

Why did the New Zealand mediation team decide to adopt formats that are radically different from conventional negotiation procedures? One immediate reason was the repeated failure of the previous attempts at conflict resolution since 1990 and a political crisis in Bougainville that was caused by the Papua New Guinean government's plan to hire a private military consultancy company (Sandline International) in 1997. New Zealand felt a sense of urgency about making a breakthrough in the peace process. New Zealand mediators wanted to achieve this goal by "invit[ing] the parties, provid[ing] for their needs, and let[ting] them find their own way" (McMillan, 1998, p. 7) without imposing any agenda or rules. At a more fundamental level, however, an important factor is the promotion of biculturalism in New Zealand, which aims to revitalize and reflect the Indigenous Māori culture in all aspects of social activities. The New Zealand Army, for instance, started to incorporate such indigenous practice into their social activities and principles as early as the first World War. Hence, adoption of indigenous forms of rituals and dialogue forms in negotiation was not new to the core New Zealand mediators. Moreover, a few people involved in the peace process like John Hayes were familiar with the social and cultural contexts in Bougainville and wider Papua New Guinea.

Hence, it was not a radical decision for New Zealand's mediation team to apply various non-Western formats of negotiation in order to make the process more compatible with the Melanesian approach to peacebuilding and the Bougainville contexts. This section reviews some of these features focusing on three broad categories. First, as the negotiation at the Burnham camp was the first occasion that the key stakeholders of the Bougainville conflicts had sat together, the New Zealand mediators' primary goal was "confidence building" between the participants. A range of cultural ceremonies and negotiation formats were used that reflected New Zealand's Indigenous Māori culture and the Melanesian cultures.

On arrival, for instance, the delegations from the Bougainville groups received a *Pōwhiri*, the New Zealand's traditional ritual for welcoming people. By observing and participating in the Māori practice for relation building, it was intended that the participants feel that they had arrived in an area of the Pacific, not an entirely alien (Western) area (Bede Corry cited in MFAT, n.d.). The next morning, the delegates were requested to engage in a *hongi*, the traditional format for greetings. Participants shook hands and pressed noses to exchange the breath of life, which symbolized shared common bonds and experience (Lees et al., n.d.). During the *hongi*, the Māori facilitators asked the delegates if they were there for peace or warfare in order to facilitate the atmosphere for conflict resolution. Moreover, to offer a more comfortable environment, the Burnham camp facilitated the negotiators to enjoy their own cultural practices like chewing betel nut as well as providing pidgin speakers to support them (Rosanowski, 2001).

Second, when the negotiation started, the mediation team decided to offer a good office by adopting nontraditional formats for dialogue. These features were contradictory to many conventional theories and diplomatic manuals that acknowledge the significant role of time pressure and encourage participants to stay away from people's emotion (Bebchick, 2002; Fisher et al., 1991; Zartman & Berman, 1982). For instance, New Zealand facilitated the negotiation without any time restriction and any set goals for achievements. The concern about time-constraint was raised by a Bougainville government official who participated in a prenegotiation meeting, who mentioned "earlier meetings had not succeeded because they had insufficient time to resolve internal difficulties" (Robert Tapi, cited in Pinfari, 2013, p. 80). The parties expressed "a strong preference for a slowly-paced negotiation process" (Pinfari, 2013, p. 80). Hence, the New Zealand mediators decided to support Bougainvilleans to "consult […] without time constraints, and once they had reached common ground, to go to PNG with proposals for more substantive peace talks" (AFP 1997, cited in Pinfari, 2013, p. 80).

Another important feature is that the New Zealand facilitators adopted *taraut*, a Bougainvillean practice "where participants voice every painful thought and feeling to the entire group" (MFAT, n.d.). The speakers were allowed to express their views in full without any interruptions; hence, the process involved long, large, and intense meetings. The *taraut* was conducted both in one group and in smaller groups. In the earlier stages of *taraut*, no agenda was set as people focused on expressing their anxiety. In the conversations, people often became emotional enough to shout at each other or attempt to commit violence. The New Zealand mediators minimized their involvement apart from intervening to prevent violence. Moreover, in order to cool down emotional tensions between individuals which intensified during *taraut* and other negotiation, the delegates took short trips to local places via bus or train and attended cultural events in between the negotiation rounds. One of the places that they visited was local *marae*, a communal and sacred place in the Māori culture, where cultural and social activities take place. There, the participants also shared *hangi* (traditional Māori meal). By creating occasions where "the casual encounters [were] inevitable," it was intended that the atmosphere gradually became "conducive to mixing, healing and the promotion of trust" (Rosanowski, 2001, p. 192).

Third, a wide range of local leaders was invited to the negotiation process, such as women's groups, the churches, and local chiefs. The role that women' delegations played is especially noteworthy. In traditional societies in Bougainville, the active involvement of women as mothers of the land in social, customary, and intraclan activities is significant although they are rarely involved in political matters. By using their extensive network and social legitimacy, women's groups had already conducted various campaigns and peacebuilding initiatives throughout the civil conflicts. Thus, the inclusion of women was not only necessary to reflect their views but also culturally important to acknowledge and utilize women's commitment. Many women participants indeed played key roles during the negotiation by using their moral legitimacy, personal connections to the leaders of the military groups, and their networking and communication skills.

For instance, in the processes of *taraut* stated earlier, women leaders were "a cooling system for the engine" to lower the emotional tensions (Page, 2012). A report on the Burnham process states: "They (women participants) would say 'Look, I am here, there is my son over there, and over there is my other son. And all of you, you are all our sons'" (Lees et al., n.d., p. 10). During the process at Lincoln, moreover, 22 women from different backgrounds conducted a story-sharing process where they talked about their personal experience and expressed an embracing of each other. After this process, those who initially attended to represent different resistance groups joined together to call for the two resistance groups to make a collective voice to represent the whole of Bougainville. Moreover, when the negotiation was dealing with the establishment of the new parliament in the post-conflict phase, the women's group collectively demanded the creation of a 12-seat quota for women. The number of seats for the women's quota eventually settled at three. After returning from the Burnham camp, some of these women leaders organized and coordinated women's groups to spread the information around Bougainville (Lees et al., n.d., p. 10).

As a result, the series of peace talks facilitated by New Zealand in 1997 and 1998 was arguably "the turning point of the Bougainville conflict and a crucial step for the development of the peace process" (Pinfari, 2013, pp. 76–77) and exceeded many people's expectation (McMillan, 1998, p. 2). While the negotiation started after the continued mutual violence and with the fear of the collapse of the peace process prior to the negotiation, the process managed to encourage the military groups in Bougainville to develop a formalized truce and produce several agreements that delineated the direction of future peace process.

Implications for teaching and training

So far, this chapter has described and examined the peace negotiations in Aceh and Bougainville to learn how transformative peace negotiation can work in practice, offering alternative or supplementary features to the conventional elite-driven and liberal formats of national negotiation. Then, what do these case studies say about new improvements to national-level peace negotiation? This section considers a few practical and theoretical implications related to this question that are critical to teaching and training about transformative peace negotiation.

First, under what circumstances can new forms of negotiation be adopted in national-level peace negotiation? Once a process is set to follow the conventional framework, it is obviously not easy to transform its key features. However, a peace process in civil conflict usually follows a long and challenging process that involves the repetition of dialogue, settlement, collapse, and renegotiation. While this is the challenging nature of conflict resolution, it may offer a suitable opportunity for wider social groups to get involved. In Aceh and Bougainville, such an opportunity came from two main factors, crises that required an urgent response and the influence of external supporters. Both factors (directly or indirectly) encouraged the elite negotiators to see the value of reflecting the support of wider society and incorporating indigenous cultural approaches.

Moreover, partly due to the urgency of the prior crises, the participating actors' genuine commitment enabled them to continue and further develop the new features of the negotiation. In Aceh, for example, one major concern related to the inclusion of the civil society was the management of confidentiality. Increasing the number of participants meant a higher risk of disseminating information. However, knowing the anxiety of GAM, the civil society representatives managed to keep an embargo on the information given to public media in the two rounds of the consultation process in Sweden.[1] Moreover, in the negotiation over Bougainville, while the participants fully committed to the *taraut* process often involving violent expressions, they also carefully managed their mutual interaction not to cause the collapse of the talks.

Second, in what sense do these new features enable peace negotiation to contribute to the promotion of sustainable peace? It is premature to present definite answers to this question in that the new features in the two case studies present many limitations to being *transformative* and the evaluation of their impact on sustainable peace requires systematic and long-term research. Nevertheless, the case studies above do present two positive changes. One noticeable point is the capacity building of the participating actors. The civil society actors in Aceh and women's groups in Bougainville learned how to behave in the negotiation and developed their communication skills as they gained more experience and, through the experience, they played even more proactive roles during the post-conflict reconstruction processes at local and national levels (Lees et al., n.d.). The second point is about the culturally reflective mediation of New Zealand, which further strengthened the Bougainville representatives' trust in New Zealand. The trusting and collaborative relationship laid the foundation for New Zealand's further involvement in post-conflict peacekeeping and development (MFAT, n.d.).

Having said this, it should be acknowledged that these examples demonstrate the limit of the *ad hoc* arrangement. Although they adopted significantly different formats and procedures in some areas, the overall structure of both negotiations still heavily relied on the liberal-rationalist framework. For instance, when the civil society actors in Aceh and women in Bougainville continued to present demands that seemed incompatible with the interests of elite negotiators, the negotiators chose to exclude the demands from the other participating actors to make the decision-making easier. The culturally reflected formats for dialogue also disappeared in the later phases of the Bougainville peace processes. This issue is partly due to the elite negotiators' attitudes prioritizing their own goals, desire to make quick settlement, and concerns about the reactions of other parties involved in the negotiation. The weakened presence of New Zealand as a mediator was another reason.

Nevertheless, at a more fundamental level, the aforementioned issue is largely attributed to the liberal-democratic paradigm itself. While the liberal democracy in principle appreciates diversity and encourages inclusive participation, it assumes that citizens' preferences or opinions can be, or should be, formed and transformed through public deliberation. According to this approach, a peace process should aim to reach agreement among the participants on the issues at stake. Hence, when the participating actors demonstrate radically different views or uncompromising attitudes, the liberal negotiation model does not offer any good methods for handling them. In other words, even in the case where the elite negotiators in Aceh and Bougainville wanted to further reflect the perspectives of the civil society and women's groups, they might not have been able to do so as long as they adopted the liberal-democratic framework of negotiation. Although the innovative efforts of the negotiators and mediators in the aforementioned case studies should be properly acknowledged, in this regard, there is a limit that such *ad hoc* arrangements cannot move beyond.

Implications for practice and policy

From a theoretical perspective, this observation calls for more systematic changes to the framework of peace negotiation in order to make it more culturally adaptive and inclusive. This has practice and policy implications for peace negotiations. The exploration of such a fundamentally alternative framework for negotiation that can be more suitable for promoting transformative peacebuilding is underresearched; various approaches can be undertaken to fill this research gap. As a proposal for future research, for example, the discourse on *agonistic pluralism* offers some insights. According to the proponents of agonistic pluralism, consensus or commonality is a difficult, fragile, and contingent achievement of political action and should not be considered a normative or ethical precondition for good relations. Instead, agonistic pluralism acknowledges and appreciates the centrality of conflict to human social actions and argues that a democratic society should allow citizens to freely contest the terms of public life (Mouffe, 1999; Schaap, 2006; Shinko, 2008). When adopting this approach, negotiation participants will not prioritize the achievement of consensus. Instead, they will pay more attention to seeking a procedure in which all actors will continue to nonviolently engage in dialogue, and will constantly select and modify what is to be discussed, agreed, and postponed for further discussion.

Note

1 In fact, the break of embargo occurred once from GoI's side, following which both GoI and GAM took prompt actions to minimize its impact (Wandi & Patria, 2015).

References

Avruch, K. (1998). *Culture and conflict resolution*. USIP Press.
Avruch, K., & Black, P. (2009). The culture question and conflict resolution. *Peace and Change, 16*(1), 22–45.
Avruch, K., Black, P., & Scimecca, J. (Eds.) (1991). *Conflict resolution: Cross-cultural perspectives*. Greenwood.
Bebchick, B. (2002). The philosophy and methodology of ambassador Dennis Ross as an international mediator. *International Negotiation, 7*(1), 115–131.
Bell, C. (2019). New inclusion project: Building inclusive peace settlements, *Accord, 28*(1), 11–17.
Brett, J. (2000). Culture and negotiation. *International Journal of Psychology, 25*(2), 97–104.
Chew, P. (2001). *The conflict and culture readers*. New York University Press.
Eriksson, M., & Kostić, R. (2013). Peacemaking and peacebuilding: Two ends of a tail. In M. Eriksson & R. Kostić (Eds.), *Mediation and liberal peacebuilding: Peace from the ashes of war?* (pp. 21–37). Routledge.
Fisher, R. (2001). *Methods of third-party intervention*. Berghof Research Center for Constructive Conflict Management.
Fisher, R., Ury, W., & Patton, B. (1991). *Getting to yes* (3rd Edition). Business Books.
Jeong, H. (2010). *Conflict management and resolution: An introduction*. Routledge.
Kingsbury, D. (2006). *Peace in Aceh: A personal account of the Helsinki peace*. Equinox Publishing. https://www.beyondintractability.org/essay/culture_negotiation
LeBaron, M. (2003). *Bridging cultural conflicts: A new approach for a changing world*. Jossey Bass.
Lederach, J. P. (1995). *Preparing for peace: Negotiating across cultures*. Syracuse University Press.
Lee, S. Y. (2011). The limit of ethnocentric perceptions in civil war peace negotiations. *Conflict Resolution Quarterly, 28*(3), 349–373.
Lees, S., Havini, M., & Murdock, J. (n.d.). *Bougainville peace agreements: The Burnham I and II dialogues*. Pacific Peace Community and UNDP.
Lehti, M. (2019). *The era of private peacemakers: A new dialogic approach to mediation*. Palgrave Macmillan.
May, B. (2008). The law on the governing of Aceh: The way forward or a source of conflicts? *Accord, 20*(1), 43–45.
McMillan, S. (1998). Bringing peace to Bougainville. *New Zealand International Review, 23*(3), 2–9.
Mouffe, C. (1999). Deliberative democracy or agonistic pluralism? *Social Research, 66*(3), 745–758.
New Zealand Ministry of Foreign Affairs and Trade (MFAT) (n.d.) A risky assignment – Bougainville. https://www.mfat.govt.nz/en/about-us/mfat75/bougainville-a-risky-assignment/
Nilsson, D. (2012). Anchoring the peace: Civil society actors in peace accords and durable peace. *International Interactions, 38*(2), 243–266.
Özerdem, A., & Lee, S. Y. (2016). *International peacebuilding: An introduction*. Routledge.
Paffenholz, T. (2016). *Inclusion and legitimacy in contemporary peace and transition process*. IHS Working Paper Series 1(2). Tufts University.
Paffenholz, T. (2015). *Broadening participation project*. Briefing Paper. The Graduate Institute of International and Development Studies.
Paffenholz, T., & Ross, N. (2015). Inclusive peace process: an introduction. *Development Dialogue, 63*(1), 28–37.
Paffenholz, T., & Zartman, I. W. (2019). Inclusive peace negotiations. *International Negotiations, 24*(1), 1–6.
Page, D. (2012). *Complexities and context: Women's peacebuilding in conflict and post-conflict Bougainville* (Master's Dissertation, Victoria University of Wellington).
Pearson D'Éstrée, T., (Ed.) (2018). *New directions in peacebuilding evaluation*. Rowman and Littlefield.
Pinfari, M. (2013). *Peace negotiations and time*. Routledge.
Rausch, C., & Luu, T. (2017). Inclusive peace processes are key to ending violent conflict. USIP Peace Brief 222. https://www.usip.org/publications/2017/05/inclusive-peace-processes-are-key-ending-violent-conflict
Rosanowski, T. (2001). *Resolving the Bougainville conflict* (Master Dissertation, University of Canterbury).
Ross, M. (2007). *Cultural contestation in ethnic conflict*. Cambridge University Press.
Schaap, A. (2006). Agonism in divided societies. *Philosophy and Social Criticism, 32*(2), 255–277.
Schirch, L. (2005). *Ritual and symbol in peacebuilding*. Kumarian Press.
Shinko, R. (2008). Agonistic peace: A postmodern reading. *Millennium, 36*(3), 473–491.

Taqwaddin, D. (2013). *The roles of civil society in Aceh conflict management* (Doctoral Dissertation, Universiti Utara Malaysia).

Ting-Toomey, S. (1999). *Communicating across cultures*. Guilford Press.

Volkan, V. (1997). *Bloodlines: From ethnic pride to ethnic terrorism*. Farrar, Straus, Giroux.

Wandi, A., & Patria, N. (2015). *The rebels, the state and the people: Inclusivity in the Aceh peace process – IPS Paper 18*. Berlin: Berghof Foundation.

Wanis-St-John, A. (2008). Peace processes, secret negotiations and civil society: Dynamics of inclusion and exclusion. *International Negotiation, 13*(1), 1–9.

Zartman, W., & Berman, M. (1982). *The practical negotiator*. Yale University Press.

Zion, J. W. (1998). The dynamics of Navajo peacemaking. *Journal of Contemporary Criminal Justice, 14*(1), 58–74.

26
EXTERNAL AID AND PEACEBUILDING

Sean Byrne and Calum Dean

External aid is an integral component of the liberal peace agenda as local everyday peacebuilders and their practices are typically excluded (Hyde & Byrne, 2015). The power remains with external donors who implement the IKEA peacebuilding model including democratic governance, elections, human rights, and security reform as local resilient networks and communities resist and negotiate their relationships with donors (Mac Ginty, 2015). The local and the international are complex and are not binary opposites containing liberal and illiberal peace modes' with resistance often directed against local elites rather than external donors (Paffenholz, 2015). What insights can applying economic aid to ethnopolitical peacebuilding provide?

Background

Foreign aid was used during the Cold War to support allies; to enhance foreign policy, development, economic, humanitarian, and peacebuilding efforts; today, it is used as part of the liberal democratic peace.

The role of economic aid

Foreign aid maintained unequal relationships with former colonies during the decolonization process; as part of the Millennium and Sustainable Development Goals as external donors determined how the agreements, conditions, and policies shaped domestic policies and which sectors the aid was channeled to (Engerman, 2018). It is critical to look at aid within the local, national, and global levels of analysis to explore geopolitical, strategic, and neoliberal economic and political interests (Bilzen, 2015). During the 1990s, humanitarian development focused on the social sector and unfettered aid as the new millennium centered on the eradication of poverty, liberalism, and neoliberal peacebuilding in contrast to the 2010s concentration on recipient's ownership and economic growth (Bilzen, 2015). The OECD Paris Declaration on Aid Effectiveness (2005) has been drafted into aid frameworks.

Recipient states' ownership of aid can boost its effectiveness in terms of human capital, labor, and productivity as well as working with civil society organizations (CSOs) and nongovernmental organizations (NGOs) that help to curtail corruption (Edwards, 2015). Aid could also be perceived as a transaction with the decision-making donor negotiating with recipients that are also influencing the bargaining process in terms of policy changes and the allocation of the aid to particular projects or to fulfill people's basic human needs (Wang, 2016).

Interdependent development partnerships between donors and recipients could go up against neoliberal hegemony opening up new possibilities for civil society actors to renegotiate power relations around equality that exploit local actors (McCann, 2015) to facilitate more joint allocation over aid disbursement so that the aid is effective in positively impacting political stability, good governance, and strong institutions as well as influencing economic growth and strong economic policies in the long term to alleviate poverty in the recipient country that impact health care, educational levels, life expectancy, and standards of living (Ishnazarov & Cevik, 2017; Saibu & Obioesio, 2017; Tang & Bundhoo, 2017).

Yet when the aid lies below a certain inception, it may not improve a country's economic growth in the Global South, as the aid must exceed 6.7 percent of Gross National Income (GNI) to be positively correlated with economic growth (Larsen, 2016). Where there is more flow of foreign direct investment, trade, and development aid into Global South countries, environmental policies must also be strictly enforced against extricating resources and pollution as often the aid does not facilitate policies to protect the local environment (Lim et al., 2015).

Or development aid is a form of "gift giving" that recipients are free to accept or decline that creates an interdependent cooperation in which donors keep order by disbursing and controlling the aid, and the recipients can create disorder by misusing the aid through corruption as typically local elites benefit to the detriment of poor local people (Furia, 2015). In addition, external aid can be tied into the "Samaritan dilemma" as the donor establishes and plans funding around a development goal as domestic governments move their funds away from that goal to attract more donor funds as donors decide whether or not to increase funding (Kumar, 2015).

Local governments often use the aid to foster economic growth to attract foreign direct investment even though the aid typically does not positively impact economic growth over the long term, and it can foster dependency on donor aid. Program aid can also nurture human capital and social development (ownership and coordination of projects) rather than economic growth compared to project aid that can stimulate economic growth yet create alignment, coordination, and planning (Janjua et al., 2018). However, contexts are complex and dynamic, and it could take a plethora of factors to impact the aid-economic policy, and economic growth connection as its effects are complex (Geng & Hernandez, 2020).

Donor motivations

The Global North maintains its hegemony and interference in recipient's domestic politics through control over resources and knowledge so that there is no real equal partnership between donors and recipients as local communities have little input in the aid distribution, and they must align their governance and institutions with the donor's ideology (Menashy, 2019). Donors support trade liberalization to open up recipient countries and establish multiple conditionalities in dispersing aid supporting internal projects in multiple sectors of society. Bilateral and multilateral aid decisions arise from a myriad of donor motivations as well as recipient need, the recipients' culture, history, policies, and level of political liberalization and donor's economic, geopolitical, security, and strategic interests (Peiffer & Boussalis, 2015).

Moreover, aid is about securing U.S. economic and security interests rather than extending democratic, humanitarian, and human rights values that are often ignored if the civil, political, and human rights violations are carried out by an ally against the needs of poor marginalized communities (e.g., Argentina and Chile during the "Dirty War") (Sandlin, 2018). The United States provides more aid to recipient states that advance U.S. national interests even if they commit human rights abuses (e.g., Hosni Mubarak's quelling of domestic unrest in Egypt during the Arab Spring) (Sandlin, 2016). The media also tends to frame aid for public opinion around the domestic ramifications of aid rather than on the needs of recipient countries' citizens, as well as the application of and the benefits of foreign aid whose support really recede during economic crises (Cawley, 2015).

Global North hegemony over aid structures has been challenged by China, an emerging global power, about whether aid is ineffective in empowering grassroots up development and peacebuilding approaches. One study found that aid-sponsored projects had little impact on local politics in sub-Saharan Africa and political support did not influence aid allocation from China and the World Bank in terms of cultural, economic, and political values (Knutsen & Kotsadam, 2020). The cultural turn in global aid also emphasizes how external norms, values, and interests are superimposed on local communities supporting development projects that facilitate economic growth and political transformation as asymmetric power relations shape how aid workers and civil servants interact with local people and their wisdom and knowledge systems as they keep control over the aid distribution and monitoring process as local people are generally omitted from participation in significant ways (Labadi, 2020).

Donors and the local

Global North donors design and own the structural aid framework with the local in a minimalist role of implementing projects and programs. Countries that have effective relationships with external development partners can better negotiate and maintain ownership of public policy while donors attempt to affect policy and curb local ownership (Aubert et al., 2018). Donors connect with local peacebuilding CSOs that are immersed in the language and ideology of the liberal peace that becomes significant intermediaries between the donors and the local (Creary & Byrne, 2014). Local actors possess a better network connection system and knowledge on local issues compared to external actors (Lee, 2015).

Critical and emancipatory peacebuilding includes a plethora of defiant grassroots voices, and peacebuilding and development practices that empower local people's agency, and ownership of their projects transforming unjust structures in the process (Thiessen, 2011). The resulting tensions between these interactions cause frictions between local and external actors as events unfold on the ground often promoting new hybrid peacebuilding processes (Björkdahl & Höglund, 2013). Hybridity creates an uncomfortable compromise between the donor's knowledge, universal norms, and resources, and local people's wisdom, practices, and human needs (Mac Ginty & Richmond, 2016). Yet a power differential remains between the local and the external especially when aid and peacebuilding and state rebuilding collide leading to conflict and disharmony (Autesserre, 2014).

Key insights

In 1985, the British and Irish governments signed the Anglo-Irish Agreement and established the International Fund for Ireland (IFI) that provided $895 million between 1986 and 2010 to finance close to 6,000 CSO projects throughout Northern Ireland (Skarlato et al., 2013, p. 221). In the wake of the 1994 reciprocal Republican and Loyalist ceasefires, the European Union (EU) created the Peace and Reconciliation Fund to support CSO projects that nurture cross-community development, peacebuilding, and reconciliation (Fissuh et al., 2012). The Peace 3 Fund (2007–2010) provided €225 million, and the EU structural funds added €108 million to aid CSOs facilitating cross-communal ties (Skarlato et al., 2016).

The following discussion flows from an exploratory case study of 120 semistructured interviews with CSO leaders, development officers, and civil servants with the IFI and the EU Peace 3 Fund that was carried out by the first author over a ten-week period in the summer of 2010 in the city of Derry or Londonderry and the Border Counties of Armagh, Cavan, Derry, Donegal, Fermanagh, Leitrim, Louth, Monaghan, and Tyrone. The research findings highlighted that real peace takes time, and it is important to develop the individual and the peace in the individual. The CSO leaders pointed out their need for resources to continue the much-needed work to transform relations and structures to make that cultural mindset shift to instill peaceful values in the people as Northern Ireland continues to remain a highly segregated society. CSOs are important vehicles in the reconciliation and peacebuilding efforts on the ground (Figueiredo et al., 2019).

Many respondents noted that the British colonial process created a dependent culture in Northern Ireland. People have become infantilized lacking the agency to be entrepreneurial and to fend for themselves relying on both funders and British governmental agencies to take care of them. The internalization of oppression and the psychological damage done to a culture and to a people ensures that ethnic groups find it difficult to transcend that experience (Fanon, 2005).

A CSO leader, Donnacha was of the opinion that Peace 2 was a deliberate weeding out process of CSOs by the statutory agencies especially in local rural areas where there was an over reliance on training people with no jobs at the end of it. The Peace and Reconciliation Fund did not plan to have sustainability as a priority and as a measure in Peace 2, and in the legacy, it wanted to leave behind in the region.

> What we always said at the times of Peace 2 funding is that there will be groups going to the wall during Peace 2 funding that won't be able to access it. And we sort of seen in the community that Peace 2 funding was like a weeding process, that groups who didn't last beyond Peace 2 will definitely not get access to what we thought would have been Peace 3 funding because the rumor and the general way of thinking at that time was Peace 3 funding was coming back to the community.

> Peace 2 funding to a certain element started to move away from the community, and started to be centralized, and delivered by statutory bodies, and to a certain extent [District] Councils. There was a train of thought that that was probably going back to the communities, and that might be a way of communities to sort of re-establish themselves. That didn't happen.

Statutory agencies saw empowered CSOs as competition and Peace 3 funding has gone to education and health boards, local Councils, and the Department of Agriculture so that the community disappeared from the equation, and it was disenfranchised and disempowered by those statutory agencies.

A CSO leader, Dearbhla reported that the Irish government plowed resources into the voluntary sector during the 1990s to do essential work on the cheap that statutory organizations were obliged to do. The government has since cut those resources. Peace 3 resources are critical in supporting CSOs to continue to do their work on the ground to address the needs of marginalized groups, and to build their capacity

> And the government would have spent huge money twenty years ago in developing the community sector in Ireland. And all along particularly when times were good in the 1990s, and into the early 2000s, money went to where the community sector was

> the thing. And it made good sense for the government because they were getting work done that they were statutory obligated to do. But they were getting it done for pittance compared to what they were being paid, you know their own executives or whatever to do it.
>
> And people, the whole volunteering aspect, I mean we would have put in here, we never estimated, we never kept a record of it. Ok, now at this moment in time the voluntary sector is taking a battering. The voluntary sector as supported by the exchequer is taking a battering. It has removed 11 million euros from the voluntary sector, the voluntary community sector, and one of the groups that is suffering is the women's group.

The Irish government needs to reinvest in the local voluntary sector especially CSOs empowering women that is contributing strongly to community development and peacebuilding in local rural communities.

Another CSO leader, Bronagh contended that CSOs apply for the funding on a competitive basis, and once the funding dries up the voluntary sector will not continue to be sustainable at the current level of providing services to the community.

> I dread to think, you know all that I have talked about has been possible because of funding because with the best will in the world you need people, their work. Because people are doing their everyday jobs, they don't have necessarily the time to invest in building these relationships. Like no matter how you look at it and no matter how idealistic you want to be about it, it does take a certain amount of facilitation and mediation work. And you need someone there leading that process, not driving the process but steering the process you know for a particular group.
>
> So, if you withdraw the funding the will is going to be there and of course you have to have a dividend from what has gone before, and you have people there who have been in a process who will want to continue it. But to what extent they can continue it without the funding its certainly going to be more difficult. And you would hope as I say that the legacy of what has gone before will continue, and there have been a lot of foundations led for building positive relations. But I think the bottom line is you need the structures, you need the money.

It is important to sustain the experience, skill sets, knowledge, and infrastructures built up over the past 20 years so that CSOs continue to change the mindsets to build trust and positive cross-community relationships. It is disheartening for the CSOs involved, and for the whole community when projects cease that have brought people together.

A CSO leader, Eleanor felt that CSOs that have become dependent on external funding have no real exit strategy when the funding ends. She articulated that some of the projects would continue due to the perseverance of ultra-loyal enthusiastic volunteers, who are committed local activists while other projects will terminate due to a lack of funding as projects need a funded dedicated staff person to ensure that the work gets done.

> At an organizational level we have other external funds as well but it would be a great loss. And it would have a very direct effect on staff that would need to be either redeployed or let go at the end of their fixed term contract, so that's from an organizational perspective. From a community perspective, it's not sustainable. I haven't

seen any really exit strategies or I mean there are encompassing the elements of the program as best practice, and they are disseminating amongst their staff, but there is an impetus that is lost when the funding goes. It may be a member of staff, or they just don't have that extra cover to disseminate that information. So, I would say, from the sustainability perspective, the future is more difficult than ever before.

There are a number of community leaders who are enthused who seem to do all the work, and there are those who are there when funding is available and programs are being run. However, it runs out of steam and the diehard activist will remain but they then feel that they are not bringing the community along with them. And the community sometimes think, "Well there's no funding. We can't do programs. We're just not going to buy into this." So, they're in search of other funding such as the lottery.

Those individuals who are driving this forward. They've seen the peace dividend. They're seeing what's happening, and as a result of both the project and the funding, and there is a willingness definitely to continue that work wherever possible. But really without the funding those programs, its very difficult to keep that going. Its more or less "We've done that and we've moved on" even within Peace because of the change of focus to anti-sectarianism and anti-racism. People kind of think, "Well that piece of work is discreet. It's finished. It's stopped." This is something new and it's mainly for those, you know, newcomer people into Northern Ireland. So, there is a definite shift in focus, and the community themselves are saying. "It's not for us. It's for them. We've moved past that now."

At some level, local people perceive that the external funding is being discontinued because the funders are framing the situation in such a way that cross-communal conflict issues appear to have been fully addressed. Attention is now focused on how new immigrants and refugees are integrated into Northern Ireland, and the Southern counties straddled along the Border.

A CSO leader, Joshua noted that the voluntary sector was quite strong in Derry before the funding arrived, and now it has become a professional class dependent on the funding, and stifled in its work by the requirements of the top-heavy funding bureaucracy

> I think the Peace program has to take on board what they are doing in the environment is that they made an intervention and they have changed the dynamics of community development in doing that some for good and some not. […] There is actually something more critical about what is happening in society, and what we think communities can do, and what they can't do.

> You know there is something wrong in the relationship between society and the state […] . There is something in Northern Ireland that's not right between citizens and the state, and between citizens and the Peace program, and between citizens and each other, and between citizens and the new Assembly. There is a democratic deficit, like "crisis" is the wrong word. There is a crisis in democracy in terms of what this community development thing means.

This leader argued that there needs to be a real injection of thinking about sustainability because there is a danger that the rigors of the Peace 3 program could erode volunteering and the relationship-building of the community sector. The professionalization of CSOs is doing them long-term damage so that there will be a future democratic deficit crisis in community development and in grassroots democracy.

Another CSO leader, Alfred noticed that the Northern Ireland government does not provide a stream of funding to support the voluntary community sector's peacebuilding work. Lack of funding limits the number and quality of programming that CSOs can offer to local communities in need.

> You have to seriously restrict the number of programs you run. And at the minute x percent of our income has to be brought in from external sources. So, you know it has literally made us have a severely restrictive impact unless there is other mainstream funding that comes into being. I mean I'm a believer that you know if you look at parts of the UK and Ireland, I mean community development is still a key element of local government funding.

> The Peace 3 monies and all other funders have let our government off the hook because there is very little other than Peace 3 monies and IFI monies, and helping organizations where there's no mainstream government funding anyway. So, they have to pick up the tab and show more responsibility for mainstreaming that stuff. Its something to say that by 2013 we will be at a position where good relations are fine. I believe that there is still a long way for us to go. But you know at the same time even if we had perfect harmony in terms of the sectarian divide we still have the right to sources to tease it out.

> This is what we're finding working in that diverse range of communities was that there isn't that much sectarian violence its all localized antisocial behavior that you know is reflective or that you could get in any city on the island or in the UK or Ireland. So, the government have to decide "Okay, well, do we ignore that or let the statutory deal with it or do we use the extremely effective and strong community infrastructure that we have built up in Northern Ireland to help deal with these problems?"

The Northern Ireland government needs to streamline the funding to make sure that CSOs on the ground continue to do the necessary work in the community to prevent the reoccurrence of sectarian violence and address localized antisocial behavior.

A CSO leader, Senan recognizes that the government's budget cuts in relation to statutory services will seriously impact local CSOs in terms of their sustainability in disadvantaged areas with a large unemployment rate. Some of the work will be sustained but not at the level that it is currently being delivered. The issue is complex, like the legacy of the past that continues to divide and polarize people, and it needs to be addressed in a sensitive manner.

> It is very frustrating, and sustainability is an ongoing dilemma. I think it is particularly difficult in the current environment of the downturn, and the cuts in expenditure that are taking place. And the fact that British and Irish governments are in economic turmoil, and they are having to look to save on expenditure. And so, the first places that they hit are organizations like ourselves that they will say is unnecessary. Having said that we are very well experienced in fighting our corner, and then scanning a horizon and seeing where the opportunities arise.

> It's not about the sustainability of organizations. Essentially it's about sustaining and addressing the need that exists and improving the quality of life and enabling people to improve their standing in life. And to become much more self-reliant and to become

less dependent on either state funding or any other funding. But these are very, very difficult issues for communities such as this. [...] I think a fundamental issue that maybe isn't addressed and maybe for political expedience reasons it is not addressed, and that is the whole notion of what colonialism does to people. And colonialism creates a dependency mindset, and its well-recognized. And that you have to then use practical intervention measures to counteract that for future generations, and that is something that we feel today.

Almost 80 percent of people living in the community are dependent on public funding in one form or another. And if that's replicated, and it is replicated within the most disadvantaged areas in the top 20 percent disadvantaged areas across the North, that's a massive cost in terms of sustainability. How do you turn it around? Well again, its about how you approach the whole issue of sustainable development and transformation, and I think it has to be done on a city-wide basis. [...]

I am only sorry that the regeneration that has taken place in this town is taking place in the current economic climate, and at a time when Peace funding and the IFI funding is running out. So, its a timing issue because that money should have really been coming in, and the back-up of a new blueprint going forward. I would also argue if we had wanted that money to make a difference in the first instance, we actually should have designed our way into a shared future and we never did that.

For this CSO leader, the issue is about creating sustainable communities with a shared future rather than sustainable peacebuilding organizations and breaking that dependency mindset created by the colonial experience. Government needs to put in place economic measures that fully include marginalized communities to improve their quality of life rather than being dependent on external funding to fill a short-term gap.

People live in disadvantaged communities with a large unemployment rate with often-intergenerational welfare recipients within families. Both funders provided an incentive to CSOs to apply for funding to provide employment opportunities in local communities. Yet the funding process is highly competitive creating a professional class as the statutory agencies weed out the CSOs, and government cutbacks ensure that there is no stream of peace and reconciliation funding available to replace Peace and IFI funding as the voluntary community sector is hijacked.

Implications for teaching and training

In our teaching and training, we really need to address the idea of dependency as donors often provide economic resources with strings attached to embed peace dividends and to buttress peace accords (Khan & Byrne, 2016). Sustainable practices of external donors require a focus on encompassing programs, addressing more than the material issues and financial needs. Politicians at the domestic macrolevel must address grievances, economic disparity, and victimhood to ensure parity between groups and continue to invest in peace processes recognizing that aid is not a panacea.

Scholars and practitioners need to use deep analytical tools like social cubism that explore the intersection and interaction of demographic, economic, historical, political, religious, and psychocultural dimensions to understand the deep roots of local conflict (Byrne et al., 2003). They should ensure that there should be an ongoing assessment of the peacebuilding process by local actors to monitor if the aid-funded projects mirror the actual situation on the ground as spoilers continue to impact the changing political terrain and the peace process could descend into a slippery slope of renewed violent conflict (Maiangwa et al., 2019). Consequently, a multimodal and multilevel intervention range of peacebuilding interventions includes track-two CSOs that work within and among grassroots communities to ensure their empowerment as they create unconventional, creative, and an innovative broad spectrum of economic, political, and peacebuilding activities as well as participation of all the key stakeholders (Byrne & Keashly, 2000).

Implications for practice and policy

New donor countries like the BRICS (Brazil, Russia, India, China, and South Africa), Qatar, and Turkey understand and intervene in peacebuilding and development differently compared to Global North neoliberal processes and practices so that the international community should approach complex conflict contexts by including multilateral donors as part of the peacebuilding architecture to improve the aid-peacebuilding policy and practice nexus (Paczyńska, 2019). When aid is increased to support peace processes the peace can last longer over the short term in terms of postpeace accord reconstruction. Yet there is often an uncoupling between local economic and political elites and the external aid architecture's interests that are empowered over sustaining peace processes (Emmanuel, 2015). Donor aid often goes to the wealthier urbanites rather than the poorer constituents in recipient countries through corruption, embezzlement, and fraud as the donors do not control the internal outlay of resources nor do they know where the poor communities reside so that the aid does not reduce poverty (Briggs, 2017). In addition, the administration of, and type of projects supported by aid must be driven by local communities that includes them as key stakeholders rather than the donors designing and affecting the types of projects they want to be implemented on the ground as they must match the needs of local communities (Dangi et al., 2015). One option is to create and funnel external aid to local foundations comprised of a broad-spectrum board of local leaders that allocate resources to local peacebuilders that they know are working hard for local communities.

Conclusion

Aid donors must balance providing resources that address inequality and conflict causes by nurturing local systems' abilities to deal with threats so that they have the wherewithal to work on future conflicts so that donors should not exacerbate conflicts and undermine local systems' resilience in adapting to escalated conflict by creating local solutions to local problems as local actors learn and are better able to cope with and address future conflicts (de Coning, 2018).

Acknowledgments

This research was supported by a grant from the Social Science and Humanities Research Council of Canada.

References

Aubert, P., Brun, M., Agamile, P., & Treyer, S. (2018). From aid negotiation to aid effectiveness: The case of food and nutrition security in Ethiopia. *Third World Quarterly, 39*(1), 104–121.

Autesserre, S. (2014). *Peaceland: Conflict resolution and the everyday politics of intervention*. Cambridge University Press.

Bilzen, G. V. (2015). *The development of aid*. Cambridge Scholars Publishing.

Björkdahl, A., & Höglund, K. (2013). Precarious peacebuilding: Friction in global-local encounters. *Peacebuilding*, *1*(3), 289–299.

Briggs, R. (2017). Does foreign aid target the poorest? *International Organization*, *71*(1), 187–206.

Byrne, S., Carter, N., & Senehi, J. (2003). Social cubism and social conflict: Analysis and resolution. *Journal of International and Comparative Law*, *8*(3), 725–740.

Byrne, S., & Keashly, L. (2000). Working with ethno-political conflict: A multi-modal approach. *International Peacekeeping*, *7*(1), 97–120.

Cawley, A. (2015). "I'd be proud to spend the sacred foreign aid budget on our poor pensioners": Representations of macro aid resourcing in the Irish, UK and US print-media during the economic crisis, 2008–2011. *International Communication Gazette*, *77*(6), 533–556.

Creary, P., & Byrne, S. (2014). Peace with strings attached: Exploring reflections of structure and agency in Northern Ireland peacebuilding funding. *Peacebuilding*, *2*(1), 64–82.

Dangi, M., Schoenberger, E., & Boland, J. (2015). Foreign aid in waste management: A case of Kathmandu, Nepal. *Habitat International*, *49*(1), 1–10.

de Coning, C. (2018). Adaptive peacebuilding. *International Affairs*, *94*(2), 301–317.

Edwards, S. (2015). Economic development and the effectiveness of foreign aid: A historical perspective. *Kyklos*, *68*(3), 277–316.

Emmanuel, N. (2015). Peace incentives: Economic aid and peace processes in Africa. *African Conflict and Peace Building Review*, *5*(2), 1–32.

Engerman, D. (2018). *The price of aid: The economic cold war in India*. Harvard University Press.

Fanon, F. (2005). *Wretched of the earth*. Grove Press.

Figueiredo, C., Dean, C., & Byrne, S. (2019). Economic aid and peacebuilding in Northern Ireland: Some critical reflections. *Journal for Peace and Justice Studies*, *28*(2), 89–111.

Fissuh, E., Skarlota, O., Byrne, S., Karari, P., & Kawser, A. (2012). Building future coexistence or keeping people apart: The role of economic assistance in Northern Ireland. *International Journal of Conflict Management*, *23*(3), 248–265.

Furia, A. (2015). *The foreign aid regime: Gift-giving, states and global dis/order*. Palgrave Macmillan.

Gellner, E. (1996). The coming of nationalism and its interpretations: The myths of nation and class. In G. Balakrishnan (Ed.), *Mapping the nation* (pp. 98–145). Verso.

Geng, X., & Hernandez, M. (2020). Aid, policies and growth: A nonlinear reassessment. *Applied Economics*, *52*(15), 1617–1633.

Girod, D. (2015). *Explaining post-conflict reconstruction*. Oxford University Press.

Hyde, J., & Byrne, S. (2015). The International Fund for Ireland and the European Union peace III fund: The impact of reconciliation and peacebuilding in Northern Ireland and the border area. *International Journal of Conflict Engagement and Resolution*, *3*(2), 93–115.

Ishnazarov, D., & Cevik, N. (2017). Foreign aid effectiveness in OIC member countries: Beyond economic indicators. *International Journal of Economics, Management and Accounting*, *25*(2), 315–336.

Janjua, P., Muhammad, M., & Usman, M. (2018). Impact of project and program aid on economic growth: A cross country analysis. *Pakistan Development Review*, *57*(2), 145–174.

Khan, S., & Byrne, S. (2016). Economic assistance, development and peacebuilding in Northern Ireland. *Development in Practice*, *26*(8), 1013–1023.

Knutsen, T., & Kotsadam, A. (2020). The political economy of aid allocation: Aid and incumbency at the local level in Sub Saharan Africa. *World Development*, *127*(1), 1–9.

Kumar, A. (2015). Samaritan's dilemma, time-inconsistency and foreign aid: A review of theoretical models. In B. M. Arvin & B. Lew (Eds.), *Handbook on the economics of foreign aid* (pp. 64–81). Edward Elgar Publishing.

Labadi, S. (2020). The future of international aid for cultural projects. In S. Labadi (Ed.), *The Cultural turn in international aid: Impacts and challenges for heritage and the creative industries* (pp. 243–252). Abingdon, UK: Routledge.

Larsen, N. (2016). Nonlinearity in the efficacy of foreign aid on economic growth. *The Journal of Applied Business and Economics*, *18*(5), 23–41.

Lee, S. Y. (2015). Motivations for local resistance in international peacebuilding. *Third World Quarterly*, *36*(8), 1437–1452.

Lim, S., Menaldo, V., & Prakash, A. (2015). Foreign aid, economic globalization, and pollution. *Policy Sciences*, *48*(2), 181–205.

Mac Ginty, R. (2015). Where is the local? Critical localism and peacebuilding. *Third World Quarterly*, *36*(5), 840–856.

Mac Ginty, R., & Richmond, O. (2016). The fallacy of constructing hybrid political orders: A reappraisal of the hybrid turn in peacebuilding. *International Peacekeeping*, *23*(2), 219–239.

Maiangwa, B., Mallon, B., Kuznetsova, A., & Byrne, S. (2019). Rethinking the impacts of IFI and EU funding in transforming paramilitarism in Northern Ireland and the Irish border counties. *Peace Research: Canadian Journal of Peace and Conflict Studies*, *51*(1), 31–65.

McCann, G. (2015). Conclusion—neoliberal decline and international development post-2015. In G. McCann & S. McCloskey (Eds.), *From the local to the global: Key issues in development studies* (pp. 321–332). Pluto Press.

Menashy, F. (2019). *International aid to education: Power dynamics in an era of partnership*. Teachers College Press.

Oloke, I., Lindsay, P., & Byrne, S. (2018). The intersection of critical emancipatory peacebuilding and social enterprise: A dialogical approach to social entrepreneurship. *Journal of Ethnic Studies: Treatises and Documents*, *81*(2), 67–86.

Paczyńska, A. (2019). *The new politics of aid: Emerging donors and conflict-affected states*. Lynne Rienner Publishers.

Paffenholz, T. (2015). Unpacking the local turn in peacebuilding: A critical assessment towards an agenda for future research. *Third World Quarterly*, *36*(5), 857–874.

Peiffer, C., & Boussalis, C. (2015). Determining aid allocation decision-making: Towards a comparative sectored approach. In B. M. Arvin & B. Lew (Eds.), *Handbook on the economics of foreign aid* (pp. 45–63). Edward Elgar Publishing.

Saibu, O., & Obioesio, F. (2017). Foreign aid, fiscal optimality and economic growth in Nigeria. *Spoudai*, *67*(4), 85–99.

Sandlin, E. (2018). Exceptional or expendable? How economic and strategic interests undermine democracy, humanitarianism, and human rights in US economic aid allocation. *Democracy and Security*, *14*(4), 358–388.

Sandlin, E. (2016). Competing concerns: Balancing human rights and national security in US economic aid allocation. *Human Rights Review*, *17*(4), 439–462.

Skarlato, O., Byrne, S., Ahmed, K., & Karari, P. (2016). Economic assistance to peacebuilding and reconciliation community-based projects in Northern Ireland: Challenges, opportunities and evolution. *International Journal of Politics, Culture and Society*, *29*(2), 157–182.

Skarlato, O., Fissuh, E., Byrne, S., Karari, P., & Ahmed, K. (2013). Peacebuilding, community development, and reconciliation in Northern Ireland: The role of the Belfast agreement and the implication for external economic aid. In T. White (Ed.), *Lessons from the Northern Ireland peace process* (pp. 198–226). University of Wisconsin Press.

Tang, K.-B., & Bundhoo, D. (2017). Foreign aid and economic growth in developing countries: Evidence from Sub-Saharan Africa. *Theoretical Economics Letters*, *7*(5), 1473–1491.

Thiessen, C. (2011). Emancipatory peacebuilding: Critical responses to (neo)liberal trends. In T. Matyók, J. Senehi, & S. Byrne (Eds.), *Critical issues in peace and conflict studies: Theory, practice, and pedagogy* (pp. 115–143). Lexington Press.

Wang, Y. (2016). The effect of bargaining on US economic aid. *International Interactions*, *42*(3), 479–502.

27
BRINGING THE INDIGENOUS INTO MAINSTREAM PEACEMAKING AND PEACEBUILDING IN FARMER-HERDER CONFLICTS: SOME CRITICAL REFLECTIONS

Surulola Eke and Sean Byrne

This chapter we hope will spark discussion of the role of traditional approaches to peacemaking and peacebuilding in farmer-herder conflicts shaping our contemporary global civic society. Often Indigenous peacemaking approaches are omitted from the dominant liberal peacebuilding process in societies transitioning out of violence (Mac Ginty, 2008a, 2011). Yet everyday peacemaking exists in Indigenous societies in urban and rural settings in Brazil (Linstroth, 2016) or in intragroup and regional conflict settings in the Philippines (Barnes & Magdalena, 2016) while traditional conflict resolution methods are often used in local disputes in Northern Ireland (Mac Ginty, 2016) or among the Iroquois in upstate New York (Rice, 2013), and in Indigenous Berom and Hausa communities in Jos, Nigeria (Eke, 2020). These peacemaking systems appear to work in a multiplicity of Indigenous societies. However, there are tensions and contradictions about the global and local context, and within the power structures of Indigenous communities. For example, international human rights law must be constructed and reframed within a grassroots context to be effective (Engle Merry, 2006) and often a patriarchal power structure works for some men and women, rather than youth and other minority groups within some Indigenous communities (Mac Ginty, 2008b).

This chapter highlights several key central themes in particular theoretical concepts, key findings, implications for training, and implications for practice and policy.

Background: Theoretical concepts

This section conceptualizes local peacebuilding, explores the origin of the transition from international peacebuilding to peacebuilding that is grounded in Indigenous customs and institutions, and examines the liberal peace debate.

Local peacebuilding and its roots

Locally driven peacebuilding is increasingly being adopted within the peacebuilding community, yet this assessment depends on how local is defined. Often, its ownership and the nature of the structure and the practices involved define the localness of peacebuilding. Local peacebuilding ownership is either minimally or maximally defined. Minimally, peacebuilding is locally owned if it involves the consultation and inclusion of the local community in the implementation of externally designed peacebuilding programs or the training of local governments to administer liberal peace-promoting institutions (Narten, 2008). When maximally defined, local ownership entails the local community's ability to envision a peaceful future through an inclusive process, and to design a peace infrastructure that is grounded solely in the cultural reality of that local community (Leonardsson & Rudd, 2015).

Local peacebuilding is also defined structurally in which case the emphasis is on the nature, location, and origin of the peacebuilding institutions. One view is that local peacebuilding exists when a community association or local government pursues it in post-peace accord societies (Hughes et al., 2015). In contrast, Mac Ginty and Richmond (2013) indicate that mere physical presence does not qualify a peacebuilding association as local. They opine that peacebuilding is local when it involves homegrown agencies that work to discover and implement peace processes in conflict societies (Mac Ginty & Richmond, 2013). Other scholars emphasize the latter part of Mac Ginty and Richmond's definition, that is, the nature of the activities undertaken. Robins (2013) and Paffenholz (2015), for example, define local as those activities that are diametrically opposed to the agenda of international peacebuilders.

Depending on which of the definitions one considers, local peacebuilding is evident in several of the contemporary peace processes but that was not always the case. The inclusion of local institutions and voices in peace processes is traceable to the scholarly works of Curle (1994), Lederach (1997), and Avruch (1998), and the positive reception of their ideas by the international peacebuilding community. Curle (1994) called for the privileging of Indigenous practices and structures since the most effective peacebuilding practices exist within the very conflict communities that require them. Hence, Lederach (1997) notes that the local people ought to be treated not as passive recipients of peace initiatives but as peacebuilding assets. Avruch's (1998) advocacy for Indigenous peacebuilding embodies both these perspectives in that he contends that sustainable peacebuilding is that which is not only based on the local customs, but it is also reliant on local community insiders for this knowledge.

The push for the inclusion of local voices and institutions in peacebuilding led to changes in the peacebuilding policy of international organizations (European Union, 2005; United Nations, 2000) and aid agencies (Department for International Development, 2010; United States Agency for Aid and Development, 2009). It also heralded an avalanche of scholarly critiques of international (liberal) peacebuilding and counter-critics.

Liberal peace debate

The critics of liberal peacebuilding have themselves received scrutiny for their conceptual and methodological inadequacies, which has produced a seemingly unending debate within the critical liberal peace literature. Here, we explore two dimensions of this debate: on the international-local dichotomy (De Heredia, 2014; Heathershaw, 2013; Philipsen, 2014; Pouligny, 2005; Rampton & Nadarajah, 2017; Roberts, 2011, 2012; Sabaratnam, 2013; Visoka & Richmond, 2017) and on the inherent dysfunction of liberal peace (Barnett, 2006; Byrne &

Thiessen, 2019; Jahn, 2007; Mac Ginty, 2008a, 2008b; Mitchell, 2010; Paris, 1997, 2010; Roberts, 2011; Visoka & Richmond, 2017).

Scholars diverge on whether liberal peacebuilding privileges the international over the local. Pouligny (2005), for example, notes that because locally oriented civil society organizations (CSOs) in post-accord societies involve a different political culture, international peacebuilders only engage with Western-styled CSOs or establish Western-styled ones in places where none exists. Relatedly, Philipsen (2014) contends that the international community constitutes the foundation of liberal peacebuilding, hence they, rather than the local population, determine institutional accountability and define success. In his critique of liberal peacebuilding, Roberts (2011) notes that the exclusion of the local population from these processes accounts for the failure of post-accord states to meet the expectations of citizens. Advancing a similar argument, Roberts (2012) avers that the local population is not only excluded from liberal peacebuilding planning, but also left vulnerable to market shocks because liberal peacebuilders constrain opportunities for economic sustenance outside the market.

The argument that liberal peace is externally oriented presupposes that it lacks local ownership. In contrast, Heathershaw (2013) notes that liberal peacebuilding cannot be devoid of local ownership since liberal peace outcomes are often the result of the interface of both the international and the local forces that are involved in the process. Similarly, Rampton and Nadarajah (2017) note that these outcomes, such as the violence that sometimes accompany peace processes, are products of local systems that are themselves offshoots of international forces. In essence, the "local" cannot be excluded from liberal peacebuilding since the lines of division between the international and the local are blurred. De Heredia (2014) holds a similar position, noting that it is implausible to distinguish between the local and the international as the local actors in post-accord societies sometimes operate in both worlds. In support of this perspective, Sabaratnam (2013) recommends a fundamental rethinking of the conceptual underpinnings of the critique of liberal peacebuilding.

Also contested is the notion that violence accompanies liberal peacebuilding because the process does not bequeath the institutions necessary for managing competition. Arguing affirmatively, Paris (1997) notes that a liberal economy is imposed on war-torn countries because it is assumed to be a prerequisite for peace. Without the right culture for healthy competition and the right institutions to manage it, liberalization tends to exacerbate rather than solve social conflicts (Paris, 1997). Barnett (2006) makes a related point but in relation to political competition. He notes that the only change that results from political liberalization is the transfer of the theatre of violence from the battlefield to the ballot box because conflict-stricken countries are not culturally suited for political competition (Barnett, 2006). In the same vein, Jahn (2007) states that the violence that accompanies new "neoliberal" states, such as Rwanda and Angola, derives from their lack of a conducive political climate. The persistence of an illiberal political infrastructure in a newly established liberal state, according to Visoka and Richmond (2017), empowers malevolent actors to appropriate the new political structures to pursue illiberal ends in post-accord states.

Other scholars, including Mitchell (2010) and Paris (2010), have challenged the notion that liberal peace is inherently dysfunctional in non-Western societies. Mitchell (2010), for example, contends that attempts at fashioning alternative visions of peace in post-accord societies are misconstrued as violent resistance to liberal peacebuilding due to the inflexibility of how the peacebuilding process is conceptualized. Similarly, Paris (2010) asserts that although liberal peacebuilding has produced unintended results in some places, it is still the most feasible pathway to stabilizing post-accord states as the African and Latin American attempts at state-controlled development have fared worse than market-controlled efforts.

Considering the scope of this debate, specifically the emphasis on the failings of liberal peacebuilding, we explore the peacebuilding practice to highlight the utility of mainstreaming local peacebuilding approaches while simultaneously identifying their own shortcomings.

Key findings

This section outlines several key central themes, specifically the roles of culture, rituals, transcultural constructive storytelling, Indigenous knowledge and peacemaking systems, and the external and internal challenges Indigenous peacemaking systems face.

Culture and indigenous peacemaking

Culture is flexible, learned, and is passed on intergenerationally through stories to groups. Culture frames "the context in which conflicts occur" (Avruch, 2008, p. 170). The role of culture in conflict can offer people an insight into the underlying dynamics providing them with "cognitive and effective frameworks" that include "images, encodements, metaphors, and schemas for interpreting the behavior and motives of others" (Avruch, 2008, p. 171). In everyday inter- and intracultural encounters, cultural markers drive conflict while Indigenous practices or "ethnopraxes" are used to manage them (Avruch, 2008, p. 174).

Lederach (1995) makes an important distinction between the prescriptive and the elicitive approaches to conflict resolution training. The prescriptive approach takes little time to pass onto trainees and for them to apply the model, however, cultural universality does not always hold in each cultural context (Lederach, 1995, p. 67). The elicitive approach perceives culture as a resource and includes local people's full participation and the forging of appropriate conflict resolution models in the context setting (Lederach, 1995, p. 67). Consequently, metaphor, proverbs, stories, and language are natural resources in the elicitive conflict training practice (Lederach, 1995, p. 79). Lederach argues that the elicitive conflict resolution process is appropriate in multicultural settings because it provides for Indigenous empowerment, conscientization, and facilitation, and it is an important integrated framework for peacemaking that are transferable across cultures (Lederach, 1995, p. 113).

There is evidence of elicitive peacebuilding in Jos. In July 2018, for example, a peacebuilding summit, partly supported by the U.S. Embassy in Nigeria, was convened to aggregate the peace initiatives of religious leaders and local chiefs (Young, 2018). Faith-based and other peacebuilders in Jos have also strived toward grounding their work in local knowledge. Yet, these organizations hinge the long-term sustainability of the program outcomes on their idea of what constitutes a viable peace infrastructure. For example, the Centre for Humanitarian Dialogue's (HD) peacebuilding work in Jos has been both elicitive and prescriptive. In establishing a framework for dialogue between the Indigenous Berom population and the non-Indigenous Hausa and Fulani groups, the HD aggregated inputs from youths, women, local chiefs, and religious and business leaders (Centre for Humanitarian Dialogue, 2021). The dialogue process culminated in a joint peace declaration, including a commitment to respect the customs and traditions of others and tolerance (Peace Agreements, 2014). The joint peace declaration was followed by the establishment of the Plateau Peacebuilding Agency in 2016 (Centre for Humanitarian Dialogue, 2021).

So, while the modalities for intercommunal dialogue were the result of grassroots consultations that involved not only community leaders but also everyday community people, the formal management of the resultant joint declaration of peace was handed over to a newly created "peace bureaucracy." While the elicitive practice is desirable, the prescriptive approach is sometimes unavoidable because post-accord communities doubt the ability of local structures to sustain dialogue, and they rely on external peacebuilders to drive the peace process. In July 2018, for example, the Dialogue, Reconciliation, and Peace (DREP) Center organized an inter-religious dialogue forum involving Christian and Muslim religious leaders from across the Plateau. Impressed with the outcome of the process, the clerics appealed to the DREP Centre to convene a follow-up session with an expanded membership that includes tribal leaders and youths (United Religions Initiative, 2018).

Rituals as peacemaking and rituals of connection

Traditional rituals are "formal and symbolic acts" that teach their members about the past and how to communicate as well as provide a critical emotive component of a group's sense of identity and memory so that they can make sense of their lived experiences, heal from past traumas, and resolve intra-and intergroup conflicts (Schirch, 2004, p. 6). Rituals can also be informal, constructive, and socializing, and can play an important role in transforming cross-cultural conflict because they connect people peacefully (Schirch, 2004, p. 19; Senehi, 2009, p. 234). For example, the Sundance sacred ceremony for North American and Canadian Indigenous peoples includes rituals to preserve the cultures and the offering of personal sacrifice of the participants for the betterment of the community.

In addition, rituals empower women in traditional societies to forge and preserve knowledge of their world (Tursunova, 2014, p. 23). In Uzbekistan, women's religious rituals played a critical role in a new post-Soviet cultural and political landscape (Tursunova, 2014, p. 23). Women's agency is reflected in these rituals to shape their understanding of local cultural nuances as well as to reclaim "sacred spaces" and to resist "discursive knowledge" about the economic context as well as Islamic practices (Tursunova, 2014, p. 23). Women perform religious rituals in female gatherings to make and remake knowledge to reclaim their "Indigenous power and knowledge," build trust and cooperation, and make action plans that empower them to defy repressive structures (Tursunova, 2014, p. 27).

Jos women have not always featured prominently in the formal peacebuilding process in the city yet they continue to demonstrate agency in their peace-related activities in Nigeria. Lacking proper representation in the formal dialogue processes, Jos women resorted to alternative nonviolent avenues to shape the Jos government's action. Following the March 2010 ethnic group clashes, for example, Jos women marched through the city center wielding mango tree leaves, wooden crosses, and Bibles, and demanding justice for slain women and children (Peace Women, 2010). Also, they draw on international symbols, like the United Nations International Day of the Family, to promote community within Jos (Epenshade, 2014). Outside their efforts to influence decision-makers, Jos women are building a network of peace through their engagements in the markets, and within other social settings (Enyiaka, 2019).

Such peace networks, which have been active in several Jos communities including Angwan Rogo, Wase, Mangu, and Riyom, have enhanced women's involvement in peacebuilding and conflict prevention (UN Women, 2017). The leader of one of these women networks, Aisha Usman, described its emancipatory effect as follows:

> Women have realized that we have so many things to speak about, but previously did not have the channels to do so. We have been enlightened on the importance of making peace right from our homes because, we, women have a significant role to play. (UN Women, 2017)

Ms. Usman's comment highlights the suppression of women's voices, which reinforces the claim that women have been "mere token presences within peacebuilding processes" in Sub-Saharan Africa (Ombati, 2015, p. 637). Further, it indicates why prescriptive peacebuilding may be desirable in some conflict zones. It shows that although the local culture should shape peacebuilding practice, peacebuilders must be sensitive to those unjust and oppressive cultural systems that silence minority groups, including women. In other words, even though the inclusion of the Indigenous may empower the local people, empowerment would be unevenly experienced if any local unjust systems are identified controlled by some local elites.

Jos women themselves recognize that there are entrenched sociocultural barriers limiting their full participation in locally driven peacebuilding. In the HD-facilitated dialogue sessions, for example, the Jos women participants issued a "peace statement" separate from the men's "peace declaration," imploring the community elders (men) to make optimal use of women's peacebuilding potentials. They urged the elders to:

> Work with *women's* strengths developed as mothers *and* caregivers, that come from the practice of holding families together [...], *inspire* change in cultural concepts on women and men as related to addressing *emerging obstacles to peace* [...], *and* [...] lead in efforts to remove *socio-cultural* barriers to women and girls' education and participation in peace processes. (Centre for Humanitarian Dialogue, 2021, emphases added)

The women recognize the obstacles to their involvement in peacebuilding as well as their limitations in inspiring change, hence they urge community elders to take the lead. Yet, as some might be beneficiaries of women's marginalization, these men may lack real incentives to champion their liberation so that external transformative prescriptions may be unavoidable.

Transcultural constructive storytellers

Traditional societies have through "constructive stories" socialized their young, shaped their sense of identity and collective memory, and passed on their knowledge and moral code over millennia (Senehi, 2010). Working with this mindset, Jos's peacebuilders in Nigeria are targeting the younger generation, with the hope that by enlightening them about the historical nature of intergroup relations, they would be oriented toward cordial interactions in the present and beyond. The Catholic Diocese of Jos, for example, created a drama unit in its Kids Ministry that has re-enacted past communal bonds in a play, "Reality." The play, which chronicles the history of intergroup relations and highlights political mischief as the root of intergroup animosity, was presented to teenage audiences across Plateau, Nigeria between 2008 and 2010 (Nyam, 2016).

The Search for Common Ground (SCG) has used the same model in its peacebuilding work in the state. SCG established and trained a group of constructive storytellers, including Indigenous Christian and settler Muslim teenage girls. The teenage girls, known as Naija Girls, shuttle between each other's schools, disseminating narratives of peace through music and drama (Search for Common Ground, 2021). As Senehi (2000, 2010) notes, "transcultural storytellers" passing on stories is a powerful means of knowledge transmission, and a critical ingredient in the reinforcement of a community's identity, and in creating a sense of who they are, and where they have come from.

Transcultural storytellers are a useful resource for rekindling a community's identity because of their knowledge. For the same reason, they are also valuable peacebuilders in local communities. As Senehi (2009, p. 234) notes, "transcultural storytellers" are local stakeholders with knowledge who are important constructive bridge builders between different groups sharing cross-cultural stories to assist in "shaping and transforming intercommunal relationships" to achieve "diversity within unity," and to "negotiate the needs for remembrance and moving on." Storytelling shares knowledge and builds a community's culture while traditionally transcultural storytellers do and have assisted minority groups in "negotiating their identity" to traverse "cross-cultural boundaries" (Senehi 2009, p. 229).

In Jos, Nigeria, the Centre for Conflict Management and Peace Studies (CCMPS), the Justice Development and Peace Commission (JDPC) as well as the SCG are made up of such local stakeholders who apply their knowledge toward constructive ends. The CCMPS has, for example, dramatized the evolution of farmer-herder relations in Jos in order to highlight the artificiality of religion and ethnicity, thereby underscoring why intergroup relations should exist independently of them (Nyam, 2016). Similarly, the SCG is educating Jos communities on intergroup tolerance using the radio (Search for Common Ground, 2021). Likewise, the JDPC uses dance improvisations and dialogue music to promote self-awareness and communication in the conflict-affected communities in Plateau, Nigeria (Nyam, 2016).

Despite the constructive ends toward which storytelling was employed in the above instances, it is important to also recognize that "destructive storytelling" can also be used for malevolent purposes to generate "enemy images of other groups," exacerbating intergroup conflict (Senehi, 2002). In fact, the farmer-herder conflicts in the Nigerian city of Jos underscore the duality of storytelling. While the conflicts are partly rooted in destructive narratives about the outgroup (Eke, 2020), enemy images are being debunked through drama, dance, and music, as the foregoing discussion shows.

Indigenous knowledge and peacemaking system

Indigenous knowledge is a complex yet commonsense understanding of one's local culture and one's place in the world that is embedded in a group's cultural "world views, values, and belief systems" that is transmitted through stories by elders to youth (Sefa Dei et al., 2002). In Australia, for example, Aboriginal people see a clear connection between "the Creator Spirit, the land, and way of being and acting in a cosmology that incorporates story, song, art, land, language, law, the bush university, stars, and birds into a world view and belief system" that has existed for millennia (Taylor, 2019). Indigenous norms, values, epistemologies, and lived experience guide people so that they can both comprehend and act on the world to address different challenges that they face on a day-to-day basis (Taylor, 2019).

The processes of globalization continue to disorient and challenge the way of being and knowing of Indigenous peoples and their ways of living. For example, the disappearance of the rainforest in Brazil due to the needs of multinational corporations like McDonald's for land is destroying the natural hinterlands of many Indigenous peoples forcing them to migrate to urban settings that in turn threatens to overwhelm their Indigenous cultures (Linstroth, 2016). In Canada, Aboriginal and First Nations peoples suffer from Continuing Traumatic Stress Disorder (CTSD) as a result of their experiences of racism, the violence of residential schools, and disappeared Aboriginal women (Battiste, 2000). However, Aboriginal and traditional teachings are empowering individuals, families, and communities to be resilient and to heal from the pain and suffering of the past as cultural gaps continue to challenge the communications and relationships of Aboriginal peoples and the dominant white Canadian settler culture (Ross, 2006).

In what is today upstate central New York, the Peacemaker brought a great way of restorative peace and reconciliation to the people of the Longhouse or the *Rotinonshonni* who were at war with each other (Rice, 2010). The Six Nations created a governing peaceful structure that both empowers and heals its peoples and influenced and shaped the development of the present-day U.S. constitutional and political system (Rice, 2013). In the Iroquois matriarchal society power ultimately, rests with the clan mothers who appoint and remove chiefs who do not follow the people's will and decide if the men are to go to war (Rice, 2013). Within the Dadin Kowa community in Jos, the Graveyard Committee and Elders Forum have also been strong peacebuilding institutions. The groups, which comprise Berom, Fulani, and Hausa elders as well as Christian and Muslim community leaders, were instrumental for preventing the diffusion of the conflict in neighboring Jos communities into Dadin Kowa (Eke, 2020). Having contributed to the nurturing of the community's children, the Dadin Kowa elders leveraged their emotional influence, and their power as community elders to control their youths (Eke, 2020).

Indigenous peacemaking works within the Indigenous community

An Indigenous peacemaking system works very well within that Indigenous community. However, what happens when security needs to be maintained and the Indigenous structures of control have either failed or are inactive? Conflicts break out not simply because there is a disputed issue. They occur when dispute management structures fail either because they are simply broken or have been suppressed. Under such a situation, a conflict management approach that is foreign to the local culture may be required. Yet, the local people remain the most useful resource for implementing such a system since they are from the community, know the terrain and are trusted by the people. Indigenous communities sometimes recognize this reality; hence they are flexible in peacemaking and peacekeeping. Barkin Ladi, in Plateau, Nigeria, is one such community where the Western security approach has been adapted to tackle the conflicts between Indigenous farmers and settler herders.

The failure of the Nigerian government to address the underlying causes of farmer-herder animosity led to full-blown conflict in the community. So, Barkin Ladi, like several other local communities in Plateau state, has had to achieve its own security using its own means. Although, as Bearak (2018) points out, Barkin Ladi employed the state policing framework to secure its people, it has relied on local resources to ensure that it is successful where the state has failed. Named Barkin Ladi's Vigilantes, the community's security architecture consists of Indigenous farmers and settler herders as well as different religions and ethnicities (Hahn & Bearak, 2018). Together, these individuals perform both security and conflict resolution duties, and, because of the inclusiveness of the group, are viewed as unbiased mediators and have become effective peacemakers (Hahn & Bearak, 2018).

These homegrown peacekeepers undertake routine security functions, such as securing the harvest of farmers and mounting checkpoints in troubled spots, as well as conflict resolution duties like mediating money and other matters (Bearak, 2018). Their identity as part of the community has facilitated their performance of their security duties as community members are open to sharing security information with them (Laurent & Hahn, 2018). They are, however, constrained by factors such as corruption within the mainstream security architecture and limited access to protective equipment (Bearak, 2018). While their effectiveness as security agents is minimal due to structural problems, the Barkin Ladi vigilantes have been impactful in their peacemaking roles. They, for example, can resolve herder-farmer disputes while they do so in ways that are satisfying to both parties (Laurent & Hahn, 2018). While their root in Barkin Ladi is the source of the community's trust in the vigilante's work, their satisfactory adjudication further bolsters their legitimacy within the community (Bearak, 2018).

Implications for teaching and training

The foregoing discussion shows the different ways in which local communities work to achieve peace. It reveals several low-tech peacebuilding practices that are being applied in post-direct violence settings. These approaches, because of their "everyday" nature, can be useful in promoting peace in different climes only if peacebuilders can identify them and recognize their value when they do. Certain individuals, for example, because of their past engagements in or status within local communities, can influence the behavior of others. Such individuals may facilitate ingroup mobilization for war. Yet, there are others who like the Dadin Kowa elders can be agents of positive change. So, peacebuilders must be trained about how to identify such benign local actors and channel their influence into peacebuilding. Considering the psychological impact of conflict on people, the role of peacebuilders must transcend identifying these peace agents. They must also orientate these individuals toward believing in their personal capacities for inspiring change.

Implications for practice and policy

In addition to harnessing local peacebuilding resources at the individual level, the broader community's confidence in their local peacebuilding resources must also be restored. Mainstreaming Indigenous practices in peacekeeping and peacebuilding is impracticable except if the local people are confident in their capacity to inspire change. Restoring that confidence cannot be the sole responsibility of the local people whose conflict experiences have dampened their resolve. Hence, external peacebuilders continue to be critical in peacekeeping and peacebuilding projects. Also, the local community is unlikely to reach this point of confidence whilst insecurity persists. Thus, the Western security approach tailored to align with the local reality, in the form of vigilantes or related systems, will continue to be valuable assets on the road to peace. Low-tech peacebuilding practices were, for example, undertaken in Jos to restore intergroup relations after, rather than during, the conflict episodes in the city.

While security must be relatively established for peace to be a realistic project, sustainable peace is achievable only when peacebuilding is grounded in Indigenous people's epistemologies and everyday practices. Yet not all Indigenous practices are just. Jos women's push for inclusion in the peacebuilding process and pursuit of peace outside the official peacebuilding channels indicate that even within the local environment, there may be factors that undermine inclusive peacebuilding. So, external peacebuilders eager to center the Indigenous culture in peacebuilding projects must be conscious of this reality in order to avoid privileging the aspects of some Indigenous cultures that facilitate the oppression of minority groups.

Conclusions

This chapter provides an important contribution about the important role of Indigenous knowledge and peacemaking and peacebuilding systems in farmer-herder conflicts taking place within our global village. It is critical to bring these groups and their unique and respectful ways of doing peace in from the margins if we are to truly include and empower all the citizens on our planet. Yet we must also be sensitive to the destructive elements of some Indigenous cultural practices that enable the oppression of minority groups, including women and youth (Mac Ginty, 2008a).

References

Avruch, K. (2008). Culture. In S. Cheldelin, D. Druckman, & L. Fast (Eds.), *Conflict: From analysis to intervention* (pp. 140–154). Continuum.

Avruch, K. (1998). *Culture and conflict resolution.* United States Institute of Peace Press.

Barnes, B. E., & Magdalena, C. (2016). Traditional peacemaking processes among Indigenous populations in Northern and Southern Philippines. In H. Tuso & M. Flaherty (Eds.), *Creating the third force* (pp. 209–229). Lexington.

Barnett, M. N. (2006). Building a Republican peace. *International Security, 30*(4), 87–112.

Battiste, M. (Ed.). (2000). *Reclaiming Indigenous voice and vision.* University of British Columbia.

Bearak. (2018). The ordinary people keeping the peace in Nigeria's deadly land feuds. *Washington Post.* https://www.washingtonpost.com/news/world/wp/2018/12/10/feature/the-ordinary-people-keeping-the-peace-in-nigerias-deadly-land-feuds/

Byrne, S. & Thiessen, C. (2019). Foreign peacebuilding intervention and emancipatory local agency for social justice. In S. Byrne, T. Matyok, I. M. Scott, & J. Senehi. (Eds.), *Routledge companion to peace and conflict studies* (pp. 131–142). Routledge.

Centre for Humanitarian Dialogue. (2021, July 13). Mediation and dialogue. https://www.hdcentre.org/activities/jos-plateau-state-nigeria/

Curle, A. (1994). New challenges for citizen peacemaking. *Medicine and War, 10*(2), 96–105.

De Heredia, M.I. (2014). Resistances and challenges to liberal peace processes. *Millennium: Journal of International Studies, 42*(2), 515–525.

Department for International Development. (2010). *The politics of poverty: Elites, citizens and states: Findings from ten years of DFID-funded research on governance and fragile states 2001–2010.* https://assets.publishing.service.gov.uk/government/uploads/system/uploads/attachment_data/file/67679/plcy-pltcs-dfid-rsch-synth-ppr.pdf

Eke, S. (2020). Community leaders as determinants of conflict and peace: Understanding the causes and spatial variation of ethnic conflict in Jos, Nigeria. [Doctoral dissertation, University of Manitoba]. MSpace. http://hdl.handle.net/1993/34802

Engle Merry, S. (2006). *Human rights and gender violence.* University of Chicago Press.

Enyiaka, C. C. (2019). *Religion, peacebuilding and human security in Africa: A case study of Jos Plateau State, Nigeria* [Doctoral thesis, Howard University]. eScholarship. https://search.proquest.com/openview/d1158cb2b58a735efbba2332667afd48/1?pq-origsite=gscholar&cbl=18750&diss=y

Epenshade, L. (2014). Tired of the violence. *Canadian Mennonite, 18*(12), 25–26.

European Union. (2005). *EU concept for ESDP support to security sector reform.* https://data.consilium.europa.eu/doc/document/ST-12566-2005-REV-4/en/pdf

Hahn, J., & Bearak, M. (2018). *Building peace in plateau state, Nigeria.* https://pulitzercenter.org/projects/building-peace-plateau-state-nigeria

Heathershaw, J. (2013). Towards better theories of peacebuilding. *Peacebuilding, 1*(2), 275–282.

Hughes, C., Öjendal, J., & Schierenbeck, I. (2015). The struggle versus the song – the local turn in peacebuilding. *Third World Quarterly, 36*(5), 817–824.

Jahn, B. (2007). The tragedy of liberal diplomacy. *Journal of Intervention and Statebuilding, 1*(2), 211–229.

Laurent, O., & Hahn, J. (2018, December 17). Meet the peacekeepers of Nigeria's plateau state. *Washington Post.* https://www.washingtonpost.com/news/in-sight/wp/2018/12/17/meet-the-peacekeepers-of-nigerias-plateau-state/

Lederach, J. P. (1995). *Preparing for peace: Conflict transformation across cultures.* Syracuse University Press.

Lederach, J. P. (1997). *Building Peace: Sustainable reconciliation in divided societies.* United States Institute of Peace Press.

Leonardsson, H., & Rudd G. (2015) The 'local turn' in peacebuilding. *Third World Quarterly, 36*(5), 825–839.

Linstroth. J. P. (2016). Conflict avoidance among the Satere-Mawme of Manaus, Brazil and peacemaking behavior among Amazonian Amerindians. In H. Tuso & M. Flaherty (Eds.), *Creating the third force* (pp. 249–279). Lexington.

Mac Ginty, R. (2016). Indigenous peacemaking in Northern Ireland. In H. Tuso & M. Flaherty (Eds.), *Creating the third force* (pp. 127–143). Lexington Press.

Mac Ginty, R. (2011). *International peacebuilding and local resistance: Hybrid forms of peace.* Palgrave Macmillan.

Mac Ginty, R. (2008a). Indigenous peace-making versus the liberal peace. *Cooperation and Conflict, 43*(2), 139–163.

Mac Ginty, R. (2008b). *No war, no peace: The rejuvenation of stalled peace processes*. Palgrave Macmillan.

Mac Ginty, R. & Richmond, O. P. (2013). The local turn in peace building. *Third World Quarterly, 34*(5), 763–783.

Mitchell, A. (2010). Peace beyond process? *Millennium: Journal of International Studies, 38*(3), 641–664.

Narten, J. (2008). Post-conflict peacebuilding and local ownership. *Journal of Intervention and Statebuilding, 2*(1), 369–390.

Nyam, E. A. (2016). *Transformative conflict resolution using forum theatre: The Jos North, Nigeria Flashpoint Paradigm* [Doctoral thesis, Kenyatta University]. https://ir-library.ku.ac.ke/bitstream/handle/123456789/17643/Transformative%20conflictre%20solution……pdf?sequence=1&isAllowed=y

Ombati, M. (2015). Women transcending "boundaries" in indigenous peacebuilding in Kenya's Sotik/Borabu border conflict. *Multidisciplinary Journal of Gender Studies, 4*(1), 637–661.

Paffenholz, T. (2015). Unpacking the local turn in peacebuilding. *Third World Quarterly, 36*(5), 857–874.

Paris, R. (2010). Saving liberal peacebuilding. *Review of International Studies, 36*(1), 337–365.

Paris, R. (1997). Peacebuilding and the limits of liberal internationalism. *International Security, 22*(2), 54–89.

Peace Agreements. (2014). *HD Jos forum inter-communal dialogue process joint declaration of commitment to peace and cooperation*. https://www.peaceagreements.org/viewmasterdocument/1536

Peace Women. (2010). *Nigerian women protest at Jos killings*. https://www.peacewomen.org/content/nigeria-nigeria-women-protest-jos-killings

Philipsen, L. (2014). When liberal peacebuilding fails. *Journal of Intervention and Statebuilding, 8*(1), 42–67.

Pouligny, B. (2005). Civil society and post-conflict peacebuilding. *Security Dialogue, 36*(4), 495–510.

Rampton, D., & Nadarajah, S. (2017). A long view of liberal peace and its European crisis. *Journal of International Relations, 23*(2), 441–465.

Rice, B (2013). *The Rotinonshonni: A traditional Iroquoian history through the eyes of Teharonhia: Wako and Sawiskera*. Syracuse University Press.

Rice, B. (2010). Restorative processes of peace and healing within the governing structures of the *Rotinonshonni* 'longhouse people.' In D. J. D. Sandole, S. Byrne, I. Sandole-Staroste, & J. Senehi (Eds.), *Handbook of conflict analysis and resolution* (pp. 409–419). Routledge.

Roberts, D. (2012). Saving liberal peacebuilding from itself. *Peace Review, 24*(3), 366–373.

Roberts, D. (2011). Post-conflict peacebuilding, liberal irrelevance and the locus of legitimacy. *International Peacekeeping, 18*(4), 410–424.

Robins, S. (2013). An empirical approach to post-conflict legitimacy. *Journal of Intervention and Statebuilding, 7*(1), 45–64.

Ross, R. (2006). *Dancing with a ghost: Exploring Aboriginal reality*. Penguin.

Sabaratnam, M. (2013). Avatars of Eurocentrism in the critique of the liberal peace. *Security Dialogue, 44*(3), 259–278.

Schirch, L. (2004). *Ritual and symbol in peacebuilding*. Kumarian.

Sefa Dei, G. J., Hall, B. L., & Goldin Rosenberg, D. (Eds.) (2002). *Indigenous knowledges in global contexts*. University of Toronto.

Search for Common Ground. (2021). *Naija girls and intergroup tolerance*. https://www.sfcg.org/naija-girls-ending-violence-in-northern-nigeria/

Senehi, J. (2009). The role of constructive, transcultural storytelling in ethnopolitical conflict transformation in Northern Ireland. In G. Irani, V. Volkan, & J. Carter (Eds.), *Regional and ethnic conflicts: Perspectives from the front lines* (pp. 227–237). Prentice Hall.

Senehi, J. (2002). Constructive storytelling: A peace process. *Peace and Conflict Studies, 9*(2), 41–62.

Senehi, J. (2000). Constructive storytelling in intercommunal conflicts. In S. Byrne & C. Irvin (Eds.) & P. Dixon, B. Polkinghorn, & J. Senehi (Assoc. Eds.), *Reconcilable differences: Turning points in ethnopolitical conflicts* (pp. 96–114). Kumarian.

Senehi, J. (2010). Building peace: Storytelling to transform conflicts constructively. In D. J. D. Sandole, S. Byrne, I. Sandole-Staroste, & J. Senehi (Eds.), *Handbook of conflict analysis and resolution* (pp. 199–212). Routledge.

Taylor, P. (2019). *Yubulyawan dreaming project*. http://ydproject.com/

Thiessen, C. (2011). Emancipatory peacebuilding: Critical responses to (neo)liberal trends. In T. Maytok, J. Senehi, & S. Byrne (Eds.), *Critical Issues in peace and conflict studies* (pp. 115–142). Lexington Press.

Tursunova, Z. (2014). *Women's lives and livelihoods in post-Soviet Uzbekistan*. Lexington Books.

United Nations. (2000). *Report of the panel on United Nations peace operations*. https://www.un.org/en/events/pastevents/brahimi_report.shtml

UN Women. (2017). *Tired of communal conflicts in northern Nigeria, women-led peace networks take-action*. https://www.unwomen.org/en/news/stories/2017/9/feature-nigeria-women-led-peace-networks-take-action

United Religions Initiative. (2018). *Interfaith dialogue follows Nigeria massacre*. https://www.uri.org/uri-story/20180731-interfaith-dialogue-follows-nigeria-massacre

United States Agency for International Development. (2009). *Security sector reform*. https://www.state.gov/documents/organization/115810.pdf

Visoka, G., & Richmond, O. (2017). After liberal peace? *International Studies Perspectives*, *18*(1), 110–129.

Young, D. (2018). Peacebuilding in Nigeria. *Reliefweb*. https://reliefweb.int/report/nigeria/peace-building-nigeria

28
FOCAL POINTS IN ETHNIC CONFLICTS: A PEACEBUILDING CONTINUUM

Jessica Senehi

Recently, in professional, personal, and classroom conversations, people have expressed great concern about a variety of social problems and society's future. This reflects an emerging pessimism in the West that characterizes our current time, perhaps crystalized by the pandemic, but building up over some years. Not only has the pandemic caused death and disease on a massive and global scale, but it also made the impact of social inequalities, in the U.S. and globally, vivid, and undeniable. During the summer of 2020, George Floyd was captured by police and murdered. This murder was captured on an iPhone by 17-year-old witness Darnella Frazier and further witnessed by millions around the world, bringing a 20/20 vision to racism often unseen and unacknowledged. This catalyzed the Black Lives Matter movement to be the biggest people's movement in U.S. history, and to also become a global movement. A group of psychiatrists from around the world have declared that global society is facing a mental health crisis; more than 1 billion people are affected by trauma as a result of political violence or natural disasters (Mollica, 2011).

While we may think of natural disasters as "acts of God" and distinct from identity-based violence, climate change is impacted by human practices and decisions (e.g., Flynn, 2015), with a greater negative impact on people affected by discrimination (e.g., Farbotko & Lazrus, 2012). The ongoing climate crisis also became even less possible to dismiss with the fires in Australia in late 2019, island nations fighting for their survival (e.g., Steiner, 2015), and young people who are vowing not to have children (e.g., Green, 2021), all during an era called "the sixth extinction" (e.g., Kolbert, 2014). On the political front, authoritarian governments and compromised democracies are on the rise (e.g., World Policy Review, 2020), global power is shifting and global economic "fault-lines" emerge (e.g., Fouskas & Gökay, 2019), and superpowers have seemed to teeter on the precipice of war. A common topic of public discourse is whether or not the democracy in the United States will endure (e.g., Bokat-Lindell, 2021; Serwer, 2021).

It seems like the mood was not always so. On November 9, 1989, the German people tore down the Berlin Wall, and for many in the West this symbolized the end of the Cold War period, and an opening up of possibilities for freedom and democracy. This validated the efforts of more than 600 academics from the United States and the former USSR who had connected in a spirit of cultural détente and citizen diplomacy, to use Harold Saunder's (1999) term, epitomized by the Dartmouth Conference, established by Norman Cousins in 1959.

The academic field of conflict resolution burgeoned in the late 1980s and 1990s, especially in the United States. This was driven in large part by funding from the William and Flora Hewlett Foundation, which funded ten academic programs on conflict resolution with the goal that those programs would become sustainable and institutionalized. The Hewlett Foundation provided more than $160 million in grants to more than 320 organizations (Kovick, 2005). In the post–Cold War era, there was increased attention to drawing on conflict resolution theory and practices to address ethnopolitical conflicts, or intercommunal conflicts, that had become more salient with the shift in global power relations.

In 1985, John Burton joined George Mason University and is credited with providing a compelling vision of world society alternative to the bleakness of Realpolitik, and a method for addressing conflicts through dialogue (Sandole, 2001). At Harvard, Herbert Kelman, Nadim Rouhana, Tamra Pearson d'Estrée, Jay Rothman, and many others applied the problem-solving methods established by Burton, especially in relation to the Israeli-Palestinian conflict (e.g., Kelman, 2015). At the University of Maryland, Ted Robert Gurr directed the Minorities at Risk Project in the Center of International Development and Conflict Management and examined 275 politically active ethnic conflicts (Gurr, 1993, 2000). Vamik Volkan, Demetrios Julius, and Joseph Montville (1990, 1991) examined the psychodynamics of international and intercommunal conflicts. At Syracuse University, research on intractable conflicts was funded by the MacArthur Foundation (Kriesberg et al., 1989). There was almost always an emphasis that sustainable conflict resolution required addressing the issues of all parties and maximizing mutual gains; positive peace requires the presence of social justice (King, 1992, [1962]; Galtung, 1969). In the early 1990s, the Hewlett Foundation, which had previously supported conflict resolution approaches within the United States, began to support projects focusing on conflict globally and on more diverse types of Track II projects (Kovick, 2005). Throughout the world, people-to-people projects addressed ethnopolitical strife (van Tongeren et al., 2005).

However, in the aftermath of the September 11, 2001, attacks in the United States, the Hewlett Foundation exited a 20-year (1984–2004) conflict resolution project for other priorities. The final report on the project concludes:

> In many ways, the field of conflict resolution has been built, no longer requiring the stewardship and support of the Hewlett Foundation. At the same time, the field faces significant challenges in the years ahead, and time will tell if the field is able to meet those challenges. (Kovick, 2005, p. 64)

Of course, no one foundation, institution, or geographical region defines conflict resolution and peacebuilding. It is almost laughable to think that the field of conflict resolution and peacebuilding would be something that would need to be established, as all human societies have had practices and ideas in place to address conflicts, and words for peace and harmony are some of the oldest in human language. However, the academic field of conflict resolution, at least in the United States, and perhaps everywhere, is inextricably linked to ideas about human nature, morality, culpability, and goals for the future, and therefore becomes fraught by the very conflicts it seeks to address.

As someone teaching peace and conflict studies in a postsecondary setting—in particular, graduate school, where people are allocating a lot of their personal energies and resources to focused study—I'm mindful of two things: first, the smallness of our field in the face of the enormity of some of the problems we seek to address; and, second, the lack of clear career paths and access to be of direct influence in these problems. This chapter seeks to address these issues and reclaim the optimism of the field (if that's needed) by emphasizing and integrating earlier peacebuilding approaches that emphasized a breadth of conflict resolution approaches, which I'm calling a intercultural peacebuilding continuum. This opens up, more explicitly, possibilities for peacebuilding and peace work.

Background: Leveraging the complexity of conflict

Conflict theory has long identified conflicts' complexity. Marc Howard Ross (1993) distinguished among structural and psychocultural dynamics in intercultural conflicts. *Social cubism* is the idea that ethnopolitical conflicts have multiple aspects that operate in interconnected ways with the result that such conflicts are resistant to resolution; these include demographic, political, economic, historical, historical, and psychocultural dimensions (Byrne & Carter, 1996). Conflicts between ethnic groups and/or defined in identity-based terms become encoded in the culture of those identity groups, and this can be a source of intractability (Northrup, 1989). For such conflicts, even when agreements are signed by states, conflicts can remain and percolate within the grassroots society; a whole social group will not likely change their perspectives at the same time, to the same degree, at the same rate, and for the same reasons. Ultimately, sustainable conflict resolution of intractable ethnopolitical conflicts that attends to social justice requires profound social change.

There will be no magic pill, nor "silver bullet," nor panacea, to create peace. Ethnopolitical and longstanding identity-based conflicts are not located in one site where they can be surgically removed. Rather, they operate throughout the social system. This complexity also suggests different access points, or focal points, for social change and sustainable conflict resolution. In 1981, Davidson and Montville (1981) coined the term "Track Two" diplomacy (Montville, 2006) to validate the efforts outside of formal diplomacy conducted by government representatives, and validated the work done by academics and others to promote mutual understanding between groups and to reduce tension through problem-solving workshops or other citizen-led or people-to-people initiatives. Building on this concept, Louise Diamond and John McDonald (1996) argued that a systemic problem requires peacebuilding initiatives differently situated, and they proposed a framework of diplomacy along multiple tracks, led by diverse actors: (1) formal negotiators; (2) professional conflict resolution third-party-facilitators, as per Davidson and Montville's Track II; (3) private citizens; (4) business actors; (5) activists; (6) researchers, trainers, and educators; (7) religious leaders and followers; (8) funders; and (9) public opinion influencers. Each of these suggests numerous roles and possibilities to address ethnopolitical conflict in sustainable ways.

John Paul Lederach and Katie Mansfield (2010) charted fourteen strategic pathways for peace. These include three core areas, which are each associated with a number of career paths: (1) achieving structural and institutional change—through law, dealing with transnational and global threats, development, and education; (2) achieving violence prevention, conflict response, and transformation—through dialogue and conflict resolution strategies, nonviolent social change, government and multilateral efforts, and humanitarian action; and (3) achiving justice and healing—through restorative justice, transitional justice, and trauma healing. Zelizer and Oliphant (2012) identified a demand for peacebuilders who are able to develop integrated programs in diverse sectors, including international development, humanitarian assistance, gender, the private sector, religion, environment, media, health, and law. Further, there is increasing recognition of Indigenous peacemaking approaches (Cormier, 2018, 2019; Tuso & Flaherty, 2016), as well as local approaches (Kroeker, 2021; Mac Ginty & Richmond, 2013), traditional approaches (Stobbe, 2015), everyday peacebuilding (Mac Ginty, 2014, 2021; McLean, 2014; Neustaeter, 2015), and hybrid approaches (Mac Ginty, 2011).

These ideas resonate with significant theories that originated outside peace and conflict studies: in particular, critical race theory and intersectionality. Structural violence almost always relates to conflict defined in ethnic terms because it involves one group getting unequal access to resources (Chasin, 1997) and/or being targeted based on their identity (Galtung, 1990). Such structural and systemic violence can become embedded in culture and therefore operate in ways of which people are largely unaware (Galtung, 1990), can serve as a rationale for the exploitation of colonized regions (Césaire, 2001 [1950]), and can be internalized in people's consciousness (Fanon, 2005 [1961]). Reflection and dialogue may be required to even bring some of these issues to consciousness where they can be addressed (Friere, 2000 [1970]). Critical race theory, originated by the lawyer Derrick Bell (1995), argues that racial inequality, based on socially constructed notions of difference, is normalized and encoded in all systems of society. This is consistent with ideas in the field of peace and conflict studies, including structural violence (Galtung, 1990), the complexity of conflict (Byrne & Carter, 1996), and the legacy of colonialism (Clarke & Byrne, 2017; Karari, 2018; Rahman et al., 2018), as well as the need for consciousness raising and/or awareness-of-self in context (Lederach, 1996). Further, the idea of intersectionality, compellingly explicated by Kimberlé Crenshaw (1989, 2019), and more recently elaborated by Patricia Hill Collins (2019) also brings forward the need to consider how intersecting social positions where one is marginalized can impact a person in damaging ways that are often unrecognized. This is consistent with the importance of providing a consideration of gender and power in the analysis of conflicts. These approaches suggest promising directions for the field and for intercommunal peacebuilding.

The academic study of peacebuilding in ethnic conflicts and the field of conflict resolution has a few key challenges. First, there is a need for a clearer codifying of peacebuilding frameworks to account for the complexity of ethnic conflicts. This is also important for addressing critiques of the field, as expressed in the Hewlett Foundation report mentioned above, that peacebuilding projects at the more grassroots level are "too diffuse and unfocused" and have not been adequately reviewed by evaluation research (Kovick, p. 17). Second, it is important to make linkages with relevant and/or overlapping social theories from other disciplines, including critical race theory and intersectionality, as well as gender studies, postcolonial studies, and critical pedagogy. Third, there is a need to better make sense of the tension between personal and political change, long identified by John Paul Lederach (1996). While this is a central dilemma of all social theory, in recent years, in the face of severe global issues, there seems to be a particular frustration with powerful and totalizing social structures among people working as peacemakers (Ahmed, 2017). Fourth, there is tension between efforts to understand the perspectives of all parties and the need for social justice and human rights. Sometimes this is reflected in the fact that peacemakers from within an affected community may call for structural change, whereas peacemakers from outside the affected community will be more engaged in humanitarian efforts and less focused on politics (Dueck-Read, 2016). Intercultural problem-solving—such as, for example, Jay Rothman's (2012) ARIA model—typically calls for understanding the perspectives of all parties in order to maximize mutual gains whereas human rights approaches may seek to name, blame, and shame. Finally, one of the challenges of peacebuilding is a lack of understanding of the work of the field. There are many people working in peacebuilding at various levels, especially the grassroots, and their work is little recognized and valued. This limits successful and innovative approaches from being applied in more contexts and in scaled-up ways, and limits envisioning what is possible.

Key insights

This chapter seeks to address some of these issues by reviewing established peacebuilding approaches in ethnic conflicts in order to bring more clarity to how particular peacebuilding efforts fit into a larger peacebuilding process. Established work in peacebuilding is organized into a peacebuilding continuum encompassing ten focal points to help manage the complexity across levels of analysis, sectors of peacebuilding, and peacebuilding roles. Second, these focal points go generally from the personal level to the structural level, that is, from personal reflexivity and considerations of the ethics of intervention to the formal peace processes and governance though in some cases peacebuilding in one focal point might involve work at multiple levels. The framework encompasses both the need to understand where each side is coming through dialogue and problem-solving approaches, as well as addressing harms and trauma caused by inequality and/or violence. The goal is that clarifying these focal points will be helpful to address concerns that the peacebuilding is diffuse and underevaluated as well as to consolidate gains in knowledge and skills.

Focal point 1: The ethics of intercultural peacebuilding

As a starting point, this level addresses the ethics of intervention in a cultural context. Essentially, intervention must not replicate a patronizing and potentially colonial relationship, but be deeply informed by decolonizing approaches. Peacebuilders must emphasize the central role of those who are being helped in an intervention, and respect their knowledge (Lederach, 1996); local knowledge is significant and critical for finding workable and sustainable solutions and preventing unforeseen harms (Scott, 1995). The United Nations (2020) provides seven recommendations for community engagement for sustainable peacebuilding, and first and foremost is a "Deeper understanding of local context through respectful, coherent and flexible engagement" (p. 8). For those working with Indigenous communities, as researchers or partners in peacebuilding, it is important to be aware of protocols that exist, as well as the ethics of intervention. Central to all research and practice should be a consideration of Indigenous relations and protocols for working with Indigenous communities. Taking intersectionality into account, and how people in different social locations may experience conflict differently and/or have different needs, it is critical to have an inclusive peacebuilding process, and include all stakeholders as well as women, young people, people with disabilities, and the LGBTQ community in identifying issues and charting a path forward.

Focal point 2: Reflexivity and positionality

Being aware of one's own cultural biases—that is, reflexivity, as per England (1994)—is critical to effective peacebuilding in ethnic conflicts. Reflection on one's practices—that is *praxis,* as per Friere (2000 [1970])—is important for developing skills and theory. Reflecting on how one's peace work is informed by one's personal and social history can help build the self-awareness necessary for intercultural work (Senehi, 2015). Knowing one's social positions also impacts how one enters into conflict. For example, Kenneth Hardy (2016) has developed a model for accounting for power in addressing racism by attending to one's position as privileged self or subjugated self, which will require different tasks. For example, a task of the privileged is "to differentiate between intentions and consequences" and starts with an acknowledgment of the latter, whereas a task for the subjugated is "to challenge silence and voicelessness" (p. 133). Our practice is not something that is produced outside of ourselves, but rather is interrelated with our identity and beliefs. In fact, Mary Anne Clarke (2015) argued that to work effectively with another culture ultimately leads to a change in one's own identity.

Focal point 3: Dialogue and problem-solving

Dialogue and problem-solving is an important aspect of peacebuilding in ethnic conflicts, especially in regard to understanding the concerns of all sides. The problem-solving approach was originally developed in the early 1960s by John Burton while he was teaching international relations at University College London (Mitchell, 2005). An articulation of this approach is interactive conflict resolution, which has been used in settings of protracted conflict, toward goals of deep understanding, mutual recognition and respect, and finding jointly acceptable and sustainable solutions—in sum, an improved relationship between the parties (Fisher, 1997, p. 241). Ronald Fisher (2005) edited a volume to review and evaluate the essential contributions of interactive conflict resolution to the Israeli-Palestinian conflict (Kelman, 2005), the Mozambique peace process (Bartoli, 2005), the Moldova conflict (Williams, 2005), Georgian–South Ossetian peacemaking (Nan, 2005), and the Peru-Ecuador peace process (Kaufman & Sosnowski, 2005). Harold Saunders (1999) introduced sustained dialogue as a type of interactive conflict resolution, which emphasized five stages: (1) deciding to engage, (2) mapping and naming problems and relationships, (3) probing problems and relationships to choose a direction, (4) scenario-building—experiencing a changing relationship, and (5) acting together to make change happen. This approach was used during the conflict in Tajikistan, during the period of 1993–1996, and is considered an example of citizen diplomacy effectively influencing the peace process (Saunders, 2005).

Focal point 4: Indigenous and local approaches

Indigenous peoples and local peacemakers hold important knowledge and skills about peacebuilding in their communities and also contribute to global knowledge of peacebuilding (Mac Ginty & Richmond, 2013). Connecting to Indigenous knowledge is a means for Indigenous peoples to reclaim culture and rediscover Indigenous peace (Cormier, 2018). Benjamin Maiangwa (2021) explores how conflicting notions of Indigeneity and belonging in Nigeria impact conflict and peacebuilding among the Fulani and other ethnic groups. In a study of peacebuilding in the Philippines, Wendy Kroeker (2021) shares peacebuilding knowledge from local peacebuilders and their motivations and strategies for peacebuilding in the aftermath of violence and trauma. Awareness and consideration of Indigenous, traditional, and local knowledges is critical for peacebuilding.

Focal point 5: Multitrack peacebuilding and community-based organizations

The importance of multitrack peacebuilding is increasingly recognized. Some peacebuilding projects leverages the joy and appeal of sports to build intercultural relationships and understanding (Sugden & Tomlinson, 2018). Arts have proven a powerful way to draw on cultural understandings, positive emotions, and create a more complex narrative that allows for shared identity (Mitchell et al., 2020).

Economic support from the European Union for bilateral projects has been used to support peacebuilding in Northern Ireland (Byrne, 2015). While business and corporate interests, e.g., resource extraction, can be a source of conflict, there is a role for business in peacebuilding; local business has an interest in peace and has diverse roles to play in promoting intergroup rapprochement and new norms (Killick et al., 2005). This focal point also encompasses civil society organizations that are involved in peace projects. To recognize innovative approaches by people across sectors to transform ethnic conflict facilitates learning from the work through evaluation, applying insights in broader context, and scaling up initiatives.

Focal point 6: Peace education

Peace education can take many forms and can refer to curriculum development about conflicts and how to resolve conflicts, as well as approaches to teaching. Peace education might refer to education in complex emergencies arising from ethnopolitical conflicts. Integrated education is one approach to peacebuilding and reconciliation in conflicts recovering from conflict (e.g., Byrne, 1997). Peace education approaches to ethnic conflict have been developed and examined in many contexts, and are recognized as an essential aspect of the systemic social change that sustainable peace requires (Bekerman & McGlynn, 2007). Facing History and Ourselves is an international organization that seeks to provide guidance about history lessons going forward to support educators; while these resources are a critical resource for educators, the implementation is not always easy and teachers need a lot of support in order to apply these lessons, especially in their own context (Murphy et al., 2016). In Canada, decolonizing education is critical for reconciliation and addressing racism toward Indigenous peoples and the legacy of colonialism; meanwhile, the implementation of this faces many barriers that are critical to address (Tennent, 2021).

Focal point 7: Nonviolent collective action and building awareness

Peacebuilding depends on the will to resolve, and nonviolent collective action has been used by groups with less power to pressure those in power to address issues (Sharp & Paulson, 2005). In Northern Ireland, in 1976, Mairead Corrigan and Betty Williams cofounded the Community of Peace and established a nonviolent movement for peace in Northern Ireland, for which work they received the Nobel Peace Prize that year. In Sri Lanka, as well as other regions, the courageous nonviolent protective accompaniment of Peace Brigades International has been an important resource for peacebuilding (Coy, 2001).

Focal point 8: Trauma-healing

Increasingly, the importance of trauma healing is recognized. In Northern Ireland, at the Junction in Derry/Londonderry, Maureen Hetherington developed a program called *Towards Understanding and Healing*, which included residencies where people affected by the conflict on both sides of the Protestant-Catholic divide met in a spirit of dialogue and encounter (O'Hagan, 2008). Currently, Healing Through Remembering is an independent organization based on five key themes: storytelling, truth recovery and acknowledgment, a living memorial museum, and commemoration (Healing Through Remembering, 2021). The Green String Network, based in Nairobi, works with communities affected by ethnic violence integrating peacebuilding and trauma-healing approaches to address the instability caused by trauma. Similarly, Pumla Gobodo Madikazela (2016) argues that addressing historical trauma is necessary to break intergenerational cycles of repetition.

Focal point 9: Transitional justice

Transitional justice encompasses a breadth of approaches for a society moving out of violence to address the harms of the past that have produced collective trauma and affected so many people that they cannot be addressed through the traditional legal system. A collective process is required for the society to go forward, and this includes truth and reconciliation commissions, and reparations programs. Transitional justice processes can be a bridge between the personal and the political, and a chance to address issues of power, human rights, and social justice in the relationship between ethnic groups.

Focal point 10: Formal peace processes

Formal peace processes can lead to important governance and legal changes, and are a form of structural redress that will in turn impact culture. Formal peace processes are critical to sustainable peace, and also interdepend with the other levels. Sustainable, inclusive, and ethical peacebuilding requires inclusion and participation of people from multiple levels and sectors of society—including civil society, young people, and people with disabilities (Mallon, 2021). Formal peace processes and accords are a major goal of peacebuilding, and, at the same time, it is valuable to see formal peace processes as one focal point in a spectrum of peacebuilding activities as the success of peace processes will interdepend with other focal points, such as relationships at the grassroots level, systemic change, trauma healing, and attention to social justice.

Implication for teaching and training

Being mindful of this framework will help locate a particular intervention or approach within a larger social system of peacebuilding. No one can be an expert in all or even many of these approaches, and yet it may strengthen people in their work to see how it may relate to other aspects of peacebuilding. Ethnic conflicts are always intercultural, and intercultural conflict resolution courses are typically part of a peacebuilding curriculum. In course curricula, using this or a similar frame allows for a consideration from the personal to the political. This framework will also emphasize one's personal reflexivity and the importance of the ethics of intervention, including an intersectional analysis that considers how different forms of marginalization may affect people, and seeks to include women, youth, the LGBTQ community, and people with disabilities.

Implications for practice and policy

One of the challenges of the field of peacebuilding in ethnic conflicts, even though so many people are engaged in this work, is how little this work is understood, and how little of the knowledge is translated to the public. If anything, society in the West is often resistant to the field as a whole. However, the academic field of conflict resolution, at least in the United States, and perhaps everywhere, is inextricably linked to ideas about human nature, morality, culpability, and goals for the future, and therefore becomes fraught by the very conflicts it seeks to address.

As is well-known, knowledge is constrained by power. Many theorists and researchers have demonstrated in detail the knowledge, wisdom, and witnessing that is often dismissed, ignored, or denied by mainstream discourses, including academic scholarship. This is one of the most sophisticated and unnoticeable ways that power and privilege operate at the expense of truth and social justice. Maybe one of the most subversive and effective ways to promote ethnopolitical peacebuilding is to visibilize, recognize, amplify, replicate, and build on peacebuilding efforts at various levels and dimensions of society.

Peacebuilding is not a matter of hope versus pessimism. Unquestioned hope can blind us to dangers; unquestioned pessimism can blind us to possibilities. Ethnic conflicts and social inequality are a global health pandemic. Clear-eyed evidence-based knowledge and best practices are needed to navigate the perils facing the world and to chart a path forward.

References

Ahmed, K. (2017). *Approaches to community-based peacebuilding initiatives: Theory and praxis on the front lines.* Lexington.
Bartoli, A. (2005). Learning from the Mozambique Peace Process: The role of the community of Saint'Egidio. In R. Fisher (Ed.), *Paving the way: Contributions of interactive conflict resolution to peacemaking* (pp. 79–104). Lexington.
Bekerman, Z., & McGlynn, C. (2007). *Addressing ethnic conflict through peace education: International perspectives.* Palgrave Macmillan.
Bell, D. A. (1995). Who's afraid of critical race theory. *University of Illinois Law Review, 4*, 893–910.
Bokat-Lindell, S. (2021, September 30). Will 2024 be the year American democracy dies? *New York Times.* https://www.nytimes.com/2021/09/30/opinion/american-democracy-2024.html?searchResultPosition=2
Byrne. S. (2015). *Economic assistance and conflict transformation: Peacebuilding in Northern Ireland.* Routledge.
Byrne, S. (1997). *Growing up in a divided society: The influence of conflict on Belfast schoolchildren.* Associated University Presses.
Byrne, S., & Carter, N. (1996). Social cubism: Six social forces of ethnoterritorial conflict in Northern Ireland and Quebec. *Peace and Conflict Studies, 3*(2), 52–71.
Césaire, A. (2001 [1950]). *Discourse on colonialism.* Monthly Review Press.
Chasin, B. H. (1997). *Inequality and violence in the United States: Casualties of capitalism.* Humanities Press International.
Clarke, M. A. (2015). *As a social worker in northern First Nations am I also a peacebuilder?* [Master's thesis, University of Manitoba].
Clarke, M. A., & Byrne, S. (2017). The three R's: Resistance, resilience and reconciliation in Ireland and Canada. *Peace Research: Canadian Journal of Peace and Conflict Studies, 49*(2), 105–132.
Collins, P. H. (2019). *Intersectionality as critical social theory.* Duke University Press.
Cormier, P. N. (2019). The paradox of complexity in peace and conflict studies: Indigenous culture, identity, and peacebuilding. In S. Byrne, T. Matyók, I. M. Scott, & J. Senehi (Eds.). *Routledge companion to peace and conflict studies* (pp. 349–358). Routledge.
Cormier, P. N. (2018). Storytelling and peace research in Indigenous contexts: Learning the peace culture of *opaaganasiniing* (place where the pipestone comes from). *Storytelling, Self, Society, 14*(2), 161–184.
Coy, P. G. (2001). Shared risks and dilemmas on a Peace Brigades International team in Sri Lanka. *Journal of Contemporary Ethnography, 30*(5), 575–606.
Crenshaw, K. (2019). *On intersectionality.* New Press.
Crenshaw, K. (1989). Demarginalizing the intersection of race and sex: A Black feminist critique of antidiscrimination doctrine, feminist theory and antiracist politics. *University of Chicago Legal Forum, 1989*(1), Article 8. https://chicagounbound.uchicago.edu/uclf/vol1989/iss1/8
Davidson, W. D., & Montville, J. V. (1981). Foreign policy according to Freud. *Foreign policy, 45*,145–157.
Diamond, L., & McDonald, J. W. (1996). *Multi-track diplomacy: A systems approach to peace.* Kumarian.
Dueck-Read, J. (2016). *Transnational activism: Intersectional identities and peacebuilding in the border justice movement* [Doctoral dissertation, University of Manitoba].
England, K. V. L. (1994). Getting personal: Reflexivity, positionality, and feminist research. *The Professional Geographer, 46*(1), 80–89.
Fanon, F. (2005 [1961]). *Wretched of the earth.* Grove Press.
Farbotko, C., & Lazrus, H. (2012). The first climate refugees? Contesting global narratives of climate change in Tuvalu. *Global Environmental Change, 22*(2), 382–390.
Fisher, R. (2005). *Paving the way: Contributions of interactive conflict resolution to peacemaking.* Lexington.
Fisher, R. (Ed.). (1997). *Interactive conflict resolution.* Syracuse University Press.
Flynn, S. E. (2015, August 24). Katrina at 10: Reflecting on a human-made disaster. *Council on Foreign Relations.* https://onlinelibrary-wiley-com.uml.idm.oclc.org/doi/full/10.1111/j.1467-8373.2010.001413.x
Fouskas, V., & Gökay, B. (2019). *The disintegration of Euro-Atlanticism and the new authoritarianism global power-shift.* Springer.
Friere, P. (2000 [1970]). *Pedagogy of the oppressed.* Continuum.
Galtung, J. (1990). Cultural violence. *Peace Research, 17*(3), 291–305.
Galtung, J. (1969). Violence, peace, and peace research. *Journal of Peace Research, 6*(3), 167–191.

Gobodo-Madikizela, P. (Ed.). (2016). *Breaking intergenerational cycles of repetition: A global dialogue on historical trauma and memory*. Barbara Budrich Publishers.

Green, E. (2021, September 20). A world without children. *The Atlantic*.

Gurr, T. R. (2000). *Peoples versus states: Why peace settlements succeed or fail*. U.S. Institute of Peace.

Gurr, T. R. (1993). *Minorities at risk: A global view of ethnopolitical conflicts*. U.S. Institute of Peace.

Hardy, K. V. (2016). Anti-racist approaches for shaping theoretical and practice paradigms. In M. Pender-Greene & A. Siskin (Eds.), *Strategies for deconstructing racism in the health and human services* (pp. 129–135). Oxford University Press.

Healing Through Remembering. (August 20, 2021). http://healingthroughremembering.org

Karari, P. (2018). Modus operandi of oppressing the "savages": The Kenyan British colonial experience. *Peace and Conflict Studies*, *25*(1), Article 2. https://nsuworks.nova.edu/pcs/vol25/iss1/2

Kaufman, E., & Sosnowski, S. (2005). The Peru-Ecuador peace process: The contributions of track-two diplomacy. In R. Fisher (Ed.), *Paving the way: Contributions of interactive conflict resolution to peacemaking* (pp. 175–202). Lexington.

Kelman, H. C. (2015). The development of interactive problem-solving: Following in John Burton's footsteps. *Psychology*, *36*(2), 243–262.

Kelman, H. C. (2005). Interactive problem solving in the Israeli-Palestinian case: Past contributions and present challenges. In R. Fisher (Ed.), *Paving the way: Contributions of interactive conflict resolution to peacemaking* (pp. 19–40). Lexington.

Killick, N., Srikantha, S. V., & Güdüz, C. (2005). The role of local business in peacebuilding. *Berghof Research Center for Constructive Conflict Management*. https://berghof-foundation.org/search/results?q=killick

King, Jr., M. L. (1992, [1963]). Letter from a Birmingham jail. In J. Fahey & R. Armstrong (Eds.), *A peace reader* (pp. 113–128). Paulist.

Kolbert, E. (2014). *The sixth extinction: An unnatural history*. Picador.

Kovick, D. (2005). The Hewlett Foundation's Conflict Resolution Program: Twenty years of field-building, 1984–204. *The Hewlett Foundation*. https://www.hewlett.org/wp-content/uploads/2016/08/HewlettConflictResolutionProgram.pdf

Kriesberg, L., Northrup, T., & Thorson, S. (Eds.). (1989). *Intractable conflicts and their transformation*. Syracuse University Press.

Kroeker, W. (2021). *Multidimensional peacebuilding: Local actors in the Philippine context*. Lexington.

Lederach, J. P. (1996). *Preparing for peace: Conflict transformation across societies*. Syracuse University Press.

Levitsky, S., & Way, L. (2010). *Competitive authoritarianism: Hybrid regimes after the Cold War*. Cambridge University Press.

Mac Ginty, R. (2021). *Everyday peace: How so-called ordinary people can disrupt violent conflict*. Oxford University Press.

Mac Ginty. R. (2014). Everyday peace: Bottom-up and local agency in conflict-affected societies. *Security Dialogue*, *45*(6), 548–564.

Mac Ginty, R. (2011). *International peacebuilding and local resistance: Hybrid forms of peace*. Palgrave Macmillan.

Mac Ginty, R., & Richmond, O. P. (2013). The local turn in peace building. *Third World Quarterly*, *34*(5), 763–783.

Maiangwa, B. (2021). *The crisis of belonging and ethnographies of peacebuilding in Kaduna State, Nigeria*. Lexington.

Mallon, B. (2021). The pieces to peace: Analyzing the role of civil society in the design and implementation of Northern Ireland's Good Friday Agreement [Doctoral dissertation, University of Manitoba].

Mansfield, K., & Lederach, J. P. (2010). Strategic peacebuilding pathways. *Kroc Institute for International Peace Studies*. https://kroc.nd.edu/alumni/strategic-peacebuilding-pathways/

McLean, L. (2014). *"If we are crying out together, then we can remain in peace": Constructing community with newcomer women* [Master's thesis, University of Manitoba].

Mitchell, C. (2005). Ending confrontation between Indonesia and Malaysia: A pioneering contribution to international problem solving. In R. Fisher (Ed.), *Paving the way: Contributions of interactive conflict resolution to peacemaking* (pp. 19–40). Lexington.

Mitchell, J., Vincette, G., Hawksley, T., & Culbertson, H. (Eds.). (2020). *Peacebuilding and the Arts*. Palgrave Macmillan.

Mollica, R., ed. (2011). *The textbook of global mental health: A companion guide for field and clinical care of traumatized people worldwide*. Harvard Program in Refugee Trauma.

Montville, J. V. (2006). Track two diplomacy: The work of healing history. *Whitehead Journal of Diplomacy and International Relations*, 7(2), 15–27.

Murphy, K., Pettis, S., & Wray, D. (2016). Building peace: The opportunities and limitations of educational interventions in countries with identity-based conflicts. In M. Bajaj & M. Hantzopouos (Eds.), *Peace education: International Perspectives* (pp. 35–50). Bloomsbury Academic.

Nan, S. A. (2005). Track one-and-a-half diplomacy: Contributions to Georgian–South Ossetian peacemaking. In R. Fisher (Ed.), *Paving the way: Contributions of interactive conflict resolution to peacemaking* (pp. 161–174). Lexington.

Neustaeter, J. R. (2015). *"Doing what needs to be done": Rural women's peacebuilding on the prairies* [Doctoral dissertation, University of Manitoba].

Northrup, T. A. (1989). The dynamic of identity in personal and social conflict. In L. Kriesberg, T. A. Northrup, & S. J. Thorson (Eds.), *Intractable conflicts and their transformation* (pp. 55–82). Syracuse University Press.

O'Hagan, L. (2008). *Training manual: Towards understanding and healing*. Yes! Publications.

Rahman, A., Ali, M., & Khan, S. (2018). The British art of colonialism in India: Subjugation and division. *Journal of Peace and Conflict Studies*, 25(1), Article 5.

Ross, M. H. (1993). *The culture of conflict: Interpretations and interests in comparative perspective*. Yale University Press.

Rothman, J. (2012). *From identity-based conflict to identity-based cooperation: The ARIA approach in theory and practice*. Springer.

Sandole, D. J. D. (2001). John Burton's contribution to conflict theory and practice: A personal view. *The International Journal of Peace Studies*, 6(1), n. p. https://www.gmu.edu/programs/icar/ijps/vol6_1/Sandole.htm

Saunders, H. H. (2005). Sustained dialogue in Tajikistan: Transferring learning from the public to the official peace process. In R. Fisher (Ed.), *Paving the way: Contributions of interactive conflict resolution to peacemaking* (pp. 143–160). Lexington.

Saunders, H. H. (1999). *A public peace process: Sustained dialogue to transform racial and ethnic conflicts*. Palgrave.

Scott, J. C. (1995). *Seeing like a state: How certain schemes to improve the human condition have failed*. Yale University Press.

Senehi, J. (2015). Our tree of life in the field: Locating ourselves in the peace and conflict studies field through the tree of life experience. *Peace Research: The Canadian Journal of Peace and Conflict Studies*, 47(1–2), 10–28.

Serwer, A. (2021, January 7). The Capitol riot was an attack on multiracial democracy. *The Atlantic*. https://www.theatlantic.com/ideas/archive/2021/01/multiracial-democracy-55-years-old-will-it-survive/617585/

Sharp, G., & Paulson, J. (2005). *Waging nonviolent struggle: 20th century practice and 21st century potential*. Extending Horizons Books.

Steiner, C. E. (2015). A sea of warriors: Performing an identity of resilience and empowerment in the face of climate change in the Pacific. *The Contemporary Pacific*, 27(1), 147–180.

Stobbe, S. P. (2015). *Conflict resolution and peacebuilding in Laos: Perspective for today's world*. Routledge.

Sugden, J., & Tomlinson, A. (2018). *Sports and peace-building in divided societies: Playing with enemies*. Routledge.

Tennent, P. (2021). *"We live in different worlds": The perspectives of educators on settler colonialism, Indigenous-settler relations, and reconciliation* [Doctoral dissertation, University of Manitoba].

Tuso, H., & Flaherty, M. P. (Eds.). (2016). *Creating the third force: Indigenous processes of peacemaking*. Lexington.

United Nations Peacebuilding. (2020). *United Nations community engagement guidelines on peacebuilding and sustaining peace*. United Nations. https://www.un.org/peacebuilding/sites/www.un.org.peacebuilding/files/documents/un_community-engagement_guidelines.august_2020.pdf

van Tongeren, P., Brenk, M., Hellema, M., & Verhoeven, J. (Eds.). (2005). *People building peace II: Successful stories of civil society*. Lynne Rienner.

Volkan, V. D., Julius, D. A., & Montville, J. V. (Eds.). (1991). *The psychodynamics of international relationships: Concepts and theories* (Vol. II). Lexington.

Volkan, V. D., Julius, D. A., & Montville, J. V. (Eds.). (1990). *The psychodynamics of international relationships: Concepts and theories* (Vol. I). Free Press.

Williams, A. (2005). Second track conflict resolution processes in the Moldova conflict, 1993-2000: Problems and possibilities. In R. Fisher (Ed.), *Paving the way: Contributions of interactive conflict resolution to peacemaking* (pp. 143–160). Lexington.

World Policy Review. (2020). What's driving the rise of authoritarianism and populism in Europe and beyond? *World Policy Review.* https://www.worldpoliticsreview.com/insights/27842/the-rise-of-authoritarianism-and-populism-europe-and-beyond

Zelizer, C., & Oliphant, V. (2012). Introduction to integrated peacebuilding. In C. Zelizer (Ed.), *Integrated peacebuilding: Innovative approaches to transforming conflict* (pp. 3–30). Routledge.

CONCLUSIONS: PEACEBUILDING AND ETHNOPOLITICAL CONFLICTS REVISITED

Jessica Senehi, Imani Michelle Scott, Sean Byrne, and Thomas G. Matyók

When a government blocks the cultural, economic, political, and social aspirations of an ethnic group, violence can result (Zariski, 1989). This especially occurs when ethnic elites feel that their talents are not being used or rewarded, and their privileges and status in the society are marginalized or neglected (Zariski, 1989). Also, conflicts can escalate into violence when a government does not negotiate in good faith, or it yields too quickly to an ethnic group's demands; and this can certainly be the case if there is a history of past violence between the state and ethnic groups (Zariski, 1989). Intergroup misperceptions result out of fear, frustration, insecurity, and lack of contact as stereotypes are used to construct the other (Zariski, 1989) and perpetuate ongoing ethnic violence.

States often use undemocratic control and suppression models to quell ethnic revolts and unrest such as partition (e.g., Cyprus, India, Ireland, Palestine), assimilation (e.g., Kurds in Turkey), and "legalized coercive force" such as shoot-to-kill and targeted assassinations (e.g., Bosnia, Chechnya, Chile, El Salvador, Northern Ireland, Palestine, South Sudan) (Zariski, 1989). States also attempt to institutionalize ethnic conflicts creating a federal system and decentralizing power providing autonomy to the local level; especially, over resources, providing parity and access to public sector employment, and allowing local media to operate and broadcast in local language(s) (Zariski, 1989). States also utilize the Swiss model of ethnic elite accommodation or consociational powersharing especially where there are multiple interlocking cleavages in the society (O'Leary, 2013). Can the Swiss liberal peace model be transplanted in other societies emerging out of violent ethnic conflict?

The recent reemergence and escalation of protracted ethnic conflicts between Russians and Ukrainians in the Crimea and in Ukraine, Azeris and Armenians in Nagorno-Karabakh, Tigrayans and the Ethiopian and Eritrean governments in Tigray, the Kurds in Turkey, Papuans and the Indonesian government in West Papua, and Houthis and the Yemeni government in Yemen stand as major threats to international peace and security. These conflicts demonstrate the interplay between governments and ethnic groups. In Eastern Ukraine—and South Ossetia—Russia used the cover of protecting ethnic Russians to justify their intervention. These state/ethnic group conflicts destabilize the global environment, and their impacts are felt beyond a conflict's geographic space.

This concluding chapter explores some of the key insights that have emerged from the collective work in each of the four parts as they relate to the underlying causes of protracted ethnopolitical conflicts as well as the challenges of peacebuilding efforts. First, a few general reflections on ethnopolitical conflicts and peacebuilding are shared. Then, the four parts are reviewed in turn.

Ethnopolitical conflicts and peacebuilding

During the Cold War, both superpowers kept ethnopolitical conflicts in check using rival ethnic groups as proxies. Ethnic conflicts escalated when the Cold War ended due to competition for resources, the existence of a plethora of small arms, a lack of international will to impose international laws and human rights, and the use of the liberal democratic peace to protect state sovereignty, deescalate tensions, and resolve conflicts in what might be termed neocolonialism (Richmond, 2016).

The adage "one person's terrorist is another person's freedom fighter" depends on who gets to write the history. In the wake of the 9/11 terrorist attacks, President Bush ushered in a global war on terror. There was a recognition that terrorist violence also shook Europe in 2016–2017, and that addressing terrorism would need to be a global counterterrorism effort. States have also used terrorism against its, or another state's, citizens such as the shoot-to-kill policy in Northern Ireland, Indonesia's illegal actions against activists in West Papua, the apartheid state's indiscriminate attacks on Black South Africans, the Sri Lankan government's extrajudicial killings, and the Myanmar army's state-sanctioned violence against the Rohingya among other ethnic groups. Also, violence is directed against Black Indigenous and People of Color (BIPOC) in the Global North through unjust structures and systems, and violent repression. In the short term, the post-Cold War reality can be unstable, unfolding with peacebuilders muddling through adjusting their strategy and framework on the fly, and as things stabilize over the long-term peacebuilders can have a long-term peace vision that facilitates inclusion of the grassroots.

Following the 1999 intervention to protect Kosovo, the onus has been placed on the international community to protect (R2P) ethnic groups like the Bosniaks that were ethnically cleansed in Bosnia or when gross acts of violence such as genocide are carried out against ethnic groups such as the recent genocide of the Rohingya in Myanmar and BIPOC people in North America. Powerful third parties use a carrot and stick approach by utilizing force or the credible threat of force to change the actions and behavior of a belligerent ethnic actor or state (Thiessen, 2011). The North Atlantic Treaty Organization bombed Serb held positions in Bosnia in 1994 and in Kosovo in 1999 to push the Serbian government to the Dayton peace table.

Nelson Mandela provided the vision for a new South Africa that reinvented national identity to be inclusive of all ethnic groups. The state can also use violence against a revolting ethnic group as it did in Northern Ireland (Bew et al., 2002) and Sri Lanka and as the Israelis are doing against the Palestinians or it can provide local autonomy to manage conflict, or it can create an ethnic elite consociational powersharing government to manage conflict or it can share resources and provide special citizenship rights as the 1998 Good Friday Agreement (GFA) did for Protestants and Catholics in Northern Ireland (O'Leary, 2013). The exploitation of 300–400 million Indigenous people around the world is an indicator of how the state has failed in providing for the interests and basic human needs of Indigenous peoples (Blanton & Kegley, 2020).

However, the liberal peace utopia has stumbled in the face of reality on the ground as former antagonists need time to address the underlying deep causes of conflict and the cycle of violence (Chandler, 2017). What occurs on the ground can become adrift in the upper echelons of external actor's bureaucracies as the translation and communication of the strategy can get lost in translation in subcommittees and planning documents so that the locals have the wrong resources, or an inadequate strategy is executed in terms of the level of substance and process with the locals expecting too much to happen too fast (Bungay, 2010).

Pragmatic critics of peacebuilding support "external intervention," good governance, societal differences, and bottom-up approaches while ignoring local people's concerns; and, in contrast critical theorists assess international peacebuilding's hegemonic interests, power, values, and lack of local knowledge (Chandler, 2017, p. 29). There is no emancipatory social transformation as peacekeepers take on new political roles, and peacebuilding is concentrated on "strengthening sovereignty" as a responsible duty of external and internal partners to build the state's capacity rather than empower local people's freedom (Chandler, 2017, p. 79). The result of the peacebuilding-statebuilding architecture is weak states with limited self-government and external actors having sovereign authority and control of states emerging from violent conflict (Chandler, 2017, p. 85). It is important for states to institutionalize Departments of Peacebuilding as integral components of their foreign policy to work with nongovernmental organizations and civil society organizations and other actors intervening in intractable ethnic conflicts.

The Global North went from imposing its ideology and will at the top to doing it in the grassroots by cloning the liberal state and these "illiberal efforts failed" because local elites resisted to maintain their power, and the lack of peacebuilding coordination and resources were left in the grassroots (Chandler, 2017, p. 147). Local elites were subsequently removed with a "turn to the local" that empowered and transformed local actors yet the tactic still involved peacebuilding and statebuilding (Chandler, 2017, p. 155). Local people's everyday practices remained hidden to external intervenors as they resisted while external intervenors shifted focus in a postliberal peace to how local practices worked, and how they and the locals could learn from each other and how they could empower these local practices to flourish as both groups learned from each other while they were doing (Chandler, 2017, p. 167).

Part 1: Key dimensions of ethnic conflicts

Part 1 focused on the complexity and intersectionality of local ethnopolitical conflicts and the roles of global actors in them. There are three insights that we can take away.

First, there are internal and external issues that are specifically relevant to the study of contemporary ethnic conflicts. Ethnopolitical conflicts are complex and include an array of interrelated internal issues (Kaufman, Chapter 1) such as the rise of populist Eurocentric nationalism (Anastasiou & Anastasiou, Chapter 7). In addition, hatred of the other is a contagious disease that can escalate into protracted ethnopolitical violence (Abuelaish, Chapter 5) while the COVID-19 pandemic has influenced the management of ethnopolitical conflicts (Žagar, Chapter 8). Heteronormative, heteromasculine, and homonational patriarchal structures extol the warrior caste (Wilmer, Chapter 2; Puar, 2007) while control over natural as well as economic and political resources escalate ethnic tensions (Figueiredo & Dean, Chapter 6). Other internal causes of ethnopolitical conflict include historical grievances and a golden past (Gurr, 2000; Smith, 2004); the legacy of colonialism and internal colonialism in the framing of traditional and progressive ethnic groups struggle for group worth (Horowitz, 2000); past traumas and fear of extinction (Volkan, 2019); cultural symbols and cultural purification that maintain ethnic divisions (Ross, 2007; Smith, 1996); religious fault lines (Abu-Nimer & Nelson, 2021); and demographic insecurity and segregation as well as external influences such as overseas diasporas (Taras & Ganguly, 2009). Consequently, peacebuilding needs to be reimagined including local wisdom and practices that emancipate everyday people (Collins & Thiessen, Chapter 4). This is critical for peacebuilding as individuals live their lives at the local level.

There are also international dimensions to the escalation of ethnic conflicts and their transformation (Olson Lounsbery & Pearson, Chapter 3).

External regional and international actors are also embroiled in ethnic conflicts using carrot and stick approaches exacerbating power asymmetry to gain their own interests. During the Cold War, both superpowers provided resources for rival ethnic groups and used counter- and pro-insurgency methods to destabilize states and regions intensifying tensions among ethnic groups (Ohanyan, 2015). States have used counterterrorism measures to control ethnic groups that have polarized communities and entrenched ethnic divisions in divided societies (Guelke, 2012). Globalism, and global capital institutions, also maintains the political and economic hegemony of the core while structural inequalities result in environmental degradation and the marginalization of people in the periphery exacerbating ethnopolitical relationships (Ritzer, 2016; Thiessen & Byrne, 2017).

Complex ethnic conflicts often lean toward external broad-based cosmopolitan approaches rather than local peacebuilding practices (Lee & Özerdem, 2015; Özerdem, 2014). Eurocentric neoliberal peacebuilding fails to address the deep roots of protracted ethnic conflicts (Philpott & Powers, 2010). It has become synonymous with statebuilding efforts that include democracy, human rights, a market economy and free trade, elections, and security reform that have failed to bring peace and social justice to ethnic conflicts because local actors resist internal powerful actors as well as external technocratic and bureaucratic domination by global actors such as international agencies, corporations, and trading blocs (Thiessen, 2011). In postwar milieu's the liberal peace is often presented as "good governance and reform" while its components are illiberal so that peace accords and elections are forced on populations without regard for local governance practices (Mac Ginty & Williams, 2009, pp. 49–51). Development in post accord societies can assist in postwar reconciliation and reconstruction as well as providing succor to impoverished and suffering people; yet, it is not sustainable. It is not solely about economic growth as development is an uneven process that can lead to the escalation of violent protracted conflict (Mac Ginty & Williams, 2009, pp. 5–7). Development assistance and humanitarian aid can for the purposes of de-escalating ethnic conflicts make bad situations worse (Mac Ginty & Williams, 2009, p. 172; Matyók & Schmitz, 2020). Local people's resilience expressed through local knowledge and practice in their everyday lived experience has ended the impasse between "liberal universalism and cultural relativism" as bottom-up peacebuilding reflects the reality of local people's experiences (Mac Ginty & Williams, 2009, p. 188).

Consequently, interim political settlements may deescalate conflicts yet end up freezing ethnic relations trapping them in a liminal stasis when more local creative and innovative solutions are required to transform ethnic groups' relationships (Wolff, 2006). In addition, external economic assistance is often used by international donors as part of the liberal peace package to nurture community capacity building. This approach can stimulate economic growth in the short run by creating employment opportunities; however, in the long term, it can prove ineffective as it ignores local challenges, wisdoms, knowledge, potential, and skills in the peacebuilding process (Awotona, 2019; Tat, 2019). Ethnic elites can access international peacebuilding resources that are embedded in hegemonic interests and values that are enmeshed in Western "neoliberal economic capitalism and security policies" that exclude local grassroots knowledge (Chandler, 2017, p. 29). Complex local systems must engage with local issues in order to be innovative and create local solutions to local problems while acclimating to conflict, pressure, and strain constructing resilience and sustainable peace with less outside intervention (de Coning, 2018).

Two, there are a number of implications for moving forward to build sustainable peace processes among ethnic groups emerging from violent conflicts. Local, micro, everyday peacebuilding actions can have a ripple effect on the ground. Empowering community-based peacebuilding approaches can assist in developing local people's capacities and resistance (Chandler, 2017, p. 188). There is no universal solution to complex ethnic conflicts. Local conflicts can be managed, and peacebuilding is no longer a distinct intervention policy nor an exclusive strategy (Chandler, 2017, p. 207). External actors must pay attention to exclusionary and inclusionary local practices (Donais, 2012), and the resiliency of local people by zooming out and having a bird's eye view of the whole conflict milieu making sure that marginalized groups like BIPOC communities, former combatants, people living with disabilities, 2SLGBTQ+ citizens, women, and youth voices are included and funded in the peace process (Byrne et al., 2018). Unjust asymmetrical power structures, epistemologies, behaviors, and privileges must be decolonized in a collaborative decision-making process between mainstream society and BIPOC people (Wallace, 2013, p. 16). Micro- and macro-reconciliation processes can rebuild trust and repair relationships between mainstream settler societies and BIPOC people in Canada, Australia, the United States, and elsewhere (Clarke & Byrne, 2017; Rahman et al., 2017). People's cultural contexts that include epistemologies, practices, and resources are critical in transforming intergroup relationships (Lederach, 2010).

Daily, people routinely live-in divided societies where the geographical space is contested and stereotypes go unchallenged (Byrne & Senehi, 2012). Consequently, peacebuilding is heterogenous and generally complex, messy, and untidy as external actors muddle through their peacebuilding strategy and framework (Mac Ginty, 2008). "Multitrack" peacebuilding interventions can link a plethora of peacebuilding societal actors in a sustainable peace system (Diamond & McDonald, 1996). As part of that process, the acknowledgment of past wrongs through truth-telling and storytelling are necessary to build trust before conflict parties can address the structural transformation and community engagement necessary to build social cohesion (Senehi, 2019). In addition, reconciliation efforts that include "truth, justice, mercy, and peace" (Lederach, 1997) are deemed critical so that citizens develop and maintain a common understanding and internalize shared memories of what took place in a violent conflict or war that needed to be conciliated (Mac Ginty & Williams, 2009, p. 109). Peace work is inherently risky and putting "historical ghosts back to sleep" may be a more appropriate strategy than reconciliation; especially, when populations are not yet ready to engage in a reconciliation process (Mac Ginty & Williams, 2009, p. 111). The inclusion of the next generation of youth and women leaders' experiences, creativity, and skillsets are critical in creating a culture of peace (Ashe, 2019; Boulding, 2000; McEvoy-Levy, 2017). Peace must be measured in terms of the quality of people's everyday lives (Autesserre, 2014; Marijan, 2017).

Third, future research and practice inquiry could include exploring the complexity of protracted ethnopolitical conflicts especially the tensions that can develop between internal and external actors, the role of ethnic identity and self-esteem, and the lack of access to key economic and political resources that creates social injustice that exacerbates relationships between ethnic groups (Byrne & Thiessen, 2019). In addition, the role of micro- and macro-reconciliation initiatives in the decolonization, healing, and repair of relationships as well as the nexus between and blending of Indigenous cosmologies, epistemologies, and practices and Western mainstream privilege, mindsets, and dominant discourses would also be worthy of further explorations.

Internal and external dynamics intersect and infuse complex protracted ethnopolitical conflicts. The successful implementation of peace accords demands a deep analysis of the causes that integrate and blend local and external actors' insights.

Part 2: Peacebuilders in ethnic conflict

Part 2 of this text speaks to the complexities peacebuilders face in working to nonviolently transform contemporary ethnopolitical conflicts. There are internal and external issues that are specifically relevant to the study of ethnic conflict. Significant to tackling those internal and external issues is an understanding of the presence of hybrid threats and asymmetric warfare vis-a-vis ethnopolitical conflicts. Yesterday's approaches to peacebuilding are not appropriate for an Age of Persistent Conflict where adversarial actors engage in ongoing struggle shifting between confrontation and conflict. Smith (2019) posits "war no longer exists." The Age of Industrial War is over. Civil peacebuilders will need to become comfortable working in unstable spaces where peace and war have been replaced by continuous ongoing confrontations between a plethora of antagonists.

The war/peace binary with clear boundaries between each is obsolete. Confrontation and conflict now occur in multidimensional spaces with no clear borders, nor limits. So, recognizing we have stepped into a world of persistent conflict, what is the big peacebuilding picture? Can we step back and imagine new peacebuilding approaches for transforming ethnic conflict? Arguably, civil and military actors, working collaboratively and coordinating efforts, will be obliged to provide coherent responses to emerging and ongoing ethnic conflicts. Responses to ethnic conflict will need to recognize the necessity of safe and secure environments that allow for sustainable approaches to conflict management while simultaneously building locally resilient populations (Lundy et al., Chapter 9; Coy, Chapter 11; Lunga & Matyók, Chapter 12). To accomplish this, peacebuilders should develop an approach to their peacebuilding activities that engages new actors, those not necessarily viewed as part of the peacebuilding community (Lee, Chapter 25). It will be necessary to integrate new dynamics not often accepted. The state has been viewed as the primary peacebuilder as well as oppressive agent of local ethnic groups sometimes (Smythe, Chapter 14). To bring in other agencies and organizations in the peacebuilding dynamic, this view will need to change when addressing the complexities of ethnic conflict (Senehi, Chapter 28).

An example of the need for Whole of Society approaches to peacebuilding is the increasing number of asylum seekers, migrants, and internally displaced people who are used to stress the capacity of nations' social systems (Matyók & Zajc, 2020). Hybrid threats transcend geography. Refugees and asylum seekers from conflicts in Syria and Afghanistan have inundated countries of the European Union stressing it and NATO allies. This conflict that ensued among states regarding refugees can be characterized as having ethnic overtones. The conflict reintroduces an East/West divide into the EU creating space for authoritarian regimes such as Viktor Orban's administration in Hungary and far right political parties like the Alternative for Germany. Altright politicians are comfortable exploiting refugees and asylum seekers exploiting ethnic tensions and creating political confrontations.

When states are stressed, the risk is governments will fail to govern expending what resources are available to maintain themselves. A failure of governance opens the space for ethnic conflicts to emerge and for bad actors to exploit divisions. Using ethnic conflict to collapse a governance structure is a cost-effective way of fighting an asymmetrical battle. For example, the Balkan war of the 1990s can provide insights into this observation. Bad actors used ethnic division to advance their agendas outside of an operating governance structure. Syria, Bosnia and Herzegovina, and Iraq provide examples of ongoing conflicts where ethnic tensions are used to stress formal governance structures (Matyók & Zajc, 2020).

Institutions are a thought collective that develop their own thought style and thought world (Douglas, 1986). How do peacebuilders participate within the *Peace Industrial Complex*? Is Peace and Conflict Studies (PACS) becoming an institution with a unique thought collective? Is there room for civil-military collaboration in working to peacefully transform ethnic conflict? These are questions that will have an impact on how PACS scholars and practitioners design the discipline's way forward. Certainly, as militaries need to change their focus from fixating exclusively on hard power approaches to confrontation management and conflict transformation, the peacebuilding community will need to understand the dynamics of a soft and hard power interface that advances societal sustainability and resilience.

Implications for moving forward

Part 2 presents several implications for moving forward. First is the need for peacebuilders to have deep understanding of governance structures and activities. Peacebuilders' knowledge of formal and competing governance structures is necessary to enlarge conflict transformation efforts engaging the Whole of Society. PACS curricula should be guided by an inclusive *design approach* (Fry, 2011; Mendoza & Matyók, 2013; Matyók, 2011). All disciplines have a role to play in peacebuilding guided by PACS. Creation of a transdisciplinary Peace Operations College bringing civil society, military, government, and academia together can be a positive step (Matyók, 2018). Not only will peacebuilding, within an ethnic conflict context setting, need to be *culturally sensitive*, but it also must be *governance sensitive*. An example is religion. Religious organizations and actors are often present in ethnic conflict zones (Abu-Nimer, Chapter 13). When formal, state governance structures collapse religious organizations frequently offer an alternative structure.

Second, there is a requirement for hybrid peacebuilding approaches. Hybrid approaches will include multiple interest groups, many of which are informal. Hybrid threats in asymmetric conflict such as "the weaponization of refugee populations as biological weapons" (Matyók & Zajc, 2020) calls for new approaches to conflict transformation and peacebuilding. Civil society (nongovernmental organizations, international organizations, host nation organizations, etc.), military, government, and academia will move beyond coordinating activities to jointly constructing seamless Whole of Society, joint methodologies employing a *Unity-of-Aim* approach to peacebuilding.

The third is the necessity of taking an expansive view of peacebuilding. Working in ethnic conflicts calls for an all-hands approach. Civil society, military, government, and academia are needed to provide holistic responses to confrontation management and conflict transformation. Civil-military interaction, interoperability, and integration will need to become the *new normal*. No longer can anyone be left outside of the peacebuilding tent. No one can claim a monopoly on peacebuilding. This will require civil and military actors to gain competency in working with each other. This will present its own issues in addressing the cultural conflicts that will arise in meshing two opposing cultures, as well as the needs of local communities embroiled in protracted conflicts.

Future research and practice inquiry

Where is academia? Academia ought to assume a greater role focusing on ethnopolitical conflict. This means moving away from analyzing the past alone to understanding the present and projecting into a desired future through future imagining to "imagine peace" (Boulding, 1989). Academia, unrestricted by structure and institutional inertia, can reach out to and influence policymakers. Questions to be investigated include:

- How can peacebuilders design an approach to confrontation management and conflict transformation that includes civil-military interaction and interoperability?
- In what ways can military peace leadership contribute to hybrid approaches of peacebuilding?
- How can the unique skill set and capacities of civil, military, government, and academic actors be blended into a unified, hybrid approach to peacebuilding?
- Before violent ethnopolitical crises occur, how can the development of joint conflict management and transformation training programs for civil, military, government, and academia break down cultural barriers to concerted peacebuilding action?

Part 3: Addressing the past and shaping the future

Part 3 of this text gives attention to the emerging role of trauma studies in peacebuilding, explores ways in which trauma manifests itself in conflict behaviors, considers the consequences of trauma to agents and their communities, and shares ideas for peacebuilders to implement trauma-informed initiatives. Three primary arenas where trauma-informed outcomes are discussed and have demonstrated relevance to contemporary peacebuilding initiatives involve the exploration of global public protests, memorialization, and iconoclasm as disdain for state-sanctioned human rights violations, the consideration of widespread and unanticipated humanitarian consequences resulting from the COVID-19 health pandemic, and the communal effects of exposure to enduring and endemic trauma and violence.

Peacebuilding amid protest

Although peacebuilding writ large has traditionally focused on conflict as a phenomenon at the interpersonal, group and/or social levels—leaving the focus on intrapersonal conflict issues to psychologists and mental health practitioners, contemporary peacebuilders have identified benefits in exploring trauma as a key component to successful peacemaking and peacekeeping initiatives. More specifically, having a better understanding of the role of trauma as it relates to cyclical and transgenerational violence and behaviors helps peacebuilders design trauma-informed resolution and transformation approaches for individuals and communities. In focusing on trauma-paradigms, 21st century peacebuilders are also seeking to generate a heightened awareness of the impacts of collective and unhealed traumas on peacebuilding efforts (Wessells, 2008).

Public protests as expressions of dissent against heavy-handed ruling classes are not new; historical records dating back to the 1200s document citizen revolts and demonstrations as responses to perceived assaults levied by governments. Accordingly, it is not unusual for officials—in their efforts to maintain power and control, to deploy police and other tactical forces to restrain protestors and crush proposals for any new protest initiatives. Another strategic ploy of power brokers to diminish the impact of protests is to widely disperse negative narratives about demonstrators messaging and behaviors to garner public contempt for those who dare publicly challenge the status quo.

In democracies like the United States where Freedom of Speech is a First Amendment right, it has long been argued that protest is a legitimate form of speech, and consequently, citizens should have the right to peaceful demonstration without government interference. However, in recent years, political demonstrations—especially those held in protest of police violence against Blacks and African Americans in this country—have been met with volatile and even deadly levels of state-sanctioned force, including military-style enforcements and attacks. The use of forceful restraint was especially apparent during the summer of 2020 which followed the police murder of George Floyd where Black Lives Matter (BLM) protests would reach heightened levels of participation and draw huge groups of demonstrators. In far too many cities where these protests occurred, the world would witness videotaped evidence of the U.S. government's targeted use of violent and even deadly police tactics in response to unarmed BLM demonstrators. The greatest irony of course is that the demonstrators were drawn together to protest the very tactics and agents against which they were met. Subsequently, protests against the trauma-inducing behaviors of state sanctioned agents only perpetuated more trauma-inducing behaviors by those agents.

Viral videos of excessively violent police attacks on noncombative protesters in the United States portrayed more than the dangerous use of state tactics as responses to peaceful demonstrations, they also highlighted the selective use of those tactics against demonstrators whose causes were to defend the rights of black and brown people. In one study, ProPublica (Buford et al., 2020) examined 400 videos of police violence across U.S. cities and concluded that the video evidence demonstrated *problematic police conduct*, including the lethal use of force which exacerbated the levels of conflict and intensified the types of behaviors between the officers and the demonstrators. Yet if the U.S. government presumed its use of "emergency powers" in the deployment of strongarm tactics would quell BLM and similar protests against racism and police brutality it was sorely mistaken. In fact, the opposite occurred as demonstrations in support of BLM and against military-style policing exploded across the world in what would become a seemingly global protest movement. Global, mass demonstrations of discontent were fortified by a multitude of individuals across the ethnic, age, gender, nationality, and religious spectrums. Ultimately, it became exceedingly apparent on the international stage—at least for a moment in time, that standing up for human rights, regardless of skin color, and against state use of force was a global rallying cry. To be sure, much of the world had visibly coalesced around the cause of human rights, and this bonding permeated demographic differences.

The role of protest as an expression of public outrage against elitist control can only be expected to increase as technology and social media continue to permit the rapid, global sharing of imagery and messaging related to state-initiated oppression. While authorities focus on control and restraint of these types of public responses, from a peacebuilding perspective there is much to be gained from understanding the deep-rooted motivations of protestors. Moving forward, it is entirely reasonable to expect that the global protest movement will become a force for the ruling class to reckon with. Consequently, opportunities for global peacebuilding and more collaborative efforts across borders will be enhanced. This presents opportunities for the work of peacebuilders and human rights workers to be increasingly fortified by international leadership and global concerns.

Implications for moving forward: Peacebuilding and the pandemic

With the advent of the COVID-19 pandemic, the world, and our personal domains in it, abruptly became smaller. Not only would the majority of the world's citizens—during at least one point in time, be required to socially isolate in some manner or fashion to avoid contamination associated with COVID-19, yet entire countries blocked their borders to prevent the entry of noncitizens into their shores. Across the globe, Coronavirus travel regulations were implemented to prohibit nonresidents from entering countries, states, and territories. And where entries were allowed, individuals were often required to quarantine, test, and be vaccinated to help prevent the spread of the disease.

For those who lived in communities where the primary threat to their health and safety was COVID-19-related and they otherwise retained a relative amount of freedom to spend their days without fear of threat and menace from external forces, the isolation and bans related to COVID-19 would be uncomfortable, but not ominous. But for those living in lands where they were enduring persecution and/or torture based on their religion, nationality, political opinion, skin color, or group membership, or where they were victims of human trafficking, survivors of environmental catastrophes, or made vulnerable by tragedies beyond their control, the COVID-19-related bans left them, their families and their communities completely outcast and exiled. Consequently, multitudes of refugees and would-be immigrants would encounter phenomenally dire realities in their efforts to seek safety and security beyond their established homelands and existence: survival would take on new meaning, as hopes and plans for a life beyond that of mere subsistence would become hollow. As a consequence of the pandemic, it became widely evident that existing conflicts were being exacerbated, that those most in need would likely go unassisted (at least for the time being), and that the existing framework for peacebuilding was ill equipped "to mitigate and prevent ongoing and new episodes of violence, to support the resilience of communities to ongoing shocks, and to ensure that health-care interventions and recovery efforts [were] sustainable" (International Alert, 2020, para. 2).

Traditionally, peacebuilding has focused on ending violence, stopping wars, resolving, and transforming conflict, promoting social justice, and more broadly, advocating for human rights. However, the advent of COVID-19 had a "profound impact on peace and conflict around the world" (International Alert, 2020, para. 1). And peacebuilders writ large, I would argue, were not ready for COVID-19; in fact, no one was. If we were ready, we would likely have been prepared with research and training to address the humanitarian crises it presented regarding care for refugees and immigrants, the policy issues associated with inequitable access to health care, and the varied impositions of power levied by state and nonstate actors on citizens. Mustasilta (2020) argues,

> The nature of the pandemic also makes it very difficult to be seized as an opportunity for peace. As global attention remains caught up in fighting the pandemic and the policy measures restricting the movement of people continue, both local and international peace efforts suffer. (para. 4)

As peacebuilders, we need to continue our work supporting the reduction of traumatized spaces, violence, and injustices in all forms. And now, having witnessed the impact of COVID-19 as an entirely new phenomenon, our work must also embrace opportunities to support the reduction of health-care biases and health inequities across the world. Add to that, we need to be flexible and versatile enough to more swiftly adapt success-proven peacebuilding paradigms and initiatives—like the healing-centered approach shared by Angi Yoder in this text, to address confrontations with the completely unanticipated and unimagined experiences such as those associated with COVID-19.

Communities as safe spaces

The 21st-century conflict dynamics, including those related to human-provoked and environmentally induced types of violence, will yield a plethora of novel lessons for peacebuilders and subsequently, opportunities for PACS scholars to approach peacebuilding. However, with the advent of new technologies leading to revolutionary forms of communication and travel, one thing is growing ever-more apparent: the world community is indeed becoming one.

This suggests that more than ever before, conflict dynamics producing traumatic outcomes and responses will saturate beyond borders to influence the world's citizens on a global scale. Consequently, the focus on healing-centered, communal responses at the local levels will become even more relevant to peacebuilding initiatives. For even though ruling-class efforts to maintain divisions between ethnic groups and segregations among populations will likely continue as a means of controlling the masses, a global recognition of the need for peacebuilding is growing at the level of communities. Subsequently, the work of conflict resolution, transformation, social justice, and trauma-recovery is being increasingly taken on at communal levels. Whether this is a primary indication of growing community distrust for governments and/or increasing regard for communal knowledge and wisdom is not clear; yet what is clear is that the grappling for resilience in the face of conflict and trauma is being increasingly accommodated by citizen-and community-led initiatives.

More out of necessity than not, the philosophy of community care has been a prominent value in and feature of traditionally marginalized groups for decades on end. In these communities, individual resilience and coping mechanisms for addressing the realities of living with both transgenerated and daily trauma have been directly located in support from the collective, through which respect, empathy, and deep-seated needs for connection can be found. Other individual benefits from connecting with community sources of support include increased opportunities for access to education and economic resources, shared values related to faith, health-care and self-care practices, and creative strategies for surmounting the complex and systemic inequities apparent in the broader society. Customarily, peacebuilding conventions and practices have supported the existence, design and sustenance of community-based initiatives and programs; and increasingly, peacebuilders are recognizing the inherent value of local wisdom, traditions, and rituals as sources for addressing violence, trauma, and other consequences of conflict. In light of the major and overwhelmingly positive impact that community care initiatives have been reported to have on the wellness of individuals, and based on increasing reports from peacebuilders of color regarding the rapid influx of expected and unexpected "trauma triggers" (especially those related to racial violence) in the 21st century, moving forward it will become imperative for the peacebuilding community to incorporate peer support and mutual aid initiatives as sources of resilience for peacebuilders of color. At the end of the day, the entire peacebuilding community will benefit from committed and healthy scholars and practitioners whose mental, spiritual, and physical wellness needs are notably and prominently supported within our circles and available to colleagues.

Questions for the future

As peacebuilders continue to move forward in their conduct of research and construct of initiatives to address long-standing and rapidly evolving concerns, Imani Scott suggests that the following issues deserve particular attention:

- Considering the global responses to issues of social justice, policing practices, health-care crises, and the mental and physical health inequities highlighted during the COVID-19 pandemic are contemporary peacebuilders obligated to become more engaged and outspoken in public discourse? If yes, why and how? What are the likely costs to those peacebuilders who take public stands and speak out (i.e., in the media, in social media, and beyond the classroom)? Should peacebuilders become involved in politics, i.e., run for political office, to effect change? If yes, at what costs? If no, why not?

- In a world where racialized assaults and social injustice are endemic, persistent, and deeply consequential, how might we support peacebuilders of color (i.e., members of traditionally marginalized and oppressed groups) who are confronted with unique challenges related to their personal exposure to repeated racialized conflict and violence?

Part 4: Approaches and cases

Part 4 focuses on specific cases and approaches to peacebuilding. Chapters 23–27 bring significant data and evidence forward on peacebuilding in ethnic conflicts from researchers who are part of or close to the communities they studied. S. I. Keethaponcalan (Chapter 23) provides a detailed analysis on how international actors and the Tamil community conceptualize reconciliation differently. Wendy Kroeker (Chapter 24) provides insights into what motivates and strengthens peacebuilders in Mindanao, in the Philippines, and the knowledge, strategies, skills, and philosophies that they bring to bear in the peace process there. Kroeker's study builds on in-depth interviews with peacebuilders whom she has known for 20 years through her own work there. SungYong Lee (Chapter 25) argues that despite the local turn in peacebuilding, it is important to examine national peace processes, and also consider transformational peacebuilding in Asia. He provides a fine-grained analysis of two peace processes, in Aceh, Indonesia, and Bougainville, Papua New Guinea. Sean Byrne and Calum Dean (Chapter 26) evaluate the role of international economic aid to peacebuilders from the European Union's Peace Fund and the International Fund for Ireland. This analysis is based on in-depth interviews with those involved in peacebuilding and development projects made possible through these funds. Surulola Eke and Sean Byrne (Chapter 27) examine Indigenous approaches to peacebuilding, highlighting examples from herder-farmer conflicts, and based on in-depth interviews and ethnographic research conducted by Eke in Nigeria.

This research brings forward knowledge that is highly contextual, and that is developed and used by people close to the conflict. This includes the Tamil community in Sri Lanka; peacebuilders in Mindanao; negotiators in Aceh and Bougainville, including civil society organizations in Aceh, and Maori third-party intervenors in Bougainville; peacebuilders in Northern Ireland; and community elders in Nigeria. This resonates with an emphasis on context-grounded practices as described by Tamra Pearson d'Estree and Ruth Parsons (2018).

This in-depth research does not examine the knowledge of these actors as if they are objects to be interpreted through a particular, e.g., Western lens, but rather includes them in the analysis. Through this research, actors in conflicts—activists, peacebuilders, negotiators, and community elders—share their knowledge. This not only creates awareness of individual and group perceptions but also their knowledge, based on the evidence of their own life experiences and reflective practice, that can inform theory held in academic texts and academia. For example, we need to consider the timing of reconciliation efforts with the process of redress of harms and underlying concerns (Keethaponcalan, Chapter 23); this is something that can be applied in other contexts. Peacebuilders in Mindanao speak to the role of a wellspring of faith, dedication to building meaningful and significant personal relationships, and strength in flexibility for addressing protracted conflicts and with the trauma of violence (Kroeker, Chapter 24); this is something that can have relevance for peacebuilders everywhere and goes beyond the linear, mechanistic how-to models of practice in the West. The peace processes developed in Aceh and Bougainville provide much guidance that can be used in other contexts on how to involve civil society organizations in a meaningfully inclusive peace process, in the case of Aceh, and how to adapt the peace process to include a set of meaningful and symbolic practices that facilitate rapprochement and resolution (Lee, Chapter 25).

Knowledge mobilization is layered. As scholars, we seek to mobilize the knowledge generated by our research through writing, presentation, and outreach so that educators, practitioners, policymakers, other researchers, and the public can be aware of, evaluate, and use that information. Activists, practitioners, and community leaders who are immersed in peacebuilding work are generating evidence-based knowledge and skills through their reflective practice, conversations and strategizing with peers, informal education in their communities, and trial and error. Research that includes and collaborates with activists, negotiators, peacebuilders, civil society organizations, and community leaders is a means by whereby they can mobilize their knowledge.

One of the ways that power operates is by controlling knowledge. This happens in so many subtle and less subtle ways through formal education and in all sectors of society. Academic scholarship is profoundly impacted by who has access to academic positions based on their region and other means, which may bring a class bias to research. The kinds of livelihoods that are available for people in academia varies drastically in different parts of the world, and may bring a cultural or regional bias to the time and resources that are possible for research. Furthermore, institutional and governmental priorities impact research support; for example, for some institutions in the West are currently requiring that scholars do research that is relevant to businesses. The formal academic process of producing knowledge may often entrench the status quo, and be blind to alternative viewpoints.

Meanwhile, much knowledge is held within a society. Research that partners with practitioners and communities affected by violence, who are not part of the formal educational process of teaching and academic scholarship, is an opportunity to decolonize knowledge production. This also has the potential to create profound awareness and abundance as the knowledge from diverse actors in diverse regions is brought forward. An important role for academics is to facilitate this process and to work for mobilizing evidence-based knowledge about conflicts and peacebuilding (Senehi, Chapter 28).

These studies are models for future research that continues to ask: After war or protracted inequality and/or oppression, how do societies balance the desire for reconciliation with communities' needs for recovering from harm and addressing concerns? How do peacebuilders continue to find strength, motivation, and success in the context of highly violent and traumatic conflicts? What approaches are third-party intervenors using for transformative negotiation at the national level? How can peace be funded, what infrastructure is needed for peacebuilding, and how can peacebuilders find a livelihood? What are the strategies community leaders use in the context of volatile interethnic conflicts? Detailed, contextual, evidence-based research in these areas is critical, as well as evaluation research of findings.

Peace is sometimes viewed as a philosophical issue: Are people inherently peaceful or aggressive? Who's thinking is correct—idealists or realists, optimists or pessimists? But these questions are a distraction. Ethnopolitical violence is a public health crisis; social and personal wellbeing requires peace. Social inequalities, hate, and bullying have health consequences (Abuelaish, Chapter 5). Research that mobilizes the knowledge of people affected by ethnic conflicts and working as peacebuilders is critical to solving some of the world's most damaging problems.

Conclusions

Local cultural wisdom and epistemologies should guide the design of the peacebuilding architecture (Lederach, 2010). In postpeace accord societies, it is important that local people's diverse stories be both heard and understood in the design and implementation of peace processes (Millar, 2014, 2020). Consequently, peacebuilding processes should be informed by local needs and knowledge that challenges external power in terms of white privilege, colonial legacy, and gender and class background (Redman-McLaren & Mills, 2015). The community's goals must be included in a democratic and inclusive transformative process because it empowers them to take control of their own circumstances to address local problems (Robins & Wilson, 2015). PACS scholars and practitioners need to take a critical and emancipatory lens with regard to ethnic conflict analysis and peacebuilding. There is a lot of work to do and pracademics and policymakers must work together and be aware of their blind spots as well as the onset of peace fatigue that can hamper peacebuilding work.

References

Abu-Nimer, M., & Nelson, R. K. (Eds.). (2021). *Evaluating interreligious peacebuilding and dialogue: Methods and frameworks*. De Gruyter.
Ashe, F. (2019). *Gender, nationalism and conflict transformation: New themes and old problems in Northern Ireland*. Routledge.
Autesserre, S. (2014). *Peaceland: Conflict resolution and the everyday politics of international intervention*. Cambridge University Press.
Awotona, A. (Ed.). (2019). *Rebuilding Afghanistan in times of crisis: A global response*. Routledge.
Bew, P., Gibbon, P., & Patterson, H. (2002). *Northern Ireland, 1921–2001: Political forces and social classes*. Interlink Publishing Group.
Blanton, S., & Kegley, C. (2020). *World politics: Trend and transformation*. Cengage Learning.
Boulding, E. (2000). *Cultures of peace: The hidden side of history*. Syracuse University Press.
Boulding, E. (1989). *Building a global civic culture: Education for an interdependent world*. Syracuse University Press.
Buford, T., Waldron, L., Syed, M., & Shaw, A. (2020). We reviewed police tactics seen in nearly 400 protest videos. Here is what we found. *ProPublica*. http://projects.propublica.org/protest-police-tactics/
Bungay, S. (2010). *The art of action: How leaders close the gaps between plans, actions and results*. Quercus.
Byrne, S., Mizzi, R., & Hansen, N. (2018). Living in a liminal peace: Where is the social justice for LGBTQ and disability communities living in post peace accord Northern Ireland? *Journal for Peace and Justice Studies, 27*(1), 24–52.
Byrne, S., & Senehi, J. (2012). *Violence: Analysis, intervention and prevention*. Ohio University Press.
Byrne, S., & Thiessen, C. (2019). Foreign peacebuilding intervention and emancipatory local agency for social justice. In S. Byrne, T. Matyók, I. M. Scott, & J. Senehi (Eds.), *Routledge companion to peace and conflict studies* (pp. 131–142). Routledge.
Chandler, D. (2017). *Peacebuilding: The twenty years crisis, 1997–2017*. Palgrave Macmillan.
Clarke, M. A., & Byrne, S. (2017). The three R's: Resistance, resilience and reconciliation in Ireland and Canada. *Peace Research: Canadian Journal of Peace and Conflict Studies, 49*(2), 105–132.
de Coning, C. (2018). Adaptive peacebuilding. *International Affairs, 94*(2), 301–317.
d'Estrée, T. P., & Parsons, R. L. (Eds.). (2018). The state of the art and the need for context-grounded practice in conflict resolution. In T. P. d'Estrée & R. J. Parsons (Eds.), *Cultural encounters and emerging practices in conflict resolution* (pp. 1–30). Palgrave Macmillan.
Diamond, L., & McDonald, J. (1996). *Multi-track diplomacy: A systems approach to peace*. Kumarian.
Donais, T. (2012). *Peacebuilding and local ownership: Post conflict consensus building*. Routledge.
Douglas, M. (1986). *How institutions think*. Syracuse University Press.
Fry, D. (2011). *Design as politics*. Berg.
Guelke, A. (2012). *Politics in deeply divided societies*. Polity.
Gurr, T. R. (2000). *People versus states: Minorities at risk in the new century*. United States Institute of Peace Press.
Horowitz, D. L. (2000). *Ethnic groups in conflict*. University of California Press.
International Alert. (2020). COVID-19 and peacebuilding. *International Alert*. https://www.internationalalert.org/news/covid-19-and-peacebuilding/
Lederach, J. P. (2010). *The moral imagination: The art and soul of building peace*. Oxford University Press.
Lederach, J. P. (1997). *Building peace: Reconciliation in divided societies*. United States Institute of Peace Press.

Lee, S., & Özerdem, A. (2015). *Local ownership in international peacebuilding: Key theoretical and practical issues.* Routledge.

Mac Ginty, R. (2008). *No war, no peace: The rejuvenation of stalled peace processes and peace accords.* Palgrave Macmillan.

Mac Ginty, R., & Williams, A. (2009). *Conflict and development.* Routledge.

Marijan, B. (2017). The politics of everyday peace in Bosnia and Herzegovina and Northern Ireland. *Peacebuilding, 5*(1), 67–81.

Matyók, T. (2018). Military peace leadership: Space and design for connectedness. In S. Amaladas & S. Byrne (Eds.), *Peace leadership: The quest for connectedness* (pp. 177–193). Routledge.

Matyók, T. (2011). Peace and conflict studies: Reclaiming our roots and designing our way forward. In T. Matyók, J. Senehi, & S. Byrne (Eds.), *Critical issues in peace and conflict studies: Theory, practice, and pedagogy* (pp. 293–309). Lexington Books.

Matyók, T., & Schmitz, C. (2020). The potential for violence in helping: Resisting the neocolonialism of humanitarian action. In A. D. Plat & S. Naisberg Siberman (Eds.), *Violence: Probing the boundaries around the world* (pp. 56–72). Brill.

Matyók, T., & Zajc, S. (2020). Joint civil-military interaction as a tool in responding to hybrid threats. *Contemporary Military Challenges, 22*(3), 27–44.

McEvoy-Levy, S. (2017). *Peace and resistance in youth cultures: Reading the politics of peacebuilding from Harry Potter to the hunger games.* Palgrave Macmillan.

Mendoza, H. R. & Matyók, T. (2013). We are not alone: When the number of exceptions to a rule exceeds its usefulness as a construct, it is time for a change. In T. Vaikla-Poldma (Ed.), *Meanings of designed spaces* (pp. 47–58). Fairchild Books.

Millar, G. (2020). *Ethnographic peace research: Approaches and tensions.* Palgrave Macmillan.

Millar, G. (2014). *An ethnographic approach to peacebuilding: Understanding local experiences in transitional states.* Routledge.

Mustasilta, K. (2020). The effects of the COVID-19 pandemic on peace and conflict. International Peace Institute. News and Press Release. http://reliefweb.int/report/world/effects-covid-19-pandemic-peace-and-conflict

Ohanyan, O. (2015). *Networked regionalism as conflict management.* Stanford University Press.

O'Leary, B. (2013). Powersharing in deeply divided places: An advocate's introduction. In J. McEvoy & B. O'Leary (Eds.), *Power sharing in deeply divided places* (pp. 1–64). University of Pennsylvania Press.

Özerdem, A. (2014). *Local ownership in international peacebuilding.* Routledge.

Philpott, D., & Powers, G. (2010). *Strategies of peace: Transforming conflict in a violent world.* Oxford University Press.

Puar, J. (2007). *Terrorist assemblages: Homonationalism in queer times.* Duke University Press.

Rahman, A., Clarke, M. A., & Byrne, S. (2017). The art of breaking people down: The British colonial model in Ireland and Canada. *Peace Research: Canadian Journal of Peace and Conflict Studies, 49*(2), 15–38.

Redman-McLaren, M., & Mills, J. (2015). Transformational grounded theory: Theory, voice and action. *International Journal of Qualitative Methods, 14*(3), 1–12.

Richmond, O. P. (2016). *Peace formation and political order in conflict affected societies.* Oxford University Press.

Ritzer, G. (2016). Introduction. In G. Ritzer (Ed.), *The Blackwell companion to globalization* (pp. 1–14). Blackwell Wiley.

Robins, S., & Wilson, E. (2015). Participatory methodologies with victims: An emancipatory approach to transitional justice. *Canadian Journal of Law and Society, 30*(2), 219–236.

Ross, M. H. (2007). *Cultural contestation in ethnic conflict.* Cambridge University Press.

Senehi, J. (2019). Theory-building in peace and conflict studies: The storytelling methodology. In S. Byrne, T. Matyók, I. M. Scott, & J. Senehi (Eds.), *Routledge companion to peace and conflict studies* (pp. 45–56). Routledge.

Smith, R. (2019). *The utility of force: The art of war in the modern world.* Penguin Random House UK.

Smith, A. D. (2004). *Chosen people: Sacred sources of national identity.* Oxford University Press.

Smith, A. D. (1996). Culture, community, and territory: The politics of ethnicity and nationalism. *International Affairs, 72*(3), 445–558.

Taras, R., & Ganguly, R. (2009). *Understanding ethnic conflict.* Routledge.

Tat, P. (2019). *Policy and governance in post-conflict settings: Theory and practice.* Routledge.

Thiessen, C. (2011). Emancipatory peacebuilding: Critical responses to (neo)liberal trends. In T. Matyók, J. Senehi, & S. Byrne (Eds.), *Critical issues in peace and conflict studies: Theory, practice, and pedagogy* (pp. 115–143). Lexington.

Thiessen, C., & Byrne, S. (2017). Proceed with caution: Research production and uptake in conflict-affected countries. *Journal of Peacebuilding and Development, 13*(1), 1–15.

Volkan, V. (2019). *Killing in the name of identity: A study of bloody conflicts*. Pitchstone Publishing.

Wallace, R. (2013). *Merging fires: Grassroots peacebuilding between Indigenous and non-Indigenous peoples*. Fernwood.

Wessells, M. (2008). *Trauma, peacebuilding and development: An Africa region perspective*. Paper presented at Trauma, Development and Peacebuilding Conference. https://citeseerx.ist.psu.edu/viewdoc/download?doi=10.1.1.519.7276&rep=rep1&type=pdf

Wolff, S. (2006). *Ethnic conflict: A global perspective*. Oxford University Press.

Zariski, R. (1989). Ethnic extremism among ethnoterritorial minorities in Western Europe: Dimensions, causes, and institutional responses. *Comparative Politics, 21*(3), 253–272.

INDEX

Page numbers in italics refer to figures. Page numbers in bold refer to tables. Page numbers followed by "n" refer to notes.

3B (Binding, Bonding and Bridging) framework 285–286
9/11 attacks 83–85, 151, 328, 340
1878–1903 Land Wars 33
1918 Spanish flu 94

Aboriginal peoples 321
Abu-Lughod, L. 289n4
abuse(s) 193; human rights 141, 271, 272, 275, 305–306; identity 165; physical 165; sexual 28, 165, 177, 187, 220
academic education in conflict resolution 126–127
accompaniment 132–133; *see also* unarmed civilian protection (UCP)
accountability 248, 249, 271; community heritage law 202; international agencies 264; issues in Sri Lanka 271, 273, 275, 277; to local communities 143; need for 274; as reconciliation mechanism 275, 277
Aceh (Indonesia), inclusive process in 295–297, 350
acting-out: categories of 192; evidence of 191–192; instance of 193; posttraumatic 195; value 195; and working-through historical trauma 193
adrenaline 262
adverse health effects of hatred 61, 65–66
advocacy: and change-making work 261; FBOs and other agencies 151, 156–157; human rights 242, 271, 348; for Indigenous peacebuilding 316
Afghanistan: ethnopolitical-armed conflicts in 20; invasion and occupation of 83; jirga in 110; war in 90

Africa, environmental security in 72
African American community 19; background 232–234; implications for practice and policy 239–240; implications for teaching and training 236–239; key insights 234–236; mental health support 238; overview 231–232
African Burial Ground National Monument 205
age-defined perspective, youth 175
agency: of civil society actors 135; defined 178; development of 259
Agenda for Peace, An (Boutros-Ghali) 269
agents of change, youth as 178–180
Age of Persistent Conflict 344
Aggestam, K. 283
aggressive nationalism 22
aggressive speeches and ethnopolitical conflict 24
agonistic pluralism 301
aid and peacebuilding; *see* external aid and peacebuilding
Albania 23
Albright, M. 244
alcohol use 261
Aleppo, Syria 210, 211, 213–214
Alfred, R. 310
Allen, J. R. 90
Alliance of Civilizations, UN 156
Al-Shabaab, charcoal trades financing in 75
Alternative for Germany 344
Altiok, A. 178–179, 180
Alzheimer's disease 61
American Academy of Pediatrics (AAP) 234
American exceptionalism 89

355

American nationalism, relapse of 83–92; implications for practice and policy 92; implications for teaching and training 91–92; security threat 83–91
American Psychiatric Association 223
American supremacy 89
amnesia, selective 277
Amnesty International 271, 273
Anan Plan 125
Anayatin, S. 289n7
Anderlini, S. 35
Anglo-Irish Agreement 306
antiestablishment polemics by leaders 84–85
antioppression toptics 66
antiracism: activism, public monuments and 191–194; movements 200–201; outrage 97–98
anti-Russian sanctions regarding Ukraine 45
anxiety 61, 253, 261, 295, 299, 300
Anzaldúa, G. E. 188
apathy 252
apolitical nature, of military 146
Appadurai, A. 214
Aquino, B., III 289n2
Arab Spring 305–306
Arbery, A. 235
Arendt, H. 164, 165, 166
Argentina 248–249, 250n18
ARIA model 330
Armenians 21; against Azerbaijan 22; genocide 31
Army of Republika Srpska (VRS) 250n6
arthritis 61
arts-based interventions, healing-centered peacebuilding 262
Ashrawi, H. 33
Asian conflict *vs* European and Middle Eastern conflicts 41
assaults, on monuments 192–193, 196
Atallah, A. 28–29
Atlanta Consulting and Psychological Services, LLC 236
Aung San Suu Kyi 32
Australia: fires in 327; indigenous knowledge and peacemaking system 321
Austria, Slovene minorities in 100–101
authoritarian leaders 84–85
autonomic nervous system (ANS) 262
Avruch, K. 114, 316

Ban Ki-moon 270, 271
Bangsamoro Autonomous Region in Muslim Mindanao (BARMM) 282
Bangsamoro Organic Law (BOL) 282, 288
Bangsamoro peace process 287–288
Banks, M. 127
Bantay Ceasefire group 286–287
Barkin Ladi 322
Barnes, C. 286

Barnett, M. N. 317
Basque separatist movement ETA 34
battered race syndrome 236
battle-related deaths 44, 46n4
Bearak, M. 322
Beckford, A. 189
Beevers, M. D. 77
being part of change, feeling of 214–215
Belgium, statues associated with figures 193, 199
Bell, D. 330
Benjamin, J. J. 114
Bercovitch, J. 42
Berents, H. 180
Berlin Wall 202–203
Berom population 318
Bethell, C., Dr. 260–261
Bhave, V. 133
biases: liberal 53; and peacemaking 111; racist 189–190, 232; toward the military and Muslims 284–285; toward wealthy elderly men 55
bicommunal peacebuilders 125–126
biculturalism, in New Zealand 298
bigotry 22
Bin Muaammar 157
Bismarck, O. von 196
Bissell, V. E. P. 202
Black, R. 273
Black Indigenous and People of Color (BIPOC) 340, 343
Black Lives Matter (2020) movement 97, 131, 187, 189, 191, 196, 200, 327, 347
Black youth 233–234
Bland, S. 235, 239
Bloom, S. 263
Body in Pain, The (Scarry) 221
Boeting, Rev. 170
Boko Haram 28
Bosnia 23; Bosniaks 340; Bosnian Muslims 33; peacebuilding efforts in 250n1, 250n2, 250n7; *see also* peace after genocide
Botcharova, O. 259
Bougainville Interim Government (BIG) 297
Bougainville peace negotiation, New Zealand and 297–300, 350
Bougainville Resistance Force (BRF) 297
Bougainville Revolutionary Army (BRA) 297
Boutros-Ghali, B. 48, 269
Brazil: disappearance of rainforest in 321; Kayapo Resistance in 111–112
Bretthauer, J. M. 72, 78
BRICS (Brazil, Russia, India, China, and South Africa) 312
Bridge Poem, The 188
Britain, statues with racist figures 192–193
Bronagh 308
Brookings Institution 90
Broome, B. J. 125, 204

Brown, L. S. 224–225
Brown, M. 23, 235
Brown, T., Dr. 236
Brubaker, R. 23
Bullard, R. D. 75–76
Burnham process 298, 299
Burrowes, R. J. 73
Burton, J. 119, 328, 332
Bush, G. W., President 340
Bush, K. D. 283
Butler, J. 226
Byrne, S. 72, 74, 350

Cabrera, M. 252
Cagoco-Guiam, R. 288–289
Cambodia, peace negotiations in 292
Cameroon (English speakers), ethnopolitical-armed conflicts in **20**
Canada: decolonizing education in 333; indigenous knowledge and peacemaking system 321; Indigenous youth, forced removals of 199
Canadian Institute for International Peace and Security (CIIPS) 125
Capitol Hill Autonomous Zone 189
cardiovascular diseases and hatred 61
caring collective, building 284–285
Carinthian Plebiscite 101
Carment. D. 40
Caruth, C. 223–224
Catalans 17
Catholic Relief Service (CRS) 284, 285
ceasefire and agreements 45
Center of International Development and Conflict Management 328
Central African Republic (CAR), religious leaders in peacebuilding 156
Centre for Conflict Management and Peace Studies (CCMPS) 321
Centre for Humanitarian Dialogue 318
Certeau, M. de 283, 289n4
Changing Lenses (Zehr) 108
Chauvin, D. 232
Chechens 45
Chigas, D. 119–120, 125
children, African American 232–234; mental and emotional dynamics of aggregated trauma 236–239; mental health support 238–239; traumatic memories 234–236; wellness needs of 238–239; *see also* African American community
Children's Defense Fund (CDF) 233
Child Trends 238–239
China: aid allocation from 306; against multilateral humanitarian relief in Syria 45; Uighur minority 21
Choucri, N. 176
Christian Peacemaker Teams 133
Christians 152–153, 281–282, 284, 285; BARMM 289n6; community leaders 321; for Peace Movement 286, 287–288, 289; religious leaders 319; representative 289n7; Settlers Peace Agenda for Bangsamoro Peace Process 288, 289n6
C-Institute for Peace and Development in Mindanao 288
circuitry of civic recognition 203
civic engagement 74
civic society movement 97
civil conflicts/war 42, 43; in Aceh, Indonesia 295–297; in Bougainville 297–300; in Côte d'Ivoire 75; external funds and armament during 39–40; external interventions in 44; and military initiatives 45–46; and poverty 21; rape during 29–31; and sanctions 41; in Sierra Leone 75; Sudan's 17; *see also specific aspects/types*
civil rights advocates 36
Civil Rights monuments 205
Civil Rights Movement 200
civil society actors, agency of 135
civil society organizations (CSOs) 73–74, 304, 306–311, 317
Civil War Mediation Data 46n1
Civil War monuments, assaults on 192
Clarke, M. A. 331
classrooms, mainstream 216
clinical anxiety and hate speech 61
Clinton, H. 86
Cohen, D. K. 29
collective healing approaches 260–261
collective identities 121, 133, 199–201
collective neuroticism 236
Collier, P. 289n1
Collins, A. E. E. 283
Collins, P. H. 190, 330
Colombia 75; Indigenous Guard civil defense organization in 110; women's participation in peace agreement 76
colonialism 192
Columbus, C. 193, 199
commemorative controversy 199
common ingroup identity model 24–25
communal violence: in India 21; in South Africa 26n1
communication 340, 348; in conflict-affected communities 321; kind of 194; low-context 293, 294; nature of 145; process, by GAM 296; skills 299, 300; without dialogue 194
community(ies): acting as change agents 76; Barkin Ladi 322; BIPOC 340, 343; community-based organizations (CBOs) 286, 332; contested community spaces 282–284; Dadin Kowa 322, 323; engagement, with monuments 204; faith 161; harmony and restorative justice 114; heritage law 202; identities 200; Indigenous, peacemaking works within 322; Jos 318–321;

LGBTQ 331, 334; Lumads 281, 282; Moros 282; Prijedor 247, 250n15; racialized 200–201; as safe spaces 348–349; sector in Ireland 307–308; Sinhala 269–270, 271, 272, 274, 276; spaces 284–285; Tamils 269–270, 271–272, 273, 274–275, 350; *see also* African American community; Christians; Muslims; Sri Lanka, postwar reconciliation in
Community of Peace 333
compartmentalization 158, 162n3
compassion 226, 227, 232
Comprehensive Agreement on Bangsamoro (CAB) 289n2
Conca, K. 72, 73, 77
Confederate monuments 198, 199, 200, 201, 202, 206
conflict(s): among participants 160; analysis 160; Bougainville 298; causes of 152, 160; ethnic/religious 176; identity 146–147; interreligious dynamics of 152; leveraging complexity of 329–330; multiethnic, Mindanao 281–282; multifactor analysis of 160; and nexus, peace 175–176; religion with 154; resolution 153, 293, 294, 295, 298, 328; and rivalry 21; in Tajikistan 332; tri-people dimension 281–282; and war 270; *see also* ethnopolitical conflicts; focal points in ethnic conflicts; Indigenous societies, peacemaking and peacebuilding; Mindanao (Philippines)
Conflict Transformation School (Lederach) 112
Congressional Black Caucus (CBC) 233
Connolly, J. 32
constitutional engineering 25
constructivist theorists 17
consultation(s): lack of 277; meetings 288, 296; with policymakers and religious leaders 162n3; process in Sweden 300
contestation 51, 52, 221, 283
contested community spaces 282–284
contextualization component, of healing-centered peacebuilding 257–259
contingency model 123–124
continuing traumatic stress disorder (CTSD) 236, 321
coordination among interveners 123–124
CORDOVA (civil society organization) 295
Corley, C. 235
Coronel-Ferrer, M. 283
Corrigan, M. 333
cortisol 262
Côte d'Ivoire, civil war in 75
counter terrorism (CT): implications of 162n2; resources in 154
counter violent extremism (CVE) 158; initiatives 155; resources in 154
Cousins, N. 327
COVID-19 pandemic 94–103; considerations and methodological issues 97–99; context 94–97; implications for practice and policy 102–103; implications for teaching and training 102; key insights 99–102; and peacebuilding 341, 347–348; related research 98–99; travel regulations 347–348
Craps, S. 223
creativity, arts-based interventions and 262
Crenshaw, K. 330
Crimes against Humanity in the Land of the Free (Brown and Wallace) 236
Cristiano, F. 283
critical environmental justice (CEJ) 75–76
critical race theory 330
critical thinking skills 66
critical trauma studies 220–222
Croatia 23, 99–100
cross-conflict team, building 119
CSOs; *see* civil society organizations (CSOs)
Cuhadar, E. 128
cultic nationalists 87, 89
culture/cultural: actors, responsibility of 67; contexts, RJ practices 113; culturally embedded programs 79; culturally reflective third-party mediation, Bougainville 297–300; "culture of peace" discourse 160; heritage, preservation of 202–203; identity 110, 120–121; and Indigenous peacemaking 318–319; missing 213–214; nationalist intellectuals 21; politics of indigeneity 113–114; strand, of trauma studies 220, 221, 222; violence 61–62, 143, 202; *see also* heritage rights, monuments, and cultural divides
Cumann na mBan (the Women's Council) 32
Curle, A. 316
curricula, hate studies 66
customization component, of healing-centered peacebuilding 257–259
Cvetkovich, A. 225–226
cycle of violence theory 259
Cyprus: conflict 119–120; ethnic conflict between Greek and Turkish Cypriots 125; youth in ethnopolitical conflicts 179
cytokines, body's balance of 61

Dadin Kowa community 322, 323
Dakota Access Pipeline, protests in response to 110
Dalby, S. 78
Danieli, Y. 249–250
Darfur-Sudan, problem-solving workshop (PSW) projects in 127
Dartmouth Conference 327
Das, V. 223
Davidson, W. D. 329
Dayton Peace Agreement 244, 245, 246, 250n4
Dean, C. 350
Dearbhla 307–308

Index

deaths: in attacks of September 11, 2001 83; attributable to radical Islamist violent extremists 86; battle-related 20, 44; gun related 90, 92; of Papuans 165
decision-making 76, 121, 125
decolonizing approach, healing-centered peacebuilding 258
De Coning, C. 283
de-escalation 4, 39, 44, 119, 121–123
Degruy, J., Dr. 232–233, 236
Democratic Party 85–86
Democratic Republic of Congo (DRC) 75; ethnopolitical-armed conflicts in **20**; sexual violence in 28, 30
demographic shifts and cultural violence 202
denialism, campaigns of 243, 249
depression 61, 253, 261
DeRouen, K., Jr. 42
d'Estrée, T. P. 328
destructive storytelling 321
Diagnostic and Statistical Manual of Mental Disorders, 3rd edition (DSM-III) 223
dialogue 119; Centre for Humanitarian Dialogue 318; humanitarian dialogue (HD) 318, 320; intrareligious dialogue, space for 161; KAICIID 156, 157, 159; meaningful 194–195; and problem-solving 332; process 318
Dialogue, Reconciliation, and Peace (DREP) Center 319
Diamond, L. 119–120, 125, 329
DiAngelo, R. 189–190
Diehl, P. F. 41
dignity 141, 167, 169, 171, 172
diplomatic initiatives 44
direct violence 110, 122, 143, 144
disabilities, people with 331, 334
disarmament, demobilization, and reintegration (DDR) 178, 180
diversity management and COVID-19 pandemic; *see* COVID-19 pandemic
Djuli, N. 296
Doctors Without Borders 39
Donais, T. 50, 289n3
Donnacha 307
donor(s): countries 312; and locals 306; motivations 305–306
double-consciousness 237
Dreyfus, E. 84
drug use 261
Du Bois, W. E. B., Dr. 237
Duterte, R., President 282
Džaferović, Š 249

Eager, P. W. 34
Eastern Revival (*Neganahira Navodaya*) 273–274
Easter Uprising of 1916 32
ecological healing, promotion 261

ecology/ecological: justice 75–76; strand of trauma studies 220, 222, 223, 225; stress 74
economic and social resources and COVID-19 95–96
Economic Cooperation and Development (BMZ) 157
Edkins, J. 248
education(al): campaigns 67; peace 333
Eke, S. 350
Eleanor 308–309
elicitive peacebuilding 318
Ellis-Petersen, H. 32
El Paso, Texas, mass shooting in 86
El Salvador 31
emancipatory intervention systems 52
emancipatory peacebuilding; *see* environment and peacebuilding; Mindanao (Philippines)
Emergency Task Force on Black Youth Suicide and Mental Health 233
emotion(al) 25, 61, 166, 167, 169, 170–171, 172, 193, 194, 195, 196, 226, 232, 238, 252; ecosystem 222; management and conflict resolution 25; tensions 299
employment, opportunities 311
empowerment ethic 136
enablers, women as 29–30
Engineers Without Borders 39
England, K. V. L. 331
Enloe, C. 28, 29
Environmental Conflict Resolution (ECR) 73
environment(al): laws and norms, implementing 79; security 71–72, 79
environment and peacebuilding 71–80; critical framework for environmental peacebuilding 73–77; environment and ethnic conflict 71–73; environment and peacebuilding 73; implications for practice and policy 79; implications for teaching and training 78–79; key insights 77–78
Equal Justice Initiative 204
Eritrea, struggle against Ethiopia 40
escalation 121–122
ethics of intercultural peacebuilding 331
ethnic cleansing: campaign 244, 245–246, 274–275; of Rohingya Muslims 32
ethnic conflict(s) 21; background 2–3; key dimensions of 341–343; peacebuilders in 344–346; *see also* focal points in ethnic conflicts
ethnicity/ethnic: activists, creating 23; exclusion 25; group, defined 18; identities 17, 18, 19, 45; positive 147–148; rebellions 21; reconciliation in Sri Lanka 271, 272, 273; riots 21; solidarity 19; *see also* Sri Lanka, postwar reconciliation in
ethnonationalist clashes 17
ethnopolitical conflicts 17–25; background 18–21; and feelings of threat 22; implications for practice and policy 24–25; implications for teaching and training 24; key insights 21–24; limiting 148;

overview 17–18; and peacebuilding 340–341; volatility of 145; *see also* peace leadership, security, and military in ethnopolitical conflicts; youth in ethnopolitical conflicts
ethnopolitical issues: armed conflicts **20**, 20–21; defined 28; identities, social construction of 17–18; violence 22
ethno-religious citizen conciliation 92
ethno-symbolist 21
European Commission 175
European migrant/refugee crisis 96
European Union (EU) 51; for bilateral projects 332; Peace and Reconciliation Fund 306; Peace Fund 350; Peace 3 Fund 306, 307
eventless theory of trauma 220
everyday peace, defined 284
evidence-based research, healing-centered peacebuilding 264
evidence-based responses 68
Eviota, D., Jr. 286
exhumation efforts, in Bosnia and Herzegovina 247–248; of Tomašica mass grave 250n16; *see also* peace after genocide
exploitation, control and 143
external aid and peacebuilding: background 304–306; donor motivations 305–306; donors and locals 306; implications for practice and policy 312; implications for teaching and training 311–312; key insights 306–311; overview 304; role of economic aid 304–305
external involvements in ethnopolitical conflict 39–46; implications for practice and policy 45–46; implications for teaching and training 44–45; key insights 41–44; overview 39–40; types of engagement 40–41
extremism, post-9/11 attack 85–87; *see also* American nationalism, relapse of
Eyerman, R. 221

Facing History and Ourselves 333
faith: -based peacebuilding 162n1; communities, responsibility of 67; groups 161; identity 153; intentional integration of 152–153; language 160–161
Faith Advisory Council 157
faith-based organizations (FBOs) 151, 155, 156–157, 158, 159
false narratives 65
familiarity, sense of 213–214
family, missing 211–213
Family Group Conferencing model (FGC) 113
farmer-herder conflicts, Indigenous peacebuilding 315, 321, 322; *see also* Indigenous societies, peacemaking and peacebuilding
Fassin, D. 220, 225, 226
fear 24; elimination 179, 193, 196; mongering 65; of otherness 36

Fearon, J. D. 19, 21
Federer, P. 120
feelings of threat 22, 24, 25
Felton, J. 235
feminism 36, 223
Ferrell, J. 235
Financial Times 87
Finn Church Aid (FCA) 156, 157, 159
Firchow, P. 289n3
firearms; *see* gun culture/violence
First Nations practices of conflict management 107–108; *see also* Indigenous societies, peacemaking and peacebuilding
Fisher, R. 118, 122, 126, 332
Fitzduff, M. 287
flexible platforms, monuments and 203–204
Floyd, G., killing of 131, 187, 189, 232, 235, 327, 347
FMLN (Salvadoran rebel force), women in 31
focal points in ethnic conflicts: background 329–330; dialogue and problem-solving 332; ethics of intercultural peacebuilding 331; formal peace processes 334; implication for teaching and training 334; implications for practice and policy 334; Indigenous and local approaches 332; key insights 330–334; multitrack peacebuilding and community-based organizations 332; nonviolent collective action and building awareness 333; overview 327–329; peace education 333; reflexivity and positionality 331; transitional justice 333–334; trauma healing 333
Fontaine, T. 165
Forbes 89
formal peace processes 334
FOR Peace Presence 133
Foucault, M. 289n4
Foundations of Rebel Group Emergence (FORGE) 42
Fox News 196
Framework Agreement on Bangsamoro (FAB) 289n2
Franco, F. 205
Frankl, V. E. 258
Frazier, D. 327
Free Aceh Movement; *see Gerakan Aceh Merdeka* (GAM)
Freire, P. 79, 194
FRELIMO regime 224
French Canadians 19
Freud, S. 191, 192, 220, 221, 222
Freyburger, H. J. 29
Friedan, B. 289n4
Friere, P. 331
frontline intervention activities 52
frustration: social 144, 148; types 147; and violence 144

Fry, D. 108
Fulani group 318, 332
Fullilove, M. 222
funding: challenges 180–181; on competitive basis 308; external 307–310; IFI 306, 307, 311, 350; MacArthur Foundation 328; organizations 204–206; Peace 2 and Peace 3 307; from William and Flora and Hewlett Foundation 328; *see also* external aid and peacebuilding

Gacaca (Rwanda) 111
Gaelic language revival program 33
Gagnon, V. P. 23
Galtung, J. 122, 202, 258
GAM (*Gerakan Aceh Merdeka*) 295–297, 300, 301n1
Gandhi, M. K. 133
Gandhi, R. 31–32, 44
Garner, E. 235, 239
Gaziantep (Turkey) 210–211, 215
gender: -based violence 41, 133, 177; equality 76
gender and ethnopolitical conflict 28–37; implications for practice and policy 36; implications for teaching and training 35–36; mothers and caregivers 33–34; rape 29–31; women combatants 31–32; women leaders 32–33; women negotiators and peacemakers 34
genocide 21, 164–165, 193, 221; cultural 199; in GPS coordinates and landscape of mass graves 243–244; in Myanmar 32–33; in Rwanda 22; of Rohingya in Myanmar 340; Srebrenica 242, 244, 245, 246–247; stages of 243; *see also* peace after genocide
geopolitics, feminist 223
George III, King 203
Georgia-South Ossetia 22; peacemaking 332; problem-solving workshop (PSW) projects 127
geotrauma 222
Gerakan Aceh Merdeka (GAM) 295–297, 300, 301n1
German women 34
Gettig, S. 110
Ghana, statues with racist figures 192–193
Gilligan, C. 35–36
Global North countries 305, 306, 312, 341
Global South countries 305
Global War on Terrorism 96
Goldman, L. 73
gold mining financing criminal groups 75
Goldstone, J. A. 176
Gonne, M. 33
Good Friday Agreement (GFA) 340
governance interventions, healing-centered peacebuilding 260
Government of Indonesia (GoI) 295–296, 297, 301n1

government response, Sri Lanka's postwar reconciliation 272–274
Goza, S. 234
GPS coordinates, genocide in 243–244
Graham, L. 233
Graveyard Committee and Elders Forum 322
Greek-Cypriot communities, peace building for 125–126
Greenblatt, J. 33
Greenham Commons Women's Peace Camp 34
Green String Network 264, 333
Grieg, J. M. 41
Grizelj, I. 178–179, 180
Gross National Income (GNI) 305
group-based hatred intervention 67
group identity 19, 21
Guidelines on Mental Health and Psychosocial Support in Emergency Settings 254
guilt, feeling of 238, 248
Gujarat riots in India 21
gun(s): culture/violence 87–90, 92; deaths related to 90, 92; mass shootings 86, 88, 89; ownership of firearms 87–89
Gunnar M. 99
Gurr, T. R. 120–121, 328
Guzman, J. M. de 287

Hadjipavlou, M. 126
Haley, N. 233
Halilovich, H. 243
hangi (traditional Māori meal) 299
Harding, S. 190
Hardy, K. 331
Harris, K. 233
Harvard Trauma Questionnaire (HTQ) 264
hate speech 61, 65, 145
hatred, as public health issue in ethnopolitical conflicts 59–69; background 59–64; components of 64; exposure to 63; conceptual framework 62; health and social consequences of 60–61; implications for practice and policy 68; implications for teaching and training 65–68; preventive measures 63; underlying causal factors 59; understanding 64
Haudenosaunee (people of the Longhouse) 33
Hausa group 318
Hayes, J. 298
Hazan, O. 34
healing and reconciliation program 68
healing-centered peacebuilding approach: arts-based interventions 262; background 252–253; breaking cycles of violence component 259; collective healing approaches 260–261; customization and contextualization component 257–259; defined 253; development, justice, and governance interventions 260; development

of agency, supporting 259; drivers of adversity, identification 263; ecological healing, promotion 261; elements and subelements 254, 256–262; evidence-based research 264; "ignore it" approach 254; implementation responses 254; implications for practice and policy 263–264; implications for teaching and training 262–263; inclusive component of 257; local peacebuilding 264; mental health approach 254; nervous system, embodied practices regulation 262; neuroscience concepts 262; objectives 263–264; psychosocial support approach 254; relationship holds and transforms space 261–262; resilience-informed 260; systems map 253–254, *255*; systems thinking component 260–261; trauma-informed organizational training 263; trauma-informed tools 261–262; victims and perpetrators 259

Healing Circles, Inc. 236
Healing Through Remembering 333
Heathershaw, J. 51, 317
helplessness 258–259
Helsinki process 295, 297
Heredia, M. I. De 317
heritage rights, monuments, and cultural divides: background 198–201; collective identity and rites of omission 199–201; commemorative controversy 199; demographic shifts and cultural violence 202; flexible platforms 203–204; implications for practice and policy 204–206; implications for teaching and training 203–204; key insights 201–203; monumental concepts in law 202–203
Herman, J. 221, 223, 225
Herzegovina 23, 250n1, 250n2; *see also* peace after genocide
Hetherington, M. 333
Hewlett Foundation 328, 330
Hezbollah, intervention for mediation 44–45
Highmore, B. 283
Hill, A. 235
Hindu groups 21, 152–153
hiring trainers from the Global South 54
Hirsch, M. 222
history/historical: strand of trauma studies 220, 222; violence 223
Hitler, A. 34
Hitler's Furies (Lower) 30
Hmong groups in Vietnam 41
Hoeffler, A. 289n1
Holocaust-based trauma 22, 221, 223
home, safe 209–210; *see also* refugees, voices of
Homer-Dixon, T. F. 72, 78
hongi (traditional form of greeting) 298
Honwana, A. 175
Hope in the Cities 204
hostility 21, 25, 61, 122, 123, 210

Hughes, F. 32
Huibregtse, A. 40
humanitarian dialogue (HD) 318, 320
human rights: abuses 141, 271, 272, 275, 305–306; suspensions of 96–97; violations 271, 273, 305
Human Rights Watch (HRW) 271, 281
Hungary 100, 344
hurricane Mitch 252
Hussein, S. 40, 203
Hutu people 22
hybrid peacebuilding 269, 306
hypothalamic-pituitary-adrenocortical axis (HPAA) 61
hysteria 220

identity(ies): abuse 165; -based conflicts 43, 121, 123, 150, 329; collective 76, 121, 133, 199–201; conflicts 146–147, 298; cultural 110, 120–121; definition 28; and ethnonational conflict 298; faith 153; group 19; national 17, 25; organizational 133; religious 19, 45; Serbian ethnic 19; social 77, 121; white 86; *see also* ethnicity/ethnic
ideological murders 86
Idris, W. 35
IES 101, 102
iftar (breaking the fast) 212
"ignore it" approach, healing-centered peacebuilding 254
IKEA peacebuilding model 304
Implementation Force (IFOR) 244, 245, 250n4
inclusions: component of healing-centered peacebuilding 257; horizontal and vertical 293; of marginalized groups 293; negotiation process 293–294; process in Aceh, Indonesia 295–297
India: Kashmiris, ethnopolitical-armed conflicts in **20**; Muslims 18
Indigenous peoples 164, 165, 192; of Brazil 111–112; history of 280–281; in Latin America/Canada 20; local approaches 332; Lumads 281; Māori culture, of New Zealand 298–299; and peacemaking, culture 318–319; peasants in El Salvador 31; racism toward 333
Indigenous societies, peacemaking and peacebuilding 110–111; background 315–318; culture and Indigenous peacemaking 318–319; defined 107–108; farmer-herder conflicts 322; implications for practice and policy 323; implications for teaching and training 323; key findings 318–322; knowledge and peacemaking system 321–322; liberal peace debate 316–318; local peacebuilding 316; overview 315; peacemaking works within Indigenous community 322; rituals as peacemaking and rituals of connection 319–320; transcultural constructive storytellers 320–321
indirect violence 164, 202

Index

Indonesia: Aceh, inclusive process in 295–297; GoI 295–296, 297, 301n1; West Papua 165, 340; *see also* West Papua (Indonesia), Mamas' resistance to annihilative violence in
information sharing 123–124
in-group/out-group male behavior 35–36
innovation, arts-based interventions and 262
insecurity and social collapse 215–216
insidious trauma 224–225
instability, cycle of violence and 142
Institute for hatred, health, well-being, and international peace (IHHWIP) 66
Institute for Multi-Track Diplomacy 125
Institute of Ethnic Studies (IES) 96
institutional entity 91
institutional racism 97
instrumentalized ("token") engagement 158
integration: of engagement with religious agencies 158, 162n4; of faith in design 152–153
interactive conflict resolution (ICR) 118–128; background 118–120; defined 119; implications for practice and policy 127–128; implications for teaching and training 126–127; key insights 120–126; role in post-conflict peacebuilding 122–123; transfer from identity of participants to the effects of transfer 124–125
Inter-Agency Standing Committee 254
Inter-Agency Task Force on Religion and Development, UN 157
intercultural(ism): conflict resolution 334; peacebuilding, ethics of 331
interdependence between groups 76
interdisciplinary environmental justice studies (EJS) 75–76
intergenerational trauma 222
intergovernmental organizations (IGOs) 51, 155
intergroup hatred 65, 67
internally displaced persons (IDPs) 252–253
international campaign, Sri Lanka's postwar reconciliation 270–272
International Commission on Missing Persons (ICMP) 245, 250n11, 250n12
international consensus about liberal norms 51
International Fund for Ireland (IFI) 306, 307, 311, 350
International Negotiation 123
International Peace and Conflict Resolution Program (IPCR) 126
international peacebuilding communities in Sri Lanka; *see* Sri Lanka, postwar reconciliation in
international ramifications of ethnopolitical conflict; *see* external involvements in ethnopolitical conflict
International Solidarity Movement 133
International Tribunal for former Yugoslavia (ICTY) 244, 245
internment camps 274

Interpeace 264
interpersonal hatred/violence 65, 66, 67, 68, 221, 223
interreligious and religious peacebuilding (IRPB) 152–154; attributes of 151–159; background 151; implications for policy and practitioners 160–161; intentional integration of faith in design 152–153; key insights 151–159; motivation 152; peacebuilding tools 161; policymaking agencies, intervention and challenges in engaging 155–157, 162n2; religious agencies in peacebuilding intervention, engagement of 158–159; third-party role in IRPB intervention 153–154; and violent extremism 154–155; *see also* religion in peacebuilding
intersectionality 330
interventions, types of external 40–41, 53
intrafaith forums 161
intrareligious dialogue, space for 161
Iran: aid to Iraqi Kurds 40; intervention for mediation 44–45
Iraq: ethnopolitical-armed conflicts in **20**; invasion and occupation of 83
Ireland: community sector in 307–308; International Fund for Ireland 306, 307, 311, 350; Irish nationalist women as combatants and terrorists 33; *see also* Northern Ireland
Irish Citizen Army 32
Iroquois: Confederacy 33; matriarchal society 322
ISIS: oil revenues sponsoring 75; Sunnis in **20**
Islamic Law 295
isolation during COVID-19 lockdown and minority communities 99–100
Israel 340; conflict over land access and water resource control 75; Israeli-Palestinian conflict 332; Jewish women in 34; water cooperation with Palestine 76
Italian minorities: in Croatia 103n7; in Slovenia 101, 103n7

Jackson, V. 236
Jaffna University Teachers for Human Rights (JUTHR) 271
Jahn, B. 317
Jalali, J. A. 287
Jews 34, 152
jihadi terrorism 90
Jim Crow period 200, 233
jirga (Afghanistan and Pakistan) 110, 111
Johansson, A. 289n4
Johnson, K. 235
joint peace declaration 318
Jones, C. 235
Jones, L. 235
Jos (Nigeria): Catholic Diocese of 320; Conflict Management and Peace Studies (CCMPS) 321;

Dadin Kowa community in 322; farmer-herder conflicts in 321, 322; peace-related activities in 318–322
Joshua 309
Journalists Without Borders 39
Julius, D. 328
justice: healing-centered peacebuilding approach 260; transitional 333–334
Justice Development and Peace Commission (JDPC) 321

Kanol, B. 126
Kantola, T. 157
Karadžiæ, R. 243, 244
Karp, A. 87
Kaufman, S. J. 22, 23–24
Kayapo Resistance in Brazil 110, 111–112
Keashly, L. 123
Keethaponcalan, S. I. 350
Kelman, H. 119, 124, 328
Kemp, G. 108
Kenya, women's movements, and communities in 76
King, M. L. 203
King Abdullah Centre for Interreligious and Intercultural Dialogue (KAICIID) 156, 157, 159
Kirksey, E. 165
knowledge: controlling 351; Indigenous 321–322, 332; and know-how 66
KontraS Aceh 295
Kosovo 23
Kroeker, W. 332, 350
Krstiæ, R. 245, 250n3, 250n9
Ku Klux Klan 200
Kurdish peshmerga combatants, women as 32
Kurdistan Workers Party (PKK) 32
Kuwert, P. 29

LaCapra, D. 191–192
Laitin, D. D. 19, 21
Lake, G. 41
Lakota tradition 110–111
Lancet, The 253
land ownership, policies ensuring 79
language of faith 160–161
Laub, D. 221
laughter, suffering and 170–171
Lawry, L. 30
Layson, B. 284, 285
leadership structure 144–145; *see also* peace leadership, security, and military in ethnopolitical conflicts
Lederach, J. P. 74, 112, 203, 252, 316, 318, 329, 330
Lee, G. 107
Lee, R. E. 202

Lee, S. 350
Lemkin, R. 165
Leopold II, King 193, 199
lesbians 225–226
Lessons Learnt and Reconciliation Commission (LLRC) 272, 273
Levy, M. 71
LGBTQ community 331, 334
LGBTQ identities 36
liberal biases 53
liberal peacebuilding: conflict-affected populations and liberal peace 49–50; critique of liberal peace 49–50; and emancipatory critique 48–56, 74; implications for practice and policy 55–56; implications for teaching and training 53–55; influence of liberal theories 51; surveying the liberal norms and practices within the peacebuilding sector 52–53
liberal peace debate 316–318
Liberation Tigers of Tamil Eelam (LTTE) 31–32, 44, 269, 270, 271, 272, 273, 274, 276, 277
Liberia, diamonds, and timber extractions in 75
Libya: peace processes in 156; post-Qaddafi 45
Lidingo (Sweden), GAM-civil society meeting 296
linguistic ties and smaller power mediators 41
lived experiences, role for 257
local ownership 50, 73–74, 77–78
local peacebuilding 53–54, 264; and donors 306; roots 316; and traditional healers 257; *see also* Sri Lanka, postwar reconciliation in
local turn, concepts of 289n3
Loken, M. 31
lost generation, concept of 177
loved ones, missing 211–213
Lower, W. 30
loyalty, dilemma of 147
LTTE; *see* Liberation Tigers of Tamil Eelam (LTTE)
Luckhurst, R. 224
Lumads Indigenous peoples 281, 282
Lundy, B. D. 114
Luu, T. 287
Luzon (Philippines) 281

Maasai tribe of East Africa 232–233, 236
MacArthur Foundation 328
MacBride, S. 33
MacDonald, J. 199, 329
Mac Ginty, R. 77, 108, 109, 284, 289n3, 289n4, 316
Madikazela, P. G. 333
Madres de Plaza de Mayo 34, 249, 251n18
Maiangwa, B. 332
Malathi Brigade (LTTE) 31–32
Malaysia: ethnic diversity in politics in 20; GAM-civil society meeting 297

Male Rape and Human Rights (Stemple) 30
male rapes 30–31
Mali mission 75
Mamas, resistance to annihilative violence in West Papua: background 164–165; effectiveness of 166; experiences of suffering 166–168; hard work of striving through suffering 166, 167, 169, 171–172; humor, voice and agency 166; key insights 166–168; Mama Bunia 169–170, 171; Mama Josefina 168, 169; Mama Koinonia 166–167, 169, 170; Mama Lula 167, 170; Mama Maybel 170; Mamaness 166; Mama Tika 171–172; Mama Viki 167–168, 169; suffering and laughter 170–171; walking through suffering 169–170; *see also* West Papua (Indonesia), Mamas' resistance to annihilative violence in
Mamasapano clash/incident 289n2
Mandela, N. 233, 340
Mandell, B. S. 126
Mansfield, K. 329
Man's Search for Meaning (Frankl) 258
Māori 108, 113, 298–299
marae (communal place in and sacred the Māori culture) 299
March of Hope 34
Markale massacre 244, 250n5
Markiewicz, C. 32
Marković, M. 33
Marshall, D. J. 227
Martin, T. 235
mass grave(s): Argentina 248–249, 251n18; in postwar Bosnia and Herzegovina 243–244, 245–246, 248; Tomašica 250n16
mass media and COVID-19 related research 98–99
mass shootings 86, 88, 89
Mato Oput (Uganda) 111
mazeways 222
Mazurana, D. 177
McArthur, A. 76
McDonald, J. W. 125, 321
McDonald, L. 239
McDoom, O. 22
McEvoy-Levy, S. 175–176, 178
McIvor, D. 203
Mckay, S. 177
media campaigns 111–112
mediation 41–42, 44, 45, 76, 119, 120–121, 123, 126, 127, 153, 156, 294, 297–300; and escalation, power 123; nongovernmental organizations (NGOs) 127
Melanesian culture 165, 298
memorials 191–194, 195
memory, trauma; *see* trauma studies
mental distress associated with racism 237
mental health and psychosocial support (MHPSS) programs 257, 263

mental health approach, healing-centered peacebuilding 254
Mesquida, C. G. 176
Mestizo peasants in El Salvador 31
Me Too! movement 187
Meyer, R. 25
military: campaign against LTTE 272, 273; efforts 144; initiatives and civil conflicts 45–46; as national institution 145–146; as security providers 147; *see also* peace leadership, security, and military in ethnopolitical conflicts
Millar, G. 50, 109
Millennium and Sustainable Development Goals 304
Milošević, S. 19, 23, 25, 33
Milstein, C. 226
Mindanao (Philippines) 350; background 280–282; Bantay Ceasefire 286–287; 3B theory, relational and structural interconnectedness 285–286; Christians for Peace Movement 286, 287–288, 289; community spaces, building caring collective 284–285; implications for practice and policy 286–288; implications for teaching and training 284–286; key peacebuilding insights 282–284; multiethnic conflict 281–282; overview 280
Minorities at Risk Project 328
Miodownik, D. 177
misleading neutrality 146–147
missing home, Syrian refugees 211–216
missing persons, in Bosnia and Herzegovina 242, 243, 245–246, 248, 250n7, 251n17
Missouri Information Analysis Center 85
mistrust 252
Mitchell, A. 317
Mitchell, C. R. 119, 127
Mladiæ, R. 244
mobilization theory 18
Mobutu Sese Sekou 22
Modi, N. 21, 199
Moldova conflict 332
Moller, H. 176
Montiel, C. J. 286
Montville, J. V. 328, 329
Monument Lab 204
monuments: Civil Rights 205; concepts in law 202–203; Confederate 198, 199, 200, 201, 202, 206; public 191–194, 195–196; removal of 201; *see also* heritage rights, monuments, and cultural divides
Moraga, C. 187, 188
moral education 66
morbidity and hatred 61
Morgana, Rev. 166
Morning After: Sexual Politics at the End of the Cold War, The (Enloe) 31
Moro Islamic Liberation Front (MILF) 282, 286, 288, 289n2

Moro National Liberation Front (MNLF) 282, 288
Moros 282
mortality and hatred 61
"Mothers Movement" during World War I 34
motivations 286; donor 305–306; interreligious peacebuilding 152; of youth involvement in violence 176
mourning 192, 199
Mozambique: peace negotiations in ethnic conflicts 292; peace process 332; War for Independence 224
Mubarak, H. 305–306
multidisciplinary nature, healing-centered peacebuilding approach 257
multiethnic conflict, Mindanao 281–282
multisectoral nature, healing-centered peacebuilding approach 257
multitrack peacebuilding and community-based organizations 332
Muñoz, J. E. 226
Murithi, T. 74
Murrey, J. 232
Muslim(s) 152, 153, 287; autonomous region for 282; Bosnian 249; communities 154, 160, 162n2; community leaders 321; Indian 18; minority 199; in Philippines 280–281, 282, 285; religious leaders 319; teenage girls 320; Uighurs 21, 45
Myanmar 156; ethnic violence in 32–33; peace negotiations in ethnic conflicts 292; Rohingya in 340
Myrdal, G. 99
myth-symbol complex 19

Nadarajah, S. 317
Naija Girls 320
Nairobi, Green String Network in 333
Nan, S. A. 123
naqba (catastrophe) 21
"*Narodni dom*," burning down of 101–102
Natasha, G. 110
national identities: in Africa 25; as ethnonational identities 17
national institution, military as 145–146
nationalism: aggressive 98; populist nationalism in America 81, 83; religious 88; *see also* American nationalism, relapse of
National Museum of African American History and Culture 205
National Rifle Association 88
national security, Sri Lanka 276
national self-determination 17
Native Americans 108; *see also* Indigenous peoples
natural resources and armed conflicts 74–75
Navajo peacemaking 107, 110
Neganahira Navodaya (Eastern Revival) 273–274
negative attitudes 121

negative emotions 61
negative peace 202
negotiations 45, 119; *see also* transformative peace negotiation
nervous system, embodied practices regulation 262
Nettelfield, L. J. 243
Network for Religious and Traditional Peacemakers 156, 159
neuroscience, healing-centered peacebuilding approach 262
neutrality, misleading 146–147
Never Again Rwanda 264
news outlets, coverage of terrorist attacks 84
New York Times 189
New Zealand 108, 297–300; *see also* Māori
Nicaragua, violence-affected regions of 252
Nigeria: farmer-herder conflicts 322; Jos, peace-related activities in 318–322; religious leaders in peacebuilding 156; schoolgirls, kidnapping of 28; youth in ethnopolitical conflicts 179
nongovernmental actors 120
nongovernmental organizations (NGOs) 51, 53, 119, 210, 211, 213, 264; and civil society organizations (CSOs) 304; international 245; mediation 127; monitoring activities of 286–287; with Palestinian survivors 226, 227; Swedish 296; tsunami-affected areas 296
nonindigenous women, clothing as identity for 110–111
nonstate actors 51
nonviolent accompaniment; *see* unarmed civilian protection (UCP)
nonviolent collective action 333
Nonviolent Peaceforce 133
Noreen, I. 166
North American peacebuilding scholarship 53
North Atlantic Treaty Organization (NATO) 51, 244, 340, 344
Northern Ireland 340; civil society organizations (CSOs) projects throughout 306, 307; Community of Peace in 333; ethnopolitical and religious conflicts in 176; government, stream of funding 310; local disputes in 315; new immigrants and refugees 309; peacebuilding in 332
Northern Provincial Council 274
Northern Spring (*Uthuru Vasanthaya*) 273–274
Norway, peace process 272
NTL Institute 125
Nuhanoviæ, H. 246–247, 248, 250n13, 250n14
Nyiramasuhuko, P. 31

Oakland Unified School District (OUSD), restorative justice in 112–113
Obama, B. 89, 200, 202, 270
Oblates of Mary Immaculate (OMI) 284
Observer Effect 134

Index

Ocalan, A. 32
Ochberg, F. 259
OECD Paris Declaration on Aid Effectiveness 304
oil revenues sponsoring ISIS 75
Olaf Palme International Center (OPIC) 296
Oliphant, V. 329
Oñate, J. de 199
Operation Deliberate Force 244
Orban, V. 344
organization(al): identities 133; training, trauma-informed 263
Organization for Security and Cooperation in Europe (OSCE) 51, 157
Organization of Islamic Cooperation (OIC) 156
Oslo Accord 124

PACS; *see* Peace and Conflict Studies (PACS)
Paffenholz, T. 122, 128, 316
Pahor, B. 101
pain: hierarchies of 226–227; of loss 169, 170–171, 172; of racialized trauma 238
Pain, R. 224
Pākehā practitioners, Family Group Conferencing model (FGC) for 113
Palestine/Palestinians 21, 226–227, 340; conflict over land access and water resource control 75; Israeli women 34; leaders, violent rhetoric against Israel 24; Palestinian-Israeli conflict 332; violence in 35
Panguna Landowners Association 297
Papua New Guinean government 298
Paris, R. 317
Paris Declaration on Aid Effectiveness 304
Partnership for Religion and Sustainable Development (PaRD) 156–157
patriarchal ideology 31, 35–36
peace: activists 36; agreements 252, 253; bureaucracy 318–319; and conflict nexus 175–176; education 333; everyday, defined 284; formal peace processes 334; liberal peace debate 316–318; negative 202; process, shift in 289n2; *see also* transformative peace negotiation
Peace Accords Matrix dataset 51
peace after genocide: after exhumation 247–248; background 242–244; to forgive and forget 246–247; implications for practice and policy 249–250; implications for teaching and training 248–249; key insights 245–248; searching for missing 245–246
Peace and Conflict Studies (PACS) 344–345, 348; peace negotiation in 293; programs 263; scholarship 91–92, 193–194, 195, 216
Peace and Development Agenda for Bangsamoro Peace Process 287–288
Peace and Reconciliation Fund 306, 307
Peace Begins with Truth (PBT) workshop 239
Peace Brigades International 133, 135, 333

peacebuilding: and COVID-19 pandemic 347–348; efforts, military 142, 143, 144, 147–148; and ethnopolitical conflicts 340–341; initiatives 180; intercultural, ethics of 331; and multitrack, community-based organizations 332; political character 48; rituals as 319–320; secular, initiatives/settings 153–154; youth contributions to 179–180; *see also specific aspects/types*
peacebuilding and public memory: background 187–191; implications for practice and policy 195–196; implications for teaching and training 194–195; key insights 191–194; public monuments, treatment 191–194
Peacebuilding Support Office 178–179
peacekeeping, failures of 242
peace leadership, security, and military in ethnopolitical conflicts: circle of conflict and peace efforts 142–143, *145*; control and exploitation, issue of 143; external influence 146; frustration and violence 144; implications for practice and policy 149; implications for teaching and training 149; key findings 148; leadership structure 144–145; military as national institution 145–146; military effort 144; misleading neutrality 146–147; overview 141; positive ethnicity in peacebuilding 147–148; power 143; theoretical concepts 142–148; youth in 179–180
pedagogical curriculum 66
Pedagogy of the Oppressed (Freire) 194
Pellow, D. 76
periodontal disease via immune dysregulation 61
perjuangan, hard work of striving through suffering 166, 167, 169, 171–172
perpetrators: and victims 259; women as 29–31
Peru-Ecuador peace process 332
Petoskey, M. 110
Pettersson, T. 21
Philippines: background 280–282; Muslims, ethnopolitical-armed conflicts in **20**; peacebuilding in 156, 332; UCP Nonviolent Peaceforce in 136; *see also* Mindanao (Philippines)
Philipsen, L. 317
physical abuse 165
physiological arousal 62–63
Pittsburg synagogue, attack on 85
Plan of Action for Religious Leaders 159, 162n5
Plateau Peacebuilding Agency 318
Plavšić, B. 33
Podrinje Identification Project 246, 250n11, 251n17
Pokagon Band of Potawatomi 110
police violence 97, 131
policymaking agencies, intervention, and challenges in engaging 155–157, 162n2; *see also* practice and policy implications

politics/political: exclusion 21–22; factors for environmental changes 72; incitement 65; *see also* gender and ethnopolitical conflict
populism/populist: nationalism in America 81, 83; politics 84–85
positionality, reflexivity and 331
positive ethnicity in peacebuilding 147–148
Post Traumatic Slave Syndrome (Degruy) 232, 236
posttraumatic stress disorder (PTSD) 191, 253, 261, 264
postwar reconciliation in Sri Lanka; *see* Sri Lanka, postwar reconciliation in
Pouligny, B. 317
poverty 21, 99, 176, 210, 215, 236, 253, 273, 312
Povinelli, E. 224
power 123, 143, 144
pōwhiri (New Zealand's traditional ritual) 298
Prabhakaran, V. 270
practice and policy implications: African American community, trauma in 239–240; American nationalism, relapse of 92; COVID-19 pandemic 102–103; environment and peacebuilding 79; ethnopolitical conflicts 24–25; external aid and peacebuilding 312; external involvements in ethnopolitical conflict 45–46; focal points in ethnic conflicts 334; gender and ethnopolitical conflict 36; hatred as public health issue in ethnopolitical conflicts 68; healing-centered peacebuilding approach 263–264; heritage rights, monuments, and cultural divides 204–206; hierarchies of pain 226–227; Indigenous peacebuilding 323; interactive conflict resolution (ICR) 127–128; interreligious peacebuilding 160–161; liberal peacebuilding 55–56; Mamas' resistance to annihilative violence in West Papua 169, 171, 172; Mindanao, case study 286–288; peace after genocide 249–250; peacebuilding and public memory 195–196; peace leadership, security, and military in ethnopolitical conflicts 149; restorative justice (RJ) and Indigenous peacemaking 113–115; Sri Lanka's postwar reconciliation 276–277; transformative peace negotiation 301; unarmed civilian protection (UCP) 138–139; voices of refugees 217; youth in ethnopolitical conflicts 180–181
prejudice 17, 22, 24, 68
prevention of violent extremism (PVE) 154, 155, 158
Price, D. 32
Price, M. 32
Prijedor community 247, 250n15
principle of inclusivity 160
problem-solving 49, 53
problem-solving workshop (PSW) 119–120; for overcoming barriers to starting negotiations 124; social-psychological rationale for 122

Promoting Reconciliation, Accountability and Human Rights in Sri Lanka 275
protests, peacebuilding amid 346–347
Provisional Irish Republican Army (PIRA) 32
psychological perspective, youth 175
psychomedicalized trauma, management 227
psychosocial support approach, healing-centered peacebuilding 254
psychotherapeutic strand, of trauma studies 220, 221
public health issue in ethnopolitical conflicts; *see* hatred, as public health issue in ethnopolitical conflicts
public monuments, treatment 191–194, 195–196
public protests, peacebuilding and 346–347
public services and systems and COVID-19 96
Pugh, M. 269
Pulse nightclub in Orlando, attack on 86

quasi-events, traumatic 224, 225–226, 227
Quebecois 17, 19
queers 225–226

Raasch, D. 110
racialized communities 200
racial violence 187, 233
racism/racist 188–191, 237, 327; antiracism movements 200–201; anti-racist activism 191–194; biases 19, 189–190; consequences of living in racialized society 238; minority populations 217; as socially transmitted disease 232–234; toward Indigenous peoples 333; in United States 216; *see also* African American community
radical efficiency 165
radical Islamist violent extremists 86
Rajapaksa, G. 276
Rajapaksa, M. 270, 272, 273, 275, 276
Ramadan 211–212
Ramirez, E. 288
Rampton, D. 317
rape, during civil war 29–31
Ratliff, B. K. 236
Rausch, C. 287
Ray, R. 233–234
Rebellious Mourning (Milstein) 226
Rechtman, R. 220, 225
reconciliation in Sri Lanka, postwar; *see* Sri Lanka, postwar reconciliation in
Redekop, V. 54
reflective interrogation 54–55
reflexivity and positionality 331
refugees, voices of: background 210–211; being part of change, missing 214–215; family and loved ones, missing 211–213; implications for practice and policy 217; implications for teaching and training 216–217; insecurity and social collapse 215–216; key insights 211–216; overview 209–210

Regan, P. M. 44
Reinares, F. 34–35
relational and structural interconnectedness 285–286
relationships, holding and transforming space 261–262
religion/religious: identities 19, 45; leaders, responsibility of 67; nationalism 88; and political violence 154–155; rituals, utilization 161
religion in peacebuilding: agencies in peacebuilding intervention, engagement of 158–159; attributes of 151–159; defined 152, 162n1; implications for policy and practitioners 160–161; intentional integration of faith in design 152–153; intervention and challenges in engaging policymaking agencies 155–157; motivation 152; overview 151; third-party role in IRPB intervention 153–154; *see also* interreligious peacebuilding
Religions for Peace (RFP) 156
repoliticizing trauma 225–226
Report of the Secretary-General's Panel of Experts on Accountability in Sri Lanka 271
Republican Action Against Drugs (RADD) 32
Republican Party 85
Republika Srpska 244, 245, 246, 247, 250n10
resilience: healing-centered peacebuilding approach 260; of Indigenous groups 112; strategies, racism-related 237
resistance to annihilative violence in West Papua, Mamas'; *see* West Papua (Indonesia), Mamas' resistance to annihilative violence in
resource scarcity and conflict 72
responsibility-to-protect (R2P) doctrine 141, 147–148
restorative justice (RJ) and Indigenous peacemaking 107–115; background 107–108; implications for practice and policy 113–115; implications for teaching and training 111–113; key insights 109–111
Results Based Management (RBM) 153
revisions, do-it-yourself 54
rhetorics and ethnopolitical conflicts 24–25
rheumatoid arthritis and stress 61
Rhodes, C. 199
Rice, B. 73
Rice, T. 235
Richards, D. A. J. 35–36
Richmond, O. P. 50, 283, 289n3, 289n4, 316, 317
Richter, E. D. 66
rioting communities 21
rites of omission, collective identity and 199–201
rituals as peacemaking and rituals of connection 319–320
Roberts, D. 317
Robins, S. 316

Rohingya Muslims, ethnic violence against 32, 298, 340
role-play approach to teaching and training 138
Roma people, during COVID-19 lockdown 100–101
Ross, M. H. 201, 329
Rotberg, F. 72
Rothberg, M. 223
Rothchild, D. 41
Rothman, J. 141, 328, 330
Rouhana, N. 328
Rubenstein, D. M. 233
Rushin, D. K. 188–189
Russia: anti-Russian sanctions regarding Ukraine 45; ethnopolitical-armed conflicts in Ukraine 20; intervention for mediation 44–45; against multilateral humanitarian relief in Syria 45
Rwanda 22; genocide and rape in 29, 68; women leaders in 35

Sabaratnam, M. 317
Sacred Stone Camp, Indigenous and non-Indigenous protesters at 110
Saideman, S. M. 40
Salbi, Z. 28–29, 33
salivary cortisol production and hate speech 61
Saltarelli, D. 283
Saltsjobaden (Sweden), GAM-civil society meeting 296
Salvadoran rebel force, women in 31
sanctions, impact on civil disputes 41, 43, 45
Sanctuary Model 263
Sandline International 298
Sands, B. 32
Sands-McKevitt, B. 32
Sands-McKevitt, M. 32
Saudi Arabia, intervention for mediation 44–45
Saunders, H. 128, 327, 332
Savage Nation 61
Scarry, E. 221, 224
Schmidt, H. 53
school-age individuals, education on hatred and health 66–67
school-to-prison pipeline and Indigenous peoples 113, 114
Scott, I. M. 231, 349
Scott, J. C. 200, 289n4
Search for Common Ground (SCG) 320, 321
secular peacebuilding initiatives/settings 153–154
securitization of peace interventions 50
security: national 146, 148; and peace leadership 142, 144, 146, 147; providers of 147, 148; receivers of 147, 148; training within military spaces 149; youth and 179–180; *see also* peace leadership, security, and military in ethnopolitical conflicts

Security Council (SC) 75
Selby, J. 50
self-determination 280, 282, 285
self-harm arising from hatred 67
self-reflection 55
Sen, D. 114
Senan 310–311
Senehi, J. 72, 74, 284, 320–321
September 11 attacks; *see* 9/11 attacks
Serbia/Serbians: and Albanian communities, ethnic conflict between 51; conservative elites in Yugoslavia 23; ethnic identity 19
sexual violence 28, 29, 30, 165, 177, 187, 220
Shakespeare, W. 142
Shanti Sena (India) 133
shared collective identity 76
Sharpton, A., Dr. 236
Sierra Leone, civil war in 75
Silber and Little 33
simulation-based approach to teaching and training 138
Sinhala community 269–270, 271, 272, 274, 276
Sjoberg, L. 31
skills training institutes 126
slavery 192, 201, 216, 221, 232–233, 234
Slovenian/Slovene minorities 99–100; in Italy and Croatia 103n7; organizations 100–102
Small Arms Survey, The 87
Smith, A. D. 18, 19, 21
Smith, M., Dr. 236
Smith, R. 344
Snitwongse, K. 282
social cognitive skills training 68
social cohesion of Indigenous groups 112
social collapse, insecurity and 215–216
social construction: of ethnic identities 19; of ethnopolitical identities 17–18
social cubism 329
social exclusion 10, 78, 97, 99
social factors for environmental changes 72
social frustration 144, 148
social groups 62, 67, 76, 90, 102, 175, 293, 294, 295, 297, 300
social identity 77, 121
social justice 68, 73–74, 75, 78, 189, 198, 199, 202, 205
socially constructed characteristics, youth 175
socially relevant diversities and COVID-19 related research 98–99
socially transmitted disease, racism as 232–234
social media 87; coverage of terrorist attacks 84; and COVID-19 related research 98–99; platforms 204–205
social mobilization theory 18, 24
social-psychological analysis of ethnopolitical conflict 121–122
social responsibility 96

social unrest 142, 176
Somalia 45, 75
Sons and Daughters of the Confederacy 206
Sousa, C. 227
South Africa: 2015 #Rhodes Must Fall student movement 199; Afrikaners' racism toward blacks 22; statues associated with figures 192–193
South African Truth and Reconciliation Commission 221
South America 110
South Sudan: Nuer, ethnopolitical-armed conflicts in **20**; UCP Nonviolent Peaceforce in 136; war with Sudan 40; youth in ethnopolitical conflicts 179
Spain, removal of statues 205
Spanovich, M. 193
spatial violence 222, 223, 226, 227
spirituality 153, 156, 160–161
Spivak, G. 190–191
Srebrenica massacre 242, 244, 245, 246–247, 249
Sri Lanka 340, 350; civil war 44; Peace Brigades International in 135; youth in ethnopolitical conflicts 179
Sri Lanka, postwar reconciliation in: background 269–270; change of strategy 275; government response 272–274; implications for practice and policy 276–277; implications for teaching and training 277; international campaign 270–272; key insights 270–276; national security 276; overview 269; Tamils 269–270, 271–272, 273, 274–275
Sri Lanka Podujana Peramuna (SLPP) 276
standpoint theory 190
Stanton, G. 243
START 84
state structures and ethnopolitical conflicts 25
Statue of Unity, The 199
statue(s): assaults on 192, 196; associated with racist figures 192–193, 199; Confederate 198, 199, 200, 201, 202; destruction of 193, 203, 205; removal of 205
Stearns, P. 194
Stemple, L. 30
stereotypes/stereotyping 22, 86, 108, 121
Stevens, M. E. 225
stigmatization 86, 154
Stoneman Douglas High School in Parkland, Florida, shooting at 88
Storr, W. 30
storytellers/storytelling: importance of 258; transcultural constructive 320–321
Strategies for Trauma Awareness and Resilience (STAR) 259
stress: and hatred 61, 63; hormones 61, 262
Strimling, A. 123
Strömbom, L. 283

structuralism 18
structural violence 143, 330
sub-Saharan African 108
Sudan: civil wars in 17; groups in Darfur, ethnopolitical-armed conflicts in **20**; Sudanese Arabs' racism against the blacks 22
sufra (gathering around a meal) 212
Suharto, authoritarian regime of 295
suicide 233, 253
suicide bombers 31, 35
Sukarno, President 295
Sunnis **20**, 210
superstitions 65, 67
sustainability/sustainable: economic practices 79; in environmental peace projects 78; peacebuilding organizations 310–311; *see also* interreligious peacebuilding
Sustainable Development Goals (SDGs), UN 157
Svensson, I. 42
Sweden 296, 300
Syria: emancipatory peacebuilding alternatives in 52–53; ethnopolitical-armed conflicts in 20; external intervention for mediation in 44–45; women brigade in 32; youth in ethnopolitical conflicts 179; *see also* refugees, voices of
systemic violence 113, 201, 330
systems thinking component, of healing-centered peacebuilding 260–261

Tajikistan, conflict in 332
Tamil National Alliance (TNA) 274
Tamils 269–270, 271–272, 273, 274–275, 350
Tanzania 25
taraut (Bougainvillean practice) 299, 300
Taylor, B. 235
Taylor, C. 194
teaching and training implications: African American community, trauma in 236–239; American nationalism, relapse of 91–92; COVID-19 pandemic 102; environment and peacebuilding 78–79; ethnopolitical conflicts 24; external aid and peacebuilding 311–312; external involvements in ethnopolitical conflict 44–45; focal points in ethnic conflicts 334; gender and ethnopolitical conflict 35–36; hatred as public health issue in ethnopolitical conflicts 65–68; healing-centered peacebuilding approach 262–263; heritage rights, monuments, and cultural divides 203–204; Indigenous peacebuilding 323; interactive conflict resolution (ICR) 126–127; liberal peacebuilding 53–55; Mamas' resistance to annihilative violence in West Papua 168–169, 170–171, 172; Mindanao, case study 284–286; peace after genocide 248–249; peacebuilding and public memory 194–195; peace leadership, security, and military in ethnopolitical conflicts 149; repoliticizing trauma 225–226; restorative justice (RJ) and Indigenous peacemaking 111–113; Sri Lanka's postwar reconciliation 277; transformative peace negotiation 300–301; unarmed civilian protection (UCP) 137–138; voices of refugees 216–217
terrorism 340; Global War on Terrorism 96; Irish nationalist women and 33; jihadi 90; by LTTE 272; terrorist attacks, social/news media coverage of 84; *see also* 9/11 attacks; counter terrorism (CT)
Thiessen, C. 283
think-tank 53
Third Party Consultation (TPC) 119
third-party role in IRPB intervention 153–154
This Bridge Called My Back: Writings by Radical Women of Color (Moraga and Anzaldúa) 188
Thomas, C. 196
Thompson, E. 195–196
Thompson, W. S. 282
Threat and Imposition of Sanctions Data (TIES) 46n2
Till, E. 236
Till, K. E. 222
Tiro, H. di 295
Tomašica mass grave 250n16
totalitarian systems, citizenship in 164
Towards Understanding and Healing 333
Track II diplomacy, (TII) projects 118, 328, 329
training 119; military 149; organizational, trauma-informed 263; *see also* teaching and training implications
transcultural constructive storytellers 320–321
transformation of space 261–262
transformative peace negotiation: background 293–295; Bougainville peace negotiation, New Zealand and 297–300; implications for practice and policy 301; implications for teaching and training 300–301; inclusive process in Aceh, Indonesia 295–297; key insights 295–300; objective 292; overview 292
transitional justice 79, 333–334
Trauma and Recovery (Herman) 221
trauma healing 333
trauma studies: background 220–222; cultural strand of 220, 221, 222; ecological strand of 220, 222, 223, 225; etiologies 222–225; floating signifier 225, 227; historical 191–194; historical strand of 220, 222; Holocaust-based 221, 223; implications for practice and policy 226–227; implications for teaching and training 225–226; insidious 224–225; intergenerational 222; key insights 222–225; nature of 191; psychotherapeutic strand of 220, 221; repoliticizing 225–226; trauma-informed

organizational training 263; trauma-informed tools 261–262; working-through 191–192, 193, 195; *see also* African American community
traumatic stress disorders 223
Tribunal, The 245
tri-people dimension 281–282
triumphalism 243, 249
Trump, D. 85, 91, 131
trust building 76, 137, 300
Turkey/Turks 21; intervention for mediation 44–45; Kurds, ethnopolitical-armed conflicts in **20**; refugees in 210–211; Turkish-Cypriot communities, peace building for 125–126
Tuso, H. 107–108
Tutsi minority in Rwanda 22
Tuzla (Bosnia and Herzegovina) 246, 250n11
Txukarramãe, M. 110

UCDP External Support Dataset 46n3
Udruzenje Prijedorcanki "Izvor" 250n8
Uighur minority, of China 21, 45
Ukraine: anti-Russian sanctions regarding 45; removal of statuary influences 205; Russians, ethnopolitical-armed conflicts in **20**
unarmed civilian protection (UCP) 131–139; background 132–134; implications for practice and policy 138–139; implications for teaching and training 137–138; key insights 134–137; Nonviolent Peaceforce 136
unemployment 176, 177, 253, 310, 311
unhealthy lifestyles 176
United Nations Development Program (UNDP) 125, 179, 194, 195
United Nations Educational, Scientific and Cultural Organization (UNESCO) 175
United Nations Human Rights Council (UNHRC) 134, 270–271, 272, 273, 274, 275, 276
United Nations Security Council (UNSC) 175, 179–180
United Nations (UN) 68, 133–134; Agenda for Peace 122; Alliance of Civilization 156; bodies 156; High Commissioner for Human Rights 271; Inter-Agency Task Force on Religion and Development 157; International Day of Family 319; Mediation Support Unit 156; missions 51; Office on Prevention of Genocide 159; Population Fund 159; recommendations for community engagement 331; Sri Lanka's postwar reconciliation 270; Strategic Learning Exchange 159; Sustainable Development Goals (SDGs) 157; World Population Prospects 174
United Network of Young Peacebuilders 179
United States: civil rights movement 23, 24; Equal Justice Initiative 204; Hope in the Cities 204; intervention for mediation 44–45; Monument Lab 204; removal of heritage sites 205

United States Agency for International Development (USAID) 125, 157, 179
United States Institute for Peace (USIP) 156
unlearning project 190, 191
Uppsala Conflict Data Program 41–42
Urdal, H. 176
Usman, A. 319–320
"us *versus* them" 24–25
Uthuru Vasanthaya (Northern Spring) 273–274
Uvaza, J. 35
Uzbekistan, women's religious rituals in 319

Vaillancourt, J. G. 71
victims: and perpetrators 259; youth as 177–178
Victor, B. 35
Victoria, Queen 199
Vinthagen, S. 289n4
violence: attempt to commit 299; breaking cycles of 136, 259; communal 21, 26n1; cultural 61–62, 143, 202; defined 63; direct 110, 122, 143, 144; ethnic, in Myanmar 32–33; ethnopolitical 22; etiologies 224; forms 164; and frustration 144; gender-based 41, 177; and gun culture 87–90, 92; and hatred 61–62; historical 223; indirect 164, 202; interpersonal 66, 68, 221, 223; military intervention 142; in Palestine 35; police 97, 131; racial 187, 233; sexual 28, 29, 30, 177, 187, 220; spatial 222, 223, 226, 227; structural 143, 330; systemic 113, 201, 330; traumatic 227, 253; against women 192; youth, role 174, 175, 176, 177–178, 179;
 see also Mamas, resistance to annihilative violence in West Papua
violence, annihilative: experiences of suffering 166–168; hard work of striving through suffering 166, 167, 169, 171–172; walking through suffering 169–170; *see also* Mamas, resistance to annihilative violence in West Papua
violent extremism/extremist: causes of 179; groups 86; and interreligious peacebuilding 154–155, 162n2
Visayas (Philippines) 281
Visoka, G. 317
Volkan, V. 19, 21, 200, 259, 328
vulnerabilities 177, 193; African American children 233; ethnic 148

Wagner, S. 243
Wahab, A. S. 111
Wallace, B., Dr. 236
Wallensteen, P. 42
Wall of Moms 132; *see also* unarmed civilian protection (UCP)
Wallstrom, M. 30
war and conflict 270

Index

Washington Post 250n13
Webster, D. 165
Weingarten, K. 169
West, H. G. 224
West Papua (Indonesia), Mamas' resistance to annihilative violence in 340; background 164–165; experiences of suffering 166–168; implications for practice and policy 169, 171, 172; implications for teaching and training 168–169, 170–171, 172; key insights 166–168; *Perjuangan*, hard work of striving through suffering 166, 167, 169, 171–172; resources 165; silence, breaking 166, 167–168, 169; suffering and laughter 170–171; walking through suffering 169–170; *see also* Mamas, resistance to annihilative violence in West Papua
White Fragility (DiAngelo) 189
white genocide 22
white identity 86
white nationalist violence 86–87
white supremacist propaganda 34
Whole of Society 344
Wickremesinghe, R. 276
Wiener, N. I. 176
William and Flora and Hewlett Foundation 328
Williams, A. 50, 72
Williams, B. 333
Williams, M. T., Dr. 234, 236
Wimmer, A. 21
Wink, W. 259
Wired 84
Witness for Peace 133
women 32–34, 76; Colombian, participation in peace agreement 76; combatants 31–32, 35; enablers, women as 29–30; FMLN (Salvadoran rebel force), women in 31; and girls trafficking of Rohingya 298; in management of natural resources and peace negotiations 79; movements and communities in Kenya 76; nonindigenous, clothing as identity for 110–111; peace activists 34; as perpetrators 29–31; rape of 29, 35; religious rituals in Uzbekistan 319; roles during negotiation 299; in Rwanda 29, 35, 68; in Salvadoran rebel force 31; suicide bombers 31; in Tamil war 31–32; violence against 192; *see also* gender and ethnopolitical conflict
Women and War (Elshtain) 31

Women for Women International (WWI) 28–29
Women in Black 34
Women's League for Peace and Freedom 34
working hypotheses 41–42
working-though trauma 191–193, 195
World Bank 306
World Council of Churches 159
World Health Organization (WHO) 63, 253
World Youth Report 177

Xi Jinping 20, 21
Xingu River dam, protests against 111–112

yahapalana government 275, 276
Yair, O. 177
Yazzie, R. 107
Yemen: ethnopolitical-armed conflicts in 20; external intervention for mediation in 44–45
Yoder, C. 259
Young, H. 73
youth: age-defined perspective 175; as agents of change 178–180; Black youth 233–234; contributions to peacebuilding 179–180; Indigenous, forced removals of 199; motivations for violence 176; psychological perspective 175; role in violence 174, 175, 176, 177–178, 179; schoolgirls, kidnapping of 28; and security 179–180; socially constructed characteristics 175; as victims 177–178
youth in ethnopolitical conflicts: as agents of change 178–180; background 175–180; defined 175, 177; implications for practice and policy 180–181; key insights 178–180; overview 174–175; peace and conflict nexus 175–176; as potential troublemakers 176–177; as victims 177–178
Yugoslavia 33; crisis in 96; Serbia's conservative elites in 23; sexual violence in 28, 29
Yugoslav People's Army (JNA) 250n6

Zartman, W. 109
Zehr, H. 108
Zelizer, C. 329
Žepa (Bosnia and Herzegovina) 242, 244
Zion, J. W. 107
Zones of Peace, development of 289n5